Interpersonal COMMUNICATION

BUILDING REWARDING RELATIONSHIPS

Second Edition

Melissa
BEKELJA WANZER
Canisius College

Kristen
CAMPBELL EICHHORN
State University of New York-Oswego

Candice
THOMAS-MADDOX
Ohio University-Lancaster

Kendall Hunt
publishing company

Book Team

Chairman and Chief Executive Officer   Mark C. Falb
President and Chief Operating Officer   Chad M. Chandlee
Vice President, Higher Education   David L. Tart
Director of Publishing Partnerships   Paul B. Carty
Senior Developmental Coordinator   Angela Willenbring
Vice President, Operations   Timothy J. Beitzel
Senior Production Editor   Sheri Hosek
Senior Permissions Editor Tammy Hunt
Cover Designer   Faith Walker

Cover image © Shutterstock.com

Kendall Hunt
publishing company

www.kendallhunt.com
Send all inquiries to:
4050 Westmark Drive
Dubuque, IA 52004-1840

Dedication

Melissa Bekelja Wanzer

For Steve, Claire and Ella—every single day with you is an adventure filled with fun, love, and laughter! Thank you for your constant support, encouragement, and unconditional love.

Kristen Campbell Eichhorn

For Eric and William—Thank you for loving me—not despite my imperfections—but because of them. For all the early mornings, late nights and everything in between—your patience, support, sense of humor and encouragement made this all possible.

Candice Thomas-Maddox

For Rick, Greyson, & Parker—With your love and support, I know that all things are possible. Thank you – for being patient when I need to work just a little bit longer, for making me laugh when I need it the most, and for believing in me…always.

brief contents

SECTION ONE : COMMUNICATION FOUNDATIONS AND UNDERSTANDING THE SELF 1

Chapter 1 Interpersonal Communication: Significance and Explanation of Key Concepts 3

Chapter 2 The Role of Interpersonal Communication in the Development of Self 29

Chapter 3 Why Do We Communicate the Way We Do? Personality and Emotion 55

Chapter 4 The Impact of Perception and Listening on Interpersonal Communication 99

Chapter 5 Verbal Communication: Words of Wisdom 135

Chapter 6 Nonverbal Communication: It's Not *What* You Said; It's *How* You Said It 165

SECTION TWO: RELATIONSHIP DEVELOPMENT AND STAGES 199

Chapter 7 Initiating Relationships: "Haven't We Met Somewhere Before?" 201

Chapter 8 Sustaining Relationships: Relationship Maintenance and Conflict Management 235

Chapter 9 The Dark Side of Relationships: Deception, Embarrassment, Jealousy, Power, and Verbal Aggression 271

Chapter 10 Terminating Relationships: Knowing When to Throw in the Towel 303

SECTION THREE: RELATIONSHIP CONTEXTS AND ENVIRONMENTS 339

Chapter 11 Mediated Communication: Understanding the Influence of Technology on Our Personal Relationships 341

Chapter 12 Intercultural Communication: Variety Is the Spice of Life 371

Chapter 13 Family Communication: It's All Relative 407

Chapter 14 Organizational Communication: Combining the Personal with the Professional 439

Chapter 15 Health Communication: Using Effective Communication to Manage Stressful Interactions 475

INDEX 503

contents

SECTION ONE : COMMUNICATION FOUNDATIONS AND UNDERSTANDING THE SELF   1

Chapter 1   Interpersonal Communication: Significance and Explanation of Key Concepts   3

Objectives 3
Scenario: Sound Familiar? 3
Overview 3
Why Study Interpersonal Communication? 4
    Significance of Interpersonal Communication (IPC) in Establishing
      Professional Relationships 4
    Significance of IPC in Establishing Personal Relationships 6
What Exactly Is Interpersonal Communication? 10
Basic Principles of Interpersonal Communication 13
History of Interpersonal Communication 16
Interpersonal Communication Theory 20
Overview of the Textbook 21
Summary 22
Discussion Questions 22
Self Assessment 23
Key Terms and Definitions 25
References 26

Chapter 2 The Role of Interpersonal Communication in the Development of Self 29

Objectives 29
Scenario: Sound Familiar? 29
Overview 29
Importance of Studying the Process of Identity Formation 30
Definition of Self 31
Self As a Process 31
Self-Complexity 31
Self-Awareness and Communication 33
The Self-System 35
    Self-Concept 35
    Self-Esteem 38
    Self-Regulation 39
Interpersonal Communication and the Development of Self 40
    Family 40
    Peer Relationships 44
    Relationship Partners 46
Summary 47
Discussion Questions 48
Self Assessment 49
Key Terms and Definitions 50
References 51

Chapter 3 Why Do We Communicate the Way We Do? Personality and Emotion 55

Objectives 55
Scenario: Sound Familiar? 55
Overview 55
The Impact of Individual Differences on Social Interaction 56
A Comparison of Trait and State Approaches to Personality Differences 58
Apprehension Traits: Communication Apprehension & Willingness to Communicate 59
    Communication Apprehension 59
    Willingness to Communicate 61
Presentation Traits: Communicator Style and Humor Orientation 62
    Communicator Style 62
    Humor Orientation 63
Adaptation Traits: Affective Orientation & Interaction Involvement 65
    Affective Orientation 65
    Interaction Involvement 66

Aggressive Traits: Assertiveness, Argumentativeness & Verbal Aggression 67
 Argumentativeness 67
 Assertiveness 68
 Verbal Aggression 69
Emotion 71
Emotions & Communication 72
Emotion Work and Emotional Intelligence 74
Emotions in Relational Contexts 75
 Emotion and Health 75
 Work and Emotion 76
 Emotions in the Classroom 77
 Diversity and the Expression of Emotion 76
Summary 79
Discussion Questions 79
Self Assessments 80
Key Terms and Definitions 82
References 93

Chapter 4 The Impact of Perception and Listening on Interpersonal Communication 99

Objectives 99
Scenario: Sound Familiar? 99
Overview 99
Perception and Interpersonal Communication 100
 Limitations in Forming Perceptions 101
Selectivity Processes 102
Organization 106
 Schemata 106
Interpretation 110
 Attribution Theory 110
 Attribution Errors 111
Individual Differences and Perceptions 113
 Sex Differences 113
 Age Differences 114
 Cultural Differences 114
The Link Between Perception and Listening 115
 Significance of Listening Skills 115
 Hearing and Listening Defined 116
 Step One: Hearing 117
 Step Two: Attending 117
 Step Three: Understanding 117

Step Four: Responding 118
Step Five: Remembering 118
Listening Styles 119
People-Oriented 119
Action-Oriented 120
Content-Oriented 120
Time-Oriented 120
Gender, Culture, and Personality Differences in Listening Styles 121
Gender 121
Culture 121
Personality 121
Common Listening Misbehaviors 122
Pseudo-Listening 122
Monopolizing 122
Disconfirming 122
Defensive Listening 123
Selective Listening 123
Ambushing 123
Best Practices for Effective Listening 123
Summary 125
Discussion Questions 125
Self Assessments 126
Key Terms and Definitions 130
References 132

Chapter 5 Verbal Communication: Words of Wisdom   135

Objectives 135
Scenario: Sound Familiar 135
Overview 135
Defining Verbal Communication 136
Rules 136
Symbols 137
Subjectivity 138
Context 139
Functions of Verbal Communication 140
Cognitive Function 140
Social Reality Function 142
Group Identity Function 143
Social Change Function 144
Verbal Communication Styles 145
Direct/Indirect 145

INTERPERSONAL COMMUNICATION: Building Rewarding Relationships

Informal/Formal 146
Clarity/Equivocation 147
Powerful/Powerless Language 147
Perceptions and Verbal Communication 148
Credibility and Status 149
Biased Communication and Language 149
Verbal Immediacy 150
Factors Affecting Verbal Communication 152
Life Span 153
Sex Differences in Verbal Communication 155
Contextual Differences 156
Best Practices: Avoid Verbal Pitfalls 156
Clarity 156
Appropriateness 157
Concreteness 157
Summary 157
Discussion Questions 158
Self Assessment 159
Key Terms and Definitions 161
References 163

Chapter 6 Nonverbal Communication: It's Not *What* You Said; It's *How* You Said It 165

Objectives 165
Scenario: Sound Familiar? 165
Overview 165
Defining Nonverbal Communication 166
Distinct Characteristics of Nonverbal Messages 167
Nonverbal Features that Are Similar to Verbal Messages 168
Eight Types of Nonverbal Communication 169
Facial Communication 170
Kinesics 171
Haptics 173
Proxemics 174
Paralanguage 175
Physical Appearance 176
Artifacts 178
Chronemics 179
Four Functions of Nonverbal Messages 180
Facilitate Cognitive Meaning 180
Encoding and Decoding Emotions 181

Express Affection and Support 183
Aid in Impression Formation/Identity Management 183
Best Practices: Avoid Common Nonverbal Communication Mistakes 184
Common Areas of Miscommunication 184
Nonverbal Messages and Social Influence 184
Practice Sending and Receiving Nonverbal Messages 186
Recognize Differences in Nonverbal Communication Perceptions 186
Future Direction for Nonverbal Communication: Electronic Paralanguage 187
Summary 189
Discussion Questions 189
Self Assessments 190
Key Terms and Definitions 194
References 196

SECTION TWO: RELATIONSHIP DEVELOPMENT AND STAGES   199

Chapter 7 Initiating Relationships: "Haven't We Met Somewhere Before?"   201

Objectives 201
Scenario: Sound Familiar? 201
Overview 202
The Role of Communication in Relationship Development 202
Relationship Defined 203
The Nature of Relationships 203
Deciding to Make the First Move: Why We Initiate Relationships 204
Interpersonal Attraction 205
Physical Attractiveness 206
Social Attractiveness 210
Task Attractiveness 211
Proximity 212
Similarity/Homophily 213
Interpersonal Goals 215
Interpersonal Communication Theories: *How* We Initiate Relationships 216
Starting the Conversation 216
Self-Disclosure 217
Social Penetration Theory 220
Uncertainty Reduction Theory 220
Predicted Outcome Value Theory 221
Social Exchange Theory 222
Stages of Relationship Development 222

Relationship Initiation Contexts 225
Relationship Initiation and Technology 225
Relationship Initiation and Culture 226
Summary 227
Discussion Questions 227
Self Assessment 228
Key Terms and Definitions 230
References 232

Chapter 8 Sustaining Relationships: Relationship Maintenance and Conflict Management   235

Objectives 235
Scenario: Sound Familiar? 235
Overview 235
Significance of Relationship Maintenance 236
Maintaining the Existence of the Relationship 236
Maintaining a Desired State in the Relationship 237
Maintaining a Satisfactory State 237
Routine and Strategic Relationship Maintenance 237
Why We Maintain Some Relationships and Not Others 238
How We Maintain Relationships: The Role of Communication Skills 240
Relationship Maintenance Strategies 242
Relationship Maintenance in Different Types of Relationships 245
Facebook and Relationship Maintenance 248
Conclusions about Relationship Maintenance 249
Conflict: A Natural Component of All Relationships 249
Definition of Conflict 250
Why Conflict Occurs 252
Conflict Can Be Productive or Unproductive for Individuals and for Relationships 253
Conflict Management Styles 254
Avoidance 255
Competitive/Distributive 255
Collaborative/Integrative 256
The Dark Side of Conflict: Verbal Aggression 258
Managing Conflict 259
Summary 262
Discussion Questions 262
Self Assessment 263
Key Terms and Definitions 265
References 267

Chapter 9 The Dark Side of Relationships: Deception, Embarrassment, Jealousy, Power, and Verbal Aggression 271

Objectives 271
Scenario: Sound Familiar? 271
Overview 271
Deception and Interpersonal Relationships 272
Why Do We Lie? 275
    Lying to Harm Others 276
    Lying to Protect Self 276
    Lying to Spare Others 276
Detecting Deception 276
Analyzing Deceptive Messages 278
Embarrassment: Why Did I Say That? 278
    Our Role in Embarrassment 279
    Responding to Embarrassment 280
Jealousy in Interpersonal Relationships 281
    Types of Jealousy in Relationships 282
    Why Does Jealousy Occur? 282
    Characteristics Associated with Jealousy and Jealousy-evoking Behavior 284
    Gender Differences and Jealousy 285
    Coping with Jealousy 286
Interpersonal Power and Verbal Aggression 288
    Types of Power 288
    Relationship between Power and Interpersonal Influence 289
    Power versus Dominance in Relationships 290
Verbal Aggression 290
    Verbal Aggression in Romantic Relationships 292
    Verbal Aggression in the Classroom 292
    Verbal Aggression in the Workplace 293
Summary 294
Discussion Questions 295
Self Assessment 296
Key Terms and Definitions 297
References 299

Chapter 10 Terminating Relationships: Knowing When to Throw in the Towel 303

Objectives 303
Scenario: Sound Familiar? 303
Overview 304

Assessing Relationship Problems: Attributions, Satisfaction, Equity 304
How Do You Determine if a Relationship Problem is Significant? 305
Investment Model: Will Your Relationship Persist or Die? 306
Duck's Process Model of Relationship Termination 307
　　　Dyadic Process 308
　　　Social Process 308
　　　Grave Dressing Process 308
　　　Resurrection Process 308
Five Stages of Relationship Dissolution 309
　　　Differentiating 309
　　　Circumscribing 310
　　　Stagnating 310
　　　Avoiding 311
　　　Terminating 311
Strategies Used to Terminate Relationships 312
　　　Positive Tone Messages 313
　　　De-escalation Messages 313
　　　Withdrawl 313
　　　Justification Messages 313
　　　Negative Identity Management Messages 313
Types of Relationships: Terminating Friendships 314
　　　Factors Prompting Friendship Termination 315
　　　Indirect Strategies for Ending Friendships 316
　　　Direct Strategies for Ending Friendships 317
Types of Relationships: Terminating Romantic Relationships 318
　　　Infidelity 318
　　　Lack of Commitment 319
　　　Dissimilarity 320
　　　Outside Pressures 321
Homosexual Relationships: Factors Influencing Relationship Quality 321
After the Breakup: Remaining "Just Friends" 322
After the Breakup: Methods of Coping 323
After the Breakup: Closure and Forgiveness 325
Summary 326
Discussion Questions 326
Self Assessment 327
Key Terms and Definitions 332
References 334

SECTION THREE: RELATIONSHIP CONTEXTS AND ENVIRONMENTS 339

Chapter 11 Mediated Communication: Understanding the Influence of Technology on Our Personal Relationships 341

Objectives 341
Scenario: Sound Familiar? 341
Overview 341
  Computer-Mediated Communication 342
How Do Face-to-Face and Mediated Communication Differ? 344
Initiating Relationships Online 349
  Information Seeking and Uncertainty Reduction 350
  Physical and Social Attraction 351
Maintaining Relationships Online 354
The Dark Side of Relationships Online 356
Terminating Relationships through the Use of Mediated Messages 357
  Expanding the Relationship Dissolution Model to SNS 358
Forming Safe and Meaningful Online Relationships: An Overview 358
  Take Your Time, Don't Rush 360
  Pay Attention to Cues 360
  Be Honest 361
  Be Inquisitive: Protecting Yourself 361
  Be Alert: Looking for Signs of Deception 362
Summary 362
Discussion Questions 362
Self Assessment 363
Key Terms and Definitions 368
References 369

Chapter 12 Intercultural Communication: Variety Is the Spice of Life 371

Objectives 371
Scenario: Sound Familiar? 371
Overview 371
Culture and Diversity Defined 373
Co-Cultures Within the United States 375
  Ethnicity 376
  Race 376
  Regional Differences 376
  Social Class 378

Characteristics of Culture 378
    Culture Is Learned 378
    Culture Is Dynamic 379
    Culture Is Pervasive 380
The Impact of Cultural Diversity on Interpersonal Relationships 381
    Understanding the Self 381
    Technological Transformations 381
    Influence of Demographic Transitions 384
Communication Competence: Four Core Concepts 385
    Knowledge 385
    Understanding 387
    Acceptance 388
    Skills 389
Personal Orientation System 389
    Needs 389
    Beliefs 391
    Values 391
    Cultural Value Orientations 392
    Attitudes: Stereotyping and Prejudice 394
Communicating Prejudice 396
    Functions of Prejudice 397
Suggestions for Effective Interpersonal Relationships with Diverse Others 398
Summary 399
Discussion Questions 399
Self Assessments 400
Key Terms and Definitions 404
References 406

Chapter 13 Family Communication: It's All Relative 407

Objectives 407
Sound Familiar? 407
Overview 407
Definition of Family 408
Types of Family Relationships 409
    Marital Relationships 409
    Parent-Child Relationships 412
    Sibling Relationships 416
    Maintenance in Sibling Relationships 417
Family Communication Theories 419
    Family Systems Theory 419

Family Communication Patterns Theory 421
Symbolic Interaction Theory 423
Creating a Family Identity 425
Family Stories 425
Family Myths 426
Family Metaphors 427
Family Themes 427
Consequences of Family Relationships 427
Difficult Communication 428
Family Stress 428
Summary 430
Discussion Questions 431
Self Assessment 432
Key Terms 434
References 436

Chapter 14 Organizational Communication: Combining the Personal with the Professional 439

Objectives 439
Scenario: Sound Familiar? 439
Overview 440
The Unique Nature of Workplace Relationships 440
Voluntary 440
Temporary 441
Hierarchy/Status Differential 441
Types of Relationships at Work 443
Superior-Subordinate Relationships at Work 443
Peer Relationships at Work 447
Friendships in Organizations 449
Mentor Relationships 451
Romantic Relationships at Work 453
Interpersonal Effectiveness: Communication in Work Relationships 455
Organizational Culture 457
Stories 457
Language 457
Rituals 458
Socialization 458
Contemporary Issues in Workplace Relationships 460
Diversity in Organizations 460
Balancing Work and Family Relationships 461
The Impact of Technology on Work Relationships 464
Summary 464

Discussion Questions 465
Self Assessment 466
Key Terms and Definitions 470
References 472

Chapter 15 Health Communication: Using Effective Communication to Manage Stressful Interactions 475

Objectives 475
Scenario: Sound Familiar? 475
Overview 476
Overview of Stress, Stressors, and Signs of Stress 476
Stress and Coping 479
Social Support 480
Communication Between Physicians and Patients 482
    Problems with Physician Communication 483
    Patient Communication 484
Potential Responses to Ineffective Provider-Patient Interactions 486
Improving Health Care Provider-Patient Communication 487
    Patient Communication 487
    Health Care Provider Communication 488
Death and Dying Communication 489
    Reasons for Anxiety when Discussing Death and Dying 490
    Responses to Death and Dying 491
    Suggestions for Improving Communication Related to Death and Dying 493
    Effective and Ineffective Death and Dying Communication 494
Summary 496
Discussion Questions 496
Self Assessments 497
Key Terms and Definitions 499
References 500

Index 503

preface

BACKGROUND AND PHILOSOPHY

It seems like only yesterday when we put the finishing touches on the manuscript of the first edition of *Interpersonal Communication: Building Rewarding Relationships*. Over the past nine years, we have cherished the feedback shared by students and colleagues, and it has inspired us to write this second edition of our book. Since that first edition, countless societal and cultural changes have influenced the ways in which we experience, discuss, and research relationships in a variety of contexts. Social media sites such as Facebook and Twitter were still in their infancy when we wrote the first edition. In 2007 (when *Interpersonal Communication* first hit college bookstore shelves), text messaging surpassed phone calls as the primary means of communicating with friends and family members. Our options for interacting with others have expanded and evolved over the past decade, creating new opportunities for communication scholars to discuss and explore relationship dynamics.

When we initially met to discuss our plans for this second edition, we knew we wanted to incorporate the historical and theoretical foundations of interpersonal communication, while introducing students to exciting and innovative research that has addressed the evolving practice of building and sustaining relationships. While the chapter titles may be the same, the book adopted a fresh approach to appeal to our current generation of students. New features include "Research in Real Life" boxes that showcase contemporary studies and news stories that apply theories and concepts discussed in each chapter. Scenarios at the beginning of each chapter were written to highlight contemporary issues encountered by college students as they navigate relationships in their personal and professional lives. A new chapter focusing on the role that emotions play in our interpersonal relationships was added, and extensive updates were made throughout the book to highlight our dependence on mobile devices and social media to create, sustain, and even terminate relationships.

Our goal is to provide both teachers and students with a text that will enhance our ability to build satisfying relationships. After all, navigating relationships is not an easy process. It requires a considerable investment of time, energy, and emotion. However, not all relationships are meant to last, and our hope is that students will be better equipped to understand and manage the "why" of relationship termination as a result of this text. Specific features of this text include:

- Integrated discussion of theory and its practical application across a variety of interpersonal contexts.
- Summaries and textboxes highlighting contemporary research conducted by leading interpersonal scholars, as well as a discussion of studies that inform our understanding of relationship communication from scholars in fields such as psychology, business, anthropology, sociology, and mediated communication.
- Focus on the evolution of communication strategies in relationship stages ranging from initiating, to maintaining, to terminating.
- Emphasis on specific skills to enhance communication in a variety of communication situations encountered in the health-care, professional, family, and cross-cultural contexts.
- Self-assessment measures at the conclusion of each chapter to provide students with the opportunity to evaluate their communication tendencies and behaviors.
- Discussion questions at the end of each chapter to engage students in application, analysis, and self-reflection of interpersonal communication theories and concepts.

ORGANIZATION OF THE TEXT

To assist instructors as they guide students on their interpersonal communication journey, this text is organized into three main areas:

Part One: Communication Foundations and Understanding the Self

Part One of the text provides an overview of the historical, conceptual, and theoretical foundations of the field and encourages students to examine how their view of self influences their relationships with others. For communication majors, Part One provides a foundation that builds on the communication models and theories typically discussed in introductory communication courses.

In Chapter One, we explore the reasons for taking a course in interpersonal communication and describe research that supports a link between interpersonal communication skills and career success, health, and relationship stability. In this chapter, we define interpersonal communication and distinguish it from other forms of communication, identify key elements of interpersonal communication, and describe important principles of interpersonal communication. A brief history of the field of interpersonal communication is included in the last section of the chapter.

Chapter Two describes the role that interpersonal communication and relationships play in the development of one's identity or sense of self. We define concepts associated with the process of identity development such as self-complexity, self-awareness, authenticity, impression management, self-concept, self-esteem, and self-regulation. This chapter also describes how interactions with family members, peers, and relationship partners contribute to our identity development. In the final section of the chapter, we describe how young adults' use of social networking sites contributes to identity development and affects self-esteem.

Contemporary research has emphasized the important role that personality differences and emotions play in our ability to communicate effectively in a variety of relationships. In Chapter Three questions such as "how" personality differences impact our communication preferences and "why" these differences influence our relationships are addressed. We discuss a variety of personality differences and explore the many emotions experienced as we navigate communication in our relationships.

Chapter Four explains the primary perceptual processes and how each affects the way we communicate with others. We discuss common perception errors such as the fundamental attribution error and the self-serving bias, and we examine how these mistakes might affect our relationships. An important skill that is closely related to information processing is listening. In the final sections of this chapter, we explain the listening process, describe listening styles, and offer suggestions for improving listening skills.

The words we use to express ourselves often have different meanings to different people. In Chapter Five, we discuss the characteristics of verbal communication and the denotative and connotative meanings that accompany them. We discuss how our verbal communication is governed by both constitutive and regulative rules through language structure and how the

words we use have many different functions. In this chapter, we describe different verbal communication styles and how they impact communication with others. In the final sections of the chapter, we discuss how differences in age and sex influence language use.

Noticeably in Chapter Six, we recognize that it is often not *what you say*, but *how you say it* that impacts how individuals interpret messages. We define nonverbal communication and explain the eight broad categories of nonverbal communication: facial communication, kinesics, haptics, proxemics, paralanguage, physical appearance, artifacts, and chronemics. We introduce nonverbal expectancy violations theory and discuss the four functions of nonverbal messages. The chapter ends with a discussion of how we can improve our ability to send and receive nonverbal messages.

Part Two: Relationship Development and Stages

Relationships don't "just happen" – they grow and evolve over time. In Part Two, the various stages of the relational lifespan are examined as we explore the "ups" and "downs" experienced in a variety of relationships including friendships, families, and platonic and romantic relationships. The three broad stages of relationship development include initiating (Chapter Seven), maintaining (Chapter Eight), and terminating (Chapter Ten). Also, it is important for students to recognize communication tendencies that can contribute to negative relational outcomes (Chapter Nine).

Chapter Seven explores "why" we pursue relationships and addresses the question of "how"

we use communication to initiate communication with others. The effectiveness of various communication strategies such as the use of pick-up lines and flirting are analyzed, and suggestions for engaging in appropriate self-disclosure are provided to help students navigate the uncertainty associated with the beginning stage of a new relationship.

Most of our time and energy are devoted to maintaining our relationships with others. Chapter Eight explains why we maintain some relationships over others, how we maintain these relationships, and individual differences that affect relationship maintenance processes. Managing conflict is not a relationship maintenance strategy; however, people need to know how to manage conflict to sustain relationship satisfaction and stability. This chapter includes a definition of conflict, an explanation of key aspects of conflict, and a description of conflict management strategies.

While it is not unusual to hear the claim "Communication is the key to success," we know that communication is a tool that can be used for good or evil purposes. Chapter Nine examines the dark side of communication in relationships. We examine communication concepts such as embarrassment, jealousy, power, and verbal aggression and how they can be used to destroy relationships or prevent them from ever developing. By understanding these concepts, students may be able to turn potentially dark relationships and conversations to be more productive and effective.

Our students often ask, "how do you know when to end a relationship?" In Chapter Ten, students will explore relationship disengagement. We introduce several theories that assist in assessing relationship problems. Students will explore the decision-making process of terminating a relationship and examine the multiple stages of relationship dissolution. This chapter includes a summary of strategies used to terminate relationships and methods of coping with relationship dissolution. In the final section we explain the importance of closure and forgiveness in terminating our relationships.

Part Three: Relationship Contexts and Environments

Interpersonal relationships are dynamic and, often, how we interact changes with our environment. Understanding different nuances of these environments can assist in our ability to develop meaningful relationships. In Part Three, we offer five different contexts and environments that impact interpersonal relationships. We will examine Mediated Communication Environments (Chapter Eleven), Intercultural Communication (Chapter Twelve), Family Relationships (Chapter Thirteen), Organizational Communication (Chapter Fourteen), and Health Communication (Chapter Fifteen).

It is no surprise that mediated communication has changed and shifted the way we initiate, maintain, and terminate interpersonal relationships. In Chapter Eleven, students will examine the influence of technology on our personal relationships. We discuss the advantages and disadvantages of mediated communication and the pervasiveness of social networking sites. Several theories are introduced to make sense of uncertainty reduction and information seeking behaviors when initiating and maintaining relationships online. Additionally, students are given instructions on how to use mediated communication to form safe and meaningful relationships.

In Chapter Twelve, students will explore the impact of cultural differences on achieving effective communication in relationships. Concepts such as stereotyping, prejudice, and ethnocentrism are addressed, and strategies for enhancing intercultural relationships are provided. Students are encouraged to engage in self-reflection throughout the chapter to identify how their values and attitudes influence their interactions with diverse others.

While many of our relationships are voluntary in the sense that we have the choice to initiate communication, family relationships present a unique set of issues to explore given that we are born into relationships that are involuntary in nature. Chapter Thirteen provides students with an overview of various family types and examines the stresses experienced by families as they grow and evolve through the family lifespan.

Since many U.S. adults spend almost as many waking hours with co-workers as they do with friends and family members, Chapter Fourteen provides students with an overview of the unique dynamics of communication in the organizational context. Topics addressed range from navigating the unique communication challenges associated with workplace friendships and romantic relationships to ensuring effective supervisor-subordinate relationships.

A significant number of our students tell us that they often feel "stressed out" and this affects their ability to succeed in school, in their jobs, and in their relationships. In Chapter Fifteen we examine the concept of "stress" and explore two of the situations most individuals label as being stressful: interacting with healthcare providers and communicating about death and dying. Our interpersonal interactions can cause us to feel stressed, but they can also help to reduce stress. In this chapter, we focus on how communication can be used more effectively to navigate difficult or stressful situations.

Overall, we are confident that this edition of *Interpersonal Communication: Building Rewarding Relationships* provides an overview of current interpersonal research and addresses the relevant relationship dynamics that influence our ability to interact in the world today. We understand the importance of student-oriented pedagogy and providing instructors with the tools they need to personalize their interpersonal communication classrooms. Therefore, in the next sections, we highlight what you can expect from all 15 chapters of this edition.

STUDENT-ORIENTED PEDAGOGY

Because we recognize the importance of assessing student learning, we have included the following features in each chapter to facilitate student learning and help instructors measure learning outcomes:

- Scenarios that illustrate the chapter theme
- Learning objectives
- Bold-faced keywords
- Definitions of key terms at the end of the chapter
- Research in Real Life text boxes that include summaries of relevant research
- Examples of classic and contemporary research throughout the chapters

- Graphics incorporated throughout to re-inforce concepts, theories, or models
- Discussion activities
- Sources at the end of chapters

ONLINE INSTRUCTOR'S ANCILLARIES

We have developed several tools, assignments, and media features that will help enhance the face-to-face, hybrid, or fully online interpersonal communication classroom. These ancillaries were created to increase teacher effectiveness and improve student engagement. We have provided tools to enhance delivery of information through chapter outlines and PowerPoint presentations. Additionally, we have provided multiple-choice items, essay questions, and media examples to assist with assessment and application of course material. With each media supplement, a link is provided to a mul-timedia example from television, film, or pop culture. A description of the clip, a list of relevant concepts from the accompanying chapter that can be applied in analysis, and discussion questions for in-class or online assignments are also provided. With each feature, we encourage instructors to personalize their interpersonal communication course with assignments that fit the mission and goals of their respective institutions.

With each chapter, we provide:

- Full sentence chapter outlines with definitions and bolded key terms
- Comprehensive, yet customizable chapter PowerPoint presentations
- Multiple-choice test quesitons
- Essay test questions
- Extended in-class, homework, or online assignments
- Brief media examples for analysis of chapter concepts

Acknowledgments

I thought writing the second edition of a textbook was supposed to be easier than writing the first! The 2nd edition of *Interpersonal Communication:Building Rewarding Relationships* reflects lots of work on behalf of the authors as well as the Kendall Hunt staff. First, I have to thank Paul and Angela at Kendall Hunt for providing us with this opportunity and for being patient with us throughout the process. We couldn't ask for better people to work with on this project! Next, I have to thank my coauthors, Candice and Kristen, for all of the laughs we shared as well as their unwavering commitment to this project. We all had the same vision for 2nd edition and we knew that achieving this task would not be easy. Finally, I have to thank my Canisius College colleagues and students for providing feedback along the way on every aspect of the book. I guess I should also thank my students for talking me out of the gnome-themed cover that I so desperately wanted.

–MBW

The 2nd edition of this book has been an enormous journey. Many individuals have provided support and encouragement along the way to bring this project to life. To my family—thank you for making me laugh and reminding me to stay balanced in my approach. To my coauthors, Melissa and Candice—I am forever grateful for your vision, feedback, and mentorship as we tackled ambitious goals for this edition. Thank you for your constant strive for excellence and your professional and personal guidance over the last decade. It has been a remarkable gift. To my SUNY Oswego family—thank you to the faculty, students, and staff that have provided feedback and support to help make this a reality. Additionally, thank you to President Deborah F. Stanley—for your unwavering support and for creating a culture for faculty to thrive in higher education. To Steve Granelli— thank you for always keeping the student's perspective alive in reviewing chapters, creating instructional support materials, and developing media supplements that will—without a doubt—enhance student engagement. To everyone at Kendall Hunt—especially Paul and Angela—Thank you for your patience, commitment, and dedication to this edition. We did this—together!

–KCE

Each time we finish a new textbook project, it is inspiring to reflect on just how many people gave so generously of their time and support to make our vision a reality. When Kristen and Melissa invited me to be part of their co-author team more than a decade ago, I never would have envisioned that we would someday work on a second edition of this text. From our vision for "gnomes" as a textbook cover to our weekly conference calls, your laughter, encouragement, and dedication to researching and teaching interpersonal communication are inspirational. To my Ohio University students who have provided me with the platform to do what I love over the past 21 years, thank you. Your questions and examples have shaped this next generation of the book. To Paul and Angela – your unwavering patience and support are second-to-none. Thank you for your support over the past decade – I cherish each of the opportunities that you have provided.

–CTM

about the
authors

Melissa Bekelja Wanzer

Melissa Bekelja Wanzer (Ed.D., West Virginia University, 1995) is Professor in the Communication Studies Department at Canisius College where she teaches graduate seminars in health communication, interpersonal communication and persuasion, and undergraduate courses in health communication, family communication, interpersonal communication, gender, and humor. Dr. Wanzer's research appears in *Communication Education, Communication Teacher, Communication Studies, Communication Quarterly, Health Communication, Journal of Health Communication, Qualitative Research Reports,* and *Communication Research Reports*. Dr. Wanzer, along with students enrolled in a Health Campaigns class, partnered with Roswell Park Cancer Institute to design and implement a comprehensive testicular cancer campaign at Canisius College. In April 2009 Dr. Wanzer received the Donald Ecroyd and Carolyn Drummond Ecroyd teaching award from the Eastern Communication Association and was recognized as a Teaching Fellow from the same association. In 2012 Dr. Wanzer received the Kenneth L. Koessler Distinguished Faculty Award from Canisius College.

Courtesy of Melissa Wanzer

Kristen Campbell Eichhorn

Kristen Campbell Eichhorn, Ph.D., is Professor of Communication Studies in the School of Communication, Media, and the Arts at the State University of New York at Oswego. Kristen received a B.A. degree in Communication Studies and Spanish from Canisius College in Buffalo ('99), M.A. in Communication Research from West Virginia University ('00), and Ph.D. in Communication Research at the University of Miami ('03). More recently, she was a 2013 participant in the American Council on Education's Regional Women's Leadership forum and a member of the 2016-2017 class of American Council on Education Fellows Program. Kristen's primary area of research is interpersonal communication within organizational, instructional, and health settings. Her research has been published in a variety of journals, including the *Journal of Computer-Mediated Communication*, *American Journal of Health Studies*, *Human Communication*, *College Student Journal*, *Communication Research Reports*, *International Journal of Leadership Studies*, and *Public Relations Review*. In the classroom, Kristen teaches courses in interpersonal communication, research methods, and communication theory. She has presented and published with over a dozen of her former students and has advised over 30 independent studies and master's theses. Kristen has been an active member of the National Communication Association (NCA) and the Eastern Communication Association (ECA) for over 15 years.

Candice Thomas-Maddox

Candice Thomas-Maddox (Ed.D., West Virginia University) is Professor of Communication Studies at Ohio University-Lancaster. Candice has taught interpersonal communication at both the graduate and undergraduate levels, as well as teaching courses in family communication, intercultural communication, and organizational communication. She is the former Executive Director and past President for both the Eastern Communication Association and the Ohio Communication Association. Candice has received a variety of teaching awards including the ECA Ecroyd Teaching Award, ECA Teaching Fellows honor, OUL Professor of the Year, and Ohio University's RHE Outstanding Professor Award. Additional co-authored textbooks that Candice has published with Kendall Hunt include *Family Communication: Relationship Foundations* and *Communicating in Your Personal, Professional and Public Lives*. She is also the co-author of *Quantitative Research Methods for Communication: A Hands-On Approach*.

Section ONE

COMMUNICATION FOUNDATIONS AND UNDERSTANDING THE SELF

Chapter 1
Interpersonal Communication: Significance and Explanation of Key Concepts 3

Chapter 2
The Role of Interpersonal Communication in the Development of Self 29

Chapter 3
Why Do We Communicate the Way We Do?: Personality and Emotion 55

Chapter 4
The Impact of Perception and Listening on Interpersonal Communication 99

Chapter 5
Verbal Communication: Words of Wisdom 135

Chapter 6
Nonverbal Communication: It's Not *What* You Said; It's *How* You Said It 165

chapter 1

Interpersonal Communication:
Significance and
Explanation of Key Concepts

OBJECTIVES

- Identify three mistakes prospective employees often make in job interview situations.

- Cite three to four examples of research that emphasize the importance of effective interpersonal communication.

- Define the term communication competence and describe the three components of Spitzberg and Cupach's component model of communication competence.

- Define interpersonal communication and distinguish it from other types of communication (e.g., intrapersonal, small group, organizational).

- Explain the four different approaches to defining interpersonal communication.

- Describe the pivotal research and historical events that contributed to the development of the field of interpersonal communication.

- Define the term theory and explain the four goals of a theory.

SCENARIO: SOUND FAMILIAR?

Emma is a business major who is required to enroll in an interpersonal communication (IPC) class at her university. As she walks to her first class, she thinks to herself, "Why do I need an interpersonal communication course? I have at least a thousand followers on Twitter and Instagram and two thousand Facebook friends." Because she exchanges hundreds of text messages regularly with her friends, family members, and boyfriend, she certainly does not need a class on how to communicate!

OVERVIEW

This scenario illustrates a phenomenon that has dramatically changed the way we establish and maintain connections with others. In Sherry Turkle's (2012) *New York Times* article, "The Flight from Conversation," she argues that many people have sacrificed meaningful face-to-face conversations for mere *connection* through different forms of technology. Turkle describes how we connect to others through technologies such as cell phones and computers and simultaneously customize our lives by controlling the images and messages we share with others. These technologies are often used strategically to manage our self-images. For example, we may post only certain pictures on Facebook or Instagram and edit tweets or text messages to be certain that we are depicted in a favorable light.

Despite all of our seemingly widespread social *connections*, Turkle notes that we often find ourselves "alone together" and, as a result of this, our interpersonal communication skills are starting to deteriorate. In the past it was important to hold eye contact while speaking with someone; today, an essential "skill" is being able to maintain eye contact with someone while sending text messages (Turkle, 2012). This example illustrates one of the many challenges we face as we attempt to learn more about what it means to be a competent communicator. Helping students become more competent communicators and establish healthy interpersonal relationships are the primary objectives of this textbook. In the next sections we examine two broad reasons to study interpersonal communication: improving our communication in professional and personal relationships.

WHY STUDY INTERPERSONAL COMMUNICATION?

Significance of Interpersonal Communication (IPC) in Establishing Professional Relationships

One probable reason for taking this course is to improve your ability to communicate in the workplace. Virtually all job applications list "strong interpersonal communication skills" as a job requirement. Prospective employees are expected to understand what it means to possess "strong interpersonal communication skills" when they apply and interview for positions. Can you identify several examples of strong interpersonal communication skills? Not surprisingly, many interviewees do not know what this entails and often fail to display appropriate interpersonal skills in the interview process. As a result of this, they are not hired.

Here are some research conclusions that highlight the importance of communication skills in the workplace:

- Personnel interviewers indicate that strong communication skills are essential for success in corporate settings; however, only 60 percent feel that applicants exhibit effective communication skills during job interviews. The five most frequently identified verbal and nonverbal communication skill inadequacies exhibited during interview situations include: topic relevance, response organization, response clarity, grammar, and response feedback (Peterson, 1997, p. 289).
- A recent Forbes.com article identified active listening skills as one of the top four skills needed to gain employment in 2013 (Casserly, 2012). If job applicants do not actively listen during interviews, they are more likely to provide responses that are irrelevant, disorganized, or inaccurate.
- Even job candidates for prestigious positions such as presidents, provosts, and deans make numerous communication mistakes. Dennis Barden (2013), a search

INTERPERSONAL COMMUNICATION: Building Rewarding Relationships

firm executive in higher education, notes that prospective job candidates make mistakes such as dressing inappropriately for the position, telling the search committee what they think they want to hear, and talking too much during interviews.

What interpersonal skills are important to exhibit during a job interview?

Once you get the job, it is important to communicate effectively to keep your job, establish strong work relationships, and move up in your organization. Regardless of the profession you enter, it is very likely that effective communication skills will be required for your success.

A number of studies point out the importance of communication skills in maintaining employment and succeeding in your chosen profession. Consider the following research:

- Health care professionals who participate in interpersonal skills training improve their ability to treat patients (Rath et al., 1998).
- Health care providers who communicate effectively (i.e., are clear, immediate, humorous, etc.) have more satisfied patients (Wanzer, Booth-Butterfield, & Gruber, 2004).

- A study published in the *Harvard Business Review* found most people would rather work with "loveable fools" than "competent jerks." Being perceived as likeable may help individuals establish relationships and succeed in the workplace, even when task competence is lacking (Casciaro & Lobo, 2005).

INACCURATE DEPICTION OF COMMUNICATION IN THE CORPORATE WORLD: USE OF THE TERM "SOFT SKILLS"

Developing strong interpersonal skills is more necessary than ever to negotiate in today's "bigger is better" business environment (Myers & Tucker, 2005). Organizations have undergone radical changes resulting in a more diverse workforce, a greater ability to obtain and process information through the Internet, and an expanding global marketplace, which makes doing business with people from other cultures easier than ever before.

Regardless of the profession you enter, it is very likely that effective communication skills will be required for your success.

> Individuals who are able to communicate effectively are not only happier and more satisfied with their relationships, but they are also healthier.

According to management professors Laura Myers and Mary Tucker, as these changes occur, more emphasis is being placed on "people skills" in business programs across the nation and the specific "soft skills" that distinguish effective from ineffective managers. Your textbook authors dislike the term "soft skills" because this label seems to imply that communication is easy, effortless, and unimportant. Communicating effectively is difficult! Instead of using the term "soft skills" to describe interpersonal communication skills, we recommend using the term "essential skills." This term illustrates the significance of IPC skills in workplace and relationship success. As we will show in Chapter 5, because language influences thought, we need to change the words we use to describe communication to influence the way people think about communication. Using more powerful language to describe interpersonal communication (i.e., "essential skills" versus "soft skills") may alter the way people perceive and approach communication.

Effective managers must be able to deliver constructive criticism, manage conflicts between employees, persuade and influence individuals at all levels, provide support and guidance, and exhibit appropriate leadership behaviors. There is nothing "soft" or easy about executing those skills in the workplace!

A number of chapters in this textbook are intended to help you to become a more effective interviewee and employee, particularly the chapters on verbal and nonverbal communication, perception and listening, relationship maintenance and conflict, and organizational communication.

Significance of IPC in Establishing Personal Relationships

Throughout your lives you will use interpersonal communication skills to establish and maintain a number of important relationships that exist outside of the workplace setting. While establishing and maintaining healthy relationships with family members, friends, relationship partners, and members of the community takes a great deal of time and effort, it is well worth the work! The interpersonal communication concepts, models, theories, and skills you will learn about in this textbook will assist you in the process of managing these different types of relationships. Individuals who are able to communicate effectively are not only happier and more satisfied with their relationships, but they are also healthier.

IPC AND HEALTH

Social science researchers have had a longstanding interest in the relationship between communication practices and health. Not surprisingly, people who have the ability to communicate effectively (i.e., express emotions, listen effectively, manage conflict) often lead healthier lives. Conversely, those who are unable to communicate effectively often experience health problems. The inability to communicate effectively and establish meaningful relationships can have deleterious effects on your mental and physical health. Several studies highlight the association between satisfying relationships and mental and physical health:

- Effective communication and rewarding relationships with others are closely connected to both mental and physical health (Burleson & MacGeorge, 2002; Omarzu, Whalen, & Harvey, 2001).
- People who report high levels of social isolation and loneliness often lack the skills needed to establish and maintain healthy relationships. Research indicates that socially isolated and lonely individuals are less likely to exercise regularly and more likely to smoke and to experience other significant health problems (Shankar, McMunn, Banks, & Steptoe, 2011).
- A meta-analysis of 32 studies (involving more than 6.5 million people) found a significant increase in risk for premature death among separated/divorced individuals over married individuals (Sbarra, Law, & Portley, 2011).
- Knowing that others will "be there" for us during stressful or traumatic times in our lives offers us a sense of perceived social support, which correlates to mental well-being (Burleson & MacGeorge, 2002).
- Daniel Goleman (2006) argues that our social brains are biologically "wired to connect" with those around us. According to Goleman (2006) "our social interactions even play a role in reshaping our brain, through 'neuroplasticity,' which means that repeated experiences sculpt the shape, size, and number of neurons and their synaptic connections" (p. 11).
- The ongoing relationships we establish can shape the intricate "wiring" or neural circuitry of our brain. To further emphasize the link between our relationships and our health, Goleman describes unhealthy or abusive relationships as "toxic" to our social brains and healthy relationships as "vitamins." Thus, when we are around individuals who love and support us, this experience is analogous to taking vitamins that assist in the functioning of our social brains (Goleman, 2006).

Many interpersonal communication scholars agree that effective communication is essential to achieving healthy relationships. When communication between individuals deteriorates or ceases to exist, relationships are often doomed to failure. A significant body of research focuses on the relationship between specific communication patterns or practices, such as emotional communication, and relationship satisfaction and longevity (see, for example, Burleson & MacGeorge, 2002; Burleson & Samter, 1996; Metts & Planalp, 2002; Noller & Feeney, 1994; Roloff & Soule, 2002).

Interpersonal communication researchers have studied nearly all aspects of romantic and platonic relationships, including how people come together to form meaningful relationships (Knapp & Vangelisti, 2000), how they maintain these relationships (Canary & Stafford, 2001), the factors individuals consider when deciding to terminate a relationship, and the methods used to disengage these relationships (Baxter, 1982; Cody, 1982). Learning about effective communication practices can assist individuals throughout every stage of relationship development, from the beginning stages when individuals are uncertain about how to proceed, to the relational maintenance stage, or to the end of a romantic relationship. In this textbook we provide you with several chapters that focus on the stages of relationship development (initiating—Chapter 7, sustaining—Chapter 8, growing dark—Chapter 9, and terminating—Chapter 10) as well as the communication practices that both contribute to and detract from a relationship's reported "health."

The following sections of this chapter highlight the broad learning objectives to be addressed throughout this textbook. While there are specific learning objectives and key terms for each chapter, the following three primary objectives are the overall purpose of this textbook.

The first objective of this textbook:

1. Students will learn about a wide range of communication concepts and theories that are central to the process of interpersonal communication.

In this chapter we define interpersonal communication and distinguish it from other forms of communication. Also, in an effort to better understand the "roots" of interpersonal communication, we discuss its history, with an emphasis on classic research and on the historical events that stimulated interest in this topic. Throughout the entire textbook you will see numerous boldfaced terms, concepts, and theories that we

consider central to understanding the process of interpersonal communication. Our hope is that you will be able to define these terms and concepts and relate them to your own experiences.

The second objective of our textbook:

2. Students will become more competent communicators.

Many of you are probably taking this course to improve your ability to send and receive messages from others, also known as communication competence.

Communication competence is defined as the ability to send messages that are perceived as appropriate and effective by receivers (Spitzberg & Cupach, 1984). The model most often used to describe communication competence is the Components Model advanced by Spitzberg and Cupach. This model highlights three key components of communication competence: knowledge, skill, and motivation.

The **knowledge** component of this model refers to understanding what reaction or action is best suited for a particular situation. Taking a class in interpersonal communication is the first step in acquiring knowledge and information about the process of forming relationships with others. The **skill** component of this model addresses the ability to utilize the appropriate behaviors in a situation. It is important to remember that there is a difference between *knowing* how to do something (e.g., knowledge of interpersonal models, theories, and concepts) and actually *being able* to do it. For example, a person may understand the principles and concepts associated with managing conflict in relationships. However, when the time comes to put that

It is not enough to have knowledge and skills. You must also have a desire to achieve communication competence.

knowledge to use, it may be difficult to engage in the appropriate behaviors. The final component of the model, **motivation**, refers to the desire to achieve results in a competent manner. It is not enough to have knowledge and skills. You must also have a desire to achieve communication competence. To assess your current level of communication competence, we suggest you complete the Communication Competence Scale found in the final pages of this chapter at the beginning of the course, and then again at the end of the semester.

While we can address the knowledge and skill aspects of communication competence, it is up to you to become more motivated and make attempts to achieve your interpersonal goals. Many of the chapters in this textbook offer valuable information about the communication process and emphasize specific communication behaviors linked to interpersonal communication competence. For example, our chapter on perception and listening highlights specific communication behaviors associated with ef-

fective communication. We often forget to focus on the process of message reception, which is why listening is often referred to as the "forgotten" communication skill. Also, in Chapters 5 and 6 we focus on the highly complex process of sending and receiving verbal and nonverbal messages. By calling attention to certain important aspects of nonverbal messages such as dress, body movements, gestures, or eye contact, we hope students will hone in on the specific skills needed to communicate more effectively.

The third and final objective of the textbook:

3. Students will achieve rewarding personal and professional relationships.

People communicate and ultimately establish different types of relationships to satisfy three universal human needs: **control**, **inclusion**, and **affection** (Schutz, 1966). We communicate with others and establish relationships to control or manage our surroundings, to be part of a group, and to fulfill the need to feel liked. Virtually every chapter in this textbook explains interpersonal communication concepts and theories that will help you understand how relationships work. By teaching you the important communication concepts that are central to understanding the process of interpersonal communication, and by helping you acquire the skills needed to communicate more effectively, we are certain that our third and final goal will be met. And so we begin our journey by clarifying what we mean when we use the term *interpersonal communication*.

WHAT EXACTLY IS INTER-PERSONAL COMMUNICATION?

Communication researchers continue to study many forms of communication, including:

- Mass or mediated communication
- Organizational communication
- Small group communication
- Intrapersonal communication
- Interpersonal communication

MASS OR MEDIATED COMMUNICATION

The study of **mediated communication** involves communicators who are typically separated by both space and time and who send and receive messages indirectly. **Mass communication** typically occurs when a small number of people send messages to a large, diverse and geographically widespread population (Cathcart & Gumpert, 1983; Kreps & Thorton, 1992).

ORGANIZATIONAL COMMUNICATION

Communication scholars also study **organizational communication**, which is recognized as communication that occurs within businesses

Often people in small groups are working to achieve a set goal.

or organizations. Organizational communication takes place between organization members within a clear hierarchical structure; individuals are typically encouraged to adhere to roles and rules established within this structure. In this text, we examine the role of interpersonal communication in organizations, and different types of relationships in this context will be discussed.

SMALL GROUP COMMUNICATION

Small group communication, another area frequently studied by communication scholars, is defined as "interaction among a small group of people who share a common purpose or goal, who feel a sense of belonging to the group, and who exert influence on one another" (Beebe & Masterson, 1997, p. 6). Small group communication is complex and often occurs between three or more people who are interdependent and working to achieve commonly recognized goals or objectives.

INTRAPERSONAL COMMUNICATION

Intrapersonal communication, the most basic level of communication, takes place inside your head and is silent and repetitive (Kreps & Thorton, 1992). Many of us talk to ourselves, which often affects our interpersonal communication decisions. Think about a time when you rehearsed what you were going to say before engaging in a conversation with someone. Perhaps it was a situation where you were building up the courage to ask someone on a date, or maybe you planned out a conversation with a colleague regarding a project at work. These examples would fall under intrapersonal communication. This type of communication is often repetitive and can be motivational. Think about a time when you were running the last few yards of a race and you told yourself, "Keep going" or "You can do it!"

© Creativa Images/Shutterstock.com

INTERPERSONAL COMMUNICATION

Interpersonal communication, sometimes referred to as *dyadic* communication or IPC, is often loosely described as communication that occurs between two individuals. While most agree that interpersonal communication typically involves at least two people (Knapp, Daly, Albada, & Miller, 2002), there is great disparity in the actual definitions advanced by interpersonal communication researchers.

There are four distinct approaches to defining IPC: **situational**, **developmental**, **interactional**, and **message-centered** (Burleson, 2010). All four definitions are important and help us understand what it means to engage in interpersonal communication.

Situational definitions of interpersonal communication were the first to emerge in the field (Miller, 1990). These definitions focus on the specific features or aspects of the communication context in defining the type of communication taking place. In offering a situational definition of interpersonal communication, the most important features are the number of interactants and the exchange of messages (Burleson, 2010). An example of a situational definition is "two people exchanging messages with each other." A criticism of situational definitions of IPC is that they seem to focus more on the number of interactants and contextual factors and less on the quality of the relationship and the specific messages exchanged (Miller, 1978).

Instead of emphasizing the number of interactants involved and the context, **developmental definitions** focus more on qualitative aspects of the relationship and

information exchanged when defining IPC. According to this approach, IPC occurs only when individuals develop a reciprocal relationship and relate to each other as unique individuals (Burleson, 2010). DeVito's (2001) definition of interpersonal communication, "communication that takes place between two persons who have an established relationship; the people are in some way connected," emphasizes the qualitative aspect of the relationship and falls under the developmental definitions.

The third type of definition, **interactional**, "treats most, if not all, cases of social interaction as instances of interpersonal communication" (Burleson, 2010, p. 150). Cappella (1987) describes interpersonal communication as one person influencing another person's behavior, above and beyond that explained by "normal baselines of action" (p. 228). We agree with Burleson and other scholars who argue that, while these approaches address the importance of interaction in IPC, they appear to neglect or

Interpersonal communication, sometimes referred to as *dyadic* communication, is often loosely described as communication that occurs between two individuals.

underemphasize the role that verbal and nonverbal messages play in creating meaning.

The **message-centered** approach to defining IPC advanced by Burleson (2010) addresses limitations in the other approaches and argues that definitions should emphasize processes involved in producing and interpreting messages. For example, Burleson's (2010) definition of IPC focuses on the importance of a communicative relationship between social interactants as well as the significance of both expressive and interpretive intent. According to Burleson (2010), IPC "is a complex, situational social process in which people who have established a communicative relationship exchange messages in an effort to generate shared meanings and accomplish social goals" (p. 151). This definition emphasizes the importance of exchanging messages (verbal and nonverbal) to reach goals or objectives during interaction and agree on what messages mean.

Working from a message-centered approach to defining IPC, we define **interpersonal communication** *as a complex process that occurs in a specific context and involves an exchange of verbal or nonverbal messages between two connected individuals with the intent to achieve shared meaning.* While there is a wide range of definitions available, we chose one that emphasizes the importance of communication as a complicated process that consists of the intentional exchange of both verbal and nonverbal messages and results in shared understandings between connected interactants. Similar to the views expressed by Burleson in the message-centered approach, our definition addresses the following key elements of interpersonal communication:

- **Process**—The process is complex and includes message production, message re-

ception, and message interpretation. All of these processes are related and must be coordinated. Communication is also described as a process because it is continuous, or ongoing (Berlo, 1960).

- **Context**—All communication occurs in a context or situation. People assume different **roles** (parts that people play) and adhere to different **rules** (guidelines for social interaction) depending on the communication situation; hence, where the communication occurs often helps us determine our roles and rules in the situation.
- **Verbal messages**—Communication involves the use of words or symbols (additional information in Chapter 5).
- **Nonverbal messages**—Communication also involves the use of nonverbal messages, which are defined as everything else other than the words exchanged (i.e., eye contact, facial expressions, gestures, clothing, artifacts, etc.) (additional information in Chapter 6).
- **Connected individuals**—When two or more people come together to communicate, they are connected by a common social goal, which is to create meaning.
- **Shared meaning**—The primary goal of interpersonal communication is to achieve shared meaning; that is, the source and receiver agree on the meaning of the verbal and nonverbal messages exchanged.

Figure 1.1 –Key elements of IPC:

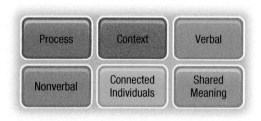

Just by looking at their expressions and gestures, can you tell what these individuals are feeling?

BASIC PRINCIPLES OF INTERPERSONAL COMMUNICATION

Now that you understand what interpersonal communication is, as well as the key elements of interpersonal communication, it is important to understand more about the nature of IPC. In the next section we highlight basic principles of interpersonal communication. These basic principles have been endorsed by numerous communication scholars and are related to a number of IPC theories, concepts, and models. As you begin your journey to becoming a more competent communicator and establishing rewarding relationships, it is important to understand these four principles as they relate to IPC:

1. Interpersonal communication is irreversible.
2. Interpersonal communication can be intentional or unintentional.
3. Interpersonal communication is dynamic.
4. Interpersonal communication is composed of content and relational components.

PRINCIPLE 1: Interpersonal communication is irreversible. First, interpersonal communication is irreversible. This means that once you say something, you cannot take it back. It is permanent. You cannot remediate or replace remarks by saying, "Oh, forget I said that." Do you remember the last time someone asked you, "How do I look?" The slightest pause or facial expression on your part cannot be taken back once it is detected by the receiver. Once we communicate something, verbally or nonverbally, it cannot be undone.

It is important to note that each interpersonal communication exchange we have affects future interactions. For example, Joe is at a party and tells a sexist joke to Kayla, who is someone he just met for the first time. Joe can't undo this interaction with Kayla and the next time Kayla sees Joe she will remember him as the guy who told the inappropriate dumb blonde joke. Since Joe can't erase his comments and the impression he made, what can he do to fix the situation and alter Kayla's impression?

If you thought that Joe should apologize to Kayla for the dumb blonde joke, you are correct. Darby and Schlenker (1982) define apologies as "admissions of blameworthiness and regret for an undesirable event" (p. 743). In order to manage your impression effectively, it is important to deliver an apology that is sincere. An effective apology typically includes the following elements: (1) admitting fault, (2) admitting damage, (3) expressing remorse, (4) asking for pardon, and (5) offering compensation (Darby & Schlenker, 1982; Schlenker & Darby, 1981).

Based on this information Joe might say to Kayla, "The joke I told you the last time we met was offensive, and I probably hurt your feelings. I feel horrible about what I said to you and I hope you will forgive me. Maybe I can buy you coffee sometime?"

PRINCIPLE 2: Interpersonal communication can be intentional or unintentional. Communication scholars often assert that "one cannot not communicate" (Watzlawick et al., 1967, p. 51) because during interpersonal encounters it is likely people will attach meaning to everything you say and do. Intentional messages

Once we communicate something, verbally or nonverbally, it cannot be undone.

are often perceived when sources exhibit nonverbal behaviors such as eye contact, gestures and body movements, facial expressions, and touch. It is often the case that receivers perceive these nonverbal behaviors exhibited by sources as intentional nonverbal communication. Remember Joe from the last scenario? Let's say his apology to Kayla was effective and they started dating. Joe decides to drop in and visit Kayla after class. When he enters her apartment, he sees Kayla slouched on the couch with a dazed look on her face and her arms hanging limply at her sides. Joe asks Kayla, "Why are you so upset?" He perceived the dazed facial expression and slouched body position as the message "I am upset" when, in actuality, Kayla was just tired and thinking about whether she passed her philosophy exam.

PRINCIPLE 3: Interpersonal communication is dynamic. Since communication in interpersonal relationships is a process and is constantly evolving, each time we speak with someone, we are building on previous messages. We are developing a history with this person and, therefore, our communication reflects this change. Think about the conversations you have with your closest friends. Because you have probably spent countless hours discussing family, friends, career goals, and other topics of mutual interest, it is not necessary to revisit these conversations in detail each time you see each other. Instead, you may make quick references to previously discussed events in your conversations.

Joe and Kayla have been dating for almost a year. Their communication, like their relationship, has changed dramatically and they now know a great deal about each other. Kayla teases Joe about their first meeting and asks, "Remember the joke you told me when we first met? Nice!" Joe does not answer this question because he knows this is an inside joke they often share with each other. Joe smiles and laughs at this comment and then asks Kayla a series of questions about her day. Joe asks about Kayla's classes, work schedule, and plans for the week. Asking these types of questions illustrates how conversations and relationships evolve over time.

PRINCIPLE 4: Interpersonal communication is composed of relational and content components. Each message exchanged between interactants is made up of two types of meaning: content and relational (Bateson, 1951). The **content**, or informational component of a message, is the verbal message you send or the specific words you choose. The **relational component** of a message is composed of information that indicates how people feel about their relationship. These signals might include nonverbal messages such as eye contact, gestures, facial expressions, and vocal inflection. The relational component of the message tells the receiver how you would like the message to be interpreted as

well as how you view your relationship (i.e., intimate, platonic, impersonal, etc.). Consider the following situation.

Joe: I just got us tickets to see the Sabres play the Penguins next Friday!

Kayla: Shut up!

Joe: I know, I really can't believe I was able to get these tickets!

Kayla: Shut up! You really are the best!

Accurately interpreting this conversation requires us to focus on both the *content* and the *relational* information in the message. By examining both the parts of the message we should be able to determine the type of relationship Joe and Kayla have with each other, their level of intimacy, and power distribution.

After Joe tells Kayla he purchased Sabres tickets, she tells him to "Shut up!" If we just examined the content or words in this exchange, we might think Kayla is more powerful, doesn't want Joe to talk anymore, and is being rude. A closer examination of this exchange requires us to also consider the relational components of this message. The relational information may be conveyed through idiosyncratic verbal (i.e., "Shut up!") and nonverbal messages (i.e. smiling, facial expressions, emphasis) that signal the type of relationship that exists between Joe and Kayla. When Kayla smiles and lightly taps Joe on the arm when she says, "Shut up!" this indicates how she feels about the message and her relationship with Joe. By examining both the content and relational information in this conversation, we might conclude that Joe and Kayla are in a close relationship where they are able to joke around with each other.

> **More often than not, people engage in metacommunication to clarify relational information to better understand message content.**

search results in millions of sources or "hits" emphasizing the importance of talking about the communication that occurs between parents and children, relationship partners, friends, co-workers, health care providers and patients, etc. Not surprisingly, the inability to communicate effectively about communication (i.e., "What did you mean when you said…?") can cause problems for both sources and receivers. This book will explore the importance of effective relationship communication in depth.

How important is it for children to feel comfortable talking with their parents?

Relational information is important because it affects how people interpret message content. A friend might say to her roommate, "What did you mean when you said 'I am fine' in that tone of voice?" Or a man might ask his significant other, "I think we need to talk about why you've been so quiet lately." Often people engage in what Gregory Bateson (1972) conceptualized as **metacommunication**, "communicating about communication," when they want to clarify a message's meaning. More often than not, people engage in metacommunication to clarify relational information to better understand message content. Metacommunication is an important tool that is often used during social interaction to increase our shared meaning and to reduce uncertainty about the status of our relationships.

How important is it to engage in metacommunication? If we Google "relationship talk," this

HISTORY OF INTERPERSONAL COMMUNICATION

In order to completely understand an academic area, you must start at its roots. In the *Handbook of Interpersonal Communication*, Knapp, Daly, Albada, and Miller (2002) provide an overview of the historical foundations of the field of interpersonal communication. The introductory chapter of the *Handbook* is dedicated to providing a framework for tracing the development of the field. Readers are presented with a timeline highlighting the accomplishments of scholars who have made prominent contributions to the understanding of relational communication.

According to Knapp and his colleagues (2002), one of the most influential studies for providing a framework for both interpersonal and organizational communication was the result of research conducted by Elton Mayo from 1927 until 1932 at the Western Electric Hawthorne Works in Chicago. Mayo, a professor at the Harvard Business School, originally designed the study to examine the impact of fatigue and monotony on work production. But while the study was designed to focus on one aspect of the work process, an interesting thing happened. Mayo discovered that social relationships and, more specifically, positive interactions between coworkers and supervisors, resulted in higher productivity. The Mayo study is an excellent example of how researchers sometimes stumble upon unexpected results that change the way we view phenomena.

During the 1930s, a series of research studies was conducted by scholars in other disciplines. These would provide the groundwork for the field of interpersonal communication. Researchers had begun to systematically study children's interactions to learn more about patterns of social interaction and role-taking behavior (see, for example, Piaget, 1926). Also during this time period, George Herbert Mead, a philosophy professor from the University of Chicago, studied the relationship between the meanings that result from our interactions with others and our sense of self. Mead is often credited with the theory that came to be known as symbolic interactionism.

Herbert Blumer, a colleague from the University of California-Berkeley, actually coined the term **symbolic interactionism** and described this concept as a "label for a relatively distinctive approach to the study of human group life and human conduct" (Blumer, 1969, p. 1). One of the first premises of this theory is that people form meanings based on the symbols used in interactions. These symbols include words or messages, roles that people play, gestures, and even rules that exist for interactions. The theory of symbolic interaction is significant because it recognizes the importance of our responses to symbols or words and the impact this has on the development of self. Consider your current role as a college student. It is likely that you gained the self-confidence to pursue a college degree as a result of the encouragement you received from parents and teachers, as well as the expectations that you and your family members have for your future education. Perhaps when you were in high school, someone asked you which college you planned to attend. All of these symbols helped shape your perception of self.

Also during this period, Abraham Maslow, a psychology professor at Brooklyn College, strove to understand the forces that cause humans to engage in certain behaviors. Beginning in 1939, he conducted research that specifically focused on human needs, resulting in the pyramid that has become widely known as **Maslow's hierarchy of needs** (See Figure 1.2). Many of these needs have been identified as forces that motivate people to form interpersonal relationships with one another. Once the basic physiological and safety needs have been fulfilled, humans seek to fulfill the love and belonging needs by interacting with other individuals. As a result of our interactions with others, self-esteem needs, the fourth level of Maslow's hierarchy, are addressed. Messages received from others are influential in forming self-esteem and tackling issues of identity (Maslow, 1943). The fifth and final need in Maslow's hierarchy of needs is self-actualization. Self-actualization is the most complicated human need to be fulfilled. When you self-actualize, you realize what you are capable of becoming—understanding your true self.

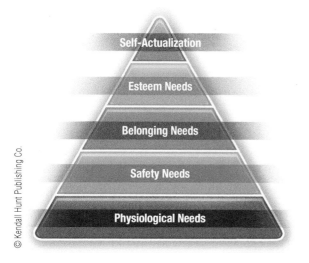

Figure 1.2 Maslow's hierarchy of needs

Progressing into the 1950s and '60s, new scholars produced significant research that began shaping and defining the field of interpersonal communication as it evolved into its own discipline. In the 1950s, anthropologist Ray Birdwhistell (1952) created the term **kinesics** to refer to the use of body movements and gestures as forms of communication. In the late 1950s and early '60s, anthropologist Edward T. Hall focused on the role of space, or **proxemics**, in shaping and influencing our interactions with others (1959). While the study of nonverbal behaviors has evolved as an intriguing aspect of interpersonal interactions, additional studies during this time contributed to our understanding of the role of self and others in relationships.

In 1959, while he was at the University of California, Berkeley, sociologist Erving Goffman published *The Presentation of Self in Everyday Life*. His work has served as the foundation for communications scholars' understanding of the role that impression management plays in our interactions with others. Goffman's work has been influential in shaping many subsequent theories of self-versus-other perceptions in interpersonal relationships.

During the late 1950s, Fritz Heider, a psychologist who taught at the University of Kansas, published work that addressed how attributions shape our interactions with others (Heider, 1958). **Attribution theory** has been influential in interpersonal studies because it addresses the judgments that we make when we communicate with others. Research on relationship initiation has drawn from Heider's work to explain the evolving process of attributions as we make decisions to pursue interactions.

While these prominent scholars provided a solid foundation for our current approaches to investigating interpersonal relationships, you may have noticed that they are not communication researchers. Scholars often cross boundaries and build on ideas initiated by researchers in other fields. Recognizing the contributions that scholars in the fields of psychology, sociology, and anthropology have made to the communication discipline is critical to understanding the interdisciplinary nature of our work. It is fascinating to explore human relationships from such a variety of perspectives! In fact, as you take classes in other disciplines, you may learn about some of the same theories and concepts that were presented in your communication classes.

While the study of communication has existed for decades, it was not until the late 1960s and into the '70s and '80s that interpersonal communication scholars began to carve out their own niche in the study of human communication and to clearly define the study of interactions in relationships. Increasing political and social unrest in the late 1960s and early 1970s caused scholars to direct their attention to individuals and their relationships. Significant historical events like the civil rights movement and the Vietnam War stimulated research activity in such areas as group dynamics, decision making, and conflict resolution.

In 1967, *Pragmatics of Human Communication* was published (Watzlawick, Beavin, & Jackson) and was one of the first books to adopt an interactional approach to communication. In the first chapter of the book, the authors acknowledge that each communication situation involves a "frame of reference." Two key concepts that have become central to the study of interpersonal communication are addressed in this initial chapter: the relationship between communication partners, and the function of the communication interaction. As a result of this groundbreaking text, colleges and universities added courses focusing specifically on the dynamics of interpersonal communication. Other textbooks soon followed (Keltner, 1970; McCroskey, Larson, & Knapp, 1971; Giffin & Patton, 1971).

As the level of interest in interpersonal communication mushroomed, scholars in the discipline turned their attention to research studies designed to explain the dynamics of relationships. Professional associations at the international, national, and regional levels formed interest groups and divisions devoted to interpersonal topics. By the late 1970s, interpersonal communication had become firmly established as a prominent field of study. During the early 1980s, it was difficult to open an issue of any leading communication journal and not find an article pertaining to research on interpersonal communication. Scholars began directing their attention to developing and testing theories directly related to interpersonal interactions.

Recognizing the contributions that scholars in the fields of psychology, sociology, and anthropology have made to the communication discipline is critical to understanding the interdisciplinary nature of our work.

How has keeping in touch with others evolved over the last 50 years?

INTERPERSONAL COMMUNICATION THEORY

Many significant theoretical contributions are provided in the historical foundations of interpersonal communication. While you may experience a heightened sense of anxiety when your instructor mentions "theory," the concepts are actually quite simple and very useful. A **theory** is nothing more than a set of statements about the way things work. Julia Wood (2000) recognizes theories as "human constructions— symbolic ways we represent phenomena" (p. 33)

and notes that we use theories to achieve one of four basic goals. The four widely recognized goals of a theory are: (1) to describe phenomena; (2) to explain how something works; (3) to understand, predict, and control occurrences; and (4) to make social change (Wood, 2000). As students of communication, you will find theories to be useful tools for explaining interactions or categorizing behaviors.

Over the past 30 years, interpersonal communication scholars have truly made their mark as a core focus in the field of communication studies. While the seeds for many of today's prominent interpersonal theories may have been planted by experts in the fields of psychology, sociology, and anthropology, the discipline has grown into an area that interpersonal researchers have defined as their own. In fact, scholars who study communication in other contexts (i.e., instructional communication, organizational communication, intercultural communication) are now applying interpersonal theories as the foundation for studying interactions in other areas.

Many different theories will be discussed throughout this text as we explore key components of interpersonal communication in a variety of contexts. Here is an overview of some of the prominent theories:

- Attribution Theory
- Symbolic Interaction Theory
- Attachment Theory
- Objective Self-Awareness Theory
- Behavioral Confirmation/Self-Fulfilling Prophecy
- Information Processing Theory
- Constructivist Theory
- Social Identity Theory

- Script Theory
- Communication Accommodation Theory
- Fundamental Attribution Error
- Self-Serving Bias
- Equity Theory
- Family Communication Patterns Theory
- Interpersonal Deception Theory
- Leader-Member Exchange Theory
- Nonverbal Expectancy Violation Theory
- Social Comparison Theory
- Social Exchange Theory
- Social Penetration Theory
- Systems Theory
- Uncertainty Reduction Theory
- Predicted Outcome Value Theory

OVERVIEW OF THE TEXTBOOK

This text is divided into three sections. Part I provides an overview of the basic concepts and theories that are central to the understanding of interpersonal communication. Chapter 1 introduces the background, fundamentals, and key components of interpersonal communication. Chapter 2 explores self-identity formation and the role that interpersonal communication plays in the development of the self. Chapter 3 discusses how our personalities and emotions influence the way we communicate and establish relationships with others. Chapter 4 explains how perception (selection, organization, and interpretation) and listening are related to interpersonal communication. Chapter 5 explains how verbal communication is used to shape meaning in others and examines how words provoke certain responses. Chapter 6 describes the significance of nonverbal communication and summarizes dimensions of nonverbal messages.

Part II explores how relationships typically develop, discussing communication practices exhibited during the outlined stages that either facilitate or hinder relationship growth and development. Chapter 7 identifies characteristics that draw us to others and examines how we communicate in initial interactions. Chapter 8 discusses relationship maintenance strategies and conflict management as a natural progression of relationships. If conflict is not managed properly, it may turn dark. Chapter 9 discusses the dark side of communication: jealousy, deception, power, and obsession. The last chapter in Part II, Chapter 10, provides a detailed overview of the relationship termination process. This chapter walks you through the process of relationship disengagement, decision making, and strategies for moving on.

Part III of our text is devoted to what Knapp and Daly (2002) identify in the *Handbook of Interpersonal Communication* as communication contexts that scholars are paying increasing attention to in their research. Some of these trends include an increased emphasis on the role of cultural differences in interpersonal interactions; an examination of interpersonal communication in applied settings such as health, family, and organizations; and the impact of technology on interpersonal communication in different communication contexts (i.e., family, organizations, health). Chapter 11 addresses the impact of mediated communication on interpersonal exchanges. Chapter 12 addresses communication with diverse populations and highlights important areas of miscommunication between individuals of different ages, sexes, races, and/or cultures. Next, Chapter 13 examines one area of applied communication research, family communication. The family communication chapter discusses communication issues that occur across the family lifespan and across family relationships. Sibling, marital, and parent-child relationships are also addressed in this chapter. Chapter 14 introduces the unique aspects of organizational communication such as the development of superior-subordinate relationships, peer relationships, friendships, mentoring, and romantic relationships. Finally, Chapter 15 focuses on the importance of interpersonal communication in health contexts.

SUMMARY

This chapter provided a framework for the interpersonal communication discipline. We defined interpersonal communication and distinguished it from other types of communication. We identified key interpersonal communication concepts and principles. Finally, we provided an overview of the history of interpersonal communication to help you understand the roots of this discipline and the contributions from scholars in other fields. Now it is time to embark on your interpersonal journey.

DISCUSSION QUESTIONS

1. Why should college students take a course on interpersonal communication?

2. Based on your interactions with your peers, what specific communication skills do most college students lack?

3. What theories do you have about how and why people use communication to establish relationships with others?

SELF ASSESSMENT

Communication Competence Scale.

Place the number on the line that best describes your agreement with the items below, using the following scale:

Strongly Agree	**Agree**	**Undecided**	**Disagree**	**Strongly Disagree**
5	4	3	2	1

_____ 1. I find it easy to get along with others.

_____ 2. I can adapt to changing situations.

_____ 3. I treat people as individuals.

_____ 4. I interrupt others too much.

_____ 5. I am rewarding to talk to.

_____ 6. I can deal with others effectively.

_____ 7. I am a good listener.

_____ 8. My personal relations are cold and distant.

_____ 9. I am easy to talk to.

_____10. I won't argue with someone just to prove he/she is right.

_____11. My conversation behavior is not "smooth."

_____12. I ignore other people's feelings.

_____13. I generally know how others feel.

_____14. I let others know I understand them.

_____15. I understand other people.

_____16. I am relaxed and comfortable when speaking.

_____17. I listen to what people say to me.

_____18. I like to be close and personal with people.

_____19. I generally know what type of behavior is appropriate in any given situation.

_____20. I usually do not make unusual demands on my friends.

_____21. I am an effective conversationalist.

_____22. I am supportive of others.

_____23. I do not mind meeting strangers.

_____24. I can easily put myself in another person's shoes.

_____25. I pay attention to the conversation.

_____26. I am generally relaxed when conversing with a new acquaintance.

_____27. I am interested in what others have to say.

_____28. I don't follow the conversation very well.

_____29. I enjoy social gatherings where I can meet new people.

_____30. I am a likeable person.

_____31. I am flexible.

_____32. I am not afraid to speak with people in authority.

_____33. People can come to me with their problems.

_____34. I generally say the right thing at the right time.

_____35. I like to use my voice and body expressively.

_____36. I am sensitive to others' needs of the moment.

Note: Items 4, 8, 11, 12, and 28 are reverse-coded before summing the 36 items.

Source: From "Explication and Test of a Model of Communicative Competence" by J.M. Wiemann, *Human Communication Research*, 3, 195–213, 1977. Reprinted with permission of Blackwell Publishing, www.blackwell-synergy.com.

KEY TERMS AND DEFINITIONS

ATTRIBUTION THEORY: a theory that explains our tendency to attribute causes or explanations to people's behaviors.

COMMUNICATION COMPETENCE: the ability to send messages that are perceived as appropriate and effective by receivers.

CONNECTED INDIVIDUALS: When two or more people come together to communicate, they are connected by a common social goal, which is to create meaning.

CONTENT COMPONENT: informational component of a message; the verbal message you send or the specific words you choose.

CONTEXT: the situation in which communication takes place.

DEVELOPMENTAL APPROACH: focuses more on qualitative aspects of the relationship and information exchanged when defining IPC.

INTERACTIONAL APPROACH: treats most, if not all, cases of social interaction as instances of interpersonal communication.

INTERPERSONAL COMMUNICATION (IPC): a complex process that occurs in a specific context and involves an exchange of verbal or nonverbal messages between two connected individuals with the intent to achieve shared meaning.

INTRAPERSONAL COMMUNICATION: takes place inside your head and is silent and repetitive.

KINESICS: refers to the use of body movements and gestures as forms of communication.

KNOWLEDGE: component of the communication competence model that refers to understanding what reaction or action is best suited for a particular situation.

MASLOW'S HIERARCHY OF NEEDS: a model that depicts our basic human needs.

MASS COMMUNICATION: involves communicators who are typically separated in both space and time and who send and receive messages indirectly; typically occurs when a small number of people send messages to a large, diverse, and geographically widespread population.

MESSAGE-CENTERED APPROACH: addresses limitations in the other approaches and argues that definitions should emphasize processes involved in producing and interpreting messages.

MOTIVATION: component of the communication competence model that refers to the desire to achieve results in a competent manner.

METACOMMUNICATION: an important tool that is often used during social interaction to increase our shared meaning and to reduce uncertainty about the status of our relationships; "communicating about communication."

ORGANIZATIONAL COMMUNICATION: communication that occurs within businesses or organizations; takes place between organization members within a clear hierarchical structure; individuals are typically encouraged to adhere to roles and rules established within this structure.

PROCESS: includes message production, message reception, and message interpretation.

PROXEMICS: refers to the role of space in IPC.

RELATIONAL COMPONENT: composed of information that indicates how people feel about their relationship.

ROLES: parts that people play.

RULES: guidelines for social interaction.

SHARED MEANING: the source and receiver agree on the meaning of the verbal and nonverbal messages exchanged; primary goal of interpersonal communication.

SITUATIONAL APPROACH: focuses on the specific features or aspects of the communication context in defining the type of communication taking place.

SKILL: component of the communication competence model that addresses the ability to utilize the appropriate behaviors in a situation.

SMALL GROUP COMMUNICATION: interaction among a small group of people who share a common purpose or goal, who feel a sense of belonging to the group, and who exert influence on one another.

SYMBOLIC INTERACTIONISM: a theory based on the premise that people form meanings based on the symbols used in interactions.

THEORY: a set of statements about the way things work.

VERBAL AND NONVERBAL COMPONENT: IPC consists of both verbal (words/symbols) and nonverbal (everything else other than the words exchanged) messages.

REFERENCES

Barden, D. M. (2013). Not dressing the part, and other interview markers. *Chronicle of Higher Education, 59,* 38–39.

Bateson, G. (1951). Information and codification: A philosophical approach. In J. Ruesch and G. Bateson (Eds.), *Communication: The social matrix of psychiatry.* New York: Wiley and Sons.

Bateson, G. (1972). *Steps to an ecology of mind.* New York: Ballantine Books.

Baxter, L. (1982). Strategies for ending relationships: Two studies. *The Western Journal of Speech Communication, 46,* 223–241.

Beebe, S. A., & Masterson, J. T. (1997). *Communicating in small groups* (5th ed.). New York: Addison-Wesley Longman.

Berlo, D. K. (1960). *The process of communication.* San Francisco: Rinehart.

Birdwhistell, R. L. (1952). *Introduction to kinesics: An annotation system for analysis of body motion and gesture.* Washington, DC: U.S. Department of State, Foreign Service Institute.

Blumer, H. (1969). *Symbolic interactionism: Perspective and method.* Englewood Cliffs, NJ: Prentice-Hall.

Burleson, B. R. (2010). The nature of interpersonal communication: A message-centered approach. In C.R. Burger, M.E. Roloff, & D.R. Roskos-Ewoldsen (Eds.), *Handbook of communication science* (2nd ed.) (pp. 145–163). Thousand Oaks, CA: Sage.

Burleson, B. R., & MacGeorge, E. L. (2002). Supportive communication. In M. L. Knapp & J. A. Daly (Eds.), *Handbook of interpersonal communication* (pp. 374–424). Thousand Oaks, CA: Sage.

Burleson, B. R., & Samter, W. (1996). Similarity in the communication skills of young adults: Foundations of attraction, friendship, and relationship satisfaction. *Communication Reports, 9,* 127–139.

Canary, D. J., & Stafford, L. (2001). Equity in the preservation of personal relationships. In J. H. Harvey & A. Wenzel (Eds.), *Close romantic relationships: Maintenance and enhancement* (pp. 133–151). Mahwah, NJ: Lawrence Erlbaum.

Cappella, J. N. (1987). Interpersonal communication: Definitions and fundamental questions. In C. R. Berger & S. H. Chaffee (Eds.), *Handbook of communication science.* Newbury Park, CA: Sage.

Casciaro, T., & Lobo, M. S. (2005). Fool vs. jerk: Whom would you hire? *HBS Working Knowledge.* N.p., 25 July 2005. Web. 10 July 2013.

Casserly, M. (2012). The student loan debt crisis is a women's issue: Here's why. *Forbes.* Forbes Magazine, 19 Nov. 2012. Web. 24 Oct. 2013.

Cathcart, R., & Gumpert, G. (1983). Mediated interpersonal communication: Toward a new typology. *Quarterly Journal of Speech, 69,* 267–277.

Cody, M. (1982). A typology of disengagement strategies and an examination of the role intimacy, reactions to inequity, and relational problems play in strategy selection. *Communication Monographs, 49,* 148–170.

Darby, B. W., & Schlenker, B. R. (1982). Children's reactions to apologies. *Journal of Personality and Social Psychology, 43,* 742–753.

DeVito, J. (2001). *The interpersonal communication book* (9th ed.). New York: Addison Wesley Longman Inc.

Giffin, K., & Patton, B. R. (1971). *Fundamentals of interpersonal communication.* New York, NY: Harper & Row.

Goffman, E. (1959). *The presentation of self in everyday life.* Garden City, NY: Doubleday.

Goleman, D. (2006). *Social intelligence: The new science of human relationships.* New York, NY: Bantam Dell.

Hall, E. T. (1959). *The silent language.* Garden City, NY: Doubleday.

Heider, F. (1958). *The psychology of interpersonal relations.* New York, NY: Wiley.

Keltner, J. W. (1970). *Interpersonal speech-communication: Elements and structures.* Belmont, CA: Wadsworth.

Knapp, M. L., & Vangelisti, A. (2000). *Interpersonal communication and human relationships.* Boston: Allyn & Bacon.

Knapp, M. L., Daly, J. A., Albada, K. F., & Miller, G. R. (2002). Background and current trends in the study of interpersonal communication. In M. L. Knapp & J. A. Daly (Eds.), *Handbook of interpersonal communication* (pp. 3–20). Thousand Oaks, CA: Sage.

Kreps, G. L., & Thorton, B. C. (1992). *Health communication: Theory & practice.* Prospect Heights, IL: Waveland Press.

Maslow, A. H. (1943). A theory of human motivation. *Psychological Review, 50,* 370–396.

McCroskey, J. C., Larson, C., & Knapp, M. L. (1971). *An introduction to interpersonal communication.* Englewood Cliffs, NJ: Prentice-Hall.

Metts, S., & Planap, S. (2002). Emotional communication. In M. L. Knapp & J. A. Daly (Eds.), *Handbook of interpersonal communication* (pp. 339–373). Thousand Oaks, CA: Sage.

Miller, G. R. (1978). The current status of theory and research in interpersonal communication. *Human Communication Research, 4,* 164–178.

Miller, G. R. (1990). Interpersonal communication. In G. L. Dahnke & G. W. Clatterbuck (Eds.), *Human communication: Theory and research* (pp. 91-122). Belmont, CA: Wadsworth.

Myers, L. L., & Tucker, M. L. (2005). Increasing awareness of emotional intelligence in a business curriculum. *Business Communication Quarterly, 68,* 44–51.

Noller, P., & Feeney, J. A. (1994). Relationship satisfaction, attachment and nonverbal accuracy in early marriage. *Journal of Nonverbal Behavior, 18,* 199–222.

Omarzu, J., Whalen, J., & Harvey, J. H. (2001). How well do you mind your relationship? A preliminary scale to test the minding theory of relating. In Harvey, J. & A. Wenzel. (Eds.), *Close romantic relationships: Maintenance and enhancement* (pp. 345–356). Mahwah, NJ: Lawrence Erlbaum.

Peterson, M. S. (1997). Personnel interviewers' perceptions of the importance and adequacy of applicants' communication skills. *Communication Education, 46,* 287–291.

Piaget, J. (1926). *The language and thought of the child.* New York: Harcourt Brace.

Rath, D., Poldre, P., Fisher, B. J., Laidlaw, J. C., Cowan, D. H., & Bakker, D. (1998). Commitment of a cancer organization to a program for training in communication skills. *Journal of Cancer Education: The Official Journal of the American Association for Cancer Education, 13,* 203–206.

Roloff, M. E., & Soule, K. P. (2002). Interpersonal conflict: A review. In M. L. Knapp & J. A. Daly (Eds.), *Handbook of interpersonal communication* (pp. 475–528). Thousand Oaks, CA: Sage.

Sbarra, D. A., Law, R. W., & Portley, R. M. (2011). *Divorce and death: A meta-analysis and research agenda for clinical, social, and health psychology.* Thousand Oaks, CA: Sage.

Schlenker, B. R., & Darby, B. R. (1981). The use of apologies in social predicaments. *Social Psychology Quarterly, 44,* 271–278.

Schutz, W. (1966). *The interpersonal underworld* (pp. 13–20). Palo Alto, CA: Science and Behavior Books.

Shankar, A., McMunn, A., Banks, J., & Steptoe, A. (2011). Loneliness, social isolation, and behavioral and biological health indicators in older adults. *NCBI.* U.S. National Library of Medicine, 30 July 2011. Web.

Spitzberg, B. H., & Cupach, W. R. (1984). *Interpersonal communication competence.* Beverly Hills, CA: Sage.

Turkle, S. (2012). The flight from conversation." *The New York Times.* N.p., 21 Apr. 2012. Web. 2 July 2012.

Wanzer, M. B., Booth-Butterfield, M., & Gruber, K. (2004). Perceptions of health care providers' communication: Relationships between patient-centered communication and satisfaction. *Health Communication, 16,* 363–384.

Watzlawick, P., Beavin, J., & Jackson, D. D. (1967). *Pragmatics of human communication.* New York: Norton.

Wood, J. T. (2000). *Communication theories in action.* Wadsworth: Belmont, CA.

chapter 2

The Role of Interpersonal Communication
in the Development of Self

OBJECTIVES

- Define the term self and explain why it is viewed as a complex process.

- Define self-complexity and explain two benefits of high self-complexity.

- Explain the three components of the self-system and discuss how each component affects interpersonal communication.

- Discuss the development of the self with special emphasis on individuals and groups of individuals who play important roles in identity formation.

- Explain attachment theory, including the three attachment styles that affect the way individuals view the self and others.

- State the importance of direct definitions and identity scripts.

- Discuss the significance of the self-fulfilling prophecy and social comparison processes in the process of identify formation.

SCENARIO: SOUND FAMILIAR?

Marcus is a student athlete who plays soccer for his university. As Marcus walks to his first class, his thoughts are focused solely on last night's devastating loss to his team's conference rival. He knows he will not be able to focus on his statistics class this morning and so he decides to skip. He glances at his phone, sees that his mother has called him and decides to ignore her call, yet again. His thoughts continually return to his team's loss last night and his performance.

OVERVIEW

This scenario depicts a student athlete who possesses a number of different sub-selves or self-aspects. Marcus is a student, an athlete, a relationship partner, and a son, among other roles, traits, or characteristics. Marcus regularly evaluates himself in these roles and, not sur-

Before we can share information about ourselves with others, *we have to be clear about who we are and how we differ from those around us.*

cause it helps us to understand who we are and why we are this way. Before we can share information about ourselves with others, *we have to be clear about who we are and how we differ from those around us.* Throughout our lives there will be many times we will need to share information about ourselves. For example, when a job interviewer says, "Tell me about yourself," it will be important for you to share relevant information about yourself. The information you share about yourself during this job interview will influence how others evaluate and perceive you. Similarly, when you go on a first date, it is very likely your date will ask you this same question. The information you choose to share with your date will influence how your date perceives you and whether or not the relationship progresses.

prisingly, these positive and negative self-evaluations affect his interpersonal communication and relationships. Similar to Marcus, all of us have different self-aspects that define who we are, what we do each day, and how we relate to those around us. Like Marcus, we also evaluate how we are performing these roles or self-aspects and make changes based on this process. In this chapter we will take a close look at important aspects of the self as well as the role of interpersonal communication in the development of the self. We define constructs related to the self that impact self-perceptions, interpersonal communication, and relationships. The primary goals of this chapter are: (1) to understand the self and how it is formed, and (2) to understand how self-perceptions affect our communication and relationships with others.

IMPORTANCE OF STUDYING THE PROCESS OF IDENTITY FORMATION

Exploring the communicative and relational processes that affect the development of the self either positively or negatively is important be-

© Blend Images/Shutterstock.com

How could her performance on the basketball court affect other aspects of this athlete's day?

Once we understand differences in how individuals develop a sense of self as well as the processes associated with the development of a more positive self-perception, we can hopefully coach individuals to interact more competently with those around them. As Houck and Spegman (1999) argue, "Given its manifestation of social competence, the development of the self is of fundamental importance not only to the well-being of individuals, but also to the well-being of others with whom they associate" (p. 2).

The next sections of this chapter offer a definition of the term self, an overview of concepts related to the self, and an explanation of individuals who affect self-perceptions. In the final sections of the chapter we offer suggestions for improving self-perceptions as well as communication and relationships with others.

DEFINITION OF SELF

While individuals use the term "self" frequently and with relative ease, it is quite challenging for researchers to offer a single consistent definition for the term (Baumeister, 1998). The self has been defined as a psychological entity consisting of "an organized set of beliefs, feelings, and behaviors" (Tesser, Wood, & Stapel, 2002, p. 10). Another way of understanding the self is as a complex system made up of a variety of interdependent elements that attain self-organization (Vallacher & Nowak, 2000). In attempting to explain the self, theorists often emphasize the origins of self, noting that it emerges through communication and established relationships with others and is constantly developing and evolving (Epstein, 1973; Park & Waters, 1988).

SELF AS A PROCESS

Take a moment to consider how your self-perceptions have changed over the years. Do you feel you are the same person you were five, ten, or fifteen years ago? You have probably changed and matured a great deal over the years and see yourself as being quite different from when you were younger. Thus, your perception of self is often described as a process because it evolves and is largely determined by ongoing communication with others. This idea is further validated by social psychologist Arthur Aron (2003) who says, "What we are and what we see ourselves as being seems to be constantly under construction and reconstruction, with the architects and remodeling contractors largely being those with whom we have close interactions" (p. 443). In later sections of this chapter we explore the specific individuals and processes that exert the greatest influence in shaping our self-perceptions.

SELF-COMPLEXITY

The self is also recognized as highly complex and multidimensional. Researchers agree that there are numerous dimensions, or aspects, of the self that make up one overall perception of the self. For example, on any given day, you may assume the roles of student, employee, son, brother, friend, teammate, or roommate. For each one of these labels, we may have additional self-aspects that further define how we see ourselves. For example, for the "teammate" self-aspect, an individual may also describe himself as "competitive" and "talented." Indeed, the process of describing oneself is a complicated one that is constantly evolving based on our experiences (Schleicher & McConnell, 2005).

Researchers have examined how individuals vary in their **self-complexity** or number of self-aspects or sub-selves. Individuals possessing higher levels of self-complexity reap a number of personal benefits. What does it mean to possess higher levels of self-complexity? Referring back to the earlier example of Marcus, the student athlete, if he views his multiple roles (son, roommate, boyfriend, athlete, teammate, friend, etc.) as separate or unique, and at the same time has encountered a number of life experiences associated with those roles, then he probably has a greater number of non-overlapping self-aspects, or higher self-complexity. On the other hand, if Marcus views himself only in two closely related roles, e.g., teammate and student, has limited life experiences associated with these roles, and is unable to separate these self-aspects and experiences, he will report lower self-complexity.

Individuals with higher self-complexity may be less prone to having mood fluctuations (Linville, 1985) and may cope better with stress (Koch & Shepperd, 2004). When individuals report lower self-complexity, they are more likely to experience negative effects in response to a negative life event than someone who reports higher self-complexity. Individuals with lower self-complexity may not be able to separate the limited roles they assume and may experience what researchers call "spillover." Thus, a student athlete who has a bad game may not be able to separate his experience on the soccer field ("me as a

soccer player") from his experience in the classroom ("me as a student"), and the negative affect from the soccer game will expand, or spill over, to other self-aspects (Koch & Shepperd, 2004).

Individuals possessing higher levels of self-complexity reap a number of personal benefits.

Higher self-complexity may actually act as a buffer for people by allowing them to mentally separate themselves from painful life events (Linville, 1987). Furthermore, the buffer effect has direct interpersonal, or relational, implications. The **buffer effect** was observed for those higher in self-complexity faced with relationship dissolution. Individuals higher in self-complexity thought about the relationship less and were less upset about their relationships ending than individuals lower in self-complexity (Linville, 1987).

The social psychology literature points to a number of self-aspects related to interpersonal communication and to relationship development processes. While there are countless constructs that could potentially be covered in the next sections (i.e., self-handicapping, self-efficacy, self-schemas, etc.), we focus on several that are closely related to interpersonal communication and relationship formation.

SELF-AWARENESS AND COMMUNICATION

Another important concept associated with the self is self-awareness or one's ability to understand the self and discriminate one's behavior from the surrounding environment (Dymond & Barnes, 1997). Acquisition of self-knowledge or self-awareness requires us to engage in communication with others. For example, when a classmate asks you, "How are you feeling?" or "What are you doing after class?" you must reflect on your feelings and behavior and respond to these questions. This process is an important one that is described as both discriminative and evaluative (Dymond & Barnes, 1997). Before we can get to know others, it is important for us to understand ourselves.

According to the theory of objective self-awareness (OSA), individuals will occasionally focus inward and engage in a process of comparing their current self with some standard or expected behavior or goal (Duval & Wicklund, 1972). This process is important because, if the current self is not measuring up to the "ideal" or expected standard of self, this results in a gap and can trigger negative feelings about the self (Silvia & Duval, 2001). OSA has been the dominant theory used to explain this process. Silvia and Duval (2001) describe the changes to OSA theory over the years that have resulted from a significant body of research in this area. They draw two important conclusions related to *when* and *why* individuals will act on a gap between the current self and the standard self:

- When individuals feel the self/standard gap is manageable and they can make sufficient progress in reducing the gap.
- The individual's causes or explanations for the self/standard discrepancy are factored into the process and whether individuals will change.

To apply OSA, think about a time when you reflected on whether or not you were a "good" relationship partner. Perhaps you felt you were not exhibiting the behaviors associated with being a good partner (i.e., there was a self/standard gap). If you attributed the gap to your own behaviors ("I am being lazy") and perceived the changes needed as reasonable ("I will call my partner more often"), you would probably make an attempt to reduce the self/standard gap.

As stated before, the concept of the "self" is complicated. Social psychologists and sociologists argue that people possess multiple perceptions of the self-concept, or different personas (Bargh, McKenna, & Fitzsimons, 2002). For example, Goffman (1959) and Jung (1953) draw distinctions between a "public" self, or the self we project during social interaction, and an "inner" self that we keep private and that may reflect how we really feel about ourselves. The public self is described as our "actual" self-concept while the inner self is presented as our "true" or our authentic self.

A construct related to self-awareness is authenticity. According to Kernis (2003) authenticity refers to "the unobstructed operation of one's true or core self in one's daily enterprise" (p. 13). Individuals who are self-aware are more likely to be authentic, which means they project an image of themselves that is real or consistent with their attitudes, beliefs, and values. Wright (2008) draws some interesting conclusions about the benefits and challenges of living an authentic life:

- Between 18 and 24 months infants become aware of their own thoughts and feelings and begin a potentially lifelong process of identifying their "true" self.
- Teens and twenty-somethings seem to be constantly experimenting with new friends, fashions, hobbies, jobs, relationship partners, and living arrangements to determine what works and what's "just not me" (p. 72).
- In addition to evaluating our own authenticity, we form judgments of others based on how "real" or "fake" people act.
- Authentic people cope better with adversity and are less likely to resort to unproductive coping methods such as drugs or alcohol.

Displaying the authentic self is not an easy task. Many people worry that if they allow others to know their true selves they may be rejected by those individuals.

Not surprisingly, the extent to which someone is authentic or not affects the way they communicate. Researchers found interesting relationships among college students' self-reported authenticity, mindfulness, and verbal defensiveness (Lakey, Kernis, Heppner, & Lance, 2008). College students who reported higher levels of authenticity also reported higher levels of mindfulness or the ability to be aware of one's surroundings and environment. In addition, the higher the college students' authenticity and mindfulness scores

were, the lower these individuals scored in verbal defensiveness. Stated simply, college students scoring high in authenticity were more likely to be mindful of their surroundings and less likely to become defensive when faced with negative information about themselves than college students scoring lower in authenticity. Authentic people are more likely to be realistic about their strengths and weaknesses and therefore are less likely to "defend" themselves when confronted with negative self-relevant information.

How do people express themselves over the Internet in ways they may not in person?

One place where some individuals may feel more comfortable expressing their true or authentic selves is on the Internet (Bargh & McKenna, 2004). According to researchers, the anonymity of the Internet gives people the chance to express self-aspects they may not feel comfortable sharing in their social groups (Bargh & McKenna, 2004). Researchers have drawn a number of interesting conclusions about how and why people use the Internet to express themselves and to establish relationships (Bargh & McKenna):

- Online relationships appear to be *highly similar* to those developed via face-to-face interaction, in terms of their breadth, depth, and quality.

- Relationships formed via the Internet *often become* face-to-face friendships.
- College students *felt more comfortable* expressing their "true" selves over the Internet than when meeting face-to-face.

While some studies point to negative effects (i.e., increased loneliness and depression for users; see Nie, 2001) of the Internet and social networking sites, others indicate the opposite. While there are clear benefits associated with forming relationships on the Internet such as relative anonymity, which allows for greater self-expression and the ability to connect with others who have similar values and interests, there are also drawbacks to this form of communication. Chapter 11 explores how and why people use mediated communication to establish relationships in much greater detail.

THE SELF-SYSTEM

We now turn our attention to the self-system. Importantly, all three parts of the self-system (self-concept, self-esteem, and self-regulation) affect how and why we communicate with others.

Figure 1. Components of the Self-System

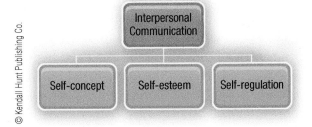

© Kendall Hunt Publishing Co.

An individual's self-concept is based on all of the feedback received from others over time.

Self-Concept

Houck and Spegman describe the **self-concept** as a cognitive construct, which is a "descriptive reference to the self, or a definition of the nature and beliefs about the self's qualities" (Houck & Spegman 1999, p. 2). In the most basic sense, self-concept refers to people's thoughts or cognitions about themselves. These thoughts or cognitions about the self are derived from life experiences and reflections on those events (Reeve, 2009).

An individual's self-concept is based on all of the feedback received from others over time. In any given day you receive feedback on everything from your choice in shoes to your personality traits! Over time this feedback is aggregated and acts as "building blocks" in the formation of the self (Reeve, 2009). For example, Marcus, our student athlete from earlier in the chapter, has the following thoughts about himself:

- Coach told me I worked really hard during practice today.

- I scored the most goals in the championship game at the end of last season, and my team carried me off the field!
- My friend Bob told me that I sacrifice a lot of time with friends and family to play soccer.
- When I have free time I like to spend it doing different outdoor activities with my family.

The above observations reflect a small sample of Marcus's life experiences that are combined to create an overall self-perception. Thus, Marcus's self-concept might be that he is a "dedicated or talented soccer player who likes to spend time with his family" (Reeve, 2009). This perception will influence every aspect of his interpersonal communication, which might range from who he talks with (e.g., coaches, fellow athletes, family members) to what he talks about with these individuals (e.g., soccer games, practices, soccer apparel, family activities).

Three of these areas of research—*the relationship between self-concept and social perception, self-concept and partner choice, and self-concept and interaction strategies*—are particularly interesting and relevant to understanding how and why our self-concept affects our interpersonal communication with others.

Much of the research on the relationship between *self-concept and social perception* concludes that people are likely to view others as relatively similar to themselves (Markus & Wurf, 1987). When you interact with your friends, family members, and coworkers, you perceive them to be more similar than dissimilar to you in attitudes, beliefs, values, goals, and behaviors. From an interpersonal communication perspective, similarity is related to interpersonal attraction and is an important variable that affects our interactions with others. Expressing similarity to another can be used strategically as an affinity-seeking behavior (Bell & Daly, 1984).

Affinity-seeking strategies are verbal and nonverbal tactics used to gain liking from others (Bell & Daly, 1984). One way to feel good about ourselves is to be liked by others. Communication researchers asked college students to generate a list of all the verbal and nonverbal behaviors they used to get others to like them. Importantly, all of the examples generated by the students had to be communicative, which meant they had to "refer to messages and/or alterations of a person's self-presentation for the purpose of achieving the liking of another" (Bell & Daly, 1984, p. 96). In addition to "expressing similarity" to gain liking, the following strategies are enacted to create more favorable impressions:

1. Altruism—helping someone by assisting them with a task.
2. Concede control—allowing the other person to have control over events or social arrangements.
3. Elicit disclosures—encouraging the other person to share opinions on different topics.
4. Openness—sharing personal information with another person.
5. Optimism—focusing on positive comments made about others and sharing positive information.

Bell and Daly identified a total of 25 different affinity-seeking strategies used by college students to gain liking with peers. Not surprisingly, teachers, coaches, and managers all use affinity-seeking strategies to increase liking and improve communication in their relationships.

36

How can a supervisor influence an employee's self-concept?

Self-concept also affects both the choice of relationship partners and subsequent behavior in those relationships (Markus & Wurf, 1987). Research on the relationship between self-perception and relationship satisfaction indicates that individuals report greater relationship satisfaction when they choose partners who validate views of themselves (Schlenker, 1984; Swann, 1985). It is not surprising to learn that we choose friends and relationship partners who will validate our self-perceptions. For example, if you view yourself as a humorous person, you probably try to surround yourself with individuals who also describe you this way. Individuals may confirm this by laughing at your jokes or saying outright that you are a funny person.

Much of the research on the role of the *self-concept in social interaction* has examined the process of impression management during interpersonal encounters (Markus & Wurf, 1987). Not surprisingly, individuals work diligently to present a particular image of themselves to others (Goffman, 1959; Greenwald & Breckler, 1985). **Impression management** is the process of controlling how one is viewed by others to achieve positive impressions (Goffman, 1959).

There are two important elements to impression management: impression motivation and impression construction (Leary & Kowalski, 1990). **Impression motivation** is defined as the extent to which people are motivated to achieve desirable impressions. Stated simply, some people are just more concerned about how others see them. **Impression construction** refers to the use of specific strategies or tactics to create desirable impressions. This would involve the use of **impression management techniques** such as deception or even altering one's appearance. Using these strategies consciously and effectively is linked to heightened self-awareness (Schlenker, 1985). When individuals have a clear idea of the image they want to project to others, they will exhibit strategies to help them achieve desired impressions. While we may not always be aware of our impression management efforts, our day-to-day choice of dress, hairstyle, accessories, and

> When individuals have a clear idea of the image they want to project to others, they will exhibit strategies to help them achieve desired impressions.

choice of words are selected strategically to project a specific desired image of ourselves to those around us. Think about the choices you make when deciding what to wear and how to style your hair in various social situations. It is highly likely that impression management played a role in your decisions.

Not surprisingly, impression management also plays a role in how people use social networking sites like Facebook. Research by Mendelson and Papacharissi (2010) examined college students' photos posted on Facebook (FB) and recorded a number of interesting observations:

- The photos posted on FB depicted college students in conventional or expected ways. For example, photos were often taken at important social events like prom or graduation.
- Females had more photos on their pages than males (female average number of photos was 337 and male was 93).
- Photos depicted the importance of relationships to college students. They were often photographed in groups of same-sex friends.

Prior to Facebook, researchers interested in impression management focused almost exclusively on face-to-face strategies. However, because people now use the computer as a means of constructing impressions, it is important understand how and why individuals use computer-mediated strategies.

Self-Esteem

The second part of the self-system is **self-esteem**, defined as the subjective perception of one's self-worth, or the value one places on the self (Houck & Spegman, 1999). Self-esteem can be measured objectively (see, for example, Rosenberg's Self-Esteem Scale; 1995), unlike self-concept, which is a highly dynamic and subjective construct. Research indicates that individuals vary in their reported levels of self-esteem. Those reporting higher levels of self-esteem feel more favorable about themselves and their behaviors than individuals with lower self-esteem.

© Andresr/Shutterstock.com

How can a teacher influence a child's self-esteem?

What is the relationship between self-esteem and interpersonal communication and relationship success? Individuals who report higher self-esteem typically indicate that they are well-liked and attractive, have better relationships, and make more positive impressions on others than those reporting lower levels of self-esteem. When researchers further investigated whether high self-esteem individuals were perceived this way by others using objective measures, the results were disconfirmed. Researchers further explain this finding by noting that individuals with high self-esteem may eventually alienate those around them by communicating in ways that are perceived by others as inappropriate and

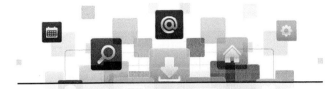

Individuals who report higher self-esteem typically indicate that they are well-liked and attractive, have better relationships, and make more positive impressions on others than those reporting lower levels of self-esteem.

ineffective (Baumeister et al., 2003). Individuals with very high self-esteem might not be as focused on others in conversations as they need to be to establish meaningful relationships.

The connection between self-esteem and the quality of romantic and platonic relationships is small to moderate, at best (Aron, 2003). Some research identified a small consistent relationship between self-esteem and marital satisfaction and success over time (see, for example, Aube & Koestner, 1992; Karney & Bradbury, 1995). Based on research conducted thus far, couples' reported self-esteem does not appear to be a major predictor of marital satisfaction or persistence.

Self-Regulation

The third and final component of the self-system, self-regulation, is regarded by some as a highly significant component of human existence (Bargh & Chartrand, 1999). **Self-regulation** is defined as individuals' ability to reflect on and monitor goals they establish (Reeve, 2009). Self-regulation

allows us to pursue and engage in goal-directed activity and keep track of our performance. It is important to study the process of self-regulation to understand how and why individuals are motivated to achieve different communication goals. Research in this area examines aspects of initiative, motivation, and decision making in relation to morality and developing a conscience. It also sets out to discover why some individuals are motivated to achieve goals and others are not. The process of self-regulation can occur at either a conscious or a subconscious level (Bargh & Chartrand, 1999). You probably exert self-regulation in all of your day-to-day interactions, whether you are aware of the process or not.

How do people acquire the ability to self-regulate? Reeve (2009) describes the four stages or phases of developing the ability to self-regulate: observation, imitation, self-control, and self-regulation. In the movie *Hitch* Will Smith's character, Alex "Hitch" Hitchens, is a professional "date doctor" who provides all types of dating advice for men who need help meeting women. Hitch's client, Albert Brennaman, played by Kevin James, must observe, imitate, exercise self-control, and self-regulate a number of "typical" dating behaviors such as dancing, kissing, touching, and talking to women. To learn more about Albert's self-regulation successes and failures, we encourage you to watch the movie *Hitch*.

What is the relationship between self-regulation and interpersonal communication and relationships? Baumeister and Vohs (2003) offer several examples of how the process of self-regulation is related to interpersonal communication and relationships. Problems such as interpersonal violence between relationship partners and infidelity are obviously linked in some way to failures in self-regulation. Self-regulation is closely related to successful maintenance of close romantic relationships (Baumeister & Vohs, 2003). Related research by Finkel and Campbell (2001) indicated that individuals reporting higher levels of self-regulation were more likely to exhibit accommodating behaviors in their romantic relationships. Not surprisingly, most individuals prefer being in relationships with partners who are accommodating, or willing to compromise, to meet each other's needs.

The extent to which one *communicates effectively and appropriately* with others is also linked to self-regulation or initiative. Recall from Chapter 1 our discussion of Spitzberg and Cupach's (1984) model of communication competence and its three components. This model advances the significance of motivation or initiative in communicating effectively with others. While individuals may possess the skills and knowledge necessary for communicating effectively, if they are not motivated to do so, they will not enact the appropriate behavior. Thus, the process of self-regulation directly affects our communication abilities and the quality of interpersonal relationships.

Now that we understand the three main components of the self-system and their relationship to interpersonal communication, we move to the discussion of the development of self. Two important questions to consider are: Which individuals or groups of individuals are most influential in forming or shaping our self-perceptions? And why?

INTERPERSONAL COMMUNICATION AND THE DEVELOPMENT OF SELF

Most scholars agree that the self emerges and develops through communication with those to whom we are close (see, for example, Aron, 2003). What exactly does this mean? This statement implies that, as infants, we do not possess a sense of self, but that one develops through our interactions with significant others (Cooley, 1902; Mead, 1934).

Cooley (1902) was the first to advance the **"looking glass self"** construct, which describes the significant impact of interpersonal communication on the development of self. This concept focuses on the role that our interactions with others play in identity formation. Researchers (Felson, 1989) extended the concept of looking glass self to include the term **reflected appraisal**, referring to the tendency to view ourselves based on the appraisals of others. Who are these significant others who affect our self-perceptions? Researchers have generally studied the influence of the following individuals in shaping our identity: (1) family, (2) peers, and (3) relationship partners. In the next sections we review the importance of interpersonal communication with family, peers, and relationship partners as it relates to the construction and reconstruction of the self over time.

Family

Family plays a significant role in the development of one's identity. One theory that has received a lot of attention from researchers interested in the connection between family, identity formation, and interpersonal relationships is **attachment theory**. John Bowlby (1969, 1973, 1980) developed attachment theory to address the significance of the relationship between children and their primary caregiver. This theory "asserts that personality (or attachment style) develops through social interaction with others in close relationships, and that attachment styles, in turn, play a life-long role in shaping behavior in close relationships" (Rholes, Paetzold, & Friedman, 2008, p. 118). Communication between the child and primary caregiver plays a pivotal role in creating the security associated with this attachment. The attachment children establish with their parents affects everything from our relationship partner selection to our relationship stability (Firestone, 2013).

How does the interaction within the family develop one's identity?

According to Firestone (2013) attachment patterns are formed in early childhood and function as a working model for different types of relationships into adulthood. Researchers describe three different attachment styles that develop out of parenting practices and affect how individuals see themselves and how they relate to others: secure, avoidant, and anxious (Ainsworth et al., 1978;

Rholes et al., 2008). These three styles were identified in Ainsworth et al.'s (1978) research, which employed the "Strange Situation Paradigm" to study how primary caregivers (often mothers) and children interact with each other after being separated from each other for a period of time. Importantly, this seminal research paved the way for many follow-up studies addressing the *significance of the parent-child bond in identity development and relationships.* Complete the measures at the end of the chapter to learn more about your attachment style.

ATTACHMENT STYLES

When the primary caregiver behaves in a loving, supportive, and nurturing way toward her child, the child is likely to develop a **secure attachment**. A secure attachment is often "characterized by intense feelings of intimacy, emotional security, and physical safety when the infant is in the presence of the attachment figure" (Peluso, Peluso, White, & Kern, 2004, p. 140). Because children raised in a secure environment typically have a history of responsive and supportive caretaking from their caregivers (Ainsworth et al., 1978), these experiences lead the children to believe others will act in a supportive and caring way as well.

Children who develop secure attachment styles are confident in their interpersonal relationships with their peers (Park & Waters, 1988). Their first exposure to relationships in the family context helps them formulate expectations for all of their subsequent relationships (Bowlby, 1973; Sroufe, 1988). Secure children, whose previous relationship experiences are generally positive, expect people in future encounters to act similarly, and therefore behave accordingly. Secure children recreate communication patterns and practices they experienced with their primary caregivers when interacting with peers, ultimately leading to more positive peer relationships (Sroufe, 1988).

In what ways is this father helping his son develop a secure attachment?

Adults reporting secure attachments tend to be happier in their romantic relationships than adults reporting insecure attachment styles (i.e., anxious and avoidant styles). Secure individuals establish productive relationships with their primary caregiver, and this provides them with the confidence needed to take risks and seek out others to form relationships (Firestone, 2013). In addition, secures are confident seeking out support from others during stressful times because they expect to receive the assistance and affirmation they need from others. Their ability to maintain a strong sense of self, manage needs for closeness and autonomy, and exhibit responsiveness in relationships contributes to their ability to maintain healthy relationships (Rholes et al., 2008).

When mothers are consistently negative or unresponsive when children need to be consoled, children develop an avoidant attachment style. In cases where children developed this attachment style, they did not seek out care or support from mothers when they were upset. These children would avoid their mothers and exhibited an unusual amount of independence for their age (Rholes et al., 2008).

Adults with avoidant attachment styles develop unhealthy or dysfunctional working models of relationships. Avoidant individuals are independent and view those who seek out support from others as weak or unstable. Not surprisingly, they do not seek out support and assistance from others during difficult times because they do not expect it to be there. These tendencies negatively affect their relationships. The psychological distance they maintain from their relationship partners during stressful times creates a number of problems in their relationships (Rholes et al., 2008).

While avoidant individuals might report higher levels of self-esteem, they tend to exhibit low levels of both trust and interdependence with relationship partners (Rholes et al., 2008). Individuals who display an avoidant attachment style may act in an unresponsive and insensitive way toward their relationship partners because they do not trust them and because they expect to be rejected by their partner at some point in the relationship (Rholes et al., 2008).

The last attachment style, anxious (also referred to as anxious ambivalent), is a result of inconsistent caregiver behavior with children. When mothers exhibit an inconsistent pattern of both responsive and attentive behavior, children develop an anxious attachment style. Similar to the avoidant attachment style, this parenting approach results in an unhealthy working model of relationships. When children were faced with this inconsistent type of caregiver behavior, they exhibited a number of negative emotional reactions. For example, children "were conflicted, hypervigilant, and angry, engaging in less exploration while making inconsistent attempts to obtain support from their mothers when they become distressed" (Rholes et al. 2008, p. 119).

Similar to individuals who display an avoidant attachment style, anxious individuals also experience problems in their interpersonal relationships. Adults with an anxious attachment style feel a great amount of anxiety at the thought of being abandoned and report low self-esteem and negative self-images (Rholes et al., 2008). Individuals with anxious attachment styles report less trust in their relationship partners than do secures. In addition, anxious individuals perceive less social support in their relationships, and this may be explained in part by their pessimistic perceptions of relationships (Collins and Feeney, 2004).

There is an extensive amount of scholarship on the relationship between attachment styles and identity development and attachment styles and relationship satisfaction. Dr. Linda Firestone (2013), clinical psychologist and author, draws a number of important conclusions and recommendations about the impact of attachment styles:

1. Sixty percent of people report secure attachments, 20 percent report avoidant, and 20 percent report anxious.
2. It is important to recognize your attachment style and, if it is insecure (anxious or avoidant), make an attempt to seek out relationships with individuals who are secure.
3. In some cases therapy can help individuals who have developed insecure attachment styles.
4. Being aware of your attachment style is an important first step in learning why you might have certain relationship challenges.
5. These styles can change in adulthood if adults challenge these poor working models of relationships and develop new ones.

DIRECT DEFINITIONS

Many of you have probably heard your parents describe your talents, personality traits, or other attributes in detail to other family members, friends, or even total strangers. **Direct definitions** are descriptions, or labels, families assign to their members that affect the way we see and define ourselves (Wood, 2001). A child who is given the nickname "Einstein" by his parents may see himself as a strong student. Similarly, a child labeled by parents as "responsible" will perceive herself as reliable and mature. Consider the impact that the nickname "trouble" would have on a child's perception. Most of us can recall the way our family

There is an extensive amount of scholarship on the relationship between attachment styles and identity development and attachment styles and relationship satisfaction.

members referred to us, and it is likely that many of these references were internalized. Researchers point out the significance of direct definitions by recognizing that positive labels can enhance our self-esteem while negative ones can have potentially deleterious effects on our self-perceptions (Wood, 2001).

IDENTITY SCRIPTS

When you reflect back on your childhood, can you recall sayings or phrases repeated in your family? How about, "money does not grow on trees," "people who live in glass houses should not throw stones," "remember the golden rule," or "a family that prays together stays together"? Do any of these sayings sound familiar to you? Can you generate a list of phrases repeated in your family? These sayings are all examples of **identity scripts**, or rules for living and for relating effectively to one another in family contexts. Identity scripts help individuals to define who they are and how to relate to others (Berne, 1964; Harris, 1969). These phrases, which most have probably heard more than once, influence the way we relate to others and also our self-perceptions.

Peer Relationships

While family relationships are important and clearly affect the development of the self, other relationships, such as peers, also play a significant role in identity development (Park & Waters, 1988). The **attachment security hypothesis**, based on Bowlby's (1973) work, states that individuals are attracted to and seek out peers and relationship partners who can provide them with a sense of security. Not surprisingly, peers, like parents, can also provide a sense of security and social support for one another. Some research

indicates that attachment-related functions are eventually transferred from parents to peers over time (Surra, Gray, Cottle, & Boettcher, 2004).

PEERS

Research by Meeus and Dekovic (1995) supports the significance of peer relationships later in life and indicates that peers, to a certain extent, are even more influential than parents in the identity development of adolescents. According to researchers, as young children age and mature they also begin the process of separation and individuation from their parents. Children begin to socialize more frequently with their peers, and to protest when they are separated from them. They begin to discover that most of their peer interactions are characterized by qualities such as equality. Peer relationships, which tend to be more egalitarian, soon become more important than parental relationships and tend to influence child-parent relationship expectations. As children grow and mature, they expect to form new relationships with their parents, also based on symmetry and equality. When these relationships do not progress as expected, adolescents become frustrated and perhaps even more bonded with their peers (Meeus & Dekovic, 1995).

Peer relationships play a significant role in identity development.

While initially researchers suspected that peers were influential only in certain areas of identity formation, research by Meeus and Dekovic (1995) illustrates the impact of peers on the formation of relational, educational, and occupational identity. Not surprisingly, best friends exerted the greatest influence on one's development of relational identity, while peers or colleagues exerted the greatest influence on occupational and educational identities. Who was most influential in your decision to select a particular major in college?

Peer relationships are also important in defining the self because individuals often use peers as a means of personal assessment. It is not unusual for individuals to compare themselves to others to determine whether they are smart, attractive, athletic, or successful. When individuals compare themselves to others to determine their abilities, strengths, and weaknesses, they are engaging in the process of social comparison. Festinger (1954) developed **social comparison theory**. This theory suggests that most individuals have a basic need, or drive, to evaluate and compare themselves to those around them. Festinger holds that one of the only ways of validating an evaluation of oneself is to find out if similar others agree with it (Tesser, 2003). Thus, if a student wants to evaluate his ability in school, he will typically compare his abilities to those of his fellow similar classmates. Do you immediately consult with your peers after receiving a test or paper grade from your professors? Social comparison theory explains why you might engage in this behavior.

Another way relationships with others affect the development of self is through a phenomenon called **behavioral confirmation**, or self-fulfilling prophecy (Aron, 2003). Aron (2003) defines **self-fulfilling prophecy** as a process in which people act to conform to the expectations of others (see, for example, Darley & Fazio, 1980). One of the classic studies illustrating self-fulfilling prophecy was conducted in the classroom. Teachers were randomly informed that their students were academic overachievers. Academic performances improved significantly for those average students whose teachers were told that they were high achievers. Why did the students improve academically? Because the teachers communicated with the students as if they were overachievers, and the students internalized these perspectives and acted accordingly (Snyder, Tanke, & Berscheid, 1977). Researchers also found that previous relationship experiences can influence our expectations of new relationship partners' behaviors (see, for example, Andersen & Berensen, 2001). Thus, if an individual experienced problems in previous relationships, he or she may expect similar negative experiences in the future and may unintentionally contribute to how the relationship progresses.

PEERS AND SOCIAL NETWORKING SITES

More recently, researchers have looked at how young adults' use of social networking sites (SNS) contributes to identity development. Young adults use SNS like Facebook to communicate with their peers; initiate, maintain, and terminate relationships; and engage in impression management. While the impact of SNS on interpersonal communication and relationship development will be examined more extensively in subsequent chapters of this textbook, it is important to point out some of the potential effects of SNS use on self-perceptions. Use of

SNS appears to have the potential to affect the way young adults view themselves both positively and negatively. Read more about the impact of SNS in the "Research in Real Life" textbox.

RESEARCH IN REAL LIFE:
Impact of SNS on self-esteem

Communication researchers Catalina Toma and Cassandra Carlson (2012) identified a number of positive outcomes associated with SNS by examining user profiles:
- Sharing Facebook profiles with friends boosts self-esteem.
- When young adults post Facebook (FB) profiles and receive positive feedback from peers, their social self-esteem increases.
- Sharing information on FB is also associated with increases in life satisfaction and perceptions of one's ability to achieve in college.
- FB users feel their profiles offer accurate, positive, and complete impressions of themselves and acknowledge making some alterations.

This research is important to communication scholars because it illustrates the power of SNS as a means of relating to others and simultaneously managing one's identity. Not surprisingly, while there is research illustrating the positive effects of FB use, there is an equal amount illustrating the negative effects:

- College students perceive that FB use has potentially more negative effects on others' relationships, potential employment, and privacy than their own (Paradise & Sullivan, 2012). This is called "the third person effect."
- Frequency and intensity of FB use was negatively associated with interpersonal competency at initiating relationships (Jenkins-Guarnieri, Wright, & Hudiburgh, 2012).

- Individuals with insecure attachment styles were more likely to use SNS to avoid face-to-face communication (Nitzburg & Farber, 2013).

Researchers should continue to study how and why individuals use SNS and offer suggestions on how to use it effectively to manage one's identity and maintain relationships.

Relationship Partners

Over time, the bond formed between partners in a romantic relationship is sure to affect the development of the self. One particularly interesting study provides further support for this statement. Researchers found that married couples come to look more alike over extended periods of time. Zajonc and his colleagues (1987) found students were more successful in matching pictures of couples married twenty-five years compared with pictures of the same couples, newly married.

Intimate relationships are also important to the development of the self because they influence how positively or negatively one views oneself over time (Aron, 2003). For example, college students in romantic relationships report greater self-esteem and body esteem than those not in romantic relationships (Pettijohn, Naples, & McDermott, 2010). Being in a relationship with someone who understands you and wants to spend time with you seems to enhance feelings of self-worth. Not surprisingly, when people feel good about themselves and their relationships, they are also happier and report greater life satisfaction. Some research indicates that married women report greater life satisfaction than single women (Borzumato-Gainey, Kennedy, McCabe, & Degges-White, 2009). In addition to providing companionship and increasing personal acceptance, relationship partners serve as an important source of social support. We seek out our relationship partners when we are stressed out and need someone to talk with about our problems. While romantic relationships are not easy to maintain and come with a number of different challenges, being in one can lead to greater self-acceptance and feelings of self-worth.

How do intimate relationships impact one's view of oneself?

According to the **similarity hypothesis**, also related to Bowlby's research on attachment theory, we are most attracted to individuals who exhibit an attachment style similar to our own (Surra et al., 2004). Not surprisingly, researchers found that college students with secure attachment styles were more attracted to relationship partners who had also developed this attachment style. As the similarity hypothesis would predict, anxious-attachment individuals were also more

likely to date anxious-attachment partners and to report being satisfied with these relationships (Surra et al., 2004). This research indicates that we often seek out individuals with similar attachment styles who also verify our perceptions of self-worth.

In addition to expressing similar attachment styles, we establish relationships with others for many different reasons. Several chapters in this textbook explore the reasons we establish both romantic and platonic relationships in much greater detail.

SUMMARY

In this chapter we explain identity formation with special attention to the role that interpersonal communication plays in this complicated process. Terms used to describe the self such as self-complexity, self-concept, self-esteem, self-regulation, authenticity, and impression management were explained to shed light on their significance in the development and refinement of the self. We also identified specific individuals who are instrumental in shaping self-perceptions. Not surprisingly, parents contribute greatly to this process with peers and relationship partners weighing in as well. The next chapters of this text explore the role of two other important self-aspects that affect communication and relationships with others: emotion and personality.

DISCUSSION QUESTIONS

1. Can you identify several individuals who were influential in your life and shaped your identity? Can you describe what these individuals said to shape your self-perceptions?

2. Please describe some positive or negative aspects of social media that you think researchers should investigate.

3. How can individuals improve their self-complexity?

SELF ASSESSMENT

Attachment Styles

These questions are concerned with your experiences in romantic love relationships.

Take a moment to think about these experiences and answer the following questions with them in mind.

Read each of the three self-descriptions below (A, B, and C) and then place a checkmark next to the single alternative that best describes how you feel in romantic relationships or is nearest to the way you feel. (Note: The terms "close" and "intimate" refer to psychological or emotional closeness, not necessarily to sexual intimacy.)

_____A. I find it relatively easy to get close to others and am comfortable depending on them and having them depend on me. I don't often worry about being abandoned or about someone getting too close to me.

_____B. I am somewhat uncomfortable being close to others; I find it difficult to trust them completely, difficult to allow myself to depend on them. I am nervous when anyone gets too close, and often, love partners want me to be more intimate than I feel comfortable being.

_____C. I find that others are reluctant to get as close as I would like. I often worry that my partner doesn't really love me or won't want to stay with me. I want to merge completely with another person, and this desire sometimes scares people away.

A = Secure, B = Avoidant, C = Anxious/Ambivalent

Hazan, C., & Shaver, P. R. (1987). Romantic love conceptualized as an attachment process. Journal of Personality and Social Psychology, 52, 511-524.

KEY TERMS AND DEFINITIONS

AFFINITY-SEEKING STRATEGIES: verbal and nonverbal messages sent strategically to gain liking from others.

ANXIOUS/ANXIOUS AMBIVALENT ATTACHMENT: an attachment style that is developed when mothers exhibit an inconsistent pattern of both responsive and attentive behavior; characterized by negative emotional reactions (i.e., hypervigilance and anger).

ATTACHMENT SECURITY HYPOTHESIS: states that individuals are attracted to and seek out peers and relationship partners who can provide them with a sense of security.

ATTACHMENT THEORY: "asserts that personality (or attachment style) develops through social interaction with others in close relationships, and that attachment styles, in turn, play a life-long role in shaping behavior in close relationships."

AUTHENTICITY: the unobstructed operation of one's true or core self in one's daily enterprise.

AVOIDANT ATTACHMENT: children develop this attachment style when mothers are consistently negative or unresponsive to their children when children need to be consoled.

BEHAVIORAL CONFIRMATION/SELF-FULFILLING PROPHECY: a process in which people act to conform to the expectations of others.

BUFFER EFFECT: higher self-complexity may actually act as a buffer for people by allowing them to mentally separate themselves from painful life events.

DIRECT DEFINITIONS: are descriptions, or labels, families assign to their members that affect the way we see and define ourselves.

IDENTITY SCRIPTS: rules for living and for relating effectively to one another in family contexts.

IMPRESSION CONSTRUCTION: the use of specific strategies or tactics to create desirable impressions.

IMPRESSION MANAGEMENT: the process of controlling how one is viewed by others in order to achieve positive impressions.

IMPRESSION MANAGEMENT STRATEGIES: the tactics or strategies individuals use to achieve positive impressions from others.

IMPRESSION MOTIVATION: the extent to which people are motivated to achieve desirable impressions.

INNER SELF: the self that we keep private and that may reflect how we really feel about ourselves; described as "authentic" self-concept.

OBJECTIVE SELF-AWARENESS: individuals will occasionally focus inward and engage in a process of comparing their current self with some standard or expected behavior or goal.

PUBLIC SELF: the self we project during social interaction; described as "actual" self-concept.

REFLECTED APPRAISAL/LOOKING GLASS SELF: the tendency to view ourselves based on the appraisals of others.

SECURE ATTACHMENT: an attachment style that is "characterized by intense feelings of intimacy, emotional security, and physical safety when the infant is in the presence of the attachment figure."

SELF: a complex system made up of a variety of interdependent elements that attain self-organization; a psychological entity consisting of "an organized set of beliefs, feelings, and behaviors."

SELF-AWARENESS: one's ability to understand the self and discriminate one's behavior from the surrounding environment.

SELF-COMPLEXITY: number of self-aspects or sub-selves.

50

SELF-CONCEPT: people's thoughts or cognitions about themselves; a cognitive construct that is a "descriptive reference to the self, or a definition of the nature and beliefs about the self's qualities."

SELF-ESTEEM: subjective perception of one's self-worth, or the value one places on the self.

SELF-REGULATION: individuals' ability to reflect on and monitor goals they establish.

SIMILARITY: related to interpersonal attraction; an important variable that affects our interactions with others.

SIMILARITY HYPOTHESIS: states that we are most attracted to individuals who exhibit an attachment style similar to our own.

SOCIAL COMPARISON THEORY: suggests that most individuals have a basic need, or drive, to evaluate and compare themselves to those around them.

REFERENCES

Ainsworth, M. D. S., Blehar, M. C., Waters, E., & Wall, S. (1978). *Patterns of attachment: A psychological study of the strange situation.* Hillsdale, NJ: Erlbaum.

Andersen, S. M., & Berensen, K. (2001). Perceiving, feeling, and wanting: Motivation and affect deriving from significant other representations and transference. In J. P. Forgas, K. D. Williams, and L. Wheeler (Eds.), *The social mind: Cognitive and motivational aspects of interpersonal behavior* (pp. 231–256). New York: Cambridge University Press.

Aron, A. (2003). Self and close relationships. In M. R. Leary & J. P. Tangney (Eds.), *Handbook of self and identity.* New York: The Guilford Press.

Aube, J., & Koestner, R. (1992). Gender characteristics and adjustment: A longitudinal study. *Journal of Personality and Social Psychology, 70,* 535–551.

Bargh, J. A., & Chartrand, T. L. (1999). The unbearable automaticity of being. *American Psychologist, 54,* 462–479.

Bargh, J. A., McKenna, K., & Fitzsimons, G. M. (2002). Can you see the real me? Activation and expression of the "true self" on the Internet. *Journal of Social Issues, 58,* 33–48.

Bargh, J., & McKenna, K. (2004). The Internet and social life. *Annu. Rev. Psychol.* 2004. 55, 573–90.

Baumeister, R. F. (1998). The self. In D. Gilbert, S. T. Fiske, and G. Lindzey (Eds.), *The Handbook of social psychology* (pp. 680–740). New York: Oxford Press.

Baumeister, R. F., & Vohs, K. D. (2003). Self-regulation and the executive function of the self. In M. R. Leary & J. P. Tangney (Eds.), *Handbook of self and identity.* New York: The Guilford Press.

Baumeister, R. F., Campbell, J. D., Krueger, J. I., & Vohs, K. (2003). Does high self-esteem cause better performance, interpersonal success, happiness or healthier lifestyles? *Psychological Science in the Public Interest, 4,* 1–44.

Bell, R. A., & Daly, J. A. (1984). The affinity-seeking function of communication. *Communication Monographs, 49,* 91–115.

Berne, E. (1964). *Games people play.* New York: Grove.

Borzumato-Gainey, C., Kennedy, A., McCabe, B., & Degges-White, S. (2009). Life satisfaction, self-esteem and subjective age in women across the lifespan. *Adultspan Journal, 8,* 29–42.

Bowlby, J. (1969). *Attachment and loss: Vol. 1. Attachment.* New York: Basic Books.

Bowlby, J. (1973). *Attachment and loss: Vol. 2. Separation anxiety and anger.* New York: Basic Books.

Bowlby, J. (1980). *Attachment and loss: Vol. 3. Loss sadness and depression.* New York: Basic Books.

Collins, N. L., & Feeny, B. C. (2004). Working models of attachment shape perceptions of social support: Evidence from experimental and observational studies. *Journal of Personality and Social Psychology, 87,* 363–383.

Cooley, C. H. (1902). *Human nature and the social order.* New York: Sage Publications.

Darley, J. M., & Fazio, R. H. (1980). Expectancy confirmation processes arising in the social interaction sequence. *American Psychologist, 35,* 867–881.

Duval, S., & Wicklund, R. A. (1972). *A theory of objective self-awareness.* New York: Academic Press.

Dymond, S., & Barnes, D. (1997). Behavior-analytic approaches to self-awareness. *The Psychological Record, 47,* 181–200.

Epstein, S. (1973). The self-concept revisited: Or a theory of a theory. *American Psychologist, 28,* 404–416.

Felson, R. B. (1989). Parents and reflected appraisal process: A longitudinal analysis. *Journal of Personality and Social Psychology, 56,* 965–971.

Festinger, L. (1954). A theory of social comparison processes. *Human Relations, 7,* 117–140.

Finkel, E. J., & Campbell, W.K. (2001). Self-control and accommodation in close relationships: An interdependence analysis. *Journal of Personality and Social Psychology, 81,* 263–271.

Firestone, L. (2013). Compassion matters. How your attachment style impacts your relationship. Retrieved from psychologytoday.com.

Goffman, E. (1959). *The presentation of self in everyday life.* Garden City, NY: Doubleday.

Greenwald, A. G., & Breckler, S. J. (1985). To whom is the self presented? In B. R. Schlenker (Ed.), *The self and social life* (pp. 126–145). New York: McGraw-Hill.

Harris, T. (1969). *I'm OK, you're OK.* New York: Harper & Row.

Houck, G. M., & Spegman, A. M. (1999). The development of self: Theoretical understandings and conceptual underpinnings. *Infants and Young Children, 12,* 1–16.

Jenkins-Guarnieri, M. A., Wright, S. L., & Hudiburgh, L. M. (2012). The relationships among attachment style, personality traits, interpersonal competency, and Facebook use. *Journal of Applied Developmental Psychology, 33,* 294–301.

Jung, C. G. (1953). *Psychological reflections.* New York: Harper and Row.

Karney, B. R., & Bradbury, T. N. (1995). The longitudinal course of marital quality and stability: A review of theory, methods, and research. *Psychological Bulletin, 118,* 3–34.

Kernis, M. H. (2003). Toward a conceptualization of optimal self-esteem. *Psychological Inquiry, 14,* 1–26.

Koch, E. J., & Shepperd, J. A. (2004). Is self-complexity linked to better coping? A review of the literature. *Journal of Personality, 72,* 727–760.

Lakey, C. E., Kernis, M. H., Heppner, W. L., & Lance, C. E. (2008). Individual differences in authenticity and mindfulness as predictors of verbal defensiveness. *Journal of Research in Personality, 42,* 230–238.

Leary, M. R., & Kowalski, R. M. (1990). Impression management: A literature review and two component model. *Psychological Bulletin, 107,* 34–47.

Linville, P. W. (1985). Self-complexity and affective extremity: Don't put all your eggs in one cognitive basket. *Social Cognition, 3,* 94–120.

Linville, P. W. (1987). Self-complexity as a cognitive buffer against stress-related illness and depression. *Journal of Personality and Social Psychology, 52,* 663–676.

Markus, H., & Wurf, E. (1987). The dynamic self-concept: A social psychological perspective. *Annual Review of Psychology, 38,* 299–337.

Mead, G. H. (1934). *Mind, self, and society.* Chicago: University of Chicago Press.

Meeus, W., & Dekovic, M. (1995). Identity development, parental and peer support in adolescence: Results of a national Dutch survey. *Adolescence, 30,* 931–945.

Mendelson, A., & Papacharissi, Z. (2010). Look at us: Collective narcissism in college student Facebook photo galleries. In Z. Papacharissi (Ed.), *The networked self: Identity, community, and culture on social network sites.* London: Routledge.

Nie, N. H. (2001). Sociability, interpersonal relations, and the Internet: reconciling conflicting findings. *Am. Behav. Sci.* 45:420–35.

Nitzburg, G. C., & Farber, B. A. (2013). Putting up emotional (Facebook) walls? Attachment status and emerging adults' experiences of social networking sites. *Journal of Clinical Psychology: In Session, 69,* 183–190.

Paradise, A., & Sullivan, M. (2012). (In)visible threats? The third-person effect in perceptions of influence on Facebook. *Cyberpsychology, Behavior and Social Networking, 15,* 55–60.

Park, K. A., & Waters, E. (1988). Traits and relationships in developmental perspective. In S. Duck (Ed.) *Handbook of personal relationships: Theory, research, and interventions* (pp. 161–176). Oxford, England: John Wiley & Sons Ltd.

Peluso, P. R., Peluso, J. P., White, J. F., & Kern, R. M. (2004). A comparison of attachment theory and individual psychology: A review of the literature. *Journal of Counseling and Development, 82,* 139–145.

Pettijohn, T. F., Naples, G. M., & McDermott, L. A. (2010). Gender, college year, and romantic relationship status differences in embarrassment and self attitudes of college students. *Individual Differences Research, 8,* 164–170.

Reeve, J. (2009). *Understanding motivation and emotion.* (5th ed.). Hoboken, NJ: John Wiley & Sons.

Rholes, W. S., Paetzold, R. L., & Friedman, M. (2008). Ties that bind: Linking personality to interpersonal behavior through the study of adult attachment style and relationship satisfaction. In F. Rhodewalt (Ed.), *Personality and Social Behavior* (pp. 117–148).

Rosenberg, M. (1995). Global self-esteem and specific self-esteem: Different concepts, different outcomes. *American Sociological Review, 60,* 141–156.

Schleicher, D. J., & McConnell, A. R. (2005). The complexity of self-complexity: An associated systems theory approach. *Social Cognition, 23,* 387–416.

Schlenker, B. (1984). Identities, identifications and relationships. In V. Derlega (Ed.), *Communication, intimacy and close relationships.* New York: Academic Press.

Schlenker, B. (1985). Identity and self-identification. In B. R. Schlenker (Ed.), *The self and social life* (pp. 65–99). New York: McGraw-Hill.

Silvia, P. J. & Duval, T. S. (2001). Objective self-awareness theory: Recent progress and enduring problems. *Personality and Social Psychology, 5,* 230–241.

Snyder, M., Tanke, E. D., & Berscheid, E. (1977). Social perception and interpersonal behavior: The self-fulfilling nature of social stereotypes. *Journal of Personality and Social Psychology, 35,* 656–666.

Spitzberg, B. H., & Cupach, W. R. (1984). *Interpersonal communication competence.* Newbury Park, CA: Sage.

Sroufe, L. A. (1988). The role of infant-caregiver attachment in development. In J. Belsky & T. Nezworski (Eds.), *Clinical implications of attachment* (pp. 18–38). Hillsdale, NJ: Erlbaum.

Surra, C. A., Gray, C. R., Cottle, N., & Boettcher, T. M. (2004). Research on mate selection and premarital relationships: What do we really know? In A. L. Vangelisti (Ed.), *Handbook of family communication* (53–82). Mahwah, NJ: Lawrence Erlbaum.

Swann, W. R. (1985). The self as architect of social reality. In B. R. Schlenker (Ed.), *The self and social life* (pp. 100–126). New York: McGraw-Hill.

Tesser, A. (2003). Self-evaluation. In M. R. Leary and J. P. Tangney (Eds.), *Handbook of self and identity.* New York: The Guilford Press.

Tesser, A., Wood, J. V., & Stapel, D. A. (2002). Introduction: An emphasis on motivation. In A. Tesser, D. A. Stapel, and J. V. Wood (Eds.), *Self and motivation: Emerging psychological perspectives* (pp. 3–11). Washington, DC: American Psychological Association.

Toma, C. & Carlson, C. (2012). *I am so much cooler online: An examination of self-presentation in Facebook profiles.* Paper presented at the International Communication Association Annual Meeting, Phoenix AZ.

Vallacher, R. R., & Nowak, A. (2000). Landscapes of self-reflection: Mapping the peaks and valleys of personal assessment. In A. Tesser, R. B. Felson, & J. M. Suls (Eds.), *Psychological perspectives on self and identity* (pp. 35–65). Washington, DC: American Psychological Association.

Wood, J. T. (2001). *Interpersonal communication: Everyday encounters.* (3rd ed.) Belmont, CA: Wadsworth Publishing Company.

Wright, K. (2008). In search of the real you. *Psychology Today,* 72–77.

Zajonc, R. B., Adelmann, R. K., Murphy, S. B., & Niedenthal, R. N. (1987). Convergence in the physical appearance of spouses. *Motivation and Emotion, 11,* 335–34.

chapter

3

Why Do We Communicate the Way We Do?:
Personality and Emotion

OBJECTIVES

- Examine the concept of personality and explain how it impacts our communication in relationships with others.

- Differentiate between state and trait approaches to examining personality.

- Identify personality differences that directly influence communication behaviors.

- Define emotion and explain its influence on communication.

- Examine research on emotion and communication across contexts.

SCENARIO: SOUND FAMILIAR?

Wyatt cringes when he hears that he is assigned to a project team to work on a proposal for his company's potential client. After all, his group project experiences up to this point have been incredibly frustrating. On every team he has worked with in college and with his new job, it seems like there is always someone who attacks everyone's ideas, while others sit around the table and never say a word. Wyatt knows that as the project deadline approaches, people's "true colors" will emerge. Over the years he has witnessed team members who inevitably get frustrated and yell at one another and some who become visibly jittery and tense, while others are cheerful and encourage the team as it works to meet deadlines.

OVERVIEW

At some point during your academic or professional career, you have probably found yourself in the same situation as Wyatt. Something as simple as communicating to share ideas can be met with a variety of reactions, both positive and negative. Learning to navigate and respond to the variety of reactions is crucial to your ability to create and sustain effective interpersonal relationships. Consider other situations where you may have encountered communication challenges:

- A conversation with a romantic partner about the current status of your relationship
- Discussions with your parents about which college you should choose
- A meeting with your boss to discuss your work performance

While communication seems like it should be an intuitively simple process, factors such as individual personality differences and emotions impact not only our communication behaviors in specific situations, but they also influence our overall communication style. In this chapter we will address two primary objectives: (1) Examine what personality is and how it shapes our personal communication style; and (2) Understand how emotion influences our perceptions of self and impacts our communication with others.

THE IMPACT OF INDIVIDUAL DIFFERENCES ON SOCIAL INTERACTION

Have you ever had a conversation with someone and labeled the person as being "difficult"? We may describe other people as being "difficult" as a result of their communication behaviors. Perhaps they responded in an unpredictable or offensive way, or we may perceive them as being demanding or inflexible. Ultimately, the "difficult" communication behavior may interfere with effective communication. A number of authors have written books about dealing with difficult people in personal and professional contexts (see, for example, Cavaiola & Lavender, 2000; Keating, 1984). One explanation that is offered for why people are identified as being "difficult" focuses on personality differences and

the challenges associated with communicating with someone whose personality is different from our own.

How does a higher level of anxiety impact your communication with others?

So why is it important to study personality differences in an interpersonal communication class? First, because our personality is an important and relatively enduring part of how we see and define ourselves, interpersonal researchers are naturally interested in learning more about the impact of individual differences on social interaction. In addition, most researchers argue that communication behaviors linked to personality differences are explained, at least in part, by social learning; that is, we learn how to communicate by observing and imitating those around us. While a number of communication scholars have argued that our genetic background best explains our personality predispositions (Beatty, McCroskey, & Heisel, 1998), it is still important to consider both explanations.

Second, by learning more about how specific personality traits influence our decisions to approach social interactions, we can make some predictions about how others will respond to us, and thus we can plan our own behaviors accordingly. You may be wondering why communication researchers don't just study self-concept and use it as the primary means for determining our behaviors. Unlike self-concept, which is subjective and could change from moment to moment, personality is relatively stable and consistent over time. For example, if you complete one of the communication trait questionnaires located in the appendices at the end of this chapter today and then complete the same survey a year from now, chances are that your scores will be identical or very similar. Learning more about communication behaviors that are trait-based helps researchers understand the impact of individual differences across various contexts.

Personality is defined as relatively long-lasting patterns of behaviors, feelings, attitudes, and characteristics that make each person unique. On a daily basis, we often analyze and describe the personalities or dispositions of others in an attempt to explain their behavior. A friend may be described as "sociable," a coworker is pronounced as being "energetic," or a sibling is labeled as "overly sensitive." Identifying unique personality characteristics helps us explain communication behaviors. Learning how to manage communication with difficult personality types is a relevant topic for a number of reasons: (1) We all have to deal with difficult people, whether at home, school, or work; (2) We might be one of those "difficult people" as a result of our own communication style that is shaped by our personality; and (3) Asking someone to change his or her personality is unreasonable and can negatively impact the relationship.

> On a daily basis, we often analyze and describe the personalities or dispositions of others in an attempt to explain their behavior.

Social psychologist John Gottman (1999) describes perpetual conflict as disagreements that occur between relational partners that are often directly related to personality issues. This type of conflict is pervasive in the relationship and not easily remedied. It often involves disagreements over matters that cannot be easily resolved, such as differences in couples' personality traits. Consider the level of frustration when someone orders you to "change your personality" in order to become a better relationship partner. This type of criticism is not only unrealistic, but it can be detrimental to your sense of self and to the relationship.

When someone asks you repeatedly to change the same aspect of your communication style (e.g., to talk more or to stop being so insensitive), perhaps what he or she is actually requesting is that you change a personality trait. Communication scholars who study personality and its impact on our interactions with others focus on two different approaches to describing personality differences: trait and state approaches.

A COMPARISON OF TRAIT AND STATE APPROACHES TO PERSONALITY DIFFERENCES

When researchers investigate differences in communication behaviors, they distinguish communication tendencies as being traits versus states. A state approach to studying communication examines how people interact with others in a particular situation or context. For example, an interpersonal researcher might examine how a person communicates right before asking someone out on a date. Specifically, the level of anxiety associated with asking someone on a date may cause you to communicate differently than you would normally behave in interactions with friends or family members. Situations, contexts, or even people can cause people to communicate in ways that aren't typical of their behavior. Thus, when scholars adopt a state approach to studying communication, they examine responses that are unique to situations or contexts (Daly & Bippus, 1998).

Does a first date raise your anxiety level?

Researchers who adopt a trait approach attempt to identify enduring, or consistent, ways that people behave. If a researcher adopts a trait approach to studying communication behaviors, it means that they are interested in examining how individuals interact the majority of the time. Daly and Bippus (1998) identify several conclusions about traits:

1. Traits define ways in which people differ.
2. Some traits address social characteristics while others emphasize cognitively oriented variables.
3. Traits can be measured by using questionnaires or by observing behaviors.

Rancer and Avtgis (2006) propose communication traits as a subset of personality traits that focus on our relatively consistent behaviors when we are either the source or the receiver of messages. Communication traits enable us to be fairly accurate in our predictions of how others will send and receive messages. Once we get to know someone, we become familiar with their communication tendencies. If you have a friend who tends to be shy, you know that it may take more effort to get your friend to open up and talk when you're around a larger group of people. Perhaps a father is prone to engaging in verbally aggressive behavior, so you can anticipate that he will likely yell at the referees during his child's basketball game.

Researchers have proposed four categories for classifying communication traits. These include: apprehension traits, presentation traits, adaptation traits, and aggressive traits (see Figure 3.1). Apprehension traits address the fear associated with communication. Predispositions that focus on the impression formation, types of information shared, and level of involvement in interactions are referred to as presentation traits. Adaptation traits refer to predispositions to be

© Antonio Guillem/Shutterstock.com

Communication traits enable us to be fairly accurate in our predictions of how others will send and receive messages.

In the following sections of this chapter, we will address the potential impact of communication traits on our interpersonal relationships.

APPREHENSION TRAITS: COMMUNICATION APPREHENSION & WILLINGNESS TO COMMUNICATE

mindful and aware of others in communication situations. A final category of communication traits, **aggressive traits**, describes tendencies to engage in forceful or potentially destructive communication.

As you reflect on your interpersonal relationships with others, consider the initial conversations that took place. Were you willing to approach the person, or did they approach you? Apprehension traits focus on our willingness to approach others and engage in communication. Understanding why some people have a tendency to avoid interactions is essential to building and maintaining effective relationships.

Figure 3.1. Categories of communication traits.

Communication Apprehension

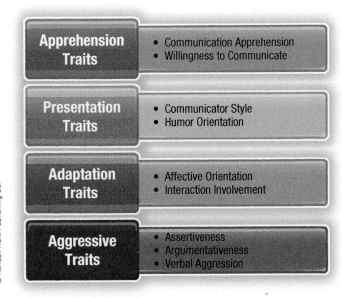

In John Maxwell's (2002) book, *The Seventeen Essential Qualities of a Team Player*, he emphasizes communication as one of the most important skills needed for succeeding in teams. Essential skills included in his list are adaptability, collaboration, enthusiasm, and the ability to establish relationships with team members. Not surprisingly, all of these qualities also require communication. Maxwell and countless other authors from a variety of academic and professional fields emphasize the relationship between communication skills and success at work. Throughout this book we will emphasize the impact of communication on your personal relationships and professional success. However, what if you are not comfortable communicating with others?

Communication apprehension is defined as an "individual's level of fear or anxiety with either real or anticipated communication with another person or persons" (McCroskey, 1978, p. 192). Approximately one in five individuals in the United States is considered high in communication apprehension (McCroskey, 2006). For someone who experiences high levels of communication apprehension, even anticipated interactions with others evoke a significant amount of stress and psychological discomfort (McCroskey, Daly, & Sorensen, 1976).

Can you identify with this group of applicants and their level of anxiety while waiting to be interviewed?

How can you identify your own level of communication apprehension? The Personal Report of Communication Apprehension (PRCA) is a 24-item questionnaire (see PRCA-24 scale at the end of this chapter) that measures a person's overall level of communication apprehension, or CA, as a trait (McCroskey, 1978). In addition, the PRCA-24 can be used to assess situational, or state, apprehension in four different contexts: public, small group, meeting, and interpersonal/dyadic situations. Recall our earlier discussion of state versus trait approaches to communication. While personality *traits* are enduring over time and across situations, personality *states* are often situational and can vary depending on the topic, receiver of the message, or the situation or context in which the interaction takes place. For example, you may experience high levels of anxiety when delivering a public speech, but you are perfectly at ease when speaking with your group about a class project. Your apprehension in the group is a temporary state that is the result of a specific context.

Individuals scoring high on the PRCA are generally very anxious about communicating with others and may attempt to avoid the interaction entirely. What are the relationship implications for those who experience trait-like communication apprehension (CA)?

- People with high CA are generally perceived by others as being less competent communicators.
- High CA is often associated with higher levels of stress and more loneliness compared to those who score lower in CA (Miczo, 2004; Zakahi & Duran, 1985).
- In the academic setting, college students with high CA are more likely to be considered "at risk" (Lippert, Titsworth, & Hunt, 2005).
- College students who experience higher levels of apprehension are less likely to emerge as leaders in work groups (Limon & La France, 2005).

Willingness to Communicate

Willingness to communicate (WTC) is similar to communication apprehension because it also taps into an individual's propensity to avoid or approach communication with others. The willingness to communicate construct does not assess fear or anxiety, only the tendency to attempt to avoid or sidestep communication across a variety of situations and with specific audiences or persons. McCroskey and Richmond (1987) coined the term *willingness to communicate* (WTC) to describe a person's tendency to initiate communication with others (McCroskey & Richmond, 1998).

A person's willingness to communicate is measured via the WTC scale, a 20-item measure that assesses an individual's willingness to interact with different individuals in a variety of situations. You can evaluate your own level of WTC by completing the scale at the end of this chapter. Individuals completing the WTC scale indicate the percentage of time they would choose to communicate in public, in meetings, in small groups, or in dyads. When individuals consistently indicate that they would not want to talk in most of the contexts listed, they are described as low in trait WTC. Conversely, individuals who indicate that they are willing to interact with others in a wide range of contexts are described as high in WTC.

What is the relationship between one's level of communication apprehension and their willingness to communicate? Individuals who are high in CA are more likely to be low in WTC. Richmond and Roach (1992) provide a summary of research that examined the benefits and drawbacks for employees who are described as low in WTC. While you may associate negative outcomes with employees who are less willing to communicate with others, research has identified some benefits. Some positive outcomes include:

- There is a decreased likelihood that those who are low WTC will initiate or perpetuate gossip.
- It's less likely that low WTC individuals will emerge as "squeaky wheels" within the organization.
- Persons who experience low WTC are less likely to take long breaks, unlike their more social high WTC counterparts.
- Employees who are low in WTC tend to be more discreet than their more talkative colleagues.

While there are benefits of employing quiet individuals, Richmond and Roach (1992) also point out potentially damaging perceptions associated with a person's low WTC in the workplace:

Approximately one in five individuals in the United States is considered high in communication apprehension .

- Quiet individuals are perceived as less competent and less intelligent because they do not contribute to discussions or share their accomplishments with others.
- Consequently, quiet employees are often mislabeled as incompetent and lacking business savvy.
- Negative impressions are associated with quiet employees and, as a result, they are often less likely to get interviewed or considered for promotions.
- Daly, Richmond, and Leth (1979) found that when individuals were described as quiet or shy in recommendation letters, they were less likely to be granted interviews than highly verbal individuals.
- People who have low WTC may be more likely to experience the "last hired" and "first fired" syndrome compared with their high WTC counterparts (Richmond & Roach, 1992).

PRESENTATION TRAITS: COMMUNICATIOR STYLE & HUMOR ORIENTATION

Presentation traits focus on awareness in presenting oneself in appropriate ways. Can you recall a time when someone was disclosing information that you perceived as inappropriate because of the topic being discussed or your relationship to the other person? In Chapter 2 we discussed several ways in which we focus on presenting our view of self to others. Presentation traits serve as our guides for impression management and reinforce how we want others to view us. Two communication traits examined by scholars that focus on our

mindfulness of the presentation of self are communicator style and humor orientation.

Communicator Style

If your friends were to describe your communicator style, what types of descriptors would they use? Would they say that you tend to be friendly, animated, or attentive? Perhaps they would describe you as being contentious or domineering. **Communicator style** refers to the verbal and nonverbal reactions that provide cues to others about how our messages should be interpreted and understood (Norton, 1978). Table 3.1 highlights the nine communication characteristics measured by Norton's (1983) Communication Style Inventory.

Other communication style instruments have been created to specifically focus on perceptions of interactions in specific interpersonal contexts. Ritchie and Fitzpatrick (1990) developed a measure to examine the styles used in parent-child interactions, and Buller and Buller (1987) focused specifically on communication styles used by physicians and their patients.

Communication scholars have examined differences between self versus others' perceptions of communicator style in a variety of contexts:

- Physicians tend to see themselves as impression-leaving, relaxed, and dramatic, while nurses view themselves as friendly and animated (Miller & Ratusnik, 1979).
- Employees experience low levels of satisfaction with employers who are dominant and dramatic, and higher levels of satisfaction with supervisors who are calm, attentive, and open (Baker & Ganster, 1985).
- In a study of perceptions of communicator styles in the classroom, teachers viewed

themselves as being more relaxed, friendly, and attentive than their students viewed them (Norton, 1977).

Humor Orientation

Booth-Butterfield and Booth-Butterfield (1991) developed the concept of **humor orientation** (HO) to explain the extent to which people use humor in their interactions with others, as well as their awareness of the appropriateness of humor in certain situations.

In what ways do you use humor to effectively communicate with others?

Table 3.1. Nine communication characteristics associated with Norton's Communicator Style Inventory.

Characteristic	Communication Style
Animated	Expressive and lively nonverbal behaviors (e.g., smiling, nodding)
Attentive	Demonstrates active listening through verbal and nonverbal acknowledgement (e.g., raising eyebrows, saying "I see!" or "Then what?")
Contentious	Argumentative and intimidating
Dominant	Controls the conversation; openly expresses opinions
Dramatic	Expressive language and exaggerated nonverbals
Friendly	Warm and encouraging; provides positive feedback
Impression-Leaving	Memorable conversational style; messages are unforgettable
Open	Shares personal information, feelings, and emotions
Relaxed	Calm and comfortable

HO can be measured using the Humor Orientation Scale, which assesses how often people use humor in their day-to-day communication and how effective they are at enacting humorous messages. You can determine your own humor orientation score by completing the HO scale at the end of this chapter. Individuals scoring higher on the HO measure (also called high HO's) incorporate a variety of humorous behaviors in their own communication, such as expressive nonverbals, language variety, and impersonation. Will people view us as being funnier in our humor attempts if we have a high HO? Research indicates that high HO's are perceived as funnier when telling jokes compared to low HO's, so our ability to deliver humorous messages effectively is impacted by our humor orientation (Wanzer, Booth-Butterfield, & Booth-Butterfield, 1995).

What are other benefits associated with having a high humor orientation? Researchers have addressed a number of positive personal outcomes for high HO's:

- High HO's are typically less lonely (Wanzer et al., 1996), more adaptable in their communication with others, and demonstrate a greater concern for eliciting positive impressions from others (Wanzer et al., 1995).
- Honeycutt and Brown (1998) found that couples that score higher on HO also experience greater levels of marital satisfaction.
- When managers are perceived as more humor-oriented by their employees, they are also viewed as more likable and effective (Rizzo, Wanzer, & Booth-Butterfield, 1999).
- Students report that they learn more from instructors whom they perceive as being more humor-oriented (Wanzer & Frymier, 1999) and also report engaging in more frequent communication outside of class with teachers who exhibit a high HO (Aylor & Opplinger, 2003).

RESEARCH IN REAL LIFE:
What Facebook cues do we use to guess one's humor orientation?

A 2014 study by Pennington and Hall asked participants to view 100 different Facebook profile pages and the eight most recent photo or status updates on each. After viewing each profile, participants guessed the humor orientation (HO) score of each Facebook profile's creator, and this number was compared with the actual HO scores provided by the page owners. In addition, a variety of potential cues to detect HO were examined. The study found that:

- An accurate estimate of one's HO can be provided after viewing a Facebook profile for 10–15 minutes.
- Status updates, photos, and the number of "likes" on a Facebook pages are the cues used most frequently in evaluating one's HO.
- Factors often associated with a lower HO include status updates that include media posts and the number of games played on Facebook.
- Three types of humor most frequently incorporated into Facebook posts include life event humor, pop culture humor, and self-related humor.

More recently, research has examined whether high HO individuals are better able to cope with stressful situations and use humor as a "coping mechanism" than those with a low HO. In studies examining nurses (Wanzer et al., 2005) and employed college students (Booth-Butterfield et al., 2007), a higher HO helped individuals cope with stressful work situations and contributed to higher levels of job satisfaction.

Can we train people to use humor more appropriately and effectively? Perhaps. We know that people often participate in improv comedy classes to improve their ability to deliver humorous messages. Based on research examining humor orientation, it seems an understanding of the appropriate use of humor and an ability to deliver funny messages could potentially improve interpersonal relationships across a variety of contexts.

ADAPTATION TRAITS: AFFECTIVE ORIENTATION & INTERACTION INVOLVEMENT

One of the hallmarks of being viewed as a competent communicator in our relationships is our ability to adapt our communication to the other person, the situation, or the context. Suppose your friend has just received a text message from a romantic interest indicating that the relationship is over. If your typical communication style with your friend involves joking and sarcasm, you may adapt your behaviors in this situation and be more responsive, empathetic, and listen more than you speak. Adap-

tation traits are those communication behaviors that are used to adjust to the topic, person, or communication context.

Affective Orientation

Affective orientation refers to the extent to which individuals are aware of their own emotional states and use them when making decisions about how to behave or respond in various situations (Booth-Butterfield & Booth-Butterfield, 1990). If you are described as affectively oriented, you tend to be quite aware of your own emotional states and consider them before responding to others. For example, you know that you experience higher levels of stress during final exam week, thus you "count to three" and carefully consider the tone of your comment to your roommate who left a bowl of tuna salad in the kitchen sink the previous night. Those who have a low affective orientation (AO) tend to be relatively unaware of their emotions and neglect to factor in the impact of their own emotions when responding to others (Booth-Butterfield & Booth-Butterfield, 1998).

If you are described as affectively oriented, you tend to be quite aware of your own emotional states and consider them before responding to others.

What are some of the benefits of having a higher AO? Individuals who exhibit higher levels of AO tend to:

- Be more nonverbally sensitive and better at providing comfort to others (Booth-Butterfield & Andrighetti, 1993; Dolin & Booth-Butterfield, 1993);
- Use humor more frequently than lower AO individuals (Wanzer et al., 1995);
- Be more romantic and idealistic in their beliefs about intimate relationships (Booth-Butterfield & Booth-Butterfield, 1994).

Interaction Involvement

Would you describe yourself as one who is generally engaged in conversations? Do you listen carefully while others speak, paying careful attention to observe their reactions to what you are saying? Or perhaps you feel uncertain of your role in conversations and find that you often become preoccupied and detached when talking to others.

Interaction involvement refers to an individual's general awareness of others' feelings, attitudes, and experiences during conversations. This involvement is demonstrated by a person's active participation throughout a conversation (Cegala, 1981). Goffman's (1967) work created the foundation for the study of this personality trait through his investigation of the alienation that occurs when a person is not actively involved, aware of the other person, or engaged during a conversation. Think about your own reaction when you're speaking to someone and they appear distracted by the television in the next room or a text message on their cell phone. You probably perceive the other person as inconsiderate and rude due to their lack of attention and dedication to your discussion. Three key factors (see Figure 3.2) used to evaluate one's involvement in interactions include:

- **Awareness** of our attitudes, feelings, and thoughts about messages that we receive from others;
- **Perceptiveness** or consideration of the intended meaning of another's message; and
- **Appropriateness** in replying to others' messages in acceptable ways.

Scholars have proposed that interaction involvement is associated with perceptions of competent communication. Key findings from these studies include:

- Interaction involvement is associated with perceptions of communication competence (Cegala, 1984).

Figure 3.2. Factors contributing to interaction involvement.

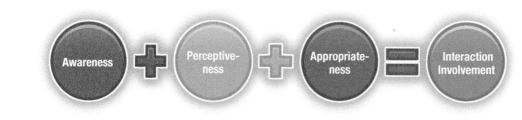

INTERPERSONAL COMMUNICATION: Building Rewarding Relationships

- Culture influences interaction involvement with low levels of perceptiveness and appropriateness reported in the initial stages of intercultural interactions (Chen, 2003).
- Higher levels of interaction involvement occur in face-to-face classes compared to those delivered via video conferencing (Umphrey, Wickersham, & Sherblom, 2008).

AGGRESSIVE TRAITS: ASSERTIVENESS, ARGUMENTATIVENESS & VERBAL AGGRESSION

Aggressive traits focus on those personality characteristics that motivate individuals to argue, debate, or speak out in conversations with others. While your first reaction may be to perceive these types of communication as being negative or destructive, it is important to note that while some aggressive traits are destructive, others may be beneficial in our personal and professional relationships.

Argumentativeness and assertiveness are described by Infante as constructive forms of aggression. Both of these behaviors are considered constructive communication because they are more active than passive, help us achieve our communication goals, and do not involve personal attacks against others (Rancer, 1998). Do you have friends or family members who argue for the sheer enjoyment? Perhaps they view these debates as challenging or intriguing. For others, arguing may result in confusion, hurt feelings, or even anger.

Argumentativeness

Individuals vary extensively in their perceptions of argumentative communication. Infante and Rancer (1982) define **argumentativeness** as a relatively consistent trait over time that predisposes people to advocate or stand up for a position on a given issue and to challenge or point out the weaknesses in the positions held by others. Argumentative individuals are prone to disagree or challenge issues and positions.

What benefits are there to being argumentative?

Infante and Rancer (1982) developed the Argumentativeness Scale, which is a 20-item Likert-type scale that asks people to record how they feel about responding to controversial issues. Ten items on the scale assess motivation to approach argumentative situations, and ten items assess motivation to avoid argumentative situations.

There are a number of benefits associated with being argumentative:

- Highly argumentative individuals are more effective in their attempts to persuade others.
- They employ a wider range of persuasion and social influence tactics and tend to

> When individuals act in an assertive way, they stand up for themselves and are able to initiate, maintain, and terminate conversations to accomplish interpersonal goals.

be more tenacious in their persuasion attempts (Boster & Levine, 1988).

- Highly argumentative individuals are more resistant to compliance attempts from others and generate more counterarguments in response to persuasive encounters (Infante, 1981; Kazoleas, 1993).
- Argumentative individuals are viewed as more credible and competent communicators who are also more interested in communicating with others (Infante, 1985).
- College students low in CA and high in argumentativeness were more likely to emerge as leaders in work groups than students high in CA and low in argumentativeness (Limon & LaFrance, 2005).

Assertiveness

Another constructive aggressive trait is **assertiveness**, which is defined as the capability to defend your own rights and wishes while still respecting and acknowledging the rights of others. When individuals act in an assertive way, they stand up for themselves and are able to initiate, maintain, and terminate conversations

to accomplish interpersonal goals (Richmond & Martin, 1998).

One way to measure assertiveness is by using the Socio-Communicative Orientation Scale developed by Richmond and McCroskey (1990). This measure includes ten assertiveness items and ten responsiveness items. Individuals are asked to report how accurately the items apply to them when they communicate with others. Some examples of assertive characteristics include: defends own beliefs, is independent, and is forceful.

There are innumerable benefits associated with the assertiveness trait:

- Assertive individuals are able to defend themselves, establish relationships, and take advantage of opportunities.
- Assertive individuals are perceived as more confident and self-assured, and are often rated as more effective teachers and managers than unassertive individuals.
- When it comes to practicing safe sex, sexually assertive males are more likely than unassertive males to use condoms to protect themselves and their partners (Noar, Morokoff, & Redding, 2002).

While argumentativeness and assertiveness are constructive in that they enable individuals to advocate for positions or issues without attacking or intentionally hurting others, not all aggressive traits are positive.

Infante (1987) recognizes a behavior as aggressive when it "applies force . . . symbolically in order, minimally to dominate and perhaps damage, or maximally to defeat and perhaps destroy the locus of attack" (p. 58). **Destructive** forms of aggression are those that can potentially damage an individual's self-esteem or, to use Infante's words, "destroy the locus of attack." The most widely recognized destructive aggressive trait is verbal aggression.

As stories of the outcomes of cyberbullying continue to make news headlines, researchers are addressing questions that focus on "how" aggressive communication is exchanged online. A 2012 study (Law, Shapka, Domene, & Gagne) of 733 middle- and high-school students employed a survey that asked students to describe why they engaged in online aggression. Results of the study found that students engage in three types of aggressive communication online:

- Sending aggressive or threatening messages, often in response to others' comments.
- Creating hostile websites; sometimes saying mean things "just for fun."
- Posting embarrassing photos of others.

The majority of participants indicated that they were aggressive online in response to others' negative communication toward them, and they felt that their retaliation was justified.

Verbal Aggression

When individuals lack the ability to argue effectively, they often resort to using verbally aggressive communication. Wigley (1998) describes **verbal aggressiveness**

as the tendency to attack the self-concept of an individual instead of focusing the communication on addressing the other person's arguments. Infante (1987, 1995) identified a wide range of messages that verbally aggressive communicators use. The following are a few examples of aggressive messages:

- Attacks on one's character or competence
- Negative comments about one's physical appearance
- Teasing, swearing, ridiculing, or threatening
- Blaming, making demands, or global rejection

As Wigley (1998) notes, "there seems to be no shortage of ways to cause other people to feel badly about themselves" (p. 192). Unfortunately, individuals who may be apprehensive about engaging in verbally aggressive behavior in the face-to-face context are willing to participate in these negative attacks in online forums or via social media.

When individuals lack the ability to argue effectively, they often resort to using verbally aggressive communication.

Infante and Wigley (1986) developed the Verbal Aggressiveness Scale, which is a 20-item self-report personality test that asks people to indicate whether they are verbally aggressive in their interactions. You can identify your tendency to engage in verbally aggressive communication by completing the scale at the end of this chapter. Since individuals may not feel that it is socially acceptable to self-report their use of aggression, the researchers designed items on the measure to make it seem like they approved of aggressive messages.

If you've ever interacted with someone who is highly verbally aggressive, one of the first questions you may have asked yourself is "Why does this person act this way?" While it seems irrational to behave in a destructive manner, two viable explanations may help us understand why some individuals possess the trait of verbal aggressiveness:

1. Individuals may be verbally aggressive because they learned this behavior from others. Thus, social learning may explain why children of verbally aggressive parents also engage in these same behaviors.
2. Verbally aggressive individuals lack the ability to argue effectively. As a result, they are more likely to become frustrated during arguments. The inability to defend one's position is frustrating and often causes the highly aggressive person to lash out at others.

There are a number of significant negative consequences for individuals who regularly communicate in verbally aggressive ways:

•   Verbally aggressive individuals are more likely to use a variety of antisocial behaviors and, as a result, are less liked (Myers & Johnson, 2003).

•   Wanzer and her colleagues (1995) found that verbally aggressive individuals are less socially attractive and more likely to target others via inappropriate use of humor. Their inapt humor may explain why acquaintances rate them as less socially attractive.

•   Individuals who are verbally aggressive are more likely to use a wide range of aggressive messages (e.g., competence attacks, teasing, and nonverbal emblems) compared with those who score low in verbal aggressiveness (Infante, Riddle, Horvath, & Tumlin, 1992).

•   Reasons offered by those high in verbal aggressiveness to explain their behavior include motives such as they were angry, did not like the target, were taught to be aggressive, were in a bad mood, or were just being humorous.

What can be done to help high aggressives? From a communication perspective, it is important to recognize when we are being verbally aggressive with others and to try to circumvent these behaviors. Have you ever had a younger sibling mimic your verbal or nonverbal messages? Recognize that when you communicate in a verbally aggressive way, others may model your behavior.

There is a substantial amount of research on this trait and the potentially negative effects of high amounts of verbal aggression on relationships in married (Infante, Chandler, & Rudd, 1989), family (Bayer & Cegala, 1992), and organizational contexts (Infante & Gorden, 1991). If you are predisposed to using verbal aggression, enroll in courses that might help you improve your ability to argue.

Understanding the four categories of personality traits can assist us in enhancing communication in our relationships in the following ways:

1. Identifying our individual personality traits can assist us in recognizing how they influence our own communication style.
2. An awareness of others' personality traits can help us better understand "why" they communicate the way that they do.

Recall our earlier description of state versus trait behaviors. While traits refer to our consistent behaviors over time, states are more transient and may result in unpredictable responses. Personality variables are relatively enduring traits that predispose individuals to respond in predictable ways. This helps us understand why some individuals always seem to be apprehensive or why we describe others as being "naturally funny." But how do we explain changes or deviations in a person's typical communication behavior? The study of emotions and emotional states offers us insight into why our communication may fluctuate depending on the situation.

EMOTION

Have you ever had a "bad day" and responded in an uncharacteristic way, and later found yourself apologizing to others for your actions? Chances are that your emotions influenced your initial response. **Emotions** are defined as intense feelings or temporary reactions that are directed toward someone or something. In essence, emotions help us answer the question, "How do I feel today?"

Figure 3.3 showcases just a few of the wide range of emotions that we experience at any given point in time. These emotions often impact our communicative responses toward others. For example, emotions such as anger or frustration may result in aggressive communication. While you may not be a verbally aggressive person, your frustration may motivate you to respond in a destructive way and blame the other person. Feeling suspicious may produce jealous communicative responses in our friendships or romantic relationships. In Chapter 9, we will discuss how jealousy and other emotional reactions contribute to the dark side of interpersonal relationships.

Figure 3.3. Examples of emotions.

Exhausted Confused Ecstatic Guilty Suspicious

Angry Hysterical Frustrated Sad Confident

Embarrassed Happy Mischievous Disgusted Frightened

Enraged Ashamed Cautious Smug Depressed

Overwhelmed Hopeful Lonely Lovestruck Jealous

Bored Surprised Anxious Shocked Shy

© Kendall Hunt Publishing Co.

Not all emotions are negative. In fact, Andersen and Guerrero (1998) point out that emotions can produce both positive and negative responses in our relationships with others. In situations where you experience feelings of confidence, your nonverbal behaviors may reflect your assurance by increased eye contact, smiling, and good posture. Excitement over your favorite team's victory may result in screaming and giving high-fives to those around you. Feelings of contentment in your romantic relationship may cause you to smile excessively and respond in overly positive ways. Emotions play an integral part in shaping how we communicate with others and their responses to us.

Communication is the means through which we both share information about our own emotions and receive clues about the emotional states of others.

EMOTIONS & COMMUNICATION

Communication is the means through which we both share information about our own emotions and receive clues about the emotional states of others. This expression of emotion is exchanged through verbal and nonverbal behaviors. While some may explicitly state their emotions through direct verbal statements as, "I'm so frustrated that you won't share any information with me!" additional clues to the intensity of emotion may be implicitly communicated through nonverbal behaviors such as shouting, shaking one's fists, or becoming teary-eyed during a conversation.

Message design logic (MDL) theory can offer insight into how we strategically structure our messages to express or suppress our emotions

(O'Keefe, 1988). Suppose you have to deliver bad news to a friend or coworker. As you prepare to deliver the message, several factors are taken into consideration: the other person's current emotional state, the potential reaction to the news, and whether the information should be shared in a public or private setting. Message design logic explains how we alter the design and delivery of a message as a result of our ability to evaluate the content of the message and organize it in such a way as to help ensure its effective delivery. The theory states that we use three types of logic in creating messages (Figure 3.4):

- Expressive logic—focuses on the source of the message and his or her level of comfort or willingness in delivering a message
- Conventional logic—addresses the appropriateness of the message delivery
- Rhetorical logic—evaluates the reactions of others and incorporates flexibility in the delivery of a message

Recall the scenario of Wyatt and his coworkers from the beginning of this chapter. He faces the task of identifying ways to communicate effectively with team members who are experiencing a variety of emotions in response to a stressful situation. Message design logic can explain Wyatt's decision to respond in a variety of ways—from shouting or frowning during a meeting to sending private emails to address individual issues about the project.

Figure 3.4. Message design logic.

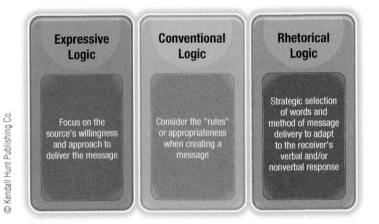

While MDL was originally developed to explain how messages are altered to influence or persuade others, the three message logics are also useful for explaining our decisions to communicate our emotions to others. Expressive logic helps us understand why some people directly tell others how they are feeling or are more emotionally expressive with their nonverbal behaviors, while others prefer to be more reserved and refrain from showing emotion. Our decisions about whether to share emotions in public or private are often guided by our conventional logic. While one couple may want the world to know that they are in love and openly express their passion through public displays of emotions, another couple may feel that these emotions should be expressed to each other in private. Rhetorical logic helps us "find the right words" to express our emotion. A parent may carefully consider her word choice to let her child know that she is disappointed by last semester's grades. While expressing the disappointment using a louder-than-normal voice, the parent may notice tears forming in the child's eyes and alter the message. The message may be carefully planned to express both the parent's disappointment in the grades and her confidence that grades will improve in the future.

Not only do we communicate our emotions through our verbal and nonverbal messages, but emotional cues are also expressed in our online messages. **Flaming** refers to the sending or posting of messages that can be perceived as attacking, hurtful, or offensive. These online expressions of perceived verbal aggression can be sent via email, posted to social media pages, or shared via discussion forums. In Chapter 11, we will take a closer look at how mediated communication is used in our relationships. It is important to note that, while flaming may be intentional, the lack of nonverbal cues in mediated communication may cause us to misperceive another's message as being verbally aggressive when that may not have been the original intent. Because of this, emoticons are often used to help clarify or explain the emotions that are being conveyed online. Figure 3.5 highlights some of the commonly used emoticons on Facebook and other social media.

Figure 3.5. Facebook codes for creating emoticons.

As you have probably experienced in both your face-to-face and online interactions with others, identifying the emotions of others requires careful thought and consideration. This effort can be explained by our own emotional intelligence and the amount of emotion work involved in our relationships.

EMOTION WORK AND EMOTIONAL INTELLIGENCE

Being able to share our own emotions effectively and read the emotions of others accurately can be challenging. **Emotion work** focuses on the effort that is required to express and interpret emotion effectively (Hochschild, 1979). Two types of emotion work that are expected in our relationships with others are evocation and suppression. **Evocation** refers to the open expression of emotion. Self-disclosure is an example of how we directly share our feelings and moods with others. **Suppression** refers to the restraint in the expression of emotion. Hiding disappointment when bad news is delivered or refraining from cheering when you win a debate competition because it is not considered appropriate behavior are examples of the suppression of emotion. In Chapter 6, we will examine various nonverbal strategies for the expression and suppression of emotion.

Why is it that some people are more effective at communicating emotion than others? A possible explanation is offered by examining the study of **emotional intelligence** (EI), which refers to one's ability to read the emotions of others while monitoring one's own emotions in an effective manner.

How do you communicate your emotions to others?

Mayer and Salovey (1997) developed an ability-focus model that identifies four key skills involved in the effective management of emotions in our interactions with others. These include:

- Identifying and perceiving the emotions experienced by self and others.
- Expressing our emotions or moods effectively in interactions with others.
- Comprehending and understanding others' emotional responses or changes in emotions.
- Regulating and managing the expression of emotion to help accomplish our relational goals.

Emotional intelligence involves careful reflection and consideration of the possible range of emotions that your friend may be experiencing. In addition, consider your own emotions and the role they play in your interactions with others. Since many of our emotions or moods are expressed via nonverbal behaviors, we need to be cognizant of the various ways emotions are communicated. Emotional intelligence equips us with the ability to choose verbal and nonverbal messages that clearly express how we are

feeling. At times, others behave in ways that we may perceive as being irrational, and we label them as being "moody." Rather than simply interpreting their behavior as being erratic, we use our emotional intelligence to help understand why they may be experiencing changes in their typical communication style. Can you recall a time when you felt like you couldn't control your emotions? While you may be incredibly frustrated with your coworkers for their lack of participation on a project, yelling and threatening may not be the most effective ways to express your frustration. Emotional intelligence enables us to carefully consider the most effective ways to control our own emotions and to manage the emotions being expressed by others.

EMOTIONS IN RELATIONAL CONTEXTS

In Chapters 12 through 15, we will focus on communication in a variety of relationship contexts including interactions with family members, coworkers, and health-care providers. Because emotion plays an integral role in our relationships with others, communication scholars have examined the impact of emotions in a variety of contexts.

Emotion and Health

Visits to physicians often produce high levels of anxiety. Even during a routine checkup, our uncertainty about what the doctor may tell us can heighten a variety of emotional responses. Not only do we experience a variety of emotions during our exam, but we also expect others to respond appropriately to our emotional states. Emotions influence our responses toward others, and they often emerge from our own health-related issues. Good health often results in happiness or other positive emotional states, while poor health triggers negative emotional responses such as frustration or depression.

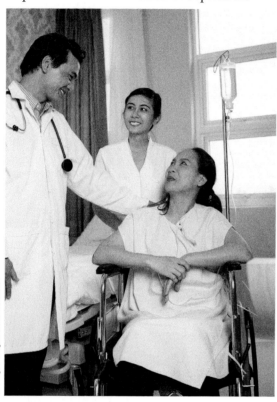

What role do our emotions play in our health?

Studies that have examined the impact of emotions in the health-care context have discovered some of the following:

• Caring for the health concerns of others affects our own emotions. For example, people tend to respond in sympathetic ways to those who experience poor health (Hatfield, Cacioppo, & Rapson, 1994).

• Patients want and expect communicative responses that demonstrate emotional support from their physicians when sharing their concerns about health-related issues (Hummert, 2009).

Emotion plays a crucial role in our health and our perceptions of health care. Not only is it important to understand the personal implications for the well-being of our health, but it is also crucial to explore the impact of emotion on our effectiveness in our professional careers.

Work and Emotion

Have you ever considered how your emotions influence your ability to perform your work responsibilities effectively? Suppose you spill a cup of coffee on your new suit as you rush to an important business meeting. The frustration experienced as a result of the fresh coffee stain may cause you to become distracted during your presentation because you perceive everyone's attention as being on your suit rather than your presentation. Because of your emotional state, a well-prepared presentation is ineffectively delivered. Not only is it important to understand the impact of our emotions on our communication, but it is also essential to consider how our personality "fits" with specific careers or organizational climates. Someone who is argumentative or who experiences high levels of communication apprehension would probably not fare well in a career in customer service that requires them to express positive and engaging emotions on a daily basis.

In Chapter 14 we will focus on communication and relationships in the workplace. Communication is an integral part of our careers, thus understanding and controlling our emotional responses at work can influence our job satisfaction and professional success. A study by Duke, Goodman, Treadway, and Breland (2009) found that employees who experience high levels of workplace stress feel less connected to the organization, while those with lower levels of workplace stress report higher levels of job satisfaction and are more likely to remain with the organization.

Goleman (1998) studied the relationship between emotional intelligence (EI) and leadership. He identified the following five key EI variables that are exhibited by those who are perceived to be effective leaders:

- **Self-awareness**—awareness of one's own emotions, motivations, and goals
- **Self-regulation**—ability to recognize and adapt one's own emotions in response to a situation
- **Social skill**—ability to manage people to achieve the organization's goals
- **Empathy**—consideration of the feelings and emotional responses of others
- **Motivation**—desire to manage moods and emotions to accomplish goals and objectives

While we may be unable to control or manage the emotions of our supervisors or coworkers, recognizing and validating their presence and impact on motivation and job satisfaction are important to enhance one's professional relationships.

Emotions in the Classroom

Not only do your emotions impact your professional success, but they can also play an important role in your academic studies. Suppose you find science to be a challenging subject, but you're required to complete a human anatomy class for your major. How do your emotions about the class influence your performance and your communication with the teacher and your classmates?

Emotional response theory (ERT) proposes that students experience positive or negative emotional responses toward learning (Mottet, Frymier, & Beebe, 2006). For example, positive emotions concerning a class may result in a student being more willing to communicate during discussions or to meet with the instructor during office hours. Research that has examined the impact of emotion in the classroom context indicates that:

- Students report more positive emotions toward a class when the teacher exhibits immediate communication behaviors such as smiling, calling students by name, making eye contact, and moving around the classroom while lecturing (Mottet, Frymier, & Beebe, 2006).
- Being able to identify and interpret an instructor's emotions is important to students. Less effort is required for students to engage in emotion work when teachers manage their emotions effectively (Titsworth, Quinlan, & Mazer, 2010).

Students react more positively in a class when the teacher engages them by smiling, making eye contact, and moving around the classroom while lecturing.

Cultures differ in their views of the appropriateness of sharing emotion.

Given the diverse backgrounds of students and teachers who communicate in face-to-face and online classrooms, it is important to consider the impact that diversity plays in shaping our expectations for communicating emotions.

Diversity and the Expression of Emotion

Recall our earlier discussion of message design logic and how societal rules or norms are taken into consideration when expressing emotion. Our culture serves as the primary source for teaching expectations for the appropriate display of emotion. In Chapter 12 we will explore how diversity shapes our communication styles and expectations. Two categories of diversity that directly influence our expression of emotion are culture and gender.

Cultures differ in their views of the appropriateness of sharing emotion. Eastern cultures, such as Japan and China, tend to encourage more reserved expression of emotion. In contrast, Western cultures, such as the United States, promote open and free expression of emotion. Not only do cultures differ in their willingness to express emotion, but there are also variations in the nonverbal channels used to communicate feelings. Western cultures tend to favor facial expressions as the preferred channel for sharing emotions, while Eastern cultures focus on the tone of voice for clues about emotional states.

While cultures may differ in terms of the preference and channels for emotion expression, Ekman and Friesen (1986) identified emotions that are nonverbally expressed and understood across cultures. Examples of these universally recognized expressions of emotion include anger, disgust, fear, happiness, sadness, and surprise. These will be discussed in more detail in Chapter 6.

The communication of emotion also differs as a result of sex differences. Multiple studies have examined emotional differences between males and females. In general, findings support the notion that women tend to be more emotionally expressive than men (Kring & Gordon, 1998). One possible explanation for the sex difference in the expression of emotion may be traced to the socialization messages received during childhood. Boys are often told, "Men don't cry!" while girls are nurtured and encouraged to openly express their feelings and moods. These messages influence our perceptions about sharing our feelings later in life.

In addition, Kring and Gordon's 1998 study found that gender roles (e.g., masculinity and femininity) influence the expression of emotion. Androgynous participants, or those who are able to be both assertive and responsive, were more expressive in their displays of emotion compared with those who had a primarily masculine or feminine gender role orientation. Both explanations (sex differences and gender role differences) help us to predict and explain "why" individuals differ in their expression of emotion.

SUMMARY

Personality and emotion are at the core of our communication behaviors. Understanding how these trait and state behaviors influence our interactions with others is essential to ensuring our ability to build and maintain effective relationships. Being able to predict and explain how others may respond in a given situation can assist us in creating messages that enhance our relationships. Communication-based personality traits such as CA, WTC, verbal aggression, argumentativeness, assertiveness, humor orientation, and affective orientation were discussed in this chapter. Some of the behaviors associated with these communication traits can be problematic for both sources and receivers. While personality enables us to make predictions about how others may respond, understanding the influence of temporary moods or feelings is also important. Emotions often change, and the potential impact of emotional reactions on interpersonal relationships is important to consider. We shared examples of research on how emotion influences communication in a variety of communication contexts: health, organizational, cultural, and educational. After reading this chapter, you now have a better understanding of these traits and how emotional states can either hinder or facilitate our communication with others.

DISCUSSION QUESTIONS

1. Why is it important to understand personality differences and their potential impact on our communication? What are some examples of careers in which various personality characteristics would be beneficial or harmful?

2. Discuss the challenges associated with communicating and detecting emotions in mediated contexts. Recall a situation in which your emotions were misunderstood in a text message or email. What steps can you take to ensure that your mediated messages convey emotions accurately?

3. Identify examples of situations where our emotions can impact our interactions with family members, friends, co-workers, and teachers/classmates.

SELF ASSESSMENTS

Personal Report of Communication Apprehension

This instrument is composed of twenty-four statements concerning feelings about communicating with other people. Please indicate the degree to which each statement applies to you by marking whether you (1) strong agree, (2) agree, (3) are undecided, (4) disagree, or (5) strongly disagree. Work quickly; record your first impression.

_____ 1. I dislike participating in group discussions.

_____ 2. Generally, I am comfortable while participating in group discussions.

_____ 3. I am tense and nervous while participating in group discussions.

_____ 4. I like to get involved in group discussions.

_____ 5. Engaging in group discussion with new people makes me tense and nervous.

_____ 6. I am calm and relaxed when participating in group discussions.

_____ 7. Generally, I am nervous when I have to participate in group discussions.

_____ 8. Usually I am calm and relaxed while participating in meetings.

_____ 9. I am very calm and relaxed when I am called upon to express an opinion at a meeting.

_____10. I am afraid to "press" myself at meetings.

_____11. Communicating at meetings usually makes me uncomfortable.

_____12. I am very relaxed when answering questions at a meeting.

_____13. While participating in a conversation with a new acquaintance, I feel very nervous.

_____14. I have no fear of speaking up in conversations.

_____15. Ordinarily I am very tense and nervous in conversations.

_____16. Ordinarily I am very calm and relaxed in conversations.

_____17. While conversing with a new acquaintance, I feel very relaxed.

_____18. I'm afraid to speak up in conversations.

_____19. I have no fear of giving a speech.

_____20. Certain parts of my body feel very tense and rigid while I am giving a speech.

_____21. I feel relaxed while giving a speech.

_____22. My thoughts become confused and jumbled when I am giving a speech.

_____23. I face the prospect of giving a speech with confidence

_____24. While giving a speech, I get so nervous I forget facts I really know.

Scoring: In order to compute the total score follow this formula: Total = 72 + (sum of the scores from items 2, 4, 6, 8, 9, 12, 14, 16, 17, 19, 21, 23) − (sum of the scores from items 1, 3, 5, 7, 10, 11, 13, 15, 18, 20, 22, 24)

The average score for college students is typically 65.6. Scores of 80 and higher indicate high levels of CA. Scores of 50 and lower indicate lower levels of CA.

Source: Richmond, V. P., & McCroskey, J. C. (1998). *Communication apprehension, avoidance and effectiveness* (5th ed.). Boston, MA: Allyn & Bacon. Copyright ©1998 by Pearson Education. Reprinted by permission of the publisher.

Willingness to Communicate Scale (WTC)

Below are twenty situations in which a person might or might not choose to communicate. Presume you have *completely free choice*. Indicate the percentage of times you would choose to *communicate* in each type of situation. Indicate in the space at the left what percent of the time you would choose to communicate.

0 = never, 100 = always

_____ 1. Talk with a service station attendant.

_____ 2. Talk with a physician.

_____ 3. Present a talk to a group of strangers.

_____ 4. Talk with an acquaintance while standing in line.

_____ 5. Talk with a salesperson in a store.

_____ 6. Talk in a large meeting of friends.

_____ 7. Talk with a police officer.

_____ 8. Talk in a small group of strangers.

_____ 9. Talk with a friend while standing in line.

_____10. Talk with a waiter/waitress in a restaurant.

_____11. Talk in a large meeting of acquaintances.

_____12. Talk with a stranger while standing in line.

_____13. Talk with a secretary.

_____14. Present a talk to a group of friends.

_____15. Talk in a small group of acquaintances.

_____16. Talk with a garbage collector.

_____17. Talk in a large meeting of strangers.

_____18. Talk with a spouse (or girl/boyfriend).

_____19. Talk in a small group of friends.

_____20. Present a talk to a group of acquaintances.

Scoring: To calculate the total WTC score follow these steps:

Step 1: Add scores from items 3, 8, 12, and 17; then divide by 4.
Step 2: Add scores from items 4, 11, 15, and 20; then divide by 4.
Step 3: Add scores from items 6, 7, 14, and 19; then divide by 4.
Step 4: Add the final scores from steps 1, 2, and 3; then divide by 3.

>82 High overall WTC
<52 Low overall WTC

Source: Richmond, V.P. and J.C. McCrosky, 1995. *Communication: Apprehension, avoidance, and effectiveness.* (4th ed.). Scottsdale, AZ: Gorsuch Scarisbrick.

Human Orientation Scale

Below are descriptions of how you may communicate in general. Please use the scale below to rate the degree to which each statement applies to your communication.

1 = strong disagree
2 = disagree
3 = neutral
4 = agree
5 = strongly agree

_____ 1. I regularly tell jokes and funny stories when in a group.

_____ 2. People usually laugh when I tell jokes or funny stories.

_____ 3. I have no memory for jokes for funny stories.

_____ 4. I can be funny without having to rehearse a joke.

_____ 5. Being funny is a natural communication style with me.

_____ 6. I cannot tell a joke well.

_____ 7. People seldom ask me to tell stories.

_____ 8. My friends would say I am a funny person.

_____ 9. People don't seem to pay close attention when I tell a joke.

_____10. Even funny jokes seem flat when I tell them.

_____11. I can easily remember jokes and stories.

_____12. People often ask me to tell jokes or stories.

_____13. My friends would not say that I am a funny person.

_____14. I don't tell jokes or stories even when asked to.

_____15. I tell stories and jokes very well.

_____16. Of all the people I know, I am one of the funniest.

_____17. I use humor to communicate in a variety of situations.

84

Step 1: Flip the responses (5 = 1, 4 = 2, 2 = 4, and 1 = 5) for questions 3, 6, 7, 9, 10, 13, 14.

Step 2: Once questions have been flipped, add up all items. Your score should fall somewhere between 17 and 85.

For college students the average on the HO measure is typically around 61.

If you score 71 or higher you are considered high in humor orientation (high HO).

If you score in the 50-70 range you are considered moderate in humor orientation.

If you score 49 and below you are considered low in humor orientation (a low HO).

Source: Booth-Butterfield, M., & Booth-Butterfield, S. (1991). Individual differences in the communication of humorous messages. *Southern Communication Journal*, 56, 32–40. Reprinted by permission of Taylor & Francis.

Affective Orientation Scale

The following statements refer to the feelings and emotions people have and how people use their feelings and emotions to guide their behavior. There are no right or wrong answers. Also realize that emotions and feelings can be positive or negative. A person can feel anger; another can feel love and tenderness. Both cases, however, are emotion. Use the following 5-point scale to indicate whether you, (5) strongly agree, (4) agree, (3) are uncertain, (2) disagree, or (1) strongly disagree with each statement.

_____ 1. I use my feelings to determine what I should do in situations.

_____ 2. I listen to what my "gut" or "heart" says in many situations.

_____ 3. My emotions tell me what to do in many cases.

_____ 4. I try not to let feelings guide my actions.

_____ 5. I am aware of and use my feelings as a guide more than others do.

_____ 6. I won't let my emotions influence how I act most of the time.

_____ 7. I follow what my feelings say I should do in most situations.

_____ 8. Most of the time I avoid letting my emotions guide what I do.

_____ 9. I usually let my internal feelings direct my behavior.

_____10. Usually my emotions are good predictors of how I will act.

_____11. My actions are often influenced by my awareness of my emotions.

_____12. My emotions provide me solid direction in my life.

_____13. How I act often depends on what my feelings tell me to do.

_____14. Even subtle emotions often guide my actions.

_____15. When I am aware of my emotional response, I listen to it to determine what to do.

Scoring: To determine the score on this scale, complete the following steps:

Step 1: Reverse the scores of 4, 6, and 8, and then add them together.
Step 2: Add the rest of the scores together.
Step 3: Total steps 1 and 2.
>60 Higher affective orientation
<44 Lower affective orientation

Source: Booth-Butterfield, M., & Booth-Butterfield, S. (1990). Conceptualizing affect as information in communication production. *Human Communication Research*, 16, 451–476. Reprinted with permission of Blackwell Publishing, www.blackwell-publishing.com.

Argumentativeness Scale

This questionnaire contains statements about arguing about controversial issues. Indicate how often each statement is true for you personally by placing the appropriate number in the blank to the left of the statement. Indicate if the statement is; (1) almost never true for you, (2) rarely true for you, (3) occasionally true for you, (4) often true for you, or (5) almost always true for you. Remember, consider each item in terms of arguing controversial issues.

_____ 1. While in an argument, I worry that the person I am arguing with will form a negative impression of me.

_____ 2. Arguing over controversial issues improves my intelligence.

_____ 3. I enjoy avoiding arguments.

_____ 4. I am energetic and enthusiastic when I argue.

_____ 5. Once I finish an argument I promise myself that I will not get into another.

_____ 6. Arguing with a person creates more problems for me than it solves.

_____ 7. I have a pleasant, good feeling when I win a point in an argument.

_____ 8. When I finish arguing with someone I feel nervous and upset.

_____ 9. I enjoy a good argument over a controversial issue.

_____10. I get an unpleasant feeling when I realize I am about to get into an argument.

_____11. I enjoy defending my point of view on an issue.

_____12. I am happy when I keep an argument from happening.

_____13. I do not like to miss the opportunity to argue a controversial issue.

_____14. I prefer being with people who rarely disagree with me.

_____15. I consider an argument an exciting intellectual challenge.

_____16. I find myself unable to think of effective points during an argument.

_____17. I feel refreshed and satisfied after an argument on a controversial issue.

_____18. I have the ability to do well in an argument.

_____19. I try to avoid getting into arguments.

_____20. I feel excited when I expect that a conversation I am in is leading to an argument.

Scoring: To compute the Argumentativeness trait score, follow these steps:

Step 1: Add scores from items 2, 4, 7, 9, 11, 13, 15, 17, 18, and 20.
Step 2: Add 60 to the sum obtained in Step 1.
Step 3: Add your scores on items 1,3,5,6,8,10,12,14,16, and 19
Step 4: To compute your argumentativeness score, subtract the total obtained in Step 3 from the total obtained in Step 2.
   73–100 High in argumentativeness
   56–72 Moderate in argumentativeness
   20–55 Low in argumentativeness

Verbal Aggressiveness Scale

This survey is concerned with how we try to get people to comply with our wishes. Indicate how often each statement is true for you personally when you try to influence others by using the following scale: (1) almost never true, (2) rarely true, (3) occasionally true, (4) often true, (5) almost always true.

_____ 1. I am extremely careful to avoid attacking individuals' intelligence when I attack their ideas.

_____ 2. When individuals are very stubborn, I use insults to soften the stubbornness.

_____ 3. I try very hard to avoid having other people feel bad about themselves when I try to influence them.

_____ 4. When people refuse to do a task I know is important, without good reason, I tell them they are unreasonable.

_____ 5. When others do things I regard as stupid, I try to be extremely gentle with them.

_____ 6. If individuals I am trying to influence really deserve it, I attack their character.

_____ 7. When people behave in ways that are in very poor taste, I insult them in order to shock them into proper behavior.

_____ 8. I try to make people feel good about themselves when their ideas are stupid.

_____ 9. When people simply will not budge on a matter of importance, I lose my temper and say rather strong things to them.

_____ 10. When people criticize my shortcomings, I take it in good humor and do not try to get back at them.

_____ 11. When individuals insult me, I get a lot of pleasure out of really telling them off.

_____ 12. When I dislike individuals greatly, I try not to show it in what I say or how I say it.

_____ 13. I like poking fun at people who do things that are very stupid in order to stimulate their intelligence.

_____ 14. When I attack a persons' ideas, I try not to damage their self-concepts.

_____ 15. When I try to influence people, I make a great effort not to offend them.

_____16. When people do things that are mean or cruel, I attack their character in order to help correct their behavior.

_____17. I refuse to participate in arguments which involve personal attacks.

_____18. When nothing seems to work when trying to influence others, I yell and scream in order to get some movement from them.

_____19. When I am not able to refute others' positions, I try to make them feel defensive in order to weaken their positions.

_____20. When an argument shifts to personal attacks, I try very hard to change the subject.

Scoring: Sum the scores all the items after reversing scoring for items 1, 3, 5, 8, 10, 12, 14, 15, 17, and 20.

Average score for college students is 49. Scores of 59 and higher indicate higher levels of verbal aggression. Scores of 39 and lower indicate lower levels of verbal aggression.

Source: Infante, D. A., & Wigley, C. J. (1986). Verbal aggressiveness: An interpersonal model and measure. *Communication Monographs*, 53, 61-69. Reprinted with permission from Taylor & Francis.

KEY TERMS AND DEFINITIONS

ADAPTATION TRAITS: category of communication traits that focuses on predispositions to be mindful and aware of others in communication situations.

AFFECTIVE ORIENTATION: an awareness of one's own emotional states that is used when making behavioral decisions.

AGGRESSIVE TRAITS: category of communication traits that focuses on the tendency to engage in forceful or potentially destructive communication.

APPREHENSION TRAITS: category of communication traits that focuses on the fear associated with communication.

APPROPRIATENESS: one of three key elements used to evaluate one's interaction involvement. Focuses on the responsiveness to others' messages in an acceptable way.

ARGUMENTATIVENESS: predisposition to advocate and defend positions in situations where differences of opinion are expressed, while verbally challenging the opinions and positions of others.

ASSERTIVENESS: the capability to defend one's rights and wishes while still respecting and acknowledging the rights of others.

AWARENESS: one of three key elements of interaction involvement that focuses on our mindfulness of our own attitudes, feelings, and thoughts about messages that we receive from others.

COMMUNICATION APPREHENSION (CA): an individual's level of fear or anxiety about real or anticipated communication with another person.

COMMUNICATOR STYLE: verbal and nonverbal reactions that provide cues to others about how our messages should be interpreted and understood.

COMMUNICATION TRAITS: a subset of personality traits that focuses specifically on our relatively consistent behaviors as a source and receiver of messages.

CONSTRUCTIVE COMMUNICATION: messages designed to achieve personal goals without attacking or demeaning others.

CONVENTIONAL LOGIC: addresses the appropriateness of the message delivery.

DESTRUCTIVE COMMUNICATION: messages designed with the intent to attack another's self-esteem in order to fulfill personal goals.

EMOTIONAL INTELLIGENCE (EI): the ability to read the emotions of others while effectively monitoring one's own emotions in communication.

EMOTIONAL RESPONSE THEORY (ERT): posits that students experience positive and negative responses toward learning.

EMOTIONS: intense feelings or reactions that are directed toward someone or something.

EMOTION WORK: effort that is required to express one's emotions effectively and to interpret the emotions of others accurately.

EMPATHY: consideration of the feelings and emotional responses of others.

EXPRESSIVE LOGIC: focuses on the source of the message and the level of comfort or willingness to deliver a message.

EVOCATION: open expression of emotion.

FLAMING: sending or posting of electronic messages that can be perceived as attacking, hurtful, or offensive.

HUMOR ORIENTATION (HO): the extent to which people use humor in their interactions with others, and their awareness of the appropriateness of humor in certain situations.

INTERACTION INVOLVEMENT: a general awareness of others' feelings, attitudes, and experiences during conversations. Involvement is demonstrated by a person's active participation during an interaction.

MESSAGE DESIGN LOGIC (MDL): ability to alter the design and delivery of a message as a result of one's ability to evaluate the content of the message and organize it in such a way as to help ensure its effective delivery.

MOTIVATION: desire to manage moods and emotions to accomplish goals and objectives.

PERCEPTIVENESS: one of three key elements in evaluating interaction involvement that involves consideration and reflection of the intended meaning of another's message.

PERPETUAL CONFLICT: ongoing disagreements between relational partners that are often directly related to personality differences.

PERSONALITY: relatively long-lasting patterns of behaviors, feelings, and attitudes that make each person unique.

PRESENTATION TRAITS: category of communication traits that focuses on the impression formation, types of information shared, and involvement in interactions with others.

RHETORICAL LOGIC: evaluate the reactions of others and incorporate flexibility in the delivery of a message.

SELF-AWARENESS: an awareness of one's own emotions, motivations, and goals.

SELF-REGULATION: the ability to recognize and adapt one's own emotions in response to a situation.

SOCIAL SKILL: ability to manage people to achieve an organization's goals.

STATE APPROACH: an approach to studying personality and communication behaviors that examines how individuals communicate in specific contexts or situations.

SUPPRESSION: refraining from the expression of emotion.

TRAIT APPROACH: an approach to studying personality and communication behavior that identifies consistent ways that people behave the majority of the time.

VERBAL AGGRESSIVENESS: the tendency to attack the self-concept of an individual instead of addressing the other person's arguments.

WILLINGNESS TO COMMUNICATE (WTC): communication trait that addresses an individual's propensity to avoid or approach communication with others.

REFERENCES

Andersen, P. A., & Guerrero, L. K. (Eds.). (1998). *Handbook of communication and emotion: Research, theory, and contexts.* San Diego, CA: Academic Press.

Aylor, B., & Opplinger, P. (2003). Out-of-class communication and student perceptions of instructor humor orientation and socio-communicative style. *Communication Education, 52,* 122–134.

Baker, D. D., & Ganster, D. C. (1985). Leader communication style: A test of average versus vertical dyad linkage models. *Group & Organization Studies, 10,* 242–259.

Bayer, C. L., & Cegala, D. J. (1992). Trait verbal aggressiveness and argumentativeness: Relations with parenting style. *Western Journal of Communication, 56,* 301–310.

Beatty, M. J., McCroskey, J. C., & Heisel, A. D. (1998). Communication apprehension as temperamental expression: A communibiological paradigm. *Communication Monographs, 65,* 197–219.

Blackhart, G. C., Fitzpatrick, J., & Williamson, J. (2014). Dispositional factors predicting use of online dating sites and behaviors related to online dating. *Computers in Human Behavior, 33,* 113–118.

Booth-Butterfield, M., & Andrighetti, A. (1993). *The role of affective orientation and nonverbal sensitivity in the interpretation of communication in acquaintance rape.* Paper presented at the Annual Convention of the Eastern Communication Association, New Haven, CT.

Booth-Butterfield, M., & Booth-Butterfield, S. (1990). Conceptualizing affect as information in communication production. *Human Communication Research, 16,* 451–476.

Booth-Butterfield, M., & Booth-Butterfield, S. (1994). The affective orientation to communication: Conceptual and empirical distinctions. *Communication Quarterly, 42,* 331–344.

Booth-Butterfield, M., & Booth-Butterfield, S. (1998). Emotionality and affective orientation. In J.C. McCroskey et al. (Eds.), *Communication and personality* (pp. 171–190). Cresskill, NJ: Hampton Press.

Booth-Butterfield, M., & Booth-Butterfield, S. (1991). Individual differences in the communication of humorous messages. *Southern Communication Journal, 56,* 32–40.

Booth-Butterfield, M., Booth-Butterfield, S., & Wanzer, M. B. (2007). Funny students cope better: Patterns of humor enactment and coping effectiveness. *Communication Quarterly, 55,* 299–315.

Boster, F. J., & Levine, T. (1988). Individual differences and compliance-gaining message selection: The effects of verbal aggressiveness, argumentativeness, dogmatism, and negativism. *Communication Research Reports, 5,* 114–119.

Buller, M. K., & Buller, D. B. (1987). Physicians' communication style and patient satisfaction. *Journal of Health and Social Behavior, 28,* 375–388.

Cavaiola, A. A., & Lavender, N. J. (2000). *Toxic coworkers: How to deal with dysfunctional people on the job.* Oakland, CA: New Harbinger Publications.

Cegala, D. (1981). Interaction involvement: A cognitive dimension of communicative competence. *Communication Education, 30,* 109–121.

Cegala, D. J., (1984). Affective and cognitive manifestations of interaction involvement during unstructured and competitive interactions. *Communication Monographs, 51,* 320–338.

Chen, L. (2003). Communication in intercultural relationships. In W.B. Gudykunst (Ed.), *Cross-cultural and intercultural communication* (pp. 225–242). Thousand Oaks, CA: Sage.

Daly, J. A., & Bippus, A. (1998). Personality and interpersonal communication. In J. C. McCroskey, J. A. Daly, M. M. Martin, & M. J. Beatty (Eds.), *Communication and personality: Trait perspectives* (pp. 1–40). Cresskill, NJ: Hampton.

Daly, J. A., Richmond, V. P., & Leth, S. (1979). Social communicative anxiety and the personnel selection process: Testing the similarity effect in selection decisions. *Human Communication Research, 6,* 18–32.

Dolin, D., & Booth-Butterfield, M. (1993). Reach out and touch someone: Analysis of nonverbal comforting responses. *Communication Quarterly, 41,* 383–393.

Duke, A. B., Goodman, J. M., Treadway, D. C., & Breland, J. W. (2009). Perceived organizational support as a moderator of emotional labor/outcomes relationships. *Journal of Applied Social Psychology, 39,* 1013–1034.

Ekman, P., & Friesen, W. V. (1986). A new pan-cultural facial expression of emotion. *Motivation and Emotion, 10,* 159–168.

Goffman, E. (1967). *Interaction ritual: Essays in face-to-face behavior.* Chicago, IL: Aldine.

Goleman, D. (1998). *Working with emotional intelligence.* New York, NY: Bantam.

Gottman, J. M., & Silver, N. (1999). *The seven principles for making marriage work.* New York, NY: Crown Publishing.

Hatfield, E., Cacioppo, J. T., & Rapson, R. L. (1994). *Emotional contagion.* New York, NY: Cambridge University Press.

Hochschild, A. R. (1979). Emotion work, feeling rules, and social structure. *American Journal of Sociology, 85,* 551–575.

Honeycutt, J., & Brown, R. (1998). Did you hear the one about?: Typological and spousal differences in the planning of jokes and sense of humor in marriage. *Communication Quarterly, 46,* 342–352.

Hummert, M. L. (2009). Not just preaching to the choir: Communication scholarship does make a difference. *Journal of Applied Communication Research, 37,* 215–224.

Infante, D. (1981). Trait argumentativeness as a predictor of communicative behavior in situations requiring argument. *Central States Speech Journal, 32,* 265–272.

Infante, D. (1985). Inducing women to be more argumentative: Source credibility effects. *Journal of Applied Communication Research, 13,* 33–44.

Infante, D. (1987). Aggressiveness. In J. C. McCroskey and J. A. Daly (Eds.), *Personality and interpersonal communication* (pp. 157–192). Newbury Park, CA: Sage.

Infante, D. (1995). Teaching students to understand and control verbal aggression. *Communication Education, 44,* 51–63.

Infante, D. A., Chandler, T. A., & Rudd, J. E. (1989). Test of an argumentative skill deficiency model of interspousal violence. *Communication Monographs, 56,* 163–177.

Infante, D. A., & Gorden, W. I. (1991). How employees see the boss: Test of an argumentative and affirming model of superiors' communicative behavior. *Western Journal of Speech Communication, 55,* 294–304.

Infante, D. A., & Rancer, A. S. (1982). A conceptualization and measure of argumentativeness. *Journal of Personality Assessment, 46,* 72–80.

Infante, D. A., Riddle, B. L., Horvath, C. A., & Tumlin, S. A. (1992). Verbal aggressiveness: Messages and reasons. *Communication Quarterly, 40,* 116–126.

Infante, D. A., & Wigley, C. J. (1986). Verbal aggressiveness: An interpersonal model and measure. *Communication Monographs, 53,* 61–69.

Kazoleas, D. (1993). The impact of argumentativeness on resistance to persuasion. *Human Communication Research, 20,* 118–137.

Keating, C. J. (1984). *Dealing with difficult people.* Mahwah, NJ: Paulist Press.

Kring, A. M., & Gordon, A. H. (1998). Sex differences in emotion: Expression, experience, and physiology. *Journal of Personality and Social Psychology, 74,* 686–703.

Law, D. M., Shapka, J. D., Domene, J. F., & Gagne, M. H. (2012). Are cyberbullies really bullies?: An investigation of reactive and proactive online aggression. *Computers in Human Behavior, 28,* 664–672.

Limon, S. M., & La France, B. H. (2005). Communication traits and leadership emergence: Examining the impact of argumentativeness, communication apprehension and verbal aggressiveness in work groups. *Southern Communication Journal, 70,* 123–133.

Lippert, L. R., Titsworth, B. S., & Hunt, S. K. (2005). The ecology of academic risk: Relationships between communication apprehension, verbal aggression, supportive communication, and students' academic risk. *Communication Studies, 56,* 1–21.

Maxwell, J. (2002). *The 17 essential qualities of a team player: Becoming the kind of person every team wants.* Nashville, TN: Thomas Nelson, Inc.

Mayer, J. D., & Salovey, P. (1997). What is emotional intelligence? In P. Salovey & D. Sluyter (Eds.), *Emotional development and emotional intelligence: Implications for educators* (pp. 3–31). New York: Basic Books.

McCroskey, J. C. (1978). Validity of the PRCA as an index of oral communication apprehension. *Communication Monographs, 45,* 192–203.

McCroskey, J. C. (2006). The role of culture in a communibiological approach to communication. *Human Communication, 9,* 31–35.

McCroskey, J. C., Daly, J. A., & Sorensen, G. A. (1976). Personality correlates of communication apprehension. *Human Communication Research, 2,* 376–380.

McCroskey, J. C., & Richmond, V. P. (1987). Willingness to communicate. In J. C. McCroskey and J. A. Daly (Eds.), *Personality and interpersonal communication* (pp. 129–156). Newbury Park, CA: Sage.

McCroskey, J. C., & Richmond, V. P. (1998). Willingness to communicate. In J. C. McCroskey, J.

A. Daly, M. M. Martin, & M. J. Beatty (Eds.), *Communication and personality* (pp. 119–132). Cresskill, NJ: Hampton Press.

Miczo, N. (2004). Humor, ability, unwillingness to communicate, loneliness, and perceived stress: Testing a security theory. *Communication Studies, 55*(2), 209–226.

Miller, L. D., & Ratusnik, D. L. (1979). *Communication between physicians and nurses: An explanatory study of self and other perceptions.* Paper presented at the International Communication Association Convention, Philadelphia, PA.

Mizco, N. (2004). Humor ability, unwillingness to communicate, loneliness, and perceived stress: Testing a security theory. *Communication Studies, 55,* 209–226.

Mottet, T. P., Frymier, A. B., & Beebe, S. A. (2006). Theorizing about instructional communication. In T. P. Mottet, V. P. Richmond, & J. C. McCroskey (Eds.), *Handbook of instructional communication* (pp. 255–282). Boston, MA: Pearson.

Myers, S. A., & Johnson, A. D. (2003). Verbal aggression and liking in interpersonal relationships. *Communication Research Reports, 20,* 90–96.

Noar, S. M., Morokoff, P. J., & Redding, C. A. (2002). Sexual assertiveness in heterosexually active men: A test of three samples. *AIDS Education and Prevention, 14,* 330–342.

Norton, R. W. (1977). Teacher effectiveness as a function of communicator style. In B. D. Rubin (Ed.) *Communication Yearbook 1* (pp. 525–542). New Brunswick, NJ: Transaction Books.

Norton, R. W. (1978). Foundation of a communicator style construct. *Human Communication Research, 4,* 99–112.

Norton, R. W. (1983). *Communicator style: Theory, applications, and measures.* Beverly Hills, CA: Sage.

O'Keefe, B. J. (1988). The logic of message design: Individual differences in reasoning about communication. *Communication Monographs, 55,* 80–103.

Orr, E. S., Sisic, M., Ross, C., Simmering, M. C., Areneault, J. M., & Orr, R. (2009). The influence of shyness on the use of Facebook in an undergraduate sample. *CyberPsychology and Behavior, 12,* 337–340.

Pennington, N., & Hall, J. A. (2014). An analysis of humor orientation on Facebook: A lens model approach. *Humor: International Journal of Humor Research, 27*(1), 1+. Retrieved from http://go.galegroup.com/ps/i.do?id=GALE%-7CA362727579&v=2.1&u=athe17405&it=r&p+LitRC&sw=w&asid+fa685a1d5605875f-cf244ff8467040f2. (NOTE: Please make sure to italicize the journal name and volume number in the citation)

Rancer, A. S. (1998). Argumentativeness. In McCroskey et al. (Eds.), *Communication and personality* (pp. 149–170). Cresskill, NJ: Hampton Press.

Rancer, A. S., & Avtgis, T. A. (2006). *Argumentative and aggressive communication: Theory, research and application.* Thousand Oaks, CA: Sage.

Richmond, V. P., & Martin, M. M. (1998). Sociocommunicative style and sociocommunicative orientation. In McCroskey et al. (Eds.), *Communication and personality.* Cresskill, NJ: Hampton Press.

Richmond, V. P., & McCroskey, J. C. (1990). Reliability and separation of factors on the assertiveness-responsiveness measure. *Psychological Reports, 67,* 449–450.

Richmond, V. P., & Roach, D. K. (1992). Willingness to communicate and employee success in U.S. organizations. *Journal of Applied Communication, 20,* 95–115.

Ritchie, L. D. & Fitzpatrick, M. A. (1990). Family communication patterns: Measuring intrapersonal perceptions of interpersonal relationships. *Communication Research, 17,* 523–544.

Rizzo, B., Wanzer, M. B., & Booth-Butterfield, M. (1999). Individual differences in managers' use of humor: Subordinate perceptions of managers' humor orientation, effectiveness, and humor behaviors. *Communication Research Reports, 16,* 370–376.

Sheeks, M. S., & Birchmeier, Z. P. (2007). Shyness, sociability, and the use of computer-mediated communication in relationship development. *CyberPsychology and Behavior, 10,* 64–70.

Titsworth, S., Quinlan, M. M., & Mazer, J. P. (2010). Emotion in teaching and learning: Development and validation of the classroom emotions scale. *Communication Education, 59,* 431–452.

Umphrey, L. R., Wickersham, J. A., & Sherblom, J. C. (2008). Student perceptions of the instructor's relational characteristics, the classroom communication experience, and the interaction involvement in face-to-face versus video conference instruction. *Communication Research Reports*, *25*(2), 102–114. doi:10.1080/08824090802021954

Wanzer, M. B., Booth-Butterfield, M., & Booth-Butterfield, S. (1995). The funny people: A source orientation to the communication of humor. *Communication Quarterly*, *43*, 142–154.

Wanzer, M. B., Booth-Butterfield, M., & Booth-Butterfield, S. (1996). Are funny people popular? An examination of humor orientation, verbal aggressiveness, and social attraction. *Communication Quarterly*, *44*, 42–52.

Wanzer, M. B., Booth-Butterfield, M., & Booth-Butterfield, S. (2005). "If we didn't use humor, we'd cry": Humorous coping communication in health care settings. *Journal of Health Communication*, *10*, 105–125.

Wanzer, M. B., & Frymier, A. B. (1999). The relationship between student perceptions of instructor humor and students' reports of learning. *Communication Education*, *48*, 48–62.

Wigley, C. J. (1998). Verbal aggressiveness. In McCroskey et al. (Eds.), *Communication and personality* (pp. 191–214). Cresskill, NJ: Hampton Press.

Zakahi, W. R., & Duran, R.L. (1985). Loneliness, communication competence, and communication apprehension: Extension and replication. *Communication Quarterly*, *33*, 50–60.

chapter

4

The Impact of Perception and Listening on
Interpersonal Communication

OBJECTIVES

- Distinguish between the three key perception processes.

- Describe the factors that affect the selective exposure, selective attention, and selective retention processes.

- Identify the four schemata that we use to interpret communication events and provide an example of each.

- Define attribution theory and distinguish between internal and external attributions.

- Explain listening styles and provide examples of four different styles.

- Identify the six common listening misbehaviors.

- Discuss strategies for listening effectively.

SCENARIO: SOUND FAMILIAR?

Jordan was looking at recent tweets posted by some of her friends and noticed that one of her closest friends had posted, "Be nice. Like, do you just feel SOOOO good when you make others feel SOOOO horrible." Jordan wondered what her friend had just tweeted about, and so she sent several text messages to her friends to find out what they thought about the tweet.

OVERVIEW

Can you relate to this example? This example represents a current trend in Twitter called "subtweeting." Subtweeting involves posting a tweet about a particular person without mentioning the individual (Knibbs, 2013). Subtweeting is a relatively common practice and is described as "calling someone out" without specifically mentioning the person (Knibbs, 2013). Interestingly, the person posting the tweet is usually attempting to avoid confrontation; however, this type of post will likely lead to

chapter 4 The Impact of Perception and Listening on Interpersonal Communication

99

misunderstandings and conflict. As if face-to-face interactions were not challenging enough to interpret, now we must attend to these types of ambiguous messages posted on social media. Jordan's perceptions will influence how she interprets this message from her friend.

In this chapter we explore the reasons why messages like this one may get misinterpreted. This chapter explains why our messages are sometimes partially interpreted, completely misinterpreted, or even ignored by others. Two processes that play a key role in how we send and receive messages in our relationships are perception and listening.

In the first part of this chapter, we examine the process of perception, paying special attention to the relationship between elements of perception and interpersonal communication. We will then turn our attention to the process of listening and how it impacts our interpersonal relationships. Can you recall a time when someone accused you of not listening? Perhaps you *heard* what the person said but did not really *listen* to what he or she was saying. In the second part of this chapter, we distinguish between the terms *hearing* and *listening,* explain the steps involved in listening, and advance a number of ways to improve listening effectiveness.

Can you recall a time when someone accused you of not listening?

Perception and listening are so closely intertwined that it is difficult to discuss one without addressing the other. As we form relationships, our perceptions impact how we view the other person as well as how we interpret their messages and behaviors.

Now consider the role that perception plays in your ability to listen. It may come as no surprise that if our perception of a situation differs from that of others, our listening skills will also differ. In fact, interpretation is a common factor present in both the processes of perception and of listening.

Our hope is that, once you gain a better understanding of the relationship between these two concepts, you will also learn why individuals view relationships, people, behaviors, and messages in different ways. An awareness of the impact of perception and listening in our relationships can increase the effectiveness of our interpersonal communication. In the next sections we focus on the primary perceptual processes and then examine the relationship between perception and interpersonal communication.

PERCEPTION AND INTERPERSONAL COMMUNICATION

Perception can be best described as the lens through which we view the world. Just as your view of color would be altered if you were to wear a pair of glasses with blue lenses, our perception impacts our view of people, events, and behaviors. One definition of **perception** is that it is the process of selecting, organizing, and interpreting sensory information into a coherent or lucid depiction of the world around us (Klopf, 1995). Stated more simply, perception is essentially how we interpret and assign meaning to others' behaviors and messages based on our background and past experiences. The word "experience" is important in understanding the overall process of perception. Consider the role perception has played in your college experience. Perhaps you enjoy writing and have kept a personal journal. If your English professor assigned daily journal entries in her class, you might tell others that the class was one of the most enjoyable ones you have ever taken. Based on your experience—and your love for writing and journaling—you perceived the class to be easy and enjoyable, and you looked forward to communicating with your professor during her office hours to discuss how you could improve your writing. But suppose there is another student in the class who has struggled with writing throughout his academic career. He might report to others that the teacher was difficult to talk with and that her assignments were unfair. Based on his perception, their conversations during office hours may have been full of criticism and confusion, and he may describe the instructor as being "uncaring" and an "impossible perfectionist." Since each student brought a unique background and set of experiences to the class, the resulting perceptions of the teacher and class were very different.

> ...perception is essentially how we interpret and assign meaning to others' behaviors and messages based on our background and past experiences.

Chances are that you have learned about perception in other classes, such as psychology or sociology. Researchers from a wide range of academic fields study perceptual processes and their impact on peoples' attitudes, beliefs, and behaviors. While psychologists conducted much of the initial research in the area of perception, communication scholars have focused specifically on the impact of perception on the meanings assigned to messages. From a communication perspective, perception is important because we often define ourselves based on our perceptions of how others see us. Recall our discussion in Chapter 2 of reflected appraisal (or looking glass self), which explains how we form impressions of ourselves based on how we think others see us. If people respond favorably toward us, we may feel more self-assured and communicate in a more confident manner. Our perception also causes us to form impressions of others, which impacts how we communicate with them. The process we use to make sense of our social world is certainly an important and complicated one.

Limitations in Forming Perceptions

Social psychologist Robert Cialdini (2001) notes that we live in an extremely complicated

How have messages from others influenced the roles you fulfill in your college experience?

society, which he describes as "easily the most rapidly moving and complex that has ever existed on this planet" (p. 7). Cialdini (2001) further states that we cannot analyze all aspects of our environment because "we haven't the time, energy or capacity for it" (p. 7).

Miller (1956) proposed **information processing theory** to explain the amount of information we can process at any given time. According to this framework, we can store five to nine (seven plus or minus two) chunks of information in our short-term memory. A chunk of information might include numbers, words, or even people's faces. This theory explains why it is so difficult to remember a large group of people's names at a social event. If it is not possible to process and recall everything we see, hear, taste, touch, or smell, then how do we make sense of the world around us?

The way humans manage all of the stimuli encountered in the environment is to limit the amount and type of information taken in. This elimination process often occurs at a subconscious level. Thus, on any given day, we put limits on what we choose to see, hear, taste, touch, or smell. Because of the innate limitations in our ability to process information, humans are often described as **limited capacity processors**. Stated simply, we consciously and subconsciously make choices about the amount and type of stimuli we perceive. To fully understand how people make sense of their environment, we need to take a closer look at three key perceptual processes: *selection*, *organization*, and *interpretation*.

The way humans manage all of the stimuli encountered in the environment is to limit the amount and type of information taken in.

SELECTIVITY PROCESSES

The first perception process is *selection*. While you might not always be consciously aware of the process of **selection**, we are continually making choices about the amount and type of information we choose to notice in our environment. It is virtually impossible to pay attention to all the things we could possibly sense at any given time. These limitations in our ability to assimilate and interpret information prevent us from "taking it all in" and so we must select certain messages or information over others. These selections we make are often done in a purposeful rather than random manner (Klopf, 1995). Three primary selectivity processes that impact our perception include selective exposure, selective attention, and selective retention. The next sections provide an overview of each of these processes and discuss variables that affect them.

Selective exposure refers to the choice to subject oneself to certain stimuli or people. Choices regarding which messages and stimuli you will subject yourself to are made each day. You choose whether to expose yourself to the messages being sent by advertisers and newscasters when you decide whether to turn on your television or radio each morning. You choose whether to subject yourself to the messages left on your voicemail, phone, social media sites, or email messages.

What messages do you choose to expose yourself to each day?

Often the choice to engage in selective exposure is based on our desire to seek information or stimuli that is comfortable or familiar to us. Culture plays a key role in determining what messages or stimuli we choose to expose ourselves to and those which we avoid. Consider the fact that some people avoid communicating with those from other cultural backgrounds. They engage in selective exposure by avoiding conversations with people from different cultures. Individuals may focus on the obvious differences of race or ethnicity and assume that they do not have anything in common with people who are so dissimilar. The choice to avoid communication in these situations may cause individuals to miss learning about all the beliefs and interests that are shared.

According to Fischer and his colleagues (2005), we are most likely to seek out information consistent with our beliefs, values, and attitudes and to avoid information viewed as inconsistent. Our propensity to seek out certain types of information and avoid others is referred to as a **biased information search** (Fischer et al., 2005). While we might not consciously be aware of this process, each day we selectively choose to associate with particular individuals or groups of people and attend to certain types of messages in a variety of contexts while ignoring others. Perhaps you purchased an expensive phone recently. To reinforce your decision to purchase the pricey phone, you might seek out friends and family members with the same phone to discuss its positive attributes. You may even search online for positive customer reviews of the phone.

There are a number of factors that affect selective exposure including: proximity, utility, and reinforcement. Not surprisingly, we are most likely to selectively expose ourselves to messages that are nearby, or close in proximity. In fact, **proximity** is the number-one predictor of whether we will develop a relationship with another person (Katz & Hill, 1958). Consider the relationships you formed with those who attended your high school. Proximity impacted your ability to selectively expose yourself to those in the same school and form relationships.

Second, we are most likely to expose ourselves to messages we perceive as being useful. **Utility** refers to the perception that particular messages are immediately useful; these messages have a much greater chance of being selected than those that are not seen as useful (McCroskey & Richmond, 1996). Expecting an important email message from your parents about your college loans will certainly influence your choice to open and read their messages to you.

Finally, most people expose themselves to messages that are consistent with their views or reinforce their attitudes and beliefs (Fischer et al., 2005). A recent study by Knobloch-Westerwick and Hoplamazian (2012) found that male and female college students were more likely to select gender appropriate magazines to read over non-gender appropriate magazines. College students' perceptions of the magazine messages' utility and consistency with their views influenced their selection choices. Read the textbox below to learn more about the study.

RESEARCH IN REAL LIFE: How does gender affect our decision to select certain magazines over others?

Researchers studied the impact of gender on magazine selection in an experimental study.

- 253 college students participated in a study to learn more about how gender influences magazine choices.
- 93 males and 160 females had the choice to select the following magazines to read: *Shape, Us Weekly, Glamour, Newsweek, National Geographic, Time, Men's Health, Game Informer,* and *Sports Illustrated.*
- "Both sexes spent about three quarters of the magazine-browsing time on 'gender appropriate' magazines, even though this category accounted for only a third of the available choices" (Knobloch-Westerwick & Hoplamazian, 2012, p. 373).

Once we have made the decision to place ourselves in a position to physically receive a message, we then focus on certain aspects or elements of the message. **Selective attention** refers to the decision to pay attention to certain stimuli while simultaneously ignoring others. Factors that affect selective attention often include the novelty, size, and concreteness of the stimuli. Novelty refers to the tendency to pay attention to stimuli that are novel, new, or different. Novel aspects are more likely to capture our attention than those with which we are familiar. For example, we tend to notice a friend's new hairstyle almost immediately.

Another factor that affects selective attention is the size, or magnitude, of the stimuli. We are more likely to pay attention to large items, objects, or people. It probably is not completely by chance that most chief executive officers in U.S. companies are at least six feet tall and that virtually every U.S. president elected since 1900 has been the taller of the two candidates.

Finally, we are more likely to pay attention to information that is concrete, or well-defined, than to information that is perceived as abstract or ambiguous. Individuals have an easier time attending to messages that are clear and straightforward. Read the textbox on the next page to learn about how communication researchers used novel, concrete, and larger messages to educate young men about testicular cancer.

Once the decision has been made to be open to and attend to stimuli, the final stage in the selectivity process involves **selective retention**, which refers to the choice to save or delete information from one's long-term memory. Two factors that affect the propensity to retain information are primacy and recency effects and utility. When studying the type of information people are most likely to retain, researchers note that arguments delivered first (**primacy**) and last (**recency**) in a persuasive presentation are more likely to be recalled and to be more persuasive (Gass & Seiter, 2003). As we form relationships, we are often concerned with the first or last impression that we make. It has been estimated that we form our initial impression of others during the first three to five seconds. Recall the last job interview you attended. You likely paid careful attention to your clothing and appearance to ensure that you would make a positive first (primacy) impression the interviewer would remember. However, if you tripped and spilled the contents of your portfolio

It has been estimated that we form our initial impression of others during the first three to five seconds.

as you exited the interview, the recency of the last impression may be the one imprinted on the interviewer's memory.

What kind of an impression do you try to make during a job interview?

A second important factor related to selective retention is **utility**, or usefulness. Almost all of us have heard the phrase, "use it or lose it." Essentially what this phrase implies is that if we do not apply the information we obtain, we may not retain it later. For example, many of you have received training in cardiopulmonary resuscitation (CPR) at one time in your life. But if one of your classmates needed CPR, would you remember the steps?

ORGANIZATION

Once we have selected information, or stimuli, we then begin the process of placing it into categories in order to make sense of it. Organization "refers to our need to place the perceived characteristics of something into the whole to which it seems to belong" (Klopf, 1995, p. 51). Organization is also described as a process that involves structuring stimuli or information in a way that helps us make sense of it.

One theory that is useful in understanding how individuals organize information in meaningful ways is **constructivism**. Kelly (1970) developed the theory of constructivism to explain the process we use to organize and interpret experiences by applying cognitive structures labeled **schemata**. Schemata are "organized clusters of knowledge and information about particular topics" (Hockenbury & Hockenbury, 2006, p. 265). Another way to describe schemata is as mental filing cabinets with several drawers used to help organize and process information.

Schemata

Schemata are the results of one's experiences and, therefore, are dynamic and often changing as we encounter new relationships and life experiences. Suppose your first romantic relationship was a disaster. The initial schema you formed to organize information about romantic relationships (which may have been obtained from television shows or movies) was likely altered to include this negative experience you encountered. But suppose your next romantic partner is incredibly thoughtful and romantic. New information is incorporated into your schema that now enables you to evaluate various aspects of romantic relationships based on both the positive and negative experiences you encountered in the past. Thus, we apply schemata to make sense of our communication experiences. More specifically, we apply four different types of schemata to interpret interpersonal encounters: prototypes, personal constructs, stereotypes, and scripts (Fiske & Taylor, 1984; Kelley, 1972; Reeder, 1985).

PROTOTYPES

Have you ever thought of your ideal romantic partner? What would he or she be like?

Prototypes are knowledge structures that represent the most common attributes of a phenomenon. These structures are used to help organize stimuli and influence our interactions with others (Fehr & Russell, 1991). Prototypes provide us with a "benchmark" that is the standard used to evaluate and categorize other examples that fall into the same category. Recall your initial encounter with someone you dated recently. It is very likely that you evaluated this individual's behaviors based on whether this person fit your "prototypical," or best, example of a relationship partner. If you were to make a list of the characteristics you desire in the "ideal" romantic partner, these preconceived ideas and expectations represent your prototype and affect how you will perceive each potential romantic partner encountered in the future.

Fehr (2004) examined prototypical examples of interactions that led to greater perceived intimacy in same-sex friendships. Not surprisingly, interaction patterns that involved increased levels of self-disclosure and emotional support were perceived by friends as being more prototypical of expectations for intimacy than other types of practical support (Fehr, 2004). Stated simply, researchers often use *prototype analysis* when they want to know "what something is" (Birnie-Porter & Lydon, 2013). The following textbox summarizes one study that examined how we use prototype analysis.

RESEARCH IN REAL LIFE: Using prototype analysis to answer the question, "What are intimacy and sexual intimacy?"

Prototype analysis helps researchers understand how individuals define constructs that may be hard to define. Birnie-Porter and Lydon (2013) asked college students to define "intimacy" and "sexual intimacy."

- 335 college students were asked to define the characteristics of intimacy and sexual intimacy.

- After the first analysis of the students' responses, 160 responses were eliminated because they were only mentioned by one, two, or three people.

- 109 features of intimacy were identified, with 57% of the participants identifying **self-disclosure** and 25% of the participants identifying **love**, **trust**, **closeness**, and **friendship** as important features of intimacy.

- "Intimacy and sexual intimacy shared 81 attributes" (Birnie-Porter & Lydon, 2013, p. 241), indicating some overlap in respondents' perceptions of these constructs.

PERSONAL CONSTRUCTS

A second type of schemata is **personal constructs**, which Kelly (1970, 1991) describes as bipolar dimensions of meaning used to predict and evaluate how people behave. Personal constructs have also been described as the "mental yardsticks" we use to assess people and social situations.

How do you use your "mental yardstick" to assess others?

Several examples of personal constructs include: responsible–irresponsible, assertive–unassertive, friendly–unfriendly, intelligent–unintelligent, and forthright–guarded. Personal constructs serve as another means of evaluating others and simultaneously influence how we approach interactions. For example, if you label your coworker as "friendly," you may smile more at this person and share more personal information than you would with another coworker labeled as "unfriendly." We monitor our personal constructs closely and keep track of how accurately they predict our life circumstances (Raskin, 2002). When necessary, we revise them when

we perceive them as unreliable. We tend to define situations and people based on the personal constructs we use regularly. Thus, it is possible that we might not be aware of qualities some people possess or situations that we do not access regularly (Raskin, 2002). We may pay close attention to whether people are perceived as "friendly" or "unfriendly" and pay less attention to whether these same individuals are "creative" or "uncreative."

STEREOTYPES

The third type of schema we use to help us organize information is stereotypes. Stereotypes are impressions and expectations based on one's knowledge or beliefs about a specific group of people, which are then applied to all individuals who are members of that group. Stereotypes greatly influence the way messages are perceived. Some researchers argue that stereotypes are often activated automatically when an individual observes a member of a group or category (Carlston, 1992) and we are likely to predict how that person will behave. For example, Hamilton and Sherman (1994) note that individuals' perceptions of different racial and ethnic groups are often "planted in early childhood by influential adults in their lives" (p. 3). Influential individuals, such as family members, and the media play important roles in shaping how we define others and how we view the world.

Why do we categorize people, events, and objects? As mentioned previously, we are limited in our ability to process the sheer number of stimuli bombarding us at any given time. Thus, we identify ways to categorize and organize stimuli to enhance "cognitive efficiency," or to make in-

Stereotypes greatly influence the way messages are perceived.

People form stereotypes about individuals based on race, culture, sex, sexual orientation, age, education, intelligence, and affiliations, among other characteristics. It is crucial that we realize that stereotypes are formed as a result of our perceptions of others and, as a result, can be accurate or inaccurate. When inaccurate or inflexible stereotypes are applied to individuals, they often divide rather than unite people. Is it possible to resist the temptation to stereotype or categorize people? While the research on changing stereotypes is not extensive, much of it is promising. Stereotyping is a normal tendency. Our desire to reduce our level of uncertainty about people and situations leads us into the stereotype "trap." We are uncomfortable in situations where we have little or no information about others, and our initial tendency is to open our schematic files in an attempt to locate any information that will help us figure out how to communicate.

formation more manageable. A second explanation for our tendency to stereotype as described by Hamilton and Sherman (1994) is "categorization as self-enhancement" (p. 6). Simply stated, we tend to evaluate those groups to which we belong more favorably than groups to which we do not belong. Recall the groups you associated with in high school. If you were a member of the student council, you may have viewed members as being strong leaders and very organized. Students who were not members of the student council may have created their own schema for evaluating its members—they may have labeled them as being "power-hungry" or aggressive.

Social identity theory offers an explanation for our tendency to evaluate in-groups more positively than out-groups. According to social identity theory, an individual's self-esteem is often connected to membership in or association with social groups (Hamilton & Sherman, 1994; Turner, 1987). In an effort to maintain a positive identity, we may overemphasize or accentuate differences between in-groups and out-groups.

The key to overcoming the negative outcomes of stereotyping is to remain open-minded and flexible. While your tendency may be to look for something to help organize and make sense of stimuli, remember that the information used to form the stereotype may be incorrect. Fortunately, there is a growing body of scholarship that suggests that the stereotypes people form can be modified over time (Hamilton & Sherman, 1994).

SCRIPTS

The last type of schema we use to organize is scripts. According to Abelson (1982), **scripts** are knowledge structures that guide and influence how we process information. Abelson (1982) describes scripts as an "organized bundle of expectations about an event sequence" (p. 134). Simply stated, we adhere to a number of different scripts throughout a day, scripts that tell us what to do and say, as well as *how* to do and say it. Very often we do not notice how scripted our day-to-day interactions are until someone deviates from the expected script. Here, a comedian makes reference to the potential embarrassment caused by scripts in his description of an encounter he had when exiting a taxi cab at the airport:

> **Taxi Driver:** Thanks! Have a nice flight!
>
> **Comedian:** You too! *(then, realizing that the taxi driver is not flying)* I mean, the next time you fly somewhere.

Script theory states that we enter into situations that we have been in before with a specific set of expectations and, when individuals violate our expectations by not adhering to the script, we are not sure what to do. From an interpersonal communication perspective, we use scripts to determine how to proceed during social interaction and form perceptions of others based on whether or not they are following the "script." Each time we approach someone for the first time we adhere to a script when we say "Hello" or "How are you?" A violation of a greeting script would be to say "I ate a cheese sandwich" before saying "Hello" or "How are you?" to a friend or acquaintance.

INTERPRETATION

After we have selected and organized information, the final step in the perception process involves interpretation. **Interpretation** is the subjective process of making sense of our perceptions. The interpretation process is described as highly subjective because individuals' interpretations of communication events vary extensively and are influenced by a wide range of factors. The following sections serve as an overview of the dominant theory used to explain how people interpret information, discuss errors in interpretive processes, and identify factors that influence the ways we interpret information.

Attribution Theory

The dominant theory that describes how people explain their own and others' behavior is known as **attribution theory** (Heider, 1958; Kelley, 1967, 1971). This theory is also known as naïve psychology because people often try to connect observable behavior to unobservable causes (Littlejohn, 1983). Can you recall a time when you have tried to explain a friend's unusual behavior? Perhaps she was supposed to phone you at a scheduled time, and the call never came. You may try to explain her lack of communication by theorizing that she overslept, the car broke down, or she had a fight with a significant other. All of these are causes that you have not directly observed, but they are used as potential explanations for the friend's behavior. Attribution theory is commonly applied to interpret the reasons for our own actions as well as the actions of others. According to Heider (1958), there are three basic assumptions to attribution theory: (1) that it is natural for people to attempt to establish the causes of their own and others' behavior, (2) that people assign causes for behavior in a systematic manner, and (3) that the attribution impacts the perceiver's feelings and subsequent communication. Thus, the causes assigned to people's behaviors play a significant role in determining reactions to interpreted behaviors.

© PathDoc/Shutterstock.com

What do you think if your BFF sends you a one-word text, "Fine!"

According to attribution theory, people assign causes to behaviors in a fairly systematic way and typically use different types of information to make these decisions. Generally, when individuals attempt to explain behaviors, they will choose among three different explanations: the situation, unintentionality or chance, and intentionality or dispositions (Heider, 1958). A person's behavior may be best explained by considering the situation and how this factor may have influenced behavior. Situational factors are often referred to as **external attributions**. For example, perhaps you are normally talkative and outgoing when in social situations. How-

ever, you go to a party with some friends and see your former relationship partner with a new "love" interest. Because you still have feelings for this person, this situation is upsetting to you, and you spend the evening moping and avoiding conversations. Hence, your behavior at the party could be best explained by situational or external attributions.

The second factor typically used to explain behavior is **unintentionality** or chance, which refers to one's inability to predict whether the behaviors will be consistent in the future (Kelsey et al., 2004). For example, a student may guess several answers on a difficult test and then claim that he may or may not be able to replicate this test performance again in the future. The student attributes his behavior to chance rather than test-taking skill (i.e., internal attribution).

The third factor, **intentionality**, or disposition, is also referred to as an internal attribution. **Internal attributions** are typically described as being stable or persistent and often refer to behaviors that are likely to be exhibited repeatedly across a variety of contexts (Heider, 1958). If your friend Sally acts quiet and reserved in almost all situations, then you would explain her quiet and reserved demeanor at your birthday party based on internal attributions or personality traits. When attempting to explain her behavior, you might say, "Sally is just that way," or tell others that she is normally very shy.

Attribution Errors

Not surprisingly, we often evaluate and explain our *own* behavior using standards that are very different from those used to evaluate and ex-

One explanation for attributing our failures to external causes is to save face.

Why do we avoid taking responsibility for our poor performance, mistakes, or shortcomings? One explanation for attributing our failures to external causes is to save face. While our tendency to protect our own self-image is understandable, it is important to realize that these distorted perceptions of self are problematic. Falsely taking credit for accomplishments and blaming others (or circumstances) for our failures can lead to distorted self-images and inaccurate representations of ourselves during social interaction (Hamachek, 1992).

plain the behavior of others. The two most common attribution errors people make are known as the self-serving bias and the fundamental attribution error. The **self-serving bias** states that we tend to manufacture, or construct, attributions that best serve our own self-interests (Hamachek, 1992). For example, when we excel in school or sports, we often explain our success based on internal factors or causes. We might think "I am smart" or "I am an incredible athlete," both of which are internal attributions.

The *self-serving bias* provides us with a viable explanation for the sources of student motivation in the classroom. Research by Gorham and her colleagues (1992) indicates that students view motivation in school as a student-owned trait or characteristic. Thus, when a student feels motivated to do well in school, he or she credits this intention to do well on internal rather than external factors. On the other hand, when a student feels unmotivated, or is unwilling to work hard in school, he or she is more likely to attribute the cause of this lack of motivation to the teacher's behavior (external attributions—the teacher did not explain the assignment clearly) rather than to the self (internal attributions).

The next question to ask is whether we attribute others' failures and successes to external or internal factors? A second common attribution error often made during the interpretation stage of perception is the **fundamental attribution error**. When attempting to explain others' negative behaviors, we tend to overestimate the internal factors or causes and underestimate the external factors or causes. For example, if you are driving to school and see someone speeding by you, you might say to your friend, "What a reckless driver" (internal attribution).

Kelsey and her colleagues (2004) used attribution theory to investigate the explanations students provided for their college instructors' classroom "misbehaviors." Examples of teacher misbehaviors include boring lectures, unfair grading, and providing too much information. The researchers found that students were more likely to attribute their teachers' inappropriate classroom behaviors to internal causes (e.g., she doesn't care about teaching and is lazy) rather than to external causes (e.g., she had a rough morning because she was in an accident). It is important to understand and acknowledge that, while the way we make sense of our own and others' behaviors is less than perfect, it greatly affects how we interact with others. To improve the way we select, organize, and interpret information, it is also essential to consider our individual differences and how these differences impact our perception.

INDIVIDUAL DIFFERENCES AND PERCEPTIONS

While there are numerous factors that affect the way we perceive information, in this section we focus on three widely researched and acknowledged variables related to perception. Sex, age, and culture impact our perceptions and the way we communicate with others. We begin our discussion by considering how sex differences affect perception and communication.

Sex Differences

Do you think men and women view the world differently? Deborah Tannen, a noted gender scholar and linguist, would answer this question with an unequivocal "Yes!" According to Tannen (1986, 1990, 1994), men and women hold different worldviews and philosophies regarding how they are expected to act in society, which evolve from early interactions with family members, peers, and society. Tannen and other gender scholars (see, for example, Wood, 1999) assert that men and women are socialized differently and, as a result, develop different perceptions of the world and their place within it. For example, women often perceive the world as a place to connect and form bonds with others. Men, on the other hand, view the world as a place to assert their independence and autonomy. These

differences in perceptions affect the ways men and women approach social interactions. Tannen says that women often engage in **rapport talk**, which is analogous to small talk or phatic communication, while men often exhibit **report talk**, which involves discussions about facts, events, and solutions. The following scenario illustrates the difference between rapport and report talk.

Elyse and Dave got a flat tire during their drive to work. As they discuss the event with friends, Elyse explains various details associated with the tire episode. "It was horrible! We were driving down the freeway when all of the sudden we heard a 'thump-thump' under the car. Of course, today would be the day that we left the cell phone at home on the table! Didn't you get a flat tire about a month ago, Janelle? I was just so scared when this happened, I couldn't even breathe!"

To improve the way we select, organize, and interpret information, it is also essential to consider our individual differences and how these differences impact our perception.

Females often respond by sharing similar stories and experiences and attempting to empathize with others (Chakrabarti & Baron-Cohen, 2008). Tannen describes this practice as "matching" problems in conversation. Not surprisingly, women engage in this behavior to establish closeness among other women. Dave, on the other hand, would provide the details of the morning's event differently.

> *"We got a flat tire on Interstate 270 this morning. We didn't have a cell phone, but the car behind us pulled over and let me use their phone to call AAA."*

In this example, Dave engages in report talk. He gives the facts and does not describe how he felt about the incident like Elyse does in her conversation. It is important to note that not all men and women communicate this way. However, because men and women may see the world differently, it affects how they perceive themselves and others and ultimately impacts their interpersonal communication.

Age Differences

A second frequently studied variable that affects perceptions is age. Recall the last time you engaged in a conversation with older relatives, friends, or coworkers. Did you notice any differences in your perspectives on various issues? One student recently shared an example of a conversation held with her mother that illustrated the impact of age on perceptual differences. Because this female student does not like to cook or clean, her mother told her, "No man will want to marry you!" The daughter argued her "case" by explaining to her mother that times have changed and women and men today often share domestic responsibilities in the home. This conversation between mother and daughter illustrates how age and experience impact our perceptions. As we grow older, we tend to build on our diverse life experiences and our perceptions often change or, in some cases, become more firmly ingrained. Some research indicates that older individuals possess more consistent and stable attitudes and are more difficult to persuade (Alwin & Krosnick, 1991). Other findings suggest that as people age they become more cognitively sophisticated and are better able to see the world from others' perspectives (Bartsch & London, 2000). Thus, it is important to consider how age affects both our own and others' perceptions.

Cultural Differences

Finally, culture affects our perceptions of the world and simultaneously influences our communication with others. In Chapter 11 we discuss the impact of cultural differences on perceptions and interpersonal communication in greater detail. However, it is important to restate the powerful impact culture can have on our perceptions. One reason for examining cultural differences is to learn more about how socialization in different cultures affects people's perceptions and behavior. For example, researchers often study perceptual and behavioral differences in individualistic and collectivistic cultures.

Collectivistic cultures emphasize group harmony and concern for others. An example of a collectivistic culture is found in China. **Individualistic cultures**, such as the dominant cultures found in the United States, tend to value individual rights, independence, and autonomy. Members of collectivistic cultures view the

Why do we say that Australians drive on the "wrong side" of the road?

world much differently than individuals from highly individualistic cultures.

There are numerous research examples that illustrate the difference between individualistic and collectivistic cultural beliefs, attitudes, behaviors, and values. One interesting study explored Chinese and U.S. managerial differences in attempts to influence employees (Yukl, Fu, & McDonald, 2003). According to Yukl and his colleagues, "the cross-cultural differences in rated effectiveness of tactics were consistent with cultural values and traditions" (Yukl et al., 2003, p. 68). Chinese managers rated informal strategies and strategies that emphasized personal relations as more effective than traditional Western strategies that emphasized being direct and task oriented. Swiss and American managers perceived more direct task-oriented tactics as being more effective than informal strategies and tactics that emphasized personal relations. This research illustrates how cultural differences explain variability in employees' perceptions of message strategy effectiveness.

It is important to remember that most of us hold more favorable perceptions of the groups we belong to than those to which we do not belong. Thus, we should be cognizant of our tendency to be favorably disposed toward people, ideas, beliefs, and concepts from our culture and our inclination to be more critical of people, ideas, and concepts from other cultural perspectives.

THE LINK BETWEEN PERCEPTION AND LISTENING

By now you should have a more sophisticated understanding of why some information is selected over others, how information is organized, and how messages are interpreted. Additionally, we have provided you with some information about common attribution errors individuals make and variables that affect the process of perception. To further understand the potential implications of perception, we must consider how our different perspectives of people and messages influence and are influenced by listening. At the beginning of this chapter, we pointed out that perception and listening are closely related to each other. Our perception of others impacts both our ability and our desire to listen in social interactions.

Significance of Listening Skills

Listening is a key element for acquiring information and for developing and sustaining our relationships. Yet, communication practitioners often refer to listening as the "forgotten" communication skill. The fact that listening skills are often neglected or undervalued is surprising since most people engage in listening more than any other type of communication activity. For example, college students report that up to 50 percent of their time is spent listening, compared to speaking (20 percent), reading (6 percent), and writing (8 percent) (Janusik & Wolvin, 2006). While colleges often require classes that emphasize competence in writing and speaking, few highlight listening as an important communication skill. To learn more about your listening skills, complete the Willingness to Listening measure at the end of this chapter.

When we engage in effective listening behaviors, we communicate a message that we comprehend and care about what the speaker has to say. Recall a time when you attempted to communicate with a friend or family member, only to receive a distracted response of "Yeah. Uh-huh. Mm-hmm." The lack of active listening behavior is extremely frustrating and may even negatively affect marital satisfaction (Boyd & Roach, 1977). A lack of awareness of ineffective listening behaviors has potential negative implications for both personal and professional relationships. Our goal in focusing on this topic is twofold: to assist you in understanding the listening process and to shed some light on how your own behaviors may be interpreted by others. Our hope is that after completing this chapter you will be able to evaluate your own listening skills and to implement some of our suggestions.

For many of you, this chapter will be the only formal training in appropriate and effective listening skills you will ever have. The implications of effective listening span a variety of interpersonal contexts. In the health-care setting, Wanzer and her colleagues (2004) found that patients who perceived their physicians as em-

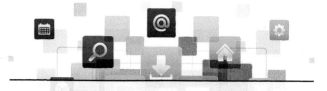

The fact that listening skills are often neglected or undervalued is surprising since most people engage in listening more than any other type of communication activity.

ploying effective listening skills were more satisfied with their doctors and the care they provided. Research has also identified a link between one's career success and effective listening skills. Employers report that listening is a top skill sought in hiring new employees, and it plays a significant role in evaluations for promotion and incentives (AICPA, 2006). In the next section we define the terms listening and hearing and describe the steps involved in listening.

Hearing and Listening Defined

Perhaps one of the most common mistakes made in the listening process is making the assumption that hearing is the same as listening. In fact, listening and hearing are two distinct processes. **Hearing** involves the physical process of sound waves traveling into the ear canal, vibrating the eardrum, and eventually sending signals to the brain. Although we often hear messages, we do not necessarily attend to them. This explains why you might be sitting in your room right now reading this text and hearing an air conditioner turn on, birds chirping outside, or friends yelling in the hallway. But, while your brain has processed these sound waves, you may not have been listening for these stimuli.

Listening not only involves the physical process of hearing, but it also involves the psychological process of attending to the stimuli, creating meaning, and responding. Listening is often described as a dynamic, multistage, and ongoing process in which individuals physically receive a message, employ cognitive processes to attribute meaning to the message, and provide verbal and/or nonverbal feedback to the source.

As you reflect on this definition, it should become quite apparent that listening is a highly complex process. Communication scholars who study listening have identified specific steps involved in this multistage process: (1) hearing, (2) attending, (3) understanding, (4) responding, and (5) remembering.

How well do you listen to others?

Step One: Hearing

As we mentioned before, hearing involves the physical process of sound waves traveling into the ear canal, vibrating the eardrum, and eventually sending signals to the brain. The first step of interpersonal communication is to physically receive the message. There are many obstacles that prevent individuals from hearing messages. A significant obstacle for 4-14% of U.S. Americans involves various hearing-related issues (www.research.gallaudet.com). Highly competent communicators are able to identify when someone has difficulty hearing and adapt their messages accordingly.

Step Two: Attending

Attending is the psychological process of paying attention to certain stimuli over others (i.e., selective attention). As mentioned earlier in the chapter, it is not possible for us to attend to all stimuli that we are exposed to in any given day. We must select information to attend to so that it can be processed.

Step Three: Understanding

The third step in the listening process is making sense of the message or reducing any uncertainty or confusion we might have about what messages mean. There are many reasons we may not understand information received from others. As stated earlier, differences in culture, race, ethnicity, age, sex, personality, and emotions may affect our ability to understand or make sense of messages. Effective listeners are motivated and willing participants who attempt to reduce uncertainty and fully comprehend the source's messages.

Step Four: Responding

Communication involves an exchange between the source and the receiver. Therefore, an important element of listening is giving some type of response to indicate that the message was received and understood. Responses can be verbal or nonverbal in nature and may include nodding one's head or giving appropriate verbal feedback. If the receiver doesn't understand the message, it is appropriate to ask questions to increase message comprehension.

Step Five: Remembering

The final step of the listening process is to retain the message. This step is particularly difficult because, in general, people do not retain much of what they hear. Communication researcher Laura Janusik (2004, 2006) created a conversational listening span measure to determine how much information people retain after reading, speaking, and hearing information. She found that when college students were exposed to 64 sentences on different topics and asked to remember and respond to them, they could recall, on average, about three items (Janusik, 2004; 2006). This research illustrates how difficult it is to retain and recall information over time. The following textbox offers suggestions for enhancing your ability to retain information.

RESEARCH IN REAL LIFE:
12 brain rules to increase retention

John Medina is a molecular biologist, research consultant, and director of the Brain Center for Applied Learning Research at Seattle Pacific University. He is also the author of *Brain Rules*, a *New York Times* bestseller that presents 12 principles for improving cognitive functioning and retaining information. His 12 principles are based on studies that have been replicated successfully a number of times. Following are five of his principles:

1. Exercise boosts brain power and helps improve our ability to think and retain information. Even exercising a few times a week is helpful.

2. Repeat information to help you remember it. Also, if possible, make an attempt to reproduce the environment where you were first exposed to the information (i.e., smells, room conditions, etc.).

3. Get enough sleep. "Loss of sleep hurts attention, executive function, working memory, mood, quantitative skills, logical reasoning and even motor dexterity" (Medina, 2008, p. 168).

4. Stressed brains have greater difficulty taking in information than non-stressed brains. Tell yourself that you have control over your situation or problem to reduce stress.

5. When possible, use pictures or images to help you recall information (in this chapter, recall a filing cabinet to help remember schemata). If you use PowerPoint presentations, be sure to include pictures and images to help people retain information.

 118

LISTENING STYLES

Reflecting on your own interpersonal relationships, did you ever notice that individuals have different listening styles? Or perhaps you have noticed that an individual's listening style changed when the topic changed. Have you considered your own listening style and how it may change with the person or topic? For example, with our friends we might pay more attention to their feelings, and when we listen to coworkers we may be more focused on the content of the message.

Seminal research on listening described four predominant listening styles (Watson, Barker, & Weaver, 1995). **Listening style** is defined as a set of "attitudes, beliefs, and predispositions about the how, where, when, who, and what of the information reception and encoding process" (Watson, Barker, & Weaver 1995, p. 2). This suggests that we tend to focus and alter our listening based on the communication context. We may pay more attention to a person's feelings, the structure or content, or particular delivery elements, such as time.

The four original listening styles are labeled people-oriented, action-oriented, content-oriented, and time-oriented and can be measured via the Listening Styles Profile (LSP-16) developed by Watson et al.

Recent scholarship by Bodie, Worthington, and Gearhart (2013) attempted to improve the LSP-16 by creating a more reliable and valid means of measuring different listening styles. The new listening styles measure is called the Listening Styles Profile-Revised (LSP-R). In the

sections below we examine the original four styles as well as the recent research by Bodie et al. that identified additional related styles of listening.

People-Oriented

First, **people-oriented** listeners seek common interests with the speaker and are highly responsive. They are interested in the speaker's feelings and emotions (Watson et al., 1995). Research shows a positive relationship between the people-oriented listening style and conversational sensitivity (Cheseboro, 1999).

A relational style of listening is very similar to the people-oriented style. **Relationally oriented listeners** attempt to understand the feelings of others and try to build and maintain relationships with others through listening. Higher scores on the relational styles of listening measure on the LSP-R were related to higher scores on empathy (Bodie et al., 2013). You probably

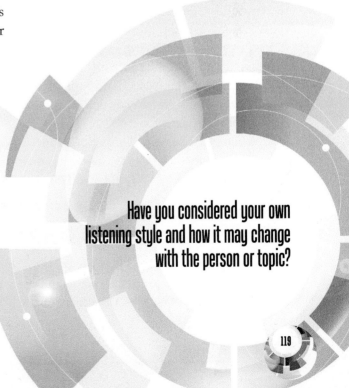

Have you considered your own listening style and how it may change with the person or topic?

adopt people-oriented and relational listening styles when you spend time with your friends and help them sort through relationship issues.

Action-Oriented

Action-oriented listeners prefer error-free and concise messages. They get easily frustrated with speakers who do not clearly articulate their message in a straightforward manner. They tend to steer speakers to be organized and timely in their message delivery (Watson et al., 1995). Action-oriented listeners are more precise, argumentative, and attentive communicators who tend to engage in arguments with others (Villaume & Bodie, 2007).

Listeners engage in a **critical listening style** when they analyze the accuracy and consistency of a source's message (Bodie et al., 2013). According to Bodie and colleagues, the critical listening style is a mix of both the action and content-oriented listening styles. People who score higher on the critical listening scale also scored higher on the need for cognition scale (Bodie et al., 2013). Critical listeners seem to have a need to fully understand information and to identify mistakes or inconsistencies in the speaker's message. Action and critical listening styles come in handy when someone is participating in a debate or engaging in an argument. These styles may not "work" as well in situations where people are sharing their feelings or discussing relationship problems.

Content-Oriented

Unlike the people-oriented listener, the **content-oriented** listener focuses on the details of the message. They pick up on the facts of the story and analyze it from a critical perspective. They decipher between credible and noncredible information and ask direct questions. A content-oriented listener will try to understand the message from several perspectives. For example, they may say, "Did you ever think they did that because . . ." or "Another way to think about the situation is . . ." (Watson et al., 1995).

An **analytical listening style** is similar to the content-oriented style (Bodie et al., 2013) because it also focuses on gathering the full meaning of the message before responding. Listeners who exhibit the analytical style engage in systematic thinking to fully comprehend the speaker's perspectives. Motivated college students who want to excel in the classroom adopt content and analytical listening styles.

Time-Oriented

Finally, **time-oriented** listeners are particularly interested in brief interactions with others. They direct the length of the conversation by suggesting, "I only have a minute," or they send leave-taking cues (such as walking away or looking at the clock) when they believe the speaker is taking up too much of their time. This type of listening is essential when time is a limited commodity.

Bodie and colleagues (2013) describe **task-oriented listeners** as similar to time-oriented listeners because they both prefer that speakers use time efficiently and refrain from rambling. Not surprisingly, people who score high on task-oriented listening are less relationally oriented and empathic (Bodie et al., 2013). A listener who engages in this style of listening may have trouble establishing relationships. However, in situations where time is limited and decisions need to be made (i.e., health care or emergencies), this style of listening could help solve problems or make decisions under pressure.

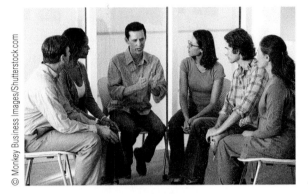

How can you become a more competent listener?

GENDER, CULTURE, AND PERSONALITY DIFFERENCES IN LISTENING STYLES

Are some communicators more or less likely to exhibit a particular listening style? Researchers have studied how individual differences such as gender, culture, and personality are related to the four different listening styles identified in the previous section (people, content, time, and action).

Gender

Some research suggests there are gender differences when it comes to listening styles. For example, Booth-Butterfield (1984) reported that "males tend to hear the facts while females are more aware of the mood of the communication" (p. 39). Just about 20 years later, researchers' findings were consistent in indicating that men score themselves higher on the content-oriented listening style and women score themselves higher on the people-oriented or relational listening style (Sargent & Weaver, 2003). In yet another, related study, college students who scored higher in masculine and lower in feminine gender roles were more likely to engage in action, content, and time-oriented listening styles (Villaume & Bodie, 2007). Interestingly, in this same study, higher masculinity and femininity scores were both associated with people-oriented listening styles. Collectively, this research suggests that people who adopt more masculine and less feminine gender roles tend to exhibit more action, content, and time orientations in their listening practices.

Culture

Listening styles also differ based on culture. Kiewitz and Weaver (1997) found that when comparing young adults from three different countries, Germans preferred the action style, Israelis preferred the content style, and Americans preferred the people and time styles.

Personality

Personality differences are also related to people's attitudes and behaviors related to listening. In a study by Villaume and Bodie (2007), college students filled out the listening styles measure and a number of personality instruments. College students who scored higher in people-oriented listening styles also scored higher in extraversion, communication competence, perceptiveness, attentiveness, and responsiveness. People-oriented listeners were also less likely to

> **Although no listening style is best, it is imperative to understand your own listening style and to recognize the listening styles of others.**

report communication apprehension and scored higher in friendly, animated, and open communicator styles (Villaume & Bodie, 2007).

Although no listening style is best, it is imperative to understand your own listening style and to recognize the listening styles of others. Depending on the situation, the individual, and the goals in communicating, you may need to adjust your listening style. In addition, recognizing the listening style in others will help direct your responding messages. For example, if you notice your boss is engaging in an action-oriented listening style, you may want to produce a clearly articulated message. He may become irritated if you include miscellaneous information or use confusing vocabulary when sharing work-related information with him.

Common Listening Misbehaviors

One way you can create a favorable impression when interacting with someone for the first time is by being an effective listener (Bodie, Cyr, Pence, Rold, & Honeycutt, 2012). To be an effective listener, you must understand which verbal and nonverbal behaviors are associated with

effective listening as well as how to enact those behaviors in conversations. This is certainly not an easy or simple task. In fact, it may be easier to identify the specific listening behaviors one should *not exhibit* when trying to create favorable impressions or build relationships. In the section below we identify the six most common listening misbehaviors listeners should avoid. After telling you the specific behaviors to avoid, we then lay out specific suggestions on what competent listeners do (Bodie et al., 2012).

Pseudo-Listening

Pseudo-listening is when we are pretending to listen. We attempt to look like we are listening by nodding our head or providing eye contact, but we are faking our attention. This is a self-centered approach to listening. Let us be honest—when we are pseudo-listening, we are not "fooling" anyone. We are not able to ask appropriate questions and we are not able to provide proper feedback.

Monopolizing

Listeners who engage in **monopolizing** take the focus off the speaker and redirect the conversation and attention to themselves. Often, monopolizers interrupt the speaker to try to "one up" the speaker. They may try to top his story by saying "That reminds me . . ." or "You think that is bad—let me tell you what happened to me. . ."

Disconfirming

Listeners who deny the feelings of the speaker are sending **disconfirming** messages. Examples of disconfirming messages include: "You shouldn't feel bad . . ." or "Don't cry . . . there is no need to cry." This misbehavior discourages the source from continuing to speak and decreases perceptions of empathy.

Defensive Listening

An individual who engages in **defensive listening** perceives a threatening environment. Defensive communication has been defined as "that behavior which occurs when an individual perceives threat or anticipates threat in the group" (Gibb, 1961, p. 141). Defensiveness includes "how he appears to others, how he may seem favorable, how he may win, dominate, impress, or escape punishment, and/or how he may avoid or mitigate a perceived or anticipated threat" (p. 141). In other words, defensiveness is a process of "saving face." The issue of face is associated with people's desire to display a positive public image (Goffman, 1967). Suppose Jordan, from the scenario in the beginning of the chapter, asks her friend to clarify the message posted on Twitter and the friend responds by saying, "What is your problem? Why do you have to read into everything I post on Twitter?"

Selective Listening

Selective listening happens when a listener focuses only on parts of the message. She takes parts of the message she agrees with (or does not agree with) and responds to those particular parts. We reduce cognitive dissonance or psychological discomfort, screening out messages that we do not agree with, to remain cognitively "stable." For example, if we recently bought a new SUV, we may choose not to pay attention to messages suggesting that SUVs are not environmentally sound. We would, however, choose to pay attention to messages suggesting SUV vehicles rated higher on safety tests than other cars.

Ambushing

Ambushers will listen for information they can use to attack the speaker. They are selectively and strategically listening for messages they can use against the speaker. Often ambushers interrupt the speaker. They do not allow the speaker to complete his thought and jump to conclusions. Ambushers make assumptions and get ahead of the speaker by finishing his sentences. They are self-motivated and lack dual perspective.

Listeners who display these listening misbehaviors frequently will experience challenges in their communication and their relationships. To become a more competent communicator, it is important to be aware of both poor listening practices and effective listening practices. In the final section of the chapter we identify some best practices for listeners.

BEST PRACTICES FOR EFFECTIVE LISTENING

What does it mean to be a competent listener? What do competent listeners actually do? This was the focus of listening research by communication researcher Graham Bodie and his colleagues. They conducted several studies to determine what college students think competent listening is as well as the specific verbal and nonverbal behaviors enacted by competent listeners (Bodie et al., 2012). They created an implicit theory of listening to help structure and guide future research in this area. Their research conclusions were:

- Competent listeners display five attributes: (1) attentiveness, (2) friendliness, (3) responsiveness, (4) conversational flow, and (5) understanding.
- Competent listeners enact specific verbal and nonverbal behaviors. Some *verbal behaviors* include: (1) responding with something related to the topic, (2) elaborating on the topic discussed, (3) offering advice, (4) asking/answering questions, and (5) paraphrasing what the speaker says. Some specific *nonverbal behaviors* include: (1) maintaining eye contact, (2) engaging in appropriate and attentive facial expressions, (3) maintaining composure, and (4) smiling and laughing appropriately.

The research by Bodie and colleagues helps us understand more about competent listening practices. Becoming an effective listener takes time and effort. Read the final textbox to learn more about additional strategies you can adopt to help you become a competent listener.

STRATEGIES FOR EFFECTIVE LISTENING

Adhere to the following strategies to improve your listening skills (remember **BIG EARS**):

- **<u>B</u>e open to receiving the message.** Display appropriate nonverbal behaviors (see list above) to show you are motivated and available to listen.
- **<u>I</u>nterpret the message.** The goal of listening is to understand the message. Ask and answer questions to make sure you understand.
- **<u>G</u>ive feedback.** Be sure to elicit appropriate verbal and nonverbal behaviors to show you understand the message.
- **<u>E</u>ngage in dual perspective.** When someone is sharing information or problems with you, try to see this information from the other's point of view or empathize.
- **<u>A</u>dapt your listening style to meet the situation.** People engage in different listening behaviors based on the communication situation. For example, we elicit different listening behaviors in class than we do when we are socializing with our friends.
- **<u>R</u>educe noise.** Noise is anything that disrupts the message. Make attempts to reduce external distractions such as your cell phone or computer. Reduce internal distractions such as hunger and fatigue by eating enough and getting enough rest so that you can listen attentively.
- **<u>S</u>tore the message.** Recall earlier suggestions such as repeating messages, getting enough rest, and exercising occasionally to assist with retaining information.

SUMMARY

In this chapter, we explained the perception process: selecting information, organizing information, and interpreting information. Additionally, we identified and explained factors related to each of the three primary selectivity processes. At this point, you should have a more detailed understanding of why certain messages or information gets selected over others.

We also learned more about the four types of schema that affect interpersonal communication. Once information has been selected and organized, the final step is interpretation. The primary theory that explains how we make sense of our own behavior and that of others is attribution theory. The way that we make sense of our own and others' behavior is quite different and flawed. In the final sections, we discussed the two primary attribution errors as well as factors that affect our interpretation process.

In the last section of this chapter, we explained the difference between hearing and listening and listed the specific steps involved in the listening process. Remember, listening refers to the dynamic process in which individuals physically hear a message, employ cognitive processes to attribute meaning to the message, and provide verbal and/or nonverbal feedback to the source. It is a highly complex process that requires focus and effort.

Not only is it important to increase your listening skills, it is also crucial to recognize different listening styles. We discussed different types of listening styles and how gender, culture, and personality are related to these styles. Finally, we recognized six common listening misbehaviors and effective listening strategies competent listeners should enact.

DISCUSSION QUESTIONS

1. Why do you think some people engage in subtweeting, and what are some of the problems that can occur as a result of this practice? Explain your response to this question.

2. Can you recall a time when you engaged in the self-serving bias? Give an example of this tendency.

3. Why do we tend to attribute others' negative behaviors to dispositional over situational factors? Can you recall a specific time when you made the fundamental attribution error to explain a friend's behavior?

4. What suggestions would you offer if you were to deliver a workshop on effective listening? Advance at least five "best practices" for being an effective listener.

SELF ASSESSMENTS

Listening Styles Profile (LSP16)

For each of the items below, indicate how well each statement applies to you using the following scale: 'Always' (4) 'Frequently' (3) 'Sometimes' (2) 'Infrequently' (1), and 'Never' (0).

_____ 1. I focus my attention on the other person's feelings when listening to them

_____ 2. When listening to others, I quickly notice if they are pleased or disappointed

_____ 3. I become involved when listening to the problems of others

_____ 4. I nod my head and/or use eye contact to show interest in what others are saying

_____ 5. 1 am frustrated when others don't present their ideas in an orderly, efficient way

_____ 6. When listening to others. I focus on any inconsistencies and/or errors on what's being said.

_____ 7. I jump ahead and/or finish thoughts of speakers.

_____ 8. I am impatient with people who ramble on during conversations.

_____ 9. I prefer to listen to technical information.

_____10. 1 prefer to hear facts and evidence so I can personally evaluate them.

_____11. I like the challenge of listening to complex information.

_____12. 1 ask questions to probe for additional information.

_____13. When hurried. I let the other person(s) know that 1 have a limited amount of time to listen.

_____14. I begin a discussion by telling others how long I have to meet.

_____15. I interrupt others when 1 feel time pressure.

_____16. I look at my watch or clocks in the room when I have limited time to listen to others.

To determine whether you enact a **People Oriented Style** add responses for questions 1,2,3, & 4.

To determine whether you enact an **Action Oriented Style** add responses for questions 5,6,7, & 8.

To determine whether you enact **Time Oriented Style** add responses for questions 9, 10, 11, & 12.

To determine whether you enact a **Content Oriented Style** add responses for questions 13, 14, 15, & 16.

For each style, scores should range from a low of 0 to a high of 16. Higher scores indicate that you are more likely to enact that particular style.

Source: Weaver, J.B., Watson, K.W., Barker, L.L. (1996). Individual differences in listening styles: Do you hear what I hear? *Personality and Individual Differences, 20*(3), 381-387.

Willingness to Listen Measure

The following twenty-four statements refer to listening. Please indicate the degree to which each statement applies to you by marking whether you:

Strongly Disagree = 1; Disagree = 2; Neutral = 3; Agree = 4; Strongly Agree = 5

_____ 1. I dislike listening to boring speakers.

_____ 2. Generally, I can listen to a boring speaker.

_____ 3. I am bored and tired while listening to a boring speaker.

_____ 4. I will listen when the content of a speech is boring.

_____ 5. Listening to boring speakers about boring content makes me tired, sleepy, and bored.

_____ 6. I am willing to listen to boring speakers about boring content.

_____ 7. Generally, I am unwilling to listen when there is noise during a speaker's presentation.

_____ 8. Usually, I am willing to listen when there is noise during a speaker's presentation.

_____ 9. I am accepting and willing to listen to speakers who do not adapt to me.

_____10. I am unwilling to listen to speakers who do not do some adaptation to me.

_____11. Being preoccupied with other things makes me less willing to listen to a speaker.

_____12. I am willing to listen to a speaker even if I have other things on my mind.

_____13. While being occupied with other things on my mind, I am unwilling to listen to a speaker.

_____14. I have a willingness to listen to a speaker, even if other important things are on my mind.

_____15. Generally, I will not listen to a speaker who is disorganized.

_____16. Generally, I will try to listen to a speaker who is disorganized.

_____17. While listening to a non-immediate, non-responsive speaker, I feel relaxed with the speaker

_____18. While listening to a non-immediate, non-responsive speaker, I feel distant and cold toward that speaker.

_____19. I can listen to a non-immediate, non-responsive speaker.

_____20. I am unwilling to listen to a non-immediate, non-responsive speaker.

_____21. I am willing to listen to a speaker with views different from mine.

_____22. I am unwilling to listen to a speaker with views different from mine.

_____23. I am willing to listen to a speaker who is not clear about what he or she wants to say.

_____24. I am unwilling to listen to a speaker who is not clear, not credible, and abstract.

Scoring: Scores can range from 24 to 120. To compute the score on this instrument, complete the following steps:

Step 1: Add scores for items 2, 4, 6, 8, 9, 12, 14, 16, 17, 19, 21, and 23
Step 2: Add scores for items 1, 3, 5, 7, 10, 11, 13, 15, 18, 20, 22, and 24
Step 3: Total score = 72 − Total from Step 1 + Total from Step 2.

Scores above 89 indicate a high willingness to listen. Scores below 59 indicate a low willingness to listen. Scores between 59 and 89 indicate a moderate willingness to listen.

Source: From *Going Public: Practical Guide To Public Talk* by Virginia Richmond & Mark Hickson III. Published by Allyn & Bacon, Boston, MA. Copyright ©1995 by Pearson Education. Reprinted by permission of the publisher.

KEY TERMS AND DEFINITIONS

ACTION-ORIENTED LISTENING STYLE: listeners who prefer error-free and concise messages.

AMBUSHING: a listening misbehavior that involves paying attention to information in order to attack the speaker.

ANALYTICAL LISTENING STYLE: focuses on gathering the full meaning of the message before responding.

ATTRIBUTION THEORY: theory that describes how people explain their own and others' behavior.

BIASED INFORMATION SEARCH: our propensity to seek out certain types of information and avoid others.

COLLECTIVISTIC CULTURES: emphasize group harmony and concern for others.

CONCRETE: factor that impacts our selective attention of stimuli; more likely to pay attention to information that is clear and well-defined as opposed to that which is abstract or ambiguous.

CONSTRUCTIVISM: the process we use to organize and interpret experiences by applying cognitive structures labeled schemata.

CONTENT-ORIENTED LISTENING STYLE: listener focuses on the details of the message.

CRITICAL LISTENING STYLE: analyzig the accuracy and consistency of a source's message

DEFENSIVE LISTENING: style listeners engage in when they perceive a threatening environment.

DISCONFIRMING: when a listener denies the feelings of the speaker.

EXTERNAL ATTRIBUTION: explaining self/others' behaviors based on situational or contextual factors.

FUNDAMENTAL ATTRIBUTION ERROR: tendency to overestimate internal factors and underestimate external factors in explaining others' behavior.

HEARING: physical process of sound waves traveling into the ear canal, vibrating the eardrum, and eventually sending signals to the brain.

INDIVIDUALISTIC CULTURES: value individual rights, independence and autonomy.

INFORMATION PROCESSING THEORY: explains the cognitive capacity of humans to recognize, interpret and remember information.

INTENTIONALITY: internal attributions that reference the role that one's disposition plays in behavior; enables us to make predictions about future behaviors.

INTERNAL ATTRIBUTION: explaining people's behavior based on personality/dispositional factors.

INTERPRETATION: the subjective process of making sense of our perceptions.

LIMITED CAPACITY PROCESSORS: people have limitations in the amount of information they can take in and store in short-term memory.

LISTENING: the physical process of hearing as well as the psychological process of attending to stimuli, creating meaning, and responding.

LISTENING STYLE: a set of attitudes, beliefs, and predispositions about the how, where, when, who, and what of the information reception and encoding process.

MONOPOLIZING: when listeners take the focus off the speaker and redirect the conversation and attention to themselves.

NOVELTY: tendency to selectively pay attention to stimuli that are novel, new, or different.

ORGANIZATION: process involving the structuring of stimuli or information in a way that is meaningful or that makes sense to us.

PEOPLE-ORIENTED LISTENING: listening type in which the listener seeks common interests with the speaker and is highly responsive; interested in the speaker's feelings and emotions.

PERCEPTION: process of selecting, organizing, and interpreting sensory information in a way that makes sense.

PERSONAL CONSTRUCTS: "mental yardsticks" that we use to assess people and social situations.

PRIMACY AND RECENCY: tendency to recall the first (primacy) and last (recency) information in a message.

PROTOTYPES: knowledge structures that represent the most common attributes of a phenomenon.

PROXIMITY: closeness between individuals and the number-one predictor of whether we will be friends or otherwise with another person.

PSEUDO-LISTENING: describes when we are pretending to listen to a source.

RAPPORT TALK: small talk or phatic communication used to build relationships with others.

REINFORCE: proposes that we selectively expose ourselves to messages that are consistent with our views or support our attitudes and beliefs.

RELATIONALLY ORIENTED LISTENERS: attempt to understand the feelings of others and try to build and maintain relationships with others through listening.

REPORT TALK: discussions about facts, events, and solutions.

SCHEMATA: organized clusters of knowledge and information about particular topics that help us process and make sense of new information.

SCRIPTS: knowledge structures that guide and influence how we process information; scripts tell us what to do and say, as well as *how* to do and say it.

SCRIPT THEORY: states that we enter into situations that we have been in before with a specific set of expectations and, when individuals violate our expectations by not adhering to the script, we are not sure what to do.

SELECTION: refers to the process of making choices about which information we select from the environment.

SELECTIVE ATTENTION: the decision to attend to certain stimuli over others.

SELECTIVE EXPOSURE: the decision to expose ourselves to certain stimuli, people, messages, etc., over others.

SELECTIVE LISTENING: happens when a listener focuses only on parts of the message.

SELECTIVE RETENTION: the process of retaining certain information or stimuli over other stimuli.

SELF-SERVING BIAS: states that we tend to manufacture, or construct, attributions that best serve our own self-interests.

SIZE: factor that impacts our selective attention of stimuli; proposes that we are more likely to pay attention to people and objects that are large or unusually small.

SOCIAL IDENTITY THEORY: theory that holds that an individual's self-esteem is often connected to membership or association with social groups.

STEREOTYPES: impressions or expectations based on one's knowledge of a group of people that is then applied to any individual who is a member of that group.

TASK-ORIENTED LISTENERS: prefer that speakers use time efficiently and refrain from rambling.

Time-oriented listening style: listening type in which the listener is particularly interested in brief interactions with others.

Unintentionality: a second factor often used to explain behavior; focuses on our inability to predict the behavior of others.

Utility: refers to our perspective of a message as being useful or beneficial.

REFERENCES

Abelson, R. P. (1982). Three modes of attitude-behavior consistency. In M. P. Zanna, E. T. Higgins, and C. P. Herman (Eds.), *Consistency in social behavior: The Ontario symposium* (Vol. 2, 131–146). Hillsdale, NJ: Lawrence Erlbaum Associates.

AICPA. (2006). Highlighted Responses from the Association for Accounting marketing survey: Creating the Future Agenda for the Profession—Managing Partner Perspective. Retrieved December 22, 2006, from http://www.aicpa.org/pubs/ tpcpa/feb2001/hilight.htm.

Alwin, D. F., & Krosnick, J. A. (1991). Aging, cohorts, and the stability of sociopolitical orientations over the lifespan. *American Journal of Sociology, 97,* 169–195.

Bartsch, K., & London, K. (2000). Children's use of state information in selecting persuasive arguments. *Developmental Psychology, 36,* 352–365.

Birnie-Porter, C., & Lydon, J. E. (2013). A prototype approach to understanding sexual intimacy through its relationship to intimacy. *Personal Relationships, 20,* 236–258.

Bodie, G. D., Cyr, K. S., Pence, M., Rold, M., & Honeycutt, J. (2012). Listening competence in initial interactions I: Distinguishing between what listening is and what listeners do. *The International Journal of Listening, 26,* 1–28.

Bodie, G. D., Worthington, D. L., & Gearhart, C. C. (2013). The listening styles profile-revised (LSP-R): A scale revision and evidence for validity. *Communication Quarterly, 61,* 72–90.

Booth-Butterfield, M. (1984). She hears . . . he hears; What they hear and why. *Personnel Journal, 63,* 36–43.

Boyd, L. A., & Roach, A. J. (1977). Interpersonal communication skills differentiating more satisfying from less satisfying marital relationships. *Journal of Counseling Psychology, 24,* 540–542.

Carlston, D. E. (1992). Impression formation and the modular mind: The associated systems theory. In L. L. Martin and A. T. Tesser (Eds.), *The construction of social justice* (pp. 301–341).

Chakrabarti, B., & Baron-Cohen, S. (2008). The biology of mindreading. In N. Ambady & J.J. Skowronski (Eds). *First impressions* (pp. 57–86). New York, NY: The Guilford Press.

Cheseboro, J. L. (1999). The relationship between listening and styles and conversational sensitivity. *Communication Research Reports, 16,* 233–238.

Cialdini, R. B. (2001). *Influence: Science and practice.* Boston, MA: Allyn and Bacon.

Fehr, B. (2004). Intimacy expectations in same-sex friendships: A prototype interaction-pattern model. *Journal of Personality and Social Psychology, 86,* 265–284.

Fehr, B., & Russell, J. A. (1991). The concept of love viewed from a prototype perspective. *Journal of Personality and Social Psychology, 60,* 425–438.

Fischer, P. E., Jonas, E., Frey, D., & Schulz-Hardt, S. (2005). Selective exposure to information: The impact of information limits. *European Journal of Social Psychology, 35,* 469–492.

Fiske, S. T., & Taylor, S. E. (1984). *Social cognition.* Reading, MA: Addison-Wesley.

Gass, R. H., & Seiter, J. S. (2003). *Persuasion, social influence and compliance gaining.* Boston, MA: Allyn and Bacon.

Gibb, J. R. (1961). Defensive communication. *Journal of Communication, 11,* 141–149.

Goffman, E. (1967). *Interaction ritual: Essays on face-to-face behavior*. New York: Pantheon Books.

Gorham, J., & Christophel, D. M. (1992). Students' perceptions of teacher behaviors as motivating and demotivating factors in college classes. *Communication Quarterly, 40,* 239–252.

Hamachek, D. (1992). *Encounters with the self* (3rd ed.). Fort Worth, TX: Harcourt Brace Jovanovich.

Hamilton, D. L., & Sherman, J. W. (1994). Stereotypes. In R. Wyer and T. Srull (Eds.), *Handbook of social cognition* (2nd ed.) (pp. 1–68). Hillsdale, NJ: Lawrence Erlbaum.

Heider, F. (1958). Attitudes and cognitive organization. *Journal of Psychology, 21,* 107–112.

Hockenbury, D. H., & Hockenbury, S. E. (2006). *Psychology* (4th ed.). New York, NY: Worth Publishers.

Janusik, L. A. (2004). Researching listening from the inside out: The relationship between conversational listening span and perceived communicative competence. *UMI Proquest: Digital dissertations.* Available at http://wwwlib.umi.com/dissertations.

Janusik, L. A., & Wolvin, A. D. (2006). 24 hours in a day: A listening update to the time studies. Paper presented at the meeting of the International Listening Association, Salem, OR.

Katz, A. M., & Hill, R. (1958). Residential propinquity and marital selection: A review of theory, method, and fact. *Marriage and Family Living, 20,* 27–35.

Kelley, H. H. (1967). Attribution theory in social psychology. In D. Levine (Ed.), *Nebraska Symposium on Motivation* (Vol. A5, pp. 192–238). Lincoln: University of Nebraska Press.

Kelley, H. H. (1971). *Attribution in social interaction.* Morristown, NJ: General Learning Press.

Kelley, H. H. (1972). Causal schemata and the attribution process. In E. E. Jones, D. E. Kanouse, H. H. Kelley, R. E. Nisbett, S. Valins, and B. Weiner (Eds.), *Attribution: Perceiving the causes of behavior* (151–174). Morristown, NY: General Learning Press.

Kelly, G. A. (1970). A brief introduction to personal construct psychology. In D. Bannister (Ed.), *Perspectives in personal construct psychology* (pp. 1–30). San Diego: Academic Press.

Kelly, G. A. (1991). *The psychology of personal constructs: Vol. 1. A theory of personality.* London: Routledge. (Original work published in 1955.)

Kelsey, D. M., Kearney, P., Plax, T. G., Allen, T. H., & Ritter, K. J. (2004). College students' attributions of teacher misbehaviors. *Communication Education, 53,* 40–55.

Kiewitz, C., & Weaver, J. B. (1997). Cultural differences in listening style preferences: A comparison of young adults in Germany, Israel and the United States. *International Journal of Public Opinion Research, 9,* 233–247.

Klopf, D. (1995). *Intercultural encounters: The fundamentals of intercultural communication.* Englewood, CA: Morton.

Knibbs, K. (2013). Subtweeting: The secret subtle art of Twitter gossip. Retrieved from http://www.digitaltrends.com/social-media/the-subtle-art-of-the-subtweet/#!3MN1X

Knobloch-Westerwick, S., & Hoplamazian, G. (2012). Gendering the self: Selective magazine reading and reinforcement of gender conformity. *Communication Research, 3,* 358–384.

Littlejohn, S. W. (1983). *Theories of human communication.* Belmont, CA: Wadsworth.

McCroskey, J. C., & Richmond, V. A. (1996). *Fundamentals of human communication.* Prospect Heights, Illinois: Waveland Press.

Medina, J. (2008). *Brain rules: 12 principles for surviving and thriving at work, home, and school.* Seattle, WA: Pear Press.

Miller, G. A. (1956). The magical number seven plus or minus two: Some limits on our capacity for processing information. *Psychological Review, 63,* 81–97.

Raskin, J. D. (2002). Constructivism in psychology: Personal construct psychology, radical constructivism, and social constructivism. In J. D. Raskin and S. K. Bridges (Eds.), *Studies in meaning: Exploring constructivist psychology* (pp. 1–25). New York: Pace University Press.

Reeder, G. D. (1985). Implicit relations between disposition and behavior: Effects on dispositional attribution. In J. H. Harvey and G. Weary (Eds.), *Attribution: Basic issues and application* (pp. 87–116). New York: Academic Press.

Sargent, S. L., & Weaver, J. B. (2003). Listening styles: Sex differences in perceptions of self and others. *International Journal of Listening, 17,* 5–18.

Tannen, D. (1986). *That's not what I meant.* New York: Ballantine Books.

Tannen, D. (1990) *You just don't understand: Women and men in conversation.* New York: Ballantine Books.

Tannen, D. (1994). *Gender and discourse.* New York: Oxford University Press.

Turner, J. C. (1987). *Rediscovering the social group: A self-categorization theory.* New York: Basil Blackwell.

Villaume, W. A., & Bodie, G. D. (2007). Discovering the listener within us: The impact of trait-like personality variables and communicator styles on preferences for listening styles. *The International Journal of Listening, 21,* 102–123.

Wanzer, M. B., Booth-Butterfield, M., & Gruber, K. (2004). Perceptions of health care providers' communication: Relationships between patient-centered communication and satisfaction. *Health Communication, 16,* 363–384.

Wanzer, M. B., Foster, S. C., Servoss, T., & LaBelle, S. (2013). Educating young men about testicular cancer: Support for a comprehensive testicular cancer campaign. *Journal of Health Communication, 19,* 303–320.

Watson, K. W., Barker, L. L., & Weaver, J. B. III. (1995). The listening styles profile (LSP-16): Development and validation of an instrument to assess four listening styles. *International Journal of Listening, 9,* 1–13.

Wood, J. T. (1999). *Gendered lives: Communication, gender, and culture* (3rd ed.). Belmont, CA: Wadsworth Publishing Co.

Yukl, G. P., Fu, P., & McDonald, R. (2003). Cross cultural differences in perceived effectiveness of influence tactics for initiating or resisting change. *Applied Psychology: An International Review, 52,* 68–82.

chapter

5

Verbal Communication:
Words of Wisdom

OBJECTIVES

- Define verbal communication and understand the characteristics of verbal communication.

- Distinguish between connotative and denotative meaning.

- Differentiate between relational and content levels of meaning.

- Explain the difference between constitutive and regulative rules.

- Describe the four functions of verbal communication.

- Explain the Sapir-Whorf hypothesis.

- Explore how uncertainty reduction is associated with verbal communication.

- Discuss the difference between direct and indirect verbal communication styles.

SCENARIO: SOUND FAMILIAR?

Lauren has been living with her partner for over a year now but they cannot seem to agree on simple household chores. Her frustration grew this morning when she stumbled over her partner's shoes and noticed the garbage was piled up by the doorway. She left their apartment in a hurry and yelled, "You are such a slob!" An hour later, she was feeling bad about what she said and called to apologize for her choice of words.

OVERVIEW

In this scenario, we can relate to Lauren's verbal reaction, which often occurs when we are frustrated. When we are not mindful of our actions and the effect they have on others, it is sometimes referred to as being on "autopilot." Being on autopilot suggests we are just reacting to situations and not thinking of how our word choice may impact others. Depending on our goals, verbal communication can be used to enhance our relationships or to destroy them. We have the power to make others feel competent, attractive, and strong. On the other hand, our words can also upset and annoy others, and our messages can cause them to feel weak. This chapter discusses how the words we use impact our interpersonal relationships.

We begin by defining verbal communication and examining several of its distinct features and functions. Next, we will examine factors that impact our verbal communication and how it is perceived by others.

DEFINING VERBAL COMMUNICATION

Verbal communication refers to the words we use during the communication process. We use words strategically to relate to the outside world and to create meaning. Have you ever tried to communicate with someone who did not speak your language? Have you ever attempted to convey a message to others without using words or played a game of charades? These two examples illustrate how difficult it can be to express ourselves without verbal communication. The words we use have a strong impact on our interpersonal relationships. What we say initially often determines whether we will have future interactions with others. There are four key characteristics of verbal communication that explain how and why we use words to create meaning: rules, symbols, subjectivity, and context.

Rules

It is important to realize that there are certain rules we must follow when using language. **Rules** are agreed-upon guidelines that provide a structure for what is socially acceptable communication in our culture. You follow certain rules when talking with your friends that are quite different than when you talk with your grandparents. There are two basic types of rules that relate to verbal communication: constitutive and regulative (Cronen, Pearce, & Snavely, 1979; Pearce, Cronen, & Conklin, 1979). **Constitutive rules** help guide our communication by identifying appropriate language and interpreting word meanings. In essence, constitutive rules address word meanings. It would probably be easy for you to come up with words to illustrate support, trustworthiness, anger, and/or respect. According to dictionary.com, the word "respect" is defined as *a certain esteem for or a sense of the worth or excellence of a person.* How do we use words to communicate respect in a classroom? Addressing your professors formally, using Dr., Mr., or Mrs., is an example of complying with constitutive rules. Constitutive rules are also in effect when students avoid using slang or swear words in classroom settings. Failure to understand word meanings and make appropriate choices in selecting words can be detrimental to a student's success as an appropriate and effective interpersonal communicator.

© imtmphoto/Shutterstock.com

What constitutive rules do parents and children have for communicating mutual respect?

Regulative rules guide our communication by identifying when, how, where, and with whom we communicate in certain situations. Regulative rules can include aspects of communication such as grammar, syntax, and age-appropriate language. Seale (1995) suggests that these regulative rules are like traffic laws because they help to create a sense of communication order. These rules help us answer questions such as: Who are we supposed to talk with and how should we speak to this person? What topics are acceptable? For how long should we talk? Think about the regulative rules in the classroom that are not explicitly stated but tell you how to interact with your classmates and professors. Students greet one another when they enter the classroom, they do not interrupt the professor, and they take turns speaking. These rules are context-bound and will change depending on the audience and context.

What regulative rules do you practice in the classroom?

Our verbal communication is governed by constitutive and regulative rules and through language structure. This makes it possible for us to create shared meaning and have a common understanding of appropriateness across contexts. There-fore, it is critical for all of us to observe, listen, research, and ask questions to understand more clearly the appropriate rules in new situations.

> Our verbal communication is governed by constitutive and regulative rules and through language structure.

Symbols

A second feature of verbal communication is that it is symbolic. **Symbols** are socially agreed-upon representations of an event, action, person, object, or phenomenon. Symbols can range from concrete to abstract. The more a symbol resembles what it represents, the more concrete that symbol is. If we were sitting in a room with a chair, a photo of a chair, and a piece of paper with the word "chair" typed on it, this would illustrate how we move from concrete to abstract symbols. **Concrete symbols** are more likely to resemble what they represent. Therefore the chair itself is the most concrete symbol. We use the chair to sit on, and this is how it is represented. **Abstract symbols** are arbitrary and nonrepresentational. Therefore, the printed word "chair" is abstract and arbitrary. The more concrete (and therefore less abstract) a symbol is, the more it is associated with its meaning. Verbal communication is made up of abstract, arbitrary, and agreed-upon concrete symbols or words.

It is difficult to discuss symbols without discussing **semantics,** or the study of meanings we attribute to each word. When people interpret words, they focus on both the denotative and connotative meanings. The **denotative meaning** refers to the universal meaning of the word, or the definition you would find in the dictionary. The denotative meaning of the word "fireplace" is *any open structure, usually of masonry, for keeping a fire, as at a campsite* (dictionary. com). The **connotative meaning** refers to the personal meaning that the source has with that word. For example, the word "fireplace" connotes hospitality and warmth. Connotative meanings are often quite difficult to explain because they can be different for everyone. This leads us to the third characteristic of verbal communication, subjectivity.

Subjectivity

Because everyone has a unique worldview, the way we use and interpret verbal communication is strongly influenced by individual biases. Verbal communication is **subjective** because we interpret the world through our own experiences, historical perspective, cultural upbringing, our physical environment, and the socio-emotional nature of relationships. Our perceptions are distinct and limited to our personal field of experience and developed schema.

The subjective meanings we place on our verbal communication have different levels of meaning. Recall our description of these two concepts from Chapter 1. The **relational level of meaning** is highly sensitive to the people involved in the conversation and indicates how people feel about the

When people interpret words, they focus on both the denotative and connotative meanings.

relationship, whereas the content level of meaning is the informational component and relies on the specific words you use. Consider the following conversation:

> **Samantha:** Do you want to come to my mom's birthday party?
> **Edgar:** Well, it's in an hour, and I'm in the middle of working on the house.
> **Samantha:** So, you don't want to come?
> **Edgar:** Well, the contractor is coming tomorrow, so I have to get this done.
> **Samantha:** You missed my sister's birthday party, also. I'm starting to think you just don't want to spend time with my family.
> **Edgar:** That is not true. I just have to get this work done.
> **Samantha:** I cannot believe you are going to miss my mom's birthday party!
> **Edgar:** Do you want me to drop everything and come?
> **Samantha:** I shouldn't have to tell you what to do; you should know what the right thing to do is!
> **Edgar:** I'm sorry, but I have to finish this project before the contractor comes.

The conversation above illustrates a common problem in interpersonal relationships: one individual is focused on the content level of meaning, and the other is interested in the relationship level of meaning. Edgar is focused on the content or the information in the message, while Samantha is concerned with how the communication process is affecting the relationship. Edgar is determined to finish working on the house and cannot understand why Samantha would be upset. Samantha feels Edgar is not really listening to what she is saying and does not understand. The content level of meaning is found in the words we use, and the relationship level of meaning is often interpreted through our nonverbal behaviors, through *how* something is said. Because of Edgar's past behavior and concern for the house, Samantha perceived his nonverbal behavior as insincere. Edgar, however, heard Samantha complaining about not going to the birthday party and offered a valid reason for not attending.

When one individual is focusing on the **content level of meaning** and the other is focused on the relationship level of meaning, conflict may often result. Verbal communication is widely subjective and is a function of our personal associations and the meanings we place on words, situations, and experiences. In order to improve our communication with others, it is important to do the following: (1) seek clarification of ambiguous messages, (2) identify areas of miscommunication, and (3) talk about ways to improve communication. **Metacommunication** is when we "communicate about our communication" and we can use it to help clarify a message's meaning. The role of metacommunication in verbal communication is a helpful strategy for relationship partners as they continuously work to improve understanding of messages.

Context

The final feature of verbal communication is the contextual framework. The **context** refers to the environment, situation, or setting in which we use verbal communication. The context may influence the interpretation, meaning, and appropriateness of the communication. For example, we may use a particular greeting with our roommates such as, "What's up?", while we may choose alternative words when we are greeting our grandparents, such as "Good morning, Grandfather!" The interpretation of our words changes when we consider the context in which they are used. In the last section of this textbook, we review five general contexts in which interpersonal communication occurs. These are: intercultural communication, family communication, organizational communication, health communication, and mediated communication.

In the next section, we will discuss two specific examples of contextually bound verbal communication: organizational jargon and expressing affection.

A person who doesn't work in the lab would have a difficult time understanding the scientists' jargon.

ORGANIZATIONAL JARGON

Organizational jargon is defined as a specialized vocabulary that is socially constructed and regularly used by members of a particular trade, profession, or organization. Jargon will differ greatly in different organizations and workplaces. Jargon is often used in technical and scientific fields to refer to concepts and terms in a universal manner. One category of jargon is the development of acronyms/abbreviations. Members of the military may use jargon such as MREs, PCDs, MEO, and CDC when communicating with each other. What is the purpose or function of jargon? These verbal shortcuts can enhance communication by increasing precision and speed during social interaction (Hirst, 2003). However, this specialized language may be abused when individuals use it with receivers who are not familiar with the vocabulary, and the speaker may be perceived as being pretentious (Nash, 1993). For example, most of us prefer our health-care providers to communicate clearly with us, and this means they avoid the use of jargon and technical language. Organizational jargon or "shop talk" is contextually bound and may be considered rude when communicating with individuals outside of the organization.

EXPRESSING AFFECTION

Another example of contextually bound verbal communication is **expressing affection**. Many of us reserve special terms for our most intimate relationships. Consider the last time you told someone "I love you." You may have contemplated these three little words for quite a while before actually saying them. That is because these few words have large implications. These expressions of affection often initiate or accelerate relational development (Floyd, 1997). We often save particular words or phrases for special individuals who impact or influence us. Communicating affection is risky. When the receiver is not on the same page as the sender, the communicative attempt may have a negative outcome. It is important that the sender considers the trust level, reciprocity, and future interactions, as well as the length of the relationship before conveying these types of messages. If the receiver does not feel the same way, they may feel manipulated or perceive the sender as imposing confusing relational boundaries (Ebert & Floyd, 2004). Once again, our verbal messages are interpreted based on the context or type of relationship we are in.

Now that we have defined verbal communication and provided its features, we can discuss the specific functions verbal messages serve in interpersonal communication.

FUNCTIONS OF VERBAL COMMUNICATION

There are four functions that help explain how we use our verbal communication. They are: cognitive function, social reality function, group identity function, and social change function. Each is discussed below.

Cognitive Function

The **cognitive function** of verbal communication can be defined as how we use language to acquire knowledge, to reason, and to make sense of the world. The cognitive function of verbal communication maintains a strong connection with culture. Our culture greatly influences our language choices. Growing up in a small town versus a large city, being a member of a quiet family versus a loud family, or growing up in the South versus the North all result in distinct language differences.

Once again, we use the cognitive function of verbal communication to acquire information. One way to do this is through the process of uncertainty reduction. Berger proposed that the main purpose of verbal communication is to "make sense" out of our interpersonal world (as cited in Griffin, 2003). Berger's **uncertainty reduction theory** suggests that human communication is used to gain knowledge and create understanding by reducing uncertainty and, therefore, increasing predictability. The more we ask questions and learn about someone new, the more we reduce our uncertainty about them. For example, when we are first introduced to someone we typically experience high levels of uncertainty. We may ask ourselves: "Who is this person?" "Where are they from?" "Are they like me?" Consider the last time you met someone new. Chances are the conversation went something like the one below.

> **James:** Hi, I'm James. What's your name?
> **Erica:** My name's Erica. Where are you from?
> **James:** I'm from New York, and you?
> **Erica:** I'm from Florida, but I'm here studying communication.
> **James:** That's my major also. Are you interested in broadcasting?

Erica: No, I'm studying communication studies. I'm interested in going to law school.

This example demonstrates how we use verbal communication to acquire knowledge through uncertainty reduction. Through the process of **self-disclosure**, or purposefully revealing personal information about ourselves, we are able to decrease the ambiguity of a situation. When we do this we increase our ability to predict future interactions. This is an example of how our verbal communication serves the cognitive function of acquiring knowledge and making sense out of the world. We will examine the concept of uncertainty and self-disclosure and their roles in relationship initiation more closely in Chapter 7.

... what appears to be real in society is socially agreed upon through our communication with others.

Social Reality Function

"The language used in everyday life continuously provides me with the necessary objectifications and posits the order within which these make sense and within which everyday life has meaning for me. I live in a place that is geographically designated; I employ tools from can openers to sports cars which are designated in the technical vocabulary of my society; I live within a web of human relationships from my chess club to the United States of America which are also ordered by means of vocabulary. In this manner, language marks the co-ordinates of my life in society and fills that life with meaningful objects." (Peter L. Berger and Thomas Luckman, *The Social Construction of Reality*, New York: Doubleday, 1966, p. 22).

In this quote from *The Social Construction of Reality*, the authors suggest that reality is socially constructed through language and vocabulary. In other words, *what appears to be real in society is socially agreed upon through our communication with others*. Consider the words that have evolved in the U.S. culture across previous decades. Throughout the 1970s and 1980's the terms "Watergate," "test-tube baby," and "Rubik's cube" became words that were widely understood in the United States because of events or products that had been introduced during that time period. Similarly, the words "AIDS" and "compact disc" were added to dictionaries in the 1980s. And words such as "selfie," "phablet," and "fauxhawk" were added in 2013. As the reality of the culture evolved, new words were created to explain and describe our

changing society. Thus, our verbal communication serves to create our **social reality**.

Two American linguists, Edward Sapir and Benjamin Lee Whorf, were interested in how we used language as a tool to make sense of the world. They developed the concept of **linguistic determinism**, which suggests that "language *determines* thought" (Whorf, 1956; Sapir, 1956). Most agree that there is a relationship between language and cognitions. You may agree that if we use certain words, it will influence what people think about. This helps us understand why particular groups are passionate about making adjustments in our language. Take, for example, the movement to more gender-neutral titles of occupations, including mail carrier (mailman); police officer (policeman); chairperson (chairman); and salesperson (salesman). If we change our language, we can start to change the way people think about these occupations. Can you think of additional examples of how changing our words can influence our cognitions?

Sapir and Whorf also conceptualized **linguistic relativity**, which proposes that distinctions encoded in one language are unique to that language alone, and that "there is no limit to the structural diversity of languages" (Whorf, 1956; Sapir, 1956). By comparing the vocabulary of Inuit and Aztec peoples they found that the Inuit have many different words for "snow." There are different words for falling snow, powdery snow, slushy snow, packing snow, and icy snow. On the other hand, in Aztec there is only one word for snow, one word for cold, and one word for ice. In addition, Sapir and Whorf were fascinated by the fact that the Hopi language did not distinguish between past, present, and future tense. Time is not considered multidimensional in their culture, whereas time is a fundamentally critical concept in Western society. Think about how we use time in such fields as physics and engineering. Also, our culture is embedded with daily planners, calendars, and appointments that rely heavily on our shared meaning of time.

The **Sapir-Whorf hypothesis** suggests that the language we learn, as well as the culture we are exposed to, is used to shape our entire reality.

Group Identity Function

Another function of verbal communication is to serve as a symbol of group solidarity. Because we have similarities in language at work, in our family, and throughout our interpersonal relationships, verbal communication fulfills an identity function. Consider the cliques that are formed in high school. Distinctions are often drawn between band members, athletes, theatrical or drama students, and student council members. Students in your school may have used labels such as "preps," "skaters," "hipsters," "emo kids," or "mean girls." Students often describe and define themselves based on their affiliations, actions/behaviors, or social groups.

Were you a part of a clique in high school? How did you treat your peers?

Within the different groups, shared "codes" develop that only members of the group might understand. These codes may be in the form of inside jokes, nicknames, abbreviations, or other specialized vocabulary. Their purpose is to form a sense of **group identification**. In other words, this function of verbal communication serves to distinguish one group from another and to provide a sense of similarity and cohesiveness for its members. This makes sense with our earlier discussion of organizational jargon. It may increase group identity with organizational members, but it may isolate individuals who do not belong or understand this language.

Families can also be considered a type of group. Think about your family. Are there inside jokes that get repeated over and over? You may hear something like, "Remember the time that Mom made Julie walk across the kitchen to get an apple, because she did not believe she had a broken leg? Or the time Shawn lied to Mom and Dad about that 'hit and run' so he could get a new bike?" We choose to let others "in" on the joke when we allow new members to enter into the group. From outside the group, nonmembers may interpret the stories, jokes, and nicknames as inappropriate, inconsiderate, and not humorous. However, group members who use verbal communication to fulfill this function feel a sense of belonging. Verbal communication used to establish group identity helps maintain the group's rituals and celebrate the history of the group.

Social Change Function

Language can "imprison us" or it can "set us free." This is how Ting-Toomey and Chung (2005) de-

---

RESEARCH IN REAL LIFE: Top ten words of 2013

The Global Language Monitor (GLM) is a San Diego-based company that tracks and analyzes trends in the English language. The GLM staff monitors the evolution and demise of language, word usage, word choices, and their impact on the various aspects of culture. GLM suggests that the September 11 attacks on America have changed forever the way we speak and interpret various words. Currently, they suggest, the numbers "9/11" are the official shorthand for the 2001 terrorist attacks, and "ground zero" stirs up thoughts of a sacred burial ground where the twin towers once stood. Also since the attacks, the word "hero" includes police, firefighters, EMTs, and any type of first responders who place their lives on the line for the public good.

Consider the Top Words of 2013 identified by GLM:

1. 404—The near-universal numeric code for failure on the global Internet.
2. Fail—The single word *fail*, often used as a complete sentence ("Fail!") to signify failure of an effort, project, or endeavor.
3. Hashtag—The "number sign" and "pound sign" reborn as the all-powerful Twitter hashtag.
4. @Pontifex—The handle of the ever-more popular Pope Franciscus (Francis).
5. The Optic—The "optic" is threatening to overtake "the narrative" as the narrative overtook rational discourse. Does not bode well for an informed political discussion.
6. Surveillance—The revelation of the unprecedented extent of spying by the NSA into lives of ordinary citizens to the leaders of the closest allies of the United States.
7. Drones—Unmanned aerial vehicles (UAV) that are piloted remotely or by onboard computers used for killing scores or even hundreds of those considered to be enemy combatants of the United States.
8. Deficit—Looks like deficit-spending will plague Western democracies for at least the next decade. Note to economists of all stripes: reducing the rate of increase of deficit spending still increases the deficit.
9. Sequestration—Middle English *sequestren*, from Old French, from Latin *sequestrare*: to hide away or isolate or to give up for safekeeping.
10. Emancipate — Grows in importance as worldwide more women and children are enslaved in various forms of involuntary servitude.

144

scribe the social change function of language. In other words, language can inhibit our abilities to perceive the world in unique ways, or it can dynamically change habits and prejudices. We often try to avoid offending others by using politically correct language. Political correctness stems from the convergence of several factors, three of which are the Sapir-Whorf hypothesis, the civil rights movement, and language reform. In addition, the feminist and racial equality movements altered our language system by attempting to eliminate gender-based and racial-based terms from our vocabulary. It is suggested that a more sensitive language will reflect a more caring society.

Now that we have explored the cognitive, social reality, group identity, and social change functions of verbal communication, we turn our attention to the different types of verbal communication styles.

VERBAL COMMUNICATION STYLES

Everyone has his or her own unique style of communicating and each comes with benefits and drawbacks. In this section we will explore four common verbal communication styles: direct–indirect, informal–formal, clarity–equivocality, and powerful–powerless. There are a number of different strengths and weaknesses associated with each of these verbal communication styles. These individual differences exist on a continuum and are not to be viewed as dichotomous. In other words, you will not necessarily be "one or the other" but you may be closer to one end of

the spectrum than the other. While some people may consider themselves to be at the midpoint between the two extremes of the spectrum, you may be more likely to describe yourself as using a particular verbal style more consistently.

Direct/Indirect

Direct communication style explicitly verbalizes inquiries and comments in a straightforward manner, while the indirect communication style relies on a more roundabout or subtle method of communicating. Individuals who rely on indirect communication often use nonverbal communication, such as facial expressions and eye contact, more often than verbal communication to convey a message. Indirect language may use ambiguous words and phrases, and the intended meaning may not be accurately interpreted by the receiver. For example, you overhear someone at work say, "This generation is lazy." Was this message intended for you?

Individuals who rely on indirect communication often use nonverbal communication, such as facial expressions and eye contact, more often than verbal communication to convey a message.

Baxter (1984) refers to the extent to which individuals are direct and indirect in her theory of relationship dissolution. She suggests individuals have different styles when it comes to ending relationships. Withdrawing, being annoying or hurtful, or suggesting "being friends" are all examples of indirect strategies used to terminate relationships. Individuals may also rely on direct strategies to end a relationship. A simple statement that "It is over" or a fight where each partner blames the other would be examples of direct strategies. Baxter (1984) suggests that apprehensive people are more likely to use indirect strategies. It is important to point out that individuals will often intentionally choose a more indirect communication style over a direct style to save face for the receiver. Picture yourself at a boring party. Instead of telling the host you are bored and are ready to leave, you may engage in a more subtle approach. Perhaps you start to yawn and hint that you did not get much sleep last night. Engaging in an indirect communication style is sometimes more considerate than directly expressing your true feelings.

© wavebreakmedia/Shutterstock.com

What strategy do you think he is using to end this relationship?

Informal/Formal

The formality of a communicated message refers to the extent to which it is "official" and "prop-er." A **formal communication style** involves an *organized* and managed message and is typically used when you are communicating with someone of higher power, such as a parent, grandparent, teacher, boss, or health professional. Formal communication uses proper words and pronunciation for the particular context and is often planned. It can be used to show respect and professionalism.

An **informal communication style** uses relaxed, casual, and familiar language. This is typically used with your peers and coworkers. In the workplace, it is best to be formal until the relationship is clearly defined. When a receiver expects a formal style and does not receive it, it significantly impacts his or her impressions of the communicator. This includes messages sent over email. Consider the research below that examines students informal email messages to instructors.

Research in real life: STUDENTS INFORMAL EMAIL MESSAGES

Researchers found that instructors are bothered by students' overly casual email messages (Stephens, Houser, & Cowan, 2009) and prefer more formalized communication to demonstrate respect and professionalism. Students in the study suggested that technology was the reason behind their informality (for example, using "RU" instead of "are you"). However, there are serious implications to sending such casual emails. Findings suggested that instructors liked students who sent informal emails less and were less likely to comply with their requests when compared to students who sent more formal emails.

Choosing between informal and formal com-

Informal communication styles are most used when speaking with peers and co-workers.

municative styles can be tricky, particularly in intercultural situations. People who live in the United States, Canada, Australia, and Scandinavia tend to be more informal in their communication styles, whereas people of Asian and African cultures tend to be more formal. Adler and Rodman (2006) suggest there are different degrees of formality for speaking with old friends, acquaintances, and strangers. The ability to use language that acknowledges these differences is the mark of a learned person in countries like South Korea. Whenever you are uncertain about a situation, it is better to be formal than informal, since most cultures value formality. Adopting a more formal communication style will demonstrate respect on your part.

Clarity/Equivocation

Another aspect of verbal communication involves the extent to which you express yourself clearly. While **clarity** refers to the simplistic, down-to-earth, and understandable nature of the communication, Bavelas and his colleagues (1990) define **equivocation** as "nonstraightforward communication . . . [that] appears ambiguous, contradictory, tangential, obscure, or even evasive" (p. 28). In other words, equivocation involves communicating by intentionally choosing words to conceal elements

of the whole truth. Equivocation may be used for different reasons. For example, equivocation allows an individual the possibility to deny events after the fact. Former President Bill Clinton denied having "sexual relations" with Monica Lewinsky. Later, Clinton stated he interpreted the agreed-upon definition of sexual relations to exclude oral sex. This example demonstrates how individuals use equivocation to protect themselves by intentionally not revealing the entire truth. However, like indirect communication, individuals may choose to act in an equivocal manner to protect someone else's feelings. For example, you may tell your date, "This lunch was very thoughtful," even though you have no intention of going on another date with this person. Be aware that sending mixed messages may lead to confusion and awkward discussions in the future.

Communicating with clarity obviously has many benefits. For example, in the classroom, researchers found that students taught by teachers with a clear communication style learned more than those taught by teachers with an ambiguous communication style. Students reported less receiver apprehension, less fear of misinterpreting, and less fear of inadequately processing information when teachers communicated clearly (Cheseboro, 2003). Finally, students indicated that they liked clear teachers and their course material more than those who were not clear (Cheseboro, 2003).

Powerful/Powerless Language

The final verbal communication style we will discuss is the extent to which your language is powerful or powerless. In our society, **powerful language** is associated with positive attributes such as assertiveness and importance, and it can be influential, commanding, and authoritative. Power-

Research has shown that we need to hear only ten to fifteen seconds of an individual's speech to form initial perceptions.

ful language combines the use of proper English, clear thoughts, organized ideas, and a persuasive structure. **Powerless language**, on the other hand, is associated with negative attributes such as shyness, introversion, timidity, nervousness, lack of confidence, and apprehension. Avoiding linguistic features that suggest powerless language may positively impact the way we are perceived by others. Types of powerless speech include hesitations, hedges, tag questions, polite forms, intensifiers, and disclaimers. See Table 5.1 for examples of each of these.

An interesting study examined the use of powerless language in health magazines (Fandrich & Beck 2012). They found that female authors and health magazines use more powerless language compared to male authors or generic types of magazines. Overall the researchers concluded that powerless language was used more often with female audiences. Can you offer any explanations for why powerless language was used more often with female audiences?

The use of powerful language has also been studied in the classroom. Haleta (1996) examined students' perceptions of teachers' use of powerful versus powerless language. Findings suggest that students' initial perceptions of powerful teachers were significantly higher in perceptions of dynamism, status, and credibility than those teachers who used powerless language. Students' level of uncertainty was significantly higher with those teachers who used powerless language. This study reminds us that it is important to be mindful of how we use language in the classroom and its impact on learning.

PERCEPTIONS AND VERBAL COMMUNICATION

One study found that we need to hear only ten to fifteen seconds of an individual's speech to form initial perceptions (Entwisle, 1970). Often

Table 5.1 Powerless Language, Interpretation, and Examples

Powerless Language	Interpreted as	Example
Hesitation	Uncertain, nervous, timid	"I think … well, yeah … I saw someone take, er, your notebook."
Hedges	Less absolute, qualifying phrases	"I guess that would be a good idea."
Tag questions	Weak assertion, less absolute	"That was a good idea, wasn't it?"
Polite forms	Subordinate	"Please pick up your dishes."
Intensifiers	Unsuccessful attempt to make words sound stronger	"It's really, really easy."
Disclaimers	Diversion of responsibility, fault, truth	"Remember, this is just what I heard …"

perceptions remain stable over time. The next section is designed to give you some insight on some typical perceptions of verbal communication. First, we explore how language choices can impact perceptions of credibility and status. We then discuss types of communication considered biased. Afterwards we explore the concept of verbal immediacy as it relates to confirming and disconfirming messages.

Credibility and Status

We can demonstrate credibility in our interpersonal relationships through our verbal communication messages. **Credibility** or believability can be defined as having three dimensions: competence, character, and goodwill (McCroskey & Young, 1981; McCroskey & Teven, 1999). **Competence** refers to your knowledge or expertise, while **character** is the extent to which you are trustworthy. The third dimension, **goodwill**, refers to your ability to care or feel concerned.

Typically, we base our perceptions of credibility on the perceived status of an individual. **Status** refers to the level of position an individual has when compared with others. This may be social, socio-economic, and/or organizational status. In addition to nonverbal behavior, we can gain an understanding of credibility through an individual's verbal comments. The degree of formality, vocabulary, accent, rate of speech, fluency of language, and articulation all play a role in our perceptions of credibility and status. Recall our earlier example of instructors perceptions of informal email messages from students. In this example, the instructor is of higher status in the educational system than students. Therefore instructors were bothered by casual emails because it did not communicate respect and professionalism. As a result, future communication with the

student was negatively impacted. Our perceptions also affect our ability to listen. We tend to listen more attentively to persons of high status than to someone we perceive as having low status. Do you think you may listen to secretaries differently than you do medical doctors? Being mindful of your own communication practices can help improve your interpersonal relationships. When we are mindful we give attention to our reactions to communication interactions. By paying attention we may be open to other types of reactions that may be more aligned with our relational goals.

How might verbal perception impact this person's credibility?

Biased Communication and Language

In the beginning of this chapter, we said that the words we choose can be used to strengthen relationships or to destroy them. When we use biased, sexist, racist, and offensive language, we are choosing to cause harm to others.

Recall the following riddle:

> A doctor and a boy are fishing. The boy was the doctor's son, but the doctor was not the boy's father. Who was the doctor?

The answer is: The doctor is the boy's mother. The punch line of this riddle is relying on the fact that we would initially assume that the doctor was male. Researchers have agreed that sexist language ultimately reinforces a sexist community. **Sexist language** refers to any speech that is degrading to males or females. Most of the research examines how females are subordinate figures in our male-geared vocabulary, with words like *chairman* and *fireman* illustrating the masculine focus of our language structure. To avoid sexist language, researchers suggest using gender-neutral words. The National Council of Teachers of English (NCTE) suggests several guidelines (see Table 5.2).

Verbally attacking individuals on the basis of their race, ethnic background, religion, gender, or sexual orientation is considered **hate speech** (Pember, 2003). As with sexist language, hate speech is used to degrade others. Hate speech includes racist language or words that dehumanize individuals from a particular ethnicity. Anthony Hudson (2003) argues, "The use of language to achieve and/or perpetuate the subordination of a group of people is well documented. Whether it be Jews in Nazi Germany, African Americans in the U.S., or slaves in Mauritania, language has been and continues to be a vital tool in the oppression and abuse of minority groups" (p. 46). Do you recall the Paula Deen controversy in 2013? Certainly you may be able to recall other media figures who have received negative press when they utilized certain words to express themselves.

It is important to be aware that we have choices in deciding our verbal communication and our words may have powerful implications.

Table 5.2 Suggestions for Avoiding Sexist Language

National Council of Teachers of English Guidelines	
Examples	**Alternatives**
mankind	humanity, people, human beings
man's achievements	human achievements
manmade	synthetic, manufactured, machine-made
the common man	the average person, ordinary people
man the stockroom	staff the stockroom
nine man-hours	nine staff-hours
chairman	coordinator, moderator, presiding officer, head
businessman	business executive
fireman	firefighter
mailman	mail carrier
steward and stewardess	flight attendant
policeman/woman	police officer
congressman	congressional representative

EXAMPLE: Give each student his paper as soon as he is finished.
ALTERNATIVE: Give students their papers as soon as they are finished.
EXAMPLE: The average student is worried about his grade.
ALTERNATIVE: The average student is worried about grades.

Adapted from http://owl.english.purdue.edu/handouts/general/gl_nonsex.html.

VERBAL IMMEDIACY

It makes sense to say that we approach things we like and avoid things we do not. Albert Mehrabian and his colleagues used this approach-avoidance theory as a basis for the concept of immediacy in the late 1960s. Mehrabian describes **immediacy** as the process of using communication behaviors purposefully to reduce psychological and physical distance (1969). Researchers have found many benefits to engaging in immediacy behaviors, including increased perceptions of liking and attraction. Immediacy may be enacted verbally and nonverbally, but we will focus on the verbal features in this chapter.

Verbal immediacy refers to using specific word choices and syntactic structures to increase perceptions of psychological closeness. Something as simple as using words such as "we" and "our" is considered more immediate than "I" and "yours." Consider this the next time you confront your roommate about the apartment being cluttered. You might say, "We should clean this apartment before dinner. Our stuff is everywhere," instead of "You should clean the apartment. I cleaned last time."

Gorham (1988) examined verbal immediacy in the classroom. She suggests that instructors can gain a psychological closeness with their students by engaging in a variety of verbal immediacy behaviors such as using humor, self-disclosing, utilizing students' names and viewpoints throughout the lecture, incorporating student suggestions into the course, and showing a willingness to work with students outside of the classroom. Teachers' use of verbally immediate messages was correlated with perceived cognitive and affective learning outcomes. Utilizing verbally immediate messages

with friends, family members, and coworkers can also increase perceptions of liking and attraction.

One way to portray verbal immediacy is through confirming messages. Research suggests we discover and establish our identity through confirming messages in interpersonal relationships (Buber, 1957). **Confirming messages** can help others feel recognized, acknowledged, valued, and respected. (Laing, 1961). Conversely, **disconfirming messages** communicate a sense of insignificance and worthlessness and act to invalidate the source (Watzlawick, Beavin, & Jackson, 1967). Research in this area has found that our self-esteem is impacted by these confirming and disconfirming messages (Cissna & Keating, 1979).

There are four functions of confirming messages: (1) to express recognition of the other's existence, (2) to acknowledge a relationship of affiliation with the other, (3) to express awareness of the significance or worth of the other, and (4) to accept or endorse the other's self-experience (Cissna & Sieburg, 1981).

In Table 5.3 we list the four functions of confirming messages, state what is being intrin-

Table 5.3 Confirming Messages

Function of Confirming Message	Expresses	Example of Confirming Message	Outcome
To express recognition of the other's existence	"To me, you exist."	"Certainly, that is upsetting."	This recognizes and validates the speaker's feelings
To acknowledge a relationship of affiliation with the other	"We are relating."	"Wow! That happened to me, too."	This recognizes that you can relate to the speaker
To express awareness of the significance or worth of the other	"To me, you are significant."	"What happened to you is terrible!"	This suggests you are attentive to their situation
To accept or endorse the other's self-experience	"Your way of interpreting the world is valid."	"Sure, I can see how you thought that."	You are increasing perceptions of value and respect

Table 5.4 Types of Disconfirming Messages

Disconfirming Message	Type	Example
Indifference response	Denying the presence of the other	Being silent when a response is expected, looking away, withdrawing, engaging in unrelated activities
	Denying the relation or involvement of the other	Using impersonal language by avoiding using the first person, avoiding feeling statements or disclosures, using nonverbal "distancing," avoiding eye contact and touch
	Rejecting the communication of the other	Talking "over" another, interjecting irrelevant comments
Imperviousness or lack of accurate awareness of others' perceptions	Denial or distortion of others' self-expression	"You don't really mean that," or "You are only saying that because . . ."
	Pseudo-confirmation	"Stop crying, there is nothing wrong with you," or "Don't be silly, of course you are not scared."
	Mystification	"No matter what you say, I know you still love me," or "You may think you feel that way now . . ."
	Selective responses	Rewarding speaker with attention and relevant responses only when he communicates in an approved fashion, while becoming silent or indifferent when the communication does not meet the responder's approval
Disqualification	Messages that disqualify the other person by direct disparagement	Insult, name-calling, or indirect disparagement (verbal or nonverbal)
	Messages that disqualify another message by transactional disqualification or tangential response	Using the speaker's remark as a starting point for a shift to a new topic to accomplish your own agenda
	Messages that are self-disqualifying	Being unclear, incomplete, ambiguous, or sending incongruent verbal–nonverbal messages

sically expressed to the other person for each function, provide examples of how to verbalize the confirming messages in interpersonal relationships, and describe possible outcomes of communicating in this manner.

Conversely, there are three groupings of disconfirming messages: indifference, imperviousness, and disqualification of the message or speaker. Are you aware of the extent to which you may rely on these behaviors? They may be the cause of unsatisfying relationships and ineffective communicative patterns. In Table 5.4 we list three disconfirming

messages, with specific types and examples. The Confirming/Disconfirming Scale located at the end of this chapter will enable you to evaluate how your own instructor uses confirming and disconfirming messages in the classroom.

FACTORS AFFECTING VERBAL COMMUNICATION

Factors such as age, sex, and context influence the words that we choose to use when communicating as well as how we interpret verbal messages from others. One factor that influences how we choose to verbally communicate and how others interpret messages is age. This includes how our communication changes and is interpreted over time or life span.

Life Span

From perceptions of control in mother-daughter relationships (Morgan & Hummert, 2000) to the meaning of friendships (Patterson, Bettini, & Nussbaum, 1993), our communicative patterns differ over our lifetime. Jon Nussbaum and his colleagues have conducted a considerable amount of research on the relationship between life-span factors and communication behaviors (see Williams and Nussbaum, 2001 for a more recent review). In the next section, we offer three examples of how our verbal communication with different age groups has an impact on our lives.

How parents *respond to their children* may impact how they view themselves. For example, those parents who are controlling and critical may threaten a child's self-esteem. As discussed in Chapter 2, self-esteem is the value we place on ourselves. Some research indicates that having high self-es-

teem has been associated with several positive attributes such as competence, assertiveness, and tenacity. Many parents struggle to establish environments where children have the opportunity to develop a heightened view of themselves through achieving goals and task completion. Some research has shown that children with low or unstable self-esteem levels reported significantly more instances of critical and psychologically controlling parent-child communication than children with high self-esteem (Kernis, Brown, & Brody, 2000). When parents are less likely to acknowledge their children's positive behaviors or show approval in value-affirming ways, children are more likely to develop low self-esteem. To improve children's perceptions of self, parents should attempt to occasionally use confirming messages and avoid disconfirming messages. Confirming messages will express recognition of the child's existence and the worth of the child. These findings suggest that parent-child verbal communication effectiveness can impact a child's level of self-esteem.

What *parents choose to talk about with their teens* and what they choose to ignore may have a serious impact on their teen's behavior. Research on parent-child communication indicates that the extent to which parents communicate with their

How do confirming messages function for parents and children?

teens about sex, birth control, and sexually transmitted diseases will directly impact the teen's sexual behavior. Specifically, research by Whitaker and Miller (2000) found that parents who spoke to adolescents about sex reduced the associations the adolescents made about their own behavior with perceptions of their peers' sexual behavior. Whitaker and Miller also found that communicating to teens about condom use correlated with adolescents' safer sexual behavior.

Finally, how some *young people communicate with the elderly* may be considered patronizing and inappropriate. Consider the following scenario.

> Patrick goes to the nursing home to visit his only living grandmother. He typically goes with his mother, but since he was leaving for college the next day, he thought he would stop in to say goodbye before he left town. Patrick walks in the room and yells, "HELLO, GRANDMA!" His grandmother acknowledges his greeting by shaking her head and smiling. "How are you feeling today?" he asks slowly. She replies jokingly, "I would be feeling better if I could get some decent food." Patrick notices his grandmother has not eaten much from the lunch tray lying over her lap. "Grandma, you really should eat . . . it's good for you," he asserts. He proceeds to pick up her fork. "Here . . . let me help you." She pushes his hand away, and snaps, "I am fine, stop talking to me like a baby!"

It appears that Patrick is going too far to accommodate his grandmother. Why does Patrick treat his grandmother like this? According to

communication accommodation theory (Giles & Wiemann, 1987):

1. During social interaction people will accommodate their speech based on the receiver.
2. People adjust their speech to gain approval and maintain positive impressions.

In most circumstances, individuals have good intentions to shift their speech patterns to more closely resemble their receiver—this is called **convergence**. This may mean they hide or emphasize a particular accent or choose slang words for particular groups of people. When individuals overdo convergence, it may backfire and end up insulting or patronizing their receiver. This is called **overaccommodation**. In this situation, it appears that Patrick is exhibiting overaccommodation. Overaccommodating can make the receiver feel degraded and underestimated. As a result, Patrick was interacting with his grandmother as if she were a baby.

The **communication predicament of aging model** (Coupland, Coupland, & Giles, 1991; Ryan, Giles, Bartolucci, & Henwood, 1986; Ryan, Hummert, & Boich, 1995) suggests that when young people communicate with the elderly, they often rely on negative stereotypes. These negative stereotypes imply that the elderly have declined in cognitive, perceptual, and emotional competence. As a result of these faulty perceptions, young people overcompensate by engaging in "patronizing communication" with the elderly. These patronizing communicative behaviors include: (1) speaking in short sentences, (2) using simple words, (3) using a high volume, (4) speaking at a slow rate, and (5) exaggerating articulation. This patronizing talk may contribute to unsatisfactory intergenerational interactions.

Although it is important to be able to communicate across age groups, it is often difficult because of the lack of homophily, or similarity. These three examples offer some insight into the problematic symptoms and implications of verbally communicating outside of your age group.

How can intergenerational interactions be improved?

Sex Differences in Verbal Communication

When it comes to communicating, are men really from Mars and women from Venus? Maltz and Borker (1982) theorize that the way in which girls and boys play at a young age impacts their speech later in life. Let us look at the type of games young children play.

Girls often enjoy games that rely on cooperative play, such as house, Barbie dolls, or school. In these types of play there needs to be a negotiation of rules. Questions like who will be Barbie and who will be the teacher need to be answered. After all, it would be difficult to play school if everyone wanted to be the teacher and no one wanted to be the students. During these childhood games, girls focus on their own and others' feelings, attitudes, and emotions. In addition, girls often discuss taking turns and decide on imaginary scenes. Therefore, girls encourage talk that emphasizes collaboration and sharing. Their conversations emphasize cooperativeness and discourage aggressiveness.

Boys, on the other hand, tend to be more competitive in their childhood games. Cops and robbers, war, sports, video games, and "king of the hill," are just a few examples of boys' games. Typically in these games, there are set rules, so there is less negotiation and, therefore, less talk. Discussions are usually driven by reiterating the rules or reinforcing them. Boys value competitiveness and aggressiveness because their games center on clear winners and losers. They value assertiveness, direct communication, and having a clear purpose.

Additionally, you may recall our discussion of rapport talk and report talk from an earlier chapter. Deborah Tannen, a professor at Georgetown University and the author of several best-selling

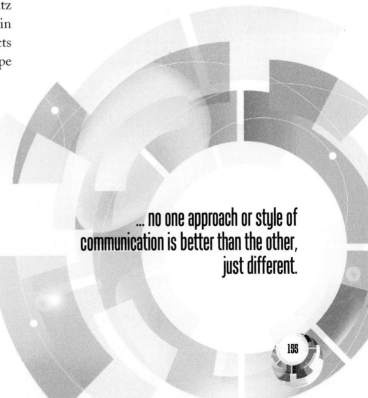

... no one approach or style of communication is better than the other, just different.

books, including *You Just Don't Understand: Women and Men in Conversations,* proposes that women engage in "**rapport talk**," or talking for the sake of talking. In other words, women talk for pleasure and to establish connections with others. In contrast, men engage in "**report talk**," or talking to accomplish goals. Males talk to solve problems and are more instrumental in their approach to communication. Over the last 20 years, Tannen has identified a number of differences in male and female perspectives in regard to communication and relationships. She emphasizes that no one approach or style of communication is better than the other, just different. To improve male-female communication, it is important to understand the differences in perspective as well as the reasons they exist.

How does rapport talk differ from report talk?

This section provides some insight into how men and women may be socialized to communicate differently. This is not to say that throughout your experiences, you have not met males who engage in rapport talk and females who engage in report talk. We acknowledge that these are research generalizations, and they certainly do not apply to everyone.

Contextual Differences

In addition to age and gender, the context of the verbal communication will impact the outcome of the message. We identified context as a characteristic of verbal communication in the beginning of this chapter. We believe this is a key feature when determining appropriate verbal communication. Therefore we have provided a more in-depth examination into how to communicate effectively within specific contexts, including within intercultural relationships (Chapter 12) and our families (Chapter 13), and with our co-workers and bosses (Chapter 14) and health-care professionals (Chapter 15). Furthermore, we will discuss how appropriate communication is used when our relationships are initiating (Chapter 7), sustaining (Chapter 8), growing dark (Chapter 9), and terminating (Chapter 10).

BEST PRACTICES: AVOID VERBAL PITFALLS

Utilizing appropriate words that are clear and direct are our best chances of reaching shared meaning in our interpersonal communication. This section will offer three strategies that will help you avoid verbal pitfalls such as misinterpretations in your interpersonal relationships.

Clarity

When you are composing a message, keep in mind the KISS acronym: **Keep It Short and Simple**. Be clear and succinct. Often we think that using large words will make us sound intelligent, but this is a risky strategy. We may confuse our audience. Direct and clear language will increase your chances of reaching *shared meaning*—your ultimate goal.

Appropriateness

Appropriateness refers to the ability to send messages that uphold the expectations for a given situation. When we send appropriate messages we are considering the contextual and personal attributes of the communication environment. Ask yourself, "What is the best way to send this message to this particular receiver?" This question will help you become more empathetic, compassionate, and sensitive over time. In order to send appropriate messages, we must try to understand the contextual and personal attributes that exist within our communication environments. One way to get better is to try different approaches and see how they work. Look for nonverbal and verbal feedback. Most people will appreciate your genuine effort to "reach" them.

Concreteness

Concreteness refers to being able to communicate thoughts and ideas specifically. In other words, choose your words wisely. Avoid jargon and superfluous words that are unnecessary. This will keep the receiver of your message "on track." Intentionally choosing words your receiver will relate to can increase your chances of being understood. Be specific and illustrative. For example, when an employer asks you to describe yourself, you might say that you are a "good leader"—but do not stop there. Offer a specific example of how you demonstrated leadership in a past role.

SUMMARY

Research on verbal communication dates back to Aristotle and continues to this day. We are fascinated with how individuals learn and use words because their impact is so powerful and significant. Catastrophes such as 9/11, Hurricane Katrina, and the Sandy Hook Elementary School shooting affect our language and change it forever. We start to think differently when we hear words like "terrorist," "gun control," and "evacuee" after such events. Television and movies also introduce new words and phrases, such as "Vote for Pedro" (*Napoleon Dynamite*), "Bazinga" (*The Big Bang Theory*), "That's what she said" (*The Office*), and "May the odds be ever in your favor," (*The Hunger Games*) into our vocabulary. In this chapter we presented definitions, features, functions, and perceptions of verbal communication. The goal of this chapter was to increase your understanding of verbal communication and how certain verbal styles are perceived by others. Heightening awareness of our own verbal communication as well as the verbal communication used by others will ultimately improve our understanding of interpersonal relationships.

DISCUSSION QUESTIONS

1. Recall the scenario in the beginning of the chapter. How could you redesign the verbal communication Lauren used to her partner to express her thoughts?

2. Are there gender differences in regulative and constitutive rules? Do men and women follow different rules? When is it socially acceptable for a male to violate a rule? What about females?

3. What is your position on the role that politically correct language plays in our interactions with others? Are we too sensitive?

4. Recall an example of a situation in which your own words (or the words of others) affected your perceptions. What strategies did/could you use to ensure that there was shared understanding of the message?

SELF ASSESSMENT

Perceived Teacher Confirmation

Directions: Complete the scale below by placing the number on the line that most accurately describes the extent you believe the following statements are true about your instructor.

Strongly Agree	Agree	Neither agree nor disagree	Infrequently	Never
5	4	3	2	1

_____ 1. Spends time to thoroughly answer students' questions.

_____ 2. Tries to become acquainted with students.

_____ 3. Responds sarcastically to some students' remarks or questions in class.*

_____ 4. Makes it known that students' remarks or questions are welcome in class.

_____ 5. Pays attention to selected students only in class and ignores everyone else.*

_____ 6. Acts in a pompous manner.

_____ 7. Shows interest by listening closely when students offer remarks or ask questions in class.

_____ 8. When students ask for extra help from the teacher, he/she criticizes.*

_____ 9. Patronized students.*

_____10. Bullies students.*

_____11. Says that he/she knows that the students are capable of succeeding in the class.

_____12. Mocks students in front of the class.*

_____13. Plays favorites.*

_____14. Is willing to answer questions outside of class.

_____15. Teaches by encouraging feedback from students.

_____16. Is willing to use different methods to help students comprehend concepts.

_____17. While lecturing, makes an effort to have eye contact with students.

_____18. He/she can improvise if needed to answer questions during a lecture.

_____19. Offers a smiling face in class.

_____20. Makes sure students comprehend material before continuing.

_____21. He/she asks students their opinion of how class is progressing, including homework.

_____22. Lectures integrate exercises if possible.

_____23. Students who don't agree get no response from the teacher.*

_____24. Assignments receive oral or written encouragement.

_____25. Tells the students that he/she can't spare the time to meet with them.

* = Recode negatively coded items. (5= 1; 4=2, 3=3, 2=4, 1= 5)

Source: Adapted from Ellis, K. 2000. Perceived teacher confirmation: The development and validation of an instrument and two studies of the relationship to cognitive and affective learning. *Human Communication Research*, 26, 264–291.

KEY TERMS AND DEFINITIONS

ABSTRACT SYMBOLS: a type of symbol that is arbitrary and nonrepresentational.

APPROPRIATENESS: refers to the ability to send messages that uphold the expectations for a given situation and that are aligned with the contextual and personal attributes of the communication environment.

CHARACTER: dimension of competence that evaluates the extent to which a source is perceived as being trustworthy.

CLARITY: refers to the simplistic, down-to-earth, and understandable nature of the communication.

COGNITIVE FUNCTION: a function of verbal communication that explains how we use language to acquire knowledge, to reason, and to make sense of the world

COMMUNICATION ACCOMMODATION THEORY: suggests that people accommodate their speech to their receivers in order to help gain approval and maintain positive impressions.

COMMUNICATION PREDICAMENT OF AGING: a model that suggests that when young people communicate with the elderly, they often rely on negative stereotypes; these negative stereotypes imply that the elderly have declined in cognitive, perceptual, and emotional competence.

COMPETENCE: the knowledge or expertise of a source.

CONCRETE SYMBOLS: a type of symbol that is more likely to resemble what they represent.

CONCRETENESS: refers to being able to communicate thoughts and ideas specifically; utilizing symbols that are likely to resemble what they represent

CONFIRMING MESSAGES: messages that communicate feelings of recognition, acknowledgement, value and respect

CONNOTATIVE MEANING: refers to the personal meaning that the source has with that word.

CONSTITUTIVE RULES: rules that help define communication by identifying appropriate word use and interpreting word meanings.

CONTENT LEVEL OF MEANING: the level of meaning in verbal communication that is primarily related to the topic at hand; often interpreted through our nonverbal behaviors (through how something is said).

CONTEXT: a particular setting or environment in which the communication takes place.

CONVERGENCE: a process referred to in communication accommodation theory that refers to shifting speech patterns to more closely resemble their receiver.

CREDIBILITY: believability; has three dimensions: competence, character, and goodwill.

DENOTATIVE MEANING: refers to the universal meaning of the word, or the definition you would find in the dictionary.

DIRECT COMMUNICATION STYLE: a communication style that explicitly verbalizes inquiries and comments in a straightforward manner.

DISCONFIRMING MESSAGES: messages that communicate a sense of insignificance and worthlessness.

EQUIVOCATION: involves communicating by choosing words that may not demonstrate the whole truth.

EXPRESSING AFFECTION: exchanging messages of liking

FORMAL COMMUNICATION STYLE: a communication style that involves an *organized* and managed message; is typically used when you are communicating with someone of higher power.

GOODWILL: dimension of credibility that refers to perceptions of one's ability to demonstrate concern for others.

GROUP IDENTIFICATION: a function of verbal communication that serves to distinguish one group from another and to provide a sense of similarity and cohesiveness for its members.

HATE SPEECH: a the act of verbally attacking individuals on the basis of their race, ethnic background, religion, gender, or sexual orientation

IMMEDIACY: the process of using communication behaviors purposefully to reduce psychological and physical distance.

INDIRECT COMMUNICATION STYLE: a communication style that relies on a more roundabout or subtle method of communicating.

INFORMAL COMMUNICATION STYLE: using a relaxed, casual, and familiar verbal communication style.

KISS: the "keep it short and simple" principle

LINGUISTIC DETERMINISM: a concept that suggests language determines thought or that there is a relationship between language and cognition.

LINGUISTIC RELATIVITY: concept that suggests distinctions encoded in one language are unique to that language

METACOMMUNICATION: an important tool that is often used during social interaction to increase our shared meaning and to reduce uncertainty about the status of our relationships; "communicating about communication."

ORGANIZATIONAL JARGON: a specialized vocabulary that is socially constructed and regularly used by members of a particular trade, profession, or organization.

OVERACCOMMODATION: a negative results referred to in communication accommodation theory when individuals shift speech patterns so severely that it insults or makes the receiver feel degraded or underestimated.

POWERFUL LANGUAGE: associated with positive attributes such as assertiveness and importance; it can be influential, commanding, and authoritative.

POWERLESS LANGUAGE: associated with negative attributes such as shyness, introversion, timidity, nervousness, lack of confidence, and apprehension.

RAPPORT TALK: talking for the sake of talking.

REGULATIVE RULES: rules that control our communication by managing or guiding interaction by identifying when, how, where, and with whom we communicate in certain situations.

RELATIONSHIP LEVEL OF MEANING: the level of meaning in verbal communication that is highly sensitive to the people involved in the conversation and the process of communicating; found in the words we use.

REPORT TALK: talking to accomplish goals.

RULES: guidelines for social interaction; agreed upon guidelines that provide a structure for what is social acceptable communication in our culture

SAPIR-WHORF HYPOTHESIS: suggests that the language we learn, as well as the culture we are exposed to, is used to shape our entire reality.

SELF-DISCLOSURE: purposefully revealing personal information about ourselves.

SEMANTICS: the study of meaning we attribute to each word

SEXIST LANGUAGE: refers to any speech that is degrading to males or females

SOCIAL CHANGE: a function of verbal communication that explains how language can inhibit or encourage change in society

SOCIAL REALITY: a function of verbal communication that explains how individuals socially construct or agree upon language that influences how we see and interact in the world.

STATUS: refers to the level of position an individual has when compared with others; this may be social, socio-economic, and/or organizational status.

SUBJECTIVE: interpreting meaning through one's own experiences, historical perspective, and cultural upbringing and/or our physical environment

SYMBOL: socially agreed-upon representations of an event, action, person, object, or phenomenon.

UNCERTAINTY REDUCTION THEORY: suggests that human communication is used to gain knowledge and create understanding by reducing uncertainty and, therefore, increasing predictability.

VERBAL COMMUNICATION: refers to the words we use during the communication process.

VERBAL IMMEDIACY: refers to using specific word choices and syntactic structures to increase perceptions of psychological closeness.

REFERENCES

Adler, R. B., & Rodman, G. (2006). *Understanding human communication*. New York: Oxford University Press.

Angelini, J. R., & Billings, A. (2010). An agenda that sets the frames: Gender, language, and NBC's Americanized Olympic telecast. *Journal of Language and Social Psychology, 29,* 363–385.

Bavelas, J. B., Black, A., Chovil, N., & Mullett, J. (1990). *Equivocal communication.* Newbury Park, CA: Sage.

Baxter, L. (1984). Trajectories of relationship disengagement. *Journal of Social and Personal Relationships, 1,* 29–48.

Berger, P. L., & Luckmann, T. (1966). *The social construction of reality: A treatise in the sociology of knowledge.* Garden City, New York: Anchor Books.

Buber, M. (1957). Distance and relation. *Psychiatry, 20,* 97–104.

Cheseboro, J. L. (2003). Effects of teacher clarity and nonverbal immediacy on student learning, receiver apprehension and affect. *Communication Education, 52,* 135–147.

Cissna, K. N., & Keating, S. (1979). Speech communication antecedents of perceived confirmation. *The Western Journal of Speech Communication, 43,* 48–60.

Cissna, K. N., & Sieburg, E. (1981). Patterns of interactional confirmation and disconfirmation. In C. Wilder-Mott & J. H. Weakland (Eds.), *Rigor and imagination: Essays from the legacy of Gregory Bateson* (pp. 253–282). New York: Praeger.

Coupland, N., Coupland, J., & Giles, H. (1991). *Language, society and the elderly.* Oxford: Basil Blackwell.

Cronen, V. E., Pearce, W. B., & Snavely, L. (1979). A theory of rule structure and forms of episodes, and a study of unwanted repetitive patterns. In D. Nimmo (Ed.), *Communication Yearbook III, New Brunswich, NJ: Transaction Press.*

Ebert, L., & Floyd, K. (2004). Affection expressions as face threatening acts: Receiver assessments. *Communication Studies, 55,* 254–270.

Edwards, A., & Shepherd, G. J. (2004). Theories of communication, human nature, and the world: Associations and implications. *Communication Studies, 55,* 197–208.

Entwisle, D. R. (1970). Semantic systems of children: Some assessments of social class and ethnic differences. In F. Williams (Ed.), *Language and poverty,* New York: Sage.

Fandrich, A. M., Beck, S. J. (2012). Powerless language in health media: The influence of biological sex and magazine type on health language. *Communication Studies, 63,* 36–53.

Floyd, K. (1997). Communicating affection in dyadic relationships: An assessment of behavior and expectations. *Communication Quarterly, 45,* 68–80.

Giles, H., & Wiemann, J. M. (1987). Language, social comparison and power. In C.R. Berger & S. H. Chaffee (Eds.), *Handbook of communication science* (pp. 350–384). Newbury Park, CA: Sage.

Gorham, J. (1988). The relationship between verbal teacher immediacy and student learning. *Communication Education, 37,* 40–53.

Griffin, E. (2003). *A first look at communication theory.* Boston: McGraw-Hill.

Haleta, L. (1996). Students' perceptions of teachers' use of language: The effects of powerful and powerless language on impression formation and uncertainty. *Communication Teacher, 45,* 16–28.

Hirst, R. (2003). Scientific jargon: Good and bad. *Journal of Technical Writing and Communication, 33,* 201–229.

Hudson, A. (2003). Fighting words. *Index on Censorship, 32,* 45–52.

Kernis, M. H., Brown, A. C., & Brody, G. H. (2000). Fragile self-esteem in children and its associations with perceived patterns of parent-child communication. *Journal of Personality, 68,* 225–252.

Laing, R. D. (1961). *The self and others.* New York: Pantheon.

Maltz, D., & Borker, R. (1982). *A cultural approach to male-female miscommunication.* In J. Gumperz (Ed.), *Language and social identity,* Cambridge: Cambridge University Press (pp. 196–216).

McCroskey, J. C., & Teven, J. J. (1999). Goodwill: A reexamination of the construct and its measurement. *Communication Monographs, 66,* 90–103.

McCroskey, J. C., & Young, T. J. (1981). Ethos and credibility: The construct and its measurement after three decades. *Central States Speech Journal, 32,* 24–34.

Mehrabian, A. (1969). Some referents and measures of nonverbal behavior. *Behavioral Research Methods and Instrumentation, 1,* 213–217.

Morgan, M., & Hummert, M. L. (2000). Perceptions of communicative control strategies in mother-daughter dyads across the life span. *Journal of Communication, 50,* 49–64.

Nash, W. (1993). *Jargon: Its uses and abuses.* Oxford: Blackwell Publishers.

Patterson, B., Bettini, L., & Nussbaum, J. F. (1993). The meaning of friendship across the life-span: Two studies. *Communication Quarterly, 41,* 145–161.

Pearce, W. B., Cronen, V. E., & Conklin, R. F. (1979). On what to look at when studying communication: A hierarchical model of actors' meanings. *Communication, 4,* 195–220.

Pember, D. (2003). *Mass media law.* Boston: McGraw-Hill.

Persing, B. (1977). Sticks and stones and words: Women in the language. *Journal of Business Communication, 14,* 11–19.

Rickford, J. (1999). *African American Vernacular English.* Malden, MA: Blackwell Publishers.

Rickford, J., & R. Rickford. (2000). *Spoken soul: The story of black English.* Hoboken, NJ: John Wiley.

Ryan, E. B., Giles, H., Bartolucci, G., & Henwood, K. (1986). Psycholinguistic and social psychological components of communication by and with the elderly. *Language and Communication, 6,* 1–24.

Ryan, E. B., Hummert, M. L., & Boich, L. H. (1995). Communication predicaments of aging: Patronising behavior towards older adults. *Journal of Language and Social Psychology 14,* 144–166.

Sapir, E. (1949). *Selected writings of Edward Sapir in language, culture, and personality.* D. G. Mandelbaum (Ed.). Los Angeles: University of California- Berkeley.

Seale, J. (1995). *The construction of social reality.* New York: The Free Press.

Stephens, K. K., Houser, M. L., & Cowan, R. L. (2009). R U able to meat me: The impact of students' overly casual email messages to instructors. *Communication Education, 58,* 303–326.

Ting-Toomey, S., & Chung, L. C. (2005). *Understanding intercultural communication.* Los Angeles, CA: Roxbury.

Watzlawick, P., Beavin, J. H., & Jackson, D. D. (1967). *Pragmatics of human communication: A study of interactional patterns, pathologies, and paradoxes.* New York: W. W. Norton & Company.

Whitaker, D. J., & Miller, K. S. (2000). Parent-adolescent discussions about sex and condoms: Impact on peer influences of sexual risk behavior. *Journal of Adolescent Research, 15,* 251–273.

Whorf, B. L. (1956). *Language, thought, and reality: The collected papers of Benjamin Lee Whorf.* J. B. Carroll (Ed.). Cambridge, MA: MIT Press.

Williams, A., & Nussbaum, J. F. (2001). *Intergenerational communication across the life span.* Mahwah, NJ: Lawrence Erlbaum.

chapter 6

Nonverbal Communication:
It's Not *What* You Said;
It's *How* You Said It

OBJECTIVES

- Define nonverbal communication and its distinct characteristics.

- Explain nonverbal expectancy violation theory.

- Recall the four functions of nonverbal messages.

- Describe three functions of facial communication.

- Explain and provide examples of the five categories of kinesics and the four types of space.

- Distinguish between the five categories of touch.

- Discuss how we use nonverbal communication to regulate our conversations.

SCENARIO: SOUND FAMILIAR?

David woke up and thought he and his partner were on the same page about saving money for an upcoming trip. His partner repeatedly said, "Sounds fine" and "Everything is good." However, their limited conversation over breakfast and the way his partner rushed out of the house suggested the conversation was anything but "fine."

OVERVIEW

This familiar scenario reminds us that our verbal communication and nonverbal communication are not always in sync. However, when *what* we are saying contradicts *how* we are saying it, we know that individuals tend to believe the nonverbal cues over what has been said. Therefore understanding nonverbal communication is critically important in initiating and maintaining healthy and effective interpersonal relationships. This chapter identifies and defines characteristics of nonverbal communication and reviews eight types of nonverbal behavior. The theories, research, and applications of nonverbal communication throughout this chapter will help you apply appropriate and effective communication with others. Furthermore, you will gain an enhanced understanding of how nonverbal communication functions and be able to consider how nonverbal communication influences our everyday interactions.

What nonverbal messages are communicated in this picture?

DEFINING NONVERBAL COMMUNICATION

There has been a vast amount of research done in the area of nonverbal communication. Scholars have examined everything from the importance of physical attractiveness in the job interview (Watkins & Johnston, 2000) to the implications of creating positive impressions in the physician-patient interaction (Street & Buller, 1987). From something as obvious as our physical appearance to a subtle pause during a conversation, we are captivated by the meanings created by others' nonverbal behaviors. While it is impossible to put a numerical value on the amount of meaning created through nonverbal and verbal communication, we know that the majority of meaning is generated through nonverbal communication. This makes sense if you think about the amount of time you spend communicating nonverbally versus verbally. Even when we are not speaking, we are constantly sending nonverbal messages to others. Consider all of the nonverbal messages you sent to your instructor today while you were sitting in class listening to the lecture. Have you thought about how online students also send nonverbal messages to their instructors?

The popular phrases "It's not *what* you said, it's *how* you said it," or "Actions speak louder than words," are examples of the emphasis our culture places on the nonverbal portion of communicating. While verbal communication refers to the words we use to express ourselves, **nonverbal communication** refers to all aspects of communication other than the words we use, including but not limited to: facial expressions, body movements and gestures, physical appearance, and voice. As explained in Chapter 1, each message we send has two components: the content level of meaning and the relationship level of meaning. While the content level of meaning is usually conveyed through the words we use, the relationship level of meaning is often created through *how* we say those words. Therefore, understanding nonverbal communication will play a critical role in understanding the relationship level of meaning in our messages.

Throughout the remaining sections of this chapter, we isolate specific types of nonverbal communication and discuss relevant research findings. However, before we do this, it is first necessary to distinguish nonverbal communication from verbal communication.

DISTINCT CHARACTERISTICS OF NONVERBAL MESSAGES

The first characteristic that is unique to nonverbal communication is that it is **continuous**. While there is a clear distinction between when we begin verbally communicating and when we stop, nonverbal communication continues beyond our words. Some say, *"You cannot not communicate."* This suggests we are continuously sending nonverbal messages that are being perceived by others. Even in the absence of others, we are sending nonverbal messages. For example, think about a high school friend you have not spoken to in a long time. She may perceive your silence and distance in several ways. Perhaps she thinks you are extremely busy or maybe she thinks that you are upset with her. What else might she think?

Our nonverbal messages may conflict with our verbal messages. We may say one thing, but behave inconsistently with our verbal message. For example, you might tell Aunty Lucy you liked the knit scarf she made for you. However, your facial expressions might tell another story as you pull the purple-and-red polka dot creation out of the package. When our nonverbal and verbal messages contradict each other, research has shown that we tend to believe the nonverbal messages. Therefore, a second unique feature of nonverbal communication is that nonverbal is more **believable** than verbal communication. Although our nonverbal communication often supplements our verbal communication, such as raising our eyebrows to help stress or emphasize certain words, we tend to believe the nonverbal more than the verbal when there is a discrep-

> When our nonverbal and verbal messages contradict each other, research has shown that we tend to believe the nonverbal messages.

ancy between the two. While Aunt Lucy heard you say you liked the scarf, she will probably interpret your facial grimace as a stronger indicator of whether it will actually become a part of your wardrobe.

While verbal communication relies solely on the words we exchange with others, nonverbal communication has many different outlets. Therefore, a third distinct feature of nonverbal messages is they are **multi-channeled**. We can use several channels to communicate something nonverbally. Doctors dress professionally, maintain eye contact, listen attentively, and hang their diplomas on the wall in an attempt to establish credibility with their patients. Likewise, day spas manipulate lighting, music, and aroma to communicate a relaxing and calm atmosphere. Because we use multiple cues to send the same message, it makes sense that we will have a higher chance of nonverbal effectiveness. Although it may seem that nonverbal and verbal messages are quite different, they do have similar characteristics. Let us discuss three similarities between verbal and nonverbal communication.

NONVERBAL FEATURES THAT ARE SIMILAR TO VERBAL MESSAGES

Just like verbal messages, nonverbal messages are rule-guided. As mentioned in Chapter 5, there are certain rules we must follow to be socially appropriate, and these rules are culturally defined. In regard to nonverbal communication, *constitutive rules* refer to the behaviors we enact to help define the appropriateness of our communication. For example, if we asked you to generate a list of nonverbal behaviors that would communicate respect in a job interview, could you do this? We can demonstrate respect and professionalism in a job interview through our choice of clothing and use of certain gestures and facial expressions. Also, we adhere to specific rules when it comes to regulating or monitoring our communication with others. Recall from Chapter 5 that we use *regulative rules* to control and/or manage our interaction. In the same way that we use words to start, maintain, or end our conversations with others, we also use nonverbal communication to control or regulate our conversations. Eye contact (or lack thereof), specific hand gestures, paralanguage, and nods are all examples of nonverbal signals that we use to indicate turn-taking cues in conversation. We can use humor to help demonstrate these concepts. In order for a joke to be funny, we must properly apply both constitutive and regulative rules. When applying constitutive rules to telling jokes, we have to ask ourselves: Is it appropriate for this environment and audience? Is it age-appropriate? When considering regulative rules, we can identify good joke tellers versus bad joke tellers based on how they utilize regulative rules. For example, to tell a good story or

joke, you must be able to take a dramatic pause before the punch line. Also, effective use of inflection, facial expressions, and eye contact are necessary to pull off a good joke.

Burgoon (1978) developed nonverbal expectancy violation theory to help understand rule-guided behavior. The theory suggests that individuals hold expectancies for nonverbal behavior and, when these expectations are violated (or the rules are not abided by), there are two common reactions, physical arousal and cognitive arousal. Physical arousal refers to the physical response a person has to nonverbal expectancies being violated. The cognitive arousal is the mental response a person has to nonverbal expectancies being violated.

Many of our behaviors are rule-guided. These rules are culturally created and maintained. Recall the last time you entered an elevator, you probably adhered to rule-guided behavior in this situation. If you are in an elevator alone and the door opens and a stranger enters, the nonverbal expectancy is that he or she will stand as far away from you as possible (in order to maximize each other's personal space). If this stranger stood directly next to you, this would be a violation of a space rule. In response to this space violation, you probably would consider stepping away (physical arousal) and also might consider the person odd (cognitive arousal) for not abiding by the "elevator rules." Nonverbal expectancy violation theory has helped shed light on our societal rules and responses to violations of these rules. Can you think of more examples of behaviors that are guided by rules? What would happen if these rules were violated?

Another similarity between nonverbal and verbal messages is that they are culturally bound. The rules we follow during social interaction are socially constructed and are restricted to a specific culture. Nonverbal gestures in the United States that imply certain meanings are not universally understood. In the United States, when we touch our forefinger to our thumb to create a circle and splay the other three fingers upward, we are signaling to others "OK" (see Figure 6.1) In France, this same gesture means "zero." In Japan it signals "money," and in Germany it is considered an obscene gesture.

Depending on the context of the nonverbal communication, it may influence the interpretation, meaning, and appropriateness of the communication.

Figure 6.1. Nonverbal symbols like this one are culturally bound.

© cmgirl/Shutterstock.com

As with our verbal language, nonverbal messages are culturally bound and do not necessarily translate to other cultures. Even within the United States, there are several subcultures that attribute their own distinct meanings to particular nonverbal behaviors. Consider gang members and their particular signs of inclusion, or social groups such as fraternities that have specific handshakes. Nonverbal communication can be unclear and confusing and may lead to many misinterpretations. Therefore, it is important to be aware of how we enact these behaviors and to be sure to confirm their meaning by asking questions when messages are perceived as ambiguous.

Finally, both verbal and nonverbal messages are contextually restricted. As we previously mentioned, we must consider the situation, environment, and setting we are in when deciding on appropriateness. Depending on the context of the nonverbal communication, it may influence the interpretation, meaning, and appropriateness of the communication. When we are pitching a new idea to our boss, we tend to dress more formally and manipulate our posture to appear more professional. However, can you imagine how surprised your friends would be if you continued this behavior while you were relaxing at home? Just like the words we use, our nonverbal behaviors should be modified to fit the situation. To gain a better understanding of these specific nonverbal behaviors, we will discuss eight types of nonverbal communication.

EIGHT TYPES OF NONVERBAL COMMUNICATION

We have grouped nonverbal communication into eight broad categories: facial communication, kinesics, haptics, proxemics, paralanguage, physical appearance, artifacts, and chronemics. In this section we will explain each type and provide insight on how the particular nonverbal behavior influences meaning during social interaction.

Facial Communication

Facial communication includes any expression on the face that sends messages. Think about the thousands of different expressions you can make with your face by raising or lowering your eyebrows, shutting or opening your eyes, wrinkling your nose, and protruding your lips. Three functions of facial communication are:

- to display emotion;
- to supplement verbal communication; and
- to reinforce verbal communication.

To begin, our face is the primary channel for expressing emotions. The most basic emotions displayed through our facial expressions are often referred to by the acronym SADFISH, which stands for sadness, anger, disgust, fear, interest, surprise, and happiness. Can you determine each of these emotions in the pictures displayed in Figure 6.2?

The second function of facial expressions is to supplement or take the place of something it is missing, such as the verbal communication. Individuals reveal their attitudes through their facial expressions in this way. Think about how we analyze facial expressions when someone opens a gift from us. We can typically tell if they like the gift by the type of facial expression revealed. Researchers Ekman and Friesen (1969) were very interested in these types of behaviors and referred to them as nonverbal leakage or deception clues. The television series *Lie to Me* (2009–2011, on FOX) was

© William Perugini/Shutterstock.com

© ArtFamily/Shutterstock.com

© Ollyy/Shutterstock.com

© Pius Lee/Shutterstock.com

© djile/Shutterstock.com

© PathDoc/Shutterstock.com

© Jeanette Dietl/Shutterstock.com

Figure 6.2.
Can you identify the emotions in these images?

INTERPERSONAL COMMUNICATION: Building Rewarding Relationships

based on Ekman's decades of research. See http://www.paulekman.com/lie-to-me/. During each episode, Dr. Cal Lightman (played by Tim Roth) would assist law enforcement by investigating whether individuals were telling the truth by analyzing microexpressions and body language.

In addition, we use facial communication to reinforce, or go along with, our verbal message. For example, when we want to emphasize a word, we tend to raise our eyebrows and open our eyes wide. This type of facial display matches the verbal portion of the message and reinforces the message. Overall, our facial movements communicate emotions, attitudes, and motivation.

One type of facial communication that has received a great deal of attention in the literature is oculesics. **Oculesics** is the study of eye behavior. Researchers are fascinated by oculesics and how it influences meaning. Eye behavior in the United States is very particular and is often perceived as an important means of showing attention, interest, and respect to others. We often encourage students to engage in eye contact during interviews for internships or jobs. However, if someone provides too much direct eye contact, it can be interpreted as disturbing and frightening. Eye contact is a perfect example of a nonverbal behavior that is culturally defined. Direct eye contact in Asian cultures is considered rude, disrespectful, and intimidating, while in the United States, eye contact during conversation is expected.

Kinesics

Another type of nonverbal communication often associated with facial expressions is **kinesics**, or body movements. Ekman and Friesen (1969) classify kinesics into five categories:

1. Emblems
2. Illustrators
3. Affect displays
4. Regulators
5. Adaptors

Let us examine each of these. **Emblems** are specific nonverbal gestures that have a particular translation. For example, extending your forefinger over your lips means to be quiet. Or if you wanted to signal to someone to "come here," you would wave your hand toward your body. Because these emblems are context-bound, they are often misinterpreted when communicating with individuals from other cultures. Kitao and Kitao (1988) explain that the emblem for "OK" in the United States is the emblem used for "money" in Japan. They write, "An American and a Japanese man wanted to meet some friends. The Ameri-

> Eye behavior in the United States is very particular and is often perceived as an important means of showing attention, interest, and respect to others.

can called from a pay phone and signaled to the Japanese man the American emblem for 'okay,' indicating that the friends would be able to meet them. The Japanese man interpreted the emblem as meaning that more coins were needed for the pay phone and rushed over to put in more money" (p. 89). Although this is a lighthearted example, you can imagine how misinterpretations during business exchanges might not be humorous and may even be costly.

Indicating something with a body gesture is an illustrator.

What is this emblem conveying?

Illustrator is the label used to indicate when you use your body to help describe or visually depict something. You have probably heard someone say, "I caught a fish this big!" while indicating the size of the fish with his or her hands. This is an example of an illustrator. We use illustrators to visually demonstrate how big our nephew is or to point someone in the right direction when he is lost. Illustrators are more universal and less ambiguous than emblems.

Regulators are any type of body movements that are used in conversation to control the communication flow. Sometimes one person is monopolizing the conversation and you want to signal to him that you have something to say.

What would you do? You have many options such as leaning forward, opening your mouth, nodding, eye rolling, eyebrow raising, and/or using your hand to gesture.

We can demonstrate our emotions nonverbally through affect displays. **Affect displays** are overt physical responses to our emotions that can be either positive or negative. Positive affect displays are constructive and encouraging. Patting or rubbing a close friend on the back when he is sad is an example of an affect display. Hugging and kissing are additional ways to display positive affect toward another. What about negative affect displays? Recall the last time someone asked you why you were angry. Perhaps it was because you were clenching your teeth or glaring with your eyes. In what ways have you physically manifested feelings of boredom, frustration, or sadness?

It is amazing how quickly infants and young children pick up on these displays. These learned behaviors are typically modeled by the infant's parent or caregiver through a process called social referencing. **Social referencing** refers to

INTERPERSONAL COMMUNICATION: Building Rewarding Relationships

the process by which individuals rely on those around them to determine how to respond to unfamiliar stimuli (Campos & Stenberg, 1988). For example, when infants are introduced to someone or something new, they look to the parent for reassurance. When the parent responds with a positive affect display, like a smile, she sends a message to the infant that this new stimuli is comforting and not threatening. It is not long before the child displays more complex emotions through nonverbal affect displays. He may roll his eyes because he is annoyed or stomp his feet and cross his arms in disgust.

Positive affect displays are constructive and encouraging.

Adaptors are body movements that are enacted at a low level of awareness and usually indicate nervousness, anxiety, or boredom. Individuals may display these types of behaviors in situations that evoke anxiety such as public speaking classes or other types of public performances. Sometimes students are not aware that while they are giving a speech they are also engaging in behaviors such as tapping a pen on the podium, cracking their knuckles, and fixing their hair. When they watch themselves on videotape later, they are surprised. Outside of the class-

room, individuals who work in human resources departments are often trained to look for adaptors during interviews and screening processes. Interviewee behaviors such as fidgeting hands, playing with paper, and postural changes are examples of adaptors that are often exhibited during interviews and considered signs of nervousness or weakness.

Do you have any nervous habits that you do unconsciously?

Haptics

An additional type of nonverbal communication is **haptics**, or touch. The amount of touch in interpersonal relationships is related to liking and status. Anderson and Sull (1985) suggest that individuals who like each other will touch each other more often than those who do not. In fact, if individuals are not fond of each other, they will actively avoid touching. Individuals with higher status, such as your boss or professor, typically choose whether to initiate touch into the relationship. They also may use touch to maintain control. For example, a middle school teacher may lead a student by physically directing him toward the corner of the room while saying, "Let's move over here." This type of touch is considered role-bound because the teacher and student are working within specific positions. Thayer (1988) offers categories of touch based on people's roles and relationships.

Functional-professional are touches that occur while accomplishing a specific task, which is performed by those working within a specific role. For example, a barber, doctor, or nail technician will perform tasks that involve touch as part of their occupation. Functional touch also includes any touch that is done while trying to accomplish a goal. Helping a player off the ice when you are playing hockey or assisting an elderly woman across the street would both be situations employing functional touch. **Social-polite** are touches that occur between business partners, acquaintances, and strangers. These include greetings and salutations, such as a handshake. **Friendship-warmth** are touches that occur between extended family members, close business associates, and friendly neighbors. This type of touch signals caring, concern, and interest between interactants. A hug and a pat on the back are examples of this type of touch. There are some gray areas between this type of touch and the "love-intimacy" category, which may be a cause of great misinterpretation. **Love-intimacy** are touches that occur between family members and friends where there is affection and a deep level of caring. Extended hugs and holding hands are often examples of this type of touch. **Sexual-arousal** are touches that occur within sexual/erotic contexts. Kissing is an example of this type of touch. Sometimes we use touch to initiate permission to enter into a "deeper" relationship with someone. If there is a discrepancy between the level of touch and your interpretation of the level of the relation-

ship, it is important to be assertive and direct in your communication about this discrepancy with your relationship partner. Touch is the most intimate type of nonverbal communication and is also the most ambiguous. We interpret touch differently depending on the context. In a crowded club, party, elevator, or subway, touch is not interpreted as intrusive. However, within different contexts, when people intentionally enter our space, we may view it as a violation. Now, let us discuss how our use of personal space contributes to nonverbal communication.

Love-intimacy touches occur between family members and friends where there is affection and a deep level of caring.

Proxemics

The fourth type of nonverbal communication is space, or **proxemics**, which refers to the invisible bubble we place around our bodies. Often this space is considered our "comfort zone." Americans are highly conscious of our space and our territory. We allow certain individuals into our space, depending on the context of the situation. Hall (1966) defined four categories of space zones as listed on the next page (See Table 6.1).

Although this chart provides us with a general idea of how individuals use space, perceptions of appropriate personal space differ among individuals. In the United States, we are generally very concerned with others infringing on what we consider to be "our space" and are very protective of it. We may even go so far as to place physical objects, or **markers**, between ourselves and others. Similar to the ways in which animals mark their territory, we may claim the territory around us by using markers to show others that this is our space. Think about all of the different ways that you may protect space that you consider yours. Have you ever spread out your books, bag, and articles of clothing in the library to purposefully take up more space? Have you ever spread out your belongings at the lunch table to discourage others from sitting next to you? Finally, have you ever had someone invade your space while conversing? A popular *Seinfeld* episode referred to this type of individual as a "close talker." They are often considered annoying and inappropriate. These are all examples of how our use of space influences our perceptions of messages and the meanings we assign to them. (See Table 6.1)

How do you react when you feel like you do not have enough space?

Table 6.1 Space, Context, and Nonverbal Communication

Type of Space	Distance	Individuals/Groups
Intimate	0 to 18 inches	Reserved for those that are closest to us (e.g., boyfriend, girlfriend, spouse)
Personal	18 inches to 4 feet	Reserved for family members and close friends
Social	4 to 10 feet	The distance that we feel comfortable conducting everyday social situations with strangers, acquaintances, and business partners
Public	10 feet and farther	The distance reserved for large audiences

Paralanguage

A fifth category of nonverbal behavior is **paralanguage**, which focuses on everything beyond the words in the verbally communicated message. Paralanguage, or vocalic components of messages, includes:

- Pitch (high—low)
- Rate (fast—slow)
- Volume (high—low)
- Pronunciation (clear—unclear)
- Inflection (high—low)
- Tempo (fast—slow)
- Accents (slight—thick)
- Vocal fillers ("ahh," "ummm")
- Hesitations (grunts, screams, laughs, gasps, sighs, and even silence) (Hickson, Stacks, & Moore, 2004, p. 258).

Have you ever thought about the ways you use silence? You may use silence to show disgust, to keep a secret, to reveal a secret, or to enhance the importance of your message. Knapp and

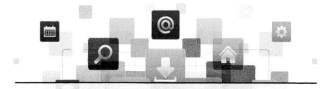

Because silence serves several functions, it is important to understand that it is often misunderstood.

Hall (2002) identified five primary functions of silence:

1. To punctuate or emphasize certain words or ideas
2. To evaluate or provide judgment of another's behavior (showing favor or disfavor, agreement, disagreement, attacking)
3. To hide or to reveal information
4. To express emotions: the silence of disgust, sadness, fear, anger, or love
5. To engage in mental activity: show thoughtfulness, reflection, or ignorance (Bruneau, 1973; Jaworski, 1993; Jensen, 1973)

Because silence serves several functions, it is important to understand that it is often misunderstood. Can you recall a time when your silence was misconstrued?

Physical Appearance

A sixth category of nonverbal communication is **physical appearance**, which includes our body, clothing, makeup, height, size, and hair. Much

of the literature on physical appearance examines the attractiveness of individuals. The literature (see, for example, McCroskey 1992) on this topic recognizes three different types of attraction: 1) physical attraction (how visibly pleasing someone is), 2) task attraction (how pleasing someone is to work with), and 3) social attraction (how pleasing someone is to interact with). We will focus primarily on physical attraction in this section. A more comprehensive discussion of all three types of attraction is provided in Chapter 7.

What is perceived as attractive in the United States may be quite different from what is considered attractive in Thailand or Egypt. Likewise, what you might find attractive, your neighbor may find repulsive. However, we know that individuals are more attracted to physically attractive people than to physically unattractive people (Sprecher, 1989). But perhaps this has more to do with **homophily**, or how similar we consider the target to be to ourselves. Although we cannot develop a global list of physically attractive attributes, we do know that there are benefits to being attractive. However, an interesting study found that when screening job applicants, attractiveness had no impact when the quality of the application was high. But attractiveness was a significant advantage when the application was mediocre (Watkins & Johnston, 2000).

Body size is one aspect of physical appearance that has been studied by researchers and is linked to how we form impressions of others. Body size is the relationship between an individual's height, weight, and muscular build, and it has received a considerable amount of attention in the nonverbal communication literature. In

1942, Sheldon and Stevens theorized that there was a link between a person's physical attributes and personality traits. After collecting data on male body types and temperament, they distinguished between three primary body types: endomorphs, mesomorphs, and ectomorphs.

The **endomorph** body type is described as being short, round, and soft. Researchers have associated the endomorph body type with being lazy, better-natured, more old-fashioned, less good-looking, more agreeable, and more dependent on others compared to the other body types. One interesting study found that self-perceived endomorphs had significantly stronger intentions to smoke cigarettes compared to the other body types (Tucker, 1983). But are all individuals with this body type lazy? Certainly former NBA player Charles Barkley, who was at one time referred to as "The Round Mound of Rebound," is not described as lazy, dependent, or even overly agreeable. It is important to be aware of our tendency to inaccurately stereotype individuals based on their appearance.

Mesomorphs are described as being physically fit, muscular, average height and weight, and athletic. Researchers have associated this body type with being stronger, better looking, more adventurous, younger, taller, and more mature compared to the other body types (Sheldon, Hartl, & McDermott, 1949). The mesomorphic body type was perceived by college students as an ideal body type for both males and females (Butler & Ryckman, 1993). Even professional clinicians have been found to stereotype based on body type. Fletcher and Diekhoff (1998) found that therapists judged more muscular males, or male mesomorphs, as more mentally healthy than endomorphs and ectomorphs.

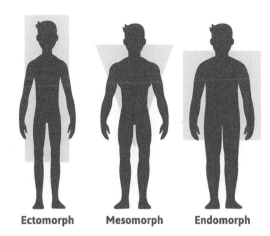

Ectomorph   Mesomorph   Endomorph

© Sudowoodo/Shutterstock.com

The three primary body types.

The **ectomorph** body type is described as being tall, thin, and frail. Characteristics associated with this body type include being tenser, nervous, quieter, taller, younger, introverted, more afraid of people, lacking confidence, and being less social when compared with the other body types (Sheldon, Hartl, & McDermott, 1949). Not all perceptions of this body type are negative. For example, our culture certainly seems to value a thin or ectomorphic body shape, especially in women. The media has been criticized for disproportionally displaying images of thin women and contributing to the problem of eating disorders in young women. More recently, you may recall that the modeling industry has adopted healthier standards for their models' body weight. As we consume media messages with models that are more representative of our culture in respect to body shape, pay attention to how you react to these messages.

In addition to body type, height has also been examined as a physical characteristic that influences meaning. Are taller people perceived as more competent? To date, Judge and Cable (2004)

> **Our subjective view of time is contingent on our personal/ psychological orientation and our cultural influences.**

have designed the most comprehensive analysis between physical height and work success. Their meta-analysis found that while controlling for sex, age, and weight, there were significant positive relationships between height and social esteem, leader emergence, performance, and income. Therefore, not only are taller people perceived as more competent, they actually get paid more. How much more? Their findings suggest that someone who is six feet tall earns, on average, nearly $166,000 more during a thirty-year career than someone who is five feet, five inches.

Artifacts

The seventh type of nonverbal communication is artifacts. **Artifacts** are defined as "the physical objects and environmental attributes that communicate directly, define the communication context, or guide social behavior in some way" (Burgoon, Buller, & Woodall 1994, p. 123). We can think about artifacts in terms of personal adornment and environmental adornment. **Personal adornment** refers to how we use artifacts on our bodies. Tattoos, jewelry, branding, scarring, painting, makeup, glasses, and body piercing are all examples of artifacts that can be

considered personal adornment. Two popular personal adornment artifacts addressed in the literature are tattoos and body piercing.

Although tattoos and body piercings are becoming more mainstream, negative perceptions are still sometimes associated with these artifacts. Some of these perceptions may be founded, since Carroll, Riffenburgh, Roberts, and Myhre (2002) noted that study participants with tattoos and body piercings were more likely to engage in high risk-taking behaviors such as disordered eating behavior, gateway drug use, hard drug use, sexual activity, suicide, and violence. Forbes (2001) also found that tattoos and piercings in college students are associated with more risk-taking behavior, greater use of alcohol and marijuana, and less social conformity. Another study found individuals with body modifications (tattoos or body piercings other than earlobes) reported more symptoms of depression and trait anxiety than individuals without body modifications (Roberti & Storch, 2005).

Environmental adornment refers to artifacts that we use in our environment to identify ourselves. Consider how much you can learn about someone just by walking through his or her bedroom. Think about the artwork on the wall, the cleanliness, the type of objects on the dresser, and the clothes hanging in the closet. The MTV show *Room Raiders* capitalized on this phenomenon. Contestants decided who to go out with based solely on the contents of the bedrooms of the prospective dates. In addition to our bedrooms, we often use artifacts in our cars, offices, and other personal spaces to reflect our identity. Try to identify the environmental adornment artifacts the next time you are in your professors' offices. Do they have any artwork? Do they have photos of their dog or children? Can you identify their alma mater?

Closely related to those artifacts are additional **environmental factors**, such as the context, room layout, lighting, and/or color. Environmental factors will influence how we interpret meaning. Consider the environmental factors inside a McDonald's. Think about the lighting, seating, and colors—do they encourage you to eat fast? Fast-food restaurants are interested in high turnover and do not typically want you to become too comfortable while eating your burger and fries. In contrast, high-end restaurants are more concerned with having their patrons relax, order more food and drinks, and stay for a long time in their establishments. These types of restaurants will often use candlelight, comfortable seating, and soft music to create an environment that says "stay awhile." Around the holidays, department stores often play specific music and try to create a certain mood to encourage shoppers to spend more money. Be aware of the setting and environment around you. Do you respond to certain colors? Is there a reason why most classrooms have white walls and very little artwork? Does certain music put you in a certain mood? What types of smells make you hungry? What scents make you calm? Being more mindful and heightening your awareness of the impact of environmental factors is critical to your success as a competent communicator.

Chronemics

The final type of nonverbal communication is referred to as **chronemics**, or how we use and perceive time. Our subjective view of time is contingent on our personal/psychological orientation and our cultural influences. Hall (1976) suggests that each culture operates on a continuum from a monochronic orientation to a polychronic orientation to time. In general,

Americans tend to be more **monochronic** because time is considered to be "linear" in nature. It spans across a "time line" and we can schedule appointments one after another in an orderly fashion. Think about how your daily planner is set up. (Or the fact that you *have* a daily planner.) You can segment time and schedule classes, appointments, and social events for each week, each day, and within each hour. Being punctual, scheduling appointments, and having strict adherence to starting times and ending times are all valued behaviors in the United States. During one of the authors' first day of graduate school, faculty stressed to the students, "Being on time is being late; being early is synonymous with being on time." This example reinforces the monochronic orientation that is valued in our culture. Being early in our culture is perceived as being organized, professional, prepared, and productive. Being late in our culture is perceived as being lazy, disorganized, uninterested, and unprofessional.

In contrast to a monochronic time orientation, **polychronic** cultures perceive time as circular. This time orientation suggests that several things can be done at the same time. Polychronic cultures do not rely as heavily on the clock as monochromic cultures do. Meetings are viewed as time to cultivate relationships, and it is more important to finish the conversation than to be "on time" for the next appointment. Time and activities are more fluid and things will "get done when they get done." Work time and personal time typically overlap in these cultures. Within the United States, this orientation has negative perceptions, such as being "nonambitious and a waste of precious time" (Hickson, Stacks, & Moore, 2004, p. 316).

In addition to our cultural norms, we must also consider individual orientations. Consider how monochronic or polychronic your parents are. Did you grow up with a curfew? Did you have daily chores? Did you eat dinner at the same time each evening? Answering these types of questions, can give us more clarity on how we interpret and react to chronemics across our interpersonal relationships.

FOUR FUNCTIONS OF NONVERBAL MESSAGES

Now that we have discussed the eight types of nonverbal communication, we will review four ways in which we use nonverbal behavior. Four primary functions of nonverbal messages are:

1. to facilitate our cognitive meaning;
2. to encode and decode emotions;
3. to express affection and support; and
4. to aid in impression formation and/or identity management.

Facilitate Cognitive Meaning

One primary function of nonverbal messages is to aid in cognitive meaning. We can use our nonverbal behavior in several ways to help create meaning. Ekman and Friesen (1969) specify five ways we aid our cognitive meaning:

1. repetition;
2. contradiction;
3. complementation;
4. accent; and
5. regulation.

First, repetition refers to both verbal and nonverbal expressions made simultaneously to reinforce each other. The nonverbal message repeats the verbal message in order to increase the accuracy of the message. For example, when a police officer is directing traffic, she may extend her hand and yell, "Stop!" In this example, the cognitive meaning of the verbal message is repeated with the nonverbal emblem. We can use this function when we want to clarify or increase the accuracy of the messages we send.

On the other hand, our nonverbal and verbal expressions may be contradictory. Oftentimes we say one thing and behave in a way that is inconsistent with our verbal message. When our nonverbal and verbal messages contradict each other, research has shown that we tend to believe the nonverbal messages. Once again, we refer to the heuristic, "It is not what you said, but *how* you said it." If someone says, "I really like your new car," you will determine the sincerity of the message by dissecting the nonverbal cues. Was it said sarcastically? What do their facial expressions reveal? After scrutinizing the nonverbal and verbal messages, we will determine whether the verbal portion of the message was genuine. If there are any discrepancies between the two messages, we will rely on the nonverbal portion of the message.

Third, complementing is a process by which our nonverbal communication is used in conjunction with the verbal portion of the message. We can determine the attitudes people hold when we examine the extent to which the verbal and nonverbal messages are complementing each other. If you want to make sure that your relationship partner knows that you are angry with her, you may glare at her and say, "I am so angry with you!"

The fourth way we aid our cognitive meaning, according to Ekman and Friesen (1969), is through accenting. **Accenting** is used when we want to stress or emphasize a particular word or phrase in our verbal message. If a friend says, "Please, do not be *late* to the party" and stresses the word "late," her use of accenting implies that it is important to her that you are on time for the party. Accenting can change the meaning of the original message, as well as the emotion conveyed (Anderson, 1999). Consider how the meaning and the emotion of the same sentence changes slightly when we accent different words in the following statements:

> *George*, will you pick up fat-free milk from the store today?
> George, will you pick up *fat-free* milk from the store today?
> George, will you pick up fat-free milk from the store *today?*

The final way to aid our cognitive meaning is to **regulate** conversations. Researchers have introduced several ways we use nonverbal communication to regulate or negotiate our conversations:

- Turn-yielding (Duncan, 1972)
- Turn-maintaining (Duncan, 1972)
- Back-channeling (Duncan, 1972)
- Turn-requesting (Wiemann & Knapp, 1975)
- Turn-denying (Burgoon, Hunsaker, & Dawson, 1994)

First, we engage in **turn-yielding** behaviors, which signal to the listener that we are going to stop talking. Some examples of these signals include placing a drawl on the final syllable, placing emphasis on a final word, saying, "do you know what I *mean*?", displaying an open and direct body position, and leaning forward. Second, we can also engage in suppressing signals or **turn-maintaining**, which suggests to the listener that we want to continue talking. These behaviors include talking more quickly and/or more loudly, using hand gestures that suggest "wait a minute" or "one last point," and filling more pauses. **Back-channeling cues** are used by listeners to signal that they are motivated to listen to us and that they are not interested in "taking over the floor." Some nonverbal behaviors they may engage in include nodding their heads, and saying "I agree" or "uh-huh." They are confirming interest in our message, but they are not interested in speaking themselves. **Turn-requesting behaviors** are utilized when listeners use buffers, short words or phrases such as, "But uhhh . . ." or "You know . . ." to signal to the speaker that they are interested in speaking (Wiemann & Knapp, 1975). These buffers may be used while the speaker is talking or during a pause in conversation. If they are used properly, the speaker should finish his thought and relinquish the floor to them. Burgoon, Hunsaker, and Dawson (1994) identified an additional turn-taking cue referred to as **turn-denying**. Listeners use this cue when they are not interested in "taking over the floor." They may signal that they are not interested by increasing space between themselves and the speaker and/or avoiding direct eye contact with the speaker.

Encoding and Decoding Emotions

A second function of nonverbal communication is to display and interpret emotions. In chapter 3 we described emotions as subjective feelings such as happiness, anger, shame, fear, guilt, sadness, and excitement that produce positive or negative reactions that are physical, psychological, and physiological. We often weigh the appropriateness of our outward emotional reaction and judge whether it is desirable and/or acceptable (see Anderson, 1999). Emotion is primarily communicated through nonverbal means.

Encoding emotions refers to an individual's ability to display feelings. Scholars have suggested that as we get older, we are better able to encode emotions such as happiness, anger, sadness, and fear (Mayo & LaFrance, 1978). Furthermore, a seminal study found that regardless of gender, young children seem to express emotions quite similarly. However, as girls become older they are more accurate in detecting affective states in others. They also are more expressive. Boys, on the other hand, are less accurate in detecting affective states in others and are less expressive encoders (Buck, 1975). Another study revealed that women were more effective in encoding emotions than men (Wagner, MacDonald, & Manstead, 1986). This research makes sense because it is more socially acceptable for women to express their emotions in the U.S. culture. U.S. men are more likely to suppress their feelings. In 1994, Kring, Smith, and Neale developed the Emotional

Expressivity Scale (EES) to measure the extent to which individuals outwardly display their emotions. You can complete the scale at the end of the chapter to determine your own emotional expressivity.

Decoding emotions refers to the ability to accurately read and interpret the emotional states of others. Most scholars agree that individuals who are skilled encoders are also skilled decoders (see Burgoon, Buller, & Woodall, 1994). Therefore, women tend to be better decoders than men (Wagner, MacDonald, & Manstead, 1986). However, research has shown that men tend to improve their sensitivity to facial expressions with individuals over time (Zuckerman, Lipets, Koivumaki, & Rosenthanl, 1975). As you can imagine, being able to appropriately encode and decode emotions can enhance our ability to connect and relate to others. This emotional skill set allows us to react with more compassion and understanding within our interpersonal relationships.

Table 6.2 Nonverbal Communication: Comforting Strategies

Comforting Strategy	Examples
Attentiveness (Showing you care)	Activing listening behaviors and head nodding
Eye contact	Maintaining direct eye contact with the person
Crying	Referencing crying or weeping, either the other person's or the comforter's
Vocalics	Using one's voice to show concern, references to tone of voice, intensity, and speaking softly
Instrumental activity (Doing something for the other person which may or may not be directly related to the distress)	Making dinner or running errands for the other person to show support
Facial expression (Showing emotional reaction through one's face)	Adapting facial features to show empathy or simply looking concerned or sad
Proxemics	Using proxemics to close up the space without touching
Gesturing	Using hand and arm movements to show empathy, anger, and/or agitation about what the person is saying
Hugs	Directly hugging the person, either a whole or half hug
Pats	Touching arm or shoulder
Increased miscellaneous touch	Any type of increase in touching that does not fall into hugging or patting category
Emotional distancing (Comforting avoidance response)	Behaviors that are self-oriented and avoidant, intended to keep distance or to remain uninvolved

What are these facial expressions saying?

Express Affection and Support

A third function of nonverbal communication is to provide affection and support. Oftentimes we will display nonverbal comforting strategies in our interpersonal relationship when some-

one is going through a difficult or stressful time. Researchers identified 12 nonverbal comforting strategies that college students employ to lend support to others (Dolin & Booth-Butterfield, 1993).

Their study revealed that females reported more nonverbal comforting strategies and more diverse comforting responses than males. This means that females not only use nonverbal comforting strategies more frequently, but they also use several different types of strategies. Males were more likely to use emotional-distancing behaviors than females. See Table 6.2 for a complete list of comforting strategies and messages.

Aid in Impression Formation/ Identity Management

Another significant function of nonverbal communication is creating first impressions. Typically, our initial perception of someone is based on observing nonverbal behavior such as physical appearance, eye contact, and facial expressions. The information gathered through these first impressions is used to predict attitudes and opinions not yet revealed. This is referred to as **proactive attribution**. This information is also used for **retroactive attribution**, or to help explain the behavior of others in hindsight (Berger, 1975). Although we gather this information quickly, it tends to remain stable over time—making these initial perceptions critical for future interactions. For example, research suggests that roommates whose initial impressions were positive had more satisfying subsequent interactions and used more productive strategies to solve conflict (Marek, Knapp, & Wanzer, 2004). However, how often do you think our first impressions are inaccurate? We do not often provide second chances, as we do not communicate long enough to find out if our first impressions were accurate.

In 2007, Houser, Horan, and Furler examined heterosexual speed daters and their impressions after 30 seconds. Their results suggest:

- Both males and females identified positive communication behaviors (example: good communication skills, acting nice, being nonverbally responsive) as being important in date prospects.
- Males identified physical attraction in simple terms, such as "cute" and "pretty," while females used more specific terms, such as "stylish clothes," "nice eyes," and "neatly groomed."
- Friendliness was identified as being an important characteristic that was displayed nonverbally, mostly through smiling. Females used descriptors such as, "great smile," "cute smile," "friendly smile," and "warm, accepting smile."
- Both males and females identified lack of attraction or negative physical qualities as primary negative judgments.
- Females reported approximately three times the negative evaluations, compared to males.

This study reminds us how quickly first impressions are formed and how detailed the interpretation of nonverbal behavior can be when we are establishing relationships.

BEST PRACTICES: AVOID COMMON NONVERBAL COMMUNICATION MISTAKES

To increase how effectively and appropriately you receive and display nonverbal communication in your interpersonal relationships, we offer suggestions in four areas. This section provides suggestions on how to monitor and adapt your nonverbal messages to your audience and context.

Common Areas of Miscommunication

First, nonverbal messages are often perceived as ambiguous and open for misinterpretation. The cultural barriers attached to many nonverbal behaviors can inhibit our interpretation of the meaning. Additionally, we do not usually have an extended period of time to create first impressions, which may have lasting results. Therefore, it is important to reinforce that nonverbal communication is not clear and is often misinterpreted. The more time we spend with others, the more accurately we can interpret their nonverbal behavior. Remember, nonverbal communication is multi-channeled and we can increase our chances of accurately interpreting others' behavior if we take all of the cues into consideration. Similarly, if we want to become more successful at getting our messages across to others, we will employ a number of different nonverbal behaviors that reinforce or clarify our verbal message. These strategies will help reduce miscommunication that often occurs within the nonverbal communication arena.

Nonverbal Messages and Social Influence

Have you ever caused someone to change a behavior or attitude without intending to do so? Can you recall a specific time when you unintentionally influenced another person's attitudes or actions by displaying certain nonverbal behaviors? The two examples below illustrate how we can unintentionally influence others through our nonverbal behaviors.

1. Perhaps you broke eye contact with your sibling while she was telling you about something that happened to her at school. As a result of this behavior, your sister stopped talking and walked away from you. When you asked her later why she walked away from you, she told you that she could tell that you were not interested in her story.

2. Several years ago a famous supermodel cut her long hair quite short and, as a result of this choice, many other women did the same. In an interview the model stated that she certainly did not intend to influence others to cut their hair short.

These examples illustrate how we may influence others' attitudes or behaviors through our nonverbal messages without intending to do so. Thus, it is important to monitor our nonverbal behaviors closely and consider how our actions may influence others. Be aware that we may unintentionally influence someone else's behavior or attitude through our nonverbal behaviors.

Of course there are also many times when we intend to influence others by exhibiting certain nonverbal behaviors. For example, each time you dress professionally for a job interview, you attempt to influence the interviewer's perceptions of you as a viable job candidate. Communication researchers have had a longstanding interest in learning more about how certain verbal and nonverbal behaviors influence those around us. Much of the research in this area suggests that you can influence individuals by displaying nonverbal behaviors associated with power and authority or kindness and liking, or both. Individuals can give the impression of authority and expertise through nonverbal cues such as wearing uniforms (e.g., military), nametags that include titles (e.g., manager), and personal artifacts. Military personnel, police officers, doctors, or managers in a retail store all have control over certain resources, and have power to reward or punish. We are more likely to obey a police officer's suggestion to move our car than the suggestion made by a stranger on the street because the officer wearing the uniform has the power to give us a ticket. Other nonverbal messages that project an image of authority and power are eye contact, touch, voice, and space. We often can tell who has the most power in an organization by the size of his or her office. Other persuasive tactics involve liking and kindness. We can persuade others by our charismatic tone, physical attractiveness, and smile. Nonverbal immediacy behaviors have also been shown to be associated with social influence.

Immediacy refers to the psychological and physical closeness we have with one another. Mehrabian (1971) developed this principle that suggests

Remember, nonverbal communication is multi-channeled and we can increase our chances of accurately interpreting others' behavior if we take all of the cues into consideration.

we are drawn to people and things that we like, prefer, and value highly. Nonverbal immediacy behaviors can indicate inclusion, approachability, involvement, warmth, and positive affect. Some examples of nonverbal immediacy behaviors that individuals might use during social interaction include: eye contact, decreasing distance, appropriate touch, positive facial expressions, open body positions, varying pitch and tempo, and spending time with another person. In general, nonverbal immediacy behaviors produce direct, positive effects on other people (Mehrabian, 1971, p. 207). This direct-effects model suggests that individuals who engage in immediacy behaviors are more likely to be perceived as warmer, friendlier, more intimate, and more attractive (Anderson, 1999). Although immediacy behaviors seem to be ultimately a good thing, can you think of a circumstance where enacting nonverbal immediacy behaviors may be detrimental to your interpersonal relationships? In other words, can you think of a time when you might want to increase the psychological space between yourself and a relation-

al partner? Anderson (1999) suggests that in less positive relationships, immediacy behaviors can be perceived as suffocating and threatening. At the end of the chapter, you can measure your own nonverbal immediacy behaviors by taking a self report measure.

Practice Sending and Receiving Nonverbal Messages

As mentioned previously, it is often quite difficult to interpret the nonverbal behavior of others. Therefore, we need to supplement our observations with questions. We can clarify our perceptions of others' nonverbal messages simply by asking questions such as: "Are you upset?", "Were you being sarcastic?", and "Are you serious?" Remember that not all nonverbal communication is intentional. Typically, the intentional nonverbal signals are emphasized. Subtle nonverbal behaviors may not be intentional. To accurately interpret others' nonverbal messages it is important to pay attention to all of the behaviors exhibited and seek clarification when verbal and nonverbal messages are contradictory.

Are you aware of the potential impact of the nonverbal messages you send to others? Because the assumption is that all nonverbal messages are intentional, we must be aware of the nonverbal messages we send. How do others interpret your facial expressions, use of space, and touch? We may never find an answer to this question unless we ask others for feedback.

Recognize Differences in Nonverbal Communication Perceptions

Sometimes individual differences can influence an individual's nonverbal behavior. One example of this is the extent to which individuals have communication apprehension. Recall our discussion of communication apprehension (CA) in Chapter 3. CA refers to the level of fear or anxiety an individual has that is associated with real or anticipated communication with another person (McCroskey, 1977). McCroskey (1976) proposes that high CAs avoid communication situations and actively try to decrease communication attempts. Therefore, he predicts that high CAs are more likely than low CAs to have increased space, to avoid eye contact, to be averse to being touched, to have less vocal variety, to have fewer kinesic movements, and to have longer pause times in conversation. The degree of CA an individual has can determine the nonverbal impact on their interpersonal communication situations.

Age is another factor that may impact how we interpret nonverbal behavior. Life span refers to how our communication changes over time. Just as our verbal communication changes over time, so does our nonverbal behavior. Because we learn most of our nonverbal communication through cultural exposure, it is common for children to lack knowledge in what is considered socially appropriate nonverbal expression. As adults, we have a good time laughing at young people when they make mistakes like making a disgusted face when they taste Grandma's signature soup. We do not expect them to have mature social skills, since those skills are acquired over time, although research has shown that throughout our life span we tend to express emotions such as SADFISH similarly. In other words, the way a child would act surprised is similar to how a 90-year-old woman would— by opening her eyes, raising her eyebrows, and dropping her jaw. While initially we may have similar ways of expressing emotions, as we grow older we tend to engage in more self-monitoring techniques, become more aware of the rules regarding nonverbal behavior, and modify our behavior to fit these socially appropriate rules.

To send and receive nonverbal messages effectively, it is important to take into consideration the ambiguous nature of nonverbal messages. To make sure that the intended message is effectively communicated to your receiver, be sure that the verbal message is accompanied by multiple nonverbal behaviors that are consistent with the verbal message. Also, be aware of the fact that you can influence others both intentionally and unintentionally by exhibiting nonverbal messages. When you are confused about the nonverbal messages someone is sending, ask questions to clarify the message's meaning. Finally, when interpreting others' nonverbal messages, always consider the impact of individual differences such as personality, age, and culture on message delivery.

FUTURE DIRECTION FOR NONVERBAL COMMUNICATION: ELECTRONIC PARALANGUAGE

A direction for future research in nonverbal communication may be how we employ nonverbal messages in the mediated environment. Current research has explored how we compensate for the lack of nonverbal cues during mediated communication. Nonverbal communication researchers know it is difficult to express emotions verbally. This is why in face-to-face situations we rely on a certain glance, smile, wink, or even tears to express our emotions. During mediated communication, we do not have the luxury of traditional

© 4zevar/Shutterstock.com

nonverbal cues. Therefore we rely on electronic paralanguage to express emotions and regulate our conversations.

Electronic paralanguage includes emoticons, acronyms, abbreviations, and flaming. **Emoticons** (short for "emotion icons") are symbols made up of combinations of keyboard keys that convey emotions. For example, :) refers to a smiley face, while :(refers to a frowning face, and ;) refers to someone winking. In addition, text messages and instant messages may insert actual artwork or emojis such as ☺ or ☹.

Researchers have examined the use of emoticons in chat rooms (Constantin et al., 2002) and email (Yoo, 2007). They have found that, in general, those individuals who utilize "smiley emoticons" have positive relational outcomes including increased perceptions of liking by the receiver. However, Walther and D'Daddario (2001) warn us that the overuse of these emoticons can cause them to lose their effectiveness. In other words, their "cuteness" factor does fade over time. We suggest individuals consider the task of the mes-

sage and the relationship with the receiver before considering the use of emoticons. Emoticons can be misinterpreted and should be used cautiously.

One difference between face-to-face nonverbal communication and engaging in electronic paralanguage is that emoticons are more deliberate and voluntary (Walther & D'Addario, 2001). In traditional face-to-face situations, our nonverbal behavior is often unintentional. However, it is impossible to insert these emoticons without intent. Research has found that emoticons may serve the function of complementing the "written" statements, but they do not necessarily enhance them (Walther & D'Addario, 2001).

Acronyms or text messaging shorthand are used to express a variety of nonverbal cues. Three functions include:

1. to express emotions;
2. to regulate conversations; and
3. to provide feedback.

Table 6. 3 Nonverbal Communication: Electronic Paralanguage

Purpose	Text Messaging Shorthand
To express emotions	LOL, laugh out loud WYWH, Wish you were here
To regulate conversations	TTYL, talk to you later BRB, be right back L8R, later PMFJI, Pardon me for jumping in OMPL, one moment please GGFN, gotta go for now
To provide feedback	IGTP, I get the point J/K, just kidding ISWYM, I see what you mean

Communicating electronically is risky because of the lack of traditional nonverbal cues. Not all electronic communication is pro-social. **Flaming** refers to antisocial electronic behavior, such as swearing, firing insults, or shouting. Shouting or expressing anger in mediated communication is usually indicated by typing in all capital letters (Krohn, 2004). All in all, it will be interesting to examine how we continue to compensate or replace traditional nonverbal messages in the mediated environment.

SUMMARY

In this chapter we have introduced nonverbal communication and highlighted the importance of nonverbal communication in our everyday lives. We identified similarities to verbal communication and characterized the unique features of nonverbal behavior. Our hope is that you will heighten your awareness of how you use and interpret the eight types of nonverbal communication and understand how they function in your interpersonal relationships. By increasing your understanding of nonverbal communication, we hope you will avoid the communication problems that often accompany our nonverbal behavior. Remember that individuals are more likely to believe our nonverbal messages, regardless of intent. Therefore it is critical we understand the messages we are sending to others and how we interpret the nonverbal communication behaviors of others.

DISCUSSION QUESTIONS

1. In what circumstances has someone violated your nonverbal expectancies? How did you respond? Under what circumstances would violating someone's expectations be considered beneficial? Could there be benefits of violating someone's expectations?

2. While our primary emotions may be inherited, our social response to these emotions have been tied to cultural upbringing. Often our response is learned through our experiences. Discuss an example of how your response to a particular emotion was different than that of a close friend or family member.

3. Do you think instant messaging, text messages, email, and other computer-mediated methods of communication contribute to a polychronic culture? Why or why not?

4. Develop a list of regulative and constitutive rules for communicating online. How do you determine turn-taking? Is there such a thing as "interrupting" online? How do you demonstrate liking, professionalism, support, and/or anger?

SELF ASSESSMENTS

Emotional Expressivity Scale

Using the following scale, place the number on the line that best describes your agreement with the following statements.

Strongly Agree	Agree	Neither Agree nor Disagree	Disagree	Strongly Disagree
5	4	3	2	1

_____ 1. I think of myself as emotionally expressive.

_____ 2. People think of me as an unemotional person.*

_____ 3. I keep my feelings to myself.*

_____ 4. I am often considered indifferent by others.*

_____ 5. People can read my emotions.

_____ 6. I display my emotions to other people.

_____ 7. I don't like to let other people see how I am feeling.*

_____ 8. I am able to cry in front of other people.

_____ 9. Even if I am feeling very emotional, I don't let others see my feelings.*

_____10. Other people aren't easily able to observe what I am feeling.*

_____11. I am not very emotionally expressive.*

_____12. Even when I am experiencing strong feelings, I don't express them outwardly.*

_____13. I cannot hide the way I am feeling.

_____14. Other people believe me to be very emotional.

_____15. I don't express my emotions to other people.*

_____16. The way I feel is different from how others think I feel.*

_____17. I hold my feelings in.*

INTERPERSONAL COMMUNICATION: Building Rewarding Relationships

* = Recode these items (5=1; 4=2; 3=3; 2=4; 1=5)

After you recode the negative items, sum all the scores together.

Range = 17–85

From "Individual Differences in Dispositional Expressiveness: The Development and Validation of the Emotional Expressivity Scale" by A.M. Kring, D.A. Smith, & J.M. Neale. *Journal of Personality and Social Psychology,* 66, 934-949. Copyright © 1994 by the American Psychological Association. Reproduced with permission. No further reproduction or distributed is permitted without written permission from the American Psychological Association and Ann M. Kring.

Nonverbal Immediacy Scale-Self Report (NIS-S)

The following statements describe the ways some people behave while talking with or to others. Please indicate in the space at the left of each item the degree to which you believe the statement applies to you. Please use the following 5-point scale:

1 = Never; 2 = Rarely; 3 = Occasionally; 4 = Often; 5 = Very Often

_____ 1. I use my hands and arms to gesture while talking to people.

_____ 2. I touch others on the shoulder or arm while talking to them.

_____ 3. I use a monotone or dull voice while talking to people.

_____ 4. I look over or away from others while talking to them.

_____ 5. I move away from others when they touch me while we are talking.

_____ 6. I have a relaxed body position when I talk to people.

_____ 7. I frown while talking to people.

_____ 8. I avoid eye contact while talking to people.

_____ 9. I have a tense body position while talking to people.

_____10. I sit close or stand close to people while talking with them.

_____11. My voice is monotonous or dull when I talk to people.

_____12. I use a variety of vocal expressions when I talk to people.

_____13. I gesture when I talk to people.

_____14. I am animated when I talk to people.

_____15. I have a bland facial expression when I talk to people.

_____16. I move closer to people when I talk to them.

_____17. I look directly at people while talking to them.

_____18. I am stiff when I talk to people.

_____19. I have a lot of vocal variety when I talk to people.

_____20. I avoid gesturing while I am talking to people.

INTERPERSONAL COMMUNICATION: Building Rewarding Relationships

_____21. I lean toward people when I talk to them.

_____22. I maintain eye contact with people when I talk to them.

_____23. I try not to sit or stand close to people when I talk with them.

_____24. I lean away from people when I talk to them.

_____25. I smile when I talk to people.

_____26. I avoid touching people when I talk to them.

Scoring:
    Step 1. Add the scores from the following items: 1, 2, 6, 10, 12, 13, 14, 16, 17, 19, 21, 22, and 25.
    Step 2. Add the scores from the following items: 3, 4, 5, 7, 8, 9, 11, 15, 18, 20, 23, 24, and 26.
    Total Score = 78 plus Step 1 minus Step 2.

Norms:

Females	Mean = 102.0	S.D. = 10.9	High = >112 Low = <92
Males	Mean = 93.8	S.D. = 10.8	High = >104 Low= <83

Source: Richmond, V. P., McCroskey, J. C., & Johnson, A. D. (2003). Development of the Nonverbal Immediacy Scale (NIS): Measures of self- and other-perceived nonverbal immediacy. *Communication Quarterly, 51,* 502-515.

KEY TERMS AND DEFINITIONS

ACCENTING: used when we want to stress or emphasize a particular word or phrase in our verbal message

ACRONYMS: text messaging shorthand; used to express a variety of nonverbal cues

ADAPTORS: body movements that are enacted at a low level of awareness and usually indicate nervousness, anxiety, or boredom

AFFECT DISPLAYS: overt physical responses to our emotions that can be either positive or negative

ARTIFACTS: the physical objects and environmental attributes that communicate directly, define the communication context, or guide social behavior in some way

BACK-CHANNELING CUES: behaviors used by listeners to signal that they are motivated to listen to us and that they are not interested in "taking over the floor"

BELIEVABLE: refers to the fact that when our nonverbal and verbal messages contradict each other, research has shown that we tend to believe the nonverbal messages

CHRONEMICS: how we use and perceive time

COGNITIVE AROUSAL: the cognitive or mental response a person has to nonverbal expectancies being violated

COMPLEMENTING: a process by which our nonverbal communication is used in conjunction with the verbal portion of the message

CONTINUOUS: refers to the fact that there is no clear distinction between when we start and stop nonverbal communication; it continues beyond our words

CONTRADICTING: when we say one thing and behave in a way that is inconsistent with our verbal message

CULTURALLY BOUND: characteristic of both verbal and nonverbal communication; states that the rules we follow during social interaction are socially constructed and are restricted to a specific culture

DECODING: refers to the ability to accurately read and interpret the emotional states of others

ECTOMORPH: a tall, thin, and frail body type

ELECTRONIC PARALANGUAGE: includes emoticons, acronyms, abbreviations, and flaming

EMBLEMS: specific nonverbal gestures that have a particular translation

EMOTICONS: short for "emotion icons"; symbols made up of combinations of keyboard keys that convey emotions

ENCODING: refers to an individual's ability to display feelings

ENDOMORPH: a short, round, and soft body type

ENVIRONMENTAL ADORNMENT: artifacts that we use in our environment to identify ourselves

ENVIRONMENTAL FACTORS: include the context, room layout, lighting, and/or color of a particular environment

FACIAL COMMUNICATION: includes any expression on the face that sends messages

FLAMING: refers to antisocial electronic behavior, such as swearing, firing insults, or shouting

FRIENDSHIP-WARMTH: touches that occur between extended family members, close business associates, and friendly neighbors

FUNCTIONAL-PROFESSIONAL: touches that occur while accomplishing a specific task that is performed by those working within a specific role

HAPTICS: nonverbally communicating through touch

HOMOPHILY: how similar we consider another person to be to ourselves

ILLUSTRATOR: when you use your body to help describe or visually depict something

IMMEDIACY: refers to the psychological and physical closeness we have with one another

KINESICS: body movements; includes emblems, illustrators, affect displays, regulators, and adaptors

LOVE-INTIMACY: touches that occur between family members and friends where there is affection and a deep level of caring

MARKERS: physical objects that we place between ourselves and others

MESOMORPH: a physically fit, muscular, average height and weight, and athletic body type

MONOCHROMIC: time is considered to be "linear" in nature

MULTI-CHANNELED: refers to the fact that we can use several senses to communicate something nonverbally

NONVERBAL COMMUNICATION: refers to all aspects of communication other than the words we use

NONVERBAL EXPECTANCY VIOLATION THEORY: suggests that individuals hold expectancies for nonverbal behavior and when these expectations are violated (or the rules are not abided by) there are two common reactions, physical arousal and cognitive arousal

OCULESICS: the study of eye behavior

PARALANGUAGE: everything beyond the words in the verbally communicated message

PERSONAL ADORNMENT: refers to how we use artifacts on our bodies

PHYSICAL APPEARANCE: includes our body, clothing, makeup, height, size, and hair

PHYSICAL AROUSAL: the physical response a person has to nonverbal expectancies being violated

POLYCHROMIC: time is perceived as circular

PROACTIVE ATTRIBUTION: formation of first impressions through the use of nonverbal cues.

PROXEMICS: space; refers to the invisible bubble we place around our bodies

REGULATE: using nonverbal communication to control our conversations

REGULATOR: any type of body movements that are used in conversation to control the communication flow

REPETITION: both verbal and nonverbal expressions made simultaneously to reinforce each other

RETROACTIVE ATTRIBUTION: process of using nonverbal cues to help explain the behaviors of others in hindsight or after-the-fact.

SEXUAL-AROUSAL: touches that occur within a sexual/erotic context

SOCIAL-POLITE: touches that occur between business partners, acquaintances, and strangers

SOCIAL REFERENCING: the process by which individuals rely on those around them to determine how to respond to unfamiliar stimuli

TURN-DENYING: behaviors used when someone is not interested in "taking over the floor"

TURN-MAINTAINING: behaviors that suggest to the listener that we want to continue talking

TURN-REQUESTING: behaviors utilized when listeners use buffers, short words or phrases to signal to the speaker that they are interested in speaking

TURN-YIELDING: behaviors that signal to the listener that we are going to stop talking

REFERENCES

Anderson, P. A. (1999). *Nonverbal communication: Forms and functions.* Mountain View, CA: Mayfield Publishing.

Anderson, P. A., & Sull, K. K. (1985). Out of touch, out of reach: Tactile predispositions as predictors of interpersonal distance. *Western Journal of Speech Communication, 49,* 57–72.

Berger, C. R. (1975). Proactive and retroactive attribution processes. *Human Communication Research, 2,* 33–50.

Bruneau, T. J. (1973). Communicative silences: Forms and functions. *Journal of Communication, 23,* 17–46.

Buck, R. (1975). Nonverbal communication of affect in children. *Journal of Personality and Social Psychology, 31,* 644–653.

Burgoon, J. K. (1978). A communication model of personal space violation: Explication and an initial test. *Human Communication Research, 4,* 129–142.

Burgoon, J. K., Buller, D. B., & Woodall, W. G. (1994). *Nonverbal communication: The unspoken dialogue.* Columbus, OH: Greyden Press.

Burgoon, J., Hunsaker, F. G., & Dawson, E. J. (1994). *Human communication* (3rd ed.). Thousand Oaks, CA: Sage.

Butler, J. C., & Ryckman, R. M. (1993). Perceived and ideal physiques in male and female university students. *Journal of Social Psychology, 133,* 751–752.

Campos, J. J., & Stenberg, C. (1988). Perceptions, appraisals, and emotion: The onset of social referencing. In M. E. Lamb and L. R. Sherrod (Eds.), *Infant social cognition: Empirical and theoretical considerations.* Hillsdale, NJ: Erlbaum.

Carroll, S. T., Riffenburgh, R. H., Roberts, T. A., & Myhre, E. B. (2002). Tattoos and body piercings as indicators of adolescent risk-taking behaviors. *Pediatrics, 109,* 1021–1027.

Constantin, C., Kalyanaraman, S., Stavrositu, C., & Wagoner, N. (2002, August). To be or not to be emotional; Impression formation effects of emoticons in moderated chatrooms. Paper presented to the Communication Technology and Policy Division at the 85th annual convention of the Association for Education in Journalism and Mass Communication (AEJMC), Miami Beach, FL.

Christophel, D. M. (1990). The relationship between teacher immediacy behaviors, student motivation, and learning. *Communication Education, 39,* 323–340.

Darwin, C. (1965). *The expression of emotions in man and animals.* Chicago: University of Chicago Press. (Original work published 1872.)

Dolin, D., & Booth-Butterfield, M. (1993). Reach out and touch someone: Analysis of nonverbal comforting responses. *Communication Quarterly, 41,* 383–393.

Duncan Jr., S. D. (1972). Some signals and rules for taking speaking turns in conversations. *Journal of Personality and Social Psychology, 23,* 283–292.

Ekman, P. (1993). Facial expression and emotion. *American Psychologist, 48,* 384–392.

Ekman, P., & Friesen, W. V. (1969). The repertoire of non-verbal behaviour: categories, origins, usage and codings. *Semiotics 1,* 49–98.

Fletcher, C., & Diekhoff, G. M. (1998). Body-type stereotyping in therapeutic judgments. *Perceptual and Motor Skills, 86,* 842.

Forbes, G. B. (2001). College students with tattoos and piercings: Motives, family experiences, personality factors, and perception by others. *Psychological Reports, 89,* 774–786.

Hall, E. T. (1966). *The hidden dimension.* NY: Doubleday.

Hall, E. T. (1976). *Beyond culture.* New York: Doubleday.

Hickson III, M., Stacks, D. W., & Moore, N. (2004). *Nonverbal communication* (4th ed.). Los Angeles, CA: Roxbury.

Houser, M. L., Horan, S. M., & Furler, L. A. (2007). Predicting relational outcomes: An investigation of thin slice judgments in speed dating. *Human Communication, 10,* 69–81.

Izard, C. E. (1992). Basic emotions, relations among emotions, and emotion-cognition relations. *Psychological Review, 99,* 561–565.

Jaworski, A. (1993). *The power of silence: Social and pragmatic perspectives.* Newbury Park, CA: Sage.

Jensen, J. V. (1973). Communicative functions of silence. *ETC, 30,* 249–257.

Judge, T. A., & Cable, D. M. (2004). The effect of physical height on workplace success and income: Preliminary test of a theoretical model. *Journal of Applied Psychology, 89,* 428–441.

Kitao, S. K., & Kitao, K. (1988). Differences in the kinesic codes of Americans and Japanese. *World Communication, 17,* 83–103.

Kleinke, C. L., & Staneski, R. A. (1980). First impressions of female bust size. *Journal of Social Psychology, 110,* 123–134.

Knapp, M. L., & Hall, J. A. (2002). *Nonverbal communication in human interaction*. United States: Wadsworth.

Kring, A. M., Smith, D. A., & Neale, J. M. (1994). Individual differences in dispositional expressiveness: The development and validation of the emotional expressivity scale. *Journal of Personality and Social Psychology, 66,* 934–949.

Krohn, F. B. (2004). A generational approach to using emoticons as nonverbal communication. *Journal of Technical Writing and Communication, 34,* 321–328.

Marek, C. I, Knapp, J. L., & Wanzer, M. B. (2004). An exploratory investigation of the relationship between roommates' first impressions and subsequent communication patterns. *Communication Research Reports, 21,* 210–220.

Mayo, C., & LaFrance, M. (1978). On the acquisition of nonverbal communication: A review. *Merrill-Palmer Quarterly, 24,* 213–228.

McCroskey, J. C. (1976). The effects of communication apprehension on nonverbal behavior. *Communication Quarterly, 24,* 39–44.

McCroskey, J. C. (1977). Classroom consequences of communication apprehension. *Communication Education, 26,* 27–33.

McCroskey, J. C. (1992). *An introduction to communication in the classroom*. Edina, MI: Burgess Publishing Division.

McCroskey, J. C., Fayer, J. M., Richmond, V. P., Sallinen, A., & Barraclough, R. A. (1996). A multi-cultural examination of the relationship between nonverbal immediacy and affective learning. *Communication Quarterly, 44,* 297–307.

McCroskey, J. C., & Richmond, V. P. (1992). Increasing teacher influence through immediacy. In V. P. Richmond and J. C. McCroskey, (Eds.), *Power in the classroom: Communication, control and concern* (pp. 101–119). Hillsdale, NJ: Lawrence Erlbaum Associates.

McCroskey, J. C., Richmond, V. P., Sallinen, A., Fayer, J. M., & Barraclough, R. A. (1995). A cross-cultural and multi-behavioral analysis of the relationships between nonverbal immediacy and teacher evaluation. *Communication Education, 44,* 281–291.

McCroskey, J. C., Sallinen, A., Fayer, J. M., Richmond, V. P., & Barraclough, R. A. (1996). Nonverbal immediacy and cognitive learning: A cross-cultural investigation. *Communication Education, 45,* 200–211.

Mehrabian, A. (1971). *Silent messages*. Belmont, CA: Wadsworth.

Roberti, J. W., & Storch, E. A. (2005). Psychosocial adjustment of college students with tattoos and piercings. *Journal of College Counseling, 8,* 14–19.

Sheldon, W. H., & Stevens, S. S. (1942). *The varieties of temperament; a psychology of constitutional differences*. Oxford, England: Harper.

Sheldon, W. H., Hartl, E. M., & McDermott, E. (1949). *The variety of delinquent youth*. Oxford, England: Harper.

Sprecher, S. (1989). Premarital sexual standards for different categories of individuals. *Journal of Sex Research, 26,* 232–248.

Street, R. L., & Buller, D. B. (1987). Nonverbal response patterns in physician-patient interactions: A functional analysis. *Journal of Nonverbal Behavior, 11,* 234–253.

Thayer, S. (1988). Close encounters. *Psychology Today, 22,* 30–36.

Tucker, L. A. (1983). Cigarette smoking intentions and obesity among high school males. *Psychological Reports, 52,* 530.

Wagner, H. L., MacDonald, C. J., & Manstead, A. S. R. (1986). Communication of individual emotions by spontaneous facial expressions. *Journal of Personality and Social Psychology, 50,* 737–743.

Walther, J. B., & D'Addario, K. P. (2001). The impacts of emoticons on message interpretation in computer-mediated communication. *Social Science Computer Review, 19,* 324–347.

Watkins, L. M., & Johnston, L. (2000). Screening job applicants: The impact of physical attractiveness and application quality. *International Journal of Selection and Assessment, 8,* 76.

Wiemann, J., & Knapp, M. (1975). Turn-taking in conversation. *Journal of Communication, 25,* 75–92.

Yoo, J. (2007) To smile or not to smile : Defining the effects of emoticons in relational outcomes. International Communication Association annual meeting, San Francisco, CA.

Zuckerman, M., Lipets, M. S., Koivumaki, J. H., & Rosenthanl, R. (1975). Encoding and decoding nonverbal cues of emotion. *Journal of Personality and Social Psychology, 32,* 1068–1076.

Section TWO
RELATIONSHIP DEVELOPMENT AND STAGES

Chapter 7
Initiating Relationships: "Haven't We Met Somewhere Before?" 201

Chapter 8
Sustaining Relationships: Relationship Maintenance and Conflict
Management 235

Chapter 9
The Dark Side of Relationships: Deception, Embarrassment, Jealousy,
Power, and Verbal Aggression 271

Chapter 10
Terminating Relationships: Knowing when to Throw in the Towel 303

chapter 7

Initiating Relationships: "Haven't We Met Somewhere Before?"

OBJECTIVES

- Explain four primary reasons people initiate interpersonal relationships.

- Identify three types of attraction: physical, social, and task. Describe the impact of demographic differences on perceptions of attraction.

- Recognize the three dimensions of similarity that influence decisions to initiate relationships.

- Describe the role of disclosure and reciprocal disclosure on relationship initiation.

- Discuss the role of question-asking in reducing uncertainty in relationship initiation.

- Explain five stages in the process of forming relationships.

SCENARIO: SOUND FAMILIAR?

Amelia went to Southwest University's first home football game with a group of friends. As she was cheering on the team with her friends, her roommate grabbed her arm and whispered in her ear, "Don't look now, but there's a cute guy seated in the next section and he keeps looking over here!" Amelia sneaked a glance and noticed a classmate from her biology class looking at her. He quickly glanced away when she caught him looking and immediately got up to go to the concession stand. As he returned, he stopped next to Amelia's seat and said, "Hey, my name is Patrick. Don't you sit behind me in BIOS 1010? Are you ready for our midterm on Monday?" They chatted about the exam for a few minutes, then Patrick asked if anyone was sitting next to Amelia. She smiled and moved over to make room on the bleacher. They spent the rest of the game talking about their love of football, discovering that they had attended rival high schools, and they made plans to get together the following day to study for their biology exam.

chapter 7 Initiating Relationships: "Haven't We Met Somewhere Before?"

201

OVERVIEW

Recalling how a relationship began often results in the telling of stories in which individuals share their perceptions of what prompted their initial interaction. As the telling of the story unfolds, partners may find that each of their views of events differs slightly. While one person may insist that it was his witty opening line that started it all, the other person may insist that she was initially attracted by a shy smile. We are intrigued by stories of "first encounters." Consider the popularity of the television series *How I Met Your Mother.* The show focuses on Ted's narrative, in which he explains to his children how he initiated his relationship with their mother.

As viewers watched Ted's story evolve during nine seasons of *How I Met Your Mother*, it became apparent that relationships aren't easy. A variety of factors cause us to be initially attracted to one another, and these ultimately influence our decision to further pursue relationships. After all, relationships require a significant amount of time and energy. Consider the fact that *every* relationship we are involved in had to start somewhere. In this chapter we take a close look at how we define the term *relationship* and how and why relationships are initially established. We also look at the communication behaviors and strategies used in the early stages of a relationship.

THE ROLE OF COMMUNICATION IN RELATIONSHIP DEVELOPMENT

The decision to begin a new relationship is filled with a myriad of emotions—confusion, excitement, anxiety, and perhaps even apprehension.

First, a person must decide whether to approach another person to initiate a conversation. Then the challenge involves determining *how* to make the initial approach in order to convey a positive image. What opening line or verbal message should be used to make the all-important first impression? In addition to finding the right words, let us not forget the impact of nonverbal messages on the relationship initiation process. After all, we form our initial perceptions about others based on nonverbal cues such as how someone is dressed and whether they make eye contact.

In addition, we also need to consider the role that self-perception plays in the process. As discussed in Chapter 2, someone with a low level of self-esteem will face unique challenges when initiating a relationship compared to a person who has a positive self-image.

As we begin our discussion of relationship initiation, it is important to define what we mean by the term *relationship*. If you are involved in a relationship at this very moment, please raise your hand. Do you have your hand up? If not, you should probably reconsider how you define this term. When we have asked this question in our interpersonal communication classes, only a few students initially raise their hands. But after much prompting with questions such as, "Are you *sure* you're not involved in *any* relationships right now?" every member of the class has a hand in the air. Our culture biases our perception about what it means to be "in a relationship." Immediately, most people think of a "relationship" as involving romance. However, we are all involved in a number of different types of relationships at any given time. Examples of these include:

- Friendships
- Family relationships

- Coworker relationships
- Teacher-student relationships
- Employee-customer relationships
- Patient-physician relationships

Throughout this chapter, we encourage you to consider how each of the concepts applies in the various relationships you have formed in your own life.

RELATIONSHIP DEFINED

We encounter countless messages about relationships on a daily basis. While waiting in the supermarket checkout line, you will see magazine covers that make claims about the status of celebrity relationships. Tweets or news stories speculating about who's dating whom are constantly updated on Internet sites. Facebook ads beckon us to "click now" to learn how to attract others with a sensuous new hairstyle, clever banter, or trendy apparel. Even if you do not venture near the magazine section or notice the Internet headlines, take a moment to consider common themes of popular songs. Many contain references to the various stages of relationships, from first encounters to breakups. Messages about relationships are everywhere!

A work relationship can start out as obligatory, but it may later transform into a voluntary friendship.

A **relationship** can be defined as a connection between two individuals that results in mutual interaction with the intent of achieving shared meaning. In this chapter, we focus primarily on voluntary relationships, which differ greatly from those that are obligatory or involuntary. Our relationships with friends, roommates, and romantic partners are considered **voluntary** because we enter into them of our own volition. Relationships with family members and coworkers are often defined as **obligatory/involuntary** because they often occur by chance and not by choice. Some relationships, like those we form with coworkers, may start out as obligatory and transform into voluntary ones. We begin by describing important elements of relationships.

THE NATURE OF RELATIONSHIPS

We often use descriptors or referents to describe and categorize the numerous relationships in which we are involved. Three categories often used to describe the nature of a relationship include references to duration, context, and roles.

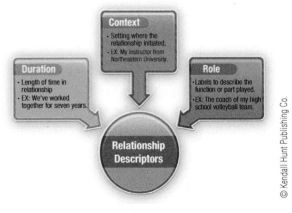

Figure 7.1. Referents used to categorize or define the nature of relationships

chapter 7 Initiating Relationships: "Haven't We Met Somewhere Before?"

203

DURATION. Duration references are used to describe the length of time we have known the other person. Statements such as "my friend from kindergarten," "my new coworker," and "an acquaintance I met last week" are used to describe the duration or how long we have known the other person. These terms provide insight as to the amount of time that the relational partners have had to share information about each other.

CONTEXT. In some instances, relationships are described by referring to the context, or setting, in which the relationship was initiated. "Friends from the soccer team," "committee members from the PTO," or "coworkers on a project team," provide information about the environment in which the relationship exists.

By making reference to the relationship context, clues are offered with regard to the **rules** or expectations for communication. Rules may be explicitly stated. A boss may openly state to employees that there is an "open door" policy in the office, indicating that employees should feel comfortable walking in without an appointment to discuss issues. Other rules are implicitly understood. Teammates have a mutual understanding that emotions have an impact on how messages are created and interpreted on game day. If a teammate has a bad game, the unspoken rule may be that it is probably not wise to discuss the errors that were made in the game. It is important to note that rules regarding the appropriateness of topics and the acceptable depth of discussions may differ from context to context. While an individual may be comfortable disclosing her intimate feelings about her newest romantic partner with a family member, such information could be viewed as highly inappropriate in the workplace.

ROLE. Finally, references to a person's **role** may be used to describe the nature of a relationship. Terms such as *mother, teacher, supervisor, friend, colleague,* or *coach* are used to describe the role an individual plays in a particular relationship. It is important to note that labels used to describe roles can provide insight into the contextual nature of the relationship and shed light on the rules and expectations for interactions. More formality is needed when a student engages in an interaction with a teacher than when calling up a family member to discuss a bad grade on an assignment. By making reference to our relationships in terms of duration, context, or roles, we let others know what our initial expectations are for communication.

What are the communication expectations associated with the role of a coach?

Deciding to Make the First Move: Why We Initiate Relationships

Think back to your first day in this class. As you walked through the door, you scanned the classroom and were faced with the decision of where to sit. Were there any familiar faces in the room? If not, you ended up sitting next to someone you had never met before. At that point, you had two decisions to make. Should you (a) initiate a conversation with that person, and if so, (b) how should you begin the interaction? As you reflect on that first day of class, consider how quickly some of these decisions were made. Even if the decision of where to sit was influenced by the fact that there were a limited number of seats available, you still had to choose whether to start a conversation, and thus, initiate a relationship with a fellow classmate. Every relationship has a unique history that includes an explanation of why we chose to initiate the relationship in the first place.

Over the years, scholars in the fields of communication, psychology, and sociology have been fascinated by the question of *why* we initiate relationships. For example, when writing about why people initiate long-term romantic relationships, interpersonal communication researcher Anita Vangelisti (2002) describes the number of factors that contribute to mate selection as "daunting." While there appear to be many different reasons, years of research have identified four common explanations for why humans begin relationships. The four primary reasons we establish relationships with others are attraction, proximity, similarity, and purpose. In the next sections, we take a closer look at each of these reasons for beginning a relationship.

INTERPERSONAL ATTRACTION

Identifying the reasons for being attracted to one person and not to another is perhaps

> The four primary reasons we establish relationships with others are attraction, proximity, similarity, and purpose.

one of the greatest mysteries in life. Researchers have dedicated countless studies to exploring the phenomenon of initial attraction. After all, attraction is perhaps one of the most influential factors in setting the relationship initiation process in motion. While references to attractiveness are often assumed to be directed toward physical characteristics, **interpersonal attraction** refers to a general feeling or desire that impacts our decision to approach and initiate a relationship with another person. Many different forms of attraction influence our decision to begin relationships.

Attraction is one of the primary determining factors for choosing to initiate relationships, and it is the basis for forming initial impressions of others. While most people may argue that forming first impressions of others simply based on their appearance is superficial and trivial, the fact remains that in the United States many of our decisions to initiate romantic relationships are rooted in our perceptions of the physical attractiveness of the other person. While our initial impressions typically focus on the physical features associated with attractiveness, other factors can come into play as well. In Chapter 6 we introduced the

chapter 7 Initiating Relationships: "Haven't We Met Somewhere Before?"

205

concept of attraction as it relates to physical attributes. McCroskey and McCain (1974) identified three dimensions of attractiveness used when deciding whether to initiate relationships: physical, social, and task attractiveness.

Why is physical attractiveness important early in a relationship?

Physical	Social	Task
based on the appeal of physical characteristics	focus is on common characteristics and shared interests	based on the need to accomplish goal or assignment

Figure 7.2. Types of interpersonal attraction.

Physical Attractiveness

More often than not, we decide whether to initiate conversations with a potential relationship partner based on our perceptions of the person's physical attractiveness (Vangelisti, 2002). According to research by Reis and his colleagues (1980), we are more likely to evaluate interactions as enjoyable when we view the person we interact with as physically attractive.

How do we determine whether someone is physically attractive? Judgments about what constitutes physical attractiveness are often answered by asking the question, "What do I think makes someone pretty or handsome?" When characteristics such as body shape or size, hair color or length, and facial features are used in making a determination of whether to initiate a relationship, this dimension is referred to as **physical attractiveness**. Aristotle recognized the value of

physical attractiveness when he stated, "Personal beauty is a greater recommendation than any letter of reference."

Recall our discussion of perception in Chapter 4. The phrase "beauty is in the eye of the beholder" addresses the perceptual nature of physical attraction and provides insight as to why one person may be attracted to blondes while another is attracted to brunettes. Sometimes we are baffled as to how individuals who appear to be so completely opposite with regard to their physical appearance could be attracted to each other. Our perception causes us to view physical characteristics in unique ways. While some studies report that men may value physical attractiveness more than women (Buss, 1989; Sprecher, Sullivan, & Hatfield, 1994), it is clear that both men and women report physical attractiveness as a factor influencing their decision to initiate relationships (Hatfield & Sprecher, 1986).

So why does physical attractiveness play such an important role in the early stages of relationship development? One explanation is that people tend to associate other positive and favorable characteristics with physical attractiveness. Take a moment and consider how much emphasis

trayed as being ugly. Hasbro's Barbie doll is presented to young children as an ideal image of female attractiveness. She has long, blond hair and blue eyes, and is big-breasted, tall, and thin. Young children are able to identify her and many idolize her. However, Barbie's bra size has been estimated to be a DDD compared to the average C cup size of most women, and her body dimensions have been translated to the equivalent of 38-18-34 if she were a real woman. Nonetheless, young girls adore Barbie! They receive the message that being physically attractive, like Barbie, is associated with having friends and receiving more attention, not to mention a host of other rewards: great clothes, cars, beach houses, and a "cool" lifestyle.

In addition to messages about physical attractiveness that are depicted in toys and media sources, messages regarding the importance of physical attractiveness are also conveyed in classrooms:

our culture places on physical attractiveness. An overwhelming amount of research (see, for example, Eagly et al., 1991) seems to support the bias that individuals have toward those perceived as physically attractive.

Several demographic factors such as age, gender, and culture influence our perceptions of physical attractiveness.

AGE AND ATTRACTIVENESS. Beginning at a very young age, we are taught that physical attractiveness is often rewarded or valued. After all, the princesses in Disney movies are always beautiful young women, while the evil characters are por-

Several demographic factors such as age, gender, and culture influence our perceptions of physical attractiveness.

chapter 7 Initiating Relationships: "Haven't We Met Somewhere Before?"

207

- Attractive children are perceived as being more popular with both classmates and teachers.
- Elementary-age students who are perceived as being physically attractive receive more attention from their teachers (Richmond, 1992).
- Attractive high school and college-age students receive higher grades than those who are perceived to be less attractive.
- Teachers provide higher evaluations and establish higher expectations for attractive students. Attractive people are perceived as being happier, more likeable, popular, and friendly (Berscheid & Reis, 1998).

As we get older, physical attractiveness impacts our own perceptions as well as the perceptions others have of us. Research has found that people under the age of 30 have been rated as being more physically attractive than people over the age of 50 (McClellan & McKelvie, 1993). In addition, various studies have examined how perceptions of physical attraction are influenced by age:

- Young and middle-age adults rate younger faces as more attractive than older faces. Older adults rate faces across all ranges as equally attractive (Foos & Clark, 2011).
- Johnson and Pittinger (1984) discovered that physically attractive males and females aged 60 to 93 were rated more positively than those in the same age group who were perceived to be less attractive.
- As males increase in age, they rate younger women as being more attractive than older women. However, the same was not true

While both men and women indicate that they view physical attractiveness as important in the initiation of romantic relationships, the level of intensity that each sex uses in expressing their value for attractiveness differs.

for women. Women in the older age categories rate males similar in age to be more physically attractive (Mathes, Brennen, Haugen, & Rice, 1985).

GENDER AND ATTRACTIVENESS. While both men and women indicate that they view physical attractiveness as important in the initiation of romantic relationships, the level of intensity that each sex uses in expressing their value for attractiveness differs.

Many research studies point to the positive and negative aspects associated with physical attractiveness:

- In the workplace, physically attractive women often encounter biases *against* them when applying for administrative or executive positions (Zebrowitz, 1997).
- In an experiment examining the impact of a female employee's physical attractiveness on the decision to terminate her, participants indicated that they would be more likely to terminate an unattractive woman

than an attractive woman (Commisso & Finkelstein, 2012).

- Lewis and Bierly (1990) examined the impact of female perceptions of male political candidates' attractiveness. Women rated physically attractive political candidates as being more competent than less attractive candidates.

Decisions to initiate dates are most often based on physical attractiveness. In a meta analysis of 2,247 personal ads, Feingold (1990) found that males are more likely than women to indicate physical attractiveness as a desired characteristic in a relationship, including descriptors of specific physical attributes as criteria for potential dates. In addition, men tend to indicate a strong preference for women who are younger than themselves. While women may identify general physical criteria such as *athletic, tall,* or *attractive* in personal ads, references to a partner's status were included more often and emerged as a stronger predictor of attraction (Davis, 1990).

CULTURE AND ATTRACTION. Culture is an influential factor in our perception of physical attractiveness. What one culture establishes as a standard of physical attractiveness may be perceived differently in other cultures. Within a culture, media play an influential role in depicting the accepted standards of beauty. Images are found on television and billboards, in magazines, movies, and books, and on the Internet. These messages influence our consumer decisions to meet the standards of beauty promoted by the media. In the United States, physical beauty is so highly valued that Americans spent more than $38 billion dollars on cosmetics in 2007, nearly double or triple the amount spent by people in other countries (see Figure 7.3).

WHO WANTS IT THE MOST?				
Total national spending on cosmetics (2007 statistics)				
	USA	JAPAN	FRANCE	GERMANY
Men	$11.059 bn	$5.927 bn	$4.163 bn	$3.879 bn
Women	$27.638 bn	$19.780 bn	$10.268 bn	$9.285 bn
Total	$38.698 bn	$25.708 bn	$14.321 bn	$13.164 bn

Figure 7.3. Money spent on cosmetics around the world

SOURCE: Americans Spend Billions on Beauty Products But Are Not Very Happy. (n.d.). Retrieved September 14, 2014, from http://jezebel.com/5931654/americans-spend-billions-on-beauty-products-and-are-still-pretty-unhappy/

Perceptions of physical attractiveness can differ across ethnic groups. A very curvaceous figure is often considered to be unattractive among Caucasian women, but African American women may not agree (Hebl & Heatherton, 1998). In fact, African American women are perceived as being more attractive by African American males if they have a curvaceous bottom, as opposed to being able to fit into a pair of size-four jeans.

As we cross cultural boundaries, it becomes apparent that there are universal perceptions of beauty as well. One particular physical feature that has been judged across cultures as a focal point for physical attraction is the human face. In particular, the more "feminine" a face appears, the greater its perceived level of attractiveness. In a study comparing the attractiveness of men and women by looking at close-up photographs of their faces, both Cau-

chapter 7 Initiating Relationships: "Haven't We Met Somewhere Before?"

209

casian and Japanese participants rated pictures of men and women whose facial features had been "feminized" or softened as being more attractive (Perrett, Lee, & Penton-Voak, 1998).

Social Attractiveness

Once we initiate a conversation with another person, it is likely that our attention shifts from the physical attributes, which drew us to start talking in the first place, to identifying commonalities. **Social attractiveness** can be defined as common interests or similar patterns of communication that cause individuals to perceive one another as someone they would like to spend time with. Questions used to identify the level of social attraction with another person might include, "Would I like to hang out with this person?" and "Is this someone who would fit in with my friends?"

While physical attraction has a substantial impact on our decision to initiate relationships with others, social attraction is equally important. Some people exert considerable effort to ensure that others perceive their social behavior favorably. Recall our discussion of **impression management** in Chapter 2, defined as the process of maintaining a positive image of self in the presence of others. Consider the time and energy dedicated to making sure our physical appearance is "just right" when we meet or approach someone for the first time. When interviewing for a job, it is essential that the suit is pressed, the shoes are polished, and the hair is neat and clean. As the expression advises, "You never get a second chance to make a good first impression."

Individuals vary greatly in the extent to which they are self-aware of the impressions that others

© Aila Images/Shutterstock.com

What questions do you ask to determine your level of social attraction to someone?

have of them. **Self-monitoring** refers to a personality construct that causes a person to respond to social and interpersonal cues for appropriate communication behaviors in a variety of situations. High self-monitors are constantly aware of behaviors others perceive to be appropriate in interpersonal situations, and continuously strive to control how they are portraying themselves. By contrast, low self-monitors dedicate little, if any, energy to responding to the cues of social appropriateness. They do not spend a lot of time worrying if they break the social rules by wearing jeans to an event where everyone else is dressed more formally, or by belching in front of a potential romantic partner.

To examine the relationship of self-monitoring and relationship initiation, participants were given file folders containing photographs and descriptions of personal attributes of potential dates. High self-monitors dedicated more time to reviewing the photographs in the folders, while low self-monitors spent more time reviewing the personal descriptions (Snyder, Berscheid, & Glick, 1985). Thus, it appears that high self-monitors place more emphasis on physical attraction when selecting a potential partner for a date, while low self-monitors focus more on social attractiveness.

While physical attractiveness plays an important role in our decision to initiate romantic relationships, social characteristics are also part of the evaluation process. Humor is one communication strategy that contributes to our perceptions of social attractiveness. When asked to describe characteristics associated with social attractiveness, descriptors such as "humorous," "low-drama," and "easygoing" are often used. While our initial attraction may be based on physical attributes, social attractiveness may emerge as we engage in conversations and share information. Wilbur and Campbell (2011) identified several gender differences in the use of humor on first dates:

- Men are more likely to use humor when getting to know a potential date.
- Women tend to evaluate "how" and "why" humor was used and then respond accordingly.
- In dating profiles, men tend to focus on describing their own sense of humor;

women indicate their desirability for humor in a potential partner.

A 2011 survey of those who posted profiles on the eHarmony online dating site examined the types of humor that males and females found to be attractive in the initial stages of a relationship (see Figure 7.4). Men indicated a preference for women who engage in a sarcastic style of humor, while women favor men with a dry sense of humor. Recall our earlier discussion of self-monitoring. Being aware of others' reactions to our use of humor is important in creating perceptions of social attractiveness.

Task Attractiveness

While physical and social attributes may be influential in the initial phase of relationships, as individuals pursue their professional goals, decisions based on attractiveness may take on a much different perspective. **Task attractiveness** refers to the characteristics or qualities that are perceived as appealing when initiating relationships in which the goal is to complete a task or

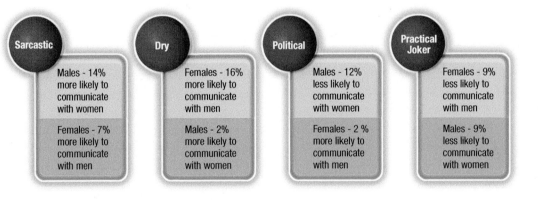

Figure 7.4. eHarmony 2011 Online Dating Survey—Gender and perceived attraction to various humor styles

chapter 7 Initiating Relationships: "Haven't We Met Somewhere Before?"

211

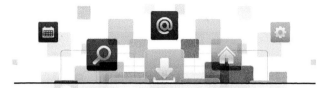

Being aware of others' reactions to our use of humor is important in creating perceptions of social attractiveness.

assignment. Suppose your professor allows you to select the team members you wish to work with on a major term project. Are you going to select the most physically attractive person to work with on this assignment? Possibly, if your goal is to get a date for Saturday night. Are you going to choose the funniest person in the class to be on your team? Maybe, if your goal is to have plenty of laughs as you work on the project. Most likely, you will seek out people with characteristics and qualities that are essential to accomplishing your goal. A question used to identify perceived task attractiveness might be, "Does this person have what it takes to help get the job done?" Depending on the task, the list of qualities used to assess task attractiveness might be very different. If you consider yourself to be "technologically challenged," you may seek someone whom you consider to be proficient with computers. Suppose there is a strict timeline for the project. In such a situation, you will probably seek a person who is dependable and organized.

While physical, social, and task attractiveness influence our decisions to initiate relationships, other variables play an important role as well.

PROXIMITY

Consider our earlier question regarding your decision to initiate a relationship with the person seated next to you in this class. In essence, the decision to begin the relationship was influenced by proximity. Proximity refers to the physical distance between two people. The fact that you sit next to the same person for an entire semester increases the chance that you will communicate with each other and ultimately choose to form a relationship. Segal (1974) supported this notion in a study that examined friendships formed in a college classroom. At the beginning of the term, students were given seat assignments. When asked to indicate the persons whom they considered to be friends in the class, most students reported that they were friends with those who were seated next to them. Relationships are often formed with our neighbors because of our close proximity to these individuals.

So why is proximity such a strong predictor of interpersonal attraction? One explanation may be found in the diminished effort required to establish relationships with those who are close in distance. It is just easier to strike up a conversation with your next-door neighbor, chat with the person who works out at the same gym, or to share stories with the coworker whose cubicle is directly adjacent to yours. Much more effort is required to start relationships with those who sit on the other side of the room or who work on different floors.

SIMILARITY/HOMOPHILY

After initiating a conversation, identifying potential topics to discuss can be the next hurdle to overcome. The goal of our discussions at this phase in a relationship is to identify common interests between ourselves and the other person. Remember the phrase, "Birds of a feather flock together?" This phrase refers to an influential element of interpersonal attraction known as **similarity**, or **homophily**.

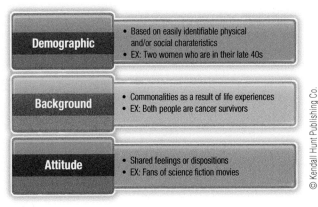

Demographic	• Based on easily identifiable physical and/or social charateristics • EX: Two women who are in their late 40s
Background	• Commonalities as a result of life experiences • EX: Both people are cancer survivors
Attitude	• Shared feelings or dispositions • EX: Fans of science fiction movies

© Kendall Hunt Publishing Co.

Figure 7.5. Categories of similarity.

Friendships may form on the basis of similar interests or hobbies.

Research confirms that we seek out relationships with those who have common interests, backgrounds, and goals, and who are similar in appearance (McCroskey, Richmond, & Daly, 1975). This phenomenon might explain why friendships are formed among people who are members of an online fan club site for a band, or how romantic relationships begin between two people who strike up a conversation after seeing each other at various political rallies. Both of these situations provide partners with common topics for discussion.

Our similarity with others can be categorized based on demographic, background, or attitude commonalities. **Demographic similarity** is based on physical and social characteristics that are easily identifiable. Consider the relationships that you have initiated with others who are of a similar age or are the same sex. **Background similarity** refers to commonalities that we share as a result of our life experiences. Chances are that many of your friendships began as a result of experiences that you had in common with others—going to the same summer camp, playing on the same athletic team, working in the same organization, or simply growing up in the same hometown. Finally, **attitude similarity** focuses on our commonly held feelings or dispositions toward people, things, or events. Some relationships are formed as a result of our cultural, religious, or political affiliations. When two friends express similar attitudes toward music, movies, or sports, they are exhibiting attitude similarity.

In their examination of interpersonal attraction and similarity, Klohnen and Luo (2003) identified four dimensions of similarity that individuals consider in initial attraction:

chapter 7 Initiating Relationships: "Haven't We Met Somewhere Before?"

213

Claiming that you have interests or beliefs in common with another person just to appear more attractive creates unrealistic expectations in the relationship.

- similarity to current self;
- complementarity;
- attachment security; and
- ideal-self similarity.

Similarity to current self refers to the belief that individuals are attracted to those who are similar to themselves. The dimensions we use to identify the congruence between ourselves and others differ from person to person. You may seek someone whose sense of humor is similar to your own, while another person may view similar levels of intelligence as being more important.

The **complementarity** hypothesis explains the saying "opposites attract." It predicts that people will be more attracted to those whose personality characteristics complement their own. This may explain why persons who have a high level of communication apprehension seek romantic relationships with those who have low levels of apprehension. To someone who is apprehensive about communicating, it is attractive to have someone who will initiate and carry out interactions.

Attachment security predicts that individuals will be most attracted to those who are secure. Thus, we find individuals who are confident and

trusting more attractive than individuals who are preoccupied by emotions of jealousy, neediness, or worry.

Finally, some individuals are most attracted to those whom they perceive to possess **ideal-self similarity** (as opposed to their actual or current self). We tend to view those who are similar to our view of how we would ultimately like to be perceived more favorably.

When we attempt to portray ourselves as being more similar to the other person than we really are just to appear more attractive, we run the risk of creating a relationship pitfall known as false homophily. **False homophily** refers to the presentation of a deceptive image of the self that appears to be more similar than it actually is. Claiming that you have interests or beliefs in common with another person just to appear more attractive creates unrealistic expectations in the relationship. While this strategy may be effective for gaining attention in the initial stages of the relationship, eventually the differences will emerge and could potentially cause problems.

Social media sites encourage us to identify commonalities with other users by posting information about music interests, favorite athletic teams, and places we have visited. We invite others to join games of Candy Crush Saga and Farmville and help one another reach goals. Online dating sites are designed to help singles quickly identify shared interests that can serve as the foundation for initiating conversations. Even in the absence of visible cues, online sites provide us with countless opportunities to identify similarities with others.

INTERPERSONAL GOALS

A final reason people choose to initiate relationships with others is to fulfill a purpose, or goal. Charles Berger (1995) defines **goals** as "desired end states toward which persons strive" (p. 143). Many of our interpersonal interactions are initiated to fulfill two primary goals: social and task.

Social goals refer to desired end states that fulfill the need for inclusion or affection. Both parties involved in the initial relationship can experience the fulfilled need. Consider the new kid in school. In order to ease some of the anxiety of starting a new school, the student might approach a table of students in the cafeteria and ask, "Is this seat taken?" One explanation for the initiation of this interaction is to fulfill a social goal—the student seeks to fulfill the need for inclusion at school.

Task goals are defined as desired end states that fulfill the need for the completion of an objective or task. Consider your current relationship with your hair stylist or barber. You initiated the relationship because the task of getting your hair cut needed to be fulfilled. A phone call was made to a local hair salon with the goal of finding a competent stylist to complete the task. As you initiated a conversation with the stylist, the task goal was to describe your desired hair cut. Consider all of the relationships you have initiated to fulfill task goals. Relationships are initiated with teachers to fulfill the task goal of achieving your educational objectives, and teachers form relationships with colleagues to accomplish tasks associated with the job. Interpersonal communication is instrumental in achieving our goals.

What social and task goals do you find in classroom relationships?

Dillard (1990) points out that our goals serve three functions in interpersonal relationships. First, goals are used to take action and fulfill an interpersonal need. Individuals determine what need to fulfill, and the goal prompts the initiation of the relationship. If your social goal is to form new friendships at school, you will introduce yourself in an attempt to take action to fulfill the need. Second, goals assist us in defining the purpose for the interaction or behaviors. Suppose a woman asks a colleague to join her for a cup of coffee to discuss an upcoming presentation for an important client. She realizes that the purpose of the interaction is to accomplish a task goal. However, if she had a romantic interest in the colleague, the ulterior motive for the meeting may have been prompted by social goals. Finally, goals provide us with a standard by which to judge the behaviors and outcomes of interpersonal interactions. We evaluate our interpersonal interactions with others and judge their effectiveness based on whether or not we

INTERPERSONAL COMMUNICATION THEORIES: *HOW* WE INITIATE RELATIONSHIPS

While attraction, proximity, similarity, and goals help explain *why* we pursue relationships, several theories are useful in understanding *how* we use communication to initiate these connections. Social penetration theory, uncertainty reduction theory, predicted outcome value theory, liking, and social exchange theory provide us with explanations to explain *how* we start relationships with others. Before we address these interpersonal theories and concepts, we will first examine the role of initial impression formation and self-disclosure in establishing relationships.

Starting the Conversation

To identify things we have in common with others, we typically need to engage in some type of communication. For some people, this is one of the most difficult tasks in a relationship. Consider the last time you attempted to start a conversation. Figuring out the most appropriate way to break the ice and create a positive initial impression can be intimidating. Should you offer a compliment or tell a joke? Mimic the shy smile or quick glances that you saw being used in a recent movie or television show? Knowing what communication behavior to use and predicting how it will be interpreted is challenging. Recall the scenario from the beginning of the chapter. Rather than using a humorous pick-up line with Amelia, Patrick initiated the conversation by asking if they were in the same class . Over the years, many of our students have shared "pick-up lines" or relational openers that have been used to initiate

accomplish our goals. After a blind date we typically evaluate the date as being "good" or "bad," based on the interaction that took place. If conversation was forced and awkward, we are likely to evaluate the date negatively.

Online interactions can also be initiated to fulfill goals. Katz and Rice (2002) pointed out that sometimes Indian parents use the Internet as a source to seek suitable mates for their children as a modern extension of their traditional matchmaking processes. Signing up to post and browse online personal ads signals a social goal—the intent to form a romantic relationship.

conversations with a potential romantic partner. Table 7.1 includes examples of pick-up lines listed on www.pickuplinesgalore.com.

Table 7.1 Sample Pick-Up Lines from www.pickuplinesgalore.com

SAMPLE PICK-UP LINES
"Do you have a sunburn, or are you always this hot?"
"Are you a camera? Because every time I look at you I smile!"
"I seem to have lost my phone number. Can I have yours?"
"Do you know what my shirt is made of? Boyfriend material."

It is important to note that pick-up lines are not necessarily the most effective conversation starters, although they may succeed in getting someone's attention. Our advice is that the next time you think about using one of these pick-up lines to begin a conversation, don't. Informal surveys of our students have revealed that the vast majority feel a simple and sincere introduction is the most effective way to initiate a conversation.

Flirtatious communication involves the use of verbal and nonverbal behaviors to indicate our interest in initiating a potential relationship. Our reasons and motives for flirting often vary depending on our relational goal. A 2008 study comparing flirting motives of students and employees identified six primary reasons that guide our decisions to engage in flirtatious communication (Henningsen, Braz, & Davies, 2008). These motives are highlighted in Table 7.2.

Table 7.2 Motives for Engaging in Flirtatious Communication

MOTIVES	GOAL
Sexual	Indicate a desire to pursue a sexual relationship
Relational	Express desire to pursue an intimate relationship that involves the sharing of personal information
Fun	Pass time; participate in playful interactions as a distraction
Exploring	Gauge the other person's interest in pursuing a relationship
Esteem	Inflate one's self esteem by seeing if the other person engages in reciprocal flirting
Instrumental	Influence or manipulate others to gain assistance or compliance with requests

The results of the study found that the motives for flirting in both work and social contexts were similar. We tend to flirt in an attempt to have fun, to build our self-esteem, and to gauge how interested the other person may be in pursuing a relationship. While flirting may be viewed as primarily a fun and innocent activity, it's important to note that miscommunication may occur as a result of misinterpretations. For example, a receiver may perceive a wink as indicating sexual interest when the intent was to communicate agreement (Hecht, DeVito & Guerrero, 1999). While flirting has been proven to be a popular strategy for gauging interest in pursuing a relationship, the sharing and exchanging of personal information provides valuable insight regarding the potential for the relationship to continue.

Self-Disclosure

While it is difficult to determine which opening line or nonverbal behavior should be used to ini-

chapter 7 Initiating Relationships: "Haven't We Met Somewhere Before?"

217

tiate our interest, continuing the conversation can be an even greater challenge. Deciding what information to share about yourself and what information you should seek from the other person can be daunting. During the early stages of relationship formation, partners will often self-disclose information in an effort to increase intimacy (Reis & Shaver, 1988; Reis & Patrick, 1996). **Self-disclosure** is "the process of revealing personal information about oneself to another" (Sprecher & Hendrick, 2004, p. 858). Sharing information results in increased attraction and liking in relationships. Self-disclosing is important not only in the initial stages, but also in sustaining relationships over time. It helps others learn who we are and our expectations for the relationship. You can assess your own preferences for disclosing information by completing the Revised Self-Disclosure scale located at the end of this chapter.

What topics do you feel comfortable disclosing in a new relationship?

Breadth of disclosure refers to the variety of topics we are willing to discuss with others. During the initial stages of a relationship, we tend to "play it safe" and stick to sharing superficial information such as our hobbies and general demographic information. For example, speed dating events provide participants with the opportunity to experience a series of multiple "mini-dates" in which they share information about a wide variety of topics in several five- to eight-minute sessions. At the end of the speed dating event, individuals indicate whom they would be interested in meeting again. The level of intimacy or the amount of detail shared about a specific topic is referred to as the **depth** of disclosure. How much detail we share is often influenced by societal or cultural norms. For example, revealing our income level, sharing our fears, or exposing details about past relationships would involve disclosing more details than we would typically expect upon meeting someone for the first time.

Once we reveal personal information about ourselves, we expect that the other person will also share similar information. **Reciprocal self-disclosure** involves the mutual sharing of information between two people. Collins and Miller (1994) identified a link between self-disclosure and liking. We like those who disclose with us, and we are more willing to disclose information to those whom we like. It is best when the disclosures of both partners are similar in terms of breadth of topics discussed and depth of disclosure. Consider the following initial disclosures between two classmates on the first day of class:

> **Sabina:** Hi, I'm Sabina. Have you ever taken a class with Dr. Yost before?
>
> **Natalie:** Hey Sabina, I'm Natalie. No, I haven't had a class with her, but my roommate took the class last semester.
>
> **Sabina:** Really, what did he say about it?
>
> **Natalie:** He said she's tough but fair.

Sabina: Ouch! That's what I was afraid of. I have to take this class for my major, and this is the only time that it fit into my schedule. If she's a difficult teacher, then why did you take this class?

Natalie: Well, even though she's tough, I've also heard that you learn a lot that will help you down the road in other classes in the major.

Sabina: Oh, are you a communication major?

Natalie: Yes, this is my second year. What year are you?

Sabina: I'm a junior, but I just transferred into the major at the beginning of the semester. I feel like I'm so far behind. Everyone else has their schedules all planned out and they know exactly who and what to take.

Natalie: Don't stress yourself out about it. We've all been there before. If you have any questions about who you should take, just ask me. Have you met with your advisor yet? They're pretty good about helping you map out your long-term schedule.

Consider the reciprocity of disclosure in this initial interaction. Both women share information about their majors as well as their fears about the class. As one asks a question, the other answers it. When one woman discloses information, so does the other. In situations where others fail to disclose similar information, we become uncomfortable and may perceive them to be hiding something, or engaging in deceptive communi-cation. Understanding the social expectations for appropriate self-disclosure is important to enhancing our relationships with others. Table 7.3 offers suggestions for both engaging in and responding to self-disclosure.

Table 7.3 Suggestions for Delivering and Receiving Self-disclosure

DELIVERING
Begin by self-disclosing information on safe or neutral topics.
During initial conversations, talk about where you went to school, hobbies, talents, etc., before sharing any private information.
If possible, attempt to match your partner's disclosures in depth.
If your partner shares intimate information (e.g., fears, future goals, insecurities), he may expect you to reciprocate. Remember that reciprocal disclosures between partners often indicate trust and liking.
Before disclosing private information, ask yourself if this is someone you can trust.
If you feel you cannot trust this person or feel this person will share this information with others, it is probably not a good idea to share private information.
RECEIVING
Do not overreact when someone shares personal information with you.
Try not to become overly emotional or provide judgmental feedback when someone shares private information with you. For example, screaming, "YOU DID WHAT?" when a friend shares information is not recommended.
Provide verbal and nonverbal support.
Make an attempt to display warm, receptive nonverbal cues during your conversation by maintaining eye contact, sitting near the person, nodding your head to indicate listening, and, if appropriate, smiling. Engage in active listening behaviors, which might include paraphrasing and appropriate empathic responses (e.g., "I can see why you would be upset").
If you do not feel comfortable discussing a topic or issue, tell your friend or relationship partner.
Rather than avoid the person and risk damaging your relationship, tell the person why you are uncomfortable discussing the topic.

chapter 7 Initiating Relationships: "Haven't We Met Somewhere Before?"

219

Social Penetration Theory

When we become more comfortable and trusting of others, the breadth and depth of our disclosures change. Altman and Taylor (1973) created **social penetration theory** to explain how self-disclosure changes as relationships move from one level to the next. It explains how and why we move from superficial topics of conversation in the initial stages of relationships to more intimate conversations as the relationship progresses.

Altman and Taylor use the analogy of an onion to describe the layers of information that are revealed as relationships become more intimate. This analogy helps illustrate the various levels of information that we share as our relationships progress from initiation to more intimate stages. There are four levels of information that we are willing to disclose depending on the nature of our relationships: superficial, intimate, personal, and private.

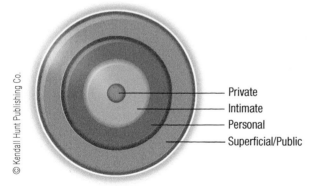

© Kendall Hunt Publishing Co.

— Private
— Intimate
— Personal
— Superficial/Public

Figure 7.6. Social penetration "onion" model.

Superficial communication is revealed in initial interactions. Communication focuses on safe topics such as one's major, occupation, or hometown. As the relationship intensifies, a layer of the onion is "peeled" away and more personal information is revealed. **Personal communication** focuses on topics of a more personal nature such as likes, dislikes, and experiences. As the relationship progresses to a more intimate level, so does the communication. **Intimate communication** topics are shared with those with whom we have a high level of trust and comfort. We may share our career concerns and aspirations with a close friend or colleague. At the innermost core of the onion model, we engage in **private communication** in which specific topics of discussion topics of discussion are reserved for our closest relationships. Topics may include our secrets, fears, hopes, and motivations.

As we disclose information with each other, we "peel" away the layers of the onion. This enables us to reduce our level of uncertainty or ambiguity about the other person.

Uncertainty Reduction Theory

Recall Amelia's initial encounter in the scenario at the beginning of this chapter. When her biology classmate chose to occupy the seat beside her at the football game, she knew very little about him. As they asked each other questions and shared information, they reduced their level of ambiguity about each other. **Uncertainty reduction theory** (Berger & Calabrese, 1975) identifies question asking as a primary communication strategy we use to encourage reciprocal disclosure and to reduce our levels of uncertainty about others. In a test to examine the relationship between our initial attraction to someone and how we use questioning or disclosure, Douglas (1990) asked pairs to engage in a six-minute initial interaction. He found that the majority of questions were asked in the initial two minutes of the conversation, and greater disclosures were made in the final two minutes of the discussion.

Nonverbal cues can also provide valuable information in the uncertainty reduction process. A quick scan of a room may reveal someone wearing a t-shirt from your alma mater, or perhaps you enter a meeting and see someone who appears to be close in age to you. We can use a variety of nonverbal cues to decrease our level of ambiguity and guide our initial encounters.

As we reduce our uncertainty about someone, we engage in a "strategy selection" process. This procedure requires us to maximize our efficiency in gaining information about others while utilizing behaviors that are viewed as socially appropriate. Speed dating is an example of a trend that provides singles with the opportunity to initiate conversations with multiple prospective dates at a singles event. The context, speed dating, itself reduces the level of uncertainty of "How long do I have to pretend to be interested?" by establishing a time limit for the interactions. If the conversation is uncomfortable, participants know that their time spent with one another will be brief.

Predicted Outcome Value Theory

Once we have reduced our level of uncertainty about a new relationship, the next step involves deciding what we expect or want from the new relationship. **Predicted outcome value theory** focuses on the perceived rewards or benefits associated with the new relationship (Sunnafrank, 1986). There is a shift from focusing on

the need for more information about the other person to analyzing the potential value that can be obtained from the relationship. Consider when you meet someone for the first time. Is this person someone you could see becoming a good friend or a potential romantic partner? Chances are you evaluate the potential for the future of the relationship without even realizing it. At some point, you make a decision regarding whether to pursue the relationship, how the relationship should progress, and what type of relationship you are interested in pursuing with the other person (e.g., friendship, romantic).

To evaluate predicted outcome value, Mottet (2000) developed a seven-question scale that asks individuals to rate future relationship potential by evaluating them using the following adjectives:

- Positive—Negative
- Good—Bad

Once we have reduced our level of uncertainty about a new relationship, the next step involves deciding what we expect or want from the new relationship.

chapter 7 Initiating Relationships: "Haven't We Met Somewhere Before?"

221

- Satisfying—Unsatisfying
- Valuable—Not valuable
- Worthwhile—Not worthwhile
- Rewarding—Unrewarding
- Comfortable—Uncomfortable

As you review the list of items used to assess the potential benefits of pursuing a relationship, consider the criteria you have used in deciding whether to pursue some of your current relationships.

Social Exchange Theory

During the process of predicting the potential value of initiating a relationship, we consider the costs and rewards associated with connecting with the other person. Have you ever heard the phrase "on the market" to refer to a person who is single and searching for a new romantic relationship? While at first this reference may seem degrading, it accurately describes the strategies we use when evaluating new relationships. This process is actually quite similar to shopping—we examine the options available and seek the best "deal."

Social exchange theory (also known as interdependence theory) refers to an assessment of costs and rewards in determining the value of pursuing or continuing a relationship (Thibaut & Kelley, 1959). **Rewards** refer to aspects that are desirable, which the recipient perceives as enjoyable or fulfilling. By contrast, **costs** are perceived as being undesirable. As we exchange information in the initial stages of a relationship, decisions are made regarding the relative value of continuing to pursue the relationship. While your initial conversation with the person seated next to you on an airplane may be rewarding in the sense that you felt comfortable

discussing common interests to pass the time on a three-hour journey, the costs of maintaining the relationship (effort involved in emailing or calling the person) may outweigh the benefits. You weigh the rewards and costs in making your prediction about the value of the relationships. As a result, you may decide to shake hands at the end of the flight, exchange pleasantries, and go your separate ways. Suppose that person seated next to you is employed at Google, an organization that you would love to work for after graduation. In that instance, the costs involved in continuing to communicate across the distance are minimal compared to the potential reward of having an inside connection when you apply for employment at the company in the future.

Stages of Relationship Development

Now that we have explored the reasons why we initiate relationships and some theoretical explanations for how we use communication, we turn our attention to understanding the process of moving from one stage of a relationship to another.

Knapp (1978) proposed a "staircase" model depicting the stages of relationship development and dissolution. The first five steps of this model, known as coming together, will be discussed here (see Figure 7.7). Chapter 9 will discuss Knapp's (1978) stages of relationship disengagement, or coming apart. Before discussing the stages of relationship initiation and development, it is important to note the following caveats about the movement from one stage to the next (Knapp & Vangelisti, 2003):

- Movement from one stage of the model to the next is typically sequential. This allows us to make predictions regarding the future of the relationship.
- Our decision to move to the next level involves an analysis of the potential benefits of continuing the relationship and increasing the level of intimacy in communication.

- At times, relationships may experience a "backward" movement to a prior stage. This is often due to a decline in the communication behaviors prescribed in the present stage.
- Movement through the stages occurs at different paces for each relationship. One may move very quickly from one stage to the next, while another may stall at one stage while the partners work through the communication challenges of that phase and make the decision of whether to progress to the next level.

INITIATION. Initiation occurs when one party decides to initiate conversation with another person. Communication during this phase typically consists of the polite formalities of intro-

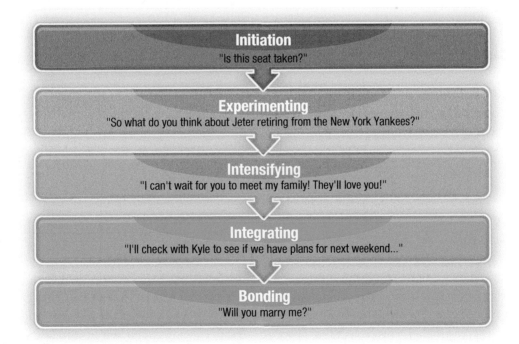

Initiation
"Is this seat taken?"

Experimenting
"So what do you think about Jeter retiring from the New York Yankees?"

Intensifying
"I can't wait for you to meet my family! They'll love you!"

Integrating
"I'll check with Kyle to see if we have plans for next weekend..."

Bonding
"Will you marry me?"

Figure 7.7. Knapp's (1978) Stages of "coming together" in a relationship.

duction. Statements such as "How are you?" or "Is anyone sitting here?" are used to break the ice. We evaluate the person's attractiveness and may scramble to come up with the perfect opening line. During this phase, impression management is essential. Our goal is to present ourselves in the most positive way possible. While some people may be tempted to use one of the pick-up lines discussed earlier in this chapter, the best strategy for making a good first impression is to be confident and sincere.

EXPERIMENTING. You know that you have reached the **experimenting** phase when the communication involves extensive questions and discussions about topics such as classes, hobbies, or other demographic information. Whereas physical attraction has a strong influence on the decision to engage in the initiation phase, social attraction is discovered during the experimenting phase. Reciprocal disclosures are common, with one person asking questions such as, "So have you lived in Los Angeles your entire life?" and the other person responding with "No, I grew up in Chicago and moved to L.A. last year to escape the cold winters. Did you grow up in California?" Uncertainty reduction is the primary goal of this stage of relationship development.

INTENSIFYING. As we progress to the **intensifying** stage of the staircase model, our disclosures with each other increase in depth. Whereas in the experimenting stage we disclosed information on a variety of topics (breadth), during this phase the information shared becomes more personal and private (depth). Messages communicated between partners involve a lot of "tests" to determine the intensity of commitment felt by the other. Knapp and Vangelisti (2003)

identify specific verbal characteristics that are common during the intensifying stage. These include using nicknames or terms of endearment to refer to each other (think "Boo Bear" or "Babe"), referring to each other through the use of first-person plural pronouns (*"We* should go to the movies with Joe and Cara on Friday"), and making explicit references to the commitment like "I think about you all the time when you're not here."

INTEGRATING. The **integrating** stage is marked by a merging of personalities and identities. Not only do the partners see themselves as a couple, but others recognize and refer to them as a unit as well. Relationship rituals that occur during this stage include exchanging personal items such as clothing, pictures, and rings that can be worn or displayed to communicate their identity as a couple to others, engaging in similar verbal and nonverbal behaviors, and identifying common "property" that is identified as special to the relationship ("our" song or purchasing a pet together). During this stage of coming together, one partner might say to the other, "What are our vacation plans for the summer?"

BONDING. **Bonding**, the final stage of coming together, is viewed as a formal contractual agreement that declares to the world that the couple has made a serious commitment to each other. This stage can be marked by performing public rituals such as exchanging class rings to show that you are "going steady," or getting engaged, or getting married. It is important to note that, while bonding can be viewed as a contract at any stage of the relationship, the message communicated between a couple during this stage is that there is a serious commitment that implies the goal of pursuing a long-term relationship.

Marriage communicates a long-term commitment to a relationship.

Relationship Initiation Contexts

Another factor impacting the decision to initiate a relationship focuses on the setting in which the initial interaction takes place. Reflect on your own relationships and recall where those relationships began. A 1981 study of college women asked them to report the settings where their significant relationships were initiated (Jason, Reichler, & Rucker, 1981). Five settings were identified by single women as the location where their significant relationships were initiated (see Table 7.4 below). Given that the women were currently enrolled in college classes, it should come as no surprise that they most often listed school as the place where their most important relationships began.

Table 7.4 Contexts of significant relationship initiation for college women

SETTING	PERCENTAGE
School	25
Work	20
Through Friends	14
Bar	9
Party	9

Source: Jason, L. A., Reichler, A., & Rucker, W. (1981). Characteristics of significant dating relationships: Male versus female initiators, idealized versus actual settings. *The Journal of Psychology, 109,* 185–190. Reprinted with permission of the Helen Dwight Reid Educational Foundation. Published by Heldref Publications, 1319 Eighteenth St., NW, Washington, DC 20036-1802. Copyright © 1981.

A study of preferred meeting places for gays and lesbians reveals a slight difference in setting choices. Gay bars are often identified as a popular place for initiating relationships, given the fact that patrons of the bars are similar in terms of their sexual preference. Among lesbians, the second most preferred meeting place is at political functions, such as feminist or lesbian rallies (Huston & Schwartz, 2003). It is important to note that some environments are not open or welcoming to the initiation of homosexual relationships. Thus, frustration in locating a common place to meet similar others is often reported by gay men and lesbians.

Relationship Initiation and Technology

ONLINE RELATIONSHIP INITIATION. As the number of people who form relationships online continues to grow, there is a greater need to understand the unique nature of interactions in cyberspace. In face-to-face interactions, the initial decision to approach another person is often based on physical characteristics. We see the person, make a decision of whether or not to approach him, and subsequently spend time getting to know each other by progressing through the relationship stages identified by Knapp and Vangelisti (2003). Online relationship initiation differs because of the absence of physical cues, which can affect the course of the relationship. Individuals meet via written messages or text. From there, they decide whether to talk with the other person via phone and, ultimately, in person. In essence, online relationship initiation could be considered a "test drive"—we can dedicate as little or as much time as we want to getting to know the person before deciding if we want to meet face-to-face.

chapter 7 Initiating Relationships: "Haven't We Met Somewhere Before?"

225

Is an on-line relationship right for me?

Table 7.5 Attraction Variables (Percentage) by Country

Attraction Variable	USA	Israel
Appearance	63	70
Status	8	0
Personality	92	94
Need filled	54	6
Propinquity	63	46
Mutual attraction	41	40
Arousal	22	25
Similarity	30	8

Source: Pines, A. M. (2001). The role of gender and culture in a romantic attraction. *European Psychologist, 6*(2), 96–102. Reproduced with permission from Hogrefe & Huber Publishers.

While we might doubt the sustainability of relationships that are initiated online, research suggests otherwise. One study examined the stability of a variety of online relationships (acquaintances, friends, and romantic partners) over a two-year period and found 75 percent of respondents indicated that they were still involved in a relationship that had been initiated online (McKenna, Green, & Gleason, 2002).

In Chapter 11, we will take a closer look at some specific ways that technologies have influenced the ways in which we initiate relationships with others.

Relationship Initiation and Culture

While you might think that perceptions with regard to relationship initiation differ across cultures, you might be surprised to find out that we are more alike than different. Pines (2001) examined the role of gender and culture in initial romantic attraction by comparing Americans with Israelis. She asked participants to describe how they met their romantic partner and indicate what attracted them to the other person initially (see Table 7.5).

The only significant differences occurred when comparing U.S. and Israeli perceptions relating to status, proximity (propinquity in Table 7.5), and similarity. Some Americans reported that they were attracted by the status of their relational partner, while none of the Israeli respondents indicated this was a factor. Physical proximity between partners was listed as being more influential to Americans who reported being more attracted to partners who lived, worked, or studied at the same place. Similarity of partners was found to be more important to Americans. Having similar experiences, values, interests, attitudes, and personalities was rated as being far more important to Americans than to Israelis.

SUMMARY

In this chapter we have answered some of the questions regarding *why* we form interpersonal relationships with others and *how* we use communication to initiate them. While each relationship is unique, the reasons we choose to interact with others are fairly similar. Our hope is that you have gained both an understanding of, and the confidence for, using effective communication behaviors to pursue new relationship journeys. Perhaps the most important piece of advice we could offer as you begin a relationship with another person, whether it is a platonic or a romantic relationship, is to just be yourself.

DISCUSSION QUESTIONS

1. Throughout this chapter, various goals and motives for initiating relationships were discussed. Which of these goals and motives do you perceive as most influential in your own decisions to initiate various relationships (e.g., friendships, romantic relationships, workplace relationships)?

2. Recall a time when you were successful at initiating a romantic relationship. Offer several suggestions or guidelines for individuals who want to be successful when initiating conversations or beginning a romantic relationship. What types of things should you avoid saying or doing during this critical time period?

3. In what context or under what circumstances did most of your important relationships begin? Do you initiate different types of relationships in different contexts? Are there similarities and differences in the questions asked/strategies employed during the initiating stages of platonic and romantic relationship development?

SELF ASSESSMENT

Revised Self-Disclosure Scale

Please refer to the specific person whom you just thought about. Indicate the degree to which the following statements reflect how you communicate with this person by circling whether you (7) strongly agree, (6) agree, (5) moderately agree, (4) are undecided, (3) moderately disagree, (2) disagree, or (1) strongly disagree.

INTENDED DISCLOSURE

_____ 1. When I wish, my self-disclosures are always accurate reflections of who I really am.

_____ 2. When I express my personal feelings, I am always aware of what I am doing and saying.

_____ 3. When I reveal my feelings about myself, I consciously intend to do so.

_____ 4. When I am self-disclosing, I am consciously aware of what I am revealing.

AMOUNT

_____ 5. I do not often talk about myself.

_____ 6. My statements of my feelings are usually brief.

_____ 7. I usually talk about myself for fairly long periods at a time.

_____ 8. My conversation lasts the least time when I am discussing myself.

_____ 9. I often talk about myself.

_____10. I often discuss my feelings about myself.

_____11. Only infrequently do I express my personal beliefs and opinions.

POSITIVE-NEGATIVE

_____12. I usually disclose positive things about myself.

_____13. On the whole, my disclosures about myself are more negative than positive.

_____14. I normally reveal "bad" feelings I have about myself.

_____15. I normally "express" my good feelings about myself.

_____16. I often reveal more undesirable things about myself than desirable things.

_____17. I usually disclose negative things about myself.

_____18. On the whole, my disclosures about myself are more positive than negative.

CONTROL OF DEPTH

_____19. I intimately disclose who I really am, openly and fully in my conversation.

_____20. Once I get started, my self-disclosures last a long time.

_____21. I often disclose intimate, personal things about myself without hesitation.

_____22. I feel that I sometimes do not control my self-disclosure of personal or intimate things I tell about myself.

_____23. Once I get started, I intimately and fully reveal myself in my self-disclosures.

HONESTY-ACCURACY

_____24. I cannot reveal myself when I want to because I do not know myself thorough enough.

_____25. I am often not confident that my expressions of my own feelings, emotions, and experiences are true reflections of myself.

_____26. I always feel completely sincere when I reveal my own feelings and experiences.

_____27. My self-disclosures are completely accurate reflections of who I really am.

_____28. I am not always honest in my self-disclosures.

_____29. My statement about my feelings, emotions, and experiences are always accurate self-perceptions.

_____30. I am always honest in my self-disclosures.

_____31. I do not always feel completely sincere when I reveal my own feelings, emotions, behaviors or experiences

NOTE: Items 5, 6, 8, 11, 13, 14, 16, 17, 24, 25, 28, and 31 are reverse scored.

SOURCE: Wheeless, L. R. (1976). Self-disclosure and interpersonal solidarity: Measurement,validation, and relationships. _Human Communication Research_, 3, 47-61.

chapter 7 Initiating Relationships: "Haven't We Met Somewhere Before?"

229

KEY TERMS AND DEFINITIONS

ATTACHMENT SECURITY: one of four dimensions of similarity considered in initial attraction. Predicts that individuals will be most attracted to those who are secure.

ATTITUDE SIMILARITY: our perception of the attitudes, beliefs, and values that we hold in common with another person(s).

BACKGROUND SIMILARITY: refers to commonalities that we share as a result of our life experiences.

BONDING: the final stage of relationship development, which involves a perceived contractual agreement of commitment between partners.

BREADTH: variety of topics that we are willing to disclose about in our discussions with others.

COMPLEMENTARITY: one of four dimensions of similarity considered in initial attraction. Often referred to as "opposites attract" and predicts that people will be more attracted to those whose personality and/or communication characteristics complement their own.

CONTEXT: references regarding the setting in which the relationship was initiated.

COSTS: perceived undesirable behaviors or outcomes that influence our decision regarding the relative value of continuing to pursue the relationship further.

DEMOGRAPHIC SIMILARITY: commonalities based on physical and social characteristics that are easily identifiable.

DEPTH: level of intimacy or amount of detail that is disclosed about a particular topic.

DURATION: references used to describe the length of time we have known the other person.

EXPERIMENTING: stage of relationship development in which partners exchange information about a variety of superficial topics and interests to identify potential commonalities.

FALSE HOMOPHILY: presentation of a deceptive image of self in an attempt to appear more similar to another person.

FLIRTATIOUS COMMUNICATION: involves the use of verbal and nonverbal behaviors to indicate our interest in initiating a potential relationship.

GOALS: refers to a desired or preferred outcome which motivates us to behave in particular ways.

IDEAL-SELF SIMILARITY: one of four dimensions of similarity considered in initial attraction. Proposes that we are attracted to those who are similar to our view of how we would like others to perceive us.

IMPRESSION MANAGEMENT: process of maintaining a positive image of self in the presence of others.

INITIATION: stage of relationship development in which one person decides to initiate conversation with another. Communication typically consists of the polite formalities of introduction.

INTEGRATING: stage of relationship development that is marked by a merging of personalities and identities. Relational partners are viewed by others as "a couple."

INTENSIFYING: stage of relationship development in which our disclosures with each other increase in depth. Messages are used to determine the intensity of commitment felt by the other person.

INTERPERSONAL ATTRACTION: a general feeling or desire that impacts our decision to approach and initiate a relationship with another person.

INTIMATE COMMUNICATION: information that is self-disclosed to those with whom we have established a high level of trust or comfort. Topics may include concerns and aspirations.

OBLIGATORY RELATIONSHIPS: often occur by chance and not by choice. Also referred to as "involuntary" relationships.

PERSONAL COMMUNICATION: self-disclosure topics that focus on personal aspects such as likes, dislikes, and experiences.

PHYSICAL ATTRACTIVENESS: characteristics such as body shape or size, hair color or length, and facial features used in making a determination of whether to initiate a relationship.

PREDICTED OUTCOME VALUE: theory that explains the process of evaluating the perceived rewards or benefits associated with a relationship.

PRIVATE COMMUNICATION: core of the social penetration theory onion model. Information that is reserved for our closest relationships.

PROXIMITY: the physical distance between two people.

RECIPROCAL SELF-DISCLOSURE: involves the mutual exchange or disclosure of information between two people. Enhances relationship satisfaction when disclosures are similar in terms of topics discussed and depth of information shared.

RELATIONSHIP: a connection between two individuals that results in mutual interaction with the intent of achieving shared meaning.

REWARDS: consist of behaviors or things that are desirable, which the recipient perceives as enjoyable or fulfilling.

ROLE: labels or descriptors used to define the nature of a relationship.

RULES: expectations for communication in relationships. May be explicitly stated or implicit.

SELF-DISCLOSURE: sharing or revealing personal information about oneself with others.

SELF-MONITORING: personality construct that causes a person to respond to social and interpersonal cues for appropriate communication behaviors in a variety of situations.

SIMILARITY: common interests, backgrounds, goals, and/or resemblances in appearance shared by two people. Also referred to as "homophily."

SIMILARITY TO CURRENT SELF: one of four dimensions of similarity considered in initial attraction. Refers to the belief that individuals are attracted to those who are similar to themselves.

SOCIAL ATTRACTIVENESS: common interests or similar patterns of communication that cause individuals to perceive each other as someone with whom they would like to spend time.

SOCIAL EXCHANGE THEORY: refers to an assessment of costs and rewards in determining the value of pursuing or continuing a relationship.

SOCIAL PENETRATION THEORY: explains how information is exchanged during relationship development. Describes the process of moving from superficial topics of conversation in the initial stages of relationships to more intimate conversations as the relationship progresses.

SOCIAL GOALS: desired end states that fulfill the need for inclusion or affection.

SUPERFICIAL COMMUNICATION: outer layer of the social penetration theory model. Information shared in the initial stages of relationships that focus on safe topics such as one's major, hometown, or occupation.

TASK ATTRACTIVENESS: characteristics or qualities that are perceived as appealing when initiating relationships in which the goal is to complete a task or assignment.

TASK GOALS: desired end states that fulfill the need for the completion of a task.

UNCERTAINTY REDUCTION THEORY: describes the process of exchanging information in an attempt to reduce ambiguity about others. Questions are a primary communication strategy used for reducing levels of uncertainty.

VOLUNTARY RELATIONSHIPS: interpersonal relationships entered into by choice or of one's own volition.

chapter 7 Initiating Relationships: "Haven't We Met Somewhere Before?"

231

REFERENCES

Altman, I., & Taylor, D. A. (1973). *Social penetration: The development of interpersonal relationships.* New York: Holt, Rinehart, & Winston.

Berger, C. (1995). A plan-based approach to strategic interaction. In D. E. Hewes (Ed.), *The cognitive bases of interpersonal interaction* (pp. 141–180). Hillsdale, NJ: Lawrence Erlbaum.

Berger, C. R., & Calabrese, R. J. (1975). Some explorations in initial interaction and beyond: Toward a developmental theory of interpersonal communication. *Human Communication Research, 1,* 99–112.

Berscheid, E., & Reis, H. T. (1998). Attraction in close relationships. In D. T. Gilbert, S. T. Fiske, & G. Lindzey (Eds.), *The handbook of social psychology* (4th ed.). New York: McGraw Hill.

Buss, D. M. (1989). Sex differences in human mate preferences: Evolutionary hypotheses tested in 37 cultures. *Behavioral and Brain Sciences, 12,* 1–49.

Collins, N. L., & Miller, L. C. (1994). Self-disclosure and liking: A meta-analytic review. *Psychological Bulletin, 116,* 457-475.

Commisso, M., & Finkelstein, L. (2012). Physical attractiveness bias in employee termination. *Journal of Applied Social Psychology, 42*(12), 2968–2987.

Davis, S. (1990). Men as success objects and women as sex objects: A study of personal advertisements. *Sex Roles, 23,* 43–50.

Dillard, J. P. (1990). A goal-driven model of interpersonal influence. In J. P. Dillard (Ed.), *Seeking compliance: The production of interpersonal influence messages* (pp. 41–56). Scottsdale, AZ: Gorsuch-Scarisbrick.

Douglas, W. (1990). Uncertainty, information seeking, and liking during initial interaction. *Western Journal of Speech Communication, 54,* 66-81.

Eagly, A. H., Ashmore, R. D., Makhijani, M. G., & Longo, L.C. (1991). What is beautiful is good, but…: A meta-analytic review of research on the physical attractiveness stereotype. *Psychological Bulletin, 110,* 109–128.

Feingold, A. (1990). Gender differences in effects of physical attractiveness on romantic attraction: A comparison across five research paradigms. *Journal of Personality and Social Psychology, 59*(5), 981–993.

Foos, P. W., & Clark, M. C. (2011). Adult age and gender differences in perceptions of facial attractiveness: Beauty is in the eye of the beholder. *The Journal of Genetic Psychology, 172*(2), 162–175.

Hatfield, E., & Sprecher, S. (1986). *Mirror, mirror: The importance of looks in everyday life.* Albany, NY: SUNY Press.

Hebl, M. R., & Heatherton, T. F. (1998). The stigma of obesity in women: The difference is black and white. *Personality and Social Psychology Bulletin, 24,* 417–426.

Hecht, M. L., DeVito, J. A., & Guerrero, L. K. (1999). Perspectives on nonverbal communication: Codes, functions, and contexts. In L. K. Guerrero, J. A. DeVite, & M. L. Hecht (Eds.), *The nonverbal communication reader: Classic and contemporary readings* (2nd ed.) (pp. 3–18). Prospect Heights, IL: Waveland Press.

Henningsen, D. D., Braz, M., & Davies, E. (2008). Why do we flirt?: Flirting motivations and sex differences in working and social contexts. *Journal of Business Communication, 45*(4), 483–502.

Houser, M. L., Horan, S. M., & Furler, L. A. (2008). Dating in the fast lane: How communication predicts speed-dating success. *Journal of Social and Personal Relationships, 25*(5), 749–768.

Huston, M., & Schwartz, P. (2003). The relationships of lesbians and of gay men. In K. M. Galvin & P. J. Cooper (Eds.), *Making connections: Readings in interpersonal communication* (3rd ed.) (pp. 171–177). Los Angeles, CA: Roxbury.

Jason, L. A., Reichler, A., & Rucker, W. (1981). Characteristics of significant dating relationships: Male versus female initiators, idealized versus actual settings. *The Journal of Psychology, 109,* 185–190.

Johnson, D. F., & Pittinger, J. B. (1984). Attribution, the attractiveness stereotype, and the elderly. *Developmental Psychology, 20,* 1168–1172.

Katz, J. E., & Rice, R. E. (2002). *Social consequences of Internet use: Access, involvement and interaction.* Cambridge, MA: The MIT Press.

Klohnen, E. C., & Luo, S. (2003). Interpersonal attraction and personality: What is attractive—self similarity, ideal similarity, complementarity, or attachment security? *Journal of Personality and Social Psychology, 85,* 709–722.

Knapp, M. L. (1978). *Social intercourse: From greeting to goodbye.* Boston: Allyn & Bacon.

Knapp, M., & Vangelisti, A. (2003). Relationship stages: A communication perspective. In K. M. Galvin and P. J. Cooper (Eds.), *Making connections: Readings in interpersonal communication* (3rd ed.) (pp. 158–165). Los Angeles, CA: Roxbury.

Lewis, K. E., & Bierly, M. (1990). Toward a profile of the female voter: Sex differences in perceived physical attractiveness and competence of political candidates. *Sex Roles, 22,* 1–12.

Mathes, E. W., Brennan, S. M., Haugen, & Rice, H. B. (1985). Ratings of physical attractiveness as a function of age. *The Journal of Social Psychology, 125,* 157–168.

McClellan, B., & McKelvie, S. J. (1993). Effects of age and gender on perceived physical attractiveness. *Canadian Journal of Behavioral Science, 25,* 135–142.

McCroskey, J. C., & McCain, T. A. (1974). The measurement of interpersonal attraction. *Speech Monographs, 41,* 261–266.

McCroskey, J. C., Richmond, V. P., & Daly, J. A. (1975). The development of a measure of perceived homophily in interpersonal communication. *Human Communication Research, 1,* 323–332.

McKenna, K. Y., Green, A. S., & Gleason, M. E. (2002). Relationship formation on the Internet: What's the big attraction? *Journal of Social Issues, 58,* 9–31.

Mongeau, P. A., Serewicz, M. C., & Therrien, L. F. (2004). Goals for cross-sex first dates: Identification, measurement, and the influence of contextual factors. *Communication Monographs, 71,* 121–147.

Mottet, T. P. (2000). The role of sexual orientation in predicting outcome value and anticipated communication behaviors. *Communication Quarterly, 48,* 233–240.

Perrett, D. I., Lee, K. J., & Penton-Voak, I. (1998). Effects of sexual dimorphism on facial attractiveness, *Nature, 394*(August, 27), 884–886.

Pines, A. M. (2001). The role of gender and culture in romantic attraction. *European Psychologist, 6,* 96–102.

Reis, H. T., & Patrick, B. C. (1996). Attachment and intimacy: Component processes. In E. T. Higgins and A. W. Kruglanski (Eds.), *Social psychology: Handbook of basic principles* (pp. 523–563). New York: Guilford Press.

Reis, H. T., & Shaver, P. (1988). Intimacy as interpersonal process. In S. Duck (Ed.), *Handbook of personal relationships: Theory, research, and interven-*

tions (pp. 367–389). Chichester: John Wiley & Sons Ltd.

Richmond, V. P. (1992). *Nonverbal communication in the classroom.* Edina, MN: Burgess.

Segal, M. W. (1974). Alphabet and attraction: An unobtrusive measure of the effect of propinquity in a field setting. *Journal of Personality and Social Psychology, 30,* 654–657.

Snyder, M., Berscheid, E., & Glick, P. (1985). Focusing on the exterior and the interior: Two investigations of the initiation of personal relationships. *Journal of Personality and Social Psychology, 48,* 1427–1439.

Sprecher, S., & Hendrick, S. (2004). Self-disclosure in intimate relationships: Associations with individual and relationship characteristics over time. *Journal of Social and Clinical Psychology, 23,* 857–877.

Sprecher, S., Sullivan, Q., & Hatfield, E. (1994). Mate selection preferences: Gender differences examined in a national sample. *Journal of Personality and Social Psychology, 66,* 1074–1080.

Sunnafrank, M. (1986). Predicted outcome value during initial interactions: A reformulation of uncertainty reduction theory. *Human Communication Research, 13,* 3–33.

Thibaut, J., & Kelley, H. (1959). *The social psychology of groups.* New York: Wiley.

Toma, C. L., & Hancock, J. T. (2010). Looks and lies: The role of physical attractiveness in online dating self-presentation and deception. *Communication Research, 37*(3), 335-351.

Vangelisti, A. L. (2002). Interpersonal processes in romantic relationships. In M. L. Knapp & J. A. Daly (Eds.), *Handbook of interpersonal communication* (pp. 643–679). Thousand Oaks, CA: Sage.

Wilbur, C. J., & Campbell, L. (2011). Humor in romantic contexts: Do men participate and women evaluate? *Personality and Social Psychology Bulletin, 37*(7), 918-929.

Zebrowitz, L. A. (1997). *Reading faces: Window to the soul?* Boulder, CO: Westview Press.

chapter 7 Initiating Relationships: "Haven't We Met Somewhere Before?"

233

chapter 8

Sustaining Relationships:
Relationship Maintenance and Conflict Management

OBJECTIVES

- Discuss the four goals of relationship maintenance.

- Explain equity theory and discuss how it is related to the process of relationship maintenance.

- Describe the five most common relationship maintenance strategies.

- Identify individual differences that affect relationship maintenance strategy choices.

- Define conflict and identify the key aspects of conflict episodes.

- Explain the three most common conflict management styles and describe advantages and disadvantages of each.

- Explain the four most typical conflict responses.

SCENARIO: SOUND FAMILIAR?

Maria was tired of fighting with her roommates. It seemed as though they were always arguing about cleaning the apartment, guests, food purchases, and a range of other roommate-related concerns. At times, the comments the roommates made to one another were verbally aggressive. Maria worked hard to maintain her relationships with her roommates, but she was becoming increasingly frustrated with their constant bickering and the lack of effort her roommates put into maintaining their friendships. She began to question whether she wanted to live with these same women next year.

OVERVIEW

In Chapter 7 we examined the process of initiating relationships. In this chapter we examine how and why individuals maintain their relationships with others and manage conflict. Perhaps you can relate to Maria's roommate situation and the frustration she is experiencing.

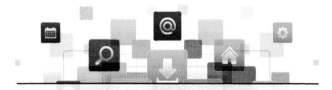

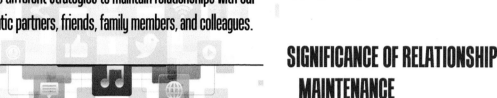

We use different strategies to maintain relationships with our romantic partners, friends, family members, and colleagues.

Some people seem to have more trouble staying together than building new bonds. The difficulty in sustaining a high level of commitment in romantic relationships is best illustrated by the current divorce rate in the United States: approximately 50 percent of current marriages will fail, and, sadly, most second marriages have an even greater chance of ending. In the first sections of this chapter we take a closer look at the goals of relationship maintenance, the reasons we maintain relationships with others, and the strategies used. We use a number of strategies to maintain relationships with our romantic partners, friends, family members, and colleagues. In this chapter we explore the use of different strategies and examine their effect on relationship maintenance.

In the second section of this chapter we examine the role of conflict in our relationships. Conflict is inevitable, and in fact, all of us experience it at one time or another in our interpersonal relationships. To maintain relationships with those we care about, it is important to manage conflict appropriately. In the conflict section of this chapter, we present information on conflict in order to help you: (1) understand what conflict is and how it can be both good and bad in relationships and (2) approach and respond to conflict situations appropriately.

SIGNIFICANCE OF RELATIONSHIP MAINTENANCE

According to Duck (1988), individuals involved in committed relationships spend much more time maintaining a relationship than in any other phase of the relationship. Relationship maintenance is not an easy task. It often takes a great deal of time, effort, and skill. To better understand the process of relationship maintenance, let us consider four common relationship maintenance goals as proposed by Dindia and Canary (1993). They state that individuals who are focusing on relationship maintenance have one of the following four goals in mind: (1) maintaining the existence of the relationship, (2) maintaining a desired state or condition in the relationship, (3) maintaining a satisfactory state in a relationship, or (4) repairing a relationship in an attempt to either restore it or sustain it in a satisfactory state (1993, p. 163). We will consider each of these goals.

Maintaining the Existence of the Relationship

Have you ever had a friend whom you call or text only once or twice a year? Or perhaps there are friends or family members who send you an annual holiday card with a letter updating the events of the past year, and that is the only communication you have with them until the next Christmas card arrives. In both of these examples, the goal of relationship maintenance is to keep the relationship in existence, or to keep it from dying.

Maintaining a Desired State in the Relationship

The second goal of relationship maintenance focuses on maintaining a desired state in a relationship. Some of you may have already experienced a situation that illustrates this goal. Perhaps you learned a close friend was interested in you romantically but you did not feel the same way about this friend. Instead of terminating the relationship with your close friend, you decided to avoid flirting with this friend, self-disclosing private information to this friend, or doing anything that might increase the level of intimacy in your relationship. To maintain your desired level of closeness with this friend, you purposely and strategically altered your communication in an effort to stay "just friends." This strategy of regulating the state of the relationship enables one partner to keep the relationship at a level that is satisfactory rather than dissolving the relationship altogether.

Maintaining a Satisfactory State

A third goal focuses on attempts made by both partners to maintain a level of relationship satisfaction that they find to be mutually agreeable. Depending on the type and status of the relationship, what partners define as "mutually

Relationship maintenance is often an ongoing task.

satisfying" can differ from one relationship to the next. In our example, Maria and her roommates might agree that, in order to maintain the quality of their relationships, they have to set time aside to have fun together. They might also agree that it is important for each of them to spend time with other friends so that they do not spend too much time together, which could negatively affect their relationships as well. The roommates find this arrangement agreeable.

Routine and Strategic Relationship Maintenance

Dindia and Canary (1993) point out that relationship maintenance involves both routine and strategic maintenance behaviors. Relationship maintenance is often an ongoing task. Just as you would seek routine maintenance to repair any issues that might keep your car from running smoothly, individuals engage in relationship maintenance to make sure that relationships run smoothly. According to researchers, **routine maintenance behaviors** "foster relational maintenance more in the manner of a 'by-product'" (Stafford, Dainton, & Haas, 2000, p. 307). Routine maintenance behaviors are performed every day in an effort to keep the relationship alive and may include behaviors such as giving advice and managing conflict (Stafford et al.; 2000). While these behaviors may seem mundane at times, they are needed to maintain relationship satisfaction.

Spending time together helps friends reconnect and maintain their friendships.

Individuals also engage in **strategic maintenance behaviors**. These behaviors are often enacted to repair or fix the relationship in some way. Perhaps you realize that your relationship with a friend has become more distant since you started a new romantic relationship. In an attempt to maintain your friendship, you realize that you have to fix some things—namely, spend more time together and engage in more communication with one another. Dindia and Canary (1993) note that it is important to remember that some aspects of these four goals can overlap with one another. Further, they point out that a relationship can be maintained even though one or both partners find it to be unsatisfactory, and even satisfactory relationships end for a number of reasons.

WHY WE MAINTAIN SOME RELATIONSHIPS AND NOT OTHERS

So why is it that we choose to maintain some relationships and not others? There are numerous factors that are central to interpersonal communication and relationship maintenance, including: intimacy, immediacy, investment, attraction, similarity, liking, commitment, and affection (see, for example, Burgoon & Hale, 1984). Rather than providing an exhaustive list of all of the characteristics that have been identified as relevant to sustaining relationships, interpersonal scholars have narrowed the list to the four relational characteristics that are generally perceived as universal to most relationships: control mutuality, trust, liking, and commitment (Canary & Stafford, 1994). Research has shown that relationships without these characteristics often lack substance, and as a result may not be able to be maintained.

Control mutuality is defined as "the extent to which couples agree on who has the right to influence the other and establish relational goals" (Canary & Stafford, 1994, p. 6). Relationships in which partners experience a high level of control mutuality are the result of both partners agreeing on who takes control in decision-making situations. Suppose two friends are planning a vacation to celebrate the end of the school year. If one of them is extremely organized, both friends may agree that he should be the one to plan their itinerary for the trip.

Trust has emerged as an equally important relationship characteristic. Individuals are often reluctant to reveal information to those they do not trust, and refusing to disclose about oneself often hinders relationship development. According to Rotenberg and Boulton (2013), individuals are considered trustworthy based on a number of different behaviors exhibited in a relationship. In order to be "trusted," a person must exhibit the following characteristics: (1) reliability, or the extent to which the individual keeps his or her promises; (2) emotional expression, or the extent to which the person does not cause any emotional pain for the partner—the individual is receptive to the partner's disclosures, does not share private information with others, and avoids saying or doing anything to embarrass the partner; and (3) honesty, or the extent to which the person is forthright with information.

Another characteristic required for sustaining a relationship is **liking**, or **affinity**. Mutual liking, or expressed affect, is a universal feature of all relationships. We prefer to be around individuals who know and like us. Not surprisingly, it is often very difficult for us to say no to requests that come from individuals we like (Cialdini, 2003).

Committed relationships are in it "for the long haul."

A fourth and final characteristic of successful relationships is **commitment**, which refers to our desire to continue a relationship. When we say we are committed to a relationship, this is usually interpreted to mean that we are in it "for the long haul" and "for better or for worse." While commitment is important in romantic relationships for obvious reasons, it is also relevant to familial and platonic relationships. Commitment, trust, control mutuality, and liking are characteristics that most of us desire in our communication and relationships.

In addition to understanding these relational characteristics, it is also important to recognize the theoretical explanations for why we choose to maintain relationships. **Equity theory** offers perhaps one of the most widely understood explanations for why some individuals engage in relationship maintenance activity and others do not (Canary & Stafford 1992). According to this the-

Overbenefited individuals may be less satisfied in their relationships because they feel guilty about not contributing equally to the relationship.

that partners who are in equitable relationships report the greatest level of satisfaction. Those who feel overbenefited are the next most satisfied, and the least satisfied individuals are those who report feeling underbenefited.

HOW WE MAINTAIN RELATIONSHIPS: THE ROLE OF COMMUNICATION SKILLS

ory, a relationship is considered equitable when the ratio of inputs to outputs is equal for both individuals involved. If, for example, you contribute more inputs compared to the outputs you receive from your partner, you will feel **underbenefited** in the relationship, possibly resulting in anger at getting less than you deserve.

Conversely, if your output to input ratio is greater than that of your relationship partner, then you will feel **overbenefited**. Some of you may wonder why those who are overbenefited in relationships report feeling dissatisfied. Is it possible that individuals who receive too much attention, affection, or gifts could possibly be unhappy in a relationship? Absolutely! Overbenefited individuals may be less satisfied in their relationships because they feel guilty about not contributing equally to the relationship. Perhaps you have a friend who is always the one who sends you text messages or who calls you. Eventually, you may feel guilty that you fail to return the friend's text messages or calls because you have failed at contributing equally to the relationship.

If we rank, in order, the level of satisfaction experienced in relationships, it is not surprising

Now that you have a better understanding of the four relational characteristics associated with maintenance and the theory explaining why we choose to sustain our relationships, let us take a closer look at the role that communication skills plays in maintaining relationships with others.

Interpersonal researchers continually explore new ways that communication can be used as a tool to maintain relationships. For example, Burleson and Samter's (1994) research emphasizes the importance of similarity in communication skills in maintaining relationships. They state, "Similarity in the nature and level of partners' social skills may be more important to relationship maintenance than the absolute level of skill sophistication of the partners" (p. 62). They propose a **skill similarity model (SSM)** that portrays relationship maintenance as a process requiring the involvement of both partners. According to the SSM, relationship partners' communication skills will not change dramatically over time; therefore, it is important for partners to possess skills perceived as similar. Across several different studies, the researchers found that relationship partners with the same level of communication skills possessed the highest levels of satisfaction (Burleson & Samter, 1996). Interestingly, both the low communication skill and the high communication skill dyads in their studies reported the same levels of relationship satisfaction. See the text box below for a summary of the results of another SSM study.

RESEARCH IN REAL LIFE: The importance of skill similarity in father-daughter relationships

Dunleavy, Wanzer, Krezmien, and Ruppel (2011) were interested in learning whether daughters and fathers with similar communication skills would report higher relationship satisfaction and more frequent communication than those with dissimilar skills. They used the skill similarity model as the framework for this research.

- 388 college-aged females completed an interpersonal communication competence measure on themselves and their fathers. Daughters also completed measures that assessed how satisfied they were in their relationships and how often they communicated with their fathers.

- As the SSM would predict, when daughters indicated their skills were different from their fathers' skills, they tended to be less satisfied in their relationships and communicate less frequently with their fathers.

- When daughters reported greater discrepancies between their skills and their fathers' skills, they were less likely to have open and ongoing conversations with their fathers about a wide range of issues.

Burleson and Samter (1994) also argue that maintaining relationships typically involves mastery of specific types of communication skills such as comforting, ego support, empathy, and face management. Those who are able to master these valuable communication skills are more likely to experience success and satisfaction in their relationships. **Comforting skills** can be verbal and/or nonverbal in nature and include the ability to reduce another's emotional distress. Comforting can be communicated verbally ("I can see why you're so upset about this situation!") or via nonverbal channels, such as with a hug or an encouraging look.

How do you comfort those who are close to you?

Ego support, which is described as the ability to make others feel positive about themselves, is another essential relationship maintenance communication skill. Giving a compliment to a close friend about his artwork is an example of ego support.

Empathy involves the ability to see things from the other person's point of view. Employing empathy communicates to others that their perspective is important in maintaining the relationship. Consider the relationship in which one partner is devoted to his religious beliefs, but the other partner was not raised to value religion. By respecting each other's differences in values and beliefs, maintenance is achieved. Perhaps the couple agrees to attend church services together for particular events, and also agrees not to force their beliefs on each other.

Face-management skills are an essential part of relationship maintenance. The concept of *face* is described as one's self-perception that they wish to portray a particular image when interacting with others. Avoiding communication that could be perceived as face-threatening can strengthen a relationship. Examples of communication facework include: being polite, avoiding topics that could potentially cause embarrassment to another, and using disclaimers to help manage the other's perception of self (e.g., "I know I may be crazy to think that this means that you don't care . . .").

Comforting, ego support, empathy, and face management skills are all important and desirable communication skills that can assist in the relationship maintenance process. Researchers have also studied a wide range of specific strategies individuals use to maintain the quality of their relationships.

RELATIONSHIP MAINTENANCE STRATEGIES

Because our relationships cannot sustain themselves, it is up to us to engage in behaviors that will prolong them. **Relationship maintenance strategies** are defined as the behaviors and activities used strategically "to sustain desired relational qualities or to sustain the current status of the relationship" (Canary & Stafford, 2001, p. 134).

What are some of the most common relationship maintenance strategies people use? Researchers Laura Stafford and Dan Canary (1991) examined all of the studies that focused on how partners maintain relationships and identified the five most common types of relationship maintenance strategies: positivity, openness, assurances, social networks, and sharing tasks. **Positivity** involves being polite, acting cheerful and upbeat, and avoiding criticism. Isn't it easier to maintain a relationship with someone who has a positive outlook on life and on the relationship than with someone who is always pessimistic? **Openness** refers to the open and ongoing discussions partners have about the status of the relationship. When individuals employ openness, they share their thoughts and feelings about the relationship. **Assurances** refer to expressions of love and commitment as well as making references to the future of the relationship. Relationship partners also sustain relationships by spending time with the mutual friends and family members who create a **social network**. The fifth and final strategy, **sharing tasks**, focuses on the extent to which partners share the chores and responsibilities associated with the relationship. Depending on the type of relationship, these tasks could include sharing responsibility for exchanging emails or phone calls, or allotting household tasks.

Sharing household tasks helps maintain a relationship.

© Minerva Studio /Shutterstock.com.

Since Stafford and Canary's initial investigation, there have been a number of follow-up studies exploring relationship maintenance strategies employed in a variety of relationships. For example, researchers have examined relationship maintenance in married adults (Dainton & Stafford, 1993; Dainton & Aylor, 2002; Ragsdale, 1996), in gay and lesbian relationships (Haas & Stafford, 1998), in dating couples (Dainton & Aylor, 2002), in same-sex (Canary et al., 1993) and cross-sex friendships (Messman, Canary, & Hause, 2000), and in family relationships (Canary et al., 1993; Myers & Weber, 2004). Once researchers began investigating the use of maintenance strategies in the various types of relationships listed above, it became apparent that there were numerous taxonomies, or ways of classifying, relationship maintenance behaviors. At this point, you will probably be happy to know that we are not going to cover all of the relationship maintenance strategies that exist. However, we will provide a brief overview of some of the additional maintenance strategies individuals might use with friends, romantic partners, family members, or coworkers such as: joint activities, mediated communication, advice, humor, no flirting, avoidance, and antisocial behaviors (Canary et al., 1993). **Joint activities** refer to those behaviors relationship partners do together: "hanging out" with each other, watching television together, and going on trips with each other. **Mediated communication** includes the exchange of email messages, letters, text messages, or phone calls to ensure a satisfying relationship. **Advice** typically involves disclosing personal information to the relationship partner or giving or seeking advice on some issue. **Humor** is

also sometimes used as a means of maintaining relationships and might include the use of jokes and sarcasm in either positive or negative ways. A positive example of using humor would be "trying to make each other laugh" (Canary et al., 1993, p. 11), while a negative example of using humor might include being sarcastic or making fun of someone's appearance or personality.

Interestingly, there are also strategies individuals use to reduce the amount of intimacy in a relationship. One such strategy is labeled **no flirting**. By not encouraging "overly familiar behaviors" in our relationships, we are able to help maintain a desired state or level of intimacy. As mentioned earlier in the chapter, if your goal is to be "friends" with someone, you would probably refrain from flirting with this person.

The relationship maintenance strategies labeled avoidance and antisocial behaviors would initially appear to be antithetical to prolonging any

> To maintain the quality of a relationship and, at the same time, preserve a sense of autonomy, it might also be necessary to establish times when we are away from our partners.

type of relationship. However, individuals employ these types of "maintenance" behaviors in certain situations. Strategies labeled **avoidant** include dodging "sore," or difficult, subjects that we should avoid discussing with our romantic partners, family members, or friends, to steer clear of conflict. To maintain the quality of a relationship and, at the same time, preserve a sense of autonomy, it might also be necessary to establish times when we are away from our partners. Hence, relationship partners might have a "girls' night" or "boys' night" out.

Partners also engage in either direct or indirect **antisocial behaviors,** which are described as behaviors that might seem unfriendly or coercive (Canary et al., 1993). To gain a relationship partner's attention or to signal something is wrong in the relationship, one partner might act moody or difficult (indirect strategy) to gain the other person's attention. Dainton and Gross (2008) identified a number of antisocial behaviors couples used to maintain their relationships. Partners in romantic relationships might start a fight (destructive conflict) or try to determine personal or private information about a partner (spying) in an effort to maintain their relationships. Not surprisingly, couples who exhibit more of these negative maintenance strategies also report lower amounts of trust, commitment, satisfaction, and liking (Goodboy, Myers, & Members of Investigating Communication, 2010). Read the textbox below to learn more about research on the use of negative relational maintenance strategies in romantic relationships.

> ### RESEARCH IN REAL LIFE:
> ### Attachment and the use of negative relational maintenance behaviors in romantic relationships
>
> Goodboy and Bolkan (2011) conducted research to understand why individuals might use negative relational maintenance strategies in their relationships. They studied the relationship between college students' **attachment styles** (Chapter 2) and use of negative relationship maintenance strategies.
>
> - 232 college students in romantic relationships completed the Attachment Style Measure and the Negative Maintenance Scale.
> - Secures were less likely to use negative relationship maintenance behaviors (i.e., jealousy induction, avoidance, destructive conflict, allowing control, spying, and infidelity) than non-secures.
> - Dismissives and fearful-avoidants, who tend to have poor working models of relationships, reported using more negative relationship maintenance strategies than secures.

See Table 8.1 for additional examples of relationship maintenance strategies.

As relationship partners become more connected, or interdependent, the use of relationship maintenance strategies generally increases (Canary & Stafford, 2001). It should come as no surprise that decreases in relationship maintenance behaviors by one or both partners often signals that a relationship is in trouble (Ayres, 1983). Canary and Stafford's (1994) research indicates that the "use of positivity, sharing tasks, and offering assurance helps sustain control mutuality, trust, liking and commitment" (p. 19). They also note that not all relationships will benefit equally from the use of these five strategies (positivity, assurances,

Table 8.1 Relationship Maintenance Strategies

Strategy	Examples
1. Positivity	Engage in cheerful communication; ask "How was your day?"
2. Openness	Solicit discussion on status of relationship; ask partner to share feelings about the relationship
3. Assurances	Emphasize commitment to one another; say "I love you" to each other
4. Social network	Express interest in spending time with mutual friends; focus on building friendships that are mutual/shared
5. Sharing tasks	Help partner with various tasks or household chores such as cooking and cleaning
6. Joint activities	Spend time hanging out with each other; go to the movies, football games, dinners
7. Mediated communication	Use email to communicate; call partner on the phone; send partner a card
8. Avoidance	Avoid talking about certain issues; avoid the relationship partner
9. Antisocial behaviors	Be mean or rude to him/her; act moody when around him/her
10. Humor	Call him/her a funny or silly name; use sarcasm when communicating
11. No flirting	Do not flirt with him/her; do not show any sign of romantic interest
12. Advice	Give/seek advice on a variety of issues (e.g., love, relationships, school, future)

Source: Adapted from Canary and Stafford (1994, 1992); Canary et al. (1993); Messman et al. (2000).

etc.). Thus, it is important to examine research that summarizes how these strategies function in different types of relationships, paying special attention to the outcomes of their use.

RELATIONSHIP MAINTENANCE IN DIFFERENT TYPES OF RELATIONSHIPS

Not surprisingly, the tactics, or behaviors, you use to maintain your friendships are different from those you use to sustain your relationship with your romantic partner. Researchers found the use of relationship maintenance strategies differs depending on relationship type. While there is a vast amount of research available on relationship maintenance in different types of relationships, we will overview a small portion to understand how relationship maintenance strategy use varies in relationships based on the *type of relationship* (i.e., romantic, platonic, family), *cultural differences*, and *sexual orientation*. We also discuss the outcomes associated with the use of these strategies.

What relationship maintenance strategies do romantic partners use?

Some strategies appear to be more effective than others in increasing relationship satisfaction and stability, but it depends on the type of relationship and the individuals involved.

Relationship maintenance has been studied extensively in different types of romantic relationships (see, for example, Canary, Stafford, Hause, & Wallace, 1993; Dainton, 2000; Dainton & Stafford, 1993). Researchers have investigated how relationship maintenance strategies differ based on (1) relationship length; (2) type of commitment, e.g., married or dating; (3) cultural differences; and (4) sexual preferences. Romantic partners use relationship maintenance strategies (e.g., positivity, openness, assurances, sharing tasks, and cards/letters) more than friends do (Canary et al., 1993). This finding is not particularly surprising since most of us put more energy into maintaining our romantic relationships. In another related study on married couples' use of relationship maintenance strategies, researchers found that married couples' use of relationship maintenance behaviors decreased over time (Dindia & Baxter, 1987; Ragsdale, 1996). Additionally, the use of relationship maintenance strategies in romantic relationships tends to become more *routine* and *less strategic* over time. In essence, we become comfortable with our partner and fall into a routine in which we use the same behaviors

that have been proven to work in the past. In newer relationships, partners usually have to devote more time and energy to thinking about how they will strategically use assurances, positivity, or even openness as a means of stabilizing their relationship. For individuals in long-term relationships, the use of these behaviors becomes part of the daily routine and is not something partners are always cognizant of doing. One example of a relationship maintenance routine exhibited in married couples or long-term relationships is an expression of affection such as "I love you." Couples who ask each other questions about their daily activities such as "How was work?" or "How was school?" are also engaging in routine relationship maintenance.

Some strategies appear to be more effective than others in increasing relationship satisfaction and stability, but it depends on the type of relationship and the individuals involved. For example, romantic relationship partners' use of assurances has been linked repeatedly to relationship satisfaction and commitment (Dainton & Aylor, 2002; Stafford & Canary, 1991). There are very few of us who do not like to hear our relationship partner say, "I love you" or "I really care about you." When comparing relationship maintenance behaviors of married couples to dating couples, married partners use more assurances and social networks, while dating couples engage in more openness than married couples (Stafford & Canary, 1991). Partners in dating relationships are still getting to know each other, and so individuals must be more open and willing to share information with each other for the relationship to develop.

Researchers have also investigated relationship maintenance in family contexts. Maintaining relationships with our grandparents, parents, siblings, aunts, uncles, and cousins takes a significant amount of time and energy. Because sibling relationships are often described as "lifelong" types of relationships, several studies have examined siblings' use of relationship maintenance strategies (Mikkelson, Myers, & Hannawa, 2011; Myers & Members of COM 200, 2001; Myers & Goodboy, 2013). From the research on siblings we can draw several conclusions:

- Adult siblings reported more positive relationships with their siblings when they used relationship maintenance strategies (i.e., positivity, assurances, openness, networks, and tasks) (Myers & Members of COM 200, 2001).
- Individuals of all ages (i.e., 18 and over 55) reported more positive relationships when their siblings engaged in relationship maintenance strategies.
- Female siblings tend to engage in relationship maintenance strategies more often than male siblings (Myers & Members of COM 200, 2001).
- Siblings who are more genetically related or share more genetic material with each other engage in relationship maintenance behavior more often than less-genetically related siblings. In other words, identical twins and fraternal twins, who share a great deal of genetic material, used positivity, openness, assurances, social networks, and shared tasks more frequently in their relationships than did adopted siblings or stepsiblings (Mikkelson, Myers, & Hannawa, 2011).

- Myers and Goodboy's (2013) research on adult sibling relationships indicated that siblings will engage in more relationship maintenance (e.g. openness) when the relationship is perceived as equitable. Siblings also report greater trust, liking, and satisfaction when the relationship is perceived as equitable.

Culture also plays a role in the types of relational maintenance strategies we employ. When comparing the impact of culture on marital partners, African American couples indicated using task-sharing as a maintenance strategy less often than European American couples (Diggs & Stafford, 1998). Researchers explain this result by pointing out that, generally, African American males and females tend to be more focused on sharing roles and responsibilities in their relationship when compared to their European American counterparts. Task-sharing might be discussed more frequently by European American couples because they have struggled historically with creating more equity in their romantic relationships. This study illustrates that partners' individual differences, which might include factors such as culture, personality, age, or even maturity, may also affect the types of relationship maintenance strategies used.

Sexual orientation also plays a role in the type of relationship maintenance strategies partners use with each other. Haas and Stafford (1998) discovered that heterosexual and homosexual couples employ many of the same strategies in their relationships. Two strategies unique to gay and lesbian relationships include (1) being "out" as a couple when communicating with their social networks, and (2) seeking out social environments supportive of gay and lesbian relationships. Additional re-

> Heterosexual and homosexual couples appear to exhibit similar behaviors in their relationships to maintain satisfaction.

search by Eldridge and Gilbert (1990) emphasizes the importance of perceived equity in relational power and high levels of emotional intimacy in enhancing relationship satisfaction in lesbian relationships. Gay men indicate a preference for low levels of conflict and high levels of cooperation as factors that help maintain a satisfying relationship (Jones & Bates, 1978). Heterosexual and homosexual couples appear to exhibit similar behaviors in their relationships to maintain satisfaction.

As researchers continue to explore the different ways partners sustain relationships, they are also turning their attention to the increasing role technology plays in how people maintain these associations. Because the impact of technology on interpersonal communication will be addressed extensively in Chapter 11, we discuss it here only briefly as it relates to relationship maintenance.

FACEBOOK AND RELATIONSHIP MAINTENANCE

Facebook, an online social networking site, has been studied extensively by researchers from a number of different academic fields. Several researchers indicate that many people use Facebook to maintain relationships with friends, family, romantic partners, and coworkers (Craig & Wright, 2012; Dainton, 2013).

Does Facebook help you maintain relationships?

College students express positivity, openness, and assurances on Facebook as a means of maintaining their romantic relationships (Dainton, 2013). Does using these behaviors on Facebook contribute significantly to romantic partners' perceptions of relationship satisfaction? Dainton (2013) examined whether college students' use of relationship maintenance behaviors on Facebook and general face-to-face relationship maintenance behaviors contributed to reported relationship satisfaction. When college students indicated their relationship partners used positivity and assurances on Facebook as a means of maintaining their romantic relationships, they reported *somewhat higher levels* of relationship satisfaction compared to college students who did not report the use of these same maintenance strategies (Dainton, 2013). However, when comparing Facebook relationship maintenance behavior with general relationship maintenance activity, the Facebook relationship maintenance behavior did not contribute meaningfully to relationship satisfaction. Dainton stated, "Facebook might not be an important tool for maintaining romantic relationships as compared to other relational types" (Dainton, 2013, p. 120). When looking at which behaviors were most instrumental in fostering satisfying romantic relationships, college students indicated that general maintenance behaviors such as "assurances" and "managing conflict" were more important to relationship satisfaction than Facebook maintenance behaviors.

CONCLUSIONS ABOUT RELATIONSHIP MAINTENANCE

There is an extensive body of research on strategic and routine relationship maintenance behaviors. Below, we highlight a number of important conclusions from the relationship maintenance literature:

- Relationships are not self-sustaining and, as such, require a significant amount of time and effort.
- Individuals are most motivated to maintain relationships in which partners exhibit high amounts of trust, commitment, control mutuality, and liking.
- Most individuals want to be in relationships that are perceived as equitable (inputs=outputs).
- Both routine and strategic relationship maintenance behaviors are used most frequently in equitable relationships.
- Five relationship maintenance strategies are used consistently regardless of the type of relationship, or whether the interactants communicate face-to-face or online: positivity, assurances, openness, sharing tasks, and social networks.

- Individuals' use of assurances, networks, and sharing tasks is consistently recognized as a significant predictor of relationship commitment.
- When researchers further examined relationship maintenance behaviors in other types of relationships, additional strategies emerged, including, among others: humor, avoidance, antisocial behaviors, mediated communication, advice, and conflict management.
- Effectiveness and frequency of strategy use depends on the type of relationship being investigated.
- Female siblings use more relationship maintenance strategies with one another than male siblings and male-female siblings.

CONFLICT: A NATURAL COMPONENT OF ALL RELATIONSHIPS

The key to sustaining our relationships often rests in our ability to manage the conflicts that arise from time to time. To maintain stability in our relationships, it is necessary to manage conflict appropriately. Many relationship scholars have identified conflict management as an important and necessary maintenance behavior. If individuals are unable to manage conflict in their different types of relationships (i.e., romantic, platonic, family, or work), it is likely that they will report less satisfaction with these relationships and may even terminate them. This section of the chapter explains what conflict is, why it occurs, how it can affect individuals and relationships (both positively and negatively), and how to manage it appropriately.

Definition of Conflict

Regardless of whether disagreements occur between two coworkers, between a husband and wife, or between two neighbors, there are aspects that all conflict episodes share. A number of definitions for conflict exist in the literature; however, we want to focus on one that approaches conflict from a communication perspective. Hocker and Wilmot (1991) define **conflict** as "an expressed struggle between at least two interdependent parties who perceive incompatible goals, scarce resources, and interference from the other party in achieving their goals" (p. 12). To understand how and why conflict occurs, it is important to examine the main components of this definition in detail. There are five consistent aspects, or components, of conflict episodes, as listed below:

Expressed struggle

Interdependence

Incompatible goals

Scarce resources

Interference

Figure 8.1 Five Components of Conflict Episodes

EXPRESSED STRUGGLE. The first consistent component of conflict is that it typically involves **expressed struggle** or open communication about the issue or problem. How do we know if a con-

flict with a friend, coworker, or family member is really a conflict? From an interpersonal communication perspective, it is important to consider the communicative interchanges that make up the conflict episode (Hocker & Wilmot, 1991).

Consider this dialogue between two roommates, Molly and Tiona:

> **Molly:** Hey Tiona, do you want to go and get some coffee after you're done studying?
>
> **Tiona:** No, thanks. *(Makes no eye contact, stares at her book.)*
>
> **Molly:** Is something wrong, you seem a little annoyed? I thought you said you wanted to go and get coffee later this evening?
>
> **Tiona:** I did, but now I really don't.
>
> **Molly:** Fine, don't tell me what is wrong!

Do you think both roommates are aware that there is a problem? It is no wonder that Molly is confused! This example illustrates the importance of expressing conflict openly. When there are joint communicative representations of conflict, that is, both partners openly express their concerns or emotions, we typically say that conflict has occurred. Some individuals might feel angry or frustrated with a relationship partner but choose not to express their concerns openly. Once people openly communicate their feelings or concerns with their relationship partners, interpersonal conflict has occurred. Interpersonal communication scholars agree that communication is an essential element in all interpersonal conflict. Additionally, they stress that communication both affects, and is affected by, aspects of relationships (Canary, Cupach, & Messman, 1995; Hocker & Wilmot, 1991).

INTERDEPENDENCE. The second key element of conflict addresses the significance of partner interdependence. Stated simply, if individuals rely on one another and are aware of how their decisions or behaviors affect one another, they are more likely to experience conflict than individuals who do not rely on one another. If you rely on your roommate to pick you up at the airport and he fails to do so, this might result in conflict. The more interdependent relationship partners are, the greater the chances are for conflict to occur (Braiker & Kelley, 1979).

INCOMPATIBLE GOALS. A third factor of conflict is incompatible goals. According to Hocker and Wilmot (1991) people are most likely to "engage in conflict over goals they often deny as being important to them" (p. 17). All of us, at one time or another, will experience opposition in trying to reach a goal. Hocker and Wilmot describe two common types of goal incompatibility that can lead to conflict. One type of goal incompatibility occurs when relationship partners want the same thing. Think about two basketball players who are both competing for the same position on the team or two employees who are both contending for the same position in a company. Another type of goal incompatibility occurs when two individuals want different things. Recall the last time you and your relationship partner disagreed on the restaurant you would go to for dinner. How long did you argue about this? Do you remember how you finally decided where you would eat? Sometimes conflict is about actual differences in restaurant choices, while other times it is about

who gets to choose the restaurant. Whether individuals perceive their goals as similar or different, perceived incompatibility in objectives is a consistent aspect of conflict episodes (Hocker & Wilmot, 1991).

PERCEIVED SCARCE RESOURCES. A fourth component of conflict is perceived scarce resources. Resources refer to anything an individual identifies as valuable or meaningful and can include, among other things: people, relationships, opportunities, material objects, or time. Hocker and Wilmot (1991) point out that "The resources might be real or perceived as real by the person. Likewise, the perception of scarcity, or limitation, may be apparent or actual" (p. 19). This is illustrated when an only child protests the addition of another sibling in the family and argues that the parents cannot possibly have enough love to go around for both children. Conflict experts say the best route to take in this situation is to try to change the child's perception of the available resource by assuring the child that there is more than enough love available for two children. Most interpersonal struggles revolve around perceived scarcity in power and self-esteem. As illustrated in the example above, the child was worried about receiving confirmation from the parents that would directly affect his or her self-esteem. Not surprisingly, when people fight or disagree, they often express sentiments that illustrate power and self-esteem struggles (Hocker & Wilmot, 1991).

INTERFERENCE. The fifth and final component of conflict is interference. Is it possible for individuals who depend on one another and perceive incompatible goals and scarce resources not to experience conflict? Yes, it is. Hocker and Wilmot (1991) point out that even when incompatible goals and limited resources are present, individuals must perceive interference from the other in their attempt to achieve a goal. As soon as someone interferes with, or blocks, your goals, it is likely that you will experience conflict. When we feel like someone is trying to stand in our way of accomplishing a goal, conflict is likely to emerge.

Remember, in order for conflict to occur between individuals, the following criteria must be evident: (1) differences must be expressed openly and recognized by both partners, (2) partners must be interdependent, (3) partners must have incompatible goals, (4) partners must perceive competition for scarce resources, and (5) partners must perceive interference in goal achievement. Next, we examine how conflict can be beneficial or detrimental to maintaining stability in a relationship.

WHY CONFLICT OCCURS

A common theme in all interpersonal conflict situations is incompatibility (Roloff & Soule, 2002). While we are often drawn to others because they are different, these differences can cause conflict. The list of reasons why conflict occurs in relationships is an endless one. In the next sections we highlight some of the more common types of relationship conflict.

- Individuals might argue about *principles*. This type of conflict has to do with discrepancies in values or ideals relationship partners possess. Perhaps one partner wants to get married in a church and have a big wedding ceremony while the other wants to continue the relationship but does not see a reason to get married.
- Individuals might have *realistic conflicts* that result from a variety of external situations or demands that the relationship partners face. Couples might argue about financial hardships, work demands, or difficult family members. These demands are all certainly stressful and can lead to conflict in relationships.
- *Personal conflict* results from one person acting based on her/his self-interests and not thinking about others. A personal conflict might occur when one roommate drinks all the milk and then places the empty container back in the refrigerator.
- Conflict also occurs when *rules* are broken in relationships. Most people establish a set of rules or expectations in their relationships and when these rules are broken, conflict occurs. For example, if you told a friend to keep certain information about you private and then she shared this information with another friend, you would probably be angry with her (Roloff & Soule, 2002).

Have differences in your relationships caused conflicts?

This is certainly not an exhaustive list of all of the types of conflict that occur in relationships; however, the common theme across these situations is incompatibility between people. Because we are all so incredibly different, conflict is an inevitable part of our relationships. We now turn our attention to the benefits and drawbacks of conflict in relationships.

CONFLICT CAN BE PRODUCTIVE OR UNPRODUCTIVE FOR INDIVIDUALS AND FOR RELATIONSHIPS

Depending upon how it is managed in interpersonal relationships, conflict can be productive or unproductive. When conflict is managed effectively, it can be good for both the relationship and the individuals involved. First, to establish meaningful relationships with others and survive in a social world, you must understand both the role of emotions (your own and others') and the social and cultural norms for conflict situations. By doing so, conflict actually becomes an important part of your personal development and growth. People's expectations and emotional states going into a conflict episode can affect the outcomes of these events (DiPaola, Roloff, & Peters, 2010). Read the textbox below to learn more about how college students' expectations of conflict intensity impacted their conflict interactions.

A second benefit of experiencing and managing conflict in interpersonal relationships is that it tests the strength and character of relationships more vigorously than other types of social interaction (Canary, Cupach, & Messman, 1995). When couples learn how to manage conflict effectively, they can strengthen their bond with each other and increase relationship satisfaction. Hence, individuals involved in the most rewarding relationships are able to manage conflict by

RESEARCH IN REAL LIFE: College students' expectations of conflict intensity: A self-fulfilling prophecy

Researchers examined how college students' expectations about conflict episodes affected their interactions. They predicted that students with more intense expectations about conflict episodes would experience more negative outcomes than those with less intense expectations (DiPaola, Roloff, & Peters, 2010).

- Working from a *self-fulfilling prophecy* perspective (see Chapter 2), the researchers argued that "individuals who expect an emotionally intense conflict engage in behavior that facilitates its occurrence" (p. 60).
- 203 college students provided information on specific aspects of the conflict episode: relationship with person, conflict topic, expectation of conflict intensity, actual conflict intensity, attacking behavior, and emotional interference.
- As expected, college students' expectations for conflict intensity were related positively to the extent to which the conflict episodes were emotionally upsetting and involved personal attacks.
- Individuals who *initiated* conflict perceived more emotional intensity and more attacking behaviors than the targets of the initiation.

using productive communication practices. For example, couples who manage conflict effectively and report higher relationship satisfaction refrain from aggression and focus more on confrontational (Cahn, 1992) and collaborative communication (Sillars & Wilmot, 1994).

Another way conflict can be good for individuals in relationships is because it exposes them to different perspectives. For example, think about the last time you and your roommate argued about politics, religion, or even your favorite band. The process of actively disagreeing with another person can be personally beneficial because it exposes us to views that are different from our own. When we encounter views or perspectives that are different from ours, we usually reexamine our perspectives and reflect on why we feel or think a certain way in order to defend our views. This process of self-reflection can help individuals to either (1) develop a better understanding of their current perspective, or (2) develop a new perspective linked to the interaction with the relationship partner. Conflict can benefit individuals and relationships in a number of different ways.

Conflicts are typically described as unproductive, or destructive, when individuals walk away feeling frustrated or cheated by the end result. One type of destructive conflict is known as **escalatory conflict spirals**. This type of conflict is "characterized by a heavy reliance on overt power manipulation, threats, coercion and deception" (Hocker & Wilmot, 1991, p. 34). In escalatory spirals, the conflict intensifies each time individuals communicate with each other and the conflict escalates with more destructive communication occurring each time the individuals encounter each other. Individuals might also engage in unfair fighting tactics and make attempts to "get even" with each other.

When it comes to conflict situations, not everyone likes to fight it out. Rather than fight, some individuals might engage in **de-escalatory conflict spirals** that often involve flight responses

(Hocker & Wilmot, 1991). Some individuals avoid volatile situations and instead adopt withdrawal types of behaviors. Why do individuals avoid or withdraw from conflict situations? As stated earlier in this section, individuals who are highly interdependent are more likely to experience conflict. Conversely, individuals who are not dependent on each other are less likely to engage in conflict. Perhaps relationship partners become bored with each other, apathetic about the relationship, or experience other problems in their relationship. If this is the case, then individuals might lose faith in the relationship, withdraw from interaction, and invest less time and effort into maintaining the relationship. Conflict in escalatory spirals is overt while conflict in de-escalatory spirals is covert. Individuals might avoid each other, or, when confronted, deny there is a problem. When conflict is not out in the open, it cannot be addressed or managed. Thus, expressing conflict in a covert or indirect way is clearly unproductive.

CONFLICT MANAGEMENT STYLES

Conflict can actually be healthy and productive in relationships if it is managed effectively. Researchers have identified a variety of strategies that are used by individuals. The strategies can be pictured on a continuum, with violence at one end and collaboration at the other (Hocker & Wilmot, 1991). When a conflict occurs, individuals typically decide whether they will avoid or confront it. Essentially, we make a decision to adopt various **conflict management styles** or habitual responses to conflict situations. The three most common conflict management styles individuals use to manage conflict are labeled *avoidance, competition (distributive),* and *collaboration (integrative).* Each of these conflict management styles has unique advantages and disadvantages, depending on how and when they are used.

Avoidance

Avoidance is often used by partners who deny having a problem in the first place, or by someone who is uncomfortable at the prospect of engaging in conflict. In an effort to avoid conflict with another person, relationship partners might directly or indirectly deny there is a problem, use equivocation or evasive comments to avoid discussing issues, change topics, act noncommittal on an issue, or use jokes or humor. While occasionally avoiding conflict might not be problematic for relationships, consistently avoiding conflict has been found to be counterproductive for individuals in any type of relationship. Avoidance styles of conflict management are generally not productive because they often indicate a low concern for self, others, and the relationship, and are perceived as ineffective in solving problems (Hocker & Wilmot, 1991).

See the textbox in the next column for examples of avoidance messages and the disadvantages and advantages of this style.

It is important to think about the benefits and drawbacks of using avoidance as a means of managing conflict. There are times when conflict should not be addressed because it is not the right time or place to discuss an issue with someone. Also, depending on an individual's culture, they may be more or less predisposed to avoid conflict with others. Finally, avoiding a conflict does not make it go away.

Avoidance Conflict Management Style

Sample Messages:
- **Direct Denial:** "There is no issue here, really."
- **Topic Shift:** "Let's not discuss this right now and instead focus on eating lunch."
- **Noncommittal Questions:** "What do you think we should do about this situation?"

Advantages:
- Buys time to contemplate issues
- Best to use with trivial or minor issues
- May protect each other's feelings

Disadvantages:
- Shows you do not really care about the relationship
- Problem will never be fixed or resolved
- Situation can escalate and relationship can end

Source: Adapted from Hocker and Wilmot (1991)

Competitive/Distributive

The second conflict management style is described as **competitive** or **distributive**. It involves the use of aggressive and uncooperative types of behaviors during conflict episodes. Individuals using this style pursue their own goals and objectives at the expense of others (Hocker & Wilmot, 1991). The primary goal when adopting this style is to win the argument using whatever means necessary. Individuals using this style view conflict as a battle or competition and address conflict situations in either assertive or aggressive ways. When individuals use a competitive style of conflict, they might offer personal criticism, rejection statements, hostile remarks, jokes or questions, presumptive remarks, or denial of responsibilities. This style of managing conflict is not always unproductive. Examine the table below for examples of this conflict style as well its as advantages and disadvantages.

Competitive/Distributive Conflict Management Style
Sample Messages:
• <u>Criticism</u>: "You have no sense of humor at all!"
• <u>Hostile Questions</u>: "Who really cares the most and works the hardest to make this relationship work?"
• <u>Rejection</u>: "You have no clue at all, do you?"
Advantages:
• May be good in emergency situations
• Can generate new and creative ideas
• Can illustrate the significance of the issue
Disadvantages:
• Can harm relationship partner's self-esteem
• People become entrenched in their positions and want to win
• Can lead to covert conflict and games
Source: Adapted from Hocker and Wilmot (1991)

As we can see in the textbox above, there are situations when using competition as a means of managing conflict can be beneficial. For example, when an individual in a work setting is in a time crunch, lacks the time to debate all available alternatives, and feels strongly about his or her position, adopting a competitive stance to "win" an argument may be necessary. Or, if an issue has been discussed extensively and the individuals experiencing conflict have not made any progress toward resolving the disagreement, adopting a competitive stance may facilitate conflict resolution. Also, when

individuals compete they often exert a great deal of energy, which sends a metamessage that the topic is important to the parties involved. However, competition can also damage relationships and isolate individuals who tend to avoid conflict situations. Unassertive or highly reticent individuals may avoid conflict situations when others adopt a competitive stance. Use of this style depends largely on the context, the goals of the interaction, and the unique characteristics of the individuals involved.

Collaborative/Integrative

The final conflict management style, **collaborative** or **integrative**, is often described as a productive means of managing conflict because it requires open and ongoing communication. When relationship partners adopt this style, they offer descriptive and disclosive statements during the conflict episode and, at the same time, make attempts to gain similar information from others (Hocker & Wilmot, 1991). Partners work

Collaboration is often described as a "win-win" approach to managing relationship issues because both parties walk away satisfied with the outcome.

together to develop solutions to their disagreements that are mutually satisfying. Collaboration is often described as a "win-win" approach to managing relationship issues because both parties walk away satisfied with the outcome. See the textbox below for an overview of this strategy.

Collaborative/Integrative Conflict Management Style

Sample Messages:
- Supportive Remarks: "I can see why you might want to do that."
- Concessions: "I promise not to interrupt you."
- Soliciting Criticism: "What are some of my communication weaknesses?"
- Disclosive Statement: "I was definitely in a bad mood last night."

Advantages:
- Best when solutions must be mutually satisfying
- Good for preserving the relationship
- Can lead to increased relationship satisfaction and solidarity

Disadvantages:
- Sometimes not worth the time and effort
- Can be used manipulatively
- Partners must have strong communication skills
- Partners must embrace this style

Source: Adapted from Hocker and Wilmot (1991)

This style of conflict management is not without its own set of constraints. For example, there are times when decisions need to be made quickly. Think about a football coach arguing with his assistant coaches about which play to run to win the game; it would not be realistic for him to consult each coach before sending out the final play. Another challenge with this approach is, because it takes time and effort, people may be reluctant to use it. Also, people might feel that by soliciting feedback from everyone and getting issues out in the open, it might "open a whole other can of worms." Collaboration, by its nature, encourages open expression of multiple perspectives. Sometimes encouraging others to openly express concerns can result in "tangents," lengthy discussion of unimportant or unrelated issues, and poor use of time. In other words, this approach could be viewed as time-consuming and challenging.

However, there are many benefits to using the collaborative/integrative approach to manage conflict management situations. When partners in romantic relationships report increased use of integrative styles of conflict management, relationship satisfaction increases (see, for example, Canary & Cupach, 1988; Canary & Spitzberg,

> **Collaboration, by its nature, encourages open expression of multiple perspectives.**

1989). Conversely, when partners in romantic relationships employ more distributive or avoiding styles of conflict, relationship satisfaction decreases significantly (Canary & Cupach, 1988; Canary & Spitzberg, 1989; Rands et al., 1981; Spitzberg et al., 1994; Ting-Toomey, 1983). It should come as no surprise that those individuals who employ integrative conflict management strategies with relationship partners are generally perceived as more communicatively competent (Canary & Spitzberg, 1989). Perceptions of relationship partners' competence mediate the relationship between conflict messages and relational outcomes. More specifically, Canary and Spitzberg (1989) note that "conflict messages are assessed as more or less appropriate, effective, and globally competent, and these assessments then affect relational features of trust, control mutuality, intimacy and relational satisfaction" (p. 644). Thus, use of integrative conflict management styles, which are generally perceived as more appropriate and effective, increases relationship partners' reported satisfaction and trust.

THE DARK SIDE OF CONFLICT: VERBAL AGGRESSION

When partners lack communication skills, they are more likely to employ verbally aggressive communication behaviors, often resulting in violent episodes (deTurck, 1987; Infante, Chandler, & Rudd, 1989; Infante et al., 1990). As discussed in Chapter 3, **verbal aggression** involves assaulting or criticizing another person's sense of self and typically involves attacks on one's character, competence, background, or appearance. These types of messages not only damage an individual's

perceptions of self-worth, but can also negatively affect relationship satisfaction. It is important for relationship partners to minimize the use of verbally aggressive messages during conflict episodes.

Are there times in a relationship when expressing aggression is acceptable?

Loreen Olsen (2002) conducted a qualitative investigation of romantic couples' conflict episodes to study the relationship between communication competence and aggression. In general, relationship partners felt the use of aggressive communication indicated a lack of communication competence. However, the researcher also found that there were times when individuals felt the use of aggressive communication in relationship disputes was justifiable. For example, participants described the use of aggressive communication as a constructive way to clear the air, gain their partner's attention, and reach a resolution faster. Some participants felt aggression was appropriate in certain situations because it became a relationship-changing event and permanently altered the way the couple managed conflict episodes. Olsen points out that her results should be interpreted with caution because most of her participants were female European Americans and because the participants recalled a conflict event that got out of hand. Thus, while these findings might not extend to all conflict episodes, they identify descriptive accounts of when relationship partners might view aggression as appropriate. In other words, because this study had participants recall conflict events, these results suggest that in hindsight there might have been productive results from aggressive behaviors.

MANAGING CONFLICT

In the final sections of this chapter, we offer a number of useful suggestions for approaching conflict productively, regardless of the communication situation. First, when approaching a conflict situation, you should consider the advantages and disadvantages of using avoidance or competitive or collaborative conflict management strategies. Each of these strategies requires a different set of communication behaviors and produces a variety of outcomes. From a relational perspective, collaboration is consistently viewed as the most competent way to manage conflict and often results in higher reported satisfaction for relationship partners. Conversely, avoidance and competition are regarded as less effective and appropriate strategies, often resulting in less relationship satisfaction.

Individuals should also consider the way they respond or react to problems in their relationships. Carl Rusbult and his colleagues (1982) found that when individuals experience problems in relationships, there are typically four different ways to react: exit, voice, loyalty, and neglect. These responses vary in the extent to which they are perceived as productive or unproductive and passive or active.

Exit responses typically involve threats of physical separation between partners. Consider a time when you had a conflict with another person and one of you physically left the room during the episode. Did you view this as a productive way to respond to the situation? Probably not. Exit is a passive strategy that is unproductive to conflict resolution.

Similarly, when relationship partners adopt a **neglect** response to conflict, they might avoid the relationship partner, refuse to discuss problems they are experiencing, and communicate with each other in a hostile or aggressive manner. This type of response is described as active and destructive. Rusbult and his colleagues (1982) found that college couples in satisfying relationships were less likely to use neglect and exit responses.

Refusing to discuss problems is unproductive to conflict resolution

Couples reporting higher satisfaction in their relationships were more likely to use *loyalty* and *voice* responses as a response to conflict (Rusbult et al.,

1982). When individuals adopt a **loyalty** response, they remain loyal to one another by not addressing the conflict. They may decide to "wait it out" in the hopes that, by doing so, the relationship will improve on its own. Loyalty is described as a passive strategy that could be viewed as productive or unproductive, depending on the situation. On the one hand, loyalty indicates that a partner is committed to the relationship and will stick with the other partner during both good and bad times. However, because the loyalty response is passive, and the partner adopting this response to a relationship problem is not actively addressing an issue, it could also be described as an unproductive response. As mentioned previously, avoiding conflict does little to bring it to a resolution.

A more productive response to problems in relationships is the **voice** response. When individuals adopt this response, they discuss relationship concerns openly and often offer suggestions for repairing the relationship transgression. Rusbult, Johnson, and Morrow (1986) noted that adopting a voice response during mild relationship transgressions assisted in stabilizing the relationship's health. Use of the voice response has been positively associated with both relationship satisfaction and commitment.

Not surprisingly, individual differences such as sex affect the way people approach and respond to conflict situations. Men and women differ in the extent to which they use voice and loyalty responses in their romantic relationships. Women, more so than men, use the voice response as a means of managing minor problems and use loyalty for a wide range of problems. Men were more likely to use neglect responses than women (Rusbult et al., 1986). These gender-based differences in conflict responses illustrate that some women might feel that they must be the "relationship experts" or the keeper of the relationship standards.

RESEARCH IN REAL LIFE: Gender differences and similarities in managing conflict in relationships

Research by Keener et al. (2012) examined gender differences and similarities in preference for conflict goals and strategies in same-sex friendship and opposite-sex romantic relationships. The researchers predicted that men and women would differ in their preference for communal or agentic conflict strategies and goals in same-sex friendship and opposite-sex romantic relationships (Keener, Strough, & DiDonato, 2012). Communal conflict strategies and goals are more receiver oriented and emphasize *collaboration* in solving problems in relationships (e.g., "I would talk with my friend about where he wanted to eat dinner"), while agentic conflict strategies and goals emphasize autonomy and *independence* in solving problems (e.g., "I would be firm about where I wanted to eat dinner and not back down"). Male and female college students completed personality measures and then read scenarios that depicted a conflict with a same-sex friend or an opposite-sex romantic partner. Study participants indicated whether they would respond to the situations using either communal or agentic conflict strategies or goals.

- As expected, the researchers found that female college students were more likely to use communal strategies than men when approaching conflict situations with same-sex friends.
- When approaching conflict situations with an opposite-sex romantic partner, female college students were more likely than male students to support the use of agentic conflict strategies.
- Males and females were very similar in their preference for using communal conflict strategies in romantic relationships.
- These findings illustrate the complex relationships among the relationship partner's sex, type of relationship, and preference for conflict strategies and goals.

Men and women differ in their preference for communal or agentic conflict strategies and goals in same-sex friendship and opposite-sex romantic relationships (Keener, Strough, & DiDonato, 2012). Communal conflict strategies and goals are more receiver-oriented and emphasize collaboration in managing problems while agentic conflict strategies and goals emphasize autonomy and independence. As expected, researchers found that female college students were more likely to use communal strategies than men when approaching conflict situations with same-sex friends.

A final suggestion for managing conflict effectively and appropriately has to do with using "fair fighting" tactics in relationships. When we use the term fair fighting, we are not referring to physical fighting in relationships. Instead, we are referring to the use of productive or competent communication practices that promote problem solving, compromise, and collaboration. The textbox below provides additional information regarding productive and unproductive communication responses to conflict.

To manage conflict in a productive and healthy way, it is important to adopt communication patterns that create an environment in which individuals feel comfortable sharing their concerns without being belittled, embarrassed, or ridiculed. It is important to choose an appropriate time and place to discuss the problem, listen actively when the other person is talking, and refrain from using negative listening behaviors such as pseudo-listening or defensive listening. Also, it is important be empathetic when communicating with the other person. Always try to understand the other person's feelings as you discuss the issue. Individuals often experience problems in their relationships because they do not really listen to one another. It is important to show individuals you are listening by using active listening behaviors, paraphrasing their messages, and asking relevant questions to help understand their perspective.

Productive and Unproductive Conflict Communication

Productive Communication:
- Active listening
- Using empathy (e.g., stating, "I can see why you might feel that way.")
- Choosing the right time and place to discuss the problem
- Communicating with respect (e.g., refraining from interruptions)
- Describing the problem clearly
- Using "I" statements versus blaming the other person (e.g., saying, "You did this to me.")
- Staying in the present
- Only focusing on issues relevant to the discussion

Unproductive Communication:
- Engaging in any of the listening misbehaviors (e.g., pseudo-listening, defensive listening, monopolizing, etc.)
- Choosing the wrong time and place to engage in conflict (e.g., in a public setting versus a private one)
- Being disrespectful and/or verbally aggressive
- Being ambiguous when describing the problem
- Bringing up the past or issues that are not relevant

SUMMARY

Relationships require work and effort! In this chapter we explored reasons for maintaining relationships, identified various maintenance strategies, and discussed the outcomes of strategy use. In the last sections of this chapter, we focused on managing conflict effectively as a means of stabilizing our relationships. More specifically, we focused on the definition of conflict, different types of conflict management strategies, conflict responses, and using productive communication during conflict episodes.

DISCUSSION QUESTIONS

1. Identify several relationship maintenance strategies you use to sustain your work relationships. Are they similar to those identified in this chapter?

2. Can you identify five or more skills needed to maintain effective relationships with family members, friends, or romantic partners?

3. Reflect on a recent conflict you experienced with a friend, roommate, or coworker. What was your approach to this situation? What conflict management style did you use? What was the outcome of this situation? In retrospect, do you feel that you could have handled this situation more effectively? What would you have done differently?

SELF ASSESSMENT

Revised Relationship Maintenance Scale

Directions: Please read the statements below and indicate the extent to which you believe your partner currently performs the behaviors listed in order to maintain the relationship, e.g., over the past two weeks. Use the following scale:

1 = Strongly Disagree
2 = Disagree
3 = Somewhat Disagree
4 = Neither Agree or Disagree
5 = Somewhat Agree
6 = Agree
7 = Strongly Agree

_____ 1. Acts positive with me.

_____ 2. Is upbeat when we are together.

_____ 3. Acts cheerfully with me.

_____ 4. Acts optimistically when he/she is with me.

_____ 5. Is understanding.

_____ 6. Is forgiving of me.

_____ 7. Apologizes when he/she is wrong.

_____ 8. Does not judge me.

_____ 9. Talks about his/her fears.

_____10. Is open about his/her feelings.

_____11. Encourages me to share my thoughts with him/her.

_____12. Encourages me to share my feelings with him/her.

_____13. Discusses the quality of our relationship.

_____14. Tells me how he/she feels about the relationship.

_____15. Has talks about our relationship.

_____16. Talks about future events (e.g., having children, or anniversaries, or retirement, etc)

_____17. Talks about our plans for the future.

_____18. Tells me how much I mean to him/her.

_____19. Shows me how much I mean to him/her.

_____20. Shares in the joint responsibilities that face us.

_____21. Performs his/her household responsibilities.

_____22. Helps with the tasks that need to be done.

_____23. Does not shirk his/her duties.

_____24. Includes our friends in our activities.

_____25. Does things with our friends.

_____26. Spends time with our families.

_____27. Asks a family member for help.

_____28. Turns to a family member for advice.

Scoring: higher scores indicate more frequent use of specific relationship maintenance strategies. Items 1-4 measure Positivity, items 5-8 measure Understanding, items 9-12 measure Self-Disclosure, items 13-15 measure Relationship Talks, items 16-19 measure Assurances, items 20-23 measure Tasks, and items 34-28 measure Networks.

Source: Stafford, L. (2010). Measuring relationship maintenance behaviors: Critique and development of the revised relationship maintenance scale. _Journal of Personal and Social Relationships, 28,_ 278-303.

KEY TERMS AND DEFINITIONS

ADVICE: relationship maintenance strategy that involves disclosing personal information to the relationship partner or giving or seeking advice on some issue.

ANTISOCIAL BEHAVIORS: relationship maintenance strategy that involves acting in an unfriendly, unkind, or coercive manner to maintain the level of desired intimacy relationship.

ASSURANCES: relationship maintenance behaviors that include expressing love and commitment as well as making references to the future of the relationship.

AVOIDANCE: a conflict management strategy that is often used by partners who deny having a problem in the first place, or by someone who is uncomfortable at the prospect of engaging in conflict.

AVOIDANT: relationship maintenance strategies that include dodging "sore" or difficult subjects that we should avoid discussing with our romantic partners, family members, or friends; to steer clear of conflict.

COLLABORATIVE/INTEGRATIVE: often described as a "win-win" approach to managing conflict because both parties walk away satisfied with the outcome. The goal of this conflict management strategy is to identify mutually satisfying solutions.

COMFORTING SKILLS: verbal and/or nonverbal messages enacted by a source to reduce another's emotional distress.

COMMITMENT: an important relational characteristic that refers to the desire to continue or maintain a relationship.

COMPETITIVE/DISTRIBUTIVE: a conflict management strategy that involves the use of aggressive and uncooperative types of behaviors to manage conflicts. Individuals using this style pursue their own goals and objectives at the expense of others. Win-lose approach to conflict.

CONFLICT: an expressed struggle between at least two interdependent parties who perceive incompatible goals, scarce resources, and interference from the other party in achieving their goals.

CONFLICT MANAGEMENT STYLES: habitual responses to conflict situations.

CONTROL MUTUALITY: the extent to which couples agree on who has the right to influence the other and establish relational goals.

DE-ESCALATORY CONFLICT SPIRALS: type of conflict where individuals might avoid each other, or, when confronted, deny there is a problem.

EGO SUPPORT: the ability to make others feel positive about themselves by giving compliments or engaging in other behaviors that increase self-esteem.

EMPATHY: involves the ability to see things from the other person's point of view.

EQUITY THEORY: states that a relationship is considered equitable when the ratio of inputs to outputs is equal for both individuals involved.

ESCALATORY CONFLICT SPIRALS: a type of conflict that intensifies each time individuals communicate with each other. Conflict escalates with more destructive communication occurring each time individuals communicate.

EXIT: responses to conflict situations that typically involve threats of physical separation between partners.

EXPRESSED STRUGGLE: open communication about the issue or problem in a conflict situation.

FACE MANAGEMENT: essential communication skills linked to relationship maintenance that involves avoiding communication with a partner that could threaten her/his self-esteem and being polite and considerate.

FAIR FIGHTING: the use of productive or competent communication practices that promote problem solving, compromise, and collaboration.

HUMOR: a relationship maintenance strategy that might include the use of jokes and sarcasm in either positive or negative ways to elicit laughter and smiling from one's partner.

INCOMPATIBLE GOALS: an important component of conflict that occurs when relationship partners experience opposition in attempting to reach a goal.

INTERDEPENDENCE: when individuals rely on one another and are aware of how their decisions or behaviors affect one another.

INTERFERENCE: an important component of conflict that occurs when a relationship partner perceives that someone is attempting to hamper or obstruct his or her ability to achieve a goal or objective.

JOINT ACTIVITIES: relationship maintenance strategy that involves partners doing activities together: for example, "hanging out" with each other, watching television together, taking dance lessons, and going on trips with each other.

LIKING (OR AFFINITY): relational characteristic that indicates partners feel positively toward one another.

LOYALTY: a response to conflict that involves remaining loyal to one's partner by not addressing the problem in the relationship.

MEDIATED COMMUNICATION: relationship maintenance strategy that includes exchanging email messages, letters, text messages, or phone calls with one's partner.

NEGLECT: response to conflict that might include avoiding the relationship partner, refusing to discuss problems they are experiencing, and communicating in a hostile or aggressive manner.

NO FLIRTING: a relationship maintenance strategy that is used to reduce the amount of intimacy in a relationship. One or both partners agree to refrain from exhibiting flirtatious behaviors.

OPENNESS: relationship maintenance strategy involving open and ongoing discussions partners have about the status of the relationship.

OVERBENEFITED: when an individual is not contributing as much to the relationship as her partner.

PERCEIVED SCARCE RESOURCES: anything an individual identifies as valuable or meaningful and can include, among other things: people, relationships, opportunities, material objects, or time.

POSITIVITY: a relationship maintenance strategy that involves being polite, acting cheerful and upbeat, and avoiding criticism.

RELATIONSHIP MAINTENANCE STRATEGIES: behaviors and activities used routinely and strategically to sustain desired relational qualities or to sustain the current status of the relationship.

ROUTINE MAINTENANCE BEHAVIORS: relationship maintenance behaviors that are performed every day in an effort to keep the relationship alive.

SHARING TASKS: a relationship maintenance strategy that focuses on the extent to which partners share the chores and responsibilities associated with the relationship.

SKILL SIMILARITY MODEL: proposes that relationship partners' communication skills will not change dramatically over time; therefore, it is important for partners to possess communication skills perceived as similar.

SOCIAL NETWORK: a relationship maintenance strategy that involves relationship partners spending time with mutual friends and family members.

STRATEGIC MAINTENANCE BEHAVIORS: relationship maintenance behaviors enacted to repair or fix the relationship in some way. These behaviors are often triggered by some type of transgression.

TRUST: an important quality of relationships; a strong belief that someone is reliable and honest.

UNDERBENEFITED: when a relationship partner contributes more to the relationship than he or she receives in return.

VERBAL AGGRESSION: communication that involves assaulting or criticizing another person's sense of self and typically involves attacks on one's character, competence, background, or appearance.

VOICE: a response to conflict that involves openly discussing relationship concerns and offering suggestions for repairing the relationship transgression.

REFERENCES

Ayres, J. (1983). Strategies to maintain relationships. *Communication Quarterly, 31*, 62–67.

Braiker, H. B., & Kelley, H. H. (1979). Conflict in the development of close relationships. In R. L. Burgess & T. L. Huston (Eds.), *Social exchange in developing relationships.* New York: Academic Press.

Burgoon, J. K., & Hale, J. L. (1984). The fundamental topoi of relational communication. *Communication Monographs, 51*, 19–41.

Burleson, B., & Samter, W. (1994). A social skills approach to relationship maintenance: How individual differences in communication skills affect the achievement of relationship functions. In D. J. Canary & L. Stafford (Eds.), *Communication and relational maintenance* (pp. 61–90). New York: Academic Press.

Burleson, B., & Samter, W. (1996). Similarity in the communication skills of young adults. *Communication Reports, 9*, 127–139.

Cahn, D. (1992). *Conflict in intimate relationships* (pp. 72–112). New York: The Guilford Press.

Canary, D. J., & Spitzberg, B. H. (1989). A model of perceived competence of conflict strategies. *Human Communication Research, 15*, 630–649.

Canary, D. J., & Stafford, L. (1992). Relational maintenance strategies and equity in marriage. *Communication Monographs, 59*, 243–267.

Canary, D. J. & Stafford, L. (1994). Maintaining relationships through strategic and routine interaction. In D. J. Canary & L. Stafford (Eds.), *Communication and relational maintenance* (pp. 3–22). San Diego, CA: Academic Press.

Canary, D. J. & Stafford, L.(2001). Equity in the preservation of personal relationships. In J. H. Harvey & A. Wenzel (Eds.), *Close romantic relationships: Maintenance and enhancement* (pp. 133–151). Mahwah, NJ: Lawrence Erlbaum Associates.

Canary, D. J., & Cupach, W. R. (1988). Relational and episodic characteristics associated with conflict tactics. *Journal of Social and Personal Relationships, 5*, 305–325.

Canary, D. J., Stafford, L., Hause, K. S., & Wallace, L. A. (1993). An inductive analysis of relational maintenance strategies: Comparison among lovers, friends, relatives, and others. *Communication Research Reports, 10,* 5–14.

Canary, D. J., Cupach, W. R., & Messman, S. J. (1995). *Relationship conflict.* Thousand Oaks, CA: Sage Publications.

Cialdini, R. B. (2003). *Influence: Science and practice* (4th ed.). International Edition. Boston: Allyn and Bacon.

Craig, E., & Wright, K. B. (2012). Computer-mediated relational development and maintenance on Facebook. *Communication Research Reports, 29,* 119–129.

Dainton, M. (2013). Relationship maintenance on Facebook: Development of a measure, relationship to general maintenance, and relationship satisfaction. *College Student Journal, 47,* 113–121.

Dainton, M. (2000). Maintenance behaviors, expectations for maintenance and satisfaction: Linking comparison levels to relational maintenance strategies. *Journal of Social and Personal Relationships, 17,* 827–842.

Dainton, M., & Aylor, B. (2002). A relational uncertainty analysis of jealousy, trust, and maintenance in long-distance versus geographically close relationships. *Communication Quarterly, 49,* 172–188.

Dainton, M., & Gross, J. (2008). The use of negative behaviors to maintain relationships. *Communication Research Reports, 25,* 179–191.

Dainton, M., & Stafford, L. (1993). Routine maintenance behaviors: A comparison of relationship type, partner similarity, and sex differences. *Journal of Personal and Social Relationships, 10,* 255–272.

deTurck, M. A. (1987). When communication fails: Physical aggression as a compliance gaining strategy. *Communication Monographs, 51,* 106–112.

Diggs, R. C., & Stafford, L. (1998). Maintaining marital relationships: A comparison between African American and European American individuals. In V. J. Duncan (Ed.), *Towards achieving MAAT* (pp. 192–292). Dubuque, IA: Kendall Hunt.

Dindia, K., & Canary, D. J. (1993). Definitions and theoretical perspectives on maintaining relationships. *Journal of Social and Personal Relationships, 10,* 163–173.

Dindia, K., & Baxter, L. (1987). Strategies for maintaining and repairing marital relationships. *Journal of Social and Personal Relationships, 4,* 143–158.

DiPaola, B. M., Roloff, M. E., & Peters, K. M. (2010). College students' expectations of conflict intensity: A self-fulfilling prophecy. *Communication Quarterly, 58,* 59–76.

Duck, S. (1988). *Relating to others.* Buckingham, PA: Open University Press.

Dunleavy, K., Wanzer, M. B., Krezmien, E., & Ruppel, K. (2011) Daughters' perceptions of communication with their fathers: The role of skill similarity and co-orientation in relationship satisfaction. *Communication Studies, 62,* 581–596.

Eldridge, N. S., & Gilbert, L. A. (1990). Correlates of relationship satisfaction in lesbian couples. *Psychology of Women Quarterly, 14,* 43–62.

Goodboy, A., & Bolkan, S. (2011). Attachment and the use of negative relational maintenance behaviors in romantic relationships. *Communication Research Reports, 28,* 327–336.

Goodboy, A., Myers, S., & Members of the Investigating Communication. (2010). Relational quality indicators and love styles as predictors of negative maintenance behaviors in romantic relationships. *Human Communication, 11,* 71–86.

Haas, S. M., & Stafford, L. (1998). An initial examination of maintenance behaviors in gay and lesbian relationships. *Journal of Social and Personal Relationships, 15,* 846–855.

Hocker, J. L., & Wilmot, W. W. (1991). *Interpersonal conflict* (pp. 4–42, 103–144). Dubuque, IA: Wm C. Brown Publishers.

Infante, D. A., Chandler, T. A., & Rudd, J. E. (1989). Test of an argumentative skill deficiency model of interspousal violence. *Communication Monographs, 56,* 163–177.

Infante, D. A., Sabourin, T. C., Rudd, J. E., & Shannon, E. A. (1990). Verbal aggression in violent and nonviolent disputes. *Communication Quarterly, 38,* 361–371.

Jones, R. W., & Bates, J. E. (1978). Satisfaction in male homosexual couples. *Journal of Homosexuality, 3*, 217–224.

Keener, E., Strough, J., & DiDonato, L. (2012). Gender differences and similarities in strategies for managing conflict with friends and romantic partners. *Sex Roles, 67*, 83–97.

Messman, S. J., Canary, D. J., & Hause, K. S. (2000). Motives to remain platonic, equity, and the use of maintenance strategies in opposite-sex friendships. *Journal of Social and Personal Relationships, 17*, 67–94.

Mikkelson, A. C., Myers, S. A., & Hannawa, A. F. (2011). The differential use of relational maintenance behaviors in adult sibling relationships. *Communication Studies, 62*, 258–271.

Myers, S., and Members of COM 200. (2001). Relational maintenance behaviors in the sibling relationship. *Communication Quarterly, 49*, 19–37.

Myers, S., & Weber, K. (2004). Preliminary development of a measure of sibling relational maintenance behaviors: Scale development and initial findings. *Communication Quarterly, 52*, 334–347.

Myers, S., & Goodboy, A. (2013). Using equity theory to explore adult siblings' use of relational maintenance behaviors and relational characteristics. *Communication Research Reports, 30*, 275–281.

Olsen, L. (2002). "As ugly and as painful as it was, it was effective": Individuals' unique assessment of communication competence during aggressive conflict episodes. *Communication Studies, 53*, 171–188.

Ragsdale, J. D. (1996). Gender, satisfaction level, and the use of relational maintenance strategies in marriage. *Communication Monographs, 63*, 354–369.

Rands, M., Levinger, G., & Mellinger, G. D. (1981). Patterns of conflict resolution and marital satisfaction. *Journal of Family Issues, 2*, 297–321.

Roloff, M. E., & Soule, K. P. (2002). Interpersonal conflict: A review. In M. L. Knapp & J. A. Daly (Eds.), *Handbook of interpersonal communication* (pp. 475–528). Thousand Oaks, CA: Sage Publications.

Rotenberg, K. J. & Boulton, M. (2013). Interpersonal trust consistency and the quality of peer relationships during childhood. *Social Development, 22*, 225–241.

Rusbult, C. E., Johnson, D. J., & Morrow, G. D. (1986). Determinants and consequences of exit, voice, loyalty, and neglect: Responses to dissatisfaction in adult romantic involvements. *Human Relations, 39*, 45–63.

Rusbult, C. E., Zembrodt, I. M., & Grunn, L. K. (1982). Exit, voice, loyalty, and neglect: Responses to dissatisfaction in romantic involvements. *Journal of Personality and Social Psychology, 43*, 1230–1242.

Sillars, A. L., & Wilmot, W. W. (1994). Communication strategies in conflict and mediation. In J. A. Daly and J. M. Wiemann (Eds.), *Strategic interpersonal communication* (pp. 163–190). Hillsdale, NJ: Lawrence Erlbaum.

Spitzberg, B. H., Canary, D. J., & Cupach, W. R. (1994). A competence based approach to the study of interpersonal conflict. In D. D. Cahn (Ed.), *Conflict in personal relationships* (pp. 183–202). Hillsdale, NJ: Lawrence Erlbaum.

Stafford, L., & Canary, D. J. (1991). Maintenance strategies and romantic relationship type, gender and relational characteristics. *Journal of Social and Personal Relationships, 8*, 217–242.

Stafford, L., Dainton, M., & Haas, S. (2000). Measuring routine and strategic relational maintenance: Scale revision, sex versus gender roles, and the prediction of relational characteristics. *Communication Monographs, 67*, 306–323.

Ting-Toomey, S. (1983). An analysis of verbal communication patterns in high and low marital adjustment groups. *Human Communication Research, 9*, 306–319.

chapter

9

The Dark Side of Relationships:
Deception, Embarrassment, Jealousy, Power, and Verbal Aggression

OBJECTIVES

- Define *deception* and explain interpersonal deception theory.

- Explain three reasons embarrassment occurs in social situations and identify three roles associated with embarrassment.

- Define *jealousy* and identify the six types of jealousy.

- Recall the five bases of power.

- Describe the three levels of influence.

- Explain how interpersonal conflicts turn dark by moving from argumentative messages to verbally aggressive messages.

- Recognize the impact of verbal aggression in romantic relationships, in the classroom, and in the workplace.

SCENARIO: SOUND FAMILIAR?

William was concerned his girlfriend, Katie, was cheating on him. One afternoon she left her cell phone on the table, and he grabbed it to see if he could find any information that would confirm his doubts. He noticed she had been texting a guy in her night class several times a day. He could tell by the messages they were more than friends. William also realized from reading the messages that Katie was not at the library the evening before as she had suggested. She had gone out to dinner. He contemplated how he should bring this issue up with Katie. Why would she lie?

OVERVIEW

This scenario reminds us that our interpersonal relationships can, and often do, experience a dark side. Friends and family members can deceive us, romantic partners may lie and cheat, and our colleagues and supervisors could attempt to abuse their power. As a result of these negative behaviors in our relationships, we can become angry, fearful, and perhaps even aggressive toward others. Although most of the research in communication is devoted to discussing appropriate and effective behavior to foster positive communicative outcomes, Cupach and Spitzberg challenged academic scholars to tackle problematic and disruptive communication patterns in their 1994 book, *The Dark Side of Interpersonal Communication*. The **dark side of communication** refers to negative communication exchanges that may contribute to dysfunctional interpersonal relationships. Some examples of dark communication that have been studied are: deception or lying, conflict, jealousy, relationship termination tactics, embarrassment, loneliness, co-dependency, and obsession or stalking (Spitzberg, 2006). This chapter recognizes that interpersonal relationships are not always filled with sunshine and smiles. People can, and do, lie, deceive, abuse power, and cheat in all types of relationships.

The goal of this chapter is to recognize the dark side of communication and to understand the motivation behind these behaviors. Although we cannot possibly attempt to discuss all of the communication behaviors that have been identified as potentially negative or dark, we have selected a few that most students in interpersonal communication are likely to encounter. Specifically, we will explore how and why individuals in romantic or platonic relationships deceive each other, become jealous, deal with social embarrassment, and engage in verbal aggression across a variety of contexts. To assist you in understanding how these concepts have been examined, we will discuss various studies that provide a clearer picture of these destructive forms of communicating. We will also provide suggestions on how to cope if you encounter these circumstances.

DECEPTION AND INTERPERSONAL RELATIONSHIPS

We do not typically enter into a relationship with the intent to be dishonest. However, engaging in deception in our interpersonal relationships is quite pervasive. Some researchers say it is just a common part of our daily lives. Feldman, Forrest, and Happ (2002) found that 60 percent of people lie at least once during a ten-minute conversation, and most told an average of two or three lies.

Results from this research also suggested:

- Men and women do not differ in the amount of lies told, but they do differ in content.
- Men typically lie to make themselves look better.
- Women lie most often to make the other person feel good.

Their study concluded that most people lie in everyday conversations when they are trying to appear likable and competent.

Do you know what you look like when you are lying?

Often times when we teach this class, we ask students to stop and think about how often they have already lied today. Students admit to telling lies about everything ranging from what they ate for breakfast to how they are actually feeling.

Deception is defined as "a message knowingly transmitted by a sender to foster a false belief or conclusion by a receiver" (Buller & Burgoon, 1996, p. 209). While we would like to believe that our relationships are built on truth and honesty, the reality is that friends, family members, and romantic partners deceive each other from time to time.

Consider this scenario:

> Jack had been infatuated with Kara since their freshman year of college. He was always extremely nervous about speaking with her and he came to terms with the fact that they would probably never be together. In the meantime, Jack started dating Kara's roommate, Laura. After three months, Jack actually started to fall for Laura, but his feelings for Kara remained unchanged. One evening, Kara asked Jack for a ride to the library. He agreed. In the car, Kara started expressing feelings for Jack. Jack was stunned. He just could not believe that this day had come. His heart raced as he tried to think of an appropriate reply. However, out of respect for his current relationship with Laura, he reluctantly told Kara that he would never have romantic feelings toward her.

> While a person may attempt to be strategic in creating a deceptive message, there are cues that alert the other person that the individual is being less than honest.

In this example, Jack protects his current relationship with Laura by deceiving Kara about his true feelings. Of course, we know that not all deception is done with such honorable intentions. Buller and Burgoon (1996) proposed **interpersonal deception theory** (IDT) to explain the strategic choices made when engaging in deceptive communication (1996). While a person may attempt to be strategic in creating a deceptive message, there are cues that alert the other person that the individual is being less than honest. At the same time, the receiver of the message attempts to mask, or hide, his knowledge of the deception. Rather than directly accuse the person who is lying, the person may nod their head, offer verbal prompts ("I see!" or "So what else happened?"), and generally behave in ways designed to keep the source from seeing his suspicion. In essence, it is a back-and-forth game between relational partners. The source tries to mask the deception, and the receiver tries to hide his suspicion of the deception. Now, consider this example:

> Julie and Robbie have been dating for two years. During the fall se-

mester of their junior year, Julie decided to study abroad in Scotland. Although Robbie was not happy that Julie was leaving, he was excited for her. At first, Julie was extremely homesick and spoke with Robbie every evening. As time passed, she met several new friends in Scotland and enjoyed going out dancing every night. Some evenings she had a little too much to drink and would end up kissing other men on the dance floor. Robbie continued to call Julie each night. He was becoming increasingly suspicious of Julie's behavior abroad. One evening he asked Julie, "Have you been with anyone since you've been there?"

There are three potentially deceptive responses that Julie can give.

1. She can tell an outright lie or resort to falsification: "No, I have been completely faithful." Oftentimes this requires the source to create a fictional story to explain the lie.
2. Alternatively, Julie might partially tell the truth while leaving out important details. This refers to concealment: "Well, when I go out, I do dance with other guys." We typically do this when we want to hide a secret.
3. Or Julie could engage in equivocation, or be strategically vague: "Just because I go out dancing does not necessarily mean I have to hook up with someone." This type of response is used to avoid the issue altogether.

In addition to managing the deceptive responses discussed previously (falsification, concealment,

and equivocation), interpersonal deception theory also suggests that deceivers manipulate their verbal and nonverbal behavior to appear more credible (Burgoon et al., 1996).

This manipulation is accomplished by varying the message along five fundamental dimensions:

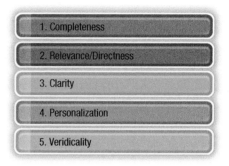

1. Completeness
2. Relevance/Directness
3. Clarity
4. Personalization
5. Veridicality

First, deceivers may vary on the completeness or extent of message details. The deceiver knows that an appropriate amount of information needs to be provided in order to be perceived as truthful by the receiver. The more practiced deceiver also realizes that specific details are probably best kept to a minimum; there is less for the receiver to challenge. When interpreting the completeness of a message, receivers may become suspicious if the information provided is too brief or vague.

A second fundamental dimension on which deceptive messages are manipulated is its relevance or directness. This refers to the extent to which the deceiver produces messages that are logical in flow and sequence, and are pertinent to the conversation. The more direct and relevant the message, the more it is perceived as truthful. Two indicators of potential deception are when a person goes off on a tangent in response to a question or is cautious in his or her response.

The extent to which the deceiver is clear, comprehensible, and concise is a third dimension of message manipulation. The **clarity** dimension varies along a continuum from very clear to completely ambiguous. The more evasive or vague a message is, the more cause there is for a receiver to probe for additional information and clarification.

A fourth dimension involves the **personalization** of the information. The extent to which the deceiver takes ownership of the information may vary. If the deceiver relies on verbal distancing or non-immediate communication, he will be perceived as less truthful. For example, the suggestions "everyone goes out during the week here" and "I just miss you so much that I am just trying to keep myself busy," are two examples that disassociate the deceiver with the behavior.

The last dimension is the extent to which the deceiver appears to be truthful, or the **veridicality** of the message. This dimension is twofold: truthfulness (verbal) and believability (nonverbal). First, the message is constructed based on the objective truth value reported by the source. In other words, to what extent does the deceiver consider the message to be truthful? Next, the believability of the message is judged by the receiver. In evaluating the truthfulness of a message, receivers often rely on nonverbal cues that are the result of our body language.

Examples of behaviors believed to signal deception include increased blinking, speech errors, higher voice pitch, and enlarged pupils (Zuckerman & Driver, 1985). These unconscious behaviors are often referred to as **leakage cues**, and while deceptive individuals attempt to control these behaviors, others may be able to detect their dishonesty.

WHY DO WE LIE?

Based on the high percentage of people who report engaging in deception, the question becomes, why are we so prone to lying? When asked, most people suggest that they lie to make themselves appear more admirable. As we stated earlier, research has found that we lie to appear competent and likable to others (Feldman, Forrest, & Happ, 2002). Therefore, it is not unusual for individuals to lie about their own personal attributes such as appearance, personality, income, career, grades, and past relational outcomes in an attempt to attract another person (Rowatt, Cunningham, & Druen, 1999).

People often tell lies to make themselves seem more attractive to someone new.

According to the deception literature (Camden, Motley, & Wilson, 1984; DePaulo, Kashy, Kirkendale, Wyer, & Epstein, 1996), there are three types of lies that people tell:

1. Lying to harm others
2. Lying to protect self
3. Lying to spare others

Understanding the ways in which messages are manipulated is one way to enhance your ability to detect deception.

Lying to Harm Others

The first type of deception, lying to harm others, is often the most damaging type of lie in interpersonal relationships. These types of lies are done to intentionally hurt others by distorting information, fabricating stories, or deliberately omitting important information. Perhaps the best example of lies designed to harm others are those seen during political campaign ads. Specific information about one's opponent is strategically distorted and manipulated in an attempt to damage his or her candidacy.

Lying to Protect Self

A more egotistical goal refers to lying to protect self. The goal of this type of lie is to make oneself look good. This can be accomplished by exaggerating praise and/or omitting weaknesses. In a study that examined sexual lies among college students, lying about the number of previous sexual partners emerged as the most frequently told lie (Knox et al. 1993). Regardless of whether the number of sexual partners was inflated to appear more experienced or reduced to appear more "pure," the goal of the lie was to enhance one's image.

Lying to Spare Others

The most common type of lie is to spare others. In the movie *A Few Good Men*, Jack Nicholson's character, Colonel Nathan R. Jessup, states, "You can't handle the truth." In this situation, Col. Jessup emphasizes that sometimes we lie in order to spare or protect others from the truth. Perhaps we want to avoid hurting the other person's feelings or damaging his self-esteem. At other times we may "stretch the truth" or omit details for the good of the relationship.

DETECTING DECEPTION

Understanding the ways in which messages are manipulated is one way to enhance your ability to detect deception. Let's discuss how we can utilize nonverbal and verbal strategies to detect deception. In a study on deceptive communication practices (Park et al., 2002), 202 college students were asked to recall a time when they had caught another person being deceptive. While a variety of discovery mechanisms were identified in the study, the three most prominent ones include the strategies labeled:

1. third-party information;
2. physical evidence; and
3. confessions.

Third-party information involves information being revealed by a person outside the relationship. Suppose a teenager wants to go to a party while his parents are out of town, but he knows his parents would not approve. He lies to his parents and tells them that he is spending the night at his friend's house in case they call home while he is at the party. When his mother speaks with the friend's mother a few days later and thanks her for allowing him to stay at their house, the friend's mother reveals that he never spent the night. Thus the lie is revealed by an outside party.

Sometimes we are able to detect deception by doing our best Sherlock Holmes impression and looking for **physical evidence** or objects/artifacts that reveal one's deception. For instance, on an episode of *Grey's Anatomy*, Addison, Dr. Shepherd's wife, discovered a pair of black panties that clearly did not belong to her in her husband's tuxedo pocket. The physical evidence swiftly revealed Derek's betrayal and finally ended the fragile marriage. The classic lipstick-on-the-collar shtick is another familiar Hollywood portrayal of deception detection.

Another method by which deception is detected is via **confessions** or a verbal acknowledgement of the transgression made by the deceiver. **Solicited confessions** are often offered as the result of direct questioning or confrontation. Suppose you heard that your best friend went on a ski trip with a group of people the same weekend that the two of you had planned to go to a professional hockey game. Initially, he told you that he could not go to the game because he was swamped with homework. When you follow up and tell him that you heard he had gone skiing that same weekend, he feels guilty and confesses his lie. While some confessions are solicited, at other times these declarations come from out of the blue. Suppose your significant other spontaneously confesses that she has been reading your emails without your knowledge. Nothing caused you to suspect that she was engaging in this behavior, yet she decided to make an **unsolicited confession**. An important point to note is that we are often able to detect deception using a combination of cues—in fact, many people report a combination of verbal and nonverbal signals as tipping them off about dishonesty.

ANALYZING DECEPTIVE MESSAGES

Deception and lying are multidimensional constructs. Key components to consider when analyzing a deceptive message include: the importance of the relationship, the importance of the information to the relationship, and the costs and rewards associated with the lie. Not all lies are created equal. Consider the following three sets of questions posed by Knapp and Vangelisti (2006):

1. What is the potential outcome of the lie? Can it potentially benefit our relationship, or one of us, individually?
2. Based on the rules we have established for our relationship, is it reasonable and just for me to tell a lie? Or am I violating one of the spoken or unspoken expectancies that we have for our relationship? What lies would we agree upon that are acceptable versus unacceptable?
3. Am I telling a lie in an attempt to protect my partner from being harmed? If I were to be caught telling the lie, would my partner understand my justification for telling the lie?

This research suggests that when we decide to lie, we must consider what will happen if my lie is detected. In other words, how will this effect the relationship? Often times, lying is a "deal breaker" for individuals in a relationship. Where is your lying threshold? Where is your partners lying threshold? What is the most important determinant in ending a relationship as a result of deception? Knapp and Vangelisti (2006) state that the more importance the receiver attaches to the information being lied about, the greater the chance that he or she will decide to end the relationship.

As you know, deception does not necessarily mean relationship termination. Interestingly, several scholars have found that despite partner deception, most romantic couples report staying together (see McCornack & Levine, 1990; Planap, Rutherford, & Honeycutt, 1988; and Bachman & Guerrero, 2006).

In all our relationships, we establish implicit and explicit rules. When these rules are violated it is considered a relational transgression. Partner deception is considered a transgression. Transgressions do not always mean there will be relationship termination. How we choose to verbally and nonverbally communicate after a transgression influences individuals' interpretation and response. For example, Horan (2012) found those individuals who receive high amounts of affection from their partners report being less hurt and ruminating less, compared to those relationships in which partners do not receive a lot of affection.

Now that you have a better understanding of the concept of deception, it is our hope that you will be strategic in your analysis of these messages and take time to understand why you and others choose to lie. Understanding these components can assist in developing healthy and effective interpersonal relationships. Now, we will turn our attention to another potential negative communication exchange, embarrassment.

EMBARRASSMENT: WHY DID I SAY THAT?

Can you remember a time when you had a huge crush on someone, and when you finally had the opportunity to talk to them and make that great first impression, something went horribly wrong and you ended up putting your foot in your mouth? Or have you ever told a joke at a party and nobody laughed? In these types of situations, we often experience social embarrassment. Recall our discussion in Chapter 2 regarding the role of self-presentation in relationships. When we perceive that our self-esteem has been threatened or if we have presented what we perceive to be a negative view of the self to others, **embarrassment** occurs. Our sense of identity is at stake if the response to our behavior is not what we expected.

Gross and Stone (1964) proposed that embarrassment emerges as the result of three factors that occur in social interaction. These can be summarized by a loss of or threat to our identity, confidence and/or poise.

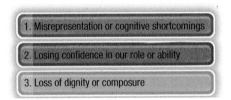

1. Misrepresentation or cognitive shortcomings
2. Losing confidence in our role or ability
3. Loss of dignity or composure

Misrepresentations or cognitive shortcomings may cause us to feel embarrassment. Have you ever called someone by the wrong name or forgotten how you know someone? Losing confidence in our role or ability in a social situation can also cause us to experience discomfort. Sometimes we script out an interaction, such as texting someone new, and the conversation does not turn out like we had anticipated. Finally, a loss of dignity, or composure, can cause us to become "red-faced." Examples of this may include tripping as you are making your way across the stage during commencement or discovering that your pants are unzipped after you have just had a conversation with your boss. More recent research by Sharkey and Stafford (1990) conceptualized six types of embarrassment. See Table 9.1 for types, examples and scenarios.

Our Role in Embarrassment

It is easy to see why we would be embarrassed in any of these situations, even if we were in control of our own behavior. We can just as easily become uncomfortable in those situations where we are the silent observer. Sattler (1965) identified three roles that exist in embarrassing social situations:

1. Agent
2. Recipient
3. Observer

Table 9.1 Sharkey and Stafford's Six Types of Embarrassment

Types of Embarrassment	Example	Scenario
Privacy Violations	Part of body is exposed accidentally; invasion of space; property;	Having a wardrobe malfunction
Lack of Knowledge or Skill	Forgetfulness; experiencing failure	Calling someone by the wrong name
Criticism and Rejection	Someone criticizes you in public and causes you to be the center of attention	Someone bullying a kid on the school bus by calling him/her names
Appropriate image	Body image, clothing or personal artifacts	Owning an outdated cell phone
Awkward Acts	Ungraceful actions; clumsiness	Falling on your way up to a stage to get an award
Environment	Being at the wrong place at the wrong time	Teenagers being seen with their parents

As an **agent**, we are responsible for our own embarrassment, perhaps by accidentally swearing in front of our grandmother or unexpectedly burping during an important interview lunch.

In other situations, we are the **recipients**, or targets, of embarrassing communication. Examples of this type of embarrassment might include your best friend revealing to your secret crush that you are attracted to him and your mother telling your friend about the time you ran naked around the neighborhood when you were three years old.

Finally, it is likely that you can recall a situation where you were simply a bystander, or **observer**, of another's embarrassment and experienced feelings of discomfort yourself. In these situations, we often offer an awkward comment, express a reassuring remark, or simply attempt to ignore the situation.

Responding to Embarrassment

How we respond to embarrassment can impact the overall impact on our interpersonal encounters. Edelmann (1985) identified three primary types of messages individuals use in response to embarrassing encounters:

1. accounts;
2. apologies; and
3. jokes.

Accounts provide a potential explanation for the cause of the embarrassing situation. Suppose you arrive at class only to discover that you forgot an important assignment that was due. You decide to speak with your instructor and explain that you have been overwhelmed with group projects in two other classes and with searching for a job. In some instances, we may feel the need to apologize for the embarrassing behavior.

Apologies are attempts to identify the source of blame for the incident. Suppose you accidentally revealed to your friend that she has not been included in the group's plans for the weekend. As you stumble over your words, you might comment, "I'm sorry. I didn't realize until now that you weren't invited," or "I didn't make the plans. They invited me along and I just assumed you were included, I'm so sorry". These responses are made with the hope that your friend will forgive you for the non-invitation.

Joking involves using humor to create a more light-hearted response to a situation. At the 2006 Academy Awards, Jennifer Garner tripped over her dress as she approached the podium. To cover her embarrassment, she joked, "I do all my own stunts." Similarly in 2013 Jennifer Lawrence tripped on her gown when she was making her way to the stage to accept her Best Actress Academy Award. The crowd gave her a standing ovation. When she arrived at the mic she stated, "You are standing up because you're feeling bad that I fell, and that's embarrassing".

Sometimes one embarrassing moment seems like it will last forever.

According to **arousal relief theory** (Berylne, 1969), use of humor in embarrassing or difficult situations often evokes positive affective responses that can help individuals diffuse anxiety or stress. The next time that you find yourself becoming embarrassed in a social situation, remember—everyone experiences this discomfort at one time or another. While at the time it may appear to be a black cloud that hangs over your head, it is likely that these feelings will be temporary and short-lived. However, there are other dark aspects of interpersonal communication the impact of which may not be so minimal on our interactions and relationships. Next, let's consider another negative communication exchange, jealousy.

JEALOUSY IN INTERPERSONAL RELATIONSHIPS

Another aspect of interpersonal relationships that has received a lot of attention in the literature is jealousy. Jealousy causes us to experience a variety of emotions and sometimes causes us to communicate or react in ways that we normally would not. Consider some of the things that can cause us to experience jealousy:

- Your best friend recently went away to college. He sends you text messages describing all the fun he is having with his new roommate and other friends he has made in the dorm.
- A coworker talks about all the activities that she does with her young children. You wonder how she is able to find the time to fin-

ish her work and spend so much time with her kids, especially because you see yourself as a neglectful parent.
- Your relationship partner has been spending a great deal of time lately with a new friend and has expressed repeatedly how much he likes this friend.

In situations like those described in the scenarios above, it is normal to experience feelings of anger or sadness. Maybe we even feel a little bit envious or resentful. **Jealousy** has been defined as "a protective reaction to a perceived threat to a valued relationship, arising from a situation in which the partner's involvement with an activity and/or another person is contrary to the jealous person's definition of their relationship" (Hansen, 1985, p. 713). It is important to point out that this definition addresses the fact that jealousy can be experienced in various types of relationships, not just romantic, and can be induced by various issues or situations.

The next time that you find yourself becoming embarrassed in a social situation, remember—everyone experiences this discomfort at one time or another.

Types of Jealousy in Relationships

Bevan and Samter (2004) examined six different types of jealousy, three that are experienced as a result of the type of the relationship, and three that are based on the issues experienced between partners.

Types of Relationships

- **Friend jealousy** is typically the result of an individual's relationship with a friend. In this situation we often become frustrated and perceive them as being "taken" away from us.
- **Family jealousy** is the result of a partner's relationship with family members. An example of this may occur when we perceive our partner is spending too much time with their sibling or parent.
- **Romantic jealousy** is the result of a partner's relationship with another person and is associated with perceived intimacy between two people.

Issues in Relationships

- **Power jealousy** arises when we believe someone else has the ability to influence our partner. For example, if our partner had to make a difficult life decision about their job and was being influenced by their boss or colleague, we may experience power jealousy.
- **Activity jealousy** emerges when our relational partner dedicates time to various hobbies or interests. Have you ever become frustrated by the amount of attention that a friend dedicates to Xbox, fraternity or sorority activities, or sports? In these instances, the activities are perceived as a threat to your relationship.
- **Intimacy jealousy** is the result of the exchange of intimate or private information that a partner may share with a third party, someone not in the relationship. Suppose your significant other reveals to his best friend that he is undergoing a series of medical tests, but says nothing to you. When his best friend asks you how your spouse is feeling, you realize that he neglected to confide in you about his health problems. Your discovery of the "concealed" information results in feelings of intimacy jealousy. Later, you may discover that your partner simply did not want you to worry, and decided not to tell you until the results of the test were returned.

© Nicoleta Ionescu/Shutterstock.com

Have you ever found information on your partners phone that he/she has been concealing from you?

Why Does Jealousy Occur?

An extensive body of research on this topic has concluded that individuals evoke or suppress feelings of jealousy to obtain a variety of goals or objectives in their personal relationships. What causes us to experience feelings of jealousy? Guerrero and Anderson (1998) suggest that there are at least six jealousy-related goals.

1. **MAINTAIN THE PRIMARY RELATIONSHIP.** First, we become jealous in situations where we wish to maintain the primary relationship. Specifically, we are concerned with preserving the relationship. When individuals are interested in maintaining a current relationship, they will often compare themselves to a rival and try to appear more rewarding to their partner by compensating for any perceived shortcomings (Guerrero & Afifi, 1999). Making oneself appear more "attractive" than the competition (also referred to as **compensatory restoration**) may be an effective maintenance strategy—up to a point. Making incessant comparisons to rivals may cause your partner to perceive you as being desperate or insecure.

2. **PRESERVING ONE'S SELF-ESTEEM.** A second goal associated with jealousy is focused on preserving one's self-esteem. This jealousy goal is concerned with maintaining one's pride and with feeling good about oneself. Individuals who are concerned about protecting their self-esteem rarely seek out circumstances that may threaten how they view themselves (Kernis, 1995). Therefore, it comes as no surprise that the more an individual is focused on preserving his or her self-esteem, the more likely he or she is to avoid or deny jealous situations (Guerrero & Afifi, 1999). Since jealousy has a negative connotation in our culture and is related to perceptions of "weakness," it makes sense that these individuals are less likely to question or scrutinize their partners' behavior or to communicate jealous feelings.

3. **REDUCING UNCERTAINTY ABOUT THE RELATIONSHIP.** Another goal of jealousy is to reduce uncertainty about the relationship. The purpose of this type of jealousy is to help an individual learn where one stands in the relationship, predict the future of the relationship, and understand how the other partner perceives the relationship. This was the only goal found to predict open and nonaggressive communication between partners (Guerrero & Afifi, 1999). If the purpose of jealousy is to reduce uncertainty and learn more about the partner, it makes sense that open and direct communication is essential to accomplishing this goal.

4. **REDUCING UNCERTAINTY ABOUT A RIVAL RELATIONSHIP.** A fourth goal involves reducing uncertainty about a rival relationship. This jealousy goal determines the threat of the competition, or how serious the rival relationship is. Individuals who focus on this goal often resort to indirect strategies, such as spying, checking up on the partner, or questioning the rival about the situation (Guerrero & Afifi, 1999). They may do this to save face with their partners so they are not perceived as "jealous" people.

5. **RE-ASSESS THE RELATIONSHIP.** When individuals are questioning the status of a relationship, they may use jealousy in an attempt to re-assess the relationship. This goal is concerned with comparing the cost with the benefits associated with the relationship. When analyzing this goal, Guerero and Afifi (1999) found that individuals typically engage in indirect strategies such as avoidance, distancing, or making the partner feel jeal-

ous. Essentially, individuals are seeking clarity on how their partners feel about them in the relationship. What does it mean when a partner responds to a jealous act? Perhaps you can use the reaction to a jealous event as a way to have further dialogue about the relationship. Certainly more direct communication is necessary to determine a partners status in a relationship.

6. RESTORING EQUITY THROUGH RETALIATION. Do you know anyone who purposely evoked jealousy to get back at someone or to make his or her partner feel bad? The last goal of jealousy refers to this idea of restoring equity through retaliation. The purpose of evoking this type of jealousy response is to show the partner what it is like to experience negative emotions and to hurt the person as retribution for something the partner has done.

There are clearly a number of different reasons that relationship partners attempt to evoke jealousy responses from their partners. Are you curious to know how you may evoke jealousy? We have included a scale at the end of this chapter to measure the extent to which individuals evoke jealousy behaviors. Not surprisingly, experiencing heightened amounts of jealousy in relationships negatively affects relationship satisfaction (Guerrero & Eloy, 1992). Thus, it is important for you to understand the reasons why we evoke feelings of jealousy in others and, at the same time, to refrain from using tactics or strategies that cause others to feel jealous.

Characteristics Associated with Jealousy and Jealousy-evoking Behavior

Researchers have examined many questions associated with jealousy, including: How does someone become jealous? What types of re-

RESEARCH IN REAL LIFE: Sex differences in jealousy at work

When a rival co-worker communicates with your supervisor, do you experience feelings of jealousy? More interestingly, would they be different for men and women? Researchers were interested in determining which attributes of a rival would induce the most jealousy (Buunk, Goor, & Solano, 2010). Following more of an evolutionary perspective, the authors assumed jealousy is more automatic and unconscious. The researchers assessed four specific attributes:

1. Social power and dominance or the extent to which one has more authority.
2. Physical attractiveness or beauty
3. Social-communal attributes, such as being a great listener
4. Physical dominance or strength

In same sex supervisors, results found that men experienced greater jealousy when their rivals had higher levels of perceived dominance or authority. For females, the level of perceived physical attractiveness of their rival resulted in higher levels of jealousy.

lationships are more likely to evoke jealousy? What are the results of feeling jealous? Researchers have identified low levels of self-esteem and feelings of insecurity to be significant predictors of jealousy (McIntosh, 1989).

Another study found that jealousy is more likely to occur in relationships of shorter duration (for less than one year) than in those of longer duration (more than one year) (Knox, Zusman, Mabon, & Shriver, 1999). What conditions are most likely to elicit jealous reactions? A 1999 study (Knox et al.) found that talking to or about a previous partner is the action or topic that is most likely to evoke jealousy.

Are you guilty of attempting to make others feel jealous? Psychologists were concerned with what motivated individuals to engage in these jealousy-induction behaviors. They define **romantic jealousy-induction** as "a strategic behavioral process to elicit reactive, romantic jealousy from a partner in order to achieve a specific goal" (Mattingly, Whitson, & Mattingly, 2012, p. 276).

Their study revealed five motivations for romantic jealousy-induction:

1. To test the partner's love or strengthen the current relationship
2. To engage in revenge against the partner
3. To gain power or control over the partner
4. Because of a preoccupation with relationship security
5. Because of low self-esteem

Similarly, communication scholars have explored specific relationship types to predict these intentional jealousy-evoking behaviors. Do affection and love influence these behaviors? Goodboy, Horan, and Booth-Butterfield (2012) found that the amount of affection received from romantic partners is inversely related with jealousy-evoking behaviors. This affection was measured by Floyd and Morman's (1998) Affectionate Communication Index, which examines the extent to which partners believed their partners provided affection across three dimensions: *verbally* (e.g., "saying I love you"), *nonverbally*, (e.g., "holding hands"), and *supportive affection* (e.g., "praising his/her with compliments"). Therefore, these jealousy-evoking behaviors are related to the amount of affection in our rela-

tionships. So, what about love? The authors further explored Lee's (1973) typology of love styles. These six styles uniquely explain how individuals experience romantic love:

1. **Eros** lovers are described as passionate and intense; they have a strong commitment to the relationship sexually and value security, physical attraction, and beauty.
2. **Ludus** lovers want to "win" as many partners as possible and see love as a "game." They value having fun and tend to have shorter relationships as a result.
3. **Storge** lovers value love that is established through common interests and friendships. They tend to see love as developing over time with a strong commitment to the relationship.
4. **Pragma** lovers are logical and realistic about their partners. They typically are looking for certain criteria that match their goals.
5. **Mania** lovers have a strong need to be loved and often develop obsessive and possessive tendencies. They value a strong attachment to their partners.
6. **Agape** lovers are described as selfless and committed to the relationship partner. They tend to put their partner's needs above their own and are described as altruistic and sacrificial.

Results from their study revealed that only the *ludus* and *mania* love styles were positive predictors of jealousy-evoking behavior.

Gender Differences and Jealousy

So, who is more jealous, males or females? Studies have found no significant differences between males and females with regard to one gender being more likely to emerge as a primary source of jealousy (Knox, Zusman, Mabon, & Shriver, 1999) or in the amount or duration of intensity of feeling jealousy (Pines & Friedman, 1998). However, research has shown that males and females do experience jealousy for different reasons.

For example:

- Males are more likely to become jealous as a result of sexual infidelity, whereas females become more jealous over emotional infidelity in heterosexual relationships (Buss et al., 1992; Frederick & Fales, 2014). **Sexual infidelity** refers to having sexual relations with someone outside of one's romantic relationship while **emotional infidelity** refers to engaging in an intense and deep emotional attachment to someone outside of the romantic relationship (Carpenter, 2012). Sexual infidelity may involve intercourse, oral sex, kissing, and sexual touch. Emotional infidelity typically involves the sharing of personal self-disclosures.
- Gay men, lesbian women, and bisexual men and women did not differ significantly on whether they were more upset over emotional or sexual infidelity (Frederick & Fales, 2014).
- Studies have found the reactions to different types of jealousy are similar for males and females (Dijkstar & Buunk, 2004). That is, emotional infidelity typically evoked responses of anxiety, worry, distrust, and suspicion, while responses to sexual infidelity were associated with feelings of sadness, rejection, anger, and betrayal.
- Women experience more jealousy in response to a physically attractive threat, while

men become more jealous when the threat is perceived as being more socially dominant (Dijkstra & Buunk, 1998). Evolutionary psychologists argue the reason for this gender difference is due to the fact that our society typically rates a female's value in a relationship as determined by her physical attractiveness, whereas the relationship value of males is often evaluated by their status or dominance (Townsend & Levy, 1990).

Therefore, examining sexual and emotional infidelity can help us understand how males and females respond to jealousy.

Coping with Jealousy

The way people initially express feelings of jealousy to a partner will ultimately influence how the partner responds. Understanding positive emotional responses can help our interpersonal relationships when dealing with jealous interactions. Yoshimura (2004) found that responses such as **integrative communication** (e.g., directly talking about the jealousy issue) and **negative affect expression** (e.g., crying) were perceived as evoking positive emotional responses by the partner (see Table 9.2). In other words, expressing your feelings openly and directly with your partner and appearing hurt by the threat produces positive emotional and behavior outcomes. This same study also found that negative emotional outcomes were more likely to produce violent behavior and manipulation attempts by the other partner. See Table 9.2 for a complete list of the ways people respond to feelings of jealousy.

While we have explored the responses to jealousy, let us take a moment to consider the role

Table 9.2 Communicative Responses to Jealousy

Strategy	Definition/Examples
1. Negative affect expression	Nonverbal expressions of jealousy-related affect that the partner can see.
	Examples: acting anxious when with the partner, appearing hurt, wearing "displeasure" on face, crying in front of the partner
2. Integrative communication	Direct, nonaggressive communication about jealousy with the partner.
	Examples: disclosing jealous feelings to the partner, asking the partner probing questions, trying to reach an understanding with the partner, reassuring the partner that "we can work it out"
3. Distributive communication	Direct, aggressive communication about jealousy with the partner.
	Examples: accusing the partner of being unfaithful, being sarcastic or rude toward the partner, arguing with the partner, bringing up the issue over and over again to "bombard" the partner
4. Active distancing	Indirect, aggressive means of communicating jealousy to the partner.
	Examples: giving the partner the "silent treatment," storming out of the room, giving the partner cold or dirty looks, withdrawing affection and sexual favors
5. Avoidance/denial	Indirect, nonaggressive communication that focuses on avoiding the jealousy-invoking issue, situation, or partner.
	Examples: denying jealous feelings when confronted by the partner, pretending to be unaffected by the situation, decreasing contact with the partner, avoiding jealousy-evoking situations
6. Violent communication/threats	Threatening or actually engaging in physical violence against the partner.
	Examples: threatening to harm the partner if he/she continues to see the rival, scaring the partner by acting as if he/she were about to hit him/her, roughly pulling the partner away from the rival, pushing or slapping the partner
7. Signs of possession	Publicly displaying the relationship to others so they know the partner is "taken."
	Examples: putting an arm around the partner and saying he or she is "taken," constantly introducing the partner as a "girl/boyfriend," telling potential rival of plans to be married, kissing the partner in front of potential rival
8. Derogating competitors	Making negative comments about potential rivals to the partner and to others.
	Examples: "badmouthing" the rival in front of the partner and his or her friends, expressing disbelief that anyone would be attracted to the rival
9. Relationship threats	Threatening to terminate or de-escalate the primary relationship or to be unfaithful.
	Examples: threatening to end the relationship if the partner continues to see the rival, threatening infidelity
10. Surveillance/restriction	Behavioral strategies designed to find out about or interfere with the rival relationship.
	Examples: spying or checking up on the partner, looking through the partner's belongings for evidence of a rival relationship, pressing the redial button to see who the partner called last

Source: Adapted from Guerrero & Anderson, 1998; Guerrero, Anderson, Jorgensen, Spitzberg, & Eloy, 1995.

that perceived influence and power can play in causing us to experience envy.

INTERPERSONAL POWER AND VERBAL AGGRESSION

A possible factor contributing to our tendency to encounter jealousy in relationships may be explained by the interpersonal power perceived by relational partners. In this section, we will take a closer look at the potential implications of power in relationships and explore power's relationship to verbal aggression and violence. **Power** can be defined as one's ability to influence others to behave in ways they normally might not. What types of power impact our relationships with others?

Types of Power

French and Raven (1960) identified five types of power that individuals typically use when they are attempting to influence others. The five classic power bases are:

1. **Reward power** is based on a person's perception that the source of power can provide rewards. Example: *I'll clean up the apartment and maybe my roommate will invite me to go with him on the ski trip with his family this weekend.*
2. **Coercive power** focuses on the perceived ability of the source to punish or to enact negative consequences. Example: *I have to finish this report today or I know my boss will make me come in this weekend.*
3. **Legitimate power** is centered on the perception that the source has authority be-

cause of a particular role that she plays in the relationship or a title that she holds. Example: *Because I'm the mommy, and I said so.*
4. **Referent power** is based on a person's respect, identification, and attraction to the source. Example: *No matter how ridiculous I feel, I will dress up in a costume and go to this Halloween party because I am really attracted to you and want you to like me.*
5. **Expert power** is grounded in the perception that the source possesses knowledge, expertise, or skills in a particular area. Example: *I will listen to what she says about our household budget because she is the financial wizard in the family.*

French and Raven propose that it is the receivers' perception of the source of the message that is the key to analyzing power. We stated in earlier chapters that effective interpersonal communication is receiver-based. Thus, it is important to consider the receiver's perception of the source to predict future interactions. But do individuals have power if we do not give it to them? Based on the important role that receiver perception plays in the communication process, probably not.

Consider the following scenario:

Alan had very little respect for his mother. At thirteen years old, he was completely out of control. He skipped school, ignored his mother's rules, and even hit his mother on several occasions when she attempted to discipline him. Finally, his mother had reached the breaking point. One night she caught Alan doing drugs with his friends in the basement. She reported Alan to the authorities and hoped that it would help him get back on track. But his misbehavior continued.

In this instance, Alan's mother should have legitimate power over him. However, his behavior is an obvious indicator that he does not perceive her to have any power in the relationship. Even when his mother attempts to utilize coercive power by calling the police, it does nothing to change Alan's perception. His inability to view his mother as having reward, coercive, or legitimate power even results in Alan's occasional use of physical violence. If you do not perceive your relational partner as having the power, then it is unlikely that you would comply with any requests he or she makes.

In Chapter 7 we discussed the distinctions between physical, social, and task attraction. Understanding the relationship between attraction and power may help explain why some influence attempts are successful whereas others fail. Depending on the perceived power base, receivers will alter their perceptions of the source's attractiveness and determine the level of acceptance or resistance in response to the request. Suppose your best friend uses a threat, or coercive power, in an attempt to influence you. This will typically decrease your level of perceived attraction for your friend, and chances are that you will resist their request. On the other hand, if you perceive that the friend has the power to reward you as a result of the request, it is likely that you would find them more attractive and would have minimal resistance to the request. These same principles can be applied in a variety of relationships. What if your mother told you that if you cleaned your room she would reward you with $5.00 and a trip to the movies? You would be more willing to agree to her request and you would find her to be more interpersonally attractive than if she would have said, "If you don't clean your room, you will have to pay me $5.00 to do it for you, and you'll be grounded from the movies for the next week." Threats and coercive behavior typically breed resentment and result in higher levels of resistance.

Relationship between Power and Interpersonal Influence

To better understand the impact of power in our decisions of whether to comply with requests made in our interpersonal relationships, we look at the three levels of influence that can be achieved. These include compliance, identification, and internalization (Kelman, 1961).

1. **Compliance** occurs when an individual agrees to a request because he can see a potential reward or punishment for doing so. This level of influence is likely to persuade someone to do something, but his motivation is typically low and the change in the behavior is usually quite temporary. When you tell your roommate that she can have your car for the weekend if she drives you to the airport and she later complies with your request, you have influenced her at the compliance level. In this example, the only reason the roommate complies with the request is to obtain a reward.

Table 9.3 Types of Power and Their Impact on Levels of Influence

Types of Power	Levels of Influence		
	Compliance	Identification	Internalization
Reward	X		
Coercive	X		
Legitimate	X		
Referent	X	X	X
Expert	X	X	X

2. If a person decides to agree to an influence attempt because she recognizes the potential benefits of doing so, or perhaps she wishes to establish a relationship with the source, then **identification** has occurred. A student agrees to his teacher's recommendation that he take honors level courses next semester to help prepare him for college instead of "cruising" in the regular classes with his friends. In this instance, individuals are typically more motivated to comply because they agree with the source's goals, interests, and values.

3. The last level of influence, **internalization**, is employed when an individual adopts a behavior because it is internally rewarding. In other words, it feels like the right thing to do. This type of influence is successful because the person sees the requested behavior as fitting within his or her existing value system. The individual agrees to the behavior because he intrinsically believes it should be done, not just because someone told him to do so. An example of this might be a spouse who takes on the responsibility of extra household or childcare duties in or-

der to assist a partner who is experiencing a difficult time at work. In this instance, the person agrees to the request because of the value placed on family and the level of commitment made to the relationship. Table 9.3 summarizes the level of influence that can be achieved as a result of each of the five types of power.

Power versus Dominance in Relationships

What is the difference between power and dominance? Burgoon and Dillman (1995) argue, "Because power is broadly defined as the ability to exercise influence by possessing one or more power bases, dominance is but one means of many for expressing power" (p. 65). In other words, power is the potential to influence another's behavior, whereas **dominance** is a mechanism typically associated with attempts to express power and take control in a relationship. What is the relationship between talking and influence? One study found that the more an individual talks, the more opportunities he has to gain influence over others (Daly, McCroskey, & Richmond, 1977). A separate study suggests that managing what individuals talk about and "controlling the floor" are perceived as forms of interpersonal dominance or control (Palmer, 1989).

VERBAL AGGRESSION

There are two primary strategies that we use to gain influence over others. First, we can make rational arguments that present reasons for why their compliance is beneficial. A second strategy involves the use of negative communication behaviors such as attacks on another person's self esteem or character in an attempt to gain their compliance. As you can see, one of these strategies is positive, and the other is negative and potentially damaging to relationships. So why do some individuals choose to present rational arguments while others choose to attack? The explanation rests in the distinction between communication traits known as argumentativeness and verbal aggression.

Recall from Chapter 3, the difference between arguementativeness and verbal aggression. **Argumentativeness** refers to the extent to which an individual challenges a position or issue (Infante & Rancer, 1982). A person can question or debate whether they should comply with a request without directly addressing the personal characteristics of the person making the request. When a request is addressed with a response that attacks the self-confidence, character, and/or intelligence of another person, **verbal aggressiveness** is being used (Infante & Wigley, 1986). Examples of verbally aggressive messages might include attacks on one's character or competence, teasing or ridiculing, or even making threats or jokes about another's appearance. It is not unusual to resort to verbally aggressive messages, when we run out of good arguments to make during a conflict situation. Just think about the last time you got into an argument. Did the conversation start calm with sound reasoning? Then what happened? Often times when we feel others are not listening or understanding we can escalate to more aggressive strategies. This is how productive conflict situations can eventually turn dark.

How did you handle your aggression in your last argument?

Loreen Olson suggests that there are four levels of aggression that are experienced in our interpersonal encounters (2004).

1. **Low aggression** is characterized by yelling, crying, refusing to talk, or stomping out of the room.
2. **Moderate aggression** involves more intense acts of verbal aggression such as verbal insults, swearing at the other, and indirect physical displays of anger such as kicking, hitting, throwing inanimate objects, or threatening to engage in these behaviors.
3. **High aggression** refers to intensive face threatening, verbal belittling, and direct physical contact with the other person in the form of slapping, shoving, or pushing.
4. The most serious level, **severe aggression**, includes intense verbal abuse and threats and involves physical attacks that include kicking, biting, punching, hitting with an object, raping, and using a weapon. Not only can verbally aggressive acts occur before relational conflicts, they can occur as a consequence to partner aggression and also serve to escalate the conflict. In relationships, struggles for power and control

are often at the heart of reciprocated and escalating aggression between partners (Olson, 2004).

Now, we will explore the impact of verbal aggression across three distinct contexts, including in romantic relationships, in the classroom, and at work.

Verbal Aggression in Romantic Relationships

Does a history of verbal aggression in our families lead to verbally aggressive romantic relationships? Communication scholars found that individuals with a history of familiar verbal aggression in childhood are more desensitized in adulthood and are more tolerant of their own and their romantic partners' verbal aggression in romantic relationships (Aloia & Solomon, 2013). These results lend support to the idea that the more we are exposed to verbal aggressive messages in childhood, the more we engage and accept verbal aggression in our adult romantic relationships. However, what role does stress and anger have in the propensity to engage in verbal aggression in romantic relationships? One study suggests that, regardless of a relational partner's coping skills, verbal aggression is likely to occur once strong emotions, such as anger, have been evoked (Bodenmann, Meuwly, Bradbury, Gmelch, & Ledermann, 2010). The authors suggest that we should focus more on reducing stress in relationships to avoid such strong negative emotions, rather than directly trying to reduce verbal aggression in an angry partner.

While our first tendency is to assume that aggression and violence are often restricted to close relationships with romantic partners or family members, this is not the case. Researchers have examined their presence and impact in a variety of relational contexts, including in the classroom and at work.

Verbal Aggression in the Classroom

Since verbal aggression is perceived as a negative communication behavior, it should come as no surprise that researchers have identified several negative outcomes associated with teachers who use words to attack students in the classroom. Students who perceive their instructors as being verbally aggressive report that they are less motivated in that class (Myers & Rocca, 2001). Also, they evaluate the teacher as being less competent and as behaving inappropriately (Martin, Weber, & Burant, 1997). In an environment where a student fears becoming the target of verbal abuse, less learning occurs (Myers, 2002)

One study suggests that, regardless of a relational partner's coping skills, verbal aggression is likely to occur once strong emotions, such as anger, have been evoked.

and the chances are greater that students will choose to avoid the situation by skipping class (Rocca, 2004). Outside the classroom, scholars have also explored the advisor-advisee relationship. One study concluded that as perceptions of the advisor's verbal aggressiveness with advisees increase, perceptions of advisor credibility decrease (Punyanunt-Carter & Wrench, 2008). When you consider that aggressiveness fosters a negative learning experience, the power of a teacher's communication becomes apparent.

How would you handle a teacher bullying your child?

Verbal Aggression in the Workplace

Another context that has been the target of research on verbal aggression is the workplace. It is important to understand the potential for verbal aggression and emotional abuse to occur in the organizational environment. Approximately 90 percent of adults report that they have been a victim of workplace bullying at some point during their professional career (Hornstein, 1996). A 2012 study found that verbal aggression by supervisors is related to employee dissatisfaction (Madlock & Dillow, 2012). The psychological impact of negative events, such as a supervisor's verbal aggression, has a lasting and more powerful impact than positive events, such as paying a compliment. These factors can impact employees' overall well-being. So why would employees stay in a position when their supervisor engages in verbal aggression? Study results suggest employees may choose to stay in a hostile work environment because of two reasons:

1. Investment size is high
2. Quality of alternatives is low

Investment size may be considered high if an employee has a significant number of years of service, non-vested portions of retirement programs, and/or several rewarding work relationships. The quality of alternatives may be considered low if an employee does not perceive there is another job opportunity available to them.

Approximately 90 percent of adults report that they have been a victim of workplace bullying at some point during their professional career.

It probably is no surprise that communication scholars (Madlock & Kennedy-Lightsey, 2010) found verbal aggression to be a negative predictor of:

- employees' communication satisfaction;
- organizational commitment; and
- job satisfaction.

However, it is interesting to note that this same study found supervisors' verbal aggression was a stronger predictor than supervisors' mentoring—suggesting once again that our negative experiences have more lasting impact than our positive experiences.

As we conclude this section on verbal aggression, we acknowledge that verbal aggression is not only enacted in face-to-face interactions. In Chapter 11 we will discuss how verbal aggression is exchanged in the mediated environment and how it may contribute to such problems as cyberbullying.

SUMMARY

While the topics discussed in this chapter may not be particularly pleasant, it is important to address their role in our communication with others. Not all relationships are enjoyable. To use the analogy of a roller coaster, virtually all relationships experience ups and downs. In this chapter we have discussed the concept of interpersonal deception and explored the potential impact of telling lies. In addition, we discussed the potential embarrassment that pops up from time to time and causes us to become "red-faced" in our interactions. In keeping with color analogies, relationships often encounter the "green-eyed monster" when jealousy emerges and causes us to respond in ways that we might not otherwise. We identified power and influence as potential sources of jealousy and as something that can affect our interactions with others. The distinction between argumentativeness and aggressiveness was made, as we offered a glimpse into the ugly side of power, when it results in verbal attacks against others.

Oftentimes we hear the phrase, "Communication is the key to success." The purpose of this chapter was to introduce a few communication situations in which communication was *not part of the solution*, but was, in fact, *part of the problem*. It is important to remember that communication is a tool that can be used for good or evil purposes.

It is up to us to understand how to use communication effectively to accomplish our goals and to become more competent in our interactions with others. By offering you a glimpse into the "dark side" of communication, it is our hope that your relationships will encounter more "ups" than "downs."

DISCUSSION QUESTIONS

1. Most people would agree that there are times when it is okay to deceive a friend, family member, or romantic partner. Have you ever been in a particular situation where you felt it was justified or acceptable to deceive someone? What were the reasons for your deception?

2. What are some ways to make sure that your partner does not feel jealous in regard to your romantic relationship? What are some suggestions for dealing with someone who often reports jealous feelings?

3. How would you recommend training individuals to use less verbally aggressive messages to influence others? What factors would you consider in this training?

4. After you complete the Evoking-Jealousy Scale, give this scale to your partner. Discuss how the discrepancy in the two scores may impact your interpersonal communication. How can the information gained from these scores help your relationship to communicate more effectively?

SELF ASSESSMENT

Evoking Jealousy Scale

Directions: Rate how often you have attempted the following items using the scale below:

**1 = Never   2 = Almost never   3 = Sometimes   4 = Neutral
5 = Often   6 = Almost always   7 = Always**

"I have tried to make my partner jealous by . . ."

_____ 1.   Dancing with someone else while he or she is around.
_____ 2.   Dressing nicely when I'm going out.
_____ 3.   Telling him or her someone flirted with me.
_____ 4.   Telling him or her I found a person attractive.
_____ 5.   Acting like it does not matter what he or she does.
_____ 6.   Pretending to be interested in another person.
_____ 7.   Talking to an ex-boyfriend or ex-girlfriend.
_____ 8.   Wearing clothing that highlights my features.
_____ 9.   Spending time doing activities without him or her.
_____ 10. Talking about activities I have been involved in.
_____ 11. Doing things he or she wants to do, but cannot.
_____ 12. Going out and not inviting him or her.
_____ 13. Talking with his or her friends.
_____ 14. Talking about a person of the opposite sex.
_____ 15. Having a person of the opposite sex answer the phone.
_____ 16. Telling him or her how much fun I had with a person of the opposite sex.
_____ 17. Having an opposite-sex friend stop by when he or she is there.
_____ 18. Flirting with members of the opposite sex.

Scoring: The possible range is 18-126. Higher scores indicate high levels of jealousy evoking behaviors.

Source: Cayanus, J. L., & Booth-Butterfield, M. (2004). Relationship orientation, jealousy, and equity: An examination of jealousy evoking and positive communication responses. *Communication Quarterly, 52,* 237–250. Reprinted by permission of Taylor & Francis Ltd., www.informaworld.com.

KEY TERMS AND DEFINITIONS

ACCOUNTS: provide a potential explanation for the cause of the embarrassing situation.

ACTIVITY JEALOUSY: emerges when our relational partner dedicates time to various hobbies or interests.

AGAPE: a love style that is often described as selfless and altruistic; these individuals tend to put their partners' needs above their own

AGENT: when we are responsible for our own embarrassment.

APOLOGIES: attempts to identify the source of blame for the incident.

ARGUMENTATIVENESS: refers to the extent to which an individual challenges a position or issue.

AROUSAL RELIEF THEORY: suggest that laughter can be used to release positive affective responses that can help individuals diffuse anxiety or stress.

CLARITY: a communication dimension that varies along a continuum from very clear to completely ambiguous.

COERCIVE POWER: focuses on the perceived ability of the source to punish or to enact negative consequences.

COMPENSATORY RESTORATION: making oneself appear more "attractive" than the competition.

COMPLETENESS: the extent of message details.

COMPLIANCE: occurs when an individual agrees to a request because he can see a potential reward or punishment for doing so.

CONCEALMENT: a form of deception that involves partially telling the truth while leaving out important details.

CONFESSIONS: a verbal acknowledgement of the transgression or deception.

DARK SIDE OF COMMUNICATION: an integrative metaphor for a certain perspective toward the study of human folly, frailty, and fallibility.

DECEPTION: a message knowingly transmitted by a sender to foster a false belief or conclusion by a receiver.

DOMINANCE: a mechanism typically associated with attempts to express power and take control in a relationship.

EMBARRASSMENT: occurs when we perceive that our self-esteem has been threatened or we have presented what we perceive to be a negative view of the self to others.

EMOTIONAL INFIDELITY: a type of infidelity that refers to engaging in an intense and deep emotional attachment to someone outside of the romantic relationship; it typically involves sharing personal self-disclosures.

EQUIVOCATION: a form of deception that involves being strategically vague.

EROS: a love style that is described as passionate and intense; these individuals have a strong commitment to the relationship sexually and value security, physical attraction, and beauty.

EXPERT POWER: grounded in the perception that the source possesses knowledge, expertise, or skills in a particular area.

FALSIFICATION: a form of deception that requires telling an outright lie.

FAMILY JEALOUSY: result of an individual's relationship with another family member, whom we perceive as being taken away from us.

FRIEND JEALOUSY: result of an individual's relationship with another friend, whom we perceive as being taken away from us.

HIGH AGGRESSION: refers to intensive face threatening, verbal belittling, and direct physical contact with the other person in the form of slapping, shoving, or pushing.

IDENTIFICATION: when a person decides to agree to an influence attempt because he recognizes the potential benefits of doing so, or if he wishes to establish a relationship with the source.

INTEGRATIVE COMMUNICATION: this refers to a specific communicative response to jealousy; it involves direct and nonaggressive communication about jealousy with a partner.

INTERNALIZATION: when an individual adopts a behavior because it is internally rewarding.

INTERPERSONAL DECEPTION THEORY (IDT): explains the strategic choices made when engaging in deceptive communication; the source tries to mask the deception and the receiver tries to hide his suspicion of the deception.

INTIMACY JEALOUSY: the result of the exchange of intimate or private information that a partner may share with a third party, someone not in the relationship.

JEALOUSY: a protective reaction to a perceived threat to a valued relationship, arising from a situation in which the partner's involvement with an activity and/or another person is contrary to the jealous person's definition of their relationship.

JOKES: involves using humor to create a more lighthearted response to a situation.

LEAKAGE CUES: unconscious behaviors believed to signal deception.

LEGITIMATE POWER: centered on the perception that the source has authority because of a particular role that she plays in the relationship or a title that she holds.

LOW AGGRESSION: characterized by yelling, crying, refusing to talk, or stomping out of the room.

LUDUS: a love style that values having fun; these individuals are interested in "winning" as many partners as possible; they see love as a "game."

MANIA: a love style that involves a strong need to be loved; these individuals often develop obsessive and possessive tendencies; they value a strong attachment to their partners.

MODERATE AGGRESSION: involves more intense acts of verbal aggression such as verbal insults, swearing at the other, and indirect physical displays of anger such as kicking, hitting, throwing inanimate objects, or threatening to engage in these behaviors.

NEGATIVE AFFECT AGGRESSION: this is a specific communication response to jealousy; it involves nonverbal expressions of jealousy-related affect that the partner can see.

OBSERVER: when we are bystanders to another's embarrassment and experience feelings of discomfort ourselves.

PERSONALIZATION: extent to which the deceiver takes ownership of the information.

PHYSICAL EVIDENCE: objects/artifacts that reveal one's deception.

POSITIVE RELATIONAL DECEPTIVE STRATEGIES: deceptive strategies that enhance, escalate, repair, and improve relationships.

POWER: one's ability to influence others to behave in ways they normally might not.

POWER JEALOUSY: associated with perceptions that a partner's other relationships or obligations are viewed as more important than your relationship with the person.

PRAGMA: a love style that involves lovers who are logical and realistic about their partners; they typically are looking for certain criteria that match their goals.

RECIPIENT: when we are targets of embarrassing communication.

REFERENT POWER: based on a person's respect, identification, and attraction to the source.

RELEVANCE/DIRECTNESS: the extent to which the deceiver produces messages that are logical in flow and sequence, and are pertinent to the conversation.

REWARD POWER: based on a person's perception that the source of power can provide rewards.

ROMANTIC JEALOUSY: the result of a partner's relationship with another person; associated with perceived intimacy between two people.

SEVERE AGGRESSION: includes intense verbal abuse and threats and involves physical attacks that include kicking, biting, punching, hitting with an object, raping, and using a weapon.

SEXUAL INFIDELITY: a type of infidelity that involves having sexual relations with some-

one outside of one's romantic relationship; this may include intercourse, oral sex, kissing, and sexual touch.

SOLICITED CONFESSIONS: often offered as the result of direct questioning or confrontation.

STORGE: a love style that involves individuals who value love that is established through common interests and friendships; they tend to see love as developing over time.

THIRD-PARTY INFORMATION: involves information being revealed by a person outside the relationship.

UNSOLICITED CONFESSIONS: declarations that are made unexpectedly or unprovoked.

VERBAL AGGRESSION: when a request is addressed with a response that attacks the self-confidence, character, and/or intelligence of another person.

VERIDICALITY: the extent to which the deceiver appears to be truthful.

REFERENCES

Aloia, L. S., & Solomon, D. H. (2013). Perceptions of verbal aggression in romantic relationships: The role of family history and motivational systems. *Western Journal of Communication, 77*(4), 411–423.

Bachman, G. F., & Guerrero, L. K. (2006). Forgiveness, apology, and communicative responses to hurtful events. *Communication Reports, 19*(1), 45–56.

Berlyne, D. E. (1969). Laughter, humor and play. In G. Lindzey and E. Aronson (Eds.), *Handbook of social psychology,* Vol. 3, (pp. 795–813). Reading, MA: Addison-Wesley.

Bevan, J. L., & Samter, W. (2004). Toward a broader conceptualization of jealousy in close relationships: Two exploratory studies. *Communication Studies, 55,* 14–28.

Bodenmann, G., Meuwly, N., Bradbury, T. N., Gmelch, S., & Ledermann, T. (2010). Stress, anger, and verbal aggression in intimate relationships: Moderating effects of individual and dyadic coping. *Journal of Social & Personal Relationships, 27*(3), 408–424.

Buller, D. B., & J. K. Burgoon. (1996). Interpersonal deception theory. *Communication Theory, 6,* 203–242.

Burgoon, J. K., Buller, D. B., Guerrero, L. K., Afifi, W., & Feldman, C. M. (1996). Interpersonal deception XII: Information management dimensions underlying types of deceptive messages. *Communication Monographs, 63,* 50–69.

Burgoon, J. K., & Dillman, L. (1995). Gender, immediacy and nonverbal communication. In P.

J. Kalbfleisch and M. J. Cody (Eds.), *Gender, power, and communication in human relationships* (pp. 63–81). Hillsdale, NJ: Lawrence Erlbaum Associates.

Buss, D. M., Larsen, R. J., Westen, D., & Semmelroth, J. (1992). Sex differences in jealousy: Evolution, physiology, and psychology. *Psychological Science, 3,* 251–255.

Buunk, A. P., Goor, J. A., & Solano, A. C. (2010). Intrasexual competition at work: Sex differences in the jealousy-evoking effect of a rival characteristics in work settings. *Journal of Social and Personal Relationships, 27*(5), 671–684.

Camden, C., Motley, M. T., & Wilson, A. (1984). White lies in interpersonal communication: A taxonomy and preliminary investigation of social motives. *The Western Journal of Speech Communication, 48,* 309–325.

Carpenter, C. J. (2012). Meta-analysis of sex differences in responses to sexual versus emotional infidelity: Men and women are more similar than different. *Psychology of Women Quarterly, 36,* 25-37.

Cupach, W. R., & Spitzberg, B. H. (1994). *The dark side of interpersonal communication.* Hillsdale, NJ: Lawrence Erlbaum.

Daly, J. A., McCroskey, J. C., & Richmond, V. P. (1977). Relationship between vocal activity and perception of communicators in small group interaction. *Western Journal of Speech Communication, 41,* 175–187.

DePaulo, B. M., Kashy, D. A., Kirkendale, S. E., Wyer, M. M., & Epstein, J. A. (1996). Lying in everyday life. *Journal of Personality and Social Psychology, 70,* 979–995.

Dijkstar, P., & Buunk, B. P. (2004). Gender differences in rival characteristics that evoke jealousy in response to emotional versus sexual infidelity. *Personal Relationships, 11,* 395–408.

Dijkstra, P., & Buunk, B. P. (1998). Jealousy as a function of rival characteristics: An evolutionary perspective. *Personality and Social Psychology Bulletin, 24,* 1158–1166.

Edelmann, R. J. (1985). Social embarrassment: An analysis of the process. *Journal of Social and Personal Relationships, 2,* 195–213.

Feldman, R. S., Forrest, J. A., & Happ, B. R. (2002). Self-presentation and verbal deception: Do self-presenters lie more? *Basic and Applied Social Psychology, 24*(2), 163–170.

Floyd, K., & Morman, M. T. (1998). The measurement of affectionate communication. *Communication Quarterly, 46*(2), 144–162.

Frederick, D. A., & Fales, M. R. (2014). Upset over sexual versus emotional infidelity among gay, lesbian, bisexual and heterosexual adults. Archives of Sexual Behavior, 43, DOI: 0.1007/s10508-014-0409-9

French, J. P. R., & Raven, B. (1960). The bases of social power. In D. Cartwright and A. Zander (Eds.), *Group dynamics* (pp. 607–623). New York: Harper and Row.

Goodboy, A. K., Horan, S. M., & Booth-Butterfield, M. (2012). Intentional jealousy-evoking behavior in romantic relationships as a function of received partner affection and love styles. *Communication Quarterly, 60,* 3, 370–385.

Gross, E., & Stone, G.P. (1964). Embarrassment and the analysis of role requirements. *American Journal of Sociology, 70,* 1–15.

Guerrero, L. K., & Afifi, W.A. (1999). Toward a goal-oriented approach for understanding communicative responses to jealousy. *Western Journal of Communication, 63,* 216–248.

Guerrero, L. K., & Anderson, P. A. (1998). Jealousy experience and expression in romantic relationships. In P. A. Anderson & L. K. Guerrero (Eds.), *Handbook of communication and emotion* (pp. 155–188). San Diego, CA: Academic Press.

Guerrero, L. K., Anderson, P. A., Jorgensen, P. F., Spitzberg, B. H., & Eloy, S. V. (1995). Coping with the green-eyed monster: Conceptualizing and measuring communicative responses to romantic jealousy. *Western Journal of Communication, 59,* 270–304.

Guerrero, L. K., & Eloy, S.V. (1992). Relationship satisfaction and jealousy across marital types. *Communication Reports, 5,* 23–41.

Hansen, G. L. (1985). Dating jealousy among college students. *Sex Roles, 12,* 713–721.

Horan, S. M. (2012). Affection exchange theory and perceptions of relational transgressions. *Western Journal of Communication, 76,* 109–126.

Hornstein, H. A. (1996). *Brutal bosses and their prey. How to overcome and identify abuse in the workplace.* New York: Riverhead Books.

Infante, D. A., & Rancer, A. S. (1982). A conceptualization and measure of argumentativeness. *Journal of Personality Assessment, 46,* 72–80.

Infante, D. A., & Wigley, C. J. (1986). Verbal aggression: An interpersonal model and measure. *Communication Monographs, 53,* 61–69.

Kelman, H. C. (1961). Processes of opinion change. *Public Opinion Quarterly, 25,* 58–78.

Kernis, M. H. (1995). *Efficacy, agency and self-esteem.* New York: Plenum Press.

Knapp, M. L., & Vangelisti, A. L. (2006). Lying. In K. M. Galvin & P. J. Cooper (Eds.), *Making connections* (pp. 247–252). Los Angeles, CA: Roxbury.

Knox, D., Schact, C., Holt, J., & Turner, J. (1993). Sexual lies among university students. *College Student Journal, 27,* 269–272.

Knox, D., Zusman, M. E., Mabon, L., & Shriver, L. (1999). Jealousy in college student relationships. *College Student Journal, 33,* 328.

Lee, J. A. (1973). *The colors of love: An exploration of the ways of loving.* Don Mills, Ontario, Canada: New Press.

Madlock, P. E., & Dillow, M. R. (2012). The consequences of verbal aggression in the workplace: An application of the investment model. *Communication Studies, 63*(5), 593–607.

Madlock, P. E., & Kennedy-Lightsey, C. (2010). The effects of supervisors' verbal aggressiveness and mentoring on their subordinates. *Journal of Business Communication, 47*(1), 42–62.

Martin, M. M., Weber, K., & Burant, P. A. (1997). Students' perceptions of a teacher's use of slang and verbal aggressiveness in a lecture: An experiment. Paper presented at the Eastern Communication Association Convention, Baltimore, MD.

Mattingly, B. A., Whitson, D., & Mattingly, M. J. B. (2012). Development of the romantic jealousy-induction scale and the motives for inducing romantic jealousy scale. *Current Psychology, 31,* 263–281.

McCornack, S. A., & Levine, T. R. (1990). When loves become leery. The relationship between suspicion and accuracy in detecting deception. *Communication Monographs, 57,* 219–230.

McIntosh, E. G. (1989). An investigation of romantic jealousy among black undergraduates. *Social Behavior and Personality, 17,* 135–141.

Myers, S. A. (2002). Perceived aggressive instructor communication and student state motivation, learning and satisfaction. *Communication Reports, 15,* 113–121.

Myers, S. A., & Rocca, K.A. (2001). Perceived instructor argumentativeness and verbal aggressiveness in the college classroom: Effects on student perceptions of climate, apprehension, and state motivation. *Western Journal of Communication, 65,* 113–137.

O'Hair, H. D., & Cody, M. J. (1994). Everyday deception. In W. R. Cupach & B. Spitzberg (Ed.), *The dark side of interpersonal communication* (pp. 181–213). Hillsdale, NJ: Lawrence Erlbaum Associates.

Olson, L. N. (2004). Relational control-motivated aggression: A theoretically-based typology of intimate violence. *Journal of Family Communication, 4,* 209–233.

Palmer, M. T. (1989). Controlling conversations: Turns, topics and interpersonal control. *Communication Monographs, 56,* 1–18.

Park, H. S., Levine, T. R., McCornack, S. A., Morrison, K., & Ferrara, M. (2002). How people really detect lies. *Communication Monographs, 69,* 144–157.

Pines, A. M., & Friedman, A. (1998). Gender differences in romantic jealousy. *The Journal of Social Psychology, 138,* 54–71.

Planap, S., Rutherford, D., & Honeycutt, J. M. (1988). Events that increase uncertainty in personal relationships II: Replication and extension. *Human Communication Research, 14,* 516–547.

Punyanunt-Carter, N. M., & Wrench, J. S. (2008). Advisor-advisee communication two: The influence of verbal aggression and humor assessment on advisee perceptions of advisor credibility and affective learning. *Communication Research Reports, 22,* 303–313.

Rocca, K. A. (2004). College student attendance: Impact of instructor immediacy and verbal aggression. *Communication Education, 53,* 185–195.

Rowatt, W. C., Cunningham, M. R., & Druen, P. B. (1999). Lying to get a date: The effect of facial attractiveness on the willingness to deceive prospective dating partners. *Journal of Social and Personal Relationships, 16*(2), 209–223.

Sattler, J. M. (1965). A theoretical, developmental, and clinical investigation of embarrassment. *Clinical Psychology Monographs, 71,* 19–59.

Sharkey, W. F. & Stafford, L. (1990). Responses to Embarrassment. *Human Communication Research, 17,* 315-342.

Spitzberg, B. H. (2006). A struggle in the dark. In K. M. Galvin & P. J. Cooper (Eds.), *Making connections* (pp. 240–246). Los Angeles, CA: Roxbury.

Townsend, J. M., & Levy, G. D. (1990). Effects of potential partners' costume and physical attractiveness on sexual and partner selection. *Journal of Psychology, 124,* 371–389.

Yoshimura, S. M. (2004). Emotional and behavioral responses to romantic jealousy expressions, *Communication Reports, 17,* 85-101.

Zuckerman, M., & Driver, R. (1985). Telling lies: verbal and nonverbal correlates of deception. In A. Siegman & S. Feldstein (Eds.), *Multichannel integrations of nonverbal behavior* (pp. 129–148). Hillsdale, NJ: Lawrence Erlbaum.

chapter
10

Terminating Relationships:
Knowing When to Throw in the Towel

OBJECTIVES

- Discuss the investment model and how it relates to relationship termination.

- Identify common reasons romantic relationships terminate.

- Describe Duck's five phases of relationship termination.

- Explain Knapp's model of relationship dissolution by describing each stage of coming apart and offer an example of typical communication that occurs in each stage.

- Explain ERA or Empathy, Rationale, Action and how it can be used in relationship termination situations.

- Identify effective strategies to "remain friends" with ex-romantic partners.

- Offer examples of strategies individuals use to cope with relationship dissolution.

SCENARIO: SOUND FAMILIAR?

Cole and Addison dated all through high school. Last year they enrolled in different colleges and found it difficult to maintain their relationship via long distance. Cole was highly involved in extramural sports, and Addison was extremely busy with clubs and organizations on campus. Cole was excited to finally visit Addison at her school and spend time with her. When he arrived on campus she was very busy with classes, volunteering, hanging out with her roommates, and talking about unfamiliar people and places. During his visit, he found that they had a difficult time connecting on anything except the past. Toward the end of his trip, he was certain that their relationship would not last. While he respected Addison for her commitment to her studies and leadership roles, he did not feel their relationship was working. He contemplated telling her before he left for home. Would this come as a shock to her? Would they maintain a friendship? He didn't want to hurt her feelings but it was clear they were evolving as individuals, but not evolving together as a couple.

OVERVIEW

The last several chapters have examined how our interpersonal relationships are initiated, maintained, and how they may turn dark. In this chapter, we turn to the process of relationship disengagement. Breaking up is not easy. It usually results in pain for one or both partners. Throughout this chapter, we examine how to assess relationship problems and how to determine if these problems are significant enough to terminate a relationship. We introduce the investment model, which can help explain why seemingly unhealthy relationships stay together much longer than they should. Next, we will introduce the stages of dissolution and discuss the type of communication that is expected across the stages. We will then explore characteristics in termination across different relationship types such as friendships, heterosexual romantic, and homosexual romantic. Finally we will discuss what happens after the breakup, including remaining friends, rebounding, and finding closure. We describe the aftermath of relationship disengagement and explore suggestions for surviving relationship disengagement and ultimately moving on.

ASSESSING RELATIONSHIP PROBLEMS: ATTRIBUTIONS, SATISFACTION, EQUITY

When considering whether to stay in a relationship or not, we often assess the trouble occurring in the relationship and the explanations for these problems. For example, we ask ourselves questions such as:

- Why does he act that way?
- Why did she say that to me?
- Why would he or she hurt me?

To address these questions, it is necessary to recall our discussion of attribution theory and the fundamental attribution error from Chapter 4. These theories provide a framework for understanding how we explain our own and others' behaviors. Recall our discussion of the **fundamental attribution error**, which holds that people tend to attribute others' negative behaviors to internal, rather than external, causes. Rather than consider external or situational causes for others' behavior (for example, "the weather"), we often tend to take the "easy" way out and attribute others' behaviors to internal factors. Internal factors we typically use to describe behavior tend to be stable over time, such as personality traits (for example, "rude," "inconsiderate," "lazy").

Not surprisingly, appraisals of our relationship partner's intentions relate to how satisfied we are in the relationship. Researchers have identified a consistent link between the attributions, or explanations, about relationship partners' intentions and reported relationship satisfaction (Waldinger & Schulz, 2006). Much of the research on attributions in romantic relationships has examined how an assessment of a partner's accountability for a relationship transgression affects relationship satisfaction (Waldinger & Schulz, 2006). It is natural to want to understand why our partner is acting a certain way, and eventually, the explanations for the partner's behavior influence our evaluation of our relationship.

Couples are happiest in relationships when there is a balance of inputs and outputs.

If you perceive you are receiving too little from the relationship compared to what you are contributing, this will impact your satisfaction.

When relationship partners offer consistently negative attributions or explanations for a partner's behavior, they are more likely to report lower relationship satisfaction (Fincham & Bradbury, 1993; Miller & Bradbury, 1995). Thus, when a relationship partner forgets to buy a birthday present or forgets to recognize an important date, the offended partner may offer negative explanations for the behavior, especially if the negative behavior has been repeated over time. The offended partner may say, "He didn't get me a present because he is lazy," or "She didn't remember our anniversary because she is so self-absorbed." When individuals view a partner's behavior as selfishly motivated and dispositional rather than situational, they are more likely to view their partner in a negative way and to report decreased relationship satisfaction (Fincham, Harold, & Gano-Phillips, 2000).

Once we assess the relational problems, we may conclude that there is some form of inequity. Recall our discussion of **equity theory** in Chapter 8, which suggests that couples are happiest in relationships when there is a balance of inputs and outputs.

If you perceive you are receiving too little from the relationship compared to what you are contributing, this will impact your satisfaction.

Alternatively, if you are receiving more outputs from the relationship than you are contributing, you will feel a sense of guilt from the imbalance. However, this process is highly subjective in terms of one's personal view of inputs, outputs, and fairness in relationships.

HOW DO YOU DETERMINE IF A RELATIONSHIP PROBLEM IS SIGNIFICANT?

Interpersonal communication researchers study relationships to shed light on significant problems or challenges that should be addressed by couples. Vangelisti (1992) examined the link between specific types of relationship problems and relational dissatisfaction. She recognized a problem as *significant* for relationship partners when it meets at least two of the following criteria:

1. The behavior has a negative effect on the relationship;
2. It occurs often in the relationship; and
3. It is important enough for one or both partners to remember it and recall it as a continuing source of dissatisfaction within the relationship.

It is important to realize that even seemingly benign behaviors can become problematic over time. For example, if your partner displays a negative behavior such as not looking at you while listening (criterion 1) and it is consistent over time (criterion 2), it may reach the point where it becomes a significant relational problem. However, a salient (criterion 1) and negative behavior that is recalled over time (criterion 3), such as kissing a colleague at happy hour, may happen only once, but may be prominent enough to continually cause displeasure in the relationship, even though the behavior was never repeated.

Interestingly, the most frequently reported communication problem in relationships concerns withholding negative emotions. These may include feelings of anger, fear, distress, disgust, and shame.

INVESTMENT MODEL: WILL YOUR RELATIONSHIP PERSIST OR DIE?

We think the investment model proposed by Rusbult, Martz, and Agnew (1998) provides the most succinct conceptualization and clear understanding of the type of relationships that continue and those that end. By examining the model in Figure 10.1, you will notice it consists of four variables that help predict the extent to which a relationship will continue. The authors define these variables as follows:

1. **Satisfaction level** Satisfaction level which is determined by how well the relationship partner fulfulls their partner's needs.
2. **Quality of alternatives** refers to the perceived desirability of the best available alternative to a relationship" (Rusbult et al., 1998, p. 359). Quality of alternatives refers to whether or not a partner's needs could be met in other ways or outside of the existing relationship.
3. **Investment size** refers to the resources attached to the relationship. Resources may include time, money, children, furniture, houses, and/or pets.
4. **Commitment** is central to a relationship's success and refers to the relationship partner's choice to stay in the relationship as well as the feeling of being connected to the other person.

Rusbult, Martz, and Agnew (1998) draw several important conclusions about how these variables are related to one another and predict relationship success and stability:

- When relationship partners report greater *commitment*, they also report feeling more *satisfied* with their relationships.
- When relationship partners feel more *committed*, they perceive *fewer alternatives* as meeting their relationship needs.
- Finally, partners who report greater *commitment* to their relationships also report greater *investments* in their bonds.

Therefore, important factors to consider when deciding whether to remain in a relationship are the level of commitment in the relationship, the

306

number of alternatives, the amount of your relationship investments, and perceived relationship satisfaction. We encourage you to examine one of your own relationships by completing the Investment Model Scale provided at the end of the chapter.

1. Intrapsychic process
2. Dyadic process
3. Social process
4. Grave dressing process
5. Resurrection process

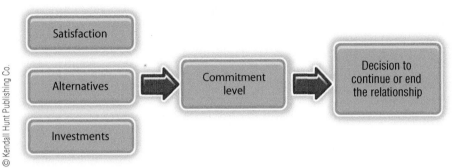

© Kendall Hunt Publishing Co.

Figure 10.1. The relationship investment model.

DUCK'S PROCESS MODEL OF RELATIONSHIP TERMINATION

Ending a relationship is stressful because of the amount of time, feelings, and energy involved in this process. Communication scholars have examined the decision-making processes involved in ending relationships and note that it is not a singular event but rather a drawn-out process that often involves a number of different individuals (Duck & Rollie, 2003; Rollie & Duck, 2006). In 1982, Duck proposed a four-phase model of decision making that impacts communication patterns, social networks, and conversational topics. In 2006, Duck and Rollie modified the model by identifying a fifth process of relationship dissolution. The five phases of this model are:

Intrapsychic Process

During the first phase, labeled the **intrapsychic process**, one partner recognizes that something is wrong in a relationship and no longer feels satisfied. The individual begins to spend more time thinking about the status of the relationship and considering the costs and rewards associated with it. There are two possible outcomes of this phase. First, the leaver may spend enough time ruminating about the negative aspects of the relationship that he is ready to move on and forgive the partner. Or, on the other hand, the leaver may spend considerable amounts of time thinking about the negative aspects of the relationship and find sufficient faults to justify ending the relationship.

© wavebreakmedia /Shutterstock.com

How did your last relationship end and what processes did you experience?

Importantly, the leaver does not express concerns directly to the partner during the intrapsychic phase; instead, the partner may vent, but only to individuals who do not know the relationship partner, such as a hairdresser or a mechanic (Duck & Rollie, 2003). Individuals in long-term relationships experience this phase often throughout the lifetime of their bonds. It is certainly not unusual for individuals to think about areas of improvement in their relationships; however, if this process becomes drawn out and more emotionally grueling, then the individual will move to the next process of relationship dissolution.

Dyadic Process

When the leaver officially announces to the partner that he or she is leaving or thinking of leaving, the **dyadic process** begins. This process opens the floodgates for discussion about the status of the relationship and justifications for ending it. This emotionally exhausting phase is characterized by long talks, conflict, and rationalizations of how the partnership "got to this place." During this phase, the other partner may make attempts to reconcile the relationship and attempt to illustrate the costs of terminating the relationship. This phase provides an opportunity for both partners to discuss the status of the relationship and, if possible, to fix it. If it does not get fixed here, the partners move to the next phase.

Social Process

If the relationship cannot be salvaged, the relationship termination then goes public. When the relationship termination is focused less on the couple and more on the relationship partners' friends and family, it is a sign that the couple has moved to the **social process**. The primary decision the couple has to make is: What are we going to tell people? Stories, blaming, and accounts of situations are shared with friends, coworkers, and family. At this time, friends will often choose sides, and the relationship partners now become socially available to others. In terms of the relationship partners, the rules and roles of their post-breakup status are discussed. Once the breakup has been shared with others, it becomes official. Sadly, many of the bonds formed with couple friends, family members, or coworkers will end.

Grave Dressing Process

The next process is **grave dressing**. This phase is called grave dressing because partners typically "dress up" the dead relationship (or grave) by promoting a positive image of their role in their particular version of the relationship story. Grave dressing also refers to "officially burying" the relationship. Relationship partners fulfill psychological and social needs through sharing their stories of the breakup (Duck & Rollie, 2003). Partners offer their explanation of the termination and save face for future relationships. Some people in this stage will engage in ceremonial burying behaviors such as burning pictures and returning, giving away, or selling items given to them by their "ex." A primary decision in this process is for individuals to create a version of the "breakup story" that depicts them in a positive light so they look desirable to others.

Resurrection Process

The last phase is called the **resurrection process** and it is characterized by trying to "enlist others as supporters for one's own view of the breakup" (Rollie & Duck, 2006, p. 236). This process focuses on the need for individuals to prepare themselves for future relationships (Rollie & Duck, 2006). Seeking advice and perspectives from others in order to "do things differently next time" is typical in this process. Individuals who have ended a relationship may actively attempt to avoid others who remind them of their ex-partner. In addition, when they start to interact with prospective relational partners, they may communicate that they are looking for anyone who does not remind them of their ex-partner.

This five-stage process model helps us understand the complexity of the relationship termination process. Duck's model sheds light on the people involved in the process as well as the communication that occurs from start to finish.

Next, we turn our attention to the actual communication between the relational partners during the process of relationship dissolution—which sometimes helps us understand the ever-so-popular relational question, "How did we get here?"

FIVE STAGES OF RELATIONSHIP DISSOLUTION

You may recall our discussion of Knapp's (1978) stages of coming together in Chapter 7; he also developed a five-stage model that depicts how relationships typically come apart, as depicted in Figure 10.2. The five stages of dissolution are labeled *differentiating, circumscribing, stagnating, avoiding,* and *terminating.* It is possible that: (1) partners could perceive that the relationships is in different stages; they don't necessarily always agree on the stage of their relationship, (2) some

stages last longer than others, and (3) partners often skip stages. It is important to note that this model seems to depict what actually happens when relationships deteriorate, not what "should" happen (Knapp, 1978).

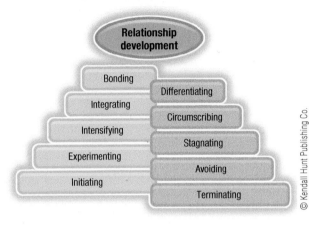

© Kendall Hunt Publishing Co.

Figure 10.2. Knapp's five stages of relationship formation and of dissolution.

Differentiating

During the stages of coming together, couples tend to emphasize hobbies, interests, and values they have in common; however, in the **differentiating** stage, partners highlight their differences. Individuals accentuate their unique attributes and use more "I" and "me" statements. During this phase of relationship dissolution, partners may engage in a great deal of conflict that often emphasizes all of the ways they differ from each other. For example, if one partner states that she likes eating out, the other partner may express a preference for cooking at home. If one person states that he likes action movies, the other person may express her affinity for romantic comedies.

When there is not a conscious decision to keep the partner involved, the relationship may drift apart.

One's independence in the relationship is the central focus of this stage, which has both positive and negative implications. On one hand, when individuals reassert their individual needs, they may choose to do things on their own, spend more time with friends, and reestablish their identity. This process can be healthy for a relationship. For example, before two individuals entered into a relationship, one partner may have enjoyed playing hockey while the other enjoyed participating in a yoga class. But as the relationship developed, there was less time for each person to enjoy his or her personal activities due to favoring more collaborative activities with the partner. As the relationship progressed, these interests were neglected. In the differentiating stage, those roots may be revisited, with hockey or yoga classes being resumed. This may provide a much-needed "spark" in the relationship and provide alternative topics for the partners to discuss. On the other hand, if the individual taking part in the activity excludes the significant other from his or her feelings and experiences, this independence may ultimately create more emotional distance in the relationship. If the partner

is kept involved, this stage may have beneficial outcomes.

Circumscribing

When there is not a conscious decision to keep the partner involved, the relationship may drift apart. The next stage of relationship dissolution is labeled the **circumscribing** stage. During this stage, the communication between the relationship partners is often described as restricted, controlled, or constrained. Akin to the "don't talk about politics or religion" standard, relationship partners in this stage only choose to talk about safe topics that will not lead to some type of argument (Vangelisti, 2002). Both the quality and quantity of information exchanged between the relationship partners deteriorates significantly as each attempts to avoid subjects that may spark a fight. Relationship partners only discuss "safe" topics such as plans for the day, current events, and the weather, which are topics that would be discussed with casual acquaintances.

Stagnating

The third stage of relationship dissolution is the **stagnating** stage. This stage is often described as two people who are merely "going through the motions" in their relationship because communication has come to a virtual standstill. There is very little interaction within the relationship, and partners continue to engage in activities separately. When partners think of bringing up any issues regarding the relationship, they tell themselves, "It will just turn into an argument," and so they resort to holding issues inside to avoid a conflict. They conserve their energy for their daily activities and do not exert any energy on preserving the relationship.

Roommates, friends, and even family members may feel stagnant in their relationships with one another. Extended time in this stage can be particularly problematic as the partners may lose their motivation to fix the relationship. Over time, the thought of having to face the partner may seem like an arduous task. Therefore, it is often easier to just avoid the partner or minimize communication in this stage of coming apart.

Avoiding

The fourth stage of coming apart is labeled the **avoiding** stage. During this stage, relationship partners will actively fill their schedules to avoid seeing their partners. Vangelisti (2002) describes this stage as particularly difficult, noting that when the partners do talk to each other, "they make it clear that they are not interested in each other or in the relationship" (p. 666). Relationship partners will arrive early to work and come home late in an effort to avoid each other. The idea of seeing the relationship partner is exhausting and any dialogue with this person is short, to the point, and often superficial. On the inside, individuals are exhausted from creating activities to avoid their partner and have increased disdain for one another. Any communication between the partners that occurs during this stage may focus on ways to avoid seeing each other. For example, one partner may ask the other, "What time will you be home from work?" in an effort to rearrange a work schedule to avoid contact.

RESEARCH IN REAL LIFE:
Complaining in heterosexual romantic couples

Hall, Travis, and Anderson (2013) attempted to examine gender differences in complaints across Knapp's relationship stages. While this study did not find significant gender differences between the stages of the model, they did find some gender differences in types of complaints overall:

- Women were more likely to complain to their significant other regarding topics that they have no power to change and that are beyond their control.
- Males were more likely to complain to their significant others regarding something they do on a regular basis or specific behaviors she may or may not do in the future.

The authors suggested that since women usually complain to others who are not the source of the problem, it could be that they are using it as a relationship-building strategy. Alternatively, perhaps males use more task-orientation approaches such as instrumental complaints because they are trying to solve problems in the relationship.

Terminating

As we grow increasingly disappointed in a relationship and in our partner, we reach a threshold and want to move on. This is when we reach the final stage of coming apart, the **terminating** stage, which marks the end of the relationship. Relationship partners may choose to divorce the partner, move out, or call an end to any type of formal or contractual commitment with the partner. When relationship partners do communicate during this stage, they make attempts to put physical and/or psychological distance between themselves and their relationship partner. Relationship partners will also make attempts to disassociate themselves from their relationship partner. Some married individuals will disassociate themselves from their partners by using their maiden names or explicitly stating to friends, coworkers, and family members, "We are not a couple anymore." See Table 10.1 for examples of typical messages that are exchanged during the stages.

Table 10.1. Sample messages in Knapp's Stages of Coming Apart

Stage	Communication Example
Differentiating	"You are just so different from me!" "I hate when you don't wash the dishes!"
Circumscribing	"It's going to rain tomorrow." "Did you let the dog out yet?" "I am not going to answer that because it will just lead to a fight!"
Stagnating	"Oh, you're home." "What is the point of discussing this anymore?" "I know, I know. The usual."
Avoiding	"I have to work nights all this week." "I will not be home for dinner." What time are you going to be at John's game?
Terminating	"I don't want to be in this relationship." "Sorry, but we can't date anymore." "I'm moving out."

As we grow increasingly disappointed in a relationship, how do we send signals that our relationship needs attention?

STRATEGIES USED TO TERMINATE RELATIONSHIPS

Determining how one should end a relationship can be quite stressful. Whether you are terminating a relationship with a romantic partner, a roommate, or a neighbor, it can create much anxiety. When we are stressed we often turn to easily accessible solutions that are not always effective.

When the relationship is not working, you may feel justification to end it.

Once the leaver decides to verbalize his or her intentions, he or she typically relies on relational disengagement tactics. During the relational disengagement period, there is obviously a great deal of conflict. Leavers will use different strategies, depending on the type of the relationship and the timing of the disengagement. For example, more polite and face-saving tactics are typically used in the beginning of the relationship termination phase. However, if the rejected partner does not respond to these tactics, or if the leaver is in a dangerous relationship and immediate action is needed, more forceful and direct tactics may be necessary. Researchers have studied what people specifically recall saying during a breakup (Baxter, 1982; Cody, 1982), and they have identified five common tactics used during relational disengagement.

Positive Tone Messages

First, **positive tone messages** are created to ease the pain for the rejected partner. These messages have a strong emotional tone and usually imply that the leaver would like to see less of the other person, but not entirely end the relationship. When individuals employ this strategy, they usually want to try to end the relationship in a positive and pleasant way. An example of a positive tone message would be, "*I really like you as a friend, but I think we perceive this relationship differently.*" In other words, the classic "It's not you, it's me." Here the leaver tries to ease the pain of the breakup by suggesting that he or she still likes the rejected partner and is interested in a friendship.

De-escalation Messages

The second tactic also involves reducing the amount of time spent with the partner. **De-escalation messages** are less emotional than positive tone messages and typically provide a rationale for wanting to see less of the rejected partner. For example, "*I think we need a break from each other,*" or "*My feelings for you have changed since the start of this relationship.*" This strategy may be problematic because it is perceived as a partial or temporary type of relationship termination strategy. Individuals who want to end the relationship for good may want to follow up with a more direct strategy for ending the relationship.

Withdrawal

A third tactic, **withdrawal**, refers to actively spending less time with the person. This includes dodging phone calls, blocking texts, and rerouting daily activities in order to avoid the individual. When you do run into the person, conversations are kept brief and shallow. This strategy is very indirect and can affect the individuals' ability to maintain a friendship in the future.

Justification Messages

A fourth way to disengage from a relationship involves utilizing **justification messages**. This tactic has three important elements. The relationship partner:

1. States that he or she needs to stop seeing the other person.
2. Provides a reason for ending the relationship with the other person.
3. Recognizes that the relationship is not salvageable and may even become worse if the relationship continues.

For example, "*I cannot live with you anymore because all we do is fight and argue. I do not see things getting any better. I am worried that if we stay roommates, things will get even worse than they are now! Therefore, we can't be roommates next year because it is just not going to work.*"

Negative Identity Management Messages

The last category of messages, **negative identity management**, is typically used as a last resort to terminate a relationship, when partners do not want to remain friends after the breakup or when one relationship partner feels a need to facilitate the disengagement. This strategy that is used to speed up the disengagement process and has little consideration for the rejected partner. The leaver may employ manipulation as part of this tactic. For example, the leaver may spark a disagreement with the partner to create an unpleasant situation and then suggest, *"See, this isn't working . . . we should see other people."*

Now that we have an understanding of the tactics that are utilized to terminate relationships, it is important to remember there is no "one size fits all" solution. In this next section we will examine relationship termination in three types of relationships, including friendships, heterosexual romantic, and homosexual romantic. Each area will offer specific research findings that help to explain these relationship types and offer some insight into their unique characteristics.

TYPES OF RELATIONSHIPS: TERMINATING FRIENDSHIPS

Friendships are some of the most enduring relationships we have. Consider your own friendships you have had since youth with a shelf life of "forever." Then there are other friends who tend to drift in and out of our lives like last season's shoes. Why do some friendships tend to outlast others? Often, friendships are forged from things we share in common with others. For example, we meet classmates who live in the same dorm, have the same major, work at the same job, share the same religion or social group, or share the same enemy or mutual friend. Friend-

ships may terminate because the very thing that brought the friends together no longer exists. People move away, change jobs, or move on to a different life stage (i.e., marriage, children, etc.) and no longer share the proximity and closeness that once protected the relationship.

There are a number of reasons individuals end friendships. For example, "Johnson and colleagues (2004) asked college students to identify why they ended a friendship. Reasons provided included the following (Johnson, Wittenberg, Haigh, Wigley, Becker, Brown, & Craig, 2004):

- Less affection (22.8 percent)
- Friend or self changed (21 percent)
- No longer participated in activities or spent time together (15.4 percent)
- Increase in distance (13 percent)

The way that someone ends a friendship depends on the intimacy, or closeness, experienced in the relationship. One study compared the differences in dissolution between casual and best friends (Rose & Serafica, 1986). *Proximity* was a strong predictor of dissolution in casual friends. This makes sense when we think of our casual friends from high school. When high school is over and we are not seeing our friends regularly, we tend to lose touch. They also found that *decreased affection* between best friends was the most important predictor in ending the relationship. Individuals have higher relationship expectations for "best" friends when it comes to displays of affection and communication; therefore, when those expectations are not met, the relationship changes.

Another reason reported for best and close friendships dissolving was the interference from

314

other relationships, such as romantic relationships. In other words, when new friendships and romantic partners enter the picture, it changes the dynamic of existing relationships. This plays a particularly detrimental role in female friendships. When one individual begins to spend more time interacting with her romantic partner's friends than with her own friends, the neglected female friends are likely to become frustrated with her behavior.

Factors Prompting Friendship Termination

One study examined *why* and *how* close and lengthy friendships come to an end (McEwan, Babin, & Farinelli, 2008). Participants in the study responded to open-ended questions about why and how they ended their friendships. Next, the researchers placed the responses into four friendship dissolution categories:

1. DISAPPROVED BEHAVIOR: friend engages in behavior that the other does not condone (example: drugs, alcohol).
2. COMPETING RELATIONSHIPS: friend spends time with family, romantic partner, or other friend(s) to the exclusion of the other partner and/or one friend does not get along with the other's family, romantic partner, or other friend(s).
3. BETRAYAL: friend engaged in deception, infidelity, malicious talk, theft, and/or exclusion that is disliked by or viewed as harmful to the other person.
4. INCREASED DISTANCE: friends "grow apart" due to increased social or proxemic distance.

Do female same-sex friendships terminate for different reasons than male same-sex friendships?

Researchers say, YES! Females were more likely to terminate same-sex friendships due to a conflict situation, whereas males were more likely to terminate same-sex friendships as a result of fewer common interests (Swain, 1989; Johnson, et al., 2004).

Next, the researchers examined how the study participants terminated their friendships. Four common methods of friendship termination were identified (McEwan, Babin, & Farinelli, 2008):

1. FADED AWAY: non-intentional loss of communication. The communication between friends ceased.
2. PURPOSEFUL AVOIDANCE: intentional reduction or stopping of communication,

Friendships may terminate because the very thing that brought the friends together no longer exists.

Rewards consist of behaviors or aspects of the relationship that are desirable, and that the recipient perceives as enjoyable or fulfilling.

no direct communication between friends about the loss of contact

3. **DIRECT REQUEST:** non-hostile, specific request to stop communication and/or end the relationships

4. **HOSTILE INTERACTION:** physical or verbal aggression leading to the end of the relationship, which may include threats, heated arguments, or actual physical violence

As friendships start to deteriorate, individuals may neglect the responsibilities of the relationships by choosing to provide less time, energy, trust, understanding, and support to their friends. Individuals may start weighing the costs and rewards of the relationship in order to determine whether they should stay in the relationship. Recall our discussion of social exchange theory in Chapter 7. To review, **social exchange theory** refers to an assessment of costs and rewards in determining the value of pursuing or continuing a relationship (Thibault & Kelley, 1959). Rewards consist of behaviors or aspects of the relationship that are desirable, and that the recipient perceives as enjoyable or fulfilling. In friendships, rewards can include how much fun you have with the person, and the extent to which he or she is trust-

worthy, honest, sincere, helpful, and supportive. Relationship costs are perceived as undesirable behaviors or outcomes. Costs in friendships may be characterized as "toxic" behaviors: the extent to which a friend may be controlling, demanding, depressing, self-absorbed, deceitful, or unfair. Also, friendships take time and energy, which may be perceived as costly when we have less time and energy to devote to them. According to social exchange theory, when the costs of the relationship outweigh the rewards, we contemplate ending the friendship. In general, people use indirect or direct methods to end a friendship, and both strategies have benefits and drawbacks.

Indirect Strategies for Ending Friendships

Indirect methods reflect your intention to gradually let go of the relationship by deviating away from a direct course of action. Baxter (1982, 1984) identified three indirect strategies used to terminate relationships:

1. **Withdrawal** of supportiveness and affection. Examples include, spending less time with the friend, sending fewer emails/texts, blocking the friend from your chat list, or defriending them from your social media.

2. **Pseudo de-escalation** or indicating the relationship will be "better off" by separating (verbally stating s/he wants to be less close). This is considered an indirect strategy because it is focused on being less close for the benefit of the relationship. For example, "Our relationship just needs a break for now so we can focus our families.

3. **Cost-escalation:** indirect attempts to make the relationship more unattractive (passive-aggressive behaviors)

Indirect methods work best if your goal is to decrease the intensity of the friendship by increasing the emotional and physical distance between you and your friend. As stated earlier, sometimes relationship partners allow the communication that sustains the friendship to just fade away (McEwan et al., 2008). If you are trying to end a relationship using an indirect strategy, it is important NOT to share your personal problems, engage in deep conversations, and be available to this person, because this will send mixed messages about the status of your friendship. This may also mean declining invitations and avoiding hangouts or shared friends until you have reached your goal of ending the relationship.

There are drawbacks to using indirect methods to weaken relationship bonds. For example, giving excuses for not hanging out may backfire. Isaacs (1999) suggests that excuses allows the other person an opportunity to overcome your refusal; your excuse of "Oh, I can't afford the gas to get out there," may be met with "That's okay, I can pick you up."

In addition, because indirect methods of terminating friendships do not include any transparency about the relationship status, the friend is often left confused about your true feelings. Recipients of this tactic may keep trying to resurrect the friendship and inaccurately interpret your indirect attempts to slow down, or even end, the friendship. If this is the case, it may be time to adopt more direct approaches to ending the relationship.

Research has shown that the type of dissolution strategy used will influence the satisfaction levels of the "left" partner. For example, Collins

and Gillath (2012) found that using open confrontation strategies such as "openly expressing" the reason were associated with greater levels of satisfaction for the "left" partner than engaging in avoidance and/or withdrawal strategies.

Therefore, if you are concerned about the satisfaction level of the individual you are leaving, it is best to be honest and open about your reasons for ending the friendship.

Direct Strategies for Ending Friendships

Direct methods involve specifically telling the friend how you feel about the status of your friendship. Direct strategies are more likely to be used in relationships when there is high intimacy/closeness and an overlap in social networks (Baxter, 1982). Direct approaches are used to end friendships when a recipient does not recognize the intent of indirect attempts or if individuals are interested in terminating the friendship abruptly due to some hurtful circumstance. If you choose to engage in this approach, be prepared to be assertive and to provide a valid reason for why you are ending the friendship. We recognize that this is not an easy task. However, understanding how to engage in assertive communication can help you navigate uncomfortable situations.

As discussed in Chapter 3, assertiveness involves defending your own rights and wishes while still respecting the rights and wishes of others. Booth-Butterfield (2006) feels individuals can maximize the effectiveness of their assertive communication by sending nonverbal messages that are consistent with the verbal. For example, you should strive to maintain eye contact, appear confident through your facial expressions, and use appropriately assertive gestures and a firm and confident tone of voice. Individuals can enhance their assertiveness and credibility by displaying confidence in their voice, gestures, posture, and facial expressions.

Booth-Butterfield offers a model of an appropriately assertive response that includes three components (**ERA**):

1. Express *Empathy*
2. State *Rationale*
3. Provide *Action* Request

Read the textbox below for an example of how to use ERA to terminate a friendship.

> ## ERA Assertive Communication Tool
>
> First, express honest and sincere empathy for the situation:
>> *"I understand we have been friends for a long time."*
>
> Second, provide a rationale for your request:
>> *"However, we have both changed a lot over the last few years and we have different interests and goals. When we get together all we do is argue the entire time and get angry with each other."*
>
> Finally, provide the action statement:
>> *"I do not think we should be friends anymore."*

TYPES OF RELATIONSHIPS: TERMINATING ROMANTIC RELATIONSHIPS

Typically, the decision to leave a romantic partner is a difficult and arduous task. For this reason, many people may recall staying in relationships much longer than they should have. In this section, we examine four common reasons individuals leave romantic relationships (adapted from Cupach & Metts, 1986). These include: (1) infidelity, (2) lack of commitment, (3) dissimilarity, and (4) outside pressures.

Infidelity

Infidelity is defined as "a secret sexual, romantic, or emotional involvement that violates the commitment to an exclusive relationship" (Glass, 2002, p. 489). As suggested in the definition, infidelity can take many forms, including physical (holding hands), sexual (kissing and other activities), and emotional (sharing intimate conversation) (Spitzberg & Tafoya, 2005).

As we discussed in Chapter 9, researchers have examined various forms of infidelity and determined that males and females differ greatly in their responses to different types of infidelity. Men are more likely to be upset with a partner's sexual infidelity, while women tend to be more upset with a partner's emotional infidelity (Glass & Wright, 1985). In other words, males are more concerned with their partners' physical transgressions, while females are more hurt by their partners' emotional disclosures with another person.

Researchers have explored whether some marriages are more prone to infidelity than others. Infidelity is more likely to exist in marriages where there are frequent arguments about trust, narcissistic attitudes and behaviors exhibited by partners, and increased time spent apart (Atkins, Yi, Baucom, & Christensen, 2005).

50–60 percent of married men and 45–55 percent of married women engage in some form of extramarital affair at some point in their marriage.

While approximately 99 percent of married persons expect sexual fidelity from their spouse (Treas & Giesen, 2000), not many couples are meeting those expectations. Although infidelity statistics are difficult to measure, some interesting findings that describe the pervasiveness of infidelity include the following:

- Atwood and Schwartz (2002) estimated that 50–60 percent of married men and 45–55 percent of married women engage in some form of extramarital affair at some point in their marriage.
- Infidelity is the most frequently cited cause of divorce (Amato & Rogers, 1997).
- 60 percent of dating relationships ended after infidelity was discovered (Feldman & Cauffman, 1999).
- Approximately 75 percent of male and 68 percent of female college students reported engaging in at least one form of infidelity, with 49 percent of men and 31 percent of women having ever engaged in a sexual infidelity (Wiederman & Hurd, 1999).
- 20–40 percent of married men and 20–25 percent of married women reported en-

gaging in extramarital sexual infidelity during their lifetimes (Greeley, 1994; Tafoya & Spitzberg, 2007).

These alarming statistics imply that although not many condone infidelity, there are a significant proportion of people engaging in these types of behaviors.

So why are heterosexual married couples cheating? Fisher (2009) suggests that men are more likely to report *sexual motivations* for infidelity and are less likely to fall in love with an extramarital partner. Women tend to have an *emotional connection* with their extramarital partner and are more likely to have an affair because they are lonely. In fact, Fisher reports that 56 percent of men (and 34 percent of women) who have affairs claim to be happy in their marriages. While this may seem high, marital dissatisfaction still appears to be the single strongest predictor of infidelity (Whisman, Gordon, & Chatav, 2007).

Lack of Commitment

Another reason individuals provide for terminating romantic relationships is a lack of commitment. **Commitment** or one's "intent to persist in a relationship" (Rusbult, Martz, & Agnew, 1998, p. 359) can be expressed and reinforced in the everyday and often mundane tasks that couples endure (Weigel, 2008). For example, relationship partners might express commitment by providing affection and support, and working together to solve problems. Commitment is what sustains romantic couples "through the ups and downs and the good times and bad times" (Weigel & Ballard-Reisch, 2014, p. 331).

Although infidelity is one way to demonstrate an individual's lack of commitment, other ways include: not spending enough time together, not prioritizing the relationship, not valuing the other's opinion, experiencing power struggles, and not nurturing the maintenance and development of the relationship. **Lack of commitment**—or the omission of expressing one's intent to persist in a relationship—can foster feelings of abandonment and loneliness. Some relationship experts argue that partners' commitment to the relationship is a stronger predictor of relationship stability than feelings of love (Lund, 1985). This research was interested in studying heterosexual dating relationships in an attempt to determine whether love or commitment served as a stronger predictor of relationship stability. She found that couples with higher levels of commitment were more likely to continue the relationship than those with high levels of love and low levels of commitment. In this study, couples' expectations of staying together proved to be more important to relationship stability than their feelings of love for each other. These findings are consistent with Fisher's (2009), who noted we may be lured outside of the relationship, even though we cite "loving" our partners.

It certainly makes sense that both our positive and negative experiences in our previous romantic relationships would affect our future relationships. Communication researchers sought to explore how closeness in previous relationships was related to current relationship commitment and satisfaction among college students in dating relationships (Merolla, Weber, Myers & Booth-Butterfield, 2004). Their results suggested the more close they felt in their past relationship, the less likely they were to report being satisfied

and committed in their current dating relationship. These findings indicate how difficult it is sometimes for people to forget the past and fully embrace new relationships.

Dissimilarity

Scholars have identified similarity as one of two components that relationship dyads consider when deciding whether to stay together or to break up (Hill, Rubin, & Peplau, 1976). A longitudinal study suggested that couples who were most similar in educational plans, intelligence, and attractiveness were most likely to remain together, whereas couples that were different in the levels of these aspects were more likely to break up.

Some may say, "opposites attract," but the truth is that great amounts of dissimilarity in significant areas create more problems than solutions over the course of a relationship. Differences in backgrounds (religion, family values), intelligence (educational goals, IQ), attitudes concerning family roles, ethics, and communicating about conflicts and temperament (argumentativeness, assertiveness) may contribute to conflict situations and misinterpretations of behavior.

Our similarity with romantic partners is often linked to our perception of solidarity with one another. **Interpersonal solidarity** refers to feelings of closeness between people that develop as a result of shared sentiments, similarities, and intimate behaviors (Wheeless, 1978). With that in mind, it makes sense that solidarity increases as relationships become more intimate, and it decreases as relationships turn toward termination (Wheeless, Wheeless, & Baus, 1984). As solidarity increases in romantic relationships, so do individuals' levels of trust, reciprocity, and self-disclosures (Wheeless, 1976). Also, the closer we feel to our partner, the more likely we are able to provide emotional support (Weber & Patterson, 1996). If individuals in romantic relationships perceive differences between themselves, there will be less trust, reciprocity, and emotional support, and fewer self-disclosures are likely to be shared.

Some may say, "opposites attract," but the truth is that great amounts of dissimilarity in significant areas create more problems than solutions over the course of a relationship.

Outside Pressures

External or **outside pressure** from friends, family, or occupations may negatively impact relationship satisfaction. Family members may put pressure on romantic relationships when they ask questions like "When are you two getting married?" or make comments such as, "You should save your money for a house!" and "I want to be a grandparent!" Friends may also exert pressure on romantic relationships by hinting that not enough time is spent with them. For couples in the public eye, the paparazzi acts as an external pressure peering over the hedge, demanding details and pushing expectations for the relationship on the couple. Additionally, work relationships or job stressors can impact the satisfaction in our romantic relationship. An increase in job demands, hours, and travel requirements are examples of significant occupational pressures that may affect relationship stability.

These outside pressures put a strain on our ability to make decisions. A theory that may help explain the link between outside pressures and relationship satisfaction is self-determination theory. According to **self-determination theory**, people have an innate psychological need to feel autonomous, or self-governing, in their behavior and relationships (Deci & Ryan, 1985; Deci, 2000, 2002). People want to feel free to choose their own paths in relationships, rather than be coerced or pressured into exhibiting certain behaviors. Ultimately, this self-initiated behavior will lead to better personal and social adjustment. Hence, those who report feeling responsible for, and in control of, their own decisions are also more secure and positive about their relationships with others.

HOMOSEXUAL RELATIONSHIPS: FACTORS INFLUENCING RELATIONSHIP QUALITY

Although scant research has addressed gay and lesbian relationship termination and whether this process differs from heterosexual relationships, one study found that cohabiting gay or lesbian partners are actually more similar when compared to married heterosexual partners (Kurdek, 1992, 1998). In a 1998 longitudinal study, he examined relationship satisfaction among partners from gay, lesbian, and heterosexual married couples over a five year period in which they completed a survey each year. Both gay and lesbian partners reported more frequent relationship dissolution compared to heterosexual spouses. Additionally, gay and lesbian partners reported more autonomy than married people. Furthermore, lesbian partners reported significantly more intimacy and equality than their married counterparts (Kurdek, 1998).

Another study examined factors that contributed to heterosexual and homosexual couples' *relationship quality* after a breakup (Lannutti & Cameron, 2002). For homosexual couples, factors that contributed to higher relationship quality included personal variables or those factors that emerged from the relationship. Some examples include the amount of liking for the ex-partner, the uniqueness of the relationship, and the hope for romantic renewal. In heterosexual couples the social environment (for example mutual friends or community) was instrumental in explaining relationship quality after a breakup, compared to homosexual couples.

Cohabitating gay or lesbian partners are more similar than different when compared to married heterosexual partners.

It makes sense that gay and lesbian relationships are influenced more by characteristics within the relationship and less by societal influences for relationship satisfaction due to their denial of legal and societal recognition over the years (Lannutti & Cameron, 2002). However, these trends may change now that homosexual marriages have become legalized.

Now that we have discussed factors related to satisfaction and dissolution in different relationship types, we turn our attention to what happens after the breakup. After a relationship ends it is normal to redefine the relationship and to determine whether or not to remain in contact with the former partner. In this section, we will review three popular areas that are addressed after a romantic breakup: (1) staying friends, (2) methods of coping, and (3) closure and forgiveness.

AFTER THE BREAKUP: REMAINING "JUST FRIENDS"

After a breakup, we sometimes want to remain friends with our "ex." This makes sense because we have self-disclosed personal information, relied on this person for emotional support and guidance, and often have a great deal in common. Think about the things that draw couples together in the first place. Research suggests that a couple is more likely to remain friends when the man has been the one who precipitated the breakup (or when the breakup was mutual) than when the woman initiated the breakup (Hill, Rubin, & Peplau, 1976).

Other research suggests that if the couple was friends prior to the romantic involvement, their

322

chances of returning to a friendship are significantly higher than those who never maintained a friendship (Metts, Cupach, & Bejlovec, 1989). Additionally, if the former partners were still receiving rewards or resources from the relationship, this could influence the impact of a partner's satisfaction with the post-breakup friendship (Busboom, Collins, & Givertz, 2002).

Have you ever tried to remain friends after a breakup?

Certain relationship disengagement strategies are more effective in creating a positive post-breakup relationship. When we ask our students how they would prefer to end a romantic relationship, most agree that they prefer an honest and direct strategy such as justification. Negative disengagement strategies, such as withdrawal, avoidance, or negative identity management have been identified as inhibiting post-dating relationship quality (Metts et al., 1989; Banks et al., 1987; Busboom, Collins, & Givertz, 2002). If relationship partners would like to remain friends, then it is a good idea to use positive tone messages, justification, or other tactics that protect the other person's feelings.

While it is certainly possible to remain friends after a breakup, it is important that both parties agree with the new relational "rules." Discuss the boundaries of the relationship and be open about what is appropriate and inappropriate behavior in this newly defined relationship. It is not unusual for post-breakup friendships to cross friendship boundaries in times of distress due to the familiarity and security of the relationship.

Some relationships cycle through development and dissolution several times and are referred to as "on-again/off-again" relationships (Dailey, Pfiester, Jin, Beck & Clark, 2009). Research has found that these relationships do experience fewer positive behaviors such as validation and understanding (Daily et al., 2009) and less relational maintenance and greater relational uncertainty (Dailey, Hampel & Roberts, 2010). So, why do individuals go back to these relationships? Research suggests it may be they have lingering feelings, more effective conversations, negative experiences with others, and/or perceptions of positive changes in the partner (Dailey, Jin Pfiester, & Beck, 2011). Overall, communication scholars are interested in how these relationships are renegotiated and redefined. Duck (2006) reminds us that relationships are constantly changing and that some relationships do not just end because they did not work out. This makes sense for romantic relationships that involve children. Co-parenting after a breakup involves negotiating the relational status.

AFTER THE BREAKUP: METHODS OF COPING

Scholars also note that the dissolution of a romantic relationship can be one of the most painful and stressful experiences people endure in their personal lives (Feeney & Noller, 1992; Simpson,

After a break-up, keep yourself busy with family or friends you many have neglected during the relationship.

1987). This section will discuss methods of coping with relationship dissolution and creating closure.

Because ending a relationship can be one of the most emotionally charged events we experience, often there is no easy or painless way to do it. No two relationships are identical in nature, and there are no scripts to terminate relationships. We are flooded with different emotions, including sadness, anger, fear, denial, guilt, and confusion. Sometimes we are relieved that the relationship is over and we are anticipating more rewarding relationships in the future. There are productive and unproductive ways to cope with the end of a relationship. Here are some of the most helpful methods of coping with relationship dissolution:

1. *Give it time.* Recognize that relationship dissolution is a process and is not just a single event (Duck & Rollie, 2003). Allow yourself time to feel a range of emotions and recognize that this is normal and healthy. Do not reject your feelings or hide them behind negative coping strategies such as binge eating (or refusing to eat), binge drinking, or drug use.

2. *Rely on your social support network to stay busy.* Discuss your feelings with friends and family. Revisit the activities that you enjoy and invite friends to join you. Explore new hobbies or schedule a vacation with friends. Research has shown that women tend to have more people to confide in during difficult times, compared to men. Therefore it is not surprising that a man is significantly "more likely to enter rebound relationships than women" (Shimek & Bello, 2014, p. 38). Reaching out to friends and engaging in activities that were neglected during your romantic relationship are healthy coping strategies.

3. *Seek out professional help or a support group.* If you feel you are burdening your friends and family by talking about the breakup, or you continue to feel depressed or angry about the breakup, talk with a professional. Additionally, the sharing of emotional support in face-to-face and online support groups offers several psychological and physical health benefits (Campbell & Wright, 2002; Cawyer & Smith-Dupre, 1995; Lin & Peek, 1999; Wellman & Whortley, 1990). Personal counseling may be covered by health insurance, and most university counseling services are provided free of charge to students. You may be able to take advantage of resources that are included in your tuition. Discussing issues with a third party who has no personal involvement in your existing relationships can provide a fresh perspective.

4. Do not engage in social media surveillance. While it may be tempting to go on to social media to seek out information regarding an ex-partner, it is not healthy

for your post break-up health. Perhaps, not surprisingly, communication scholars have found that young people who have engaged in higher levels of internet surveillance experience more breakup distress (Lukacs & QUan-Haase, 2015). Certainly, you may be able to recall a time you consoled a friend who found something disturbing online regarding an ex-partner. Perhaps an effective coping strategy would be to hide or avoid social media messages that may mention your ex-partner.

AFTER THE BREAKUP: CLOSURE AND FORGIVENESS

Closure refers to a level of understanding, or emotional conclusion, to a difficult life event, such as terminating a romantic relationship. In this situation, closure often includes the rationale for the breakup. Some research suggests that individuals need a certain level of closure in their breakup before they can effectively move on (Weber, 1998). The purpose of closure is to discuss things with your former partner that "worked" in the relationship as well as to discuss the challenges of the relationship in order to learn from them. Remember, the purpose of this discussion is to make future relationships more effective, and not to resurrect the terminated relationship. Therefore, blaming, accusations, and name-calling are counterproductive. If properly executed, this discussion is helpful in understanding what went wrong in the relationship, providing some direction for future relationships.

Granting forgiveness is one strategy used during closure. Forgiveness does not mean you forget, accept, understand, or excuse the behavior; it simply implies that you will not hold your partner in debt for his or her wrongdoing. Granting forgiveness is a powerful tool. When you forgive someone that you are terminating a relationship with, you set yourself free from harboring negative feelings. Negative feelings are detrimental to your ability to nurture future relationships. All in all, granting forgiveness is an investment in you!

Self-forgiveness refers to giving yourself permission and an opportunity to heal and move forward. You give yourself permission to shed yourself of the burden, guilt, pain, and anger that

RESEARCH IN REAL LIFE:
Do "rebound relationships" actually work?

Could focusing on someone new or "rebounding" be helpful in letting go of an ex-partner? The following study was determined to answer this question.

Using attachment theory, researchers designed an experimental study that examined those individuals who were most likely to have the most emotional connection to ex-partners.

They found that their longing for their ex-partner was disrupted when they attempted to focus their attention on a new partner. In other words, they experienced less emotional pain from their previous relationship, when their attention was placed on someone new.

This research helps explain why individuals often turn to rebound relationships. Rebound relationships are described by the researchers as "an adaptive behavior" or a strategy that helps us adjust to another type of situation.

The authors also add that "focusing on new relationship options—either a new relationship or an optimistic outlook on relationships—decreases attachment" to an ex-partner (Spielmann, MacDonald, & Wilson, 2009, p. 1391).

is held inside of you. Once you grant yourself forgiveness you can focus on how to become a better person and make healthier choices in the future.

Creating closure optimally involves getting together with your "ex" face-to-face to discuss the good times and the bad. In most situations, this option is impossible because either it is too difficult to sit in the same room or a partner has physically moved away. Therefore, closure is often difficult and not easily attainable.

One way to create an emotional conclusion to a relationship is to reframe the event. Frequently, this is a way individuals can create a sense of closure without relying on the ex-partner. **Reframing** is a psychological process in which you change the way you look at the romantic termination in order to foster a more productive resolution. For example, if you are angry and hurt that your partner cheated on you, you may reframe the event by thinking about how dishonest the partner was. Instead of focusing on your hurt and anger, you psychologically emphasize that untruthfulness is not a characteristic of a person you want to share a romantic relationship with. You focus on recognizing signs of the cheating behavior and predictors of his or her behavior so you can be more

aware in future relationships. By reframing the event, you are looking at the event in a different light, which enables you to move forward.

SUMMARY

This chapter reviewed how to assess relationship problems and factors that individuals consider when ending a relationship. In addition, we described the complex processes involved in ending our relationships by explaining Duck's four-phase process of decision making during relationship termination and Knapp's five stages of relationship deterioration. Research specific to different types of relationships such as friendships and romantic relationships was summarized. Finally, we discussed the processes involved in redefining the relationship, closure, and forgiveness after relationship termination. Ending a relationship with someone you cared about is often a difficult and challenging task. Understanding the key concepts and natural process of dissolution discussed in this chapter will help you determine when and how to end unhealthy relationships and accept termination as a natural progression.

DISCUSSION QUESTIONS

1. Were you able to remain friends with an ex-romantic partner? If so, what were some of the challenges as your relationship shifted from romantic to platonic?

2. What are some effective tactics that you have used to terminate friendships? Discuss the effectiveness (or ineffectiveness) of the strategies you selected.

3. Can you recall a time when you were able to reframe a difficult or challenging event in your life? Can you describe the event and how you applied reframing to understand it?

SELF ASSESSMENT

Investment Model Scale

Satisfaction Level

1. Please indicate the degree to which you agree with each of the following statements regarding your current relationship (circle an answer for each item).

   (a) My partner fulfills my needs for intimacy (sharing personal thoughts, secrets, etc.)

   | Don't Agree At All | Agree Slightly | Agree Moderately | Agree Completely |

   (b) My partner fulfills my needs for companionship (doing things together, enjoying each other's company, etc.)

   | Don't Agree At All | Agree Slightly | Agree Moderately | Agree Completely |

   (c) My partner fulfills my sexual needs (holding hands, kissing, etc.)

   | Don't Agree At All | Agree Slightly | Agree Moderately | Agree Completely |

   (d) My partner fulfills my needs for security (feeling trusting, comfortable in a stable relationship, etc.)

   | Don't Agree At All | Agree Slightly | Agree Moderately | Agree Completely |

   (e) My partner fulfills my needs for emotional involvement (feeling emotionally attached, feeling good when another feels good, etc.)

   | Don't Agree At All | Agree Slightly | Agree Moderately | Agree Completely |

2. I feel satisfied with our relationship (please circle a number).

   | 0 | 1 | 2 | 3 | 4 | 5 | 6 | 7 | 8 |

   Do Not Agree At All   Agree Somewhat   Agree Completely

3. My relationship is much better than others' relationships.

   | 0 | 1 | 2 | 3 | 4 | 5 | 6 | 7 | 8 |

   Do Not Agree At All   Agree Somewhat   Agree Completely

4. My relationship is close to ideal.

   | 0 | 1 | 2 | 3 | 4 | 5 | 6 | 7 | 8 |

   Do Not Agree At All   Agree Somewhat   Agree Completely

5. Our relationship makes me very happy.

0	1	2	3	4	5	6	7	8
Do Not Agree At All				Agree Somewhat				Agree Completely

6. Our relationship does a good job of fulfilling my needs for intimacy, companionship, etc.

0	1	2	3	4	5	6	7	8
Do Not Agree At All				Agree Somewhat				Agree Completely

Quality of Alternatives

1. Please indicate the degree to which you agree with each statement regarding the fulfillment of each need in alternative relationships (e.g., by another dating partner, friends, family).

   (a) My needs for intimacy (sharing personal thoughts, secrets, etc.) could be fulfilled in alternative relationships

Don't Agree At All	Agree Slightly	Agree Moderately	Agree Completely

   (b) My needs for companionship (doing things together, enjoying each other's company, etc.) could be fulfilled in alternative relationships

Don't Agree At All	Agree Slightly	Agree Moderately	Agree Completely

   (c) My sexual needs (holding hands, kissing, etc.) could be fulfilled in alternative relationships

Don't Agree At All	Agree Slightly	Agree Moderately	Agree Completely

   (d) My needs for security (feeling trusting, comfortable in a stable relationship, etc.) could be fulfilled in alternative relationships

Don't Agree At All	Agree Slightly	Agree Moderately	Agree Completely

   (e) My needs for emotional involvement (feeling emotionally attached, feeling good when another feels good, etc.) could be fulfilled in alternative relationships

Don't Agree At All	Agree Slightly	Agree Moderately	Agree Completely

2. The people other than my partner with whom I might become involved are very appealing (please circle a number).

0	1	2	3	4	5	6	7	8
Do Not Agree At All				Agree Somewhat				Agree Completely

3. My alternatives to our relationship are close to ideal (dating another, spending time with friends).

0	1	2	3	4	5	6	7	8
Do Not Agree At All				Agree Somewhat				Agree Completely

4. If I weren't dating my partner, I would do fine—I would find another appealing person to date.

0	1	2	3	4	5	6	7	8
Do Not Agree At All				Agree Somewhat				Agree Completely

5. My alternatives are attractive to me (dating another, spending time with friends or on my own, etc.).

0	1	2	3	4	5	6	7	8
Do Not Agree At All				Agree Somewhat				Agree Completely

6. My needs for intimacy, companionship, etc., could easily be fulfilled in an alternative relationship.

0	1	2	3	4	5	6	7	8
Do Not Agree At All				Agree Somewhat				Agree Completely

Investment Size

1. Please indicate the degree to which you agree with each of the following statements regarding your current relationship (circle an answer for each item).

		Don't Agree At All	Agree Slightly	Agree Moderately	Agree Completely
(a)	I have invested a great deal of time in our relationship	Don't Agree At All	Agree Slightly	Agree Moderately	Agree Completely
(b)	I have told my partner many private things about myself (I disclose secrets to him/her)	Don't Agree At All	Agree Slightly	Agree Moderately	Agree Completely

<table>
<tr><td>(c)</td><td>My partner and I have an intellectual life together that would be difficult to replace</td><td>Don't Agree At All</td><td>Agree Slightly</td><td>Agree Moderately</td><td>Agree Completely</td></tr>
<tr><td>(d)</td><td>My sense of personal identity (who I am) is linked to my partner and our relationship</td><td>Don't Agree At All</td><td>Agree Slightly</td><td>Agree Moderately</td><td>Agree Completely</td></tr>
<tr><td>(e)</td><td>My partner and I share many memories</td><td>Don't Agree At All</td><td>Agree Slightly</td><td>Agree Moderately</td><td>Agree Completely</td></tr>
</table>

2. I have put a great deal into our relationship that I would lose if the relationship were to end (please circle a number).

0	1	2	3	4	5	6	7	8
Do Not Agree At All				Agree Somewhat				Agree Completely

3. Many aspects of my life have become linked to my partner (recreational activities, etc.), and I would lose all of this if we were to break up.

0	1	2	3	4	5	6	7	8
Do Not Agree At All				Agree Somewhat				Agree Completely

4. I feel very involved in our relationship—like I have put a great deal into it.

0	1	2	3	4	5	6	7	8
Do Not Agree At All				Agree Somewhat				Agree Completely

5. My relationships with friends and family members would be complicated if my partner and I were to break up (e.g., partner is friends with people I care about).

0	1	2	3	4	5	6	7	8
Do Not Agree At All				Agree Somewhat				Agree Completely

6. Compared to other people I know, I have invested a great deal in my relationship with my partner.

0	1	2	3	4	5	6	7	8
Do Not Agree At All				Agree Somewhat				Agree Completely

Commitment Level

1. I want our relationship to last for a very long time (please circle a number).

0	1	2	3	4	5	6	7	8
Do Not Agree At All				Agree Somewhat				Agree Completely

2. I am committed to maintaining my relationship with my partner.

0	1	2	3	4	5	6	7	8
Do Not Agree At All				Agree Somewhat				Agree Completely

3. I would not feel very upset if our relationship were to end in the near future.

0	1	2	3	4	5	6	7	8
Do Not Agree At All				Agree Somewhat				Agree Completely

4. It is likely that I will date someone other than my partner within the next year.

0	1	2	3	4	5	6	7	8
Do Not Agree At All				Agree Somewhat				Agree Completely

5. I feel very attached to our relationship—very strongly linked to my partner.

0	1	2	3	4	5	6	7	8
Do Not Agree At All				Agree Somewhat				Agree Completely

6. I want our relationship to last forever.

0	1	2	3	4	5	6	7	8
Do Not Agree At All				Agree Somewhat				Agree Completely

7. I am oriented toward the long-term future of my relationship (for example, I imagine being with my partner several years from now).

0	1	2	3	4	5	6	7	8
Do Not Agree At All				Agree Somewhat				Agree Completely

SOURCE: Rusbult, C. E., Martz, J. M., & Agnew, C. R. (1998). The Investment Model Scale: Measuring commitment level, satisfaction level, quality of alternatives, and investment size. *Personal Relationships, 5,* 357–391.

KEY TERMS AND DEFINITIONS

AVOIDING: relationship partners will actively fill their schedules to avoid seeing their partners.

CIRCUMSCRIBING: communication between the relationship partners is often described as restricted, controlled, or constrained.

CLOSURE: refers to a level of understanding, or emotional conclusion, to a difficult life event, such as terminating a romantic relationship.

COMMITMENT: the extent of our dedication to continue a relationship.

COST ESCALATION: indirect strategy to terminate a friendship in which attempts are made to make the relationship appear burdensome or unappealing due to the amount of effort the other person has to invest.

DE-ESCALATION MESSAGES: less emotional than positive tone messages and typically provide a rationale for wanting to see less of the rejected partner.

DIFFERENTIATING: partners highlight their differences.

DIRECT METHODS: refers to specific and straightforward strategies used in telling a friend how you honestly feel.

DISSIMILARITY: the differences between relationship dyads such as backgrounds, intelligence, attitudes, ethics, and temperament.

DYADIC PROCESS: when the leaver officially announces to the partner that he or she is leaving or thinking of leaving.

EQUITY THEORY: couples are happiest in relationships when there is a balance of inputs and outputs.

ERA: model that outlines three components of appropriately assertive responses - empathy, rationale, and action.

FUNDAMENTAL ATTRIBUTION ERROR: when attempting to explain others' negative behaviors, we tend to overestimate the internal factors or causes and underestimate the external factors or causes.

GRANTING FORGIVENESS: a powerful tool used to set yourself and your partner free from harboring negative feelings toward each other and perceptions of the relationship.

GRAVE DRESSING PROCESS: partners are able to articulate the explanation of the termination and create their own versions of the relationship, whether truthful or not.

INDIRECT METHODS: methods to decrease the intensity of the friendship by increasing the emotional and physical distance between you and your friend.

INFIDELITY: behaving in a way that crosses the perceived boundary and expectation of an exclusive relationship.

INTERPERSONAL SOLIDARITY: feelings of closeness between people that develop as a result of shared sentiments, similarities, and intimate behaviors.

INTRAPSYCHIC PROCESS: initial phase in the relationship termination process where the leaver spends considerable time contemplating whether the relationship is worth saving.

INVESTMENT MODEL: identifies four factors that can be used to assess or predict the likelihood of a relationship continuing and prospering, or terminating.

INVESTMENT SIZE: includes the tangible and intangible qualities that are associated with being involved in a relationship; the resources that are invested in continuing the relationship.

JUSTIFICATION MESSAGES: stating that he or she needs to stop seeing the other person; provides a reason for ending the relationship and recognizes that the relationship is not salvageable.

LACK OF COMMITMENT: neglecting to express one's intent to continue or persist in the current relationship.

NEGATIVE IDENTITY MANAGEMENT: a strategy used to hurry the disengagement process; has little consideration for the rejected partner.

OUTSIDE PRESSURE: stress that stems from a relationship as a result of people external of the relationship such as friends, family, or coworkers.

POSITIVE TONE MESSAGES: created to ease the pain for the rejected partner.

PSEUDO DE-ESCALATION: indirect strategy to terminate a friendship in which the benefits of spending less time together are emphasized.

QUALITY OF ALTERNATIVES: addresses the potential for fulfilling one's needs by someone outside of the current relationship.

REFRAMING: a psychological process in which you change the way you look at the romantic termination in order to foster a more productive resolution.

RESURRECTION PROCESS: final phase of relationship termination in which one seeks the support of others to rationalize the end of the partnership in an effort to prepare for future relationships.

SATISFACTION LEVEL: the level of positive or negative emotions or feelings toward the partner or the relationship.

SELF-DETERMINATION THEORY: people have an innate psychological need to feel autonomous, or self-governing, in their behaviors.

SELF-FORGIVENESS: refers to giving yourself permission and an opportunity to heal and move forward.

SOCIAL EXCHANGE THEORY: an assessment of costs and rewards in determining the value of pursuing or continuing a relationship.

SOCIAL PROCESS: relationship termination goes public and focuses less on the relationship and more on the relationship partners' friends and family.

STAGNATING: two people who are merely "going through the motions" in their relationship because their communication has come to a virtual standstill.

TERMINATING: this stage marks the end of a relationship.

WITHDRAWAL/AVOIDANCE TACTICS: actively spending less time with the person.

REFERENCES

Amato, P. R., & Rogers, S. J. (1997). A longitudinal study of marital problems and subsequent divorce. *Journal of Marriage and the Family, 59,* 612–624.

Atkins, D. C., Yi, J., Baucom, D. H., & Christensen, A. (2005). Infidelity in couples seeking marital therapy. *Journal of Family Psychology, 19,* 470–473.

Atwood, J. D., & Schwartz, L. (2002). Cyber-sex: The new affair treatment considerations. *Journal of Couple and Relationship Therapy, 1,* 37–56.

Banks, S. P., Altendorf, D. M., Green, J. O., & Cody, M. J. (1987). An examination of relationship disengagement: Perceptions, breakup strategies and outcomes. *The Western Journal of Speech Communication, 52,* 19–41.

Baxter, L. (1982). Strategies for ending relationships: Two studies. *Western Journal of Speech Communication, 46,* 233–242.

Booth-Butterfield, M. (2006). *Influential health communication.* Littleton, MA: Tapestry Press.

Busboom, A. L., Collins, D. M., & Givertz, M. D. (2002). Can we still be friends? Resources and barriers to friendship quality after romantic relationship dissolution. *Personal Relationships, 9,* 215–223.

Campbell, K. L., & Wright, K. B. (2002). Online support groups: An investigation of relationship among source credibility, dimensions of relational communication, and perceptions of emotional support. *Communication Research Reports,* 19, 183–193.

Cawyer, C. S., & Smith-Dupre, A. (1995). Communicating social support: Identifying supportive episodes in an HIV/aids support group. *Communication Quarterly, 43,* 243–259.

Cody, M. (1982). A typology of disengagement strategies and an examination of the role intimacy reactions to inequity and relational problems play in strategy selection. *Communication Monographs, 49,* 148–170.

Collins, T. J. & Gillath, O. (2012). Attachment, breakup strategies, and associated outcomes: The effects of security enhancement on the selection of breakup strategies. *Journal of Research in Psychology, 46,* 210–223.

Cupach, W. R., & Metts, S. (1986). Accounts of relational dissolution: A comparison of marital and non-marital relationships. *Communication Monographs, 53,* 311–334.

Dailey, R. M., Hampel, A. D., & Roberts, J. (2010). Relational maintenance in on-again/off-again relationships: An assessment of how relational maintenance, uncertainty, and relationship quality vary by relationship type and status. *Communication Monographs, 77,* 75-101.

Dailey, R. M., Jin, B., Pfiester, R. A., & Beck, G. (2011). On-again/off-again relationships: What keeps partners coming back? *Journal of Social Psychology, 151,* 417-440.

Dailey, R. M., Pfiester, A., Jin, B., Beck, G., & Clark, G. (2009). On-again/Off-again dating relationships: How are they different from other dating relationships. *Personal Relationships, 16,* 23-47.

Deci, E. L., & Ryan, R. M. (1985). *Intrinsic motivation and self determination in human behavior.* New York: Plenum Press.

Deci, E. L. (2000). The "what" and "why" of goal pursuits: Human needs and the self-determination of behavior. *Psychological Inquiry, 11,* 227–268.

Deci, E. L. (2002). Self-determination research: Reflections and future directions. In E. L. Deci & R. M. Ryan (Eds.), *Handbook of self-determination research* (pp. 431–441). Rochester, NY: University of Rochester Press.

Duck, S. W. (1982). A topography of relationship disengagement and dissolution. In S. W. Duck (Ed.), *Personal relationships 4: Dissolving personal relationships* (pp. 1–30). London: Academic Press.

Duck, S. & Rollie, S. (2003). Relationship Dissolution. In J. J. Ponzetti (Ed), *International encyclopedia of marriage and the family* (2nd ed.) (pp. 1297–1300). New York: Macmillan.

Feeney, J. A., & Noller, P. (1992). Attachment style and romantic love: Relationship dissolution. *Australian Journal of Psychology, 44,* 69–74.

Feldman, S. S., & Cauffman, E. (1999). Sexual betrayal among late adolescents: Perspectives of the perpetrator and the aggrieved. *Journal of Youth and Adolescence, 28,* 235–258.

Fincham, F. D. (1994). Cognition in marriage: Current status and future challenges. *Applied and Preventative Psychology: Current Scientific Perspectives, 3,* 185–198.

Fincham, F. D., & Bradbury, T. N. (1993). Marital satisfaction, depression and attributions: A longitudinal analysis. *Journal of Personality and Social Psychology, 64,* 442–452.

Fincham, F. D., Harold, G. T., & Gano-Phillips, S. (2000). The longitudinal association between attributions and marital satisfaction: Direction of effects and role of efficacy expectations. *Journal of Family Psychology, 14,* 267–285.

Fisher, H. (2009). *Why him? Why her?: Finding real love by understanding your personality type.* NY: Holt, Henry & Company, Inc.

Glass, S. P. (2002). Couple therapy after the trauma of infidelity. In A. S. Gurman & N. S. Jacobson (Eds.), *Clinical handbook of couple therapy* (3rd ed.) (pp. 489–507). New York: Guilford.

Glass, D. P., & Wright, T. L. (1985). Sex differences in type of extramarital involvement and marital dissatisfaction. *Sex Roles, 12,* 1101–1120.

Greeley, A. (1994). Marital infidelity. *Society, 31,* 9–13.

Hall, E. D., Travis, M., Anderson, S., & Henley, A. (2013). Complaining and Knapp's relationship stages: Gender differences in instrumental complaints. *Florida Communication Journal, 41,* 49–61.

Hill, C. T., Rubin, Z., & Peplau, L. A. (1976). Break-ups before marriage: The end of 103 affairs. *Journal of Social Issues, 32,* 147–168.

Isaacs, F. (1999). *Toxic friends/true friends: How your friends can make or break your health, happiness, family and career.* Scranton: William Morrow & Co.

Johnson, A. J., Wittenberg, E., Haigh, M., Wigley, S., Becker, J., Brown, K., & Craig, E. (2004). The process of relationship development and deterioration: Turning points in friendships that have terminated. *Communication Quarterly, 52,* 54–67.

Knapp, M. L. (1978). *Social intercourse: From greeting to goodbye.* Boston: Allyn & Bacon.

Kurdek, L. A. (1998). Relationship outcomes and their predictors: Longitudinal evidence from heterosexual married, gay cohabiting, and lesbian cohabiting couples. *Journal of Marriage and the Family, 60,* 553–568.

Kurdek, L. A. (1992). Relationship stability and relationship satisfaction in cohabiting gay and lesbian couples: A prospective longitudinal test of the contextual and interdependence models. *Journal of Social and Personal Relationships, 9,* 125–142.

Lin, N., & Peek, M. K. (1999). Social networks and mental health. In A. V. Horwitz & T. L. Scheid (Eds.), *A handbook for the study of mental health: Social contexts, theories, and systems.* New York: Cambridge.

Lund, M. (1985). The development of investment and commitment scales for predicting continuity of personal relationships. *Journal of Social and Personal Relationships, 2,* 3–23.

Lannutti, P. J., & Cameron, K. A. (2002). Beyond the breakup: Heterosexual and homosexual post-dissolutional relationships. *Communication Quarterly, 50*(2), 153–170.

Lukacs, V. & Quan-Haase, A. (2015). Romantic breakups on Facebook: new scales for studying post-breakup behaviors, digital distress, and surveillance. *Information, Communication, and Society, 18,* 492, 508.

McEwan, B., Babin, G. B., & Farinelli, L. (2008). The end of a friendship: Friendship dissolution reasons and methods. Conference paper presented at the National Communication Association annual meeting. San Diego, CA.

Merolla, A. J., Weber, K. D., Myers, S. A., & Booth-Butterfield, M. B. (2004). The impact of past dating relationship solidary on commitment, satisfaction, and investment in current relationships. *Communication Quarterly, 52,* 251–264.

Metts, S., Cupach, W. R., & Bejlovec, R. A. (1989). "I love you too much to ever start liking you": Redefining romantic relationships. *Journal of Social and Personal Relationships, 6,* 259–274.

Miller, G. E., & Bradbury, T. N. (1995). Refining the association between attributions and behavior in marital interaction. *Journal of Family Psychology, 9,* 196–208.

Rollie, S. S., & Duck, S. W. (2006). Divorce and dissolution of romantic relationships: Stage models and limitations. In J. H. Harvey & M. A. Fine (Eds.), *Handbook of divorce and relationship dissolution* (pp. 223-240). Mahwah, NJ: Lawrence Erlbaum Associates.

Rose, S., & Serafica, F. C. (1986). Keeping and ending casual, close, and best friendships. *Journal of Social and Personal Relationships, 3,* 275–288.

Rusbult, C. E., Martz, J. M., & Agnew, C. R. (1998). The Investment Model Scale: Measuring commitment level, satisfaction level, quality of alternatives, and investment size. *Personal Relationships, 5,* 357–391.

Shimek, C., & Bello, R. (2014). Coping with breakups: Rebound relationships and gender socialization. *Social Sciences, 3,* 24–43.

Simpson, J. A. (1987). The dissolution of romantic relationships: Factors involved in relationship stability and distress. *Journal of Personality and Social Psychology, 53,* 683–692.

Spielmann, S. S., MacDonald, G., & Wilson, A. E. (2009). On the rebound: Focusing on someone new helps anxiously attached individuals let go of ex-partners. *Personality and Social Psychology Bulletin, 35,* 1382–1394.

Spitzberg, B., & Tafoya, M. (2005). Explorations in communicative infidelity: Jealousy, sociosexuality, and vengefulness. Paper presented at the International Communication Association annual meeting in New York, NY.

Swain, S. (1989). Covert intimacy: Closeness in men's friendships. In B. J. Risman & P. Schwartz (Eds.), *Gender in intimate relationships: A microstructural approach.* Belmont, CA: Wadsworth.

Tafoya, M. A., & Spitzberg, B. H. (2007). The dark side of infidelity: Its nature, prevalence, and communicative functions. In B. H. Spitzberg & W. R. Cupach (Eds.), *The dark side of interpersonal communication* (2nd ed.) (pp. 201-242). Mahwah, NJ: Lawrence Erlbaum Associates.

Thibault, J. W., & Kelley, H. H. (1959). *The social psychology of groups.* New York: Wiley.

Treas, J., & Giesen, D. (2000). Sexual infidelity among married and cohabiting Americans. *Journal of Marriage and the Family, 62,* 48–60.

Vangelisti, A. L. (2002). Interpersonal processes in romantic relationships. In M. L. Knappand & J. A. Daly. (Eds.), *Handbook of interpersonal communication* (pp. 643–679). Thousand Oaks, CA: Sage Publications.

Vangelisti, A. L. (1992). Communicative problems in committed relationships: An attributional analysis. In J. H. Harvery, T. L. Orbuch, & A. L. Weber (Eds.), *Attributions, accounts, and close relationships* (pp. 144–164). New York: Springer-Verlag.

Waldinger, R. J., & Schulz, M. S. (2006). Linking hearts and minds in couple interactions: Intentions, attributions, and overriding sentiments. *Journal of Family Psychology, 20,* 494–504.

Weber, A. L. (1998). Losing, leaving, and letting go: Coping with nonmarital breakups. In B. H. Spitzberg & W. R. Cupach (Eds.), *The dark side of close relationships* (pp. 267–306). Mahwah, NJ: Erlbaum.

Weber, K., & Patterson, B. R. (1996). Construction and validation of a communication based emotional support scale. *Communication Research Reports, 13*(1), 68–76.

Weigel, D. J. (2008) A dyadic assessment of how couples indicate their commitment to each other. *Personal Relationships, 15,* 17–39.

Weigel, D. J., & Ballard-Reisch, D. S. (2014). Constructing commitment in intimate relationships: Mapping interdependence in the every-day expressions of commitment. *Communication Research, 41,* 311–332.

Wellman, B., & Wortley, S. (1990). Different strokes for different folks: Community ties and social support. *American Journal of Sociology, 96,* 558–588.

Wheeless, L. (1976). Self-disclosure and interpersonal solidarity: Measurement, validation, and relationships. *Human Communication Research, 3*(1), 47–61.

Wheeless, L. (1978). A follow-up study of the relationships among trust, disclosure, and interpersonal solidarity. *Human Communication Research, 4*(2), 143–157.

Wheeless, L. R., Wheeless, V. E., & Baus, R. (1984). Sexual communication, communication satisfaction, and solidarity in the developmental stages of intimate relationships. *Western Journal of Speech Communication, 48,* 217–230.

Whisman, M. A., Gordon, K. C., & Chatav, Y. (2007). Predicting sexual infidelity in a population-based sample of married individuals. *Journal of Family Psychology, 21,* 320-324.

Wiederman, M. W., & Hurd, C. H. (1999). Extradyadic involvement during dating. *Journal of Social and Personal Relationships, 16,* 265–274.

Section THREE

RELATIONSHIP
CONTEXTS AND
ENVIRONMENTS

Chapter 11

Mediated Communication: Understanding the Influence of
Technology on Our Personal Relationships   341

Chapter 12

Intercultural Communication: Variety Is the Spice of Life   371

Chapter 13

Family Communication: It's All Relative   407

Chapter 14

Organizational Communication: Combining the Personal with
the Professional   439

Chapter 15

Health Communication: Using Effective Communication to Manage
Stressful Interactions   475

chapter

11

Mediated Communication:
Understanding the Influence of Technology on Our Personal Relationships

OBJECTIVES

- List advantages and disadvantages of computer-mediated communication (CMC)

- Discuss similarities and differences between face-to-face and mediated relationships

- Identify three sets of concerns held by online dating participants that contribute to uncertainty reduction behaviors

- Explain the hyperpersonal model of CMC

- Identify functions of social media sites

- Examine the benefits and drawbacks of mediated communication as a means of initiating and maintaining relationships

- Identify best practices for developing safe and meaningful online relationships

SCENARIO: SOUND FAMILIAR?

Olivia stared at her computer in disbelief. She could not believe it. Her friend Kathryn met a guy through an online dating site just three months ago. They have never met in person. Kathryn's online status was now "engaged." *How is this even possible?*, she thought. Olivia met her husband in college, and they dated several years before getting engaged. How could Kathryn decide to pursue a life partnership with someone she had never actually "met" in person?

OVERVIEW

While this scenario may sound a bit shocking, it is not unusual for individuals to initiate and develop relationships online. While getting engaged before actually meeting a person face-to-face is rare, research suggests that relationships that are initiated online may be more successful than their conventional counterparts. Cacioppo et al. (2013) examined a nationally representative sample of approximately 19,000 respondents who married between 2005 and 2012. Their research suggests that approximately one-third of marriages begin online. These marriages are slightly less prone to breakup compared to those who met offline. These encouraging findings may help Olivia resolve some of her doubt about her friend Kathryn—however, how could someone want to marry someone that they have never met in person? Why do we accept "friend requests" from people we have never met? We will try to answer these questions as we explore different aspects of mediated communication in our interpersonal relationships.

Computer-Mediated Communication

Computer-mediated communication (CMC) has captured the attention of interpersonal communication scholars. We are fascinated by how this medium influences how we construct messages and how it fulfills our relational needs. Spitzberg (2006) developed the Computer-Mediated Communication Competence measure (see scale at end of chapter) to investigate how well individuals are able to converse with others via mediated channels. While some aspects of

How many times a day do you text, surf or catch up on social networking?

communicating online are similar to our face-to face interactions, others are different.

Mediated communication is integral throughout all stages of interpersonal relationships—from initiating, sustaining, growing dark, and terminating. Consider how much you rely on text messages, instant messaging, email, blogs, and social networking sites in your own relationships. Recent studies suggest that we spend between 6.5 to 10 percent of our leisure time online (Cacioppo et al., 2013).

Online social networking sites (SNS) provide people with a place to come together to identify and discuss common interests or causes. According to a Pew Research Report, almost three-quarters (72 percent) of U.S. adults indicate that they use social networking sites (Brenner & Smith, 2013). The practice has become part of many individuals' "daily rituals," and this has added to the complexity of our relational communication. Users of these sites suggest that, while they may be used to initiate new relationships, their primary purpose is to maintain existing relationships.

Social networking sites provide an avenue to reconnect with high school friends or former neighbors, and also maintain communication with current friends and relatives (Cummings, Lee, & Kraut, 2006; Ellison, Steinfield, & Lampe, 2007). Millennials will make SNS sharing a lifelong habit, according to a 2010 Pew Research Internet Report. Sixty-seven percent of survey respondents agreed that by 2020, Millenials will continue to be ambient broadcasters who disclose a great deal of personal information in order to stay connected and to take advantage of social, economic, and political opportunities. All of these benefits align with our interpersonal needs of control, inclusion, and affection.

Why have mediated channels become more popular as a means of establishing and maintaining relationships with others? First and foremost, more people have access to technologies today and regularly use them for a variety of purposes. Most people keep a cell phone within close proximity at all times. For individuals in established relationships who want to communicate with friends, family members, and relationship partners, mediated communication is often less expensive and time-consuming than calling or writing letters. Technology allows individuals who study abroad, are on military assignments, or are in long-distance relationships to maintain constant communication. For some, the anonymity of mediated communication is comforting, especially when seeking answers to embarrassing or difficult questions. Finally, the asynchronous nature of technologies such as email and text messaging allows individuals time to create and respond to messages at their convenience.

Using our phones to communicate gives us time to think about what we want to say and edit our messages before sending them.

Top 5 Most Popular Dating Sites (January 2015)		
Match.com	OkCupid	Zoosk
PlentyofFish	eHarmony	

For the most current list, check out: http://www.ebizmba.com/articles/dating-websites

Top 15 Most Popular Social Networking Sites (SNS) (January 2015)		
Facebook	Tumblr	Meetup
Twitter	Instagram	Tagged
LinkedIn	Vk	Ask.fm
Pinterest	Flickr	meetMe
Google +	Vine	ClassMates

For most current list checkout: http://www.ebizmba.com/articles/social-networking-websites

Alternatively, mediated communication has its share of frustrating characteristics. Sometimes technology malfunctions. Can you recall a time when the "auto-correct" function in email or text-messaging caused problems in conveying a message? For those who are uncomfortable with technological innovations, the constant addition of new apps and social networking sites can be intimidating. Mediated channels provide us with limited exposure to nonverbal cues that provide valuable insight into the true meaning of a message. Can you recall a time when you perceived someone as being upset with you simply because an email response was brief? The lack of nonverbal cues may cause you to misperceive a message as being negative when circum-

Table 11.1 Advantages and Disadvantages of Mediated Communication

Advantages	Disadvantages
Is instantaneous and frequent; may be used to enhance communication flow and collaboration	Not everyone has access to the same devices, platforms, and programs
Ability to review messages to enhance cognitive processing and ability to store/save messages	Time required to learn the technology and different platforms; assumes a working knowledge of technology and the social norms of use
Reduce potential barriers to communication due to proximity	Frustration, stress, and potential communication overload; the inability to "unplug"
Reduce personal bias and stereotyping	Credibility issues (who is the source of the message?)
Accessibility to information and people	Lack of nonverbal cues
Sharing of multiple ideas and viewpoints	Trust issues (is the information accurate?)
Convenient/flexible	Confidentiality issues (is it safe to share this information online?)
Foster independent learning	Decrease in face-to-face interaction

stances may have required a brief response. An absence of nonverbal cues creates challenges in understanding the intended meanings behind messages.

Table 11.1 provides a more complete list of advantages and disadvantages of mediated communication.

HOW DO FACE-to-FACE and MEDIATED COMMUNICATION DIFFER?

Several important distinctions can be made when comparing the impact of face-to-face versus mediated communication on our interpersonal relationships. Table 11.2 highlights several of the distinctions between these two forms of communication. In particular, the level

of communication activity, nonverbal cues, language style, synchronicity, and media richness are altered when we move from communicating in person to using technology to convey our messages.

LEVEL OF COMMUNICATION ACTIVITY. The vast majority of our face-to-face interactions require us to be active or engaged participants in a conversation. Of course, there are times when we engage in passive communication behaviors (e.g., responding "uh-huh" to a question while watching a game on television), but our physical presence typically requires us to be actively involved in face-to-face interaction. We expect others to be actively engaged when we are in their physical presence. Consider how those expectations are violated when someone constantly views their cell phones while dining with you or a job candidate glances at a text-message that appears on

Table 11.2 Comparisons of Face-to-Face and Mediated Communication

Qualities	Face-to-Face (FTF)	Mediated Communication
Level of communication activity	Active	Active & Passive (lurking, viewing)
Nonverbal cues	Real	Artificial
Language style	Elaborate and more formal	Restricted and less formal
Synchronicity	Synchronous	Asynchronous and Synchronous
Richness of interaction	High	Low
Social presence	High	Low

their phone screen in the middle of an interview. A negative impression is often formed based on our expectations for giving one another our full attention when we are together. In the mediated environment, our communication activity can range from active to passive. Active participation may include overt feedback, such as sending a text to a friend or commenting on a blog. Mediated environments afford us more opportunities to engage in passive communication. Examples of passive activity include scrolling through sites

In FTF interactions, one look at someone's face can tell you how that person is reacting to your message.

such as Pinterest to see who shares your interests and scanning Twitter updates. Our expectations for interpersonal communication change in the mediated context. Recall our earlier discussion of the asynchronous nature of online communication. Since we can't see one another when we communicate using technology, our communication may be considered to be more passive. One example of this passive communication is **lurking**, which involves viewing posts in mediated channels without responding or providing feedback. Online developers are incorporating innovative features that are specifically designed to expose "lurkers." For example, you can subscribe to services that allow you to track who has viewed your photos, social networking sites, and blogs. Adding these types of features helps reduce some of the uncertainty about who is following or reading our online posts.

NONVERBAL CUES. Online rules for nonverbal communication are drastically different from the rules in face-to-face interactions. One theory developed to explain the absence of nonverbal cues in online interactions is **reduced social cues the-**

tive symbols are used to compensate for the lack of nonverbal cues expressed:

- Emoticons are used to communicate emotion: ☺
- Emojis, which literally means "picture" (e) + "letter" (☺) are used to graphically represent emotions:
- Capital letters are used to indicate the INTENSITY of emotion associated with the message
- Acronyms or abbreviations are inserted in messages to indicate a playful or informal tone (LOL, TTYL, YOLO, SMH, or IDK)

Examples of these artificially created nonverbal cues are included in Table 11.3.

With reduced nonverbal cues, the way we engage with others and how we interpret messages is different. For example, students are more willing to share negative information online than in face-to-face interactions. Often they feel protected in the online world because they cannot see the nonverbal responses of others in response to their negative messages. This explains why instructors may receive negative information about a course through email rather than during class or office hours.

Additionally, the social norms and constraints that typically guide our behavior are modified online. For example, students often admit to downloading illegal music online but would never consider actually stealing a CD from a store. According to the Recording Industry Association of America (RIAA), "Since peer-to-peer file-sharing site Napster emerged in 1999, music sales in the U.S. have dropped 53%, from 14.6 billion to 7 billion

ory (Sproull & Kiesler, 1986). According to this theory, we rely on social cues such as a person's appearance, attire, facial expressions, and gestures to help interpret received messages. Many of the social cues that we depend on in face-to-face interactions are absent in mediated contexts. One look at another person's facial expression reveals a myriad of cues about the mood or intent of a message. During face-to-face interactions, we often check to see whether the other person is smiling, whether they look confused, or if the person is focused on the message. The absence of cues makes the process of managing and interpreting online interactions more challenging. As a result, alterna-

in 2013." Additionally, they state, "From 2004–2009 alone, approximately 30 billion songs were illegally downloaded on file-sharing networks" (for more information, see http://www.riaa.com/facts/).

This is consistent with classic studies of deindividuation, or losing one's self-awareness while in group settings. **Deindividuation theory** suggests that the anonymity provided by being part of a group enables individuals to engage in anti-normative or aggressive behaviors they normally would not do. Sometimes this is referred to as "crowd behavior" or "mob behavior" to authority. Can crowd behavior also produce pro-social behaviors? Recent research suggests that not all crowd behavior is negative, particularly in online groups in which we choose to form relationships. For example, DoSomething.org is an example of a global organization that enlists members to promote social action. The site tackles social issues ranging from homelessness, texting while driving, and cruelty to animals. According to Lea and Spears's (1991) **social identity model of deindividuation effects (SIDE)**, the lack of nonverbal cues in mediated communication forces us to form impressions based on perceptions of social groups rather than on individual qualities or characteristics. This theory shifts our attention from just looking at anonymity to also examine the salience of the group. In online environments, we may reduce our self-awareness in order to align ourselves with group norms.

LANGUAGE STYLE. Due to the tedious nature of typing, it is often easier to take "shortcuts" when composing written messages. As a result, our mediated messages are often more *informal* in terms of language style compared to the *formal* characteristics of face-to-face messages. However, this casual language may have negative consequenc-

Deindividuation theory suggests that the anonymity within groups provides and enables individuals to participate in anti-normative or aggressive behavior they would not normally engage in.

RESEARCH IN REAL LIFE:
Students send casual emails to their instructors: Does it Matter?

Students rely heavily on email to communicate with their instructors outside of class. Understanding the implications of constructing appropriate email messages is important to their success. In 2009, Stephens, Houser and Cowan examined the informal tone of emails sent by students to their instructors. Results found overly casual email messages cause instructors to:

- like the student less;
- view them as less credible;
- form a less positive opinion of message quality;
- decrease their willingness to comply with student requests sent via email

Results of the study found that instructors attributed this poor email behavior to a lack of training while students tend to blame the technology.

Mediated communication is different from face-to-face communication because people exhibit passive behaviors that go unnoticed by active participants.

es for relationships we are trying to establish or maintain.

Social information processing theory (Walther, Anderson, & Park, 1994; Walther, 1996) suggests that individuals will find ways to utilize contextual cues in online environments to compensate for the lack of nonverbal cues. These contextual cues focus on typographic and/or language use. In other words, misspellings, poor grammar, overly casual language, or excessive use of exclamation points may result in negative perceptions of the sender.

SYNCHRONICITY. Another notable distinction between face-to-face and mediated interactions involves the synchronicity, or the rate at which responses occur in the exchange of messages. In face-to-face interactions, the sending and receiving of messages is synchronous, or simultaneous. As a source sends a message, feedback cues are received that help interpret the receiver's response. Online environments provide opportunities for both synchronous and asynchronous communication. Forums such as chat rooms or instant messaging create an expectation that once a message is received, an immediate response will be provided. Asynchronous communication involves a time lapse between when a message is received and feedback is sent. Examples of asynchronous online messages include emails, texting, or discussion board postings. The "appropriate" amount of time that can elapse before responding to messages depends on the context of the communication and the relationship between the source and receiver. In professional settings, 24-hours is a standard "courtesy rule" courtesy rule for responding to a message. However, individuals in different types of relationships may expect a quicker response time. Consider your own expectations for receiving a response to a text or email message that you sent to a close friend or a romantic partner. Rules for responding to emails and text messages are often discussed in relationships when individual expectations have not been met.

© Kendall Hunt Publishing Co.

Less ◄ Effectiveness of communication ► **More**

Medium

| Unaddressed documents | Written, addressed documents | 2-Way radio | Telephone | Video conferencing | Face-to-Face |

Fig. 11.1 Information richness of different mediums

RICHNESS OF INTERACTION. Another distinction to consider between face-to-face and mediated communication focuses on the richness of the channel used to share information. For decades, scholars have address the question of "What is the best way to send this message?" Daft and Lengel (1984) examined media choices to develop **media richness theory** (Daft & Lengel, 1984) to describe the capability of a communication channel to convey a variety of cues. This theory suggests that communication media vary in their ability to effectively share messages based on the level of "richness". The less time it takes to convey the meaning of a complex message in a coherent and clear manner, the richer the medium. Overall, we are less likely to misinterpret a message if it comes from a richer medium.

Information richness, refers to the channel's:

- synchrony;
- availability of social cues;
- ability to use natural language (as opposed to text or symbols); and
- ability to convey emotions using the channel.

Using a web camera can heighten interactive richness because you can see the other person(s) nonverbal cues.

In other words, the richer the medium, the greater the clarity of the messages being exchanged via that channel. Refer to Figure 11.1 to examine effectiveness of communication across mediums.

Face-to-face interaction is considered to be the richest communication channel because (1) it is synchronous, (2) it incorporates nonverbal cues, (3) uses natural language, and (4) it conveys emotion. Email is rated low in richness because (1) it lacks nonverbal cues, (2) it is asynchronous, (3) text is used instead of natural language, and (4) it is more difficult to convey emotion. Fortunately, new technologies are introduced that allow us to enhance the richness of communication channels. Suppose you were to have a conversation with a friend via a web-camera attached to your computer. The camera allows you to observe a number of your friend's nonverbal cues and increases the level of richness in the interaction.

INITIATING RELATIONSHIPS ONLINE

Now that we examined differences between mediated and face-to-face communication, we turn our attention to how various mediated environments, such as online dating sites and social networking sites, have influenced how we approach and navigate the various relationship stages. First, we will discuss the process of information seeking and uncertainty reduction on initiating relationships, and then we will explore how physical and social attraction is evaluated online.

Information Seeking and Uncertainty Reduction

Recall our discussion in uncertainty reduction theory in earlier chapters and the role it plays in alleviating the ambiguity associated with forming new relationships. Berger and Calabrese (1975) posit that individuals need information about others in order to reduce their uncertainty. This theory applies to mediated communication because it is typical for individuals to try to reduce uncertainty by gathering information about others online. Information-seeking strategies within the mediated context tend to be passive, by scanning sites or posts to collect information about others. Information seeking online takes many different forms. We can review pictures, likes, hobbies, posts, tweets, blogs, and other online indicators to reduce our uncertainty about another person's likes, dislikes, attitudes, and behaviors. **Cognitive uncertainty** refers to an individual's beliefs and attitudes toward certain objects or subject matter. **Behavioral uncertainty** refers to the ability to predict how individuals will react in a certain situation or circumstance. Researching and scanning online information helps us to learn more about the beliefs and attitudes of others so we have a better understanding of how to relate in face-to-face interactions.

Just as similarity is a significant predictor in our decisions to initiate relationships in face-to-face contexts, it also plays an important role when we decide to pursue an online relationship. Online dating sites enable us to search for similarities in age, cultural background, sexual orientation, religion, educational level, and interests. Sites such as eHarmony or Match.com provide users with the opportunity to indicate their preferences for a variety of demographic categories. Some sites target specific demographic characteristics, including silversingles.com for seniors, eSPIN-the-Bottle for tweens, Farmersonly.com for those who share a common interest in agriculture, and Jdate for singles

of the Jewish faith. Consider the popularity of the online dating service, Match.com. Created in 1995, the site advances "a simple mission: to take the lottery out of love" (www.match.com). The creators of this website boast that more than 250,000 marriages per year result from relationships that are initiated on their site. With over 15 million members, Match.com offers a number of choices for identifying potential relationship partners. Individuals simply log on to the site to view photos and read descriptive information about members of this online community. The site enables others to do the "searching and matching for them."

As in face-to-face relationships, similarity plays a strong role in deciding whether to initiate a relationship with someone online

Gibbs, Ellison, and Lai (2011) suggest that individuals who engage in online dating categorize their uncertainty reduction within three sets of concerns:

1. **PERSONAL SECURITY CONCERN:** the extent to which meeting individuals through online dating sites will impact personal safe-

ty (for example, cyberstalking or sending threatening messages or images).

2. MISREPRESENTATION CONCERN: the extent to which an individual met through an online dating site is drastically different from the profile they created to describe themselves to potential dates.

3. RECOGNITION CONCERN: the extent to which an individual believes his or her online dating profile will be seen by friends, family, and colleagues (Gibbs, Ellison, & Lai, 2011).

These concerns became more prevalent after society was introduced to the concept of catfishing. **Catfishing** is a phenomenon in which scammers fabricate online identities and social circles to deceptively pursue online romances. This term was coined in a 2010 American documentary of a young man who searched for the woman he formed a romantic relationship with online. During his search, he discovered that the woman was 20 years older than she indicated online, and she used fake photographs and fabricated friendship connections to deceive him.

As the demand for online dating websites increases, services offered by these sites have become more sophisticated and cater specifically to users' needs. If a person is concerned about the honesty of a potential date, there are sites that conduct background checks. Criminal background investigations and public record screenings have been added as a feature to many popular online dating sites such as eHarmony and Match.com to ensure the safety and integrity of potential dates. Sites such as truedater.com allow subscribers to read reviews posted by others who have met the potential date through a dating website.

It is important to understand this medium and be able to reduce uncertainty effectively. Your self-efficacy in forming effective relationships via dating sites can influence your outcome. In other words, the more an online dater believes in his or her own capabilities to organize information and find a good match online, the more likely he or she is to engage in uncertainty-reduction strategies (Gibbs, Ellison, & Lai, 2011).

Physical and Social Attraction

Relationship initiation and maintenance relies heavily on interpersonal attraction. In Chapter 7 we discussed the role of physical and social attraction in initiating relationships. Physical attraction refers to the extent to which others are perceived as being attractive based on characteristics such as body shape or size, hair color or length, and facial features. Social attraction refers to sharing common interests and similar patterns of communication. In a study that examined impression formation on Facebook, maintaining positive impressions of physical and social attraction was important in terms of sustaining these online relationships (Walther et al., 2008).

When answering the question "What attracts people to each other online?" qualities and characteristics similar to those that attract us to others in face-to-face relationships are considered to be important. Most individuals highlight their best physical characteristics in their online profiles. Profile pictures are edited to ensure that the best possible visual image is presented to others.

What attracts people to each other online?

Through our online social networks we can control and manage the impressions others have of us. By selectively presenting aspects of ourselves to others, we shape how others see us. Recall our discussion of impression management from Chapter 2. Just as we use a variety of impression management techniques in our face-to-face interactions to project the best possible image, we should carefully consider everything we post online with regard to the impression we wish to portray. Have you ever gone out with friends to a great party and wanted to share pictures online to show the world your "exciting and fun" time? Pictures, links, quotes, comments, blogs, "likes," and information provided on online social networks contribute to our overall online image. An exploratory study conducted by college students found a correlation between the number of "likes" or lack of "likes" and how students see themselves and others on Instagram (Quinones, Fuller, & Wilson, 2015).

As we pursue relationships through a variety of social networking sites (SNS), we readily self-disclose information that otherwise would take time to be revealed in face-to-face conversations with others. Background, attitude, and demographic similarities—information that often requires extensive small talk on a first date—can easily be determined by browsing an online profile. **Online self-disclosure** extends the traditional definition of verbally revealing information about yourself to include publicly posting pictures, favorite links, and other likes and dislikes directly on your profile or in your posts(Kim & Dindia, 2011).

A primary concern with the transparent disclosure of information on on SNS is personal safety. A 2013 Pew Internet and American Life Survey indicated that teenagers are now sharing more information online than ever before:

- 91 percent post a photo of themselves
- 92 percent share their real name
- 20 percent post their cell phone numbers
- 71 percent include their school, city, or home town in personal online bios
- 82 percent share their birth date
- 62 percent post their relationship status
- 16 percent set up their profiles to automatically include their location in posts

Overall, males and females were similar in their willingness to share first names, school names, or IM screen names. However, females tended to post more photos (both of themselves and of their friends) compared to males, while males were more likely to post videos or to reveal their hometowns and last names in their online profiles. Females were more likely than males to delete friends from their network (82 percent vs. 66 percent) and block people (67 percent vs. 48 percent) from information disclosed online.

Consider the rate at which self-disclosure occurs in face-to-face relationships compared to mediated contexts. Walther (1996) advances a **hyperpersonal model of CMC**, noting that online communication often facilitates relationship development and perceptions of intimacy. As part of his hyperpersonal model, Walther offers several explanations for why online communication facilitates rapid relationship development:

1. *Ability to construct a specific and desired image of him/herself.* The sender can create an image that reflects an "ideal" versus the "real" self. Unlike face-to-face interactions where physical flaws or idiosyncratic personality traits may be readily apparent, personal weaknesses are not on display or are often omitted from the personal description in mediated contexts.

2. *Ability to alter message content prior to posting or sending it.* The sender can create messages, review them, and then alter them as needed when using mediated channels of communication. This process may improve the quality of the information exchanged and elicit more favorable responses from receivers.

3. *The receiver's propensity to create positive impressions of the partner.* Because the sender has created an ideal or desired image and has carefully monitored and edited the information exchanged, the receiver is likely to form more favorable impressions via mediated channels than through face-to-face contexts.

4. *The increased depth and breadth of self-disclosure exchanged between the relationship partners.* Similar to face-to-face interactions, when the initial exchanges between individuals are positive, this leads to increased disclosure. In mediated contexts the rate at which individuals exchange private information tends to be much faster than in face-to-face contexts (Walther 1996; Anderson & Emmers-Sommer 2006).

Walther (1996) and other scholars agree that greater levels of intimacy can be established through mediated contexts than in similar types of face-to-face interactions. Follow-up research has substantiated this claim, attributing the rapid pace of relationship development to the higher frequency of interaction (Hian, Chuan, Trevor, & Detenber, 2004). In the beginning of the chapter we described a scenario where Kathryn was able to establish an intimate relationship online in a very short period of time. The hyperpersonal model of CMC explains how use of social media may have facilitated her relationship development.

Relationship development and maintenance relies heavily on interpersonal attraction.

MAINTAINING RELATIONSHIPS ONLINE

Now that we have examined relationship initiation online and the influence of attraction and similarity, let us turn our attention to unique aspects of relationship maintenance in mediated contexts.

One of the clear benefits of mediated communication is that we can communicate regularly with family members, friends, coworkers, or a romantic partner to maintain healthy relationships. However, simply being in a relationship doesn't mean we are necessarily happy. Relational satisfaction is often determined by our communicative actions and behaviors. What are we saying? How are we saying it? Where are we saying it?

Technology is used to assist us in maintaining a variety of relationship types.

The Internet and SNS provide countless communicative opportunities

- to expand personal networks;
- to connect with individuals with similar interests;
- to engage in romantic offline dating; and
- to deepen our existing relationships.

However, what kind of communication is really transpiring online? This question was examined by Coyle and Vaughn (2008), who examined undergraduate students and the reasons they use online communication. A summary of the study's findings is provided in Table 11.4.

Table 11.4 Purposes of Online Communication

Categories of Responses	% Respondents
To keep in touch with friends	41
Fun; entertainment; amusement	17
To post or look at photos	12
Alleviate boredom	12
To respond to others who have initiated contact online	10
Everyone is doing it	10
To communicate with others in the absence of alternate contact information	7
To communicate with multiple people simultaneously	3
Other	19

NOTE: Total percentage of respondents is greater than 100 percent because respondents could list multiple reasons.

Overall, results of their study indicated that social networking sites are primarily used for trivial and/or unimportant messages with friends, and the primary use of these sites is to maintain friendships.

However, we can probably all agree that not all social networks are created equal. There are distinctions in the structure, content or goal intention, and the attitude/tone that the user brings to the site. For example, consider the different purposes and the content when updating a Facebook status compared to Tweeting or posting on Snapchat. Likewise, as social networking sites evolve they will offer more specific sites for more specialized topics and relationships. It is critical to analyze a social networking site's goals, purpose, and intended audiences in order to locate an appropriate platform to maintaining our interpersonal relationships.

MAINTENANCE STRATEGIES. Once we have initiated relationships, the majority of our time and energy shift to maintaining our relational satisfaction. Recall our discussion of relational maintenance strategies in Chapter 8. Stafford and Canary (1991) identified specific relational maintenance behaviors or strategies that contribute to our overall relational satisfaction. Just as we devote time and energy to maintaining our face-to-face relationships, we also depend on mediated communication to sustain our relationships. One study suggests that "the mere act of designating someone as a Facebook friend maintains a relationship to the extent that communication lines remain open and might therefore prevent a relationship from falling into the dormant category" (Bryant & Marmo, 2009, p. 145).

Are there maintenance strategies that can be used in either face-to-face or mediated interactions? Absolutely—in fact, most translate very well across contexts. While maintenance strategies were discussed in more detail in Chapter 8, we will briefly review two specific maintenance behaviors:

- **Showing positiveness:** expressing favorable attitudes and being cheerful, upbeat, humorous, polite, cooperative, and optimistic.

- **Demonstrating openness:** sharing feelings, declaring affection, expressing wants and needs freely, and an attitude of acceptance of the wants and needs of others.

Craig and Wright (2012) suggest that these two relational maintenance strategies (positivity and openness) may be a function of attitude similarity and social attraction. In their study, attitude similarity was a significant predictor of social attraction within social networking sites. Feelings of friendliness encourage others to discuss a wide range of topics (breadth) with greater intimacy (depth), which contributes to the health of the interpersonal relationship online.

Bryan and Marmo (2009) argue that, in addition to serving as an information-seeking tool, the act of *surveillance* can be considered a relational maintenance behavior. Maintaining relationships by monitoring what others are doing, but not directly communicating one-on-one about the activities, is a form of maintenance that occurs via social networking sites. Elphinston and Noller (2011) take an opposing view of SNS surveillance and conceptualized Facebook monitoring as an intrusion behavior that can be linked to jealousy and result in relationship dissatisfaction.

While mediated communication plays an important role in the initiation and maintenance, relationships that utilize mediated communication can also experience negative outcomes. In the next section, we will discuss some of the negative aspects of relying on mediated communication in relationships.

Relational Maintenance: Who Uses What?

- Relatives use email more than friends and significant others do to maintain relationships.
- Friends reported using social networking sites more than significant others and relatives do.
- Women use more maintenance strategies than men while communicating online.
- Positivity is used most often by those who use email and social networking sites.
- Openness is used more through IM and texting.
- Overall, maintenance strategies are consistent online and offline.

Houser, M. L., Fleuriet, C., & Estrada, D. (2012). The cyber factor: An analysis of relational maintenance through the use of computer mediated communication. *Communication Research Reports, 29*, 34–43.

THE DARK SIDE OF RELATIONSHIPS ONLINE

While adjusting to the different forms of technologies to communicate in our relationships, we need to consider potential pitfalls and cautions of this medium, including:

- Cyberbullying which has been defined as behaviors intended to inflict "willful and repeated harm" such as cyberstalking, exclusion, harassment over a mediated platform, such as computers and/or phones (Hindja & Patchin, 2009, p.5).
- Internet/Smart Phone Addiction
- Failure to employ proper online etiquette, resulting in potential communication breakdowns and misunderstandings
- Anonymity that creates a false sense of security that lures people to share private information willingly OR, to express or post negative comments online that would never be shared.
- Deceptive behavior, such as misrepresenting personal attributes, failing to share important personal information, an overreliance on an "online" persona, or accelerated intimacy

Internet addiction disorder (IAD) or **problematic Internet use** (PIU) refers to excessive Internet use that interferes with one's daily life. According to Young (1998), Internet addiction is defined as spending six hours or more online at a time, craving online interaction, and experiencing feelings of anxiousness and irritation when offline. Young identified five categories of online addictive behaviors:

1. Compulsive use of adult websites
2. Over-involvement in online relationships
3. Obsessive online gambling, shopping, or day trading
4. Compulsive web surfing or database searches
5. Obsessive computer game playing

Young (1998) contends that Internet addiction can negatively affect our lives in many areas, including our relationships, as it often leads to a greater focus on a virtual life and less focus on reality.

Our dependence on technology has also been linked to an obsession with our mobile devices. Scholars have noted that the growing dependence of teens on mediated channels to communicate in their relationships will likely impact their ability to effectively interpret nonverbal cues and effectively engage in face-to-face interactions during adulthood (Clemmitt, 2013). The pervasiveness of social media, access, ease of technology, and

How many hours a day do you spend on the Internet?

inefficiency at work or lack of interaction with others. Not having access to technology can result in communication that takes on an aggressive or irritable tone.

TERMINATING RELATIONSHIPS THROUGH THE USE OF MEDIATED MESSAGES

the fear of "missing out" on something important are leading factors that cause students to pay partial, yet continuous, attention to multiple stimuli simultaneously. Most of us can relate to some level of addiction to our mobile devices. We know this because we probably have caught ourselves on our phone when we know we should be doing something else (working, studying, making dinner). How many of us sleep next to or with our phones? Often times it is the first thing we look at in the morning and the last thing we look at in the evening. Recall the panic you felt the last time you forgot or misplaced your cell phone. Figure 11.2 summarizes some of the emotional responses we experience when we lose track of our mobile devices. This may lead to loss of sleep,

Individuals use social networking sites to announce the beginning or end of a relationship and to publicly declare a change in relational status. However, how appropriate or ethical is it to receive notification over SNS or via a text message about relationship dissolution? A 2013 study suggested only about 5 percent of relationships are terminated via a public announcement via social media or through a text message. When mediated communication is used to end a relationship, text messaging is the most often used channel (38 percent) for termination (Weisskirch & Delevi, 2013). These findings also suggest that relationships of less than one year in duration are more likely (85 percent) to be terminated via technology compared to relationships that have endured for longer periods of time.

HOW DID YOU FEEL WHEN YOU MISPLACED YOUR PHONE?

| 73% | 14% | 7% | 6% |
| PANICKED | DESPERATE | SICK | RELIEVED |

Figure 11.2 Almost all of us have some level of smartphone addiction.

Expanding the Relationship Dissolution Model to SNS

In Chapter 10, we introduced Rollie and Duck's (2006) five processes of relationship dissolution:

1. Intrapsychic process
2. Dyadic process
3. Social process
4. Grave dressing process
5. Resurrection process

Researchers have used this model to help explain online behaviors on SMS after a breakup, including "defriending," limiting access, and posting emotional messages. LeFebvre, Blackburn, and Brody (2015) identified specific online behaviors that overlapped with this dissolution model. Some of these behaviors include:

1. Virtually mourning the end of the relationship by posting an emotional status update or mentioning an ex-partner online;
2. Relational cleansing behaviors, such as updating status to "single" or hiding or removing status information from your personal SMS;
3. Continuing to ruminate about the ex-partner and the future through surveillance behaviors;
4. Self-regulating behaviors, including distancing oneself from communicating with previous partners.

Table 11.5 aligns specific online behaviors to Rollie and Duck's (2006) last three processes of relationship dissolution: social, grave dressing, and resurrection. The findings of this study help explain how and when individuals engage in these online behaviors following a breakup.

FORMING SAFE AND MEANINGFUL ONLINE RELATIONSHIPS: AN OVERVIEW

Technology can be an important channel to develop and maintain healthy and meaningful relationships. Some positive aspects associated with its use include:

- Communicating online allows people to gradually build their level of intimacy be-

Table 11.5 During and After Relationship Termination: Online Behaviors in the Relationship Dissolution Model

Category	Behavior
Social	**Relational cleansing** (EX: hide, remove, or update relationship status; untag self in pictures/albums)
	Relational transgressions (EX: write negative disclosures about breakup or relationship secrets; expose unflattering/fabricated information; reveal cheating or infidelity
	Social networking support (EX: discuss, seek, or receive relational support)
	Virtual mourning (EX: post emotional statuses or mention ex-partner)
Grave Dressing	**Account modification** (EX: change individual privacy settings)
	Impression management (EX: post about fun activities and positive statuses)
	Relational cleansing (EX: hide, remove, or update relationship status; untag self in pictures/albums)
	Self-regulation from Facebook (EX: take a vacation from Facebook; limit personal postings)
	Self-regulation from partner (EX: avoid viewing partner's profile and mutual friends' profiles; unsubscribe from ex-partner's newsfeed)
	Virtual mourning (EX: post emotional statuses or mention ex-partner)
	Virtual reconciliation (EX: refriend ex-partner or try to refriend ex-partner)
Resurrection	**Impression management** (EX: Post on fun activities and positive statuses)
	New relationship interest (EX: review partner's albums, new partner's previous profile pictures, mutual friends, or previous relationships)
	Self-regulation from partner (EX: avoid viewing partner's profile and mutual friends' profiles; unsubscribe from ex-partner's newsfeed)
	Withdraw access (EX: defriend, delete, or block ex-partner, ex-partner's family, and ex-partner's friends)

fore they meet, which may result in more meaningful relationships.

- Ability to save face in mediated rejection compared to a face-to-face rejection.
- Decreased geographic limitations and barriers that potentially inhibit relationship initiation.
- Less confrontation with unwanted admirers, and expanded opportunities to connect with potential relationship prospects (Anderson & Emmers-Sommer, 2006; Walther, 1993, 1996).
- Certain personality traits, including shyness, can benefit from the opportunity to meet others in a non-threatening environment.
- Little to no cost associated with maintaining regular and frequent communication.
- Convenience of communicating in the comfort of your own home.

Mediated communication affords us the opportunity to build and develop effective interpersonal relationships. We are reminded that when partners communicate on a more consistent basis they tend to develop a stronger attraction to each other (Hendrick & Hendrick, 1983). The instantaneous nature of mediated communication allows us to interact more frequently and across a large range of topics.

In this last section, we offer five suggestions for forming meaningful relationships in a safe way:

1. Take your time.
2. Pay attention to cues.
3. Be honest.
4. Be inquisitive: Protect yourself.
5. Be alert: Look for signs of deception.

Take Your Time, Don't Rush

It is important to be patient and dedicate *time* to develop meaningful online relationships (Walther, 1992; Rintel & Pittam, 1997). Given that many individuals readily disclose in-depth personal information on social networking and dating sites, we may think we have achieved intimacy in an online relationship when in fact it may not be as intimate as we imagine. Allowing ample time for forming relationships using mediated communication and allowing for adequate impression formation is critical.

If used effectively, mediated communication can allow a relationship to form gradually. However, Trafford (1982) and Greenfield (1999) have both called attention to a phenomenon they often observe in online relationships known as **coup de foudre** (bolt of lightning), or accelerated intimacy. When comparing individuals who establish relationships online to those who establish relationships primarily via face-to-face communication, those established online often experience significant increases in the amount

of intimate information exchanged. Trafford (1982) and Greenfield (1999) agree that the accelerated amount of intimacy experienced in online relationships may not always benefit individuals or relationships. It takes time and effort to establish trust and intimacy in relationships. Individuals may need time to process information about the relationship partner, observe the relationship partner for consistency in their behaviors, and then determine whether there is potential for the relationship to move forward.

Pay Attention to Cues

Research shows that even the "small stuff" counts online. Ellison, Heino, and Gibbs (2006) interviewed individuals who were currently active on a large online dating site to learn more about how they managed their online impressions. Participants indicated that they often paid close attention to small online cues. For example, one participant described the significance of profiles that were well-written, stating, "I just think if they can't spell or . . . formulate a sentence, I would imagine that they are not that educated" (Ellison et al., 2006, p. 10). Another participant commented that she did not want to come across at all as being sexual in her profile because she "didn't want to invite someone who thought I was going to go to bed with them [as soon as] I shook their hand" (Ellison et al., 2006, p. 10). Individuals indicated that they also tried to be brief when responding to potential partners so as not to appear "too desperate for conversation" (Ellison et al., 2006, p. 10). All of these examples illustrate how individuals monitor behavioral cues to display a certain image online. Individuals must not only understand how to use effective behavioral cues, but also how to assess the behavioral cues of others.

Be Honest

Honesty is an important element for effective online communication. Conley and Bierman (1999) contend that honesty is a crucial component of successful online relationships. One should not exaggerate personal attributes and must always be specific about self-attributes and the desired attributes one is looking for in others. Ellison et al. (2006) describe the tendency for people to describe their ideal self, not their actual self, when attempting to find a relationship partner. For example, one woman using online dating services noted that the picture she posted on her profile was from five years ago and the picture depicted her as a thinner version of her current self (Ellison et al., 2006). Because the picture was dated and depicted her ideal, not her actual, self, the woman expressed a desire to lose weight so that her online and face-to-face personas were consistent. This example illustrates the relationship between online behavior, face-to-face interactions, and the potential for relationship development. When individuals are deceptive online about aspects of their appearance, likes, dislikes, or hobbies, they risk being "caught" in a lie once actual face-to-face interactions occur.

Be Inquisitive: Protecting Yourself

It is important to "do your homework" when deciding to date online or to sign up for a social networking site. The Privacy Rights Clearing House offers these recommendations for those wishing to protect themselves online:

Honesty is a crucial component of successful online relationships.

1. *Consider electronic privacy:* Recall the information you provide online is permanent and even if we think we have deleted something, we are often reminded by cybersecurity specialists that these files can be found.

2. *Read the terms of service and privacy policy:* Oftentimes these sites can harvest personal information and sell your information to third parties, usually without us even recognizing it. Are you able to "opt out"? Will they delete your information after you close the account?

3. *Share photographs with caution.* Digital photos contain metadata, such as when and where the image was taken. This information may be used by scammers. Photos are often cached and "tagged."

4. *Consider getting a free email account for online usage.* This may allow you to manage your information more gradually and appropriately for new relationships.

5. *Respect your instincts.* Trust your gut about mischievous and strange behavior. Be sure not to reveal too much personal information in the beginning of the relationship. For more information, see https://www.privacyrights.org/perils-and-pitfalls-online-dating-how-protect-yourself.

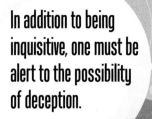

In addition to being inquisitive, one must be alert to the possibility of deception.

cautious in forming relationships with Internet strangers" (Beebe et al., 2002, p. 389).

SUMMARY

In this chapter, we explained the advantages and disadvantages of computer-mediated communication. Additionally, we identified similarities and differences in face-to-face communication and computer-mediated communication.

We also learned how relationships are formed and maintained and some potential dark sides to this medium. We touched on how mediated communication may be utilized in terminating relationships and discussed safe tips in developing meaningful relationships online.

Overall, mediated communication can aid in the formation and maintenance of healthy interpersonal relationships. We hope that the information in this chapter will help guide healthy online relationships that contribute to your overall well-being.

Be Alert: Looking for Signs of Deception

In addition to being inquisitive, one must be alert to the possibility of deception. Beebe, Beebe, and Redmond (2002) believe "the detection of deception in face-to-face encounters is aided by the presence of nonverbal cues. However, online such deception is almost as easy as simply typing the words" (p. 389). Thus, one must "be

DISCUSSION QUESTIONS

1. Choose three social media sites and explain appropriate communication behaviors in each of the sites. Discuss appropriate communication behaviors to use when texting. When emailing?

2. What communication advice would you offer to a friend who has decided to post a profile to an online dating site?

3. Describe cues that you use to convey or to detect emotions and moods in email messages? How does these cue differ from those used in text messages? In SMS posts?

SELF ASSESSMENT

Computer-Mediated Communication Competence Measure

Instructions: This instrument is interested in how people use various computer-mediated communication (CMC) technologies for conversing with others. For the purpose of this questionnaire, please consider CMC to include all forms of e-mail and computer-based networks (e.g., instant messaging, social networking sites, etc.) for sending and receiving written messages with other people. For this survey, indicate the degree to which each statement regarding your use of various CMC media is true or untrue of you, using the following scale:

1 = NOT AT ALL TRUE OF ME
2 = MOSTLY NOT TRUE OF ME
3 = NEITHER TRUE NOR UNTRUE OF ME; UNDECIDED
4 = MOSTLY TRUE OF ME
5 = VERY TRUE OF ME

MOTIVATION

_____ 1. I enjoy communicating using computer media.

_____ 2. I am nervous about using the computer to communicate with others. [R]

_____ 3. I am very motivated to use computers to communicate with others.

_____ 4. Communicating through a computer makes me anxious. [R]

KNOWLEDGE

_____ 5. I am very knowledgeable about how to communicate through computers.

_____ 6. I am never at a loss for something to say in CMC.

_____ 7. I am very familiar with how to communicate through email and the internet.

_____ 8. I always seem to know how to say things the way I mean them using CMC.

_____ 9. When communicating with someone through a computer, I know how to adapt my messages to the medium.

EFFICACY

_____ 10. I don't feel very competent in learning and using communication media technology.

_____ 11. I feel completely capable of using almost all currently available CMCs.

_____ 12. I am confident I will learn how to use any new CMCs that are due to come out.

_____ 13. I'm nervous when I have to learn how to use a new communication technology.

_____ 14. I find changes in technologies very frustrating.

_____ 15. I quickly figure out how to use new CMC technologies.

_____ 16. I know I can learn to use new CMC technologies when they come out.

_____ 17. If a CMC isn't user friendly, I'm likely not to use it.

SKILLS COORDINATION

_____ 18. I know when and how to close down a topic of conversation in CMC dialogues.

_____ 19. I manage the give and take of CMC interactions skillfully.

_____ 20. I am skilled at timing when I send my responses to people who email me.

_____ 21. I am skilled at prioritizing (triaging) my email traffic.

ATTENTIVENESS

_____ 22. I ask questions of the other person in my CMC.

_____ 23. I show concern for and interest in the person I'm conversing with in CMC.

_____ 24. I can show compassion and empathy through the way I write emails.

_____ 25. I take time to make sure my emails to others are uniquely adapted to the particular receiver I'm sending it to.

EXPRESSIVENESS

_____ 26. I am very articulate and vivid in my CMC messages.

_____ 27. I use a lot of the expressive symbols [e.g., for "smile"] in my CMC messages.

_____ 28. I try to use a lot of humor in my CMC messages.

_____ 29. I am expressive in my CMC conversations.

COMPOSURE

_____ 30. I display a lot of certainty in the way I write my CMC messages.

_____ 31. I use an assertive style in my CMC writing.

_____ 32. I have no trouble expressing my opinions forcefully on CMC.

_____ 33. I make sure my objectives are emphasized in my CMC messages.

_____ 34. My CMC messages are written in a confident style.

_____ 35. I am skillful at revealing composure and self-confidence in my CMC interactions.

SELECTIVITY

I choose which medium (i.e., computer, phone, face-to-face, etc.) to communicate based on . . .

_____ 36. how quickly I need to get a message out to people.

_____ 37. how much benefit there would be to having the other(s) present face-to face.

_____ 38. how lively the interaction needs to be.

_____ 39. how much access the person I need to communicate with has to the medium.

_____ 40. how much information is involved in the message I need to communicate.

_____ 41. how much access I have to the channel or medium.

_____ 42. how long I need people to hang on to or remember the message.

_____ 43. how many different uses and forms are needed (e.g., hardcopy, image processing, voicemail, computer language, etc.)

_____ 44. how personal or intimate the information in the message is.

_____ 45. how quickly the receiver needs to react to the message.

_____ 46. the extent to which I need to get some "back and forth," "give and take," and interchange of ideas.

_____ 47. the extent to which I need some creative brainstorming.

APPROPRIATENESS

_____ 48. I avoid saying things through that might offend someone.

_____ 49. I pay as much attention to the WAY I say things as WHAT I say.

_____ 50. I never say things that offend the other person.

_____ 51. I am careful to make my comments and behaviors appropriate to the situation.

EFFECTIVENESS

_____ 52. I generally get what I want out of interactions.

_____ 53. I consistently achieve my goals in interactions.

_____ 54. My interactions are effective in accomplishing what I set out to accomplish.

_____ 55. I am effective in my conversations with others.

CLARITY

_____ 56. I get my ideas across clearly in conversations with others.

_____ 57. My comments are consistently accurate and clear.

_____ 58. My messages are rarely misunderstood.

_____ 59. I feel understood when I interact with others.

SATISFACTION

_____ 60. I am generally satisfied with my communication encounters.

_____ 61. I enjoy my interactions with others.

_____ 62. I feel good about my conversations.

_____ 63. I am generally pleased with my interactions.

ATTRACTIVENESS

_____ 64. If I can engage someone in conversation, I can usually get them to like me.

_____ 65. I come across in conversation as someone people would like to get to know.

_____ 66. I make friends easily.

_____ 67. People generally enjoy my company when interacting with me.

EFFICIENCY/PRODUCTIVITY

_____ 68. I get a tremendous amount accomplished through CMC.

_____ 69. My CMC interactions are more productive than my face-to-face interactions.

_____ 70. I am more efficient using CMC than other forms of communication.

_____ 71. CMC technologies are tremendous time-savers for my work.

GENERAL USAGE/EXPERIENCE

_____ 72. I rely heavily upon my CMCs for getting me through each day.

_____ 73. I use computer-mediated means of communication almost constantly.

_____ 74. I can rarely go a week without any CMC interactions.

_____ 75. I am a heavy user of computer-mediated communication.

_____ 76. If I can use a computer for communicating, I tend to.

[R] = needs to be reverse coded.

Scores on the CMC competence scale range from a low of 76 to a high of 380. Higher scores indicate greater self-perceived competence in use of CMC.

Source: Spitzberg, B. H. (2006). Preliminary development of a model and measure of computer-mediated communication (CMC) competence. *Journal of Computer-Mediated Communication*, 11, 2, 629-666.

KEY TERMS AND DEFINITIONS

ACTIVE ACTIVITY: refers to being an engaged participant in a conversation; includes overt feedback, such as sending a text to a friend or commenting on a blog.

ASYNCHRONOUS: involves a time lapse between when a message is received and when a response is made.

BEHAVIORAL UNCERTAINTY: the ability to predict how individuals will react in a certain situation or circumstance

CATFISHING: a phenomenon of Internet scammers who fabricate false online identities and social circles to pursue deceptive online romances.

COGNITIVE UNCERTAINTY: an individual's beliefs and attitudes toward certain objects or subject matter.

COMPUTER-MEDIATED COMMUNICATION (CMC): messages sent via mediated channels.

COUP DE FOUDRE: bolt of lightning, accelerated intimacy.

DEINDIVIDUATION THEORY: this theory suggests that the anonymity within groups provides and enables individuals to participate in antinormative or aggressive behavior they would not normally engage in.

DEMONSTRATING OPENNESS: sharing feelings, declaring affection, expressing wants and needs freely, and an attitude of acceptance of the wants and needs of others.

HYPERPERSONAL MODEL OF CMC: proposes that online communication often facilitates relationship development and perceptions of intimacy in online environments.

INTERNET ADDICTION DISORDER/PROBLEMATIC INTERNET USE: excessive Internet use that interferes with one's daily life.

LURKING: involves viewing posts made on a discussion board or forum without responding.

MEDIA RICHNESS THEORY: describes the capability of a communication channel to convey a variety of cues.

ONLINE SELF DISCLOSURE: extends traditional face-to-face disclosure to include publicly sharing information with others through the posting of photos, links, personal interests, etc. online.

PASSIVE ACTIVITY: less obvious activity, such as scrolling through sites such as Pinterest and Twitter news feeds.

REDUCED SOCIAL CUES THEORY: states that we depend on social cues such as a person's appearance, attire, facial expressions, and gestures to help interpret received messages and that many of the social cues that we depend on in face-to-face interactions are absent in CMC.

SELF-EFFICACY: the extent to which an individual believes in his or her own capabilities to achieve a task

SELF-PRESENTATION: process of selectively presenting aspects of ourselves to others

SHOWING POSITIVENESS: expressing favorable attitudes and being cheerful, upbeat, humorous, polite, cooperative, and optimistic.

SOCIAL IDENTITY MODEL OF DEINDIVIDUATION EFFECTS: suggests the lack of nonverbal cues in computer-mediated communication forces us to form impressions that are based on social groups rather than individual features that we may share.

SOCIAL INFORMATION PROCESSING THEORY: suggests that individuals will find ways to utilize contextual cues in online environments to compensate for the lack of nonverbal cues.

SYNCHRONOUS: messages are sent simultaneously.

REFERENCES

Anderson, A. T., & Emmers-Sommer, T. M. (2006). Predictors of relationship satisfaction in online romantic relationships. *Communication Studies, 57,* 153–172.

Beebe, S. A., Beebe, S. J., & Redmond, M. V. (2002). *Interpersonal communication: Relating to others* (3rd ed.). Boston, MA: Allyn & Bacon.

Berger, C. R., & Calabrese, R. J. (1975). Some exploration in initial interaction and beyond: Toward a developmental theory of communication. *Human Communication Research, 1,* 99–112.

Brenner, J., & Smith, A. (2013, May). 72% of online adults are social networking site users. Pew Research Internet Project. http://www.pewinternet. org/files/old-media//Files/Reports/2013/PIP_ Social_networking_sites_update_PDF.pdf

Bryant, E. M., & Marmo, J. (2009). Relational maintenance strategies on Facebook. *The Kentucky Journal of Communication, 28,* 129–150.

Casey Johnston is the Culture Editor at Ars Technica. She covers business, privacy, the Internet, and new media. Read the full article here: http://arstechnica.com/staff/2013/07/19/ why-i-hate-read-receipts/

Cacioppo, J. T., Cacioppo, S., Gonzaga, G. C., Ogburn, E. L., & VanderWeele, T. J. (2013, May). Marital satisfaction and break-ups differ across on-line and off-line meeting venues. *Proceedings of the National Academy of Sciences, 10*(25), 10135–10140.

Clemmitt, M. (2013, January 25). Social media explosion. *CQ Researcher, 23,* 81-104. Retrieved from http://library.cqpress.com/

Conley, L., & Bierman, J. (1999). *Meet me online: The #1 practical guide to Internet dating.* Webster, NC: Old Mountain Press, Inc.

Coyle, C. L., & Vaughn, H. (2008). Social Networking: Communication revolution or evolution?, *Bell Labs Journal, 13,* 13–18.

Craig, E., & Wright, K. B. (2012). Computer-mediated relational development and maintenance on Facebook. *Communication Research Reports, 29,* 119–129.

Cummings, J. N., Lee, J. B., & Kraut, R. (2006). Communication technology and friendship during the transition from high school to college. In R. Kraut, M. Brynion, & S. Kiesler (Eds.), *PC's, phones, and the Internet: The social impact of information technology.* Oxford, UK: Oxford University Press.

Daft, R. L., & R. H. Lengel. (1984). Information richness: A new approach to managerial behavior and organization design. *Research in Organizational Behavior, 6,* 191–233.

Ellison, N., Heino, R., & Gibbs, J. (2006). Managing impressions online: Self-presentation processes in the online dating environment. *Journal of Computer-Mediated Communication, 11,* 1–28. Retrieved online June 19, 2007, from www. blackwell-synergy.com.

Ellison, N. B., Steinfield, C., & Lampe, C. (2007). The benefits of Facebook "Friends": Social capital and college students' use of online social network sites. *Journal of Computer Mediated Communication, 12,* Retrieved from http:// jcmc.indiana.edu/vol12/issue4/ellison.html

Elphinston, R. A., & Noller, P. (2011). Time to face it! Facebook intrusion and the implications for romantic jealousy and relationship satisfaction. *Cyberpsychology, Behavior, and Social Networking, 14,* 631–635.

Gibbs, J. L., Ellison, N. B., & Lai, C. (2011). First comes love, then comes Google: An investigation of uncertainty reduction strategies and self-disclosure in online dating. *Communication Research, 38*(1), 70–100.

Greenfield, D. N. (1999). *Virtual addiction: Help for netheads, cyberfreaks, and those who love them.* Oakland, CA: New Harbinger Publications.

Hendrick, C., & S. Hendrick. (1983). *Liking, loving and relating.* Monterey, CA: Brooks/Cole.

Hian, L. B., Chuan, S. L., Trevor, T. M. K., & Detenber, B. H. (2004). Getting to know you: Exploring the development of relationship intimacy in computer-mediated communication. *Journal of Computer-Mediated Communication, 9,* Retrieved June 24, 2007 from http://www. ascusc.org/jcm/vol9/issue3/detenber.html.

Hindja, S. & Patchin, J. W. (2009). Bullying, cyber-bullying and suicide. *Archives of Suicide Research, 14* (3)

Kim, J., & Dindia, K. (2011). Online self-disclosure: a review of research. In Wright, K. B., & Webb, L. M. (Eds.), *Computer-mediated communication in personal relationships.* New York: Peter Lang.

Lea, M., & Spears, R. (1991). Computer-mediated communication, de-individuation and group decision making. *International Journal of Man Machine Studies, 34,* 283–301.

LeFebvre, L., Blackburn, K., & Brody, N. (2015). Navigating romantic relationships on Facebook: Extending the relationship dissolution model to social networking environments. *Journal of Social and Personal Relationships, 32*(1), 78–98.

Pew Research Center. (2006; 2010; 2013). Pew Internet and American Life Project. http://www.pewinternet.org

Quinones, A., Fuller, K., & Wilson, N. (2015). All it takes is a like for me to be happy: Instagram and its impact on self-concept. Paper presented at the annual convention of the Eastern Communication Association, Undergraduate Scholars Conference, Philadelphia, PA.

Recording Industry Association of American (2016). Retrieved from http://www.riaa.com/facts/

Rintel, S. E., & Pittam, J. (1997). Strangers in a strange land: Interaction management on internet relay chat. *Human Communication Research, 23* (4), 507–534.

Rollie, S. S., & Duck, S. W. (2006). Stage theories of marital breakdown. In J. H. Harvey and M. A. Find (Eds.), *Handbook of divorce and dissolution of romantic relationships* (176–193). Mahwah, NJ: Lawrence Erlbaum Associates.

Spitzberg, B. H. (2006). Preliminary development of a Model and Measure of Computer-Mediated Communication (CMC) Competence. *Journal of Computer-Mediated Communication, 11,* (2), 629-666.

Sproull, L., & Kiesler, S. (1986). Reducing social context cues: Electronic mail in organizational communication. *Management Science, 32,* 1492–1512.

Stafford, L., & Canary, D. J. (1991). Maintenance strategies and romantic relationship type, gender, and relational characteristics. *Journal of Social and Personal Relationships, 8,* 217–242.

Stephens, K. K., Houser, M. L., & Cowan, R. L. (2009). R U able to meet me: The impact of students' overly casual email messages to instructors. *Communication Education, 58,* 303–326.

Trafford, A. (1982). *Crazy time: Surviving divorce.* New York: Bantam Books, Inc.

Walther, J. B. (1992). Interpersonal effects in computer-mediated interaction: A relational perspective. *Communication Reports, 19,* 52–90.

Walther, J. B. (1993). Impression development in computer-mediated interaction. *Western Journal of Communication, 57,* 381–389.

Walther, J. B. (1996). Computer-mediated communication: Interpersonal, intrapersonal, and hyperpersonal interaction. *Communication Research, 19,* 52–90.

Walther, J. B., Anderson, J. F., & Park, D. W. (1994). Interpersonal effects in computer-mediated interaction: A meta-analysis of social and antisocial communication. *Communication Research, 21* (4), 460–487.

Walther, J. B., Van Der Heide, B., Kim, S., Westerman, D., & Tong, S. T. (2008). The role of friends' behavior on evaluations of individuals' Facebook profiles: Are we known by the company we keep? *Human Communication Research, 34,* 28–49.

Weisskirch, R. S., & Delevi, R. (2013). Attachment style and conflict resolution skills predicting technology use in relationship dissolution. *Computers In Human Behavior, 29*(6), 2530–2534.

Young, K. S. (1998). *Caught in the net.* New York: John Wiley & Sons, Inc.

chapter

12

Intercultural Communication:
Variety Is the Spice of Life

OBJECTIVES

- Identify three reasons for studying the impact of diversity on interpersonal relationships.

- Distinguish between the concepts of culture and diversity.

- Explain three characteristics of culture.

- Explore factors that affect our perceptions of others: needs, beliefs, values, and attitudes.

- Recognize how stereotypes and prejudices influence interpersonal relationships.

- Describe the impact of Hofstede's four dimensions of cultural values on interpersonal communication.

SCENARIO: SOUND FAMILIAR?

Mariella and Tadashi had been dating since the beginning of fall semester. As their relationship grew more serious, they decided that Tadashi would go home with Mariella during spring break to meet her parents and siblings. Mariella was embarrassed by her family's behavior as she introduced Tadashi to them. Her brother and father raised their eyebrows as they opened the door to greet them, and Mari's little sister asked if he could show her some karate moves. To make matters worse, Mariella's mother apologized as they sat down to dinner, saying, "If Mari had told us you weren't American, I would have made something Chinese." Tad smiled and gently explained that while his parents were originally from Japan, he had been born and raised in Seattle.

OVERVIEW

Throughout this text, we have discussed various aspects of interpersonal communication and the role that it plays in our relationships. As we approach the end of our journey of exploring the specifics of interpersonal communication, we would be remiss if we failed to discuss the one variable that *all* interpersonal relationships have in common: they are composed of diverse individuals. Typically, discussions of diversity focus on things that we can see: race, ethnicity, and gender are the most commonly identified elements when defining diversity.

Focusing our attention exclusively on obvious physical characteristics and differences may cause us to fail to recognize the important role that cultural attitudes, values, and norms play in our interpersonal relationships. These are only a few of the factors that create challenges for relational partners when trying to achieve shared meaning. Consider friends who argue with one another simply because they differ in their religious or political beliefs. Maybe you have had a difficult time with a teacher who doesn't seem to understand that your questions are not intended to "challenge authority," but are simply attempts to better understand the information being presented in class.

Our cultural attitudes can be hidden from the world if we carefully monitor our words and actions. However, there are numerous examples of celebrities whose prejudices were publicly expressed and recorded for the world to see:

- On July 28, 2006, actor Mel Gibson was pulled over while speeding on Pacific Coast Highway in Malibu, California. As officers were questioning Gibson, he began yelling at them, making anti-Semitic and sexist comments toward the arresting officers.

- Celebrity chef Paula Deen was fired by the Food Network in 2013 following charges of racial harassment that were filed by one of her employees. During television interviews regarding the case, Deen admitted to reporters that she had used racial slurs in the past.

- During the 2015 Academy Awards red carpet telecast, host Giuliana Rancic made a stereotypical and racist comment about singer Zendaya's dreadlocks as she arrived for the award show.

What causes individuals to engage in such negative behavior? Why do people express such hurtful words and actions? One reason may be our inability to engage in effective interpersonal communication with those who are different. Understanding how our cultural background influences our communication preferences and our reactions to those who are different is an important first step to enhancing our interpersonal relationships.

Our cultural attitudes can be hidden from the world if we carefully monitor our words and actions.

Our decisions about how to communicate with others are typically grounded in our beliefs, values, and attitudes. If our beliefs or attitudes toward someone are negative, our communication may be negative as well. Our lack of knowledge about cultural differences results in uncertainty about what is considered appropriate or effective communication when we encounter cultural differences. In these situations, many people simply avoid communicating with diverse others. In this chapter we will explore a variety of concepts that help explain how culture and diversity influence our relationships with others.

CULTURE AND DIVERSITY DEFINED

Culture has been defined by scholars in a number of different ways. In fact, a 1952 book identified 156 different definitions of culture (Kroeber & Kluckhohn). In the 60+ years since these definitions were compiled, attention to the increasing diversity in our societies has prompted scholars to create even more descriptions to capture the changes in our world. Anthropologists have broadly defined culture as being composed of perceptions, behaviors, and evaluations. Other researchers have adopted a descriptive approach to explaining culture. Their definitions include characteristics such as knowledge, morals, beliefs, customs, art, music, law, and values. In this text, we define **culture** as shared perceptions that shape the communication patterns and expectations of a group of people.

While the concept of culture focuses on aspects that are shared by groups, **diversity** refers to the

Focusing our attention exclusively on obvious physical characteristics and differences may cause us to fail to recognize the important role that cultural attitudes, values, and norms play in our interpersonal relationships.

unique qualities or characteristics that distinguish individuals or groups from one another. Awareness of the impact of diversity on communication can help you understand the challenges encountered in relationships. Consider the various levels of diversity that potentially impact our diverse views of relationships and communication (Figure 12.1).

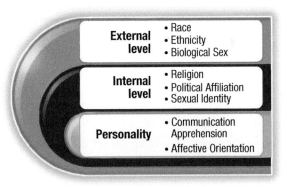

Figure 12.1 Levels of diversity.

© Kendall Hunt Publishing Co.

External factors include those aspects of diversity that are readily visible, such as skin color or ethnic styles of dress. Since these are the things that we can see, we often use them to form our initial impressions about others. However, many of the differences that significantly impact on our communication with others are found at the internal level. These may include beliefs and attitudes associated with our religious or political affiliation. These attitudes and beliefs may be shared by cultures, or they may be more individualized. At the core of what makes each of us unique is our personality. In Chapter 3, we discussed some of the many personality characteristics that guide our communication with others.

Now more than ever, we have opportunities to form relationships with many different people.

Unfortunately, many of our initial decisions to form relationships with others are based on assumptions and impressions formed by external-level factors. Upon closer analysis, you may find that you actually have *more* in common at the internal and personality levels with those who are different on the external level. Just because we may *look* different doesn't mean that we will *think* or *perceive* differently. Communication provides us with valuable information to determine how different we actually are from others.

THINK ABOUT IT. . .

In what ways do the following aspects of diversity impact communication in your relationships with others?

- Age
- Educational background
- Family status
- Geographical residence
- Military experience
- Physical and mental ability
- Sexual orientation
- Socioeconomic status
- Spiritual practice
- Work experience

Consider the characteristics that you share with your closest friend. You probably formed a friendship based on similarities in some of the factors listed above. Perhaps you are close in age and have similar educational backgrounds. Stop for a moment and consider the relationship implications as a result of differences in these factors. Consider how diversity impacts communication in the following relationship scenarios:

- A couple with different spiritual backgrounds needs to negotiate whose religious beliefs will be followed in raising their children.
- A son who is gay finds it difficult to communicate his feelings about his romantic partner to his heterosexual parents.
- A soldier tries to convey her beliefs about war and her value of freedom to her friends back home who have never served in the military.

When considering the many aspects of diversity, it is easy to see why many relationships encounter stumbling blocks as individuals attempt to navigate differences in knowledge, experiences, beliefs, and values. To evaluate how cultural differences impact your level of apprehension when communicating with others, complete the Personal Report of Intercultural Communication Apprehension (PRI-CA) scale at the end of this chapter.

Our culture shapes our perceptions and teaches us the preferred ways of behaving. For example, democracy is valued by many in the United States. Beginning in elementary school, students are taught the meaning of democracy. Later in life, they may witness people defending their rights to free speech via tweets or protests. Socialization refers to the process of learning about cultural norms and expectations. This is critical for an individual to become a functioning member of society. Keep in mind that our perceptions are highly individualized, so much so that we may not consider that others see things differently. It may be easy to overlook the impact that diversity has on our communication patterns.

Communication behaviors are often unique to a culture, allowing us to easily identify members of various cultural groups. For example, an employee from Georgia assigned to work on a project with a team from Ohio may be easily identified by her accent. Culture is not only reflected in our behavior or language; it also influences our expectations. We form assumptions about how individuals *should* behave and what we should expect in our relationships with them. For example, Japan is considered to be a collectivistic culture that values and encourages group goals over individual achievement. A student from Japan who studies in the United States where individualism is valued may be uncomfortable in situations where he is "singled out" for his individual academic achievements and prefer to be acknowledged with his class.

While we each have diverse characteristics that make us unique, we also share some aspects in common with other members of our larger culture. These shared characteristics allow us to identify with various groups or co-cultures that help further define our identity.

CO-CULTURES WITHIN THE UNITED STATES

Within the larger cultural context, numerous co-cultures exist, each distinguishable by unique characteristics. It is important to note that you are a member of multiple co-cultures. Consider the man who identifies as a long-time employee of

It may be easy to overlook the impact that diversity has on our communication patterns.

Quest Pharmaceuticals, in addition to being an adult, African-American Texan with Republican views, and of the Methodist faith. A total of seven co-cultures are claimed in this one example.

Our multiple memberships may contribute to confusion and miscommunication in our relationships. Suppose you assume that because one of your soccer teammates likes sports, she would not be interested in classical music or the theatre. As you pass a poster announcing the upcoming cultural arts series on campus, you make some negative comments about "artsy geeks." What you do not know is that your teammate has studied classical music since a young age, and her mother is a trained opera singer. While this is an extremely simplified example, assuming that membership in one group precludes an individual from having interests in other groups can lead to embarrassing situations that can impact relationships. There are several examples of co-cultures that potentially shape our perceptions and our interactions.

Ethnicity

While the terms *race* and *ethnicity* have often been used synonymously, these two categories are unique. **Ethnicity** refers to the common heritage, or background, shared by a group of people. Categories may be established to identify the culture from which one's ancestors came. These include Irish-American, German-American, or Mexican-American. While there has been some debate over the connotations associated with the labeling of some of these groups, the intention of naming is simply for identification purposes.

Race

Race is the term used to refer to genetically inherited biological characteristics such as hair

texture and color, eye shape, skin color, and facial structure. Terms used to describe different racial categories include Caucasian, African-American, and Asian.

The diverse population of the United States continues to produce more interracial and interethnic relationships.

An increase in the number of interracial and interethnic relationships prompted the U.S. government to update the categories one could choose to record their race on the U.S. Census. Prior to 2000, U.S. citizens were forced to choose one category to represent their racial or ethnic identity. Today, options have been added so people can more accurately report their identity. Figure 12.2 includes some of the categories included on the 2010 U.S. Census form to enable people to report those racial and ethnic groups with which they identify. Citizens can now identify as a member of multiple racial groups rather than being restricted to only one identity.

Regional Differences

Within a given culture, speech patterns, attitudes, and values may differ significantly depending on the geographic location that an individual calls home. Northern Germans ex-

→ NOTE: Please answer BOTH Question 8 about Hispanic origin and Question 9 about race. For this census, Hispanic origins are not races.

8. Is Person 1 of Hispanic, Latino, or Spanish origin?

☐ **No,** not of Hispanic, Latino, or Spanish origin
☐ Yes, Mexican, Mexican Am., Chicano
☐ Yes, Puerto Rican
☐ Yes, Cuban
☐ Yes, another Hispanic, Latino, or Spanish origin — *Print origin, for example, Argentinean, Colombian, Dominican, Nicaraguan, Salvadoran, Spaniard, and so on.* 🖊

[ ][ ][ ][ ][ ][ ][ ][ ][ ][ ][ ][ ][ ][ ][ ][ ][ ][ ]

9. What is Person 1's race? *Mark* ☒ *one or more boxes.*

☐ White
☐ Black, African Am., or Negro
☐ American Indian or Alaska Native — *Print name of enrolled or principal tribe.* 🖊

[ ][ ][ ][ ][ ][ ][ ][ ][ ][ ][ ][ ][ ][ ][ ][ ][ ][ ]

☐ Asian Indian   ☐ Japanese   ☐ Native Hawaiian
☐ Chinese   ☐ Korean   ☐ Guamanian or Chamorro
☐ Filipino   ☐ Vietnamese   ☐ Samoan
☐ Other Asian — *Print race, for example, Hmong, Laotian, Thai, Pakistani, Cambodian, and so on.* 🖊   ☐ Other Pacific Islander — *Print race, for example, Fijian, Tongan, and so on.* 🖊

[ ][ ][ ][ ][ ][ ][ ][ ][ ][ ][ ][ ][ ][ ][ ][ ][ ][ ]

☐ Some other race — *Print race.* 🖊

[ ][ ][ ][ ][ ][ ][ ][ ][ ][ ][ ][ ][ ][ ][ ][ ][ ][ ]

Figure 12.2 Sample categories to identify racial and ethnic identity from the 2010 U.S. Census form.

Source: http://www.pewresearch.org/fact-tank/2014/05/05/millions-of-americans-changed-their-racial-or-ethnic-identity-from-one-census-to-the-next/

press values that are quite different from those of southern Germans. Those who reside in northern Brazil communicate using nonverbal gestures that are unrecognizable to those from southern Brazil. Accents within a culture also vary depending on the geographic region. Japanese spoken in Okinawa takes on different tones when spoken in Tokyo. English spoken by those who live in the Amish region of Pennsylvania may be different from those living in Texas.

Dodd (1998) observed a variety of **regional differences** in communication styles within the boundaries of the United States. These include variety in the amount of animation, perceived openness,

informal rapport, and rate of speech delivery. In 2003, the Harvard Dialect Survey identified a variety of regional differences in vocabulary and pronunciation within the United States (Vaux & Golder). While we may think we speak the same language, the potential for misunderstandings exists even within our nation's boundaries. Figure 12.3 highlights differences in regional dialects that are found as you travel across the United States.

How would you address a group of two or more people?	You all Y'all Yinz Yous
What do you call a big road on which you drive fast?	Highway Freeway Expressway Parkway
What do you call the sweet spread that is put on a cake?	Frosting Icing
What do you call a large motor vehicle used to carry freight?	Semi Tractor-trailer 18-wheeler Rig/Big Rig
What do you call the long sandwich that contains deli meat, lettuce and so on?	Sub Grinder Hoagie Poor Boy Hero
What do you call the rubber-soled shoes worn in gym class or for athletic activities?	Sneakers Gym Shoes Jumpers Tennis Shoes Trainers
What do you call a sweetened carbonated beverage?	Soda Pop Coke Soft Drink

Figure 12.3 Sample questions from the 2003 Harvard Dialect Survey.

In addition to regional differences in language, distinctions in values also impact relationships. Consider distinctions between rural and urban co-cultures. Rural co-cultures tend to approach decisions more cautiously, while members of urban co-cultures are more willing to take risks and reach decisions more quickly.

Social Class

Communication challenges may be influenced by social class. Co-cultural categories are created on the basis of educational, occupational, or financial backgrounds, resulting in perceived status differentials. While many are hesitant to discuss their own social status or to address potential implications of class differentials on communication, research has identified some potential effects:

- Nearly 38 percent of patients indicated that they lacked confidence in understanding medical statistics. Many of these patients identified themselves as being low-income or low-education (Smith, Wolf, & Wagner, 2010).
- In a 2014 study examining socioeconomic status (SES) and parent-child communication regarding task completion, low-SES families tended to exhibit traditional gendered patterns. Mothers conveyed supportive messages and fathers focused on task completion. The opposite was true with high-SES families: mothers were more task-oriented and fathers were more focused on the relationship with the child (Grebelsky-Lichtman, 2014).

Stratification in our relationships often occurs on the basis of homophily, the idea that we choose to be with people who are similar to us. When initiating relationships, we seek out those in similar careers, with similar educational experiences, and of similar financial status. While social status may be considered a "taboo topic" for discussion, understanding its impact on our interactions is important.

CHARACTERISTICS OF CULTURE

Understanding what culture *is*, as well as the ways we identify with various co-cultures, is an important first step in exploring its impact on our relationships. In the next sections we explain the three primary characteristics of culture and *how* it becomes such an influential factor in our lives.

Culture Is Learned

The preferred ways of behaving as a member of a society are learned at a young age. Consider the learning experiences of children. Adults teach them how to say words, which foods can be eaten with the fingers and which should be eaten with utensils, and songs and rituals that are part of the culture. They may be taught that profanity is not acceptable and be rewarded for saying the Pledge of Allegiance. Children are even taught biases and prejudices. Expectations about the nature of relationships and communication are also learned at a young age. For example, in the United States it is viewed as unacceptable for male friends to hold hands in public. In some Arab cultures it is not uncommon to see two men engage in this behavior. Society teaches us the behaviors that are accepted by most members of the culture, and, at the same time, instills within us a response mechanism for reacting to violations of cultural norms. Figure 12.4 highlights examples of learned cultural expectations for appropriate use of nonverbal communication.

What is acceptable behavior in a culture is learned both explicitly and implicitly. **Explicit learning** involves actual instructions regarding the preferred way of behaving. A school may create a brochure that specifies the dress code required of all students, or a teacher may instruct students to raise their hand before speaking in class. **Implicit learning** occurs via observation. We are not directly told what behaviors are preferred; rather we learn by observing others. Our choices of what to wear for a first date or for the first day of work may be influenced by our observations of others or by scanning various media sources. We learn the preferred ways of a culture so as to be accepted.

Culture Is Dynamic

Over time, events occur that cause cultures to change. Consider how relationships were altered in the United States after the events of September 11th. In the days and months following the tragedy, people reported that they engaged in more frequent communication and open expressions of affection with family and friends.

Cultures and their members also change as a result of "borrowing" from other cultures. It is quite common to open a fashion magazine and see examples of trends being borrowed from other cultures. For

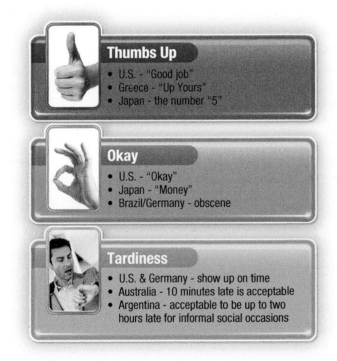

Thumbs Up
- U.S. - "Good job"
- Greece - "Up Yours"
- Japan - the number "5"

Okay
- U.S. - "Okay"
- Japan - "Money"
- Brazil/Germany - obscene

Tardiness
- U.S. & Germany - show up on time
- Australia - 10 minutes late is acceptable
- Argentina - acceptable to be up to two hours late for informal social occasions

Figure 12.4 Cultural norms for nonverbal behaviors that are learned.

example, U.S. stores and catalogues showcase Asian-inspired t-shirts and jewelry that include Chinese or Japanese writing.

Depending on a culture's approach to uncertainty, change may occur at different rates. Within the last decade, change has occurred at a rapid rate within the United States. Technological advances make some computers obsolete a year or two after purchase. Food, music styles, and exercise trends experience changes as each generation identifies new preferences. Not only do cultures change with regard to food and clothing styles, but popular culture also undergoes transitions. Reflect on how your own conversations are focused on or influenced by cultural trends. Figure 12.5 provides examples of trends for 2015 as identified by *The Washington Post*. After all, what we talk about one week may be "old news" the next.

Changes in our culture provide us with new topics for discussion and debate in our personal relationships. However, not all cultures embrace change. In fact, some cultures are reluctant to implement change and emphasize the importance of tradition and stability. This can create challenges when those who welcome change attempt to form relationships with those who are resistant to change.

Culture Is Pervasive

Culture is everywhere. Take a moment and look around you. Chances are that you see numerous examples of your culture's influence with one simple glance. Is there a smartphone on your desk? Perhaps there are posters, photos, or artwork on the walls. Is there a television turned on

The Washington Post's 2015 In/Out List	
WHAT'S OUT	**WHAT'S IN**
Black Friday	Black November
Minimalist running shoes	Thick-cushioned soles
Binge watching	Binge listening
Hashtag activism	T-shirt advocacy
Zombie apocalypses	Climate change dystopias
Swiping right	Saying "hello"
"Yasss"	"On fleek"

Figure 12.5 Predictions for 2015 U.S. cultural trends.

Source: http://www.washingtonpost.com/wp-srv/artsandliving/features/2014/year-in-review/the-list.html

or music playing? Maybe you are on campus and there are other students nearby. Take a look at the style of their clothes and listen to the words they are saying to one another. Each of these things demonstrates the pervasive nature of culture. It surrounds us—in fact, we cannot escape the influence of our culture.

If one were to adopt a descriptive definition of culture, this prevalence could be seen as influencing everything: our expectations for relationships, the clothing we wear, the language we speak, the food we choose, and even our daily schedules. Culture is represented not only in our material possessions, but also in the values, beliefs, and attitudes that comprise our personal orientation system. It shapes virtually every aspect of our lives and influences our thoughts and actions.

By taking a moment to consider the impact that culture has on our lives, it becomes clear that culture and communication are inseparable. Our verbal and nonverbal messages are shaped by our culture's influence, and we learn about our culture through the messages we receive from others.

Becoming a competent communicator across cultures requires you to develop a game plan. Knowing that each person's communication is guided by his or her unique set of values, beliefs, and attitudes will prepare you for differences in your approaches to conversations. Just as a sports team needs to study plays, people need to study and understand the various elements that create confusion and miscommunication in cross-cultural encounters. If you discover that you offend or confuse someone, you may need to alter your verbal or nonverbal messages. This chapter will help you to develop a personal game

plan for becoming a competent communicator in diverse interpersonal relationships.

THE IMPACT OF CULTURAL DIVERSITY ON INTERPERSONAL RELATIONSHIPS

Recent changes in political and social policy, evolving demographics, and technological advances have provided us with countless opportunities for forming relationships with diverse others. Figure 12.6 highlights three of the many reasons for exploring the impact of diversity on communication in interpersonal relationships, including: (1) increased awareness of self, (2) appreciation for technological transformations, and (3) understanding of demographic transitions.

Understanding the Self

Perhaps the simplest and most overlooked reason for studying the impact of diversity on our relationships is the opportunity it provides for exploring and understanding our own cultural background and identity. By delving into the cultural factors that influence communication patterns, we begin to gain an awareness of our own reasons for thinking and behaving as we do.

Technological Transformations

In the 1960s, McLuhan introduced the notion of a "global village" (McLuhan & Powers, 1989). He predicted that mass media and technology would bring the world closer together, a notion considered to be farfetched at that time.

Cultural influence on dating expectations

Culture affects how we initiate and maintain our interpersonal relationships. In many European cultures, it is common for teenagers to go out on large "group" dates. Females in Australia may ask out males and offer to split the cost of a date. In China and Japan, dating is typically reserved for those who are older, usually in their twenties. Dating was discouraged in India until recently. Families were expected to introduce couples and help them get to know each other socially in preparation for marriage. While online dating has grown in popularity in the United States and many European countries, this method of initiating romantic relationships would be frowned upon in cultures that view dating as a time for getting to know one's potential future in-laws.

- In what ways does culture influence our expectations for other relationships (e.g., marital partners, sibling/parent relationships, co-workers)?

Understanding the self

Technological Transformations

Demographic Trends

Figure 12.6 Reasons for exploring diversity and communication.

But a quick inventory of today's technologies, which provide opportunities for forming diverse relationships, reveals that McLuhan's vision was quite accurate. Airline travel, television, cell phones, and the Internet are just a few of the technologies that have changed the way we communicate. We now have the capability to travel around the world in a matter of hours, simultaneously view events as they occur in other cities and countries, and interact with persons from around the globe.

THINK ABOUT IT. . .

Janelle had grown up in a small town with a population of approximately 350. The population was entirely Caucasian, and the overwhelming majority of the residents were middle-class and Methodist. When she moved to a major metropolitan area, she encountered challenges associated with understanding cultural differences. Shortly after moving into her new apartment, she saw a neighbor in her building struggling to bring several bags of groceries from the parking garage. Janelle hurried to help her neighbor as she introduced herself and attempted to take a couple of bags from her neighbor's car. She was quickly told that her assistance was not needed. Later that evening, Janelle discussed the incident with her roommate, who pointed out, "You have to understand that people in large cities don't just walk up and help one another. Don't be offended. City folks need time to build the level of trust that you're accustomed to." As she reflected on why her first few weeks in the city were so frustrating, Janelle realized that she had been focusing on how "strange" other people were instead of considering how her *own* cultural background influenced her perceptions and expectations.

- Recall a time when you formed impressions based on your initial impressions of someone.
- How did your own cultural background influence your perceptions?

Internet Users in the World Distribution by World Regions - 2014

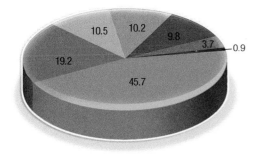

- Asia 45.7%
- Europe 19.2%
- Lat Am / Carib. 10.5%
- North America 10.2%
- Africa 9.8%
- Middle East 3.7%
- Oceania / Australia 0.9%

© Kendall Hunt Publishing Co.

Figure 12.7 Global Internet usage statistics.

Opportunities provided by technology for forming relationships with diverse persons have increased exponentially over the past 20 years. The 2013 U.S. Census reported that nearly 84 percent of U.S. households owned a computer, and nearly 75 percent of homeowners reported that they had an Internet connection (File & Ryan, 2014). Figure 12.7 provides a summary by continent of the more than 3 billion Internet users worldwide (*http://www.internetworldstats. com/america.htm*). In the United States alone, nearly 310 million people use the Internet to find information and to form relationships with others. This is an increase of 187 percent from 2000–2014. Relationships can be initiated and maintained online with ease. Online assignments designed to connect students from diverse cultures, corporate meetings via Skype with colleagues from around the globe, and online video games that enable players to collaborate and compete from across the country are just a few examples of the ways in which the Internet has eliminated geographic boundaries for making connections.

How has the Internet made it easier for us to know about world events as they occur?

©Andrey_Popov /Shutterstock.com

Airline travel, television, cell phones, and the Internet are just a few of the technologies that have changed the way we communicate.

Due to increased opportunities for interactions with those from diverse backgrounds, relationship success depends on the ability to demonstrate communication competence across cultures.

As corporate America expands its boundaries to include many overseas partners, work teams will be composed of members from diverse cultures. People come to the workplace with varied beliefs, experiences, and expectations about the role of communication in relationships at work. Technology provides us with opportunities to communicate with persons who come from backgrounds different from our own.

Influence of Demographic Transitions

Over the past 30 years, the demographic composition of the United States has changed dramatically. Medical advancements have extended the life expectancy of Americans, so we have more generational differences to navigate. Immigration patterns have changed dramatically since the 1960s, when most immigrants came primarily from European countries. Today, nearly 90 percent of immigrants arrive from Latin American and Asian nations. Figure 12.8 highlights the predicted racial and ethnic composition of the United States.

Over the past decade, the number of interracial and interdenominational marriages has increased, and the U.S. workplace has seen a shift from the predominance of white male employees to a more diverse workforce that is also composed of women and racial and ethnic groups. Opportunities to expand our linguistic, political, and social knowledge abound.

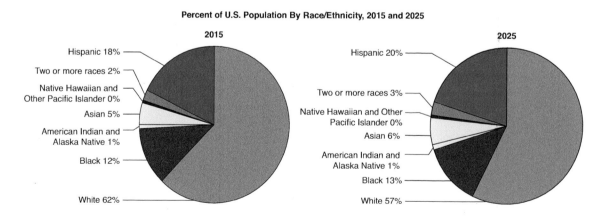

Percent of U.S. Population By Race/Ethnicity, 2015 and 2025

2015

- Hispanic 18%
- Two or more races 2%
- Native Hawaiian and Other Pacific Islander 0%
- Asian 5%
- American Indian and Alaska Native 1%
- Black 12%
- White 62%

2025

- Hispanic 20%
- Two or more races 3%
- Native Hawaiian and Other Pacific Islander 0%
- Asian 6%
- American Indian and Alaska Native 1%
- Black 13%
- White 57%

Figure 12.8. Predicted U.S. demographic trends from 2015–2025.

However, not all intercultural encounters are viewed as opportunities. While these demographic shifts create opportunities for diverse relationships, it is important to recognize that they present communication challenges as well. Uncertainty about other individuals creates tension, and the consequences of changing demographics are being felt in many social institutions. Consider the potential communication challenges faced in 2013 when students at Wilcox County High School in Georgia hosted the school's first racially integrated prom, despite protests and criticism from members of the local community. The debate over diverse beliefs about racial segregation resulted in heated debates and gained the attention of national media.

Due to increased opportunities for interactions with those from diverse backgrounds, relationship success depends on the ability to demonstrate communication competence across cultures. After all, achieving communication competence should be the ultimate goal in our interpersonal relationships. When the source and receiver are from diverse backgrounds and have unique expectations of communication, this goal may be a bit more difficult to achieve. Four core concepts that may assist us in enhancing cultural communication competence are: knowledge, understanding, skills, and acceptance. Let us examine each of these concepts more closely.

COMMUNICATION COMPETENCE: FOUR CORE CONCEPTS

Knowledge

Knowledge refers to the theoretical principles and concepts that explain behaviors occurring within a specific communication context. In other words, increasing your knowledge of communication theories and concepts will enhance your ability to understand and appreciate differences in intercultural relationships. You have already increased your knowledge base as a result of reading this textbook up to this point. Each of the concepts and theories that have been introduced has enhanced your understanding of the factors that impact communication in interpersonal relationships.

Consider how knowledge of communication theories can enhance our intercultural relationships. In Chapter 7, we introduced Berger and Calabrese's **uncertainty reduction theory** (URT). This theory describes how we exchange information in an attempt to reduce ambiguity about others. Questions are asked to gain new knowledge about the other person and to assist us in forming effective interpersonal relationships. If we can predict the attitudes, behaviors, and emotions of others, we have reduced our uncertainty about the other person (Berger & Calabrese, 1975).

When crossing cultural lines, alleviating this ambiguity becomes a bit trickier. For example, the notion of what constitutes acceptable disclosures in interpersonal relationships in the United States might differ from what is considered proper in other cultures. Is it acceptable to ask about another person's occupation? About her family? How does the other person view status differentials, and what rules does he or she adopt for communicating with someone of different status? Berger (1979) identified three primary communication strategies used to reduce uncertainty in relationships (Figure 12.9). These are: passive strategies, active strategies, and interactive strategies.

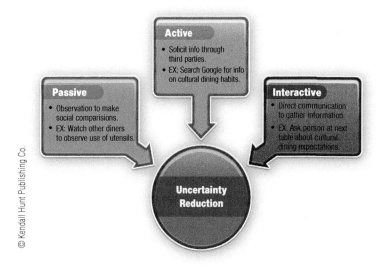

Figure 12.9 Uncertainty reduction strategies.

Passive strategies typically involve observation and social comparison. We observe members of other cultures and make assessments as to the differences that exist. When one of your authors arrived in Hong Kong to teach summer classes, she did not speak Chinese. She spent many hours during her first weekend there sitting at the busy harbor, browsing through shopping areas and walking around campus to observe how people interacted with one another. Through her observations, she learned the cultural rules for personal space, noticed styles of dress and forms of nonverbal greetings, and became familiar with the protocol for communication between students and teachers on campus.

Active strategies require us to engage in interactions with others to learn additional information about the other person. Suppose your professor assigns you to have weekly conversations with an international partner during the semester. Prior to your first meeting, you may decide to ask other international students what they know about

your conversation partner's culture, or you may go online and search for information about your conversation partner's culture.

Interactive strategies typically involve a face-to-face encounter between two individuals to reduce uncertainty. Typically, partners engage in **self-disclosure** as a means of sharing information about themselves with others. When examining cultural differences in disclosure, it was found that American college students disclose about a much wider range of topics—and to more people outside the family—whereas college students in Korea self-disclose mostly to immediate family members (Ishii, Thomas, & Klopf, 1993). Consider the following example:

Alicia was excited to learn that she had been selected to live with an international student in the dorm during her freshman year. She had been fortunate enough to travel with her parents on business trips to various countries for the past several years and found learning about other cultures to be fascinating. Her new roommate, Kyon, was from Korea. As they were unpacking their things, Alicia told Kyon about her hometown, her summer vacation to Hilton Head Island, and about all of her friends from high school who were attending their college. She shared how frightened she was about the first day of classes, and she laughed as she told Kyon how she had taken her schedule and walked around campus to locate her classrooms for the first day of class. Eventually, Alicia noticed that she had been doing all the talking, so she began asking Kyon questions. While Kyon was willing to discuss the classes she would be taking and the plane trip from Korea, she seemed reluctant to talk about her family, friends, or even her fears about starting college.

Without knowledge of cultural differences in communication styles, Alicia may have become easily frustrated by Kyon's lack of disclosure. After all, in the United States it is common to engage in question-asking and self-disclosure to reduce our uncertainty about others. But understanding that expectations for self-disclosure in Korea are different from those held by Americans will help alleviate the potential frustration and hurt feelings that could occur otherwise.

Schools teach children the cultural expectations for acceptable classroom behaviors.

Knowledge of one's own culture is learned. Cultures teach their members preferred perceptual and communication patterns. Beginning at a very young age, this learning process instills knowledge about the culture's accepted behaviors. Communication is the channel for teaching these lessons.

Gaining cultural knowledge can remove some of the barriers that can create communication challenges in relationships with diverse people. But knowledge in and of itself is insufficient for achieving competence. We also need to gain an understanding of why others communicate the way they do.

Understanding

Understanding involves applying knowledge to specific situations in an attempt to explain the behaviors that are occurring. While you may know the definition of uncertainty reduction theory (URT), it is important to gain an understanding of *how* it impacts a particular interaction. Understanding involves exploring the roots, or sources, of communication, rather than simply explaining the behavior. Consider two coworkers who attempt to influence each other on a project on which they are collaborating. Joe is assertive and tries to persuade Maynae by directly disagreeing with her proposal. Maynae's cultural background is one that values saving face in front of others. Thus, she avoids directly disagreeing with Joe— rather, she nods her head and proceeds with the project as she originally planned. Both of them end up frustrated. Joe cannot understand why Maynae did not follow their game plan. Had she not nodded her head and agreed with him? Joe attributes Maynae's actions to her shyness. Maynae is frustrated by Joe's confusion. Did he not understand that she did not want to embarrass him in front of their colleagues?

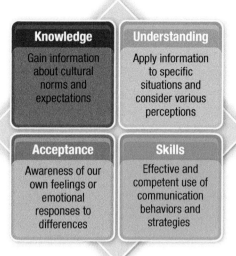

A room full of students appearing to be similar on the surface could have many different cultural backgrounds.

Figure 12.10 Core elements of intercultural communication competence.

Broadening our study of culture and diversity to understand the influence of elements such as race, ethnicity, language differences, and religious beliefs is essential for relationship success. But it is also important to understand that what works in one relationship may not work in another. Consider the example of the coach and her team. They know and understand multiple plays so they can choose the most effective one to enhance their chances of winning the game. Just as it would be ineffective to run the same play over and over again in a game, communicating with diverse persons in the same manner would not result in satisfying relationships. While this chapter will assist you in building knowledge and understanding of communication differences, acceptance of differences is also a key to interpersonal success.

Acceptance

Acceptance refers to our awareness of our feelings and emotions in response to diverse approaches to relationships and communication. It encompasses our willingness to understand the behavior of others. Accepting differences in behavior enables us to be less judgmental and to reject ethnocentric thinking. At times our intercultural apprehension inhibits us from seeing and perceiving things from the other person's point of view. **Ethnocentrism** refers to the tendency to perceive our own ways of behaving and thinking as being correct, or acceptable, and judging the behaviors of others as being "strange," incorrect, or inferior. You can assess your own level of ethnocentrism by completing the scale at the end of this chapter. A study of 107 college students found that ethnocentrism and intercultural apprehension prompted people to avoid intercultural conversations (Neuliep, 2012). By expanding our knowledge of other cultures and understanding the reasons for reactions to cultural differences, we will develop a more accepting attitude toward these unique tendencies. The only element remaining is to hone our communication and relational skills.

Skills

We have discussed many of the specific skills that are central to interpersonal communication throughout this text. **Skills** are the specific communication behaviors that contribute to competent and effective interpersonal relationships. Effective listening, assertiveness, responsiveness, nonverbal sensitivity, language comprehension, and conflict management are just a few of the many skills required in diverse relationships. It is important to note that there is a difference between *knowing* how to communicate effectively across cultures, and actually *engaging* in the appropriate behaviors. You might understand that the Chinese culture values silence, but because you are an extremely talkative person and are ineffective in practicing silence, you may be perceived as being rude when interacting with members of that culture.

Research points to the benefits of practicing intercultural communication skills through an examination of interactions that occur among college students. Those students who engage in frequent interactions with students of different racial backgrounds have positive discussions about race and ethnicity, tend to have a higher self-concept, and report that they are more satisfied with college (Smith & Associates, 1997).

By expanding our knowledge of other cultures and understanding the reasons for reactions to cultural differences, we will develop a more accepting attitude toward these unique tendencies.

and are commonly referred to as our **personal orientation system**. Communication plans and relationship expectations are developed and organized based on these characteristics.

Many of the components of the personal orientation system are learned within the cultural context. This learning begins at a young age. Messages are shared by parents, teachers, and friends who teach the younger members of society to perceive certain actions as good or bad, fair or unfair. For example, Chinese children are taught to value history and tradition, and stories of the past are viewed as lessons to guide their behavior. Children in the United States tend to view stories of the past as entertaining, but rather than focusing on tradition, they are encouraged to find new and innovative ways of doing things. When faced with decisions regarding the proper way to respond in situations, our needs, beliefs, values, and attitudes assist us in guiding our perception of a situation.

PERSONAL ORIENTATION SYSTEM

Each individual has a set of predispositions that serves as a guide for thoughts, actions, and behaviors. These predispositions are composed of needs, beliefs, values, and attitudes

Needs

All individuals have **needs** that result in strong feelings of discomfort or desires. These needs motivate us to achieve satisfaction or comfort. A strong relationship exists between needs and interpersonal communication, with communication serving as the primary mechanism through which we satisfy needs. If a student needs to have an assignment explained more clearly, he or she must communicate that need to the instructor. If an employee needs assistance in obtaining a copy of a company report, communication with the human resources director or with a supervisor can satisfy the need.

As discussed in Chapter 1, Maslow's hierarchy of needs (1954) organizes the needs that humans must fulfill. A hierarchical structure helps us to understand the importance and priority of having some needs achieved before others.

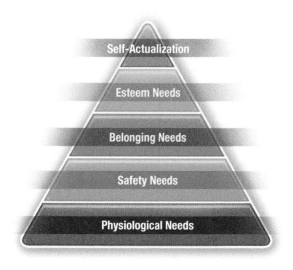

Figure 12.11 Maslow's hierarchy of needs.

Source: http://www.researchhistory.org/wp-content/uploads/2012/06/maslows-hierarchy-of-needs.gif

At the most basic level are the **physiological needs** of humans. These include the need for food, clothing, and shelter. While most cultures are able to devote adequate attention to meeting these needs, others cannot. The next level includes **safety and security needs**. Individuals possess a motivation to feel safe and secure in their surroundings. However, cultures differ in their methods for satisfying this need.

At the middle of the hierarchy is the need for **love and belonging**. Schutz (1958) identified three basic needs across cultures: affection, control, and inclusion. We have a need to love and to be loved. **Esteem needs** are located at the next level of Maslow's hierarchy. Humans have a need to feel good about themselves. Interpersonal communication with others is one mechanism for meeting this need. Things that cultural members say and do impact the fulfillment of these needs. At the highest level of Maslow's hierarchy is **self-actualization**. This level is achieved when an individual feels that he or she has accomplished all that can be achieved in a lifetime. As the U.S. Army's motto implies, self-actualization is fulfilled when an individual feels that the goal "be all that you can be" has been met.

When applying Maslow's hierarchy to our interpersonal relationships, it becomes apparent that communication is the means through which we fulfill most of our needs. It is also the key to understanding the needs of others. Considering the importance of the needs of others can help us alleviate some misunderstandings. Cultural differences may cause one person to have a need for power and status, while another may possess a strong need for friendship and affection. The intensity with which each of these needs is experienced may cause these two people to interact in very different ways.

Beliefs

A second component of culture that guides our thoughts and behaviors is our belief system. **Beliefs** are an important part of understanding our interactions with diverse others because not only do they influence our conscious reactions to situations, but they dominate our subconscious thoughts as well. We are constantly influenced by our beliefs. They are our personal convictions regarding the truth or existence of things. In Chapter 2, we discussed how interactions with others shape our view of ourself.

When crossing cultural borders, an examination of the beliefs possessed by a culture's members yields some fascinating differences. People from Malaysia believe that it is bad luck to touch someone on the top of the head as it is believed to be the location of the center of spiritual energy. Hawaiians possess a number of beliefs about the messages indicated by the appearance of a rainbow. Consider the superstitious beliefs held by members of the American culture. Walking under a ladder, having a black cat cross your path, and the groom seeing the bride on the wedding day prior to the ceremony are all believed to be signs of bad luck. These diverse beliefs impact our interpersonal communication.

Because most people do not question social institutions, many of the beliefs of a culture are perpetuated from generation to generation without any thought being given to the reasons for the existence of the beliefs. Some individuals have reported that reactions to their questioning of beliefs have been so negative that they feared rejection in their relationships and simply adopted the accepted beliefs into their own personal orientation system.

Values

Values serve as the guide for an individual's behavior. They dictate what we should and should not do. Kluckhohn (1951) describes **values** as a personal philosophy or set of standards that influences the choice of alternative actions that may be available. This definition highlights the relationship between values and communication in that values are communicated both explicitly and implicitly through our behaviors. The majority of our actions are reflective of the values that are firmly established in our personal orientation system.

Consider the values that are communicated in proverbs across cultures:

- "A stitch in time saves nine": communicates the value placed on addressing issues or problems when they are small rather than waiting until they grow bigger.
- "A bird in the hand is worth two in the bush": emphasizes the importance of practicality and being satisfied with what you have.
- "Friendship doubles our job and divides our grief": a Swedish proverb that highlights the value placed on friendships.

Nonverbal communication may be a more subtle means for communicating values. Many Asian cultures practice the custom of giving a gift to demonstrate the values of reciprocity and friendship. It is not unusual for students to offer their teachers gifts in exchange for the lessons that are learned. In the American culture, many teachers would be extremely uncomfortable accepting these gifts because they could be perceived as bribes. The rejection of gifts could potentially result in confusion in the student-teacher relationship, and make subsequent interactions uncomfortable. It is important to gain an understanding not only of the values held by a culture's members, but also the ways in which individuals communicate these values. By doing so, misunderstandings may be avoided.

Cultural Value Orientations

To understand the values shared by a culture's members, a number of scholars have developed models for studying value orientations. These models pose questions designed to measure the intensity with which a culture's members value specific characteristics.

How might this diverse group of college students differ in terms of their communication styles and preferences?

Kluckhohn and Strodbeck (1961) developed one of the first models of cultural value orientation, and it is still being used in research today. Questions are designed to gain insight into such perceptions regarding relationships between humans and humans and nature. Sample questions include:

- What is the basic nature of human beings? Are they inherently evil and incapable of being trusted, or do most humans have a good heart?
- How are social relationships organized? Are relationships viewed as being hierarchical with divisions of power? Or should equal rights be present in all social relationships?

As discussed earlier in the text, Hall's model of cultural values (1976) represents a continuum of characteristics associated with high-context and low-context cultures. These differences are characterized by distinct differences in communication styles. Cultures which fall at the **low-context** end of the continuum exhibit high verbal tendencies. This style is associated with a direct approach and verbal expressiveness. A philosophy of "say what you mean" is embraced. **High-context cultures**, on the other hand, prefer a more indirect style; cues about the intended message are interpreted through nonverbal channels. Whereas persons from a low-context culture expect messages to be direct, those from a high-context culture search the environment for cues. Rather than asking a person whether he or she is happy, high-context cultures would infer these feelings from other cues such as posture, facial expressions, and disposition. Consider the difficulties experienced by a couple who have different cultural backgrounds:

Alec was confused. He and Miki had been living together for the past year and were engaged to be married in a few months. One evening, Miki was silent as they ate dinner. He knew something was upsetting her, but she kept insisting that things were fine. Miki was extremely frustrated as well. Why did Alec always insist that she tell him what was wrong? Did she always have to put her feelings into words? Why couldn't Alec be more in tune with her nonverbal behaviors and understand that things were not quite right?

This example illustrates the difference between the influence of the low-context approach of the United States on Alec's behavior and the high-context approach of Miki's Japanese upbringing. Miki expects Alec to be more aware of the messages that are being communicated via nonverbal channels, while Alec expects Miki to say what is bothering her.

A final model of cultural values that was touched on earlier is presented by Hofstede (1980). Dimensions of values were identified by examining the attitudes of employees in more than 40 cultures. These dimensions include individualism/collectivism, power distance, masculinity/femininity, and uncertainty avoidance.

INDIVIDUALISM/COLLECTIVISM. Individualism/collectivism describes the relationship between the individual and the groups to which he or she belongs. **Individualistic** cultures, such as in the United States, focus on individual accomplishments and achievements. **Collectivism**, or value and concern for the group, is the primary value of many Asian cultures. Consider the cultural differences portrayed in *Gung Ho*, a movie about an automobile manufacturing plant. In the film, Asian managers took great pride in their work. After all, their own performance ultimately reflected on the group. They would never dream of taking time off for personal reasons. Ameri-

can workers, whose behaviors reflected individualism, placed their individual needs over those of the company. Employees expected time off to be at the birth of a child or to keep a medical appointment. These differences in the values of the group versus the self had disastrous outcomes, with the company facing the risk of closing as a result of conflicting cultural values.

POWER DISTANCE. **Power distance** refers to the distribution of power in personal relationships as well as within organizations. **Low power distance** cultures have a flat structure with most individuals being viewed as equals. The tendency

---

RESEARCH IN REAL LIFE

How does our uncertainty about relationships influence perceptions of the interactions we have with our romantic partners? A 2013 study by Theiss and Nagy of 294 college students from Korea (N=138) and the United States (N=156) examined cultural differences and the potential impact on relationship uncertainty. Participants in the study were asked to report their *self-uncertainty* about the relationship (their own commitment and liking in the relationship), *partner uncertainty* (the other's perceived commitment and liking), and *relationship uncertainty* (longevity of relationship and expectations for behaviors). Results of the study found that U.S. Americans indicated higher levels of all three types of certainty compared to Korean students. A possible explanation for these differences may be rooted in cultural tendencies toward collectivistic versus individualistic values. As a collectivistic culture, Koreans may not question or doubt their relationships as much as their individualistic U.S. counterparts. Americans are also more likely to use direct questioning (low-context) to inquire about the relationship status compared to Koreans (high-context).

> In order to become more competent in our interactions with diverse others, it is important to realize that stereotypes can and do impact our perceptions and our communication.

to show favoritism to individuals based on their age, status, or gender is minimized. **High power distance** cultures are depicted by a tall hierarchical structure with distinct status differences.

Imagine the frustration experienced by a young intercultural couple who had been married for only a few months. The husband, who was Hispanic, was raised in a culture that places the man as the head of the household (high power distance). His wife, who was raised by a single working mother in New York City, valued her independence. The power differential in her family of origin was low, thus she anticipated that her husband would view her as an equal partner in their relationship. As a result of their differing values for status and power based on their roles as husband and wife, the couple experienced many arguments.

MASCULINE/FEMININE. Prevalence of masculine and feminine traits in a culture characterizes Hofstede's (1980) dimensions of masculinity and femininity. **Masculine** cultures demonstrate a preference for assertiveness, ambition, and achievement. Characteristics of responsiveness, nurturance, and cooperation are associated with

cultures at the **feminine** end of this dimension. Gender roles in these cultures are perceived to be more equal. Cultures such as those found in Japan and Mexico exhibit more masculine tendencies, while those found in Brazil, Sweden, and Taiwan are more feminine.

UNCERTAINTY AVOIDANCE. **Uncertainty avoidance** refers to the willingness of a culture to approach or to avoid change. Cultures high in uncertainty avoidance demonstrate a preference for avoiding change. They embrace tradition and order. China and Germany are examples of countries with cultures that avoid uncertainty and embrace tradition. Cultures low in uncertainty avoidance welcome the possibility of change and are more willing to take risks. The United States and Finland are more open to change and are more tolerant of taking risks and adopting new and innovative approaches.

Understanding these dimensions can provide cues as to which values are promoted among members of a culture. This information is useful for determining the appropriate methods to approach interpersonal communication and for providing valuable information that assists in checking the accuracy of one's perceptions.

Attitudes: Stereotyping and Prejudice

Throughout our lives, each of us develops learned predispositions to respond in favorable or unfavorable ways toward people or objects. These tendencies are known as **attitudes**. A primary goal of this chapter is to assist you in identifying your responses to differences as well as to help you to understand your internal orientations guiding these reactions. When we interpret another's cultural customs or actions as being "wrong" or "offensive," it is important to understand how our culture has influenced our own attitudes. Two types of attitudes to consider are stereotypes and prejudices.

STEREOTYPING. Stereotyping results from our inability to see and appreciate the uniqueness of individuals. When generalizations about a group are made and are then attributed to any individuals who either associate with, or are members of, a specific group, the process of stereotyping evolves. Three steps have been identified in the process of stereotyping.

The first step involves categorizing a group of people based on observable characteristics that they have in common. Consider the impressions of U.S. lifestyles that are conveyed on American movies and television shows. Many of these shows have gained global audiences, and members of other cultures use them as resources to increase their knowledge of the United States. In 2011, former U.S. Secretary of State Hillary Clinton cautioned about the stereotypes generated from our media as she shared, "I remember having an Afghan general tell me that the only thing he thought about Americans is that all the men wrestled and the women walked around in bikinis because the only TV he ever saw was *Baywatch* and *World Wide Wrestling*." (http://www.businessinsider.com/hillary-clinton-al-jazeera-2011-3)

The second step in stereotyping involves assigning characteristics to a group of people. An example of this would be a popular magazine characterizing mothers who are employed outside the home as being less dedicated to their children.

Finally, we apply those characteristics to any individual who is a member of that group. An example would be the teacher who assumes that a student-athlete is not serious about academic studies. Since the events of 9/11, some members of Arab cultures have reported that they have been subjected to racial profiling. **Racial profiling** occurs when law enforcement or other officials use race as a basis for investigating a person for criminal involvement. This is a result of applying the single characteristic of race in determining whether a person should be viewed as threatening.

While stereotyping can be irrational, it is actually quite normal. Because humans are uncomfortable with uncertainty, stereotyping enables us to make predictions about our potential interactions with others. In order to become more competent in our interactions with diverse others, it is important to realize that stereotypes *can* and *do* impact our perceptions and our communication.

PREJUDICE. Another form of attitude that involves negative reactions toward a group of people based on inflexible and inaccurate assumptions is commonly known as **prejudice**. In essence, prejudice involves "pre-judging" individuals. Some of the most common forms of prejudice in the United States include racism, sexism, and ageism.

Racism. **Racism** refers to prejudice against an individual or group based on racial composition. Recall from the first part of this chapter that race is a term used to refer to inherited biological characteristics such as skin color, eye color and shape, hair texture, and facial structure.

Ageism. Negative communication toward persons based on their age is referred to as **ageism**. In the United States, some people assume that senior citizens are incapable of making contributions to society and can be considered helpless. In 1967, Congress passed the ADEA (Age Discrimination in Employment Act) to protect older workers against age discrimination. According to the law, an employer cannot replace an employee over the age of forty with a younger person if the current employee is able to satisfactorily perform her or his job. Assumptions that shape faulty attitudes about older workers include:

- They are "set in their ways" and resist change.

- Older people resist or have difficulty adjusting to new technology.
- They are slower than younger workers or can't perform demanding tasks.

Chances are you know many people over the age of 65 who debunk these myths. Prejudicial attitudes such as these can be damaging to workplace relationships if we fail to open our eyes to individual abilities.

Sexism. Sexism refers to negative communication directed toward persons of a particular sex. In the United States, sexist attitudes have traditionally been directed toward females. As a result, females have experienced discrimination in the workplace and in other walks of life. While stories of sexism frequently focus on the prejudices against females, men also are subject to sexist behaviors. Consider the father who stays at home and raises the children. As he shops for groceries with the children in the cart or plays with them at the park on a sunny weekday afternoon, he may hear a comment such as, "It's so nice that he's babysitting the children!" Not surprisingly, he may become offended because it is assumed that he is not capable of being the primary caregiver for his children.

COMMUNICATING PREJUDICE

There are three primary ways that we communicate prejudice. Verbal abuse refers to the process of engaging in comments or jokes that are insulting or demeaning to a targeted group. Consider the impressions that we form of people as a result of their negative verbal behaviors toward others. For example, the racist comments made by Paula Deen may have caused some of her fans to question their positive attitudes toward the celebrity chef.

Discrimination involves denying an individual or group of people their rights. While prejudice involves negative cognitions, or thoughts, discrimination is displayed when behaviors are used to express one's negative cognitions. Typically, discrimination is expressed through negative verbal comments made toward a group or an individual, with physical avoidance being the ultimate goal.

The most severe form of prejudice is **violence** which often results in physical harm or excessive force. On November 24, 2014, the jury in the trial involving a Ferguson, Missouri, police officer decided not to indict him for shooting an African American teen. As word of the verdict spread, riots erupted throughout the city. During the next week, the world watched as physical attacks, arson, protests, and looting occurred throughout the city. In the end, more than 25 businesses were burned, 80 arrests were made the first night of the riots, and the city suffered over $5 million in damages from the buildings that were destroyed. This violence demonstrates the potentially extreme outcome of prejudice.

Functions of Prejudice

While prejudice is often based on false, irrational, and inflexible generalizations, it is often considered "normal."

Why do individuals form prejudices? Figure 12.12 highlights three of the primary reasons expressed by others for forming prejudices.

ACCEPTANCE. **Acceptance** is when a person communicates negative feelings toward a particular group in order to fit in within a desired group. An example of this is when a fraternity member expresses hatred for another fraternity's members. When asked why he has these strong feelings, the only reason offered is "because all Alpha Betas dislike them."

EGO-DEFENSIVE. Another reason for communicating prejudice is to defend the ego. By expressing negative feelings and attitudes toward a group of people, individuals create a scapegoat for their own misfortunes. An employee was overheard expressing his prejudice against women being selected for administrative positions. Upon further questioning, he admitted that he did not actually harbor any ill feelings toward women supervisors. Rather, he was frustrated by the fact that a woman had been offered the position rather than him.

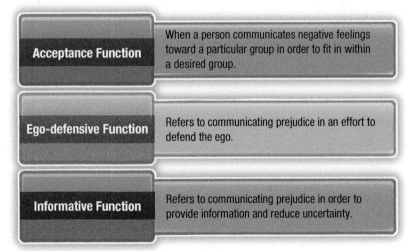

Acceptance Function	When a person communicates negative feelings toward a particular group in order to fit in within a desired group.
Ego-defensive Function	Refers to communicating prejudice in an effort to defend the ego.
Informative Function	Refers to communicating prejudice in order to provide information and reduce uncertainty.

Figure 12.12. Functions of prejudice.

INFORMATIVE. A final reason for prejudice is to provide information. As was stated earlier, humans have a need to reduce uncertainty. Unfortunately, many individuals form prejudices as a means for forming knowledge about a group of people with whom little or no contact has been made. The information provided by our prejudices may serve the purpose of allowing us to make sense of the world. For example, you may form a bias against members of a culture that you've never met or visited in order to help you anticipate or predict how you should communicate in your initial interactions.

Our needs, values, beliefs, and attitudes are extremely influential in guiding our expectations for our own and for others' communication. Careful consideration of the impact of these variables is required in order to engage in effective intercultural relationships.

Culture surrounds our lives and its influence is everywhere.

©Rawpixel /Shutterstock.com

SUGGESTIONS FOR EFFECTIVE INTERPERSONAL RELATIONSHIPS WITH DIVERSE OTHERS

As shown throughout this chapter, culture causes us to perceive things in unique ways. But there are strategies that can assist us in avoiding misunderstandings. Each of the suggestions below requires us to dedicate effort to understanding and practicing better interpersonal communication.

- Engage in careful listening and clear communication. Focus on listening for what is really being said, not what you want to hear. Be clear and explicit in your communication.

- Refrain from judging people based on observable differences such as race, ethnicity, or gender. Remember, internal factors contributing to diversity may be more influential than the external factors that we can readily see.

- Be patient with yourself. Remember that becoming an effective cross-cultural communicator requires skill and knowledge. It takes time to practice those skills. You may make mistakes, but there are lessons to be learned from those faux pas.

- Seek out opportunities to interact with those from diverse cultures. Be willing to take risks and to make mistakes.

- Practice patience with others. Cultural influences are powerful, and making the transition from one culture's way of thinking and behaving to another's takes time.

- Check for understanding. Do not be afraid to ask for clarification or to ensure that you understood what was being communicated. One simple question now can save offending someone later.

SUMMARY

Throughout this chapter we have discussed the prevalence of diversity in *all* of our interpersonal relationships. While diversity is most frequently identified based on observable characteristics such as race, ethnicity, or sex, it is important to consider additional variables that influence our communication choices as we interact with others. Individual beliefs, attitudes, and values have a significant impact on the messages we send as well as on our reactions to the messages that we receive. At this point we would like to reiterate the importance of studying and understanding the impact of cultural diversity on our interpersonal interactions—by taking a moment to enhance your own knowledge and skills, you are better equipped to understand the reasons underlying your own communication preferences as well as the communication choices of others.

DISCUSSION QUESTIONS

1. Reflect on your cultural background. Identify five ways that you are different from your friends and from your co-workers. Discuss how these differences may lead to miscommunication in your personal and professional relationships.

2. What are some ways that you explicitly and implicitly learned about your culture's expectations for communication and expected behaviors?

3. Identify strategies for enhancing your own intercultural communication competence in your personal relationships. What strategies could be used to enhance competence in your professional relationships?

SELF ASSESSMENTS

Personal Report of Intercultural Communication Apprehension (PRICA)

Directions: The 14 statements below are comments frequently made by people with regard to communication with people from other cultures. Please indicate how much you agree with these statements by marking a number representing your response to each statement using the following choices: **Strongly Disagree = 1; Disagree = 2; are Neutral = 3; Agree = 4; Strongly Agree = 5**

_____ 1. Generally, I am comfortable interacting with a group of people from different cultures.

_____ 2. I am tense and nervous while interacting with people from different cultures.

_____ 3. I like to get involved in group discussion with others who are from different cultures.

_____ 4. Engaging in a group discussion with people from different cultures makes me nervous.

_____ 5. I am calm and relaxed with interacting with a group of people who are from different cultures.

_____ 6. While participating in a conversation with a person from a different culture, I get nervous.

_____ 7. I have no fear of speaking up in a conversation with a person from a different culture.

_____ 8. Ordinarily I am very tense and nervous in a conversation with person from a different culture.

_____ 9. Ordinarily I am very calm and relaxed in conversations with a person from a different culture.

_____10. While conversing with a person from a different culture, I feel very relaxed.

_____11. I am afraid to speak up in conversations with a person from a different culture.

_____12. I face the prospect of interacting with people from different cultures with confidence.

_____13. My thoughts become confused and jumbled when interacting with people from different cultures.

_____14. Communicating with people from different cultures makes me fee uncomfortable.

Scoring: To compute the PRICA score, complete the following steps:

Step 1. Add the scores for the following items: 1, 3, 5, 7, 9, 10, and 12

Step 2. Add the scores for the following items: 2, 4, 6, 8,11,13, and 14

Step 3. Complete the following formula: PRICA score = 42 - Total from Step 1 + Total from Step 2.

Scores can range from 14 to 70. Scores below 32 indicate low intercultural CA. Scores above 52 indicate high intercultural CA. Scores ranging between 32 and 52 indicate a moderate level of intercultural CA.

Source: Neuliep, J. W., & McCroskey, J. C. (1997). The development of intercultural and interethnic communication apprehension scales. *Communication Research Reports*, 14, 385-398.

Ethnocentrism Scale

Below are items that relate to the cultures of different parts of the world. Work quickly and record your first reaction to each item. There are no right or wrong answers. Please indicate the degree to which you agree or disagree with each item using the following five-point scale:

Strongly Disagree = 1; Disagree = 1; Neutral = 3; Agree = 4; Strongly Agree = 5

_____ 1. Most other cultures are backward compared to my culture.

_____ 2. My culture should be the role model for other cultures.

_____ 3. People from other cultures act strange when they come to my culture.

_____ 4. Lifestyles in other cultures are just as valid as those in my culture.

_____ 5. Other cultures should try to be more like my culture.

_____ 6. I am not interested in the values and customs of other cultures.

_____ 7. People in my culture could learn a lot from people in other cultures.

_____ 8. Most people from other cultures just don't know what's good for them.

_____ 9. I respect the values and customs of other cultures.

_____10. Other cultures are smart to look up to our culture.

_____11. Most people would be happier if they lived like people in my culture.

_____12. I have many friends from different cultures.

_____13. People in my culture have just about the best lifestyles of anywhere.

_____14. Lifestyles in other cultures are not as valid as those in my culture.

_____15. I am very interested in the values and customs of other cultures.

_____16. I apply my values when judging people who are different.

_____17. I see people who are similar to me as virtuous.

_____18. I do not cooperate with people who are different.

_____19. Most people in my culture just don't know what is good for them.

_____20. I do not trust people who are different.

_____21. I dislike interacting with people from different cultures.

_____22. I have little respect for the values and customs of other cultures.

Recode questions 4, 7, & 9 with the following format:

1=5

2=4

3=3

4=2

5=1

Drop questions 3, 6, 12, 15, 16, 17, 19

After you have recoded the previous questions, add all of the responses to the remaining 15 items together to get your composite ethnocentrism score.

Source of original scale: Neuliep, J. W., & McCroskey, J. C.(1997).The development of a U. S. and generalized ethnocentrism scale. *Communication Research Reports*, 14, 385-398.

KEY TERMS AND DEFINITIONS

ACCEPTANCE: refers to our cognizance of the feelings and emotions involved in our willingness to understand the behavior of diverse others.

ACTIVE STRATEGIES: strategies used to reduce uncertainty about others. Requires interacting with third parties to learn additional information about another person.

AGEISM: prejudice in which discrimination or negative communication is directed toward persons based on their age.

ATTITUDES: learned predispositions to respond in favorable or unfavorable ways toward people or objects.

BELIEFS: personal convictions regarding the truth or existence of things.

COLLECTIVISM: emphasizes value and concern for the group.

CULTURE: shared perceptions that shape the communication patterns and expectations of a group of people.

DISCRIMINATION: denying an individual or group of people their rights.

DIVERSITY: refers to the unique qualities or characteristics that distinguish individuals and groups from one another.

ESTEEM NEEDS: includes the need to accomplish goals and to attain prestige, respect, and status.

ETHNICITY: the common heritage, or background, shared by a group of people.

ETHNOCENTRISM: tendency to perceive our own ways of behaving and thinking as being correct or acceptable while evaluating the behaviors of others as incorrect or inferior.

EXPLICIT LEARNING: involves direct instructions regarding a culture's preferred or expected ways of behaving.

FEMININE CULTURES: demonstrate a preference for responsiveness, nurturance, and cooperation; gender roles are more equal.

HIGH-CONTEXT CULTURES: cultures that place emphasis on the meanings that are conveyed via nonverbal cues.

HIGH POWER DISTANCE CULTURES: cultures are depicted by tall hierarchical structures with distinct status differential. Strict adherence to rules and procedures.

HOMOPHILY: stratification that occurs on the basis of similarity.

IMPLICIT LEARNING: learning about a culture's preferred or expected norms for behavior through indirect methods (e.g., observation).

INDIVIDUALISM: emphasizes individual accomplishments and achievements.

INTERACTIVE STRATEGIES: strategies used to reduce uncertainty about others. Typically involves a face-to-face encounter between two individuals to directly exchange information.

KNOWLEDGE: theoretical principles and concepts that explain behaviors occurring within a specific communication context.

LOVE AND BELONGING NEEDS: addresses our need to form interpersonal relationships to provide intimacy, love, and affection.

LOW-CONTEXT CULTURES: cultures that emphasize the meanings conveyed via spoken words. Emphasis is on verbal communication.

LOW POWER DISTANCE: cultural orientation in which members of a culture are viewed as being equals with little differential in status.

MASCULINE CULTURES: demonstrate a preference for assertiveness, ambition, and achievement.

NEEDS: strong feelings of discomfort or desire that motivate individuals to achieve satisfaction or comfort.

PASSIVE STRATEGIES: strategies used to reduce uncertainty about others. Typically involves observing and making social comparisons.

PERSONAL ORIENTATION SYSTEM: predispositions that serve as a guide for thoughts, actions, and behaviors; comprises one's needs, beliefs, values, and attitudes.

PHYSIOLOGICAL NEEDS: most basic needs identified in Maslow's Hierarchy of Needs. Includes food, clothing, and shelter.

POWER DISTANCE: refers to the distribution of power in personal relationships as well as within organizations.

PREJUDICE: attitude or "pre-judgment" that involves negative reactions toward a group of people based on inflexible and inaccurate assumptions.

RACE: genetically inherited biological characteristics such as hair texture and color, eye shape, skin color, and facial structure.

RACIAL PROFILING: occurs when race is used as a basis for investigating a person for criminal involvement.

RACISM: prejudice against an individual or group based on racial composition.

REGIONAL DIFFERENCES: variety in the communication styles within the larger culture. Examples may include the level of nonverbal animation, perceived openness, informal rapport, and rate of speech delivery.

SAFETY AND SECURITY NEEDS: second level of Maslow's Hierarchy. Addresses need to ensure feelings of safety and security and may include laws, freedom, order, and protection from those things that can cause harm.

SELF-ACTUALIZATION: the highest level of Maslow's hierarchy of needs. Involves the realization of achieving one's full potential in terms of personal growth and experiences.

SELF-DISCLOSURE: sharing or revealing personal information about oneself with others.

SEXISM: prejudice in which discrimination or negative communication is directed toward persons of a particular sex.

SKILLS: specific communication behaviors that contribute to competent and effective interpersonal communication. Examples include effective listening, nonverbal sensitivity, and conflict management.

SOCIAL CLASS: classifications used by members of a culture to group members on the basis of educational, occupational, or financial backgrounds, resulting in classifications and status differentials.

SOCIALIZATION: process of learning about one's cultural norms and expectations.

STEREOTYPING: generalizations about a group that are attributed to any individuals who either associate with, or are members of, the group.

UNCERTAINTY AVOIDANCE: willingness of a culture to approach or to avoid change.

UNCERTAINTY REDUCTION THEORY (URT): describes the process of exchanging information in an attempt to reduce ambiguity about others. Asking questions is a primary communication strategy used for reducing levels of uncertainty.

UNDERSTANDING: involves applying knowledge to specific situations in an attempt to explain the behaviors that are occurring.

VALUES: serve as guides for an individual's behavior and indicate what one views as being important or ethical.

VERBAL ABUSE: process of engaging in comments or jokes that are insulting or demeaning to a targeted group.

VIOLENCE: most severe form of prejudice, which often results in physical harm or excessive force.

REFERENCES

Berger, C. (1979). Beyond initial interactions. In H. Giles and R. St. Clair (Eds.), *Language and social psychology* (122–144). Oxford: Basil Blackwell.

Berger, C., & Calabrese, R. (1975). Some explorations in initial interaction and beyond: Toward a developmental theory of interpersonal communication. *Human Communication Research, 1,* 99–112.

Dodd, C. (1998). *Dynamics of intercultural communication* (5th ed.). San Francisco, CA: McGraw-Hill.

Grebelsky-Lichtman, T. (2014). Parental patterns of cooperation in parent-child interactions: The relationship between verbal and nonverbal communication. *Human Communication Research, 40*(1), 1–29.

File, T., & Ryan, C. (2014). Computer and Internet Use in the United States: 2013. Retrieved May 21, 2015, from http://www.census.gov/content/dam/Census/library/publications/2014/acs/acs-28.pdf

Hall, E. T. (1976). *Beyond culture.* Garden City, NY: Anchor.

Hofstede, G. (1980). Motivation, leadership, and organizations: Do American theories apply abroad? *Organizational Dynamics, Summer,* 42–63.

Ishii, S., Thomas, C., & Klopf, D. (1993). Self-disclosure among Japanese and Americans. *Otsuma Review, 26,* 51–57.

Kluckhohn, C. (1951). Values and value-orientation in the theory of action. In T. Parsons and E. Shils (Eds.), *Toward a general theory of action* (pp. 388–433). Cambridge, MA: Harvard University Press.

Kluckhohn, C., & Strodbeck, F. (1961). *Variations in value orientations.* Evanston, IL: Row, Peterson.

Kroeber, A. L., & Kluckhohn, C. (1952). *Culture: A critical review of concepts and definitions.* Cambridge, MA: Harvard University Press.

Martin, J. D., Trego, A. B., Nakayama, T. K. (2010). College students' racial attitudes and friendship diversity. *The Howard Journal of Communication, 21*(2), 97–118.

Maslow, A. (1954). *Motivation and personality.* New York, NY: Harper.

McLuhan, M., & Powers, B. (1989). *The global village: Transformations in world life and media in the 21st century.* New York: Oxford University Press.

Neuliep, J. W. (2012). The relationship among intercultural communication apprehension, ethnocentrism, uncertainty reduction, and communication satisfaction during initial intercultural interaction: An extension of Anxiety and Uncertainty (AUM) Theory. *Journal of Intercultural Communication Research, 41*(1), 1–16.

Schutz, W. (1958). *FIRO: A three dimensional theory of interpersonal behavior.* New York: Holt, Rinehart & Winston.

Smith, S. G., Wolf, M. S., & Wagner, C. (2010). Socioeconomic status, statistical confidence, and patient-provider communication: An analysis of the Health Information National Trends Survey (HINTS 2007). *Journal of Health Communication, 15,* 169–185.

Smith, D., & Associates. (1997). *Diversity works: The emerging picture of how students benefit.* Washington, DC: Association of American Colleges and Universities.

Theiss, J. A., & Nagy, M. E. (2013). A relational turbulence model of partner responsiveness and relationship talk across cultures. *Western Journal of Communication, 77*(2), 186–209.

Vaux, B., & Golder, S. (2003). *The Harvard Dialect Survey.* Cambridge, MA: Harvard University Linguistics Department.

chapter 13

Family Communication:
It's All Relative

OBJECTIVES

- Identify sibling relational maintenance strategies.

- Describe elements of systems theory and examine their impact on family interactions.

- Explain family communication patterns theory.

- Identify family types identified by Koerner and Fitzpatrick.

- Discuss ways in which families form their own identity (stories, myths, metaphors, themes).

- Explain the ABCX model of stress as it applies to family interactions.

SOUND FAMILIAR?

As the end of the semester approached, Bailey felt more stress than he had ever experienced in his life. He knew that his parents were going to be less than pleased when he told them about his decision to change his major, and he was worried about how he would break the news to them that his roommate got him a summer job with his father's company and he wouldn't be coming home this summer. A few minutes after he tweeted, "Stressed to the max—parental units are NOT going to be happy!" his cell phone rang. As he glanced and saw his mother's Caller ID, he groaned and considered letting the phone go to voice mail. "That's what I get for accepting my parents' requests to follow me on Twitter," he thought to himself as he reluctantly answered the call.

OVERVIEW

Of all the relationships we form throughout our lifetime, our family relationships are the most enduring. We begin this chapter by advancing an important question about family communication: What makes family relationships unique from the other types of interpersonal relationships we experience in a lifetime? Vangelisti (2004) describes the significance of the family by labeling it "the crucible of society" (p. ix). These relationships are unique from other types of interpersonal relationships because they are described as both voluntary and involuntary and play a significant role in shaping self-perceptions. After all, our family relationships offer our first glimpse into what it means to form an intimate connection with another person.

> "The family. We were a strange little band of characters trudging through life sharing diseases and toothpaste, coveting one another's desserts, hiding shampoo, borrowing money, locking each other out of our rooms, inflicting pain and kissing to heal it in the same instant, loving, laughing, defending, and trying to figure out the common thread that bound us all together" (p. 9).
>
> Source: Bombeck, E. (1987). *Family: The ties that bind...and gag!* New York: McGraw-Hill.

Consider the fact that families have unique communicative features. After all, you have a frame of reference for understanding communication in families since these are the first and likely to be the longest-lasting relationships formed in your life. Perhaps the best way to understand family relationships is to take a look at the role of interpersonal communication in the family and how it shapes our sense of identity and serves as a model for communication choices. Even in situations where relationships with family members have become strained, the bonds shape an individual's sense of self, serve as a model for desirable or undesirable communication, and shape expectations for future relationships. In this chapter we examine classic and contemporary family communication research, theories, and concepts. We will also address interpersonal communication concepts as they apply across the family life span.

DEFINITION OF FAMILY

If you were asked to list the number of people you consider to be part of your family, who would you include? Would you list in-laws, close family friends, close personal friends, neighbors, siblings' spouses, stepfamilies, or even co-workers? Would you include only those relatives related by blood or marriage? When students are asked this question, they often include a wide range of individuals in their list of family members. Most family relationships are described as *involuntary* because we do not get to choose our parents, siblings, cousins, aunts, uncles, grandparents, and so on. Some family relationships may be formed of *voluntary* members. An example of this is the television series *Friends,* which showcases how non-biological relationships can fulfill family roles.

As we grow older, our choices of who we include in our "family" expand. Voluntary families are created as a result of conscious decisions made to include others in the familial relationship. For example, we select our spouse or life partner. We all have experience with family relationships, but have you considered the unique nature of these bonds? A scene from the 2005 film *The Family Stone* illustrates this sense of family ob-

Most family relationships are involuntary because we don't get to choose who to include.

Even in situations where relationships with family members have become strained, the bonds shape an individual's sense of self, serve as a model for desirable or undesirable communication, and shape expectations for future relationships.

ligation. Sarah Jessica Parker portrays a young woman struggling to be accepted by her fiancé's close-knit family. At one point she becomes frustrated and asks her future mother-in-law, "What's so great about you guys?" Diane Keaton replies, "Uh, nothing . . . it's just that we're all that we've got." Each family member recognizes other family members' idiosyncrasies, but also realizes that the strength of the family bond surpasses all other relationships.

TYPES OF FAMILY RELATIONSHIPS

It is difficult to describe a "typical" family in the twenty-first century. Over the years, the structure of the typical American family has changed. The *Handbook of Family Communication* explores several different family types such as intact families, divorced or single parent families, stepfamilies, and gay or lesbian families. But while the types may have changed, core family relationships continue to exist and

have provided scholars with opportunities to take a glimpse into how communication develops in these relationships. While we do not have the space to discuss all family types, three specific interpersonal relationships that exist in the family structure will be discussed: marital relationships, parent-child relationships, and sibling relationships.

Marital Relationships

According to family communication researchers Turner and West (2002), "marriage is often seen as the most important intimate relationship two people can share" (p. 232). Some research indicates that individuals in healthy marriages tend to be both healthier and happier than unmarried individuals or those in unhealthy relationships. The longstanding question posed by researchers from a variety of academic and professional fields has always been how to obtain and maintain an enduring marital relationship.

Individuals in healthy marriages tend to be healthier and happier than others.

Each life partner brings his or her own set of expectations to the marital relationship. Tune into a television talk show and at some point you will likely see a couple asking the host to solve their marital problems. It is not unusual for the host to identify differing expectations as the root of the problem. Earlier in this text, we mentioned that messages have both content and relational dimensions. The same is true of our expectations for marital relationships—couples hold content expectations and relational expectations for their partners.

CONTENT EXPECTATIONS. **Content expectations** focus on how the relationship is defined by the role each partner plays. Roles are defined by the expectations held for a position in the family. The ABC television show *Wife Swap* focused on the role expectations established for wives in two different types of families. In each episode, the wives switched families for two weeks. Clashes ensued over differing content expectations for husbands' and wives' roles in housekeeping and child-rearing. It is important to note that one of the difficult tasks involved in the marital relationship is ensuring that the two sets of expectations are congruent.

RELATIONAL EXPECTATIONS. **Relational expectations** refer to the similarity, or correspondence, of the emotional, or affective, expectations each partner has for defining the relationship. In one episode of *Wife Swap,* the Kraut and Hardin wives exchange households. One wife spends considerable time shopping and focusing on current fashion trends while her husband tends to the household duties. She is perceived to focus on herself rather than on the emotional needs of family members. The other wife expects all family members to participate in household chores, and the couple has formed the expectation that the role of the wife will include being responsible for homeschooling the children. She is extremely involved in every aspect of the children's lives and is aware of any changes in their emotional states. When the two families swap wives for the two-week period, they discover that their relational expectations are incongruent in the new environment. This often causes the sparks to fly! When the wives are in their own homes, communication is more satisfying because their spouses and children have congruent expectations for the relationship. They have become comfortable with the communication expectations associated with the maternal roles. Marital satisfaction is greater in relationships where couples discuss their expectations for the relationship—failure to talk about expectancies is often equated to playing "guess what's inside my mind."

To explain the various expectations that couples have for communication and for the relationship, Fitzpatrick (1987) developed a model to distinguish each couple type and how they view role conventionality, interdependence, and their approach to conflict. Three couple types were identified: traditionals, separates, and independents (see also Figure 13.1). Characteristics that distinguish the various couple types from one another are their expectations for sex roles and their approach to conflict in the relationship.

TRADITIONALS. Those who exhibit a high level of interdependence and sharing are considered **traditional couples.** Conventional sex roles are adopted in traditional couples, with males performing tasks such as lawn care, automobile maintenance, and taking out the garbage. Women fulfill the role of nurturing caregiver and are responsible for housekeeping and childcare duties. In her research, Fitzpatrick (1987) found that traditionals tend to be the most satisfied of the three couple types. A 2009 study of 210 couples found that traditional couples reported the highest level of commitment to the relationship compared to other couple types (Givertz, Segrin, & Hanzal). Clear expectations for the roles partners will play and for their relationship result in dedication to the relationship.

Traditionals	• Demonstrate a high amount of interdependence and sharing • Adopt traditional or conventional sex roles
Separates	• Emphasize each other's individual identity over relational maintenance • Typically avoid conflict
Independents	• Respect the need for autonomy • Negotiate a high level of communication and sharing • Adopt nonconventional sex roles (husband stays home and wife works outside of home)

Figure 13.1 Description of marital types.

Traditional couples adopt conventional sex roles in their marriages.

Marital satisfaction is greater in relationships where couples discuss their expectations for the relationship.

SEPARATES. Separate couples tend to emphasize each individual's identity and independence over maintaining the relationship. In addition to maintaining conventional sex roles in the relationship, this couple is characterized by their avoidance of conflict. As is evident, this couple type typically reports a low level of marital satisfaction. Givertz, Segrin, and Hanzal (2009) found that separate couples experience the lowest levels of marital satisfaction and commitment of the three couple types.

INDEPENDENTS. Independent couples simultaneously respect the need for autonomy and engage in a high level communication and sharing with one another. Sex roles in the independent relationship are unconventional. Individual freedom is a priority, and partners are willing to engage in conflict when they disagree on issues and tend to be assertive in expressing and defending their position on issues.

Parent-Child Relationships

Consider for a moment that the first family relationship formed is between a parent and a child. As well as having a legal responsibility to care for and protect their children, parents are responsible for the moral and character development of their children— not an easy task. In his book, *Family First,* Dr. Phil McGraw (2004) discusses the role that parents play in preparing children for life's challenges, and points out that parents need to realize the influence they have as a result of the messages they communicate to their children.

A parent's role is complicated; biological and emotional attachments create a special bond that makes communication both rewarding and frustrating at times. Television shows such as *Nanny 911* and *Super Nanny* provide parents with advice for managing interactions with their children. They also provide a glimpse into the parenting challenges experienced by others, offering support to parents who can see that others are enduring the same, or worse, situations.

Young children assert their independence when they state they want to "do it all by myself."

Over the course of the family life cycle, communication between parents and children evolves as new events occur. It is during this time that the dialectical tensions between autonomy and connection are perhaps the strongest. In the beginning of their lives children are totally dependent on the parents to provide for them and look out for their best interests. In the United States, many parents begin teaching children at a young age to become independent. Children are encouraged to learn to eat by themselves, pick out their own clothes, and to explore their individual interests in sports and other extracurricular activities. But even while encouraging independence, many parents simultaneously reinforce the message that they are still connected to their children. Providing children with cellular telephones is one strategy currently used by parents to stay connected as their children explore autonomy.

As children progress through adolescence, a new set of communication issues needs to be considered. Up to this point, children have been encouraged to become independent, but eventually the dialectical tension between autonomy and connection kicks in and parents may begin to feel that children are becoming too independent. Adolescence is often a difficult transition period for both children and parents alike, and it is not uncommon for conflicts to occur during this time in the family life cycle. A common communication issue during this period involves the negotiation of rules, with new guidelines for behavior being added on a regular basis as parents and children clash over preferences for clothes, manners, curfews, and activities. As the occurrence of parent-child conflict increases during adolescence, issues that once seemed unimportant now take on new relevance. Consider the issues you and your parents disagreed on during your adolescence. Why do you think communication surrounding these issues was so problematic?

As children grow up, identify their aspirations, and pursue their goals, families may find that their time is divided, and this provides yet another source of tension in the household. A 2015 study examining the impact of the time mothers spend with young children (ages 3–11) and teens (ages 12–18) found that the time spent directly engaged together during younger years does not have a significant impact on the child's behavior or academic success. However, there are important social and academic implications for increased mother-child time during the teen years. Teens who spend time with their mothers are less likely to engage in risky behaviors, and time spent with both parents together enhanced the teen's sense of well-being (Milkie, Nomaguchi, & Denny, 2015). Figure 13.2 highlights some of the trends in the amount of time parents spent with their children from 1965 to 2010.

Spending time with the kids

The average number of hours parents spent with their children each week rose since 1985.

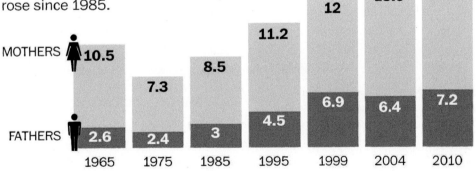

Figure 13.2 The average number of hours U.S. parents spent with their children each week, 1965–2010.

Source: http://www.washingtonpost.com/local/making-time-for-kids-study-says-quality-trumps-quanti-ty/2015/03/28/10813192-d378-11e4-8fce-3941fc548f1c_story.html

During adolescence, issues that once were insignificant can result in conflict.

While many adult privileges are granted to children when they reach the age of eighteen, parents and children view and negotiate the transition to adulthood in different ways. The period when children begin the separation process from their parents is often referred to as the **launching stage**. However, this term is often misleading because many families continue to experience a sense of interdependence in their lives for a period of time after the child reaches legal age. For example, after returning to college after Christmas break, one student was overheard saying, "It was kind of nice being back home and knowing that my mom would stay up and wait for me to come in at night. I guess I have to admit that I missed that during my first semester at college." While some may find comfort in the old routines, others may find that new rules need to be negotiated during the launching stage. Statistics reported on forbes.com indicate that approximately 13 percent of adult children move back home with their parents after living on their own for a period of time. Researchers have coined the term **boomerang children** to refer to young adults who return home to live with their parents after living on their own for a period

of time. Daily chores, financial contributions, and respect for household rules are only a few of the topics that require negotiation between boomerang children and their parents as they readjust to living under the same roof again.

Divorce and remarriage create additional issues to consider in parent-child interactions. Stepfamilies face unique challenges that revolve around issues relating to discipline, resources, and ties to the biological family unit. According to a 2011 Pew Research Center report, almost 42% of American adults are part of a steprelationship, as a stepparent, a stepsibling, or a stepchild. Should stepfamilies and stepchildren expect communication and relationships to be similar to those between biological parents and children? Family communication scholars use the analogy of starting a novel halfway through the book to describe the experience of negotiating the stepfamily relationship (Coleman, Ganong, & Fine, 2004).

Images of stepfamilies portrayed in stories and the media often depict these relationships as filled with challenges and negative communication. In the 1998 film *Stepmom*, a conversation between a biological mother (Jackie) and her daughter (Anna) about her stepmother (Isabel) illustrates one of many potential communication issues associated with stepfamily relationships.

Anna:	I think Isabel's pretty.
Jackie:	Yeah, I think she's pretty too . . . if you like big teeth.
Anna:	Mom?
Jackie:	Yes, sweetie?
Anna:	If you want me to hate her, I will.

(*Stepmom*, directed by Chris Columbus, 2hr. 4 min., 1492 Pictures, 1998.)

Anger or guilt can impact communication about the relationship, and both children and parents may find it difficult to be open about their true feelings. Not only are families required to negotiate nuances (such as children addressing stepparents as "Mom" or "Dad"), but the role of step grandparents in the blended family is also a consideration. Gold (2015) offers suggestions to assist stepgrandparents in adapting to the new family structure. These include:

- Respect the rules established by the new stepparent. Resist the temptation to "take sides" in situations involving the stepparent and stepchild.
- Be flexible and understand that the new family needs to create their own traditions. Have a conversation with the new spouse and their children about your traditions to see where they might "fit" into the new family's plans.
- Realize that stepgrandchildren have tremendous adjustments in their lives. Do not force affection (hugs, kisses) until they are ready. Learn about and support the stepgrandchildren's interests before expecting them to become interested in you. (Gold, 2015)

RELATIONAL MAINTENANCE IN PARENT-CHILD RELATIONSHIPS. Parents and children often find the need to increase efforts in maintaining their relationship as children grow older and gain more autonomy. Activities, new friends, and, eventually, the process of starting a new family can detract from the time and energy available for relationships with parents. In some instances, the onset of these maintenance challenges begins much earlier when parents decide to divorce. Non-custodial parents are faced with identifying new strategies to maintain their relationship with their children in the absence of the close physical proximity they once shared.

Parents and children often find the need to schedule special time together to maintain their relationship as children grow older.

While many strategies used to maintain the relationship are similar to those found in other types of relationships, a 1999 study by Thomas-Maddox identified several strategies unique to this context:

- Non-custodial parents indicated that they depend on mediated communication (sending letters, emails, phone calls) and material/monetary offerings (sending gifts, taking children on "exciting" trips) to maintain their relationship.
- Children identified strategies for maintaining their relationship with non-custodial parents that include mediated communication, proximity (living with non-custodial parent during summer vacations and breaks by choice), and suggesting joint activities (proposing ideas such as going to the movies).

While being physically separated as a result of this difficult decision may not be easy for par-

Parents and children often find the need to increase efforts in maintaining their relationship as children grow older and gain more autonomy.

ents and children, there are communication strategies that can be used to continue the relationship from a distance.

Sibling Relationships

Relationships with siblings generally last the longest, given that our brothers and sisters are often still with us long after our parents are gone. Approximately 80 percent of individuals have siblings and, with the exception of firstborn children, sibling relationships are simultaneously formed with parent relationships. In their younger years, siblings often spend more time playing and interacting

---

RESEARCH IN REAL LIFE: The impact of overinvolved parenting

Is it possible for parents to become too controlling and involved in their children's lives? A 2014 study by Givertz and Segrin of 339 college students and their parents asked a series of questions to explore the role that parenting style plays in shaping family satisfaction and a child's sense of identity and entitlement. The study concluded that:

- Both parents and children report higher levels of family satisfaction when parents adopt an authoritative communication style that is open.
- Parents reported using authoritarian and permissive styles less frequently than their children perceived them using them.
- Families that exhibit high levels of adaptability and cohesion report greater levels of satisfaction.
- Children whose parents exhibited controlling (authoritarian) behaviors reported lower levels of self-efficacy and higher levels of perceived entitlement.

Overall, parents perceived their family as higher in cohesiveness and more effective in communicating with one another compared to the evaluations of their children.

- Do you think your evaluations of family satisfaction, cohesion, and parenting styles would be similar to your parents' evaluations? Why or why not?
- What factors do you think impact the different ways in which parents and children view the family relationship?

---

with one another than they do with their parents. But that does not necessarily mean these relationships are always positive. One minute siblings may be collaborating to "team up" against their parents, and the next minute they may be fighting like cats and dogs.

Communication in the sibling relationship often reflects both negative and positive characteristics. As family resources such as time, parents' attention, or physical objects are perceived to be scarce, siblings may engage in conflict or competition. Same-sex siblings tend to be more competitive than opposite-sex siblings. In some instances, siblings may be expected to fulfill the role of teacher or "co-parent." If you have siblings, chances are you have probably been instructed to "Watch out for your brother (or sister)" at some point in time. Often this occurs in single-parent families or in families where both parents are employed outside the home.

As siblings approach adolescence, their relationship experiences new transformations. Perhaps the competition for resources may become more intense, or siblings experience frustration when they are compared to one another. In these instances, a sibling may seek deidentification from other siblings. **Deidentification** is defined as an individual's attempt to create a distinct identity that is separate from that of their siblings. Have you ever had a teacher compare you to an older sibling? Or perhaps you have had friends at school who point out how similar or different you are compared to your brother or sister. When siblings are constantly evaluated against one another, they may experience a desire to create a unique identity and sense of self. Perhaps your ability to play soccer was often compared to one of your siblings who also played soccer.

In an effort to distinguish yourself from your sibling, you quit playing soccer and played basketball instead.

Maintenance in Sibling Relationships

Recall our discussion of the importance of relationship maintenance in Chapter 8. Relational maintenance is of particular importance in the sibling relationship, since these typically last longer than any other family relationship. In a study designed to investigate unique maintenance strategies employed by siblings, six behaviors were identified (Myers & Weber, 2004). These include the following (see also Figure 13.3):

- CONFIRMATION. **Confirmation** consists of messages used to communicate the importance or value of siblings in one's life. Statements such as, "I'm lucky to have you as my brother" or "I really appreciate having you here to support me" are often viewed as validating the relationship.
- HUMOR. Often siblings use **humor** as a way to bring amusement or enjoyment to their relationship. Sharing private jokes about family members or making fun of their behaviors are ways siblings use humor to strengthen their bond.
- SOCIAL SUPPORT. Siblings provide **social support** to one another by using comforting strategies to assist one another through difficult times. Asking a sibling for advice or sharing information about difficulties in other relationships illustrates the trust that is present in the relationship.
- FAMILY EVENTS. Siblings often maintain and strengthen their relationships with

each other and other family members through participation in **family events**. They may agree to visit their parents at the same time during the summer or holidays to spend time together.

- ESCAPE. Siblings approach the time and communication spent with one another as an **escape** or diversion during difficult situations.

- VERBAL AGGRESSION. While the final strategy, **verbal aggression**, may seem counterintuitive to maintaining a relationship, this maintenance mechanism allows siblings to vent their frustrations with one another. Yelling at one another may be the most effective method for having their concerns heard in a specific situation.

Additional research on adult sibling maintenance identified verbal statements, nonverbal gestures, and social support as additional options for strategies that are often used when siblings make purposeful or strategic attempts to maintain a relationship, as opposed to using messages and behaviors that are more habitual or routine (Myers, Byrnes, Frisby, & Mansson, 2011).

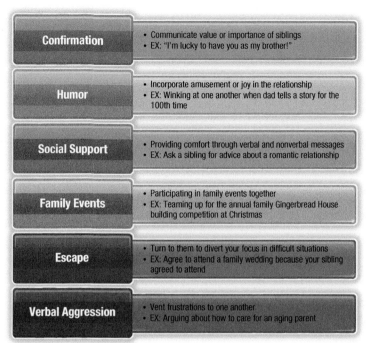

Confirmation	• Communicate value or importance of siblings • EX: "I'm lucky to have you as my brother!"
Humor	• Incorporate amusement or joy in the relationship • EX: Winking at one another when dad tells a story for the 100th time
Social Support	• Providing comfort through verbal and nonverbal messages • EX: Ask a sibling for advice about a romantic relationship
Family Events	• Participating in family events together • EX: Teaming up for the annual family Gingerbread House building competition at Christmas
Escape	• Turn to them to divert your focus in difficult situations • EX: Agree to attend a family wedding because your sibling agreed to attend
Verbal Aggression	• Vent frustrations to one another • EX: Arguing about how to care for an aging parent

© Kendall Hunt Publishing Co.

Figure 13.3 Sibling relational maintenance strategies.

©Volt Collection /Shutterstock.com

Often siblings use humor as a strategy to maintain their relationship with one another.

FAMILY COMMUNICATION THEORIES

Several theories can be applied to the study of communication in family relationships. Recall the definition of interpersonal communication: a process that occurs in a specific context and involves an exchange of verbal or nonverbal messages between two connected individuals with the intent to achieve shared meaning. The family is one context of connected individuals in which these interactions occur. Scholars of family communication have applied a variety of interpersonal theories to explain these interactions. In essence, virtually any theory of interpersonal communication could be applied to the study of families. Three theories that have specific implications for the family relationship include systems theory, family communication patterns theory, and symbolic interactionism.

Family Systems Theory

Systems theory has been employed by family scholars to explore a variety of interactions, including children's attitudes about their single parent dating (Marrow-Ferguson & Dickson, 1995), family involvement in addressing children's problems at school (Walsh & Williams, 1997), and adolescent abuse of their parents (Eckstein, 2004).

Family systems theory is one of the most frequently used theories in family communication scholarship (Stamp, 2004).

In essence, virtually any theory of interpersonal communication could be applied to the study of families.

The basic premise behind this theory is that family relationships can be treated as systems and can include the study of systemic qualities such as wholeness, interdependence, hierarchy, boundaries, calibration, and equifinality (Stamp, 2004). Each of the elements of systems theory is particularly relevant in explaining how and why

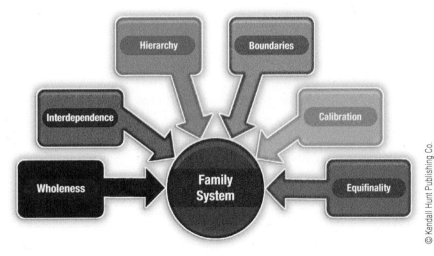

© Kendall Hunt Publishing Co.

Figure 13.4 Elements of family systems.

family members relate to one another (See Figure 13.4).

WHOLENESS. Wholeness implies that a family creates its own personality or culture, and that this personality is unique from that of each family member. Many studies that have applied systems theory recognize that in order to understand the dynamics of families, the role of individual family members must be considered as well.

INTERDEPENDENCE. Interdependence proposes that the family system comprises interrelated parts, or members. A change experienced by one family member is likely to result in changes that impact all other family members. Suppose a child catches the flu and cannot attend school for several days. If both parents work outside the home, one will have to make adjustments to his or her work schedule to stay at home with the child. To protect other family members from being exposed to the illness, family routines such as sharing dinner or watching television together may be altered.

HIERARCHY. All systems have levels, or a **hierarchy**, present. Typically, parents take on the powerful roles in the family and are responsible for seeing that children's needs are fulfilled and that discipline and control are maintained in the system. It is important to note that power is often linked to respect among family members. We may differ in how we perceive power structures in the family. A 2008 study surveyed 133 African American, European American, and Latina girls and their mothers to explore how culture influences the display of respect for power in families. Results indicated that:

- European American girls showed the lowest levels of respect for their mothers com-

pared with the other two groups.
- In situations where conflict was present, African American and Latina mothers indicated that arguments were more intense than reported by European American mothers (Dixon, Graber, & Brooks-Gunn, 2008).

Parents often assume primary responsibility for childcare and discipline in the family.

BOUNDARIES. Families create **boundaries** that facilitate communication with members who are considered to be part of the system. These boundaries are often flexible as the family expands to include friends and pets. **Ambiguous boundaries** often create confusion about who family members perceive as being part of the system. Some families may view close friends as part of their family even in the absence of biological or legal connections. In these situations, even though the bonds are not biological, individuals may view one another as an important part of the family.

CALIBRATION. The system element of **calibration** is the mechanism that allows the family to review communication in their relationships and decide if any adjustments need to be made to the system. For example, reality shows that feature families interacting with one another may provide examples of effective (or ineffective) family interactions that we can use as a reference or basis for comparison. Feedback communicated through messages received from others can also be taken into consideration. While waiting in line at the grocery store, a mother might receive a compliment about her well-behaved children. This provides her with feedback to gauge her performance as a parent.

EQUIFINALITY. The final system element, **equifinality**, refers to a family's abilities to achieve the same goal by following different paths or using different communication behaviors. For example, one family may teach the children independence by communicating the expectation that the children are responsible for getting themselves up and getting ready for school in the morning. In another family, the mother might enter the bedroom and gently sing "Good Morning" to the children, lay out their school clothes, and have breakfast ready for them. Both families accomplish the same goal: working through the morning routine of getting to school on time. However, each family has a different method for accomplishing the goal.

Family Communication Patterns Theory

Perhaps one of the most complicated phenomena to factor into the family communication equation is the role that intrapersonal communication plays in the process. **Family communication patterns theory** is a comprehensive theory that focuses on the cognitive processes used to shape and guide our interpersonal interactions. Originally developed by McLeod and Chaffee (1972, 1973) as a way for explaining family

members' interactions associated with television viewing, the goal of the theory was to explain how parents help children to understand messages received from multiple sources through mediated channels. But consider for a moment all of the different messages received from outside the family that are processed on a daily basis. Ritchie and Fitzpatrick (1990) expanded the focus of this theory beyond mediated messages to focus on how a variety of messages are processed and discussed within the family to create shared meaning. This revised theory identified two primary orientations used by families: conversation and conformity

Conversation orientation refers to the level of openness and the frequency with which a variety of topics are discussed. Families who adopt a high conversation orientation encourage members to openly and frequently share their thoughts and feelings with one another on a wide variety of topics. It is rare that a topic is "off limits" for discussion in families who have a high conversation orientation. On the other hand, families with a low conversation orientation experience less frequent or less open interactions, and sometimes there are limits with regard to what topics can be discussed.

The second dimension of the communication pattern analysis focuses on the family's conformity orientation. **Conformity orientation** refers to the degree to which a family encourages autonomy in individual beliefs, values, and attitudes. Families who emphasize a high level of conformity in interactions encourage family members to adopt similar ways of thinking about topics, often with the goal of avoiding conflict and promoting harmony in the family. At the other end of the conformity continuum, family members are encouraged to form independent beliefs and attitudes, and these differing opinions are often perceived as having equal value in discussions and decision making.

To explain the interrelationship between conversation orientation and conformity orientation, Koerner and Fitzpatrick identified four different family types (2002). These include pluralistic, consensual, laissez-faire, and protective families. See Figure 13.5 for an integration of the family types into the two family orientations.

Parents who encourage their children to form relationships outside the home and couples who believe that each partner should pursue his or her own network of friends typically do so in an effort to broaden the perspectives of individuals within the family. Complete the Family Communication Patterns scale located at the end of this chapter to find out what you perceive your family orientation to be.

PLURALISTIC. **Pluralistic families** adopt a high conversation orientation and a low conformity orientation. Almost anything goes in this family! A wide range of topics are discussed, and family members are encouraged to have their own opinions without feeling the pressure to agree with one another. Children in pluralistic families are often encouraged to participate in decision-making on topics ranging from where the family should go for vacation to the establishment of family rules.

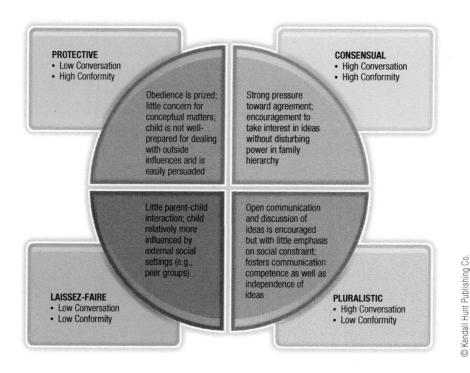

PROTECTIVE
• Low Conversation
• High Conformity

Obedience is prized; little concern for conceptual matters; child is not well-prepared for dealing with outside influences and is easily persuaded

CONSENSUAL
• High Conversation
• High Conformity

Strong pressure toward agreement; encouragement to take interest in ideas without disturbing power in family hierarchy

Little parent-child interaction; child relatively more influenced by external social settings (e.g., peer groups)

LAISSEZ-FAIRE
• Low Conversation
• Low Conformity

Open communication and discussion of ideas is encouraged but with little emphasis on social constraint; fosters communication competence as well as independence of ideas

PLURALISTIC
• High Conversation
• Low Conformity

© Kendall Hunt Publishing Co.

Figure 13.5 Family types as identified by family communication patterns theory.

CONSENSUAL. Consensual families adopt both a high conversation and a high conformity orientation. These families often encourage members to be open in their interactions with one another, but they expect that family members will adopt similar opinions and values. Parents in consensual families promote open conversations, but they still believe that they are the authority when it comes to decisions in the family.

LAISSEZ-FAIRE. Laissez-faire families adopt both a low conversation and low conformity orientation. Rarely will family members talk with one another, and when conversations do occur, they are focused on a limited number of topics. Children are encouraged to make their own decisions, often with little or no guidance or feedback from their parents, in the laissez-faire family.

PROTECTIVE. Protective families score low on conversation orientation and high on conformity. The phrase "Children should be seen but not heard" is characteristic of this family type. Parents are considered to be the authority, and children are expected to obey the family rules without questioning them.

Identifying and understanding the approaches used to communicate and to promote autonomy and independence is beneficial to understanding how these interactions shape both individual and family identities.

Symbolic Interaction Theory

Symbolic interactionism is perhaps one of the most widely applied theories in the study of family life. In Chapter 2 we discussed the role that messages play in assigning meaning to our experiences, and in how we perceive others and ourselves.

RESEARCH IN REAL LIFE:
Family communication patterns and students' decisions to "friend" parents on Facebook

How likely would you be to "friend" your parent on Facebook? If you do provide them with access to your posts, would you change your privacy settings to limit what they could access or what others could post to your page? A 2013 study (Ball, Wanzer, & Servoss) asked 189 college students to report on their Facebook use and evaluate their family's communication patterns. Results found the following:

- A total of 154 students (82 percent) reported that they were Facebook friends with their parents.
- Females were 2.5 times more likely to friend their parents than males.
- Participants who perceive their families as having a higher conversation orientation were more likely to accept friend requests from their parents.
- Only 25 percent of the students who are Facebook friends with their parents adjusted their privacy settings to limit access to profile information.

Mead's (1934) five concepts of symbolic interactionism (mind, self, I, me, and roles) are particularly useful in understanding the impact that family interactions have on shaping your identity. In his discussion of the concept of "mind," Mead explains the role that symbols play in creating shared meaning. Children interact with family members and learn language and social meanings associated with words. Similarly, Mead points out that our sense of "self" is developed through interactions with others. Families are influential in shaping this view of self through the messages and their reactions to one another. Members gain a sense of how they are viewed by others from messages that are exchanged. Statements such as "You're such a good husband!" or "He's such a rotten kid" shape how individuals see themselves.

It is important to note that individual differences, such as personality traits or communication predispositions, may cause family members to view the same situation in very different ways. Consider the following scenario:

Families are influential in shaping this view of self through the messages and their reactions to one another.

Kaija was quiet as Jay drove up the driveway. Jay smiled at her and said, "Trust me, they'll love you!" Kaija was meeting Jay's family for the first time since he had proposed. As they entered the front door, she was bombarded with hugs and kisses from various aunts, uncles, grandparents, and cousins. During dinner the talking never stopped! Kaija felt so left out—and nobody even seemed to care enough to ask her questions about herself. At one point, she slipped out to the back patio just to have a few moments of peace and quiet. As they drove back to campus, Jay commented, "Wasn't it a great evening! Everyone thought you were awesome!" Kaija couldn't believe what she had just heard. How could Jay have come to the conclusion that his family liked her? After all, they didn't take the time to find out anything about her. And the hugs and kisses were so intimidating. Kaija's family would have never shown such open displays of affection the first time they met Jay. She was confused—how could Jay have thought the evening went so great when she thought it had been horrible?

Who was correct in his or her assessment of the evening's events? Symbolic interactionism would indicate that both Jay and Kaija formed accurate perceptions. Each of them had formed his or her own meaning of the event based on their individual interpretations of the messages and behaviors. We learn in the scenario that Kaija's family would not have displayed affection so openly, while Jay's family background shaped his acceptance of effusive greetings. Our experiences in our family of origin shape the meanings we see in events, messages, and behaviors. The fact that Jay's family did not ask Kaija about herself caused her to perceive them as being uninterested. But suppose Jay had shared with his family that Kaija was an only child and tended to be shy around large groups. He may have asked them to refrain from bombarding her with questions that might cause her to feel uncomfortable. To better understand how symbolic interactionism applies to this scenario, it might be useful to examine the three underlying assumptions of the theory (LaRossa & Reitzes, 1993).

First, *our interactions with family members influence the meanings we assign to behaviors and messages.* Children determine if they should evaluate experiences as being positive or negative by watching the reactions of family members to various events and messages. A child whose parents avoid conflict may believe that conflict is a negative behavior that should be avoided at all costs. Coming from a family that shows caring through conversation, Kaija assigned a negative meaning to Jay's family's failure to ask her questions about herself.

Next, *individuals create a sense of self, which serves as a guide for selecting future behaviors.* We assess situations and take into consideration whether others will perceive behaviors and messages in a positive or negative way. This assumption goes beyond our own evaluation of events to include the perceptions of others. A child whose father has told him "You're a rotten kid" and "You'll never amount to anything" has learned to misbehave. As the negative messages are repeated, he comes to believe that others expect him to misbehave.

Finally, symbolic interactionism posits that the *behavior of family members is influenced by culture and society.* Perhaps this assumption sheds light on the reasons families are reluctant to admit that they experience conflict from time to time. Based on media portrayals of family life and from listening to the happy stories of other families, an expectation has been established that "normal" families do not fight.

CREATING A FAMILY IDENTITY

While Chapter 2 focused on how individuals form their own identities, the family as a unit also creates a collective identity. Communication is the primary mechanism for creating this family identity, with various messages and behaviors providing insight as to how the family views itself as a group. Four ways that families create and sustain an identity as a unit are through stories, myths, themes, and metaphors (see Figure 13.6). As we discuss each of these elements, reflect on your own family of origin and how these communicative acts shaped your sense of what it means to be a part of your family.

Family Stories

Family stories are narratives recounting significant events that have been shared by members. In essence, family life is composed of a series of stories. Because they are about shared experiences, these stories are often personal and emotional; they may evoke positive or negative feelings in family members. Individuals often use these stories to shape their own sense of identity. One of the authors of this textbook had a difficult time gaining confidence in her driving ability. Do you think it might be due in part to the fact that her family members enjoyed telling and retelling the story of how she was responsible for wrecking the family car when she was four years old?

Three types of family stories that have been studied by family scholars in an attempt to explain how families define their experiences are birth stories, courtship stories, and stories of survival.

- **Birth stories** describe how each person entered the family and can define how members "fit" into the system. One woman shared a story of enduring a 42-hour labor prior to the birth of her son. She stated, "I guess I should have known then that he would always be challenging me because he gave me such a difficult time from the beginning!"
- **Courtship stories** provide a timeline for tracing romance in the family. They are often used to describe how parents and grandparents met and how they decided that they were right for one another. When asked how he met his wife, a grandfather explained that she was working in the fields on her family farm and that it was love at first sight. He joked, "I knew she was a hard worker, so I asked her to marry me!" He then went on to explain that he knew she was devoted to helping her family and that she would be dedicated to her own family.
- **Stories of survival** are narratives used to explain how family members have overcome difficult times. They are often told to help family members cope with challenges. Three sisters who, at a young age, were physically abused by their father, discussed how they shared their stories with one another to assist in coping with their similar experiences. The sisters viewed the stories as therapeutic; they reinforced the notion that if they could survive the abuse of their father, they were strong enough to face any situation.

Family Myths

Family myths are created to communicate the beliefs, values, and attitudes held by members to represent characteristics that are considered important to the family. These myths are often fictional as they are based on an ideal image the family wishes to convey to others. Consider the following example:

> "I couldn't believe what I was hearing! At my grandfather's funeral, my dad's family members were all talking about what a great man my grandfather was and how much they would miss him. My grandmother sobbed as she whispered, 'He was such a loving and caring man. I don't know what I'll do without him.' After the service, I asked my father why they were all referring to my grandfather that way. For years I had heard stories of the physical abuse that had taken place in the family during my dad's childhood, and I had heard my grandfather yell at my grandmother on numerous occasions. My dad responded, 'It's just easier on your grandmother if we all remember him in a positive way.'"

In this scenario, the family creates a myth that portrays the grandfather as a loving, caring man. Doing so enables them to protect the grandmother and to perpetuate the belief that he was a good father and husband. In the movie, *Doing Time on Maple Drive*, a family goes to great lengths to portray the image of the "perfect family" to their friends and neighbors. At one point, the son reveals to his parents that he attempted to commit suicide because he would rather be dead than admit to them that he is gay. This scene illustrates the power of family myths and the tremendous amount of pressure placed on family members to live up to the expectations communicated in these myths.

Family Metaphors

Sometimes families create **family metaphors** to assist in communicating how family life as a system is experienced by members. These metaphors make reference to specific objects, events, or images to represent the family experience and a collective identity. The metaphor of a "three-ring circus" may be used to describe the chaos and disorganization that exists within one family, while the "well-oiled machine" can depict the emphasis on control and organization that is the norm for another family. Metaphors can provide those within the family and outside of the family with an understanding of what behaviors are valued as well as how family members are expected to behave. A person from a "well-oiled machine" family can use the metaphor to understand the expectations associated with being a member of the family.

Family Themes

Family themes represent important concerns regarding the expected relationship between family members and can assist family members in understanding how to direct their energy as a family unit. These themes often emerge from two primary sources—the background or experience of the parents, and the dialectical pulls experienced by the family. Suppose Joe and Marnie are having a difficult time managing the tensions of autonomy and connection as their children grow older, begin dating, and spend more time with friends than with family members. In an attempt to communicate their concern for the growing independence of family members, they remind the children that "Blood is thicker than water" and "Friends may come and go, but family is forever." These themes are intended to remind the children that, while they may form many relationships outside the unit, the strongest ties should be reserved for those in their family.

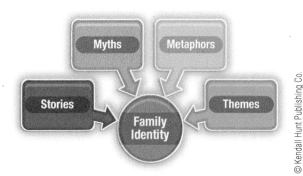

Figure 13.6 Communication strategies used to shape and sustain family identity.

© Kendall Hunt Publishing Co.

CONSEQUENCES OF FAMILY RELATIONSHIPS

Throughout this text, various communication variables have been identified as being both beneficial and harmful to our interpersonal relationships. Because families play such a vital role in the development of our self-identity, understanding how specific communication behaviors can enhance and damage our relationships and our sense of self is important.

©wong yu liang .com

Offering encouragement fosters the development of intimacy in family relationships.

> Understanding and supportive communication are related to family satisfaction. If we perceive family members as being there for us, we are more willing to exert energy toward developing a more intimate relationship.

Families can serve as the primary source of understanding and support for individuals. As we grow older, we receive messages that let us know that we are cared for and accepted. These perceptions are often shaped by the types of verbal and nonverbal cues we receive from others and are often linked to the formation of our sense of self. Three types of messages are often used to indicate whether family members view us in the same way we see ourselves:

- **Confirming communication** occurs when we treat and communicate with family members in a way that is consistent with how they see themselves. A child who perceives himself to be independent is confirmed when a parent gives him responsibility and allows him to make his own decisions.
- **Rejection** occurs when family members treat others in a manner that is inconsistent with how they see themselves. Can you recall a time when you felt like you were "grown up" but your parents treated you as though you were still a child?

- **Disconfirming communication** occurs when family members fail to offer any type of response. We often get caught up in our busy schedules and fail to communicate with family members. Even though our response is neither positive nor negative, it can cause others to feel dissatisfied with the relationship.

Understanding and supportive communication are related to family satisfaction. If we perceive family members as being there for us, we are more willing to exert energy toward developing a more intimate relationship.

DIFFICULT COMMUNICATION

It is important to note that families are not immune to difficult communication. Just as romantic partners and friends experience highs and lows in relationships, so do families. Because families evolve as members grow and encounter new life experiences, additional communication challenges emerge. The key to managing these issues effectively and maintaining a positive relationship is to understand the role of communication in guiding us through the muddy waters.

Family Stress

Reuben Hill developed the **ABCX model** to study the stress experienced by families during war (1958). Each component of this model provides a glimpse into how different families cope with stress.

- "A" represents the stressor event and resulting hardship.

- "B" refers to the resources a family has available to manage the stress.
- Given that different families define stress in unique ways, "C" is used to explain how the family defines the stress.
- Depending on how a family defines "A," "B," and "C," the perception of an event as a crisis is represented by "X."

The model is useful for understanding how and why families label situations as stressful and cope with stressors. Consider the stress experienced by a military family when a mother is deployed and won't be home for months.

The mother has a young child who is left behind while she is stationed in Iraq. Her three-year-old son is confused and upset that his mother is away. His grandmother does her best to comfort him when he mistakes another woman for his mother and runs to her. His grandmother tries to explain that mommy is still far away, flying helicopters, soothing him until he falls asleep. Once he is tucked in bed, she must try to calm her own fears for her daughter's safety, knowing that she is in a hostile land. This is the life of a soldier's family.

"A" represents the stressor event of a young mother stationed with the U.S. military in Iraq. In this story, extended family members serve as resources to assist with the care of a three-year-old child in the absence of his mother, representing the "B" in the model. The confusion experienced by the grandmother as she tries to help her grandson cope with the separation causes her to define the stressor as emotionally draining (C). While the family knows that the daughter will return home eventually, they also understand that she chose to serve her country and realize the danger associated with this respon-

sibility. This may keep the family from evaluating the stress as a crisis (X). Take a look at Figure 13.7 to review each step of the ABCX model.

Stressor events can take many forms; Boss (1988) developed a typology of stressors that families face. Table 13.1 lists these various types of stressors.

Table 13.1 Types of Stressors

TYPES OF STRESSORS	
Internal • Originate with a family member	**External** • Originate outside the family
Normative • Expected; part of family life cycle	**Non-normative** • Unexpected
Voluntary • Stress that is sought out	**Involuntary** • Events that simply occur
Chronic • Long-term	**Acute** • Short-term

Internal stressors are those that evolve from a family member. Examples might include a daughter's upcoming wedding or a teen who has tried to run away from home. External stressors, on the other hand, are often the result of an event that occurs outside the family, such as a hurricane destroying a family's home or even just an increase in the price of gasoline.

Normative stressors are those that are expected to occur at some point during the course of the family life cycle. The birth of a child or the death of an elderly parent are events that families anticipate dealing with at some point in time. Non-normative stressors are unpredictable and often catch families "off guard." While most people think that winning the lottery would be

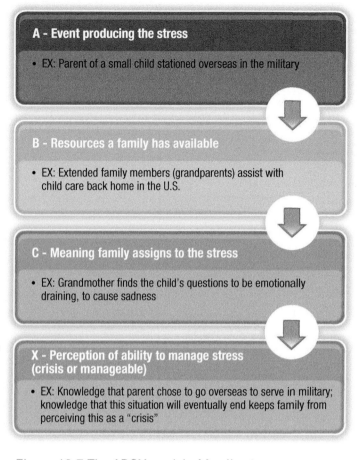

A - Event producing the stress

- EX: Parent of a small child stationed overseas in the military

B - Resources a family has available

- EX: Extended family members (grandparents) assist with child care back home in the U.S.

C - Meaning family assigns to the stress

- EX: Grandmother finds the child's questions to be emotionally draining, to cause sadness

X - Perception of ability to manage stress (crisis or manageable)

- EX: Knowledge that parent chose to go overseas to serve in military; knowledge that this situation will eventually end keeps family from perceiving this as a "crisis"

Figure 13.7 The ABCX model of family stress.

a great stressor to experience, families do not typically anticipate having difficulty dealing with the new challenges posed by their good fortune.

Some families make decisions that bring about voluntary stressors, or those events that family members seek out on their own accord. Examples of these types of stressors may include changing careers and moving to a new city or deciding to run for political office. Involuntary stressors are events that simply occur—a family member who is unexpectedly injured in a car accident or the announcement of an unplanned teen pregnancy.

Illnesses such as cancer or alcoholism are examples of chronic stressor events that require families to cope with the situation for an extended period of time. Acute stressors are relatively short-lived and include events such as a student getting suspended for misbehaving or losing the only set of keys to the family car.

SUMMARY

While we form countless interpersonal relationships throughout our lifetime, the relationships and interactions with family members are perhaps the most influential. Beginning at a young age, messages received from family members shape our identity and influence our own choice of communication behaviors. In addition to the individual identities that are shaped by these interactions, the family itself begins to create an identity that is shared by members.

Throughout this chapter we have discussed the importance of interpersonal communication throughout the family life cycle. Various interpersonal theories can be applied to the study of family communication to illustrate the dynamic nature of these relationships. While we often assume that "family is forever," it is important to recognize that just as other types of interpersonal relationships experience a "dark side," family relationships can experience challenging communication as well. By exploring the

Identifying the right time and way to reveal a secret that has long been kept from family members can be stressful. In a 2009 study by Afifi and Steuber, 629 members from 171 different families were asked to describe a secret they were keeping from a family member and describe how they would reveal the secret if they were to share it. Six specific strategies for revealing secrets were identified in the study:

- **Directness**: tell the person face-to-face; reveal the secret if asked about it
- **Indirect mediums**: share the secret via email, letter, or text
- **Third-party revelation**: share the secret with someone else and let them reveal it
- **Incremental disclosure**: reveal small parts of the secret or share a similar secret from someone else to gauge reactions
- **Preparation and rehearsal**: plan a script or practice telling the secret to others
- **Entrapment**: leave clues or evidence about the secret and allow them to draw conclusions

role that interpersonal communication plays in families, we are better able to understand our own family's communication tendencies, both when interacting with each other and when interacting with people from outside the family group.

DISCUSSION QUESTIONS

1. How would you define "family"? Who would you include in your family? Explain why these individuals are included. What individual differences affect how you define this term (e.g., sex, culture, age, your family of origin, relationship experiences) and who you include in your family?

2. Identify a family from one of your favorite television shows. Use systems theory to analyze the characters' communication patterns and relationships with one another (e.g., interdependence, wholeness, etc). Would you describe the family members' communication and relationships as healthy or unhealthy? Defend your response to this question and be sure to use specific examples to support your arguments.

3. Identify what you think are the "Top 5" issues facing families today. If you were to offer advice to families for communicating about these issues, what would you tell them?

SELF ASSESSMENT

Revised Family Communication Patterns Instrument

Respond to the following statements as they apply to your communication with your parents while you were growing up. Place a number on the line that best describes your agreement with the statements below, using the following scale:

5 = Strongly Agree, 4 = Agree, 3 = Neither Agree nor Disagree, 2 = Disagree, 1 = Strongly Disagree

_____ 1. My parents often said things like, "You'll know better when you grow up."

_____ 2. My parents often asked my opinion when the family was talking about something.

_____ 3. My parents often said things like, "My ideas are right and you should not question them."

_____ 4. My parents encouraged me to challenge their ideas and beliefs.

_____ 5. My parents often said things like, "A child should not argue with adults."

_____ 6. I usually told my parents what I was thinking about things.

_____ 7. My parents often said things like, "There are some things that are just not to be talked about."

_____ 8. I can tell my parents almost anything.

_____ 9. When anything really important was involved, my parents expected me to obey without question.

_____10. In our family we often talk about our feelings and emotions.

_____11. In our home, my parents usually had the last word.

_____12. My parents and I often had long, relaxed conversation about nothing in particular.

_____13. My parents felt that it was important to be the boss.

_____14. I really enjoyed talking with my parents, even when we disagreed.

_____15. My parents sometimes became irritated with my views if they were different from theirs.

_____16. My parents often say something like "you should always look at both sides of an issue."

_____17. If my parents don't approve of it, they don't want to know about it.

_____18. My parents like to hear my opinions, even when they don't agree with me.

_____19. When I am at home, I am expected to obey my parents' rules.

_____20. My parents encourage me to express my feelings.

_____21. My parents tended to be very open about their emotions.

_____22. We often talk as a family about things we have done during the day.

_____23. In our family we often talk about our plans and hopes for the future.

_____24. In our family we talk about topics like politics and religion where some persons dis agree with others.

_____25. My parents often say something like "Every member of the family should have some say in family decisions."

_____26. My parents often say something like "You should give in on arguments rather than risk making people mad."

SCORING DIRECTIONS:

Items 1, 3, 5, 7, 9, 11, 13, 15, 17, 19, 26 represent the Conformity items. Add these items and divide by 11 to determine your Conformity score.

Items 2, 4, 6, 8, 10, 12, 14, 16, 18, 20, 21, 22, 23, 24, 25 represent the Conversation items. Add these items and divide by 15 to determine your Conversation score.

Scoring—Your scores will range from 1–5 and the higher score is more likely to be the perceived communication pattern in your family.

Source:)."Revised Family Communication Pattern Instrument" by L. D. Ritchie from Roloff, M. E. (1990). Family communication patterns: Measuring interpersonal perceptions of interpersonal relationships. *Communication Research*, 17(4), 523–544. Reprinted by permission of Sage Publications Inc.

KEY TERMS

ABCX MODEL: includes various elements to examine the stress experienced by families and the various ways in which they cope with stress.

ACUTE STRESSOR: relatively short-lived or temporary stress-producing events encountered by families.

AMBIGUOUS BOUNDARIES: vague or indistinguishable boundaries that may create confusion about who family members perceive as being part of the family system.

BIRTH STORIES: one type of family stories that describes how a person entered the family and defines how members "fit" into the system.

BOOMERANG CHILDREN: young adults who return home to live with their parents after living on their own for a period of time.

BOUNDARIES: created by families to indicate who is considered part of the family system. May be flexible to include the addition of new family members, friends, or even pets.

CALIBRATION: a component of family systems theory that allows the family to review the communication in their relationships and decide if any adjustments need to be made to the system.

CHRONIC STRESSOR: events that require families to cope with a stressful situation for an extended period of time.

CONFIRMATION: relational maintenance strategy in which messages are designed to communicate the importance or value of a family member in one's life.

CONFIRMING COMMUNICATION: messages that indicate that we see family members in a way that is consistent with how they see themselves.

CONFORMITY ORIENTATION: focuses on the degree to which a family encourages autonomy in individual beliefs, values, and attitudes.

CONSENSUAL FAMILIES: promote open conversations while still maintaining control and authority when it comes to decisions in the family.

CONTENT EXPECTATIONS: focus on how the relationship is defined by the role each partner plays in the family.

CONVERSATION ORIENTATION: refers to the level of openness and the frequency with which a variety of topics are discussed.

COURTSHIP STORIES: one type of family stories that provides a timeline for tracing romance in the family. Often used to describe how parents and grandparents met and how they decided that they were compatible.

DEIDENTIFICATION: an individual's attempt to create a distinct identity that is separate from that of their siblings.

DISCONFIRMING COMMUNICATION: occurs when family members fail to acknowledge or offer any type of feedback or response to another family member.

ESCAPE: relational maintenance strategy in which family members turn to one another to divert one's focus during difficult situations.

EQUIFINALITY: a component of family systems theory that refers to a family's ability to achieve the same goal by following different paths or employing different communication behaviors.

EXTERNAL STRESSOR: the result of an event that occurs outside the family.

FAMILY COMMUNICATION PATTERNS THEORY: focuses on how messages are processed and discussed within the family to create shared meaning. Includes the two primary orientations of conversation and conformity.

Family events: relational maintenance strategy in which family members participate in events together as a means of sustaining their relationship.

Family Metaphors: references to specific objects, events, or images to represent the family experience and a collective identity.

Family Myths: created to communicate the beliefs, values, and attitudes held by members to represent characteristics that are considered important to the family; are often fictional as they are based on an ideal image the family wishes to convey to others.

Family stories: narratives recounting significant events that have been shared by members.

Family systems theory: proposes that family relationships can be treated as systems and includes the study of six elements to explain how and why family members relate to one another.

Family Themes: represent important concerns regarding the expected relationship between family members and can assist family members in understanding how to direct their energy as a family unit.

Hierarchy: perceived levels of power or control associated with roles in the family.

humor: relational maintenance strategy in which family members incorporate amusement or joy to sustain the relationship.

Independent couple: describes a couple that simultaneously respects the need for autonomy and engages in a high level of communication and sharing with one another.

Interdependence: proposes that the family system is composed of interrelated parts, or members, and a change experienced by one family member is likely to result in changes that impact all other family members.

Internal stressor: family stressors that result from within the family.

Involuntary stressor: stress-producing events that unexpectedly occur within a family.

Laissez-faire families: adopt both a low conversation and low conformity orientation. Family members rarely talk with one another, and when conversations occur they focus on a limited number of topics.

Launching stage: the period when children begin the separation process from their parents.

Non-normative stressor: unpredictable and often catches families "off guard."

Normative stressor: stress-producing events that are expected to occur at some point during the course of the family life cycle.

Pluralistic families: adopt a high conversation orientation and a low conformity orientation. Children are encouraged to participate in decision-making.

Protective families: adopt a low conversation orientation and a high conformity orientation. Parents are considered to be the authority, and children are expected to obey the family rules without questioning them.

Rejection: occurs when family members treat others in a manner that is inconsistent with how they see themselves.

Relational expectations: refer to the similarity, or correspondence, of the emotional, or affective, expectations each partner has for defining the relationship.

Separate couples: tend to emphasize each individual's identity and independence over maintaining the relationship.

Social support: relational maintenance strategy in which family members provide comfort for one another via verbal and/or nonverbal messages.

STORIES OF SURVIVAL: narratives used to explain how family members have overcome difficult times; often, they are told to help family members cope with challenges they face.

SYMBOLIC INTERACTIONISM: proposes that one's sense of self is developed through interactions with others; families are influential in shaping this view of self through the messages and reactions to one another.

TRADITIONAL COUPLES: couples who exhibit a high level of interdependence and sharing in their relationships with one another.

VERBAL AGGRESSION: relational maintenance strategy in which family members vent or express their frustrations with one another.

VOLUNTARY STRESSOR: those events that family members seek out (such as changing careers or moving to a new home) that result in stress.

WHOLENESS: implies that a family creates its own personality or culture, and that this personality is unique from that of each family member.

REFERENCES

Afifi, T., & Steuber, K. (2009). The Revelation Risk Model (RRM): Factors that predict the revelation of secrets and the strategies used to reveal them. *Communication Monographs, 76*(2), 144–176.

Ball, H., Wanzer, M. B., & Servoss, T. J. (2013). Parent-child communication on Facebook: Family communication patterns and young adults' decision to "friend" parents. *Communication Quarterly, 61*(5), 615–629.

Boss, P. (1988). *Family stress management.* Newbury Park, CA: Sage.

Coleman, M., Ganong, L., & Fine, M. (2004). Communication in stepfamilies. In A. Vangelisti (Ed.), *Handbook of family communication.* (215–232). Mahwah, NJ: Lawrence Erlbaum Associates.

Dixon, S. V., Graber, J. A., & Brooks-Gunn, J. (2008). The roles of respect for parental authority and parenting practices in parent-child conflict among African American, Latino, and European American families. *Journal of Family Psychology, 22*(1), 1–10.

Dunn, A. (2015). Failure to launch: Adult children moving back home. Retrieved May 29, 2015, from http://www.forbes.com/sites/moneywise-women/2012/06/06/failure-to-launch-adult-children-moving-back-home/

Eckstein, N. J. (2004). Emergent issues in families experiencing adolescent-to-parent abuse. *Western Journal of Communication, 68*(4), 365-388.

Fitzpatrick, M. A. (1987). Marital interaction. In C. Berger & S. Chaffee (Eds.), *Handbook of communication science* (564–618). Newbury Park, CA: Sage.

Givertz, M., Segrin, C., & Hanzal, A. (2009). The association between satisfaction and commitment differs across marital couple types. *Communication Research, 36*(4), 561–584.

Givertz, M., & Segrin, C. (2014). The association between overinvolved parenting and young adults' self-efficacy, psychological entitlement, and family communication. *Communication Research, 41*(8), 1111–1136.

Gold, J. M. (2015). Intergenerational attachments in stepfamilies: Facilitating the role of step-grandparents. *The Family Journal: Counseling and Therapy for Couples and Families, 23*(2), 194–200.

Hill, R. (1958). Generic features of families under stress. *Social Casework, 49,* 139–150.

Koerner, A. F., & Fitzpatrick, M. A. (2002). Toward a theory of family communication. *Communication Theory, 12,* 70–91.

LaRossa, R., & Reitzes, D. C. (1993). Symbolic interactionism and family studies. In P. G. Boss,

W. J. Doherty, R. LaRossa, W. R. Schumm, & S. K. Steinmetz (Eds.), *Sourcebook of family theories and methods: A contextual approach* (135–163). New York, NY: Plenum Press.

Marrow-Ferguson, S., & Dickson, F. (1995). Children's expectations of their single-parent's dating behavior: A preliminary investigation of emergent themes relevant to single-parent dating. *Journal of Applied Communication Research, 23*, 1–17.

McGraw, P. (2004). *Family first: Your step-by-step plan for creating a phenomenal family.* New York: Free Press.

McLeod, J. M., & Chaffee, S. H. (1972). The construction of social reality. In J. Tedeschi (Ed.), *The social influence process* (pp. 50–59). Chicago, IL: Aldine-Atherton.

McLeod, J.M., & Chaffee, S.H. (1973). Interpersonal approaches to communication research. *American Behavior Scientist, 16*, 469–499.

Mead, G. H. (1934). *Mind, self and society.* Chicago: University of Chicago Press.

Milkie, M.A., Nomaguchi, K. M., & Denny, K. E. (2015). Does the amount of time mothers spend with their children or adolescents matter? *Journal of Marriage and Family, 77*, 355–372.

Myers, S. A., & Weber, K. D. (2004). Preliminary development of a measure of sibling relational maintenance behaviors: Scale development and initial findings. *Communication Quarterly, 52*, 334–346.

Myers, S. A., Byrnes, K. A., Frisby, B. N., & Mansson, D. H. (2011). Adult siblings' use of affectionate communication as a strategic and routine relational maintenance behavior. *Communication Research Reports, 28*(2), 151–158.

Ritchie, L. D. (1990). Family communication patterns: Measuring interpersonal perceptions of interpersonal relationships. *Communication Research, 17*(4), 523–544.

Ritchie, L. D., & Fitzpatrick, M. A. (1990). Family communication patterns: Measuring interpersonal perceptions of interpersonal relationships. *Communication Research, 17*, 523–544.

Stamp, G. H. (2004). Theories of family relationships and a family relationships theoretical model. In A. Vangelisti (Ed.), *Handbook of family communication.* (1–30). Mahwah, NJ: Lawrence Erlbaum Associates.

Thomas-Maddox, C. (1999). *Keeping the relationship alive: An analysis of relational maintenance strategies employed by non-custodial parents and their children following divorce.* Paper presented at the National Communication Association convention, Chicago, IL.

Turner, L. H., & West, R. (2002). *Perspectives on family communication.* McGraw-Hill: Boston, MA.

Ungricht, M. (2006, February 17). MSNBC Citizen Journalist Reports: Stories from front line families. Retrieved from http://msnbc.com/id/7012316/.

Vangelisti, A. (2004). *Handbook of family communication.* Mahwah, NJ: Lawrence Erlbaum Associates.

Walsh, W. M., & Williams, R. (1997). *School and family therapy: Using systems theory and family therapy in the resolution of school problems.* Springfield, IL: Charles C. Thomas.

Organizational Communication:
Combining the Personal with the Professional

OBJECTIVES

- Distinguish among five types of work relationships (superior-subordinate, peer/co-worker, friendship, mentoring, romantic) and discuss communication practices in each type of relationship

- Explain three approaches to communication in organizations (classical, human relations, human resources) and identify how each addresses interpersonal communication

- Explain factors influencing leader-member relationships in organizations.

- Identify factors that influence peer relationships at work

- Describe the three stages of organization socialization and the role of communication in each of these stages

- Identify strategies for balancing work and family relationships

- Describe the impact of technology on interpersonal communication at work

SCENARIO: SOUND FAMILIAR?

Ben had been looking forward to his promotion as manager of the campus bookstore. Unlike most new managers, he felt comfortable about his new position. After all, he would still be working with the team of colleagues he had been working with for the past three years, many of them he considered to be close friends. As he reviewed schedules, he discovered that some of the bookstore's employees had been taking advantage of the system. It became apparent that a few of them often extended their lunch hours by an extra twenty to thirty minutes to run errands. Ben called a meeting to discuss organizational policies and to address some of the issues he had witnessed during his first few weeks as manager. As he discussed the need to adhere to company policies, many of his employees began to complain. "What's going on here? Have you become 'Mr. Big Shot' and forgotten that we're friends?" Others chimed in with similar comments. Frustrated, Ben ended the meeting by stating, "Look, I think you're trying to take advantage of the situation here!

I'm your supervisor now, and you need to listen." As he walked away from the meeting, Ben was dumbfounded. How could his friends turn on him like that? Had that much really changed just because of his promotion?

OVERVIEW

From popular television shows such as *The Office*, *The Apprentice*, and *Undercover Boss* and films such as *Office Space*, work relationships are depicted as everyday encounters in our lives. Throughout this text, we have discussed the theoretical foundations and concepts central to understanding the role communication plays in interpersonal relationships. As we continue to examine how and why our relationships are impacted by contextual issues, it is important to take a closer look at one context where many adults spend the majority of their time with others—the workplace. Many Americans spend more than the average forty hours per week at their jobs (Figure 14.1). Add to this the fact that many employees take work home with them, and the amount of time dedicated to work relationships increases. For some individuals, this may mean that they could potentially spend more time engaged in communication in their work relationships than in any other context.

In this chapter, we address the unique aspects of interpersonal communication in relationships associated with your professional career or membership in various organizations. We will examine how and why organizational relationships differ from other types of interpersonal bonds, and explore different types of work relationships, as well as diversity in the workplace.

Few employees remain at their first job for a long period of time. As a result our work relationships are sometimes temporary in nature.

THE UNIQUE NATURE OF WORK-PLACE RELATIONSHIPS

Each relationship is characterized by unique features, and the bonds formed with others at work are no exception. As we begin our discussion of interactions at work, we first need to consider the characteristics of these relationships. How are workplace relationships different from relationships we form with friends, family, and at school? Sias, Krone, and Jablin (2002) defined workplace relationships as "any relationship one has with a coworker, such as a supervisor-subordinate, peer, or mentoring relationship" (pp. 489-490). These relationships can be characterized as being voluntary or involuntary, temporary, and are influenced by the presence of a hierarchy or status differential.

Voluntary

Very few employees remain at their first job for their entire lives. A 2015 study conducted by the U.S. Bureau of Labor Statistics found that employees have held an average 11.7 different jobs by the time they reach age 48 (http://www.bls.gov/nls/nlsfaqs.htm#anch41). Consider the fact that the majority of our work relationships are **voluntary** in the sense that individuals have the choice to interview with the organization and, if offered a job, they have the choice to accept the position or not. Deciding to become a member of an organization indicates that a person is interested in pursuing the relationships associated with membership.

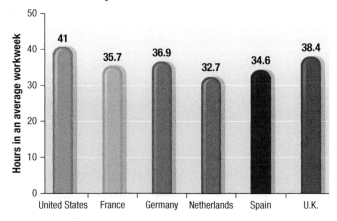

Figure 14.1 Average hours worked per week across cultures.

While the initial decision to join an organization is voluntary, some tasks assigned to an employee may result in the formation of involuntary relationships. **Involuntary relationships** exist between members who did not have a desire to initiate a relationship. If you have ever been appointed by your supervisor to work on a project or a team, the relationship between you and the new team members was likely involuntary.

Within the workplace, both implicit and explicit rules and norms for communicating with those of different status exist.

Temporary

Work relationships are also often **temporary** in nature. While family bonds are long-lasting, employees have the option to continue the relationships with those at work or to seek employment and, therefore, new coworkers, elsewhere. Further, some of the relationships formed in the workplace may be temporary in nature due to the task associated with them. For example, if Martha is assigned to work on a project that is scheduled to be completed six months from now, chances are the relationships formed during the term of the project are likely to be temporary.

Hierarchy/Status Differential

A final characteristic of work relationships is that the interactions are often regulated by a hierarchy or status differential. Our relationships with others in the workplace are impacted by status differentials between members in the organization. Some organizations are **tall structures** with many levels of supervisors, administrators, and employees, while others have relatively **flat structures** and few hierarchical levels separating supervisors from employees.

Within the workplace, both implicit and explicit rules and norms for communicating with those of different status exist. For example, persons of lower status understand that they are expected to wait for those of higher status. Have you ever waited for your academic advisor or professor to show up for office hours to discuss an assignment that is due? Chances are you are willing to wait 15–20 minutes if she is late. It is not likely that the professor would be willing to wait that amount of time for a student to show up for an appointment.

Organizational hierarchies form the backbone and/or foundation for a company. Managers and their employees must form relationships to meet mutually agreed-upon goals, coworkers are required to interact with one another to accomplish tasks and fulfill the goals, and numerous relationships are formed with individuals and other organizations that the company depends upon for its success.

Have you ever stopped to consider the number of organizations that influence your life each and every day? Given that you are a student, you are obviously influenced by your school. To ensure your physical care, relationships have been formed with health care providers' offices. If you work while going to school, add one more organization you may interact with on a daily basis. In essence, we all exist in an organizational world. As you reflect on the relationships that you have formed in organizations, chances are that many of the communication variables we have discussed in this text have been influential.

THINK ABOUT IT. . .
Multiple relationships formed by organizations

Clear Mountain Bank is a small community bank with nine branch offices located in several surrounding communities. The bank's officers and branch managers interact with one another to ensure that they fulfill the organization's overall goals. If the bank is to succeed, its tellers must establish satisfactory relationships with its customers. Taking a look beyond the confines of the bank buildings, several other relationships are initiated and maintained. In order to attract new customers, the bank forms relationships with the local media and supports events in each of the communities where its branches are located. To ensure that the bank is complying with federal regulations, interactions are held with those responsible for insuring that regulations are met. Additionally, Clear Mountain forms relationships through sponsorship of the local elementary schools and several youth athletic teams.

Consider the number of relationships that are formed in organizations of which you are a member.
- How many different types of relationships can you identify that must be formed by your college or university?
- What communication strategies are most effective in initiating and maintaining those relationships?

Whether the task involves building trust, listening to colleagues, providing feedback to your manager or clients, or initiating and maintaining relationships, communication plays a pivotal role. Let us take a closer look at the different types of relationships formed in organizations.

TYPES OF RELATIONSHIPS AT WORK

As you can see from the Clear Mountain example, there are a variety of relationships that can be formed within a single organization. Research that has focused on communication in organizations has primarily focused on two types of work relationships: superior-subordinate relationships and coworker relationships.

Organizational hierarchies create the foundation for communication expectations in a company.

Superior-subordinate relationships are characterized by a status differential between individuals, and focus on the interactions that take place between supervisors or managers and their employees or subordinates. **Coworker, or peer, relationships** evolve as a result of interactions between members of an organization at the same status level. Regardless of the type of relationship, communication factors play a vital role in achieving interpersonal effectiveness. Factors such as trust, listening, and feedback are critical.

Superior-Subordinate Relationships at Work

Superior-subordinate relationships differ from other types of interpersonal bonds because of the explicit status differential that is present. Factors impacting relationships between organizational leaders and members include channels of communication, emphasis on task versus relational needs, and communication flow. As we take a closer look at the relationships between supervisors and subordinates, it is important to trace the theoretical foundations that have guided managers in developing various styles of communication.

Early theories of organizational communication focused on information being communicated downward from supervisor to subordinate. **Classical theories** viewed communication as being primarily one-way. Managers send information down the channels to employees, and messages are typically formal and focus almost exclusively on task issues. Hierarchies in organizational

Whether the task involves building trust, listening to colleagues, providing feedback to your manager or clients, or initiating and maintaining relationships, communication plays a pivotal role.

© Pressmaster/Shutterstock.com

relationships are demonstrated by Taylor's **scientific management theory**. Taylor's theory (1911) asserts that there are distinct differences between managers and employees. The manager's role is to plan and direct the workers to do things the "correct" way as they complete tasks. Over time, researchers realized that something was missing from this communication model. Meeting the interpersonal needs of workers emerged as an essential element in achieving high productivity and worker satisfaction.

In earlier chapters, we introduced the concept of Maslow's Hierarchy of Needs. Maslow's (1943) hierarchy of needs was one of the first theories used to specifically acknowledge the higher-level needs of organizational employees. While previous theories had acknowledged the pres-ence of workers' physiological and safety needs, Maslow's theory addressed needs for affilia-tion, esteem, and self actualization. Affiliation or social needs are placed at the third level of Maslow's hierarchy. These needs are often ful-filled through interpersonal relationships with managers and coworkers. Figure 14.2 provides specific examples of how some of the needs represented by Maslow's theory are fulfilled by organizations. As you review these examples, consider the role that communication plays in ensuring that these needs are fulfilled in organizations.

Maslow's theory paved the way for scholars to ex-amine the relationship between work factors, em-ployees' higher-order needs, job satisfaction, and productivity. Human relations theories focus on

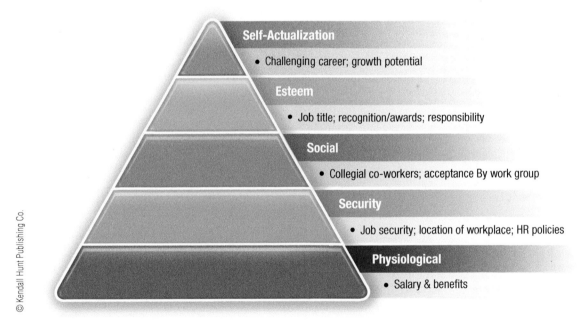

© Kendall Hunt Publishing Co.

Figure 14.2 Examples of individuals' needs in the organizational context.

the importance of social interactions in the workplace. Rather than focusing solely on communicating to accomplish tasks, managers engage in more informal communication with employees to learn about their personal needs and goals. While many of the **human relations** theories of management provided valuable insight into the value of social relationships at work, one weakness was the overemphasis on informal communication and the assumption that face-to-face interactions were most effective.

As organizational theories evolved, the importance of the superior-subordinate relationship became more evident. In the 1960s, researchers began to explore the impact that interactions between supervisors and subordinates had on organizational efficiency, effectiveness, and satisfaction. Many of the theories developed during this time period are classified as **human resources** approaches. What distinguishes these theories from their earlier counterparts in the classical and human relations approaches is their focus on multi-directional communication and an appreciation for both formal and informal communication styles. Human resources managers recognize that while relationships are an essential part of organizational success, in order to effectively operate as a team, task messages are also crucial to accomplishing goals. A unique feature of the human resources approach is its focus on teams in organizations. Communication is no longer viewed as being strictly upward or downward. After all, employees need to interact not only with their supervisors, but they also may rely on communication with leaders and members of other teams in the organization, or even peers on their own teams. See Table 14.1 for a summary of the three approaches to superior-subordinate relationships.

Table 14.1 Theoretical Approaches to Communication Flow and Message Focus

Theoretical Perspective	Direction of Communication	Focus of Message
Classical	Downward	Task
Human Relations	Upward & Downward	Relational
Human Resources	Upward, Downward, Across, & Diagonal	Task & Relational

Leader-member exchange theory, or LMX, explains the process of relationship development between superiors and subordinates (Graen, 1976). In essence, this theory states that leaders in an organization develop relationships with all the members of their organization, but that there are qualitative differences in these bonds. Relationships exist on a continuum ranging from perceptions of "in-group" to "out-group" status. According to LMX, high-quality, or "in-group," relationships are the result of supportive messages from supervisors to subordinates. Managers consult with employees on organizational decisions and they are provided with greater responsibility. High LMX relationships are often characterized by trust, liking, and support by both superiors and subordinates (Dansereau, Graen, & Haga, 1975). Obvious outcomes of these positive factors are greater amounts of interaction and, ultimately, higher levels of satisfaction.

Low-quality, or "out-group," relationships are characterized by little supervisory support and limited influence in decision making. In this low LMX context, communication can be compared to that of a secret club—one in which informa-

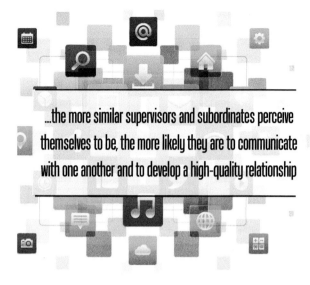

...the more similar supervisors and subordinates perceive themselves to be, the more likely they are to communicate with one another and to develop a high-quality relationship

tion is only shared by those in control or power. Interactions are guided by strict adherence to roles and rules in the hierarchy. Members of low-LMX organizations are often less satisfied and the organization often experiences higher levels of employee turnover. It is quite possible that you have experienced high- or low-quality LMX relationships within educational organizations.

So what factors contribute to the development of high-quality exchanges among superiors and subordinates? You might be surprised to discover that concepts we have been discussing throughout this text play an influential role in forming these relationships. These concepts include similarity, attraction, and trust. First, the more similar supervisors and subordinates perceive themselves to be, the more likely they are to communicate with one another and to develop a high-quality relationship (Turban & Jones, 1988). Recall our discussion of similarity and attraction in Chapter 7. The more similar two people perceive themselves to be, the more attractive they may be to one another. Next, task attraction, which is based on factors that have the potential to help accom-

plish a goal, is influential in the development of quality LMX. Finally, similarity and task attraction result in increased communication among leaders and members, thus enhancing the level of trust between them. Supervisors trust in-group subordinates and allow them to contribute to decision making by delegating responsibility.

Leader-member communication has been the focus of studies designed to identify its impact on workplace relationships and productivity. A variety of outcomes have been associated with the level of LMX, including:

- Stronger leader-member (LMX) communication is associated with increased levels of communication among coworkers (CWX) and more positive organizational citizenship behaviors (Baker & Omilion-Hodges, 2013).
- Employees whose managers use more person-centered communication that considers their perspectives report higher levels of job satisfaction and higher-quality relationships with their supervisors (Fix & Sias, 2006).

As organizations become increasingly diverse, cultural competence is critical for the development of high-quality LMX relationships. Both superiors and subordinates need to engage in the process of perspective taking. We can avoid falling into the trap of stereotyping one another by being open-minded and committed to learning from the other's perspective. Doing so potentially increases the chances for high-quality LMX relationships to emerge. Suppose a manager from a U.S.-based organization was working with employees in Japan. It would be important for the manager to keep in mind that her Japanese employees are uncomfortable being "singled-out" from the group and prefer to adopt a collectivistic approach to communication with employees. By acknowledging the contributions of the group as opposed to those of specific individuals, the manager will likely enhance the LMX relationship.

Peer Relationships at Work

Managers and scholars have recognized that perhaps the most influential relationships in the workplace are those that form among coworkers, or peers. Several types of peer relationships have been examined by communication scholars. These include friendships, mentoring relationships, and romantic relationships. Stop for a moment and consider the number of times you interact with peers in your workplace in a given day. These relationships are often a central focus for understanding organizational life because, in many cases, we interact with peers in the workplace more frequently than we do with supervisors.

How does tele-work impact the relationships that are formed among organizational members?

To understand the evolution of peer interactions in organizations, it is important to consider the factors that cause these relationships to form and strengthen. As we take a closer look at various types of peer relationships, the impact of factors such as physical proximity, communication climate, task/goal dependence, and dual meanings on relationship development will become evident (Figure 14.3).

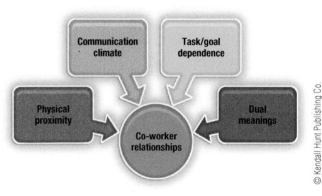

Figure 14.3 Factors impacting peer relationships in organizations.

PHYSICAL PROXIMITY. First, physical proximity affects relationship development among coworkers. Several studies have found that proximity increases opportunities for interaction (Fine, 1986; Monge & Kirste, 1980). The more opportunities for interaction that exist, the greater the chance that peer relationships will be formed. Colleagues whose cubicles are located next to each other are more likely to form relationships and interact with one another than are those who are located on different floors of the building. One employee who describes his office as a "rat maze" of cubicles explains the impact

Studies have found that coworkers come together to provide social support in situations where managers are perceived to be unfair or untrustworthy

of proximity as, "Sometimes I just roll my office chair into the next cubicle and blow off steam after a meeting. It's like having a neighbor you can vent to when things get rough." Remember that most employees report spending more than forty hours per week at work. More time together provides greater opportunities to share.

COMMUNICATION CLIMATE. A second factor influencing the development of peer relationships is the communication climate between superiors and subordinates. An inherent hierarchical structure often contributes to the development of an "us versus them" mentality. Studies have found that coworkers come together to provide social support in situations where managers are perceived to be unfair or untrustworthy (Odden & Sias, 1997; Sias & Jablin, 1995). High levels of employee cohesiveness often result from these negative communication climates. Consider a time when you have been frustrated by something that happened at work or at school. You probably chose to communicate your frustrations to a coworker or classmate who could relate to the situation you were experiencing because of

their familiarity with the environment. While family and friends listen and offer support, they may not be able to understand the actual organizational climate as well as a workplace colleague does.

TASK/GOAL DEPENDENCE. Task or goal dependence is a third factor influencing the development of peer relationships. By their very definition, organizations exist for the purpose of accomplishing a specific task or goal. Its members must work together to carry out its mission. Peer influence is an essential factor in fulfilling these goals. As we discuss team relationships in organizations later in this chapter, you will learn how shared tasks bring organizational members together. Team members depend on one another to meet the goals. If one team member "drops the ball," other members may communicate pressure in an attempt to encourage compliance. In some instances, coworkers may even have more influence over peer behaviors than supervisors do. In essence, peer influence in organizations is not that different from peer influence witnessed among teens in today's society.

DUAL MEANINGS. A final factor that plays a key role in understanding the formation of relationships in organizations is the dual meanings communicated in messages. Messages exchanged between peers often contain "clues" to help define the nature of the relationship. Suppose you are the chairperson of a student organization that is hosting a blood drive on campus. If you advise members that, "We're going to have to kick it into high gear if we hope to meet our goal for this project," you are sending a message that you perceive yourself as being in a position to evaluate the performance of the group. The content dimension is clear—the number of donors needs to increase in order to meet the group's goal, and an implied relational message is present as well. By referencing the group through the use of pronouns such as "we," you communicate to the members that there is a bond that links everyone together.

As stated earlier, there are three types of coworker relationships that have gained the interest of communication scholars: friendships, mentoring relationships, and romantic relationships. Let us take a closer look at the communication dynamics in each of these relationships in organizations.

FRIENDSHIPS IN ORGANIZATIONS

Reflecting on the proximity principle of peer relationships, it should come as no surprise that many friendships are formed as a result of organizational affiliations. As we explore the prevalence of these relationships, consider the friendships you have formed as a result of your membership in work, education, volunteer, or social organizations. Some individuals may create labels to describe these relationships by identifying a person as "a friend from work" or "a friend from my church." Our decision to form friendships at work is voluntary. While you may not have any choice regarding those you form relationships with at work, you do have options when it comes to forming friendships.

Friendships provide organizational members with social support and assistance throughout the socialization process. Communication scholars have realized the prevalence of these types of relationships and have applied theories to explain the dynamics of friendships at work. Bridge and Baxter (1992) identified five dialectical tensions

Workplace friendships are unique due to the need to balance both the personal and professional relationships.

experienced by friends in organizations, three of which are new to the study of struggles experienced in other types of interpersonal relationships. They point out that friendships in the workplace are unique, due to the blending of "personal" and "professional" role expectations. Tensions emerge because of the struggle between the behaviors we expect of someone as a friend and behaviors expected of that same person in his or her role as coworker. The familiar tensions of autonomy/connection and openness/closedness that are typically experienced in intimate relationships occur as a result of friendships formed at work. Tensions that are unique to organizations include struggles between equality/inequality, impartiality/favoritism, and judgment/acceptance (Bridge & Baxter, 1992).

EQUALITY/INEQUALITY. A unique tension experienced by friends at work focuses on the contradictory struggle between **equality** versus **inequality**. Earlier, we discussed the fact that organizational relationships are characterized by status differentials created by the presence of a hierarchical structure. As friends, two employ-

ees may view themselves as being equal in their relationship status. However, when role status as an organizational member is factored into the equation, inherent inequalities may emerge. One person may be placed in the position of reviewing the performance of the friend, and the inequities in the relationship become evident.

IMPARTIALITY/FAVORITISM. Friends at work may experience tensions between being **impartial** and treating all members the same, and showing **favoritism** to friends. This is complicated by the fact that friends trust that each one will look out for the other's best interests. Recall the scenario at the beginning of the chapter. Brad may have experienced a struggle between strictly enforcing company procedures and ignoring the misbehaviors of coworkers who are also his friends. While an inherent characteristic of friendship is to provide support, ethical or moral codes may prescribe the equal treatment of all employees.

WHAT WOULD YOU DO?

As manager of the restaurant, Abbey was responsible for providing feedback on the performance of servers. One of the servers, Janelle, had become friends with Abbey over the past several months. Janelle, a single mother of two young children, had been a source of support when Abbey found herself in the midst of a divorce, wondering how she could juggle work and raise her children alone. Recently, Janelle's daughter had been having some problems at school. Janelle was often called to meet with teachers during the day, requiring her to call off from work at the last minute. Abbey knew that she had to address Janelle's absences in the performance report, but she felt horrible about giving her a low evaluation because she knew all of the issues Janelle had been struggling with lately. If you were Abbey, what would you do?

JUDGMENT/ACCEPTANCE. A final tension encountered at work is the struggle between **judgment** and **acceptance**. Friends are expected to provide support and understanding to one another without judgment. However, depending on the role expectations associated with their position in an organization, colleagues may be required to assess one another's work or performance. Consider Abbey and Janelle's situation. As a manager, Abbey knows that she needs to address the attendance issues with Janelle. But as Janelle's friend, she is reluctant to say anything because she is sympathetic to her situation. Providing and taking criticism in a performance review from a friend may form a tension that otherwise may not exist in the workplace.

In an attempt to understand how friendships evolve in the workplace, Sias and Cahill (1998) interviewed nineteen pairs of friends in organizations. Individuals were asked to indicate the changes that occurred in their friendships between the initial meeting and the present time. Results of the study support the notion that there are three distinct phases of friendship development at work:

- *Phase One* - transition from acquaintances to friends. This is experienced as the result of two employees working in close proximity for a period of time. Often results from commonalities or similarities that are discovered through conversations at work.
- *Phase Two* - transition from friends to close friends. This is often the result of supportive messages exchanged as friends socialize more outside the workplace and experience more opportunities for personal disclosures. On average, this transition occurs approximately 31 months after their first meeting.

- *Phase Three* - transition from close friends to "almost best" friends (Sias & Cahill, 1998). As the level of intimacy in the relationship increases and as more personal information is disclosed, friends experience an intense level of trust and support. Participants indicated that they reach this stage approximately four years after their first meeting.

MENTOR RELATIONSHIPS

Friendship is only one type of workplace relationship that provides organizational members with support. **Mentor relationships** are those in which a more experienced member serves as a role model, teacher, or guide for a colleague who is less experienced. Establishing a relationship with a mentor has repeatedly been linked to an individual's career progress, organizational influence, and upward mobility within an organization (Ragins & Cotton, 1991). Additional benefits of mentoring include providing new employees with both social support and professional guidance (Van Emmerik, 2004). Examples of mentoring in today's workplace range from an experienced employee who is formally assigned to be a mentor for a new colleague to a successful woman whose efforts at balancing work and family have inspired colleagues to seek her support and advice.

Mentoring partnerships may be formed on a voluntary or involuntary basis. When organizational members seek out mentors who possess qualities or characteristics they admire, they form a voluntary or **informal mentoring** relationship. Similarity in personality, goals, attitudes, or background is often a force that guides

Establishing a relationship with a mentor has repeatedly been linked to an individual's career progress, organizational influence, and upward mobility within an organization.

the decision to pursue voluntary mentor relationships. Other members may establish these relationships through involuntary or **formal mentoring** programs available in their organization. These involuntary, or assigned, mentoring partnerships may involve formal, written agreements that address the expectations for each person.

Those who establish a relationship with a mentor often achieve greater career success.

Regardless of the method for initiating the relationship, several communication characteristics are common. Just as other types of relationships involve highs and lows, so does the mentor relationship. Mentors and protégés may have dif-ferent goals that need to be negotiated, and the differences have the potential to result in jealousy or conflict. Trust is an essential part of the relationship, as both parties expect the other to be honest and open in their assessment and advice. Due to the time invested in this relationship, the concept of social exchange may become an issue to be resolved.

In their study of organizational mentoring, DeWine, Casbolt and Bentley (1983) identified five types of mentors (Figure 14.4). While the relationship is generally perceived as being supportive and nurturing, organizational members should be aware of the fact that some mentors approach their responsibility in less sensitive ways.

- **Parent mentors** are those who are considered to be "older and wiser" as a result of their tenure in the organization. Protégés often describe the parent mentor as having significant influence on their career.
- The **cheerleader mentor** is one who provides encouragement, and the mentor often describes the pride resulting from the protégé's success.
- **Groom mentors** are those who hold positions of power in an organization and are viewed as "grooming" a protégé for specific responsibilities or roles.

Not all mentor relationships result in positive experiences for the protégé. The following are some more problematic types of mentors.

- **Self-promoter mentors** are described as those who want to work with the best new members in order to surround themselves with high-quality colleagues.
- The **guilt-trip producer** is a mentor who motivates a protégé by communicating

messages of disappointment when performance fails to meet expectations. Phrases such as "I expected more from you" or "You know you can do better than that" are often associated with this type of mentor.

The outcomes of mentoring relationships can be beneficial for the individuals involved as well as for the organization. Mentors report a sense of satisfaction in seeing protégés achieve their goals, and protégés often credit their career success to the advice provided by mentors. Studies have found that employees who are mentored report more desirable occupational outcomes and advance more quickly in their professions (Ragins & Cotton, 1991). An obvious benefit for organizations is the job satisfaction that results from mentoring relationships. While many mentoring relationships evolve as a result of friendships at work, it is important to remember their purpose and refrain from confusing the roles of friend and mentor.

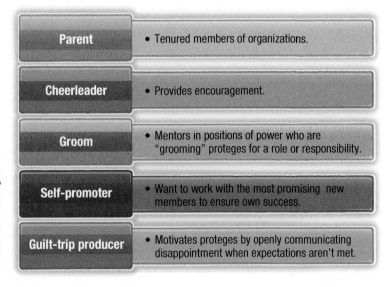

Parent	• Tenured members of organizations.
Cheerleader	• Provides encouragement.
Groom	• Mentors in positions of power who are "grooming" proteges for a role or responsibility.
Self-promoter	• Want to work with the most promising new members to ensure own success.
Guilt-trip producer	• Motivates proteges by openly communicating disappointment when expectations aren't met.

Figure 14.4 Types of mentors in organizations.

ROMANTIC RELATIONSHIPS AT WORK

With more women in the workplace and employees working longer hours, it should come as no surprise that romantic relationships have captured the attention of communication scholars. One employee explained the decision to pursue romantic relationships at work, "How can I help being attracted to colleagues at my office? I know they're goal-oriented, and it's just easier to date someone at work than to spend time hanging out at bars where everything is so uncertain." A 2014 survey by vault.com stated that fifty-six percent of employees reported that they have been involved in an office romance. Approximately 20% of women surveyed indicated that they have dated a supervisor, while nearly 25% of men reported a romantic relationship with a subordinate. A 2014 study by CareerBuilder found that nearly 12% of workers indicate they have a **work spouse**. While these relationships are not romantic in nature, they serve as a source of support and candor similar to that provided by an actual spouse. Support ranges from telling jokes during stressful times to allowing one another to vent.

The communication strategy often used to initiate romantic relationships is flirting. **Flirting** can be defined as "ambiguous goal motivated behaviors that can be, but are not restricted to being, interpreted as sexually motivated" (Henningsen, Braz, & Davies, 2008, p. 484).

While some flirting behaviors may be innocently used to explore interest in pursuing a romantic relationship, these behaviors have also been used for more manipulative purposes in organizations. Employees may flirt with coworkers for self-serving purposes such as seeking assistance on a project or even advancing their careers (Keyton & Rhodes, 1999). Colleagues need to pay careful attention to the reciprocal communication and realize that unwanted or excessive flirting in the workplace can be perceived as sexual harassment.

The Civil Rights Act of 1964 made sexual harassment illegal in the workplace. While the main goal of the Act was to prevent organizations from discriminating against minorities and women, it also addressed the legalities associated with making sexual relationships a condition for employment. In 1986, the definition of sexual harassment was further refined to address behaviors that contributed to an unpleasant or uncomfortable work environment. Berryman-Fink (1997) cites the Equal Employment Opportunity Commission (EEOC)'s definition of **sexual harassment** as "any unwelcome sexual advances, requests for sexual favors, and other verbal or physical conduct of a sexual nature" (p. 272). Sexual harassment is distinguished from flirting and other types of physical, verbal, or sexual behavior because it is perceived as unwelcome by the recipient and is reoccurring.

©BlueSkyImage/Shutterstock.com

Co-workers may flirt for romantic reasons or in an effort to advance their career.

RESEARCH IN REAL LIFE: Flirting in social vs. workplace contexts

Are there differences in the communicative goals that motivate us to flirt in various contexts? A 2008 study by Henningsen, Braz, and Davies explored the reasons by examining motives provided by 199 students and 89 workers. Six (6) flirting motivations examined in the study include:

- **Sexual** – to pursue a sexual encounter
- **Relational** – to pursue a closer interpersonal relationship
- **Fun** – view flirting as a "game" which encourages playfulness
- **Exploring** – to identify if there is reciprocal interest
- **Esteem** – to feel more attractive or positive about the self
- **Instrumental** – to get others to do things or to provide assistance

Students were more likely to engage in flirting for sexual goals, while workers report using flirting to accomplish instrumental goals. While both students and workers report flirting for exploring reciprocal interest, men in both groups were more likely to list this as a goal.

The EEOC identifies two primary types of sexual harassment that typically occur in the workplace: quid pro quo harassment and hostile work environment harassment. Quid pro quo is a Latin term that translates as "something for something." An example of this type of harassment might include a boss telling his subordinate that she will not receive a promotion, raise, or opportunity at work unless she engages in a sexual act with him. The second form of sexual harassment, hostile work environment, is less clearly defined and might include employees exchanging sexual jokes, stories, or materials in front of other employees, or ongoing unwanted sexual behavior from a coworker. While the majority of sexual harassment claims are filed by women, it is important to note that nearly 16% of harassment charges filed with the EEOC in 2013 were made by men (http://www.eeoc.gov/eeoc/statistics/enforcement/sexual_harassment.cfm). Understanding the interpretations of flirting and other communicative behaviors is important to distinguish between behavior that are intended to be playful as opposed to harmful.

What are the implications of workplace relationships for productivity and employee morale? Organizational romance can lead to negative perceptions about your job performance (Pierce, 1998), decreased productivity (Quinn & Lees, 1984; Lowndes, 1993), a loss of trust and decreased communication between coworkers (Horan & Chory, 2009), and diminished credibility (Horan & Chory, 2011). For those employees watching the romance from the sidelines, the relationship may become a distraction, and time and energy is spent focusing on the relationship rather than on issues relevant to work. Consider the climate when relationships between coworkers are terminated. The emo-

tional aftermath has the potential to impact not only those formerly involved in the romance, but also coworkers who are inclined to "take sides." Studies examining the impact of workplace romance have found:

- Employees report that they are more likely to engage in information manipulation by being less honest in disclosures and more likely to engage in deceptive communication with peers who are dating their superiors (Malachowski, Chory, & Claus, 2012).
- Employees perceive peers who date superiors more negatively than peers who date other peers (Horan & Chory, 2011).

The close proximity of work relationships and the difficulty of terminating them and moving on are important considerations when deciding whether to pursue workplace relationships.

INTERPERSONAL EFFECTIVENESS: COMMUNICATION IN WORK RELATIONSHIPS

Many of the communication concepts and theories discussed throughout this text can be applied in our analysis of relationships in the workplace. The study of relationships across communication contexts often requires scholars to apply fundamental concepts in new ways. Concepts such as similarity and attraction can be used to explain the initiation process between friends, colleagues, or romantic partners. Trust and disclosure are fundamental to strengthening relationships regardless of whether the relationships are between coworkers, family members, or friends. Persuasion, listening, and feedback are essential communication tools for organizational effectiveness.

In Chapter 3, we discussed the impact of individual differences. These differences shape our communication behavior in our personal and professional relationships. Effective superiors are almost always seeking ways to enhance organizational effectiveness. While several studies have shown that cognitive ability is a strong predictor of job performance, communication scholars have realized the impact of addressing individual differences in achieving effectiveness. **Organizational orientation** theory identifies three types of individual differences and the approaches used by each to enact their work roles (McCroskey, Richmond, Johnson, & Smith, 2004; See Figure 14.5).

- **Upward mobiles** refers to those members who demonstrate a high level of dedication toward accomplishing the organization's goals. They are easily identified by their demonstrated respect for roles and rules and they are often described as giving "110 percent" to tasks and the organization.

- **Indifferents**, on the other hand, view work as a means to earn a living. They are motivated to work simply to obtain a paycheck, and dedication to the organization is low on their list of personal goals. They are typically reluctant to participate in organizational activities not directly related to their job, and topics of discussion typically revolve around their personal lives rather than work. It should come as no surprise that indifferents make up the majority of organizational orientations at work.

- **Ambivalents** are those who openly express their frustration and focus on issues that need to be changed in the organization. If things fail to be resolved to their satisfaction, they often decide to seek employment elsewhere. In essence, the ambivalent can be described as the employee who is always looking for a better opportunity. The best advice for communicating with ambivalents is to focus on neutral topics to keep the conversation from turning into a gripe session about the organization's weaknesses.

Being able to identify each of these organizational orientations and their expectations for communication can be crucial to identifying effective communication strategies to manage each type of personality.

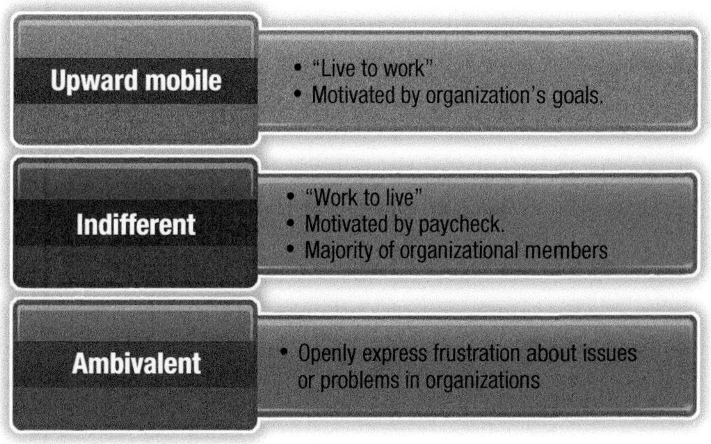

Upward mobile
- "Live to work"
- Motivated by organization's goals.

Indifferent
- "Work to live"
- Motivated by paycheck.
- Majority of organizational members

Ambivalent
- Openly express frustration about issues or problems in organizations

Figure 14.5 Organizational orientations.

ORGANIZATIONAL CULTURE

We introduced the concept of culture in Chapter 12, focusing on how members share common beliefs, values, and attitudes. Organizations can be considered cultures as well; after all, organizations aspire for supervisors and subordinates to share a common vision for the company that is guided by similarities in beliefs and values. Scholars have begun exploring organizational cultures to understand how members construct their organizational realities. **Organizational culture** can defined as the shared systems of symbols, meanings, values, and beliefs that shape and guide behaviors in organizations. To better understand how this meaning is exchanged, researchers have focused their attention on how communicative elements such as stories, language, and rituals are used to help members understand their role in the organization's culture.

Trust and disclosure are fundamental to strengthening relationships regardless of whether the relationships are between coworkers, family members, or friends.

Stories

Organizational members exchange stories about events that have shaped the history of the organization and help provide a rationale for the beliefs and values shared by supervisors and subordinates. An administrative assistant at Wendy's corporate headquarters in Ohio told the following story shared by one of her colleagues to describe how the company's founder, Dave Thomas, interacted with his employees during office visits:

"One day Mr. Thomas came into the office and I was swamped! As the phone was ringing off the hook I greeted him and asked if I could get him a cup of coffee. He smiled and stated that I was the one who was busy and he went to get me a cup of coffee."

The story was used to communicate the value that Dave Thomas had for employees, and how he viewed the organization as a team effort.

Narrative paradigm theory is often used to explain how organizations share information that communicates the values held by an organization. The sharing of these stories is beneficial for building trust among organizational members (Jarvenpaa & Leidner, 1999) and enhancing the cohesiveness among teams (Miner, 2005).

Language

Organizational culture is also shaped by the specialized language, or vocabulary, used by members. This shared language serves to strengthen the bonds between colleagues, sometimes creating a means for distinguishing between members and non-members. For example, students and faculty at Ohio University share a common language to refer to transcripts during the academic advising process. When a faculty member asks a student to bring his DARS (degree audit reporting system) to an advisory meeting, the student knows that he should bring a copy of the transcript. This specialized language helps students, faculty, and staff communicate more efficiently. As you review the examples of technical jargon in Figure 14.6, consider the ways in which this specialized language shapes the culture of an organization.

What types of rituals do the employees at your workplace engage in?

Powerful messages are exchanged through these routine behaviors, and they serve the function of promoting relationships among organizational members.

Android	• Google's mobile operating system
BitTorrent	• Internet file-sharing protocol
Malware	• Malicious software
SEO	• Search Engine Optimization

© Kendall Hunt Publishing Co.

Figure 14.6 Specialized language used in technology industries.

Rituals

Rituals and routines are mechanisms used by organizational members to make sense of their membership. Daily coffee breaks, annual Christmas parties, quarterly employee recognition ceremonies, or even simple greetings used to acknowledge colleagues each morning provide insight as to how members of an organization define their place in the organization.

In a landmark study of organizational rituals and the meanings attributed by members, Roy (1960) describes the strategic use of everyday rituals such as Coke breaks, banana breaks, and opening the window at a particular time to break up the monotony of work at an assembly plant. Because employees spend so much of their time at work, collective attempts are often made by managers or groups of employees to improve employee morale and job satisfaction.

SOCIALIZATION

Just as new members of cultures must assimilate to the different environment, newcomers to an organization experience a similar introductory process to learn information about the expectations for organizational behavior. The following story was shared by an employee in a large consulting firm who described the value of socialization to her success in the organization:

> "I accepted the job offer two weeks before I graduated from college. Boy, was I in for a surprise! There was no syllabus to tell me what was expected and when things were due. I quickly learned that if I wanted to figure out what was expected I better open my eyes and ears and start asking questions."

Jablin (1984) describes the process of organizational **assimilation** as the means by which individuals learn role expectations and what it means to be a member of an organization. Employees may be formally or informally socialized on the expectations of membership. Organizations that conduct formal orientation programs or assign mentors to new employees apply more formal methods for ensuring that employees learn the ropes. Informal socialization may result from an employee joining colleagues for lunch and learning through the sharing of stories that the supervisor sets strict deadlines and gets angry with those who do not meet goals.

Socialization typically evolves through three stages: anticipatory socialization, organizational encounter, and metamorphosis (Jablin 2001). These phases are shown in Figure 14.7. In the **anticipatory socialization phase** new members form expectations regarding their role in the organization. These expectations can be formed as early as childhood, as when a young girl creates beliefs about what it is like to be a lawyer by watching her mother, or they can evolve through research about organizations or through stories portrayed in the media. Once a newcomer enters the organization, the **encounter phase** begins. While technically an employee, the newcomer may find that she may not yet be considered part of the group. Organizations use a variety of formal and informal methods to socialize members

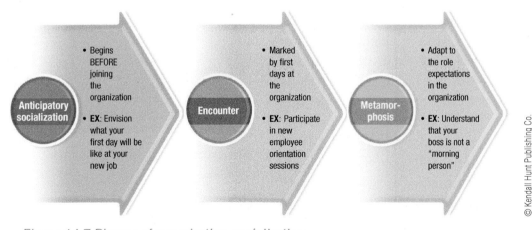

Figure 14.7 Phases of organization socialization.

© Kendall Hunt Publishing Co.

during this phase. Examples may include orientation or training programs, mentoring, and Internet sites designed for employees to seek information. In a study of first-year medical students, friendships with older students were identified as a means for assimilating into and navigating the medical school culture (Zorn & Gregory, 2005). The final stage of socialization, **metamorphosis**, involves changes in the new employee's behavior to adapt to the role expectations in the new environment. At this point, the employee begins to be viewed as an "insider." Unspoken expectations are often discovered during this phase. While a manager may say that attendance at weekly update meetings is optional, an employee may soon learn that important information is shared during these sessions, and managers expect all employees to be present.

CONTEMPORARY ISSUES IN WORK-PLACE RELATIONSHIPS

As we reflect on the changes that have evolved in the ways supervisors, subordinates, and peers communicate with one another in the workplace, contemporary trends become apparent. Interpersonal relationships are the key to organizational success in industries. As the demographics of our work population continue to change, so does our need to address issues that will demand the attention of communication scholars in the twenty-first century. Three areas for focus are: diversity in the workplace, balancing work and family, and the impact of technology on interactions at work.

DIVERSITY IN ORGANIZATIONS

Many organizations have found themselves faced with the task of conducting business with partners from around the world. Globalization has increased the potential for interactions with clients and colleagues from other countries and cultures. Effective communication requires an understanding of cultural differences, and those who understand these differences can avoid embarrassing or insulting others. In Chapter 12 we explored communication concepts designed to enhance interactions across cultural differences. Employers have realized the importance of these concepts as they address the changing face of the workplace. As we consider cultural differences, it is important to note the role of organizational culture that was discussed earlier. As larger corporations buy out smaller organizations, employees from diverse organizational cultures are often expected to not only adapt to one another, but also to be satisfied and productive.

©wavebreakmedia /Shutterstock.com

Increasingly there is a wider age range among employees working together in organizations.

Age diversity has created a new set of issues for organizations. According to a 2014 Gallup report, the average age of retirement for U.S. Americans has increased from 57 in 1993 to 62 in 2014 (Riffkin, 2014). Older employees decide to postpone retirement, and many more have decided to pursue part-time employment after retirement. The result is a wider age range among employees, often with older workers being supervised by those who are younger. This role reversal may produce an uncomfortable situation for employees, with younger managers experiencing reluctance to give orders to their elders.

Effective organizations understand the value of addressing the contributions that diversity can offer. Those of diverse cultural backgrounds can be valuable resources to assist in training others to do business in their native cultures. Managers should recognize the value of diverse backgrounds and viewpoints in brainstorming and decision making, and encourage openness and respect. However, it is important to note that diverse opinions could potentially result in conflict, requiring organizations to explore new approaches to conflict management. As our opportunities for interacting with those around the world increases with the emergence of new technologies and globalization, an organization's success depends on its ability to manage diverse interpersonal relationships.

Communication scholars argue that "training could be the key to unlocking the potential of diversity in the organization" (Gonzalez, Willis, & Young, 1997, p. 290). During the last few years, diversity training has become a "buzz word" in many organizational circles. For this training to be truly effective at building effective interpersonal relationships in the workplace, three steps are required.

- First, members should be encouraged to explore the differences that *do* exist in the workplace. Rather than assume that everyone is similar based on the fact that they chose to become members of the same group, organizations could benefit from encouraging the exploration of differences among coworkers.
- Next, diversity training should address the presence of differences in communication styles and address how these unique approaches impact the organization's goals.
- Finally, training should encourage individuals to identify ways in which cultural differences in communication can be integrated to create a work team that is both cohesive and satisfying.

BALANCING WORK AND FAMILY RELATIONSHIPS

We all strive to achieve balance in our work and family relationships. After all, achieving balance in our personal and professional lives contributes to our self-esteem and relational satisfaction. Our self-esteem is often linked to having well-established roles. When our resources for fulfilling personal roles are limited, stress results and we start to question our identity as a good parent or a productive employee. The struggle appears to be more prevalent among female employees.

So what can organizations do? Employees who perceive their supervisors as being supportive of their efforts to balance work and family often report higher levels of job satisfaction. Some organizations are addressing these issues and pro-

> **Employees who perceive their supervisors as being supportive of their efforts to balance work and family often report higher levels of job satisfaction.**

viding resources to help employees achieve balance in their personal and professional lives. Child and elder care opportunities are provided at some work sites, and options are being made available for flexible work schedules through job sharing, compressed work weeks, and telecommuting.

Achieving balance in our personal and professional lives contributes to our self-esteem and relational satisfaction.

Communication scholars have realized the value of peer, or coworker, relationships and are addressing strategies to assist organizational members in achieving balance in different areas of their lives. Farley-Lucas (2000) discovered that valuable social support can be offered to working mothers through conversations with coworkers about child rearing, and employers who encouraged these dialogues were perceived as being more supportive of working mothers. To understand the strategies used to manage the stress of balancing work and family, Medved (2004) interviewed thirty-four mothers and asked them to describe their "typical" day balancing work and family life. Medved discovered that two types of actions, routinizing and improvising, are used to balance work and family responsibilities and illustrate the role that interpersonal communication plays in effectively managing multiple demands. Table 14.2 summarizes each of the two categories of strategic communication used to manage work-family life balance. **Routinizing actions** incorporate recurring patterns or interactions to plan and organize daily routines. Examples of these communication strategies include the following:

- Women report that they use the communicative strategy of **connecting** to coordinate childcare plans. Daily calls to coordinate schedules with a partner, or contacting the childcare facility to check in on the child are examples of this management strategy.
- **Alternating** involves interactions between parents to exchange tasks in the daily routine. One parent may be responsible for taking the children to school one week and the other parent picks them up after school and takes them to extracurricular activities. The next week, their duties may switch.
- To help alleviate the chaos of morning departures for work, **prepping** is a nightly strategy used to maintain order in the routine. Children may be asked what homework needs to be accomplished each evening, school lunches may be packed in

the evening, and coats and shoes may be lined up next to the door in anticipation of the morning rush to catch the bus.

- **Reciprocating** strategies often involve conversations to coordinate the exchange of childcare issues on a regular basis. Coordinating carpools to sports practice so that a working mother only has to leave work early one evening each week is an example of this strategy.

As much as we like predictability in our lives, there are times when events occur that are beyond our control. In these situations, working mothers may use **improvising action** messages to help coordinate the impromptu or unpredictable demands of balancing work and family. These spur-of-the-moment strategies include:

- **Requesting assistance** and asking others for work accommodations or childcare assistance as a result of last-minute circumstances. A single mother taking college classes may approach an instructor and ask for an extension on an assignment due to the illness of her children, or a neighbor may be asked to watch the children when mom is delayed by a traffic jam.
- **Trading off** is a strategy that involves negotiating responsibilities between spouses when unique situations arise. One spouse may agree to pick up a sick child from school one day with the agreement that the other parent assumes the responsibility the next time the situation arises.

Dual career couples often share responsibility for child-care tasks such as school pick-up.

Table 14.2 Routinization and Improvisation Strategies to Balance Work-Family Demands

ROUTINIZING ACTIONS		
Connecting	Strategy used by working parents to coordinate regular childcare plans	EX: Call childcare provider daily at naptime to check on the child
Alternating	Negotiate "trade-offs" or exchange tasks in the daily routine of childcare	EX: One parent drops child off at school; the other picks up from sports practice
Prepping	Advance communication to maintain order in the daily routine	EX: Laying out clothes and packing lunches for the next day prior to bedtime
Reciprocating	Coordinate favors in exchange for childcare issues on a regular basis	EX: Coordinating carpool schedules with other families
IMPROVISING ACTIONS		
Requesting Assistance	Ask others for work accommodations or childcare assistance as a result of last-minute circumstances	EX: Ask a colleague to cover your shift at work so you can pick up a sick child from school
Trading Off	Negotiate responsibilities between working parents when unique situations arise	EX: Coordinate with your partner to pick up a child today so you can attend an important meeting, then you will resume the normal schedule
Evading	Withhold information, or intentionally deceive others, as a means for managing multiple demands	EX: Claim that you are sick as an excuse for missing work rather than admitting that it is your child who is sick

- A final improvising strategy, *evading*, involves withholding information, or intentionally deceiving others, as a means for managing multiple demands. A mother may decide that it is easier just to call in sick to work rather than risk explaining to her supervisor that she needs to stay home to care for an ill child.

As more women enter the workplace, there will be a greater need for communication scholars to explore how both men and women use communication to balance their relationships at work and at home.

THE IMPACT OF TECHNOLOGY ON WORK RELATIONSHIPS

There is no escaping the impact of technology on how we interact with others at work. Many organizations have replaced live humans at the switchboard with automated voice systems that answer and direct calls. As many as seventy-five percent of business calls do not reach a person—instead, the game of "phone tag" ensues. Email has alleviated some of the frustrations of calling on the phone by providing colleagues with the convenience of asking and answering questions at times that are convenient for them. Some organizations have limited the ability of applicants to interact with a human resources representative by requiring them to submit applications online.

Our work lives have become so busy that many of us depend on smart phones to organize our schedules and to stay connected to work-related tasks away from the office. While these technologies have enabled us to organize our work lives and to enhance our task efficiency, some may question their impact on interpersonal relationships. Indeed, technology has provided employees with the opportunity to telecommute, or to work from home. Individuals report that technology has caused a "blurring of the lines" between their work and personal lives, and this has made the task of balancing these relationships more difficult. Employees report a struggle to establish boundaries between work time and personal time. Decreases in face-to-face contact pose new issues for researchers in understanding the role that technology plays in our interpersonal communication at work.

SUMMARY

Considering the fact that you may spend the majority of your adult life interacting with individuals at work, it is essential that you understand the various types of relationships that are present in the workplace and the accompanying expectations for communication. While we may all aspire to be "the boss" someday, the reality is that we have to "pay our dues" to earn promotions and earn higher status within the workplace. Understanding the relationship dynamics between supervisors and subordinates is essential to our success. In addition, positive relationships with coworkers contribute to employee motivation and satisfaction. After all, we might not necessarily like our jobs, but if we enjoy our interactions with coworkers, often the task becomes a bit more bearable.

Given that so much time is spent at work, it should come as no surprise that friendships evolve and grow in organizations. But like all of our interpersonal relationships, these friendships are not without issues that need to be addressed. Dialectical tensions can emerge and create a struggle between professionalism and friendship. As our workplaces become increasingly diverse, the communication issues to be addressed will change. Technology will continue to change the way that we work and the ways in which we interact with those at work. In essence, your ability to build effective interpersonal relationships at work just might make the difference between waking up and looking forward to your job each morning, or wishing that you could stay at home.

DISCUSSION QUESTIONS

1. Interview a manager in either a large or mid-sized organization and ask some of the following questions: (1) How much of your day is devoted to dealing with relationship or communication problems or issues? (2) Provide examples of typical relationship-type issues that you had to manage and how you addressed this situation. (3) How important are peer relationships to your employees? (4) What does your organization do to help foster healthy peer relationships?

2. Conduct research on some of the ways that organizations are addressing the issues addressed in this chapter (e.g., sexual harassment, dating in the workplace, impact of technology on communication, diversity in the workplace and work life balance). What are the organization's policies, procedures, and opinions on these issues? How do the organizations that are recognized as some of "The Best Places to Work in the U.S." address these issues?

3. Reflect on your socialization experiences as a new member of your college or university. What messages did you receive from others to assist you in building effective relationships with peers and instructors?

SELF ASSESSMENT

Organizational Orientations

Organizational Orientations are trait-like ways that people approach work in contemporary organizations. The measures reported below are designed to measure the degree to which an individual employs one or more of these orientations in their own work environment.

Upward Mobile Orientation Measure

Instructions: Please indicate the degree to which you agree or disagree with each of the statements below by recording your response in the space before each item. Use the following response options: **5 = Strongly Agree; 4 = Agree; 3 = Undecided; 2 = Disagree; 1 = Strongly Disagree.**

_____ 1. I generally try my best to do what an organization I work for wants me to do.

_____ 2. If I had the choice, I would take a promotion over the acceptance of my peers any time.

_____ 3. One of my goals is to get a good job and excel at it.

_____ 4. Eventually, I would like to be the "big boss" in an organization.

_____ 5. I firmly believe that if I work hard enough, one day I will be right up at the top.

_____ 6. I am good at my job and I love it.

_____ 7. Most of all, I really want to be recognized for the excellent work I do.

_____ 8. *I think moving up in an organization is not worth all the work you have to do.

_____ 9. Sometimes I think I am a "workaholic."

_____ 10. I want a job where what I do really counts for something.

_____ 11. Everyone tells me I am a really good worker.

_____ 12. I want work which has a lot of intangible rewards.

_____ 13. Ordinarily, I feel good about what I have accomplished when I am done with my day's work.

_____ 14. I would be willing to work hard to be the top person in an organization.

_____ 15. Since I am really good at what I do, I will move up in the organization.

_____ 16. What I want most in a job is the possibility of really doing something important.

_____ 17. Any job worth doing is worth doing as well as I can.

_____ 18. I am a very creative worker.

* Reverse scoring.

Ambivalent Orientation Measure

Instructions: Please indicate the degree to which you agree or disagree with each of the statements below by recording your response in the space before each item. Use the following response options: **5 = Strongly Agree; 4 = Agree; 3 = Undecided; 2 = Disagree; 1 = Strongly Disagree.**

_____ 1. Other than a paycheck, the organizations I have worked for have had little to offer me.

_____ 2. The product/service produced by organizations where I have worked are of very low quality.

_____ 3. *I have generally been quite satisfied with jobs I have had.

_____ 4. The organizations I have worked for couldn't care less whether I live or die--and I feel the same way about them.

_____ 5. I really dislike the rules and regulations I am forced to live with in organizations.

_____ 6. I am usually unhappy wherever I work.

_____ 7. Everywhere I have worked, I have had an incompetent supervisor.

_____ 8. Wherever I work, I wish I were working somewhere, almost anywhere, else than where I am.

_____ 9. *The procedures and regulations of organizations I have worked for have generally been quite reasonable.

_____ 10. I find it difficult to adapt to the demands of most organizations.

_____ 11. Generally, I don't like the rules that organizations make me follow.

_____ 12. I don't really like most of the people I have worked with.

_____ 13. *I have worked for really good organizations.

_____ 14. Most organizations have unreasonable expectations for workers like me.

_____ 15. Most of the time, a halfhearted effort is all I feel I need to give in a job.

_____ 16. I really hate most organizations I have worked for.

_____ 17. One supervisor is about like any other, a pain in the backside.

_____ 18. What I want most in a job is to be left alone.

_____ 19. Frankly, I am smarter than most of the people I have worked for.

_____ 20. I have been unhappy just about everywhere I have worked.

* Reverse scoring.

Indifferent Orientation Measure

Instructions: Please indicate the degree to which you agree or disagree with each of the statements below by recording your response in the space before each item. Use the following response options: **5 = Strongly Agree; 4 = Agree; 3 = Undecided; 2 = Disagree; 1 = Strongly Disagree.**

_____ 1. My life begins when I get off work.

_____ 2. If I were offered a job that paid better, I would take it in a "New York Minute."

_____ 3. A job is a job--everyone has to work somewhere.

_____ 4. I am generally indifferent to where I work. One job is about the same as another.

_____ 5. Generally, I just do as much as is required by my job.

_____ 6. Since I am entitled to them, I take all of my sick days whether I am sick or not.

_____ 7. I don't much care where I work, so long as the pay is good.

_____ 8. When work is over, life begins.

_____ 9. One job is pretty much like any other job.

_____ 10. If I found out the organization I worked for was in trouble, I would quickly look for a job in another organization.

_____ 11. Work is something I have to do, not something I want to do.

_____ 12. When it comes to choosing a job, "show me the money!"

Source: McCroskey, J. C., Richmond, V. P., Johnson, A. D., & Smith, H. T. 2004. Organizational orientations theory and measurement: Development of measures and preliminary investigations. *Communication Quarterly,* 52, 1-14.

KEY TERMS AND DEFINITIONS

ALTERNATING: involves interactions between working spouses to negotiate "trade-offs" or exchange tasks in the daily routine of childcare.

AMBIVALENTS: openly express their frustration and focus on issues that need to be changed in the organization. May decide to leave organization if things are not resolved.

ANTICIPATORY SOCIALIZATION PHASE: socialization phase in which new members form expectations regarding their role in the organization before officially becoming a part of the organization.

ASSIMILATION: means by which individuals learn role expectations and what it means to be a member of an organization.

CHEERLEADER MENTOR: a mentor who provides encouragement to an organizational member; openly expresses pride resulting from the protégé's success.

CLASSICAL THEORIES: proposed that communication is primarily one-way from upper-levels to lower-levels. Messages tend to be formal and task-focused.

CONNECTING: strategy used by working parents to coordinate regular childcare plans.

COWORKER (PEER) RELATIONSHIPS: workplace relationships that evolve as a result of interactions between members of the same status level.

ENCOUNTER PHASE: socialization phase marked by the initial days as an organizational member. May include socialization methods such as orientation programs or mentoring.

EQUALITY/INEQUALITY: dialectical tension experienced by friends in organizations in which role status results in inherent or perceived inequalities among friends.

EVADING: withholding information, or intentionally deceiving others, as a means for managing multiple demands of work-family life.

FLAT STRUCTURE: few hierarchical levels separating organizational administrators from employees.

FLIRTING: goal-motivated communicative behaviors that may accurately or inaccurately be interpreted as indicating sexual interest.

FORMAL MENTORING: involuntary, or assigned, mentoring partnerships which may involve written agreements or guidelines to address the expectations for each person.

GROOM MENTOR: a mentor who holds a position of power in an organization and is "grooming" or preparing a protégé for specific responsibilities or roles.

GUILT-TRIP PRODUCER MENTOR: motivates a protégé by communicating messages of disappointment when performance fails to meet expectations.

HOSTILE WORK ENVIRONMENT: a type of sexual harassment that may include the sharing of sexual jokes or materials in front of other employees, or ongoing unwanted sexual behavior from a coworker.

HUMAN RELATIONS: theoretical approach that emphasizes the important of social relationships and informal communication in organizations.

HUMAN RESOURCES: theoretical approach that focuses on multi-directional communication in organizations; emphasis on both task and relationship messages.

IMPARTIALITY/FAVORITISM: dialectical tensions experienced by friends in organizations in which status differentials result in conflicting desires to be fair to all employees or show preferential treatment to employees with whom they are friends.

IMPROVISING ACTION: messages to help coordinate the impromptu or unpredictable demands of balancing work and family.

INDIFFERENTS: view work as a means to earn a living. Dedication to the organization is low on their list of personal goals or priorities.

INFORMAL MENTORING: voluntary partnerships in which organizational members solicit advice, guidance, or support. Typically formed on the basis of similarities.

INVOLUNTARY RELATIONSHIPS: exist between organizational members who did not have a choice or a voice in the decision to work with one another.

JUDGMENT/ACCEPTANCE: dialectical tension experienced by friends in the workplace in which the desire to provide acceptance and support to one another without judgment is in tension with assessing one another's work or performance.

LEADER-MEMBER EXCHANGE THEORY (LMX): qualitative differences in relationships formed between leaders and members as a result of communication.

MENTOR RELATIONSHIPS: more experienced members serve as role models, teachers, or guides for colleagues who are less experienced.

METAMORPHOSIS: socialization phase that involves changes in the new employee's behavior to adapt to the role expectations in the new environment. Employee begins to be viewed as an "insider."

NARRATIVE PARADIGM THEORY: explains how organizations share information that communicates the values held by an organization.

ORGANIZATIONAL CULTURE: shared systems of symbols, meanings, values, and beliefs that shape and guide behaviors in organizations.

ORGANIZATIONAL ORIENTATION: theory that explains three types of individual differences and the approaches used by each to enact work roles.

PARENT MENTOR: a mentor who is considered to be "older and wiser" as a result of his or her tenure in the organization.

PREPPING: nightly communication by working parents to prepare for childcare needs and to maintain order in the daily routine.

QUID PRO QUO HARASSMENT: a form of sexual harassment in which one member of an organization makes promises or threats in exchange for a sexual relationship.

RECIPROCATING: conversations to assist working parents in coordinating the exchange of childcare issues on a regular basis.

REQUESTING ASSISTANCE: asking others for work accommodations or childcare assistance as a result of last-minute circumstances.

ROUTINIZING ACTIONS: recurring communication patterns or interactions that are used to plan and organize daily routines to assist parents in balancing the demands of work-family life.

SCIENTIFIC MANAGEMENT THEORY: approach that emphasized the distinct differences between managers and employees. Manager's role is to direct and plan workers to complete tasks the "correct way." Communication is top-down.

SELF-PROMOTER MENTORS: those mentors who want to work with the best new members in order to surround themselves with high-quality colleagues.

SEXUAL HARASSMENT: verbal or physical conduct of a sexual nature that causes coworkers to feel uncomfortable.

SUPERIOR-SUBORDINATE RELATIONSHIP: workplace interactions characterized by a status differential between individuals.

TALL STRUCTURE: organizational hierarchy that includes many levels of administration and reporting units.

TEMPORARY RELATIONSHIPS: refers to the short-lived nature of some workplace relationships. Employees have the option of maintaining or terminating workplace relationships due to reassignment of tasks or relocation to another job.

TRADING OFF: alternating or negotiating responsibilities between working spouses when unique situations associated with childcare arise.

UPWARD MOBILES: organizational members who demonstrate a high level of dedication toward accomplishing the organization's goals. Characterized by their respect for roles and rules.

VOLUNTARY RELATIONSHIPS: refers to the notion that individuals have the choice to interview with an organization and, if offered a job, they have a choice of whether to accept the position.

WORK SPOUSE: non-romantic relationships in the workplace in which coworkers provide support and candor similar to that typically provided by a spouse.

REFERENCES

Baker, C., R., & Omilion-Hodges, L. M. (2013). The effect of leader-member exchange differentiation within work units on coworker exchange and organizational citizenship behaviors. *Communication Research Reports, 30*(4), 313–322.

Berryman-Fink, C. (1997). Gender issues: Management style, mobility and harassment. In P. Y. Byers (Ed.), *Organizational communication: Theory and behavior* (259–283). Boston, MA: Allyn and Bacon.

Bridge, K., & Baxter, L. A. (1992). Blended relationships: Friends as work associates. *Western Journal of Communication, 56*, 200–225.

Dansereau, F., Graen, G. B., & Haga, W. (1975). A vertical linkage dyad approach to leadership within formal organizations: A longitudinal investigation of the role making process. *Behavior and Human Performance, 13*, 46–78.

DeWine, S., Casebolt, D., & Bentley, N. (1983). Moving through the organization: A field study assessment of the patron system. Paper presented at the International Communication Association, Dallas, TX.

Farley-Lucas, B. (2000). Communicating the (in) visibility of motherhood: Family talk and the ties to motherhood within the workplace. *The Electronic Journal of Communication, 10*. Available: *http://www.cios.org/www.ejcrec2.htm.*

Fine, G. A. (1986). Friendships in the work place. In V. J. Derlega and B. A. Winstead (Eds.), *Friendship and social interaction* (185–206). New York: Springer-Verlag.

Fix, B. & Sias, P. M. (2006). Person-centered communication, leader-member exchange, and employee job satisfaction. *Communication Research Reports, 23*(1), 35–44.

Gonzalez, A., Willis, J., & Young, C. R. (1997). Cultural diversity and organizations. In P. Y. Byers (Ed.), *Organizational communication: Theory and behavior.* (284–304). Boston, MA: Allyn and Bacon.

Graen, G. B. (1976). Role-making processes within complex organizations. In M. D. Dunnette (Ed.), *Handbook of industrial and organizational psychology* (1201–1245). Chicago, IL: Rand McNally.

Henningsen, D. D., Braz, M. E., & Davies, E. (2008). Why do we flirt? Flirting motivations and sex differences in working and social contexts. *Journal of Business Communication, 45*, 483–502.

Horan, S. M., & Chory, R. M. (2009). When work and love mix: Perceptions of peers in workplace romances. *Western Journal of Communication, 73*, 349–369.

Horan, S. M., & Chory, R. M. (2011). Understanding work/life blending: Credibility implications for those who date at work. *Communication Studies, 62*, 563-580.

Jablin, F. M. (1984). Assimilating new members into organizations. In R. N. Bostrom, (Ed.), *Communication yearbook 8.* Beverly Hills, CA: Sage Publications.

Jablin, F. M. (2001). Organizational entry, assimilation, and disengagement/exit. In F. M. Jablin & L. L. Putnam, (Eds.), *The new handbook of organizational communication* (732–818). Thousand Oaks, CA: Sage Publications.

Jarvenpaa, S. L., & Leidner, D. E. (1999). Communication and trust in global virtual teams. *Organization Science, 10,* 791–815.

Keyton, J. & Rhodes, S. C. (1999). Organizational sexual harassment: Translating research into application. *Journal of Applied Communication Research, 27,* 158–173.

Lowndes, L. (1993). Dangerous office liaisons. *Legal Assistant Today,* 64–70.

Madlock, P. E., & Booth-Butterfield, M. (2012). The influence of relational maintenance strategies among coworkers. *Journal of Business Communication, 49*(1), 21-47.

Malachowski, C. C., Chory, R. M., & Claus, C. J. (2012). Mixing pleasure with work: Employee perceptions of and responses to workplace romance. *Western Journal of Communication, 76*(4), 358–379.

Maslow, A. H. (1943). A theory of human motivation. *Psychology Review, 50,* 370–396.

McCroskey, J. C., Richmond, V. P., Johnson, A. D., & Smith, H. T. (2004). Organizational orientations theory and measurement: Development of measures and preliminary investigations. *Communication Quarterly, 52,* 1–14.

Medved, C. (2004). The everyday accomplishment of work and family: Exploring practical actions in daily routines. *Communication Studies, 55,* 128–145.

Miner, J. B. (Ed.). (2005). *Organizational behavior 1: Essential theories of motivation and leadership.* London, UK: M. E. Sharpe.

Monge, P. R., & Kirste, K. K. (1980). Measuring proximity in human organizations. *Social Psychology Quarterly, 43,* 110–115.

NLS FAQs. (2015). Retrieved June 1, 2015, from http://www.bls.gov/nls/nlsfaqs.htm#anch41.

Odden, C. M., & Sias, P. M. (1997). Peer communication relationships and psychological climate. *Communication Quarterly, 45,* 153–166.

Quinn, R. E., & Lees, P. L. (1984). Attraction and harassment: Dynamics of sexual politics in the workplace. *Organizational Dynamics, 13,* 35–46.

Ragins, B. R., & Cotton, J. L. (1991). Easier said than done: Gender differences in perceived barriers to gaining a mentor. *Academy of Management Journal, 34,* 939–951.

Riffkin, R. (2014). *Average U.S. retirement age rises to 62.* US: Gallup. Retrieved from http://www.gallup.com/poll/168707/average-retirement-age-rises.aspx

Roy, D. (1960). Banana time: Job satisfaction and informal interaction. *Human Organization, 18,* 158–168.

Sias, P. M., & Cahill, D. J. (1998). From co-workers to friends: The development of peer friendships in the workplace. *Western Journal of Communication, 62,* 279–299.

Sias, P. M., & Jablin, F. (1995). Differential superior-subordinate relations, perceptions of fairness, and coworker communication. *Human Communication Research, 22,* 5–38.

Sias, P. M., Krone, K. K., & Jablin, F. M. (2002). An ecological systems perspective on workplace relationships. In J. Day & M. L. Knapp (Eds.), *Handbook of interpersonal communication* (3/e, pp. 615–642). Newbury Park, CA: Sage.

Taylor, F. W. (1911). *The principles of scientific management.* New York: Harper & Row.

Turban, D. B., & Jones, A. P. (1988). Supervisor-subordinate similarity: Types, effects and mechanisms. *Journal of Applied Psychology, 73,* 234–238.

VanEmmerick, I. J. (2004). For better and for worse: Adverse working conditions and the beneficial effects of mentoring. *Career Development International, 9,* 358–373.

Weissmann, J. (2014, September 11). Americans, ever hateful of leisure, are more likely to work nights and weekends. *Slate.* Retrieved from http://www.slate.com/blogs/moneybox/2014/09/11/u_s_work_life_balance_americans_are_more_likely_to_work_nights_and_weekends.html

Zorn, T. E., & Gregory, K. W. (2005). Learning the ropes together: Assimilation and friendship among first-year medical students. *Health Communication 17*(3), 211–31.

chapter

15

Health Communication:
Using Effective Communication to Manage Stressful Interactions

OBJECTIVES

- State the definition of stress, stressors, and coping.

- Explain emotion-focused and problem-focused coping.

- Define health communication.

- State several potential outcomes of ineffective physician-patient communication.

- Describe at least five suggestions for improving health care provider-patient communication and relationships.

- Explain the stages of death and dying and provide an example of typical communication in each stage.

- Define comforting communication and describe the least and most effective types of comforting messages.

- Discuss effective and ineffective ways to communicate with someone who is terminally ill or recently lost a loved one.

SCENARIO: SOUND FAMILIAR?

Allison was at the student health center again. Her roommates all had the flu, and she was quite sure that she had it as well. Even though she'd visited the health center at least ten times this semester, she was still nervous about talking with the physician. As she sat waiting for the doctor in one of the exam rooms, she realized she was going to have to cancel her appointment at the counseling center today and call in sick for work because the doctor was running late. She was upset about missing her counseling appointment because she really needed to talk with someone about how overwhelmed she felt this semester. If her loan did not come through in the next week, she might have to take a semester off from school and work full-time. She did not even want to look at her phone to see the 50 text messages she had received. At least 45 of them were from her mother!

OVERVIEW

Do Allison's problems sound familiar to you? A survey of over 200,000 incoming full-time college students was conducted to determine how the emotional health and stress levels of students in 2010 compared to students in 1985 (Pryor, Hurtado, DeAngelo, Blake, & Tran, 2011). Results of the survey were quite discouraging and illustrated the changes in college students' lifestyles and well-being: "Self-rated emotional health for incoming first-year students is at the lowest point since we first asked the questions 25 years ago in 1985" (Pryor et al., 2011, p. 1). College students, and especially female students, report feeling more overwhelmed by their responsibilities than those surveyed in the past. While there are numerous factors that explain this dramatic increase in college students' stress levels, one of the most significant stressors is the cost of attending college today compared to 25 years ago. More students, like Allison in the scenario at the beginning of this chapter, are taking out loans and receiving grants or scholarships to attend college, and this places additional pressure on today's students. In this chapter, we describe other types of stressors that are unique to college students and offer suggestions for managing stress.

First, we take a closer look at stress and how it affects young adults. It is important to understand what stress is, how to know when you are experiencing stress (i.e., signs and symptoms), and productive ways of coping with stress. After providing a general overview of stress, the next sections of the chapter focus on specific situations that most people find stressful: communicating with health care providers and communicating about death and dying.

To become a more competent communicator, it is important to learn more about why these types of interactions are difficult for most people. Since most of us will likely encounter these interactions, it is important to understand and control our fears to better manage these situations. In this chapter we present research on these topics to help you understand why people find these conversations to be difficult and offer suggestions to improve communication in each of these situations. For each of the challenging areas, the following questions are addressed: (1) Why do these situations often produce stress or anxiety for one or both of the interactants, (2) What are some typical responses or reactions to these situations, and (3) How can we improve communication in these situations? First, we take a closer look at stress and related concepts.

OVERVIEW OF STRESS, STRESSORS, AND SIGNS OF STRESS

Stress is defined as "the experience of a perceived threat (real or imagined) to one's mental, physical, or spiritual well-being, resulting from a series of physiological responses and adaptations" (Seaward, 2012, p. 3). Today, it is common to hear friends, family members, classmates, or coworkers say, "I am so stressed out." However, this has not always been the case (Seaward, 2012). The "stress phenomenon" is a relatively new occurrence, and its effects have changed dramatically over the years. Ask your parents and grandparents how often they recall saying that they were "stressed out" when they were your age. In the past, feeling stressed or anxious was essential to human survival. Today, stress is often described as a "killer" that is associated with heart disease, cancer, lung ailments, accidents, cirrhosis, and suicide (Seaward, 2012).

It is important to take a closer look at the causes of stress, known as stressors, as well as the signs or symptoms of stress. According to Seaward (2012), a **stressor** is any particular situation or event that causes stress. Indeed, there are an infinite number of potential events or circumstances that could be identified as stressors. People vary greatly in their perceptions of events that they label stressful. For example, you may think that riding a rollercoaster is fun and exciting while your friend labels that activity as stressful. There are different types of stressors. For example, **rapid-onset stressors** are situations or events that occur suddenly, like losing your phone or being in a car accident. **Chronic stressors** are those situations or circumstances that we have to manage daily, such as a poor work environment or an unhealthy relationship. While people seem to recover quickly from rapid-onset stressors, exposure to chronic stressors affects the body over time (Seaward, 2012).

Feeling stressed out seems to be a way of life for many.

The "stress phenomenon" is a relatively new occurrence, and its effects have changed dramatically over the years.

College students face unique stressors that can be managed with effective communication practices. For each of these common stressors, there are a number of specific communication skills addressed in this textbook that can be used to reduce stress and improve outcomes in these situations:

- *Roommate communication challenges*: disagreements between roommates are common. To manage these situations, apply the following skills: assertiveness (Chapter 10), listening (Chapter 4), and conflict management (Chapter 8).
- *Career decisions*: college students experience stress when selecting majors and deciding what career they want to pursue. College students need to seek out resources on campus such as advisors, career center staff, professors, and other students to help them make these decisions. To manage these situations, apply the following skills: assertiveness (Chapter 10) and asking questions and listening (Chapter 4).
- *Friendships and intimate relationships*: college students establish a number of close bonds that provide them with companion-

ship and social support. Maintaining these relationships is not always easy. We hope that chapters on initiating relationships (Chapter 7), maintaining relationships (Chapter 8), dark communication (Chapter 9), and terminating relationships (Chapter 10) will help you navigate relationship stressors that you might experience.

STRESS SIGNS AND SYMPTOMS

Cognitive Symptoms
- Memory problems
- Inability to concentrate
- Poor judgment
- Seeing only the negative

Emotional Symptoms
- Moodiness
- Irritability or short temper
- Agitation, inability to relax

Physical Symptoms
- Aches and pains
- Diarrhea or constipation
- Nausea, dizziness

Behavioral Symptoms
- Eating more or less
- Sleeping too much or too little
- Isolating yourself from others

Visit Helpguide.org to take a stress test that will help you determine how stressed you feel. According to Helpguide.org these symptoms may be associated with other psychological or medical problems. It is important to visit a physician to talk about these symptoms if you are concerned.

Other common stressors that college students experience include financial aid and school loans, budgeting finances, lifestyle choices, and exploring sexuality (Seaward, 2012). We hope this textbook provides you with the interpersonal communication skills needed to manage all of the unique stressors you face throughout college.

How do you know when you are stressed out? According to the American Institute of Stress, there are 50 common signs and symptoms of stress. These signs can include, among others: frequent headaches, grinding teeth, stuttering or stammering, neck pain, and dry mouth (www.stress.org). See the textbox to the left for a list of different types of symptoms. When people experience more of these different types of symptoms, they also tend to feel more stressed or overloaded.

Now that you know what stress is as well as its causes, we turn our attention to research that focuses on how to cope effectively with stress.

© kryzhov/Shutterstock.com

It is important to recognize the cognitive, emotional, physical and behavioral signs of stress.

STRESS AND COPING

To manage stressful situations, individuals apply different types of coping strategies. **Coping** is defined as a response to something novel or to changes in one's environment or relationships (Infante, Rancer, & Avtgis, 2009). **Coping strategies** are the specific behaviors or messages enacted to manage emotions associated with the stressful or novel situation. There is a significant amount of research on how individuals cope with adversity and whether certain types of coping strategies are more effective than others in reducing negative affective states (Folkman, Lazarus, Dunkel-Schetter, DeLongis, & Gruen, 1986; O'Brien, DeLongis, Pomaki, Putterman, & Zwicker, 2009; Riley & Park, 2014). The most widely used explanation of how individuals cope is the **two-function model of coping** (Riley & Park, 2014). According to this model, individuals employ either problem-focused or emotion-focused methods of coping in difficult situations. **Problem-focused coping** involves changing the situation or fixing the problem while **emotion-focused coping** "involves processing and expressing feelings arising from the stressor" (Riley & Park, 2014, p. 588).

Researchers have compared the effectiveness of problem-focused and emotion-focused coping methods in reducing stress. Not surprisingly, the type of coping method applied depends on the situation. When individuals perceive that they have more control over the situation, problem-focused coping is more effective than emotion-focused coping (Lazarus & Folkman, 1984; Riley & Park, 2014). Problem-focused coping or solution-oriented coping strategies seem to work well with specific types of stressors. For example, if your work schedule is causing stress for you and eating into your school time, you might use an appropriately assertive response (ERA-empathy, rationale, action) to communicate with your manager and reduce the number of hours you work. In general, problem-focused coping strategies have been associated with lower amounts of physiological and psychological stress than emotion-focused coping (Riley & Park, 2014). College students who employ problem-focused coping strategies tend to be more optimistic and resilient (Sarid, Anson, Yaari, & Margalith, 2004). Avoiding stressors or putting tasks off that most students find stressful, such as writing papers or dealing with a roommate conflict, often results in greater amounts of stress for college students (Chao, 2011).

What are the strategies you use to cope with stress?

Emotion-focused coping strategies address the affective responses that people experience in stressful or difficult situations. These coping strategies are varied and while some strategies might help in managing affective responses to situations, others could make the situation worse. For example, individuals might engage in maladaptive emotion-focused coping strategies such as binge drinking or overeating in response to situations that evoke anger, sadness, or anxiety. On the other hand, using an emotion-focused coping strategy, such as reframing, could help individuals manage stress more effectively. **Reframing** involves viewing the problem or stressor in a different manner. Instead of labeling a situation such as taking an exam as "stressful," the individual might reframe it as "personally challenging." If you are someone who likes challenges, then reframing a test as a challenge can help you manage the emotional response to this event (Scott, 2015). Other effective ways to manage stress include: meditation, journaling, positive thinking, and spending time with your friends.

More recently, researchers have pointed out the significance of social support in managing stress. In the next sections we explain social support and describe its significance for individuals and relationships. See the textbox below for research on the relationships among stress, social support, and coping.

SOCIAL SUPPORT

Social support can include a wide range of activities but often refers to the resources people have available to provide them with assistance during times of adversity (duPré, 2009). These resources include individuals who are not counselors but who provide support through informal support groups or personal relationships. Resources might include relationships such as friends, family members, coworkers, classmates, neighbors, or members of religious groups. In times of stress or adversity, what is most important is that people *believe* they have resources available to them to offer the support they need. The perception of social support has been repeatedly proven to be more important than actual social support received in relationship to mental and physical well-being (Cohen & Willis, 1985). If individuals do not think that they can talk to friends or family members during stressful or difficult times, then these resources cannot be utilized to cope (Malinauskas, 2010).

Social support resources might include relationships such as friends, family members, coworkers, classmates, neighbors, or members of religious groups.

Perceived social support has been linked to numerous positive outcomes such as mental and physical health (Merianos, Nabors, Vidourek, & King, 2013), life satisfaction (Brannan, Biswas-Diener, Mohr, Mortazavi, & Stein, 2013), and decreased mortality (Barger, 2013). When individuals feel they have the support they need from their friends, family members, relationship partners, etc., they report greater physical and mental health, greater life satisfaction, and they are likely to live longer. Research on social support consistently demonstrates that individuals benefit greatly from knowing they have others whom they can count on in times of need.

Not surprisingly, college students adjust better to college life when they have support from their family members (Jenkins, Belanger, Connally, Boals, & Durón, 2013). Jenkins et al. (2013) found that first-generation college students report less support from family members than non-first-generation college students. While there are a number of significant cultural and socioeconomic factors that explain differences in first-generation and non-first-generation students' college experiences, another issue is a lack of ongoing communication between first-generation college students and parents. First-generation students often refrain from sharing college stressors with their parents, which affects the amount of social support they receive (Jenkins et al., 2013). First-generation students might feel that their parents would not be able to relate to the problems they experience at school because they did not attend college. In addition, parents of first-generation students, who often come from racial and ethnic minority cultures or from lower socioeconomic status, must deal regularly with a wide range of stressors that might limit the amount of support they can provide to their children in college. On the other hand, too much parental support can also be detrimental in different ways for college students. Read the textbox on the next page to learn more about helicopter parents and the effects of over-controlling parents on college students' well-being.

In addition to college-specific stressors, individuals face a variety of situations in life that evoke stress responses. In the next section we take a closer look at interpersonal communication in health and bereavement situations. Both of these situations offer a variety of challenges for communicators.

In times of stress or adversity, what is most important is that people *believe* they have resources available to them to offer the support they need.

COMMUNICATION BETWEEN PHYSICIANS AND PATIENTS

Researchers from a variety of academic fields are fascinated with physician-patient communication and have been studying it extensively for quite some time (Ainsworth-Vaughn, 1998; Burgoon et al., 1987; Burgoon et al., 1990a; Burgoon et al. 1990b; Kreps & Thorton, 1992; Thompson, 1986; Smith, 2013). Interpersonal scholars interested in physician-patient communication study an area called **health communication**, "an area of study concerned with human interaction in the health care process" (Kreps & Thorton, 1992, p. 2). Interpersonal researchers study communication in health care settings by examining verbal and non-verbal messages exchanged between health care providers and patients, and the outcomes of these interactions. Health communication scholars have been particularly interested in research areas such as physician-patient communication and patient compliance (Burgoon et al., 1987; Burgoon et al., 1990a; Burgoon et al., 1990b), physician and health care provider communication practices as they relate to patient satisfaction (Wanzer, Booth-Butterfield, & Gruber, 2004), health literacy and health care provider communication (Leung, Cheung & Chi, 2014), and the impact of patient anxiety on physician-patient interactions (Richmond, Smith, Heisel, & McCroskey, 2001).

Communication researchers study health care provider-patient interactions for a variety of reasons. By studying interactions between health care providers and patients, researchers learn more about why patients are anxious and can determine how to reduce this anxiety to improve communication and patient compliance (Thompson, 1986). Patient anxiety often acts as a substantial barrier that can inhibit patients' communication with their health care providers. Booth-Butterfield (2006) and others (Richmond et al., 2001; Thompson, 1986) noted that patients' communication anxiety can create serious problems for the patient and the physician/health care provider. Patients with high communication anxiety might avoid making appointments with their doctors even when they have symptoms of a health problem. Also, when highly apprehensive patients finally do visit their physicians, they are more likely to rush through their appointments and to refrain from asking questions or seeking additional necessary information (Booth-Butterfield, Chory, & Benyon, 1997). Not surprisingly, patients with higher communication apprehension tend to be less satisfied with their physicians and the medical care received (Richmond et al., 2001). When patients and physicians do not establish a "good doctor-patient relationship," patients are much more likely to sue their health care providers (Ostrum, 2004).

If patients feel less anxious, they are more likely to have satisfying relationships with their physicians.

There are often physiological signs that indicate that patients are anxious about visiting their physicians. While some medical professionals say there is no real explanation for the "white coat effect," also referred to as white coat hypertension (WCHT), patients often experience surges in their blood pressure during visits to their doctors' offices. WCHT is said to happen when a patient's blood pressure is higher than normal in the doctor's office but within normal range at home (Celis & Fagard, 2004). Many medical professionals suspect that their white coats may trigger anxiety in patients, leading to increases in blood pressure.

To determine your level of fear about visiting the physician, complete the Fear of Physician scale at the end of the chapter. Scores on this scale may help you determine just how anxious you are about visiting your health care provider. Read on to determine steps that you can take to make the most out of your doctor visits.

Problems with Physician Communication

People often report experiencing a great deal of anxiety about visits to physicians. In one study, 85 percent of patients indicated feeling quite distressed when they had to visit their physician (Bertakis, Roter, & Putnam, 1991). Why is this often the case? Some reasons patients cite for not wanting to visit the physician are obvious ones: they might receive bad news about their health, be subjected to painful procedures or tests, or feel embarrassed. Other reasons patients might give for feeling stressed include: (1) patient did not adhere to the physician's recommendations (e.g., lose weight, quit smoking, etc.), (2) patient does not want to talk about private or personal issues (e.g., number of sexual partners, "gyn

More recently, there is greater emphasis on communication between physicians and patients, with many physicians participating in communication skills training during medical school and beyond.

apprehension"), and (3) patient feels exposed during the examination when wearing the always popular and very attractive medical gowns.

Patient anxiety may also be explained by the physician's lack of supportive, patient-centered communication practices. In one study trained coders observed residents' interactions with patients and noted that 38 percent of the physicians did not specify the amount of medicine they prescribed and 50 percent did not indicate the length of treatment (Falvo & Tippy, 1988). In a related study, physicians often interrupted (Beckman & Frankel, 1984) when patients were attempting to express concerns to them. Beckman and Frankel (1984) found that physicians, on average, only allowed patients 18 seconds to express themselves and self-disclose information before interrupting them. In an article in the online version of the *Seattle Times*, patients stated that the main reason they sued their health care provider when problems occurred "was because their health professionals showed no concern, warmth, wouldn't listen, or wouldn't talk or wouldn't answer questions" (Ostrum, 2004, p. 2).

More recently, there is greater emphasis on communication between physicians and patients, with many physicians participating in communication skills training during medical school and beyond. Researchers conducted a systematic review of different communication skills programs for physicians to determine which types were the most effective (Berkhof et al., 2011). Successful physician training programs were those that last for at least one day, were learner-centered in their approach, and focused on practicing specific communication skills. Role-play, feedback, and small group instructional strategies worked the best to help physicians improve their communication skills with patients and family members (Berkhof et al., 2011). It is likely that patients would also benefit from these types of instructional strategies in learning to communicate more effectively with their health care providers.

Patient Communication

In targeting physicians' lack of communication skills, we are only addressing part of the problem. Researchers and health care providers agree that patients could also improve their communication practices during health care visits and, at the same time, make a greater effort to adhere to their health care providers' requests as a means of improving relationships and patient outcomes (Cegala, Gade, Broz, & McClure, 2004).

As defined in Chapter 1, and discussed throughout this text, interpersonal communication is a transaction that occurs between two individuals. The patient also has the potential to either contribute to or detract from the quality of the patient-physician relationship. One of the most significant and frequently cited ways the patient can affect the patient-physician relationship is by not complying with the physician's requests. Patient noncompliance and noncooperation are significant problems in health care (Thompson, 1986). And while there are numerous reasons patients do not comply with physician requests, "patient cooperation depends on how the health care provider communicates more than on anything else" (Thompson, 1986, p. 111). Kreps and Thorton (1992) identify common areas of patient noncompliance such as clients not keeping appointments, not following health care regimens, and not using prescribed drugs correctly.

Being a patient in a hospital can be an especially overwhelming situation.

Another problem linked to ineffective communication between patients and physicians is the unrealistic expectations some patients might have of their health care providers' abilities to cure their illness (Kreps & Thorton, 1992). Patients might even expect their physicians to perform amazing miracles like those seen in soap operas or movies. Soap operas, particularly, regularly have characters slip into "hopeless" comas only to recover a few days later. It is not unusual for patients to

expect too much from their health care providers and to view their own health care concerns as more significant or serious than the problems of other patients (Kreps & Thorton, 1992).

Recently, patients have started bringing information they gather from the Internet to physician visits and questioning their providers' decisions based on the information (Ahmad, Hudak, Bercovitz, Hollenberg, & Levinson, 2006). Physicians report feeling overburdened by this trend because they are expected to be familiar with, and receptive to, Internet information. In a study of primary care physicians, the physicians expressed concern with patients self-diagnosing and self-treating based on information located via online sources (Ahmad et al., 2006). Physicians may not react well to this trend and may even become defensive when patients question their treatment decisions. When these problems occur, patients are more likely to communicate ineffectively with their health care provider and establish poor relationships. As Kreps and Thorton (1992) point out, physician-patient miscommunication, lack of cooperation, and unrealistic expectations are all problematic and can lead to a tumultuous physician-patient relationship.

A patient needs to possess appropriate assertiveness to help improve communication with a health care provider.

Many individuals experience difficulty performing their "patient" roles because they are often uncertain about what being a patient entails (Northouse & Northouse, 1998). When they enter a health care setting, individuals shed the familiar roles (as wife, mother, father, employee) and assume the unfamiliar role of patient. Hospital settings are especially overwhelming for patients. When patients enter the hospital they encounter numerous health care professionals, each with a different role in providing patient care. These health care experiences cause anxiety for most patients. Read the textbox to the right to learn more about what physicians want their patients to know. This information can help patients understand what physicians need from them during medical visits.

Potential Responses to Ineffective Provider-Patient Interactions

When physician-patient communication is ineffective, a variety of problems can occur. Outcomes of poor health care provider and patient communication may include one or more of the following:

1. Poor health outcomes for patients
2. Malpractice law suits
3. Patient dissatisfaction
4. Provider dissatisfaction and burnout
5. Lack of patient compliance and cooperation

Incomplete, inaccurate, ambiguous, or deceptive communication between health care providers and patients can result in poor health outcomes for patients. When patients are not forthcoming about their health practices, symptoms, or reasons for visiting their providers, physicians may provide the wrong treatment (Palmieri & Stern, 2009) and patients' health may deterio-

RESEARCH IN REAL LIFE: What physicians want patients to know

Consumer Reports conducted an online poll of 660 primary-care physicians to learn more about what challenges physicians faced as well as how they felt patients could get the most out of the physician-patient relationship. Some of the conclusions from the survey were as follows:

1. Physicians take the long view: establishing a long-term relationship with a primary-care physician is beneficial for both patients and physicians.
2. Respect is a two-way street. Physicians feel that patients have become less appreciative and respectful. Therefore, it is important to express thanks and be courteous during physician visits (turn off your phones!).
3. Take your medications. Physicians emphasized the importance of taking medications as instructed and adhering to treatment plans for optimal patient health outcomes.
4. Track your medical history. Physicians emphasized the importance of tracking your medical history, bringing a friend or relative to your appointments, and taking notes.

For more information on the survey results, go to http://www.consumerreports.org/cro/2012/04/what-doctors-wish-their-patients-knew/index.htm

rate. Providers are not deception detection experts, and research indicates that patients often lie about a wide range of health issues (Lewis, Matheson, & Brimacombe, 2011; Palmieri & Stern, 2009). As stated previously, patients need to improve their communication practices and provide truthful and descriptive information to their health care providers.

As Levinson (1994) notes, while physician mistakes are not common, poor communication practices along with physician mistakes are perceived as a recipe for litigation. Malpractice law suits are a significant problem in health care that affect all of us in some way. Approximately 70 percent of malpractice claims are linked in some way to health care providers' ineffective communication skills (Levinson, 1994; Levinson, Roter, Mullooly, Dull, & Frankel, 1997).

A significant and expected outcome of communication problems in this context is widespread dissatisfaction for both the health care providers and the clients. What happens when patients are less than satisfied with their health care experiences? They avoid getting professional assistance, even when they really need it (Kreps & Thorton, 1992). What happens when patients avoid visits to their physicians? This decision affects us all, either directly or indirectly. If a patient does not get regularly screened for certain types of diseases, then potentially curable diseases or illnesses persist undetected.

Patients are not the only ones who are dissatisfied with the current state of our health care. Health care professionals, frustrated with the lack of patient compliance and other work-related stressors, are more likely to experience burnout and leave the profession (Kreps & Thorton, 1992).

Ineffective, or poor, communication between physicians and patients affects patient compliance and cooperation. The research has indicated that both patient and physician behaviors can explain patient noncompliance and noncooperation. Rates of patient noncooperation have been estimated to be as high as 70 percent (Thompson, 1986)! Patients might not comply with physician requests because they are lazy, apathetic, scared, ignorant, or defiant. On the other hand, physicians also contribute to patient noncompliance by employing either ineffective or negative tactics to gain patient compliance (Thompson, 1986). Regardless of whether the patient, the physician, or both are to blame for problems with patient noncompliance, it is another significant problem that can potentially affect a patient's health and rate of recovery.

IMPROVING HEALTH CARE PROVIDER-PATIENT COMMUNICATION

While much of this chapter has focused on physician-patient studies and related information, we want to expand our discussion to include suggestions for improving communication between all types of health care providers (e.g., physicians, nurses, technicians, physical therapists, and pharmacists) and patients. In the following sections, we advance several suggestions for improving communication between health care providers and patients to reduce the incidence of patient noncompliance, reduce the prevalence of lawsuits, and increase patient and health care provider satisfaction with communication and relationships.

Patient Communication

While there is a great deal of information available for physicians and health care providers who want to improve their communication with their patients (see, for example, Klingle, 2004), there is considerably less available for patients who want to improve communication in health settings. Additionally, patients and physicians seem to have quite different views of what constitutes competent patient communication (Cegala, Gade, Broz, & McClure, 2004). For example, patients want physicians to express empathy and concern during medical interactions, but physicians might not always see this type of communication as necessary for achieving their goals.

According to Booth-Butterfield (2006), one of the most important communication skills for a patient to possess is appropriate assertiveness. Recall our definition of **assertive communication**: defending your own rights and wishes while still respecting the rights and wishes of others. In addition to using an appropriately assertive response, the style of delivery is also important. Booth-Butterfield (2006) feels individuals can maximize the effectiveness of their assertive communication by sending nonverbal messages that are consistent with their verbal ones. For example, individuals should strive to maintain eye contact and appear confident through their facial expressions, use appropriately assertive gestures, and a firm and confident tone of voice. Individuals can enhance their assertiveness and credibility by displaying confidence in their voice, gestures, posture, and facial expressions. Remember to apply ERA in medical interactions to assure fair and equitable treatment in health care situations.

Maintaining eye contact and projecting confidence maximize the effectiveness of assertive communication.

Cegala, health communication researcher and communication professor (patcom.jcomm.ohio-state.edu), offers several helpful suggestions for patients preparing for medical interviews. One key piece of advice for patients is to *prepare* for medical interactions by writing down physical symptoms or questions prior to the appointment. His advice, expressed as the acronym **PACE**, is easy to remember and can help patients to communicate more effectively with their physicians. His suggestions are listed in Table 15.2 below.

Table 15.2 Preparing Communication for Medical Interviews

P	Present detailed, descriptive information about how you are feeling to your health care provider. Be sure to describe your symptoms and any irregularities in your health. This information will help the care provider diagnose and treat you.
A	Ask questions if appropriate information is not provided by your health care provider. If you are confused about the information, seek clarification by *asking questions*.
C	Check your understanding of information that is given to you (e.g., paraphrasing information back to your health care provider, "*So what you are saying is . . .*")
E	Express any concerns that you may have about the recommended treatment. If necessary, be appropriately assertive (ERA).

Health Care Provider Communication

Health care providers can use a number of communication strategies to establish good relationships with their patients. For example, Levinson and her colleagues (1997) found that physicians who laughed and smiled more and used more facilitation statements (e.g., *First I am going to take your blood pressure . . .*) with their patients were less likely to be sued than those who used these behaviors less often. Wanzer and her colleagues (2004) tested a preliminary model of health care providers' use of patient-centered communication in relationship to patient satisfaction. The patient-centered communication model, CHILE, can be used by health care providers to improve communication between care providers and patients and increase patient satisfaction. See the textbox below for an explanation of CHILE and see the scale at the end of the chapter for a measurement used to assess health care providers' patient-centered communication practices.

RESEARCH IN REAL LIFE:
Patient-centered communication

Wanzer, Booth-Butterfield, and Gruber (2004) investigated the relationship between pediatric providers' (physicians, nurses, and hospital staff) use of patient-centered communication and parent/guardian satisfaction with medical care and communication. Parent/guardians were asked to complete surveys on providers' use of the following behaviors (CHILE).

1. **Clarity:** was clear and refrained from using medical jargon.
2. **Humor:** used appropriate humor.
3. **Introductions:** introduced her/himself to parent/guardian and patient and stated title.
4. **Immediacy:** used nonverbal immediacy behaviors—eye contact, appropriate gestures, etc.
5. **Listening:** engaged in active listening behaviors.
6. **Empathy:** expressed empathy and concern to the parent/guardian and/or patient.

Wanzer and her colleagues found a significant positive correlation between parent/guardians' perceptions of providers' use of these behaviors and reported satisfaction with communication and medical care. It was especially important for physicians to be immediate, to listen, and to exhibit empathic messages with the parents/guardians of child patients as a means of increasing satisfaction with medical care and communication.

Other researchers have identified four best practices that can be used to assess physicians' communication during medical interviews (Krupat, Frankel, Stein, & Irish, 2006). The researchers created the "Four Habits Coding Scheme," which is a tool used to assess health care providers' communication skills and help them improve communication during medical interviews. Krupat and his colleagues (2006) identified the following four habits or best practices that health care providers should adopt:

1. Invest in the beginning: greet the patient warmly and engage in small talk.
2. Elicit the patient's perspective: elicit information from patients to identify shared goals for the visit.
3. Demonstrate empathy: encourage the patient to identify and express feelings.
4. Invest in the end: give clear explanations about diagnosis and treatment and make sure the patient understands the information.

These suggestions should help both patients and care providers improve their interactions, leading to better relationships, increased patient compliance, and increased satisfaction for both physicians and patients.

DEATH AND DYING COMMUNICATION

The information presented in the last sections of this chapter will help you understand why it is so difficult to talk about death and dying and how to negotiate your way through similar difficult situations.

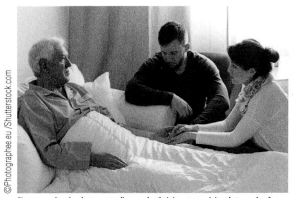

Given our culture's reluctance to discuss death, it is not surprising that people often avoid the topic.

The topic of death and dying is an extremely difficult subject for most individuals, even professionals who deal with death and dying on a regular basis. In this section, we discuss the reasons individuals find this to be a difficult topic and the typical responses to situations involving death and dying. Suggestions for improving communication about death and dying from both the dying person's perspective and the family member's or loved one's perspective are offered in the final sections of this chapter. After reading this chapter, we hope you will be able to manage conversations about this topic more effectively and provide appropriate comforting communication to individuals who are either ill or have recently experienced the death of a loved one.

Reasons for Anxiety when Discussing Death and Dying

There are a number of reasons individuals become anxious or uncomfortable when discussing death and dying. For many of us, we wonder how and when we will die. Will we die of old age? Will our death include suffering or pain? Will we

die suddenly? Where do we go after we die? Another significant worry often triggered by discussions about death and dying is the potential loss of our loved ones. We fear losing the ones we love or leaving them behind when we die.

Another reason that death, even aging, is not discussed is because it is a subject that is "evaded, ignored, and denied by our youth-worshipping, progress-oriented society" (Kubler-Ross 1975, p. x). Kubler-Ross (1975), also known as the "death and dying lady," discusses our culture's inability to approach aging and death as a natural part of life. Instead, she notes, we often treat death as an illness or disease we should be able to conquer. For a number of years Kubler-Ross interviewed terminally ill patients in front of medical students, physicians, nurses, social workers, and clergy, to provide care providers with greater insight into the perspective of the dying patient. As a result of her research and others' on this topic (e.g., Kastenbaum, 1992), professionals who treat terminally ill patients now know more about the thoughts, feelings, and behaviors exhibited by the terminally ill and are better equipped to treat them and to help them make end-of-life decisions.

Despite the work by Kubler-Ross and others, it is not unusual for dying patients to continue to experience communication problems with their health care providers, often leading to poor care (Hines, Babrow, Badzek, & Moss, 2001). Because approximately 80 percent of people die in institutional settings such as hospitals, nursing homes, or retirement facilities, it is likely that they will interact with health care professionals who are poorly equipped to discuss issues related to death and dying (Servaty, Krejci, & Hayslip, 1996). Thus, health care providers, who deal with death on a regular basis, have become the focus of much of the more recent research (Servaty et al., 1996).

Both doctors and patients are reluctant to talk about death for various reasons (Hines et al., 2001). Physicians are not typically trained to talk about death with patients, and even with training, they are usually not willing to talk about death and dying due to reluctance on the patient's behalf. Even family members of the terminally ill are unwilling to talk about death with their loved ones. Hines and his colleagues note that family involvement with the terminally ill patient may often be counterproductive or even contradict the patient's needs (Hines et al., 2001). While family members can be a great source of support and comfort, they may also become overly emotional and agitated, hindering their ability to help a loved one make important end-of-life care decisions. Given our culture's reluctance to discuss death, it is not surprising that health care providers, patients, and patients' family members often avoid discussing end-of-life issues.

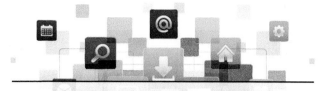

Physicians are not typically trained to talk about death with patients, and even with training, are usually not willing to talk about death and dying due to reluctance on the patient's behalf.

for every person, (2) some individuals might not go through every stage of the process, and (3) some patients exhibit two or three stages simultaneously. Kubler-Ross notes that, ideally, both the dying patient and the patient's family should reach the stage of acceptance before death occurs, although this is not always possible. Some individuals may stay in one stage throughout the process due to unique personality traits, emotional states, or individual coping styles. It is important to know what individuals experience during each of these stages to communicate more effectively with them throughout the process.

Responses to Death and Dying

How do people typically react when they are faced with the topic of death? According to Kubler-Ross, there seem to be several stages that both individuals who are dying and loved ones of the terminally ill go through. The stages of death and dying are denial, anger, bargaining, depression, and acceptance (Kubler-Ross, 1974; 1975). Kubler-Ross draws a number of important conclusions regarding the stages: (1) the stages do not always occur in the same order

DENIAL. The first stage of death and dying is typically the **denial** stage. In the denial stage, the patient may "deny the bad news and continue to work as if he were as well and as strong as before" (Kubler-Ross, 1975, p. 1). Family members or friends of the loved ones may deny that the individual is sick as well and continue to interact with the individual as if he or she is healthy. Denial is viewed as an unproductive stage for both the dying patient and loved ones because it may either prevent treatment of the illness, hasten death, or prevent the terminally ill person and loved one from talking about end-of-life issues and engaging in grief work.

ANGER. The next stage of death and dying is **anger**. During this stage individuals might ask "Why me?" and become angry with everyone around them. Individuals might lash out at loved ones, possibly resulting in isolation from the very people they need the most. Similar to denial, this stage is also unproductive and prevents individuals from enjoying the time they have left, engaging in grief work, and dealing with end-of-life issues. If the terminally ill person or loved one remains in this stage for an extended period of time, social support from others may dwindle significantly.

BARGAINING. During the **bargaining** stage of death and dying, individuals try to strike deals with others in order to recover from their illnesses. It is not unusual for people to bargain with God, promising good behavior or increased church attendance in exchange for an extension of life or to escape pain and suffering. Similar to the other two stages, this phase is generally considered unproductive for both the terminally ill individual and the loved ones because it may prevent further treatment, create a sense of false hope, or prevent individuals from facing end-of-life issues. Some terminally ill individuals and family members may be taken advantage of by those who promise miracle or "quack" cures.

DEPRESSION. During the **depression** stage the terminally ill individual or loved one may lose interest in the outside world and significantly reduce his or her contact with other people. It is difficult to observe the patient or loved one in this stage. Patients may abuse drugs or alcohol or

contemplate suicide because they are depressed. It is important to help individuals move through this stage. A patient's family members or friends might seek or recommend professional help or other means of helping the patient manage depression and begin the grieving process.

ACCEPTANCE. According to Kubler-Ross, if the dying person is afforded the opportunity to grieve and his family members have learned to let go, then he will be able to die in a stage of **acceptance**. Patients would typically reach the acceptance stage of death and dying if it were not for members of the helping professions who are reluctant to admit defeat and family members who are reluctant to let go of their loved one (Kubler-Ross, 1974). Kubler-Ross feels that the acceptance stage is the most realistic goal a dying person can work toward, since all of us have to die eventually. Once someone has reached this stage, he has a much better chance to focus all of his energies on working with the physician and treatment team to prolong his life and to spend time with loved ones.

Not surprisingly, individuals cope differently with death and dying situations. Most people are fairly resilient following the death of a loved one and do not grieve in a dysfunctional or unhealthy manner (Bonanno, 2004). Most people are able to maintain a sense of resilience during bereavement situations. **Resilience** refers to an individual's ability to sustain healthy levels of physical and psychological functioning when faced with adversity (Booth-Butterfield, Wanzer, Weil, & Krezmien, 2014). Researchers studied individual differences associated with resilience during bereavement situations and found that humor-oriented individuals often cope better (Booth-Butterfield et al., 2014). Read the textbox be-

492

low to learn more about this research and how humor helps individuals cope with death and dying situations.

In the next section we explore ways to help individuals cope with death and dying situations. It is important to note that everyone copes differently, and we should never force someone to grieve or cope a certain way.

Suggestions for Improving Communication Related to Death and Dying

It is important for all of us to help our friends, relatives, coworkers, or relationship partners during difficult times. One way to help those we care about is by providing appropriate and effective comforting communication. Burleson's (1984) definition of comforting communication is "the type of communication behavior having the intended function of alleviating, moderating, or salving the distressed emotional states of others" (p. 64). Comforting communication can include verbal messages such as "I am really sorry this happened to you," or nonverbal behaviors such as eye contact, attentiveness, crying, hugs, or gestures (Dolin & Booth-Butterfield, 1993).

What types of messages are perceived as the most effective comforting strategies? Effective comforting messages are those that are described as more person-centered (Burleson & MacGeorge, 2002). Person-centered comforting messages are strategies that help a person explain how he or she is feeling at the moment, recognize and validate the expressed feelings, and illustrate how those feelings fit in a broader social context. Person-centered messages are often perceived as the most effective means of helping others deal with difficult situations because they "tend to be more listener-centered, accepting, emotionally focused, and evaluatively neutral" (Burleson & MacGeorge, 2002, p. 395). To illustrate the stark contrast between comforting messages that are high and low in person-centeredness, let us imagine that your friend's grandmother died recently in a car accident. An example of a comforting message that is high in person-centeredness would be, "How

It is important for all of us to help our friends, relatives, coworkers, or relationship partners during difficult times. One way to help those we care about is by providing appropriate and effective comforting communication.

are you feeling right now? I can see why you would be upset. Anyone who has been through a situation as difficult as yours would probably feel like you do right now. Is there anything I can do to help you get through this difficult time?" By contrast, a comforting message that is low in person-centeredness would be, "Why are you so upset? Don't you think that you are overreacting right now? You really need to stop moping around and move on with your life. Let's just go out tonight and drink some beers!" These not-so-subtle examples illustrate the difference between comforting messages that help individuals feel better and messages that do not help, and may even make others feel worse.

Some people are better at providing comfort and social support than others. Interpersonal researchers have studied the relationship between individual differences and comforting abilities. For example, individuals described as **cognitively complex** possess more highly abstract and differentiated construct systems (e.g., schema) and are more likely to enact sophisticated comforting messages compared to individuals low in cognitive complexity (Burleson & Samter, 1990). Individuals higher in cognitive

complexity can access a variety of different comforting strategies and, as a result, are more likely to employ more sophisticated person-centered messages than those low in cognitive complexity. Dolin and Booth-Butterfield (1993) studied how individual differences such as sex and **affective orientation** affect the types of nonverbal comforting individuals provide. They found that females tended to be more affectively oriented than males, which meant they were more likely to use their emotions to guide communication decisions. In addition, females who were high in affective orientation employed more diverse nonverbal comforting strategies than individuals scoring low in affective orientation (Dolin & Booth-Butterfield, 1993). Affectively oriented individuals also employed more diverse **nonverbal comforting strategies** (e.g., hugging, patting the person on the back, and showing concern through their voices), which seems to indicate greater cognitive complexity as well. Not surprisingly, age is also associated with comforting communication skills (Burleson, 1984). As children age they develop more sophisticated communication skills and engage in more prosocial behaviors. Thus, age and maturity are also connected to your ability to provide comfort to another person.

Effective and Ineffective Death and Dying Communication

What are some of the best ways to provide comfort to individuals who are terminally ill? First and foremost, Kubler-Ross (1974; 1975) encourages those caring for the terminally ill to meet the individual's support needs by spending time with him or her, acknowledging that death is imminent, and addressing any needs or immediate concerns he or she may have. It seems most important to spend time with the terminally ill person, listen, and allow the person to express his or her feelings. Additionally, experts recommend allowing the individual to grieve and mourn on his own terms and not to force him to reach a particular stage of death and dying. While it is most beneficial to help him reach the acceptance stage, forcing the person to feel or think a certain way is not productive. It is extremely important to be supportive and to listen actively, always letting the person know you are available. Being available, listening, taking care of the person's needs, and nonverbal comforting strategies are all valuable ways of helping individuals manage this difficult time. From the patient's perspective, it is important for those caring for the dying individual to be honest and compassionate and, when necessary, to allow the patient to express fears about the situation.

©glenda./Shutterstock.com

It's important to comfort and support a grieving friend and validate feelings of loss.

What about after the terminally ill person has died—what is the *best* thing to say to someone who has lost a loved one? There are some support attempts that are recognized as unhelpful by the recipient; much of what people say after some-

one has died is not helpful and does not alleviate the pain associated with the loss. Davidowitz and Myrick (1984) found that 80 percent of the statements made to individuals who had recently lost a loved one were not helpful. Commonly delivered statements such as, "She led a full life," "Be thankful you have another son," or "Don't question God's will," are not comforting for the recipient. In similar research conducted by Lehman and his colleagues (1986), those who had lost a spouse or a child in a motor vehicle accident in the last four to seven years were asked to identify the least helpful support tactics. The strategies identified as the least helpful in providing comfort included giving advice, encouragement of recovery, minimization/forced cheerfulness, and identification with feelings. From Lehman's research, the most helpful strategies included contact from a similar other, expressions of concern and caring, allowing the person to vent his or her feelings, involvement in social activities, and just being available.

Range, Walston, and Pollard (1992) also identified a number of effective and ineffective verbal comforting strategies delivered to loved ones after a suicide, homicide, accident, or natural death. The most helpful statements were, "If there is anything I can do, please let me know, and I am here if you need someone to talk to."

In death and dying situations, it is important to let the other person know that you are available for him or her and are willing to help if needed. When faced with death, individuals handle situations differently and experience varied emotions and feelings. It is important to support them and validate their feelings without minimizing their grief or concern. As validated by Lehman's research, a highly ineffective comforting strategy would be to state, "I know exactly how you feel because my dog just died." Why is this statement an example of ineffective comforting communication? Because the source does not know *exactly* how the individual is feeling, and providing the example of losing a pet as being similar to losing a parent is not appropriate or reassuring.

It is comforting to know that sophisticated communication strategies are not required in these situations. It is important for the person providing support to listen, allowing the other person time to vent, and to ask how he or she can help make the situation better. Effective comforting communication would not include the use of trite, or common, phrases such as "Doesn't life seem unfair?" "God needed another angel," or "Heaven is a nice place." Virtually everyone who has lost a loved one would agree that these statements are not usually helpful in death and dying situations.

SUMMARY

In this chapter, we provided an explanation of stress and related terms and then described how people cope with stress. Next, we identified two situations most individuals describe as stressful or challenging. Interacting with health care providers and communication during death and dying situations often evoke anxiety for either one or both of the interactants. Now that you are more aware of why these situations are difficult and the strategies available for communicating effectively in each of these situations, we hope you will approach these experiences with greater confidence. In addition, there is one final important piece of advice we would like to offer: Do not be afraid of making mistakes in these situations, because everyone does! If you say the wrong thing when interacting with your physician or with someone who recently lost a loved one, provide a genuine apology for your mistake. Try not to make the same mistake again, but do not avoid these interactions in the future. As we mentioned in Chapter 1, communication is a skill that individuals can improve upon over time. Now that you understand *why* these situations are challenging and *how* you can manage these difficult situations, we hope you will make a conscious effort to employ some of the strategies recommended in this chapter.

DISCUSSION QUESTIONS

1. Your health care provider prescribes medication that has several dangerous side effects. You are concerned about taking this medication. Using ERA, develop an appropriately assertive response to this situation.

2. Recall your last visit to your primary-care physician. Can you evaluate your visit to the health care provider by describing specific examples of the four habits or CHIILE?

3. Discuss some problem-focused coping strategies that you have used in the past to manage stressors. Can you recall examples of times when you used emotion-focused coping strategies? Were these strategies effective or ineffective in managing your stress levels?

SELF ASSESSMENTS

The Patient-Centered Communication Scale

The Patient-Centered Communication Scale employs a 5-point Likert-type format to assess the extent to which caregivers exhibit the positive behaviors (1 = Never; 2 = Rarely; 3 = Occasionally; 4 = Often; and 5 = Very Often. Also note that items 6 and 11 are reverse coded for analysis.) Scores range from a low of 13 to a high of 65. Scores over 50 indicate more frequent use of PCC while scores below 39 indicate less frequent use of PCC.

_____ 1. The physician/nurse/staff member introduced her/himself to me.

_____ 2. When the physician/nurse/staff member approached me he/she provided her/his title/position to me.

_____ 3. The physician/nurse/staff member used gestures while speaking with me.

_____ 4. The physician/nurse/staff member used appropriate humor when communicating with me.

_____ 5. The physician/nurse/staff member looked at me while talking to me.

_____ 6. The physician/nurse/staff member had a tense body position while talking to me.*

_____ 7. The physician/nurse/staff member smiled at me as he/she approached me.

_____ 8. The physician/nurse/staff member listened intently during our conversation.

_____ 9. The physician/nurse/staff member communicated in a clear and direct manner when talking to me.

_____10. I felt comfortable expressing any worries or concerns to this physician/nurse/staff member.

_____11. When I stated any worries or concerns that I had, the physician/nurse/staff member directed the conversation away from my statement.*

_____12. If I expressed emotions such as anxiety or fear, the physician/nurse/staff member invited discussions about my concerns.

_____13. The physician/nurse/staff member asked me to express any concerns that I might have.

SOURCE: Wanzer, M.B. & Booth-Butterfield, M. (2015). An overview of the Patient-Centered-Communication Scale. In D.K. Kim & J. Dearing (Eds). *Health Communication Measures*. Peter Lang Publishing.

Directions: There are five statements below which are common comments made by patients concerning their physicians. Please indicate how well each statement describes how you feel when communicating with your physician, employing the following scale:

1 = not at all; 2 = somewhat; 3 = moderately so; 4 = very much so

_____ 1. When communicating with my physician, I feel tense.

_____ 2. When communicating with my physician, I feel calm.

_____ 3. When communicating with my physician, I feel jittery.

_____ 4. When communicating with my physician, I feel nervous.

_____ 5. When communicating with my physician, I feel relaxed.

Scoring:
> Step 1: Add the scores for items 1, 3, and 4.
> Step 2. Add the scores for items 2 and 5.
> Step 3. Complete the following formula: FOP = 15 + total for Step 1 - total for Step 2.

Scores above 13 indicate high fear of physician. Scores below 7 indicate low fear of physician. Scores between 7 and 13 indicate moderate fear of physician.

Source: From "The impact of communication apprehension and fear of talking with a physician and perceived medical outcomes" by V.P. Richmond, R.S. Smith, A.M. Heisel and J.C. McCroskey, *Communication Research Reports*, 1998, 15, 344-353. Reprinted by permission of the publisher Taylor & Francis Ltd., www.informaworld.com.

KEY TERMS AND DEFINITIONS

ACCEPTANCE: stage of dying where the dying person is afforded the opportunity to grieve and his or her family members have learned to let go.

AFFECTIVE ORIENTATION: the level to which an individual is likely to use emotions to guide communication decisions.

ANGER: an unproductive stage of death where individuals become angry and lash out at loved ones.

ASSERTIVE COMMUNICATION: defending your own rights and wishes while still respecting the rights and wishes of others.

BARGAINING: an unproductive stage of death where individuals try to strike deals with others in order to recover from their illness.

CHRONIC STRESSORS: situations or circumstances that we have to manage daily such as a poor work environment or an unhealthy relationship that affect the body over time.

COGNITIVELY COMPLEX: individuals who possess more highly abstract and differentiated construct systems and are more likely to enact sophisticated comforting messages compared to individuals low in cognitive complexity.

COMFORTING COMMUNICATION: the type of communication behavior having the intended function of alleviating, moderating, or salving the distressed emotional states of others.

COPING: a response to something novel or to changes in one's environment or relationships.

COPING STRATEGIES: the specific behaviors or messages enacted to manage emotions associated with the stressful or novel situation.

DENIAL: first stage of death and dying where the patient may deny the bad news and continue to work as well and as strong as before.

DEPRESSION: stage of death and dying where interest in the outside world is lost and contact with other people is significantly reduced.

EMOTION-FOCUSED COPING: method of coping involving processing and expressing feelings arising from the stressor.

HEALTH COMMUNICATION: an area of study concerned with human interaction in the health care process.

NONVERBAL COMFORTING STRATEGIES: hugging, patting the person on the back, and showing concern through the voice when communicating about death.

PERSON-CENTERED COMFORTING: strategies that help a person explain how he is feeling at the moment, recognize and validate the expressed feelings, and illustrate how those feelings fit in a broader social context.

PROBLEM-FOCUSED COPING: method of coping involving changing the situation or fixing the problem.

RAPID-ONSET STRESSORS: situations or events that occur suddenly, like losing your phone or being in a car accident.

REFRAMING: viewing the problem or stressor in a different manner.

RESILIENCE: an individual's ability to sustain healthy levels of physical and psychological functioning when faced with adversity.

SOCIAL SUPPORT: the resources people have available that provide them with assistance and help them manage different types of problems.

STRESS: the experience of a perceived threat (real or imagined) to one's mental, physical, or spiritual well-being, resulting from a series of physiological responses and adaptations.

STRESSORS: any particular situation or event that causes stress.

TWO-FUNCTION MODEL OF COPING: a widely used explanation of how individuals cope with adversity.

REFERENCES

Ahmad, F., Hudak, P. L., Bercovitz, K., Hollenberg, E., & Levinson, W. (2006). Are physicians ready for patients with Internet-based information? *Journal of Medical Internet Research, 8,* e22.

Ainsworth-Vaughn, N. (1998). *Claiming power in doctor-patient talk.* New York: Oxford University Press.

American Institute of Stress. 50 common signs and symptoms of stress. Retrieved on April 1, 2015 from http://www.stress.org/stress-effects/

Barger, S. D. (2013). Social integration, social support and mortality in the US National Health Interview Survey. *Psychosomatic Medicine, 75,* 510–517.

Beckman, H. B., & Frankel, R. M. (1984). The effect of physician behavior on the collection of data. *Annals of Internal Medicine, 101,* 692–696.

Berkhof, M., van Rijseen, J., Schellart, A., Anema, J., & van der Beek, A. (2011). Effective training strategies for teaching communication skills to physicians: An overview of systematic research. *Patient Education and Counseling, 84,* 152–162.

Bertakis, K. D., Roter, D., & Putnam, S. M. (1991). The relationship of the physician's medical interviewing style to patient satisfaction. *Journal of Family Practice, 32,* 175–181.

Bonanno, G. (2004). Loss, trauma, & human resilience. *American Psychologist, 59,* 20–28.

Booth-Butterfield, M. (2006). *Influential health communication.* Littleton, MA: Tapestry Press.

Booth-Butterfield, S., Chory, R., & Beynon, W. (1997). Communication apprehension and health communication behaviors. *Communication Quarterly, 45,* 235–250.

Booth-Butterfield , M., Wanzer , M., Weil, N., & Krezmien, E. (2014) Communication of humor during bereavement: Intrapersonal and interpersonal emotion management strategies. *Communication Quarterly, 62,* 436–454.

Brannan, D., Biswas-Diener, R., Mohr, C., Mortazavi, S., & Stein, N. (2013). Friends and family: A cross-cultural investigation of social support and subjective well-being among college students. *Journal of Positive Psychology, 8,* 65–75.

Burgoon, J. K., Pfau, M., Parrott, R., Birk, T., Coker, R., & Burgoon, M. (1987). Relational communication, satisfaction, compliance-gaining strategies, and compliance in communication between physicians and patients. *Communication Monographs, 54,* 307–324.

Burgoon, M., Parrott, R., Burgoon, J. K., Birk, T., Pfau, M., & Coker, R. (1990a). Primary care physicians' selection of verbal compliance gaining strategies. *Health Communication, 2,* 13–27.

Burgoon, M. (1990b). Patients' severity of illness, noncompliance, and locus of control and physicians' compliance gaining messages. *Health Communication, 2,* 29–46.

Burleson, B. (1984). Age, social-cognitive development, and the use of comforting communication strategies. *Communication Monographs, 51,* 140–153.

Burleson, B. R., & MacGeorge, E. L. (2002). Supportive communication. In M. L. Knapp & J. A. Daly (Eds.), *Handbook of interpersonal communication* (374–424.) Thousand Oaks, CA: Sage Publications.

Burleson, B. R., & Samter, W. (1990). Effects of cognitive complexity on the perceived importance of communication skills in friends. *Communication Research, 17,* 165–182.

Cegala, D., Gade, C., Broz, S., & McClure, L. (2004). Physicians' and patients' perceptions of patients' communication competence in a primary care medical interview. *Health Communication, 16,* 289–305.

Celis, H., & Fagard, R. H. (2004). Whitecoat hypertension: a clinical review. *Eur J Intern Med, 15*(6), 348–357.

Chao, R. (2011). Managing stress and maintaining well-being: Social support, problem-focused coping, and avoidant coping. *Journal of Counseling & Development, 89,* 338–348.

Cohen, S., & Willis, T. A. (1985). Stress, social support, and the buffering hypothesis. *Psychological Bulletin, 98,* 310–357.

Davidowitz, M., & Myrick, R. D. (1984). Responding to the bereaved: An analysis of "helping" statements. *Death Education, 8,* 1–10.

Dolin, D. J., & Booth-Butterfield, M. B. (1993). Reach out and touch someone: Nonverbal comforting communication. *Communication Quarterly, 41,* 383–393.

duPré, A. (2009). *Communicating about health: Current issues and perspectives.* New York: Oxford University Press.

Falvo, D., & Tippy, P. (1988). Communicating information to patients—Patient satisfaction and adherence as associated with resident skill. *Journal of Family Practice, 26,* 643–647.

Folkman, S., Lazarus, R. S., Dunkel-Schetter, C., DeLongis, A., & Gruen, R. J. (1986). Dynamics of a stressful encounter: Cognitive appraisal, coping and encounter outcomes. *Journal of Personality and Social Psychology, 50,* 992–1003.

Hines, S., Babrow, A. S., Badzek, L., & Moss, A. (2001). From coping with life to coping with death: Problematic integration for the seriously ill elderly. *Health Communication, 13,* 327–342.

Infante, D. A., Rancer, A. S., & Avtgis, T. (2009). *Contemporary communication theory.* Dubuque, IA: Kendall Hunt.

Jenkins, S. R., Belanger, A., Connally, M. L., Boals, A., & Durón, K. M. (2013). First-generation undergraduate students' social support, depression and life satisfaction. *Journal of College Counseling, 16,* 129–142.

Kastenbaum, R. (1992). *The psychology of death* (2nd ed). New York: Springer Publishing Company.

Klingle, R. (2004). Compliance gaining in medical contexts. In Gass and Seiter (Eds.), *Perspectives in persuasion, social influence, and compliance gaining* (289–315). Boston, MA: Allyn & Bacon.

Kreps, G. L., & Thorton, B. C. (1992). *Health communication: Theory and practice* (2nd ed). Prospect Heights, IL: Waveland Press.

Krupat, E., Frankel, R., Stein, T., & Irish, J. (2006). The four habits coding scheme: Validation of an instrument to assess clinicians' communication behavior. *Patient Education & Counseling, 62,* 38–45.

Kubler-Ross, E. (1974). *Questions and answers on death and dying.* New York: Macmillan Publishing Co.

Kubler-Ross, E. (1975). *Death: The final stage of growth.* Englewood Cliffs, NJ: Prentice Hall.

Lazarus, R. S., & Folkman, S. (1984). *Behavior therapy & beyond.* New York: McGraw-Hill.

Lehman, D. R., Ellard, J. H., & Wortman, C. B. (1986). Social support for the bereaved: Recipients' and providers' perspectives on what is helpful. *Journal of Consulting and Clinical Psychology, 54,* 438–446.

Leung, A., Cheung, M., & Chi, I. (2014). Relationship between patients' perceived capacity for communication, health literacy, and diabetes self-care. *Journal of Health Communication, 19,* 161–172.

Levinson, W. (1994). Physician-patient communication: A key to malpractice prevention. *Journal of the American Medical Association, 272,* 1619–1620.

Levinson, W., Roter, D. L., Mullooly, J. P., Dull, V. T., & Frankel, R. M. (1997). Physician-patient communication: The relationship with malpractice claims among primary care physicians and surgeons. *Journal of the American Medical Association, 227,* 553–559.

Lewis, C., Matheson, D., & Brimacombe, C. (2011). Factors influencing patient disclosure to physicians in birth control clinics: An application of the communication privacy management theory. *Health Communication, 26,* 502–511.

Malinauskas, R. (2010). The associations among social support, stress, and life satisfaction as perceived by injured college athletes. *Social Behavior and Personality, 38,* 741–752.

Merianos, A. L., Nabors, L. A., Vidourek, R. A., & King, K. A. (2013). The impact of self-esteem and social support on college students' mental health. *American Journal of Mental Health Studies, 28,* 27–34.

Northouse, L. L., & Northouse, P. G. (1998). *Health communication: Strategies for professionals* (3rd ed.). Stamford, CT: Appleton & Lange.

O'Brien, T., DeLongis, A., Pomaki, G., Putterman, E., & Zwicker, A. (2009). Couples living with stress: The role of empathic responding. *European Psychologist, 14,* 18–28.

Ostrum, C. M. (2004). Good medicine begins with good doctor-patient relationship. *The Seattle Times.* Retrieved 12/11/2006 from http://archives.seattletimes.nwsource.com

Palmieri , J., & Stern , T. (2009). Lies in the doctor-patient relationship. *Primary Care Companion to The Journal of Clinical Psychiatry, 11*(4), 163–168.

Pryor, J. H., Hurtado, S., DeAngelo, L., Blake, P. L. & Tran, S. (2011). *The American freshman: National norms fall 2011.* Los Angeles: Higher Education Research Institute, UCLA.

Range, L., Walston, A., & Pollard, P. (1992). Helpful and unhelpful comments after suicide, homicide, accident or natural death. *OMEGA, 25,* 25–31.

Richmond, V. P., Smith, R. S., Heisel, A. D., & Mc-Croskey, J. C. (1998). The impact of communication apprehension and fear of talking with a physician and perceived medical outcomes. *Communication Research Reports, 15,* 344–353.

Richmond, V. P., Smith, R. S., Heisel, A. D., & Mc-Croskey, J. C. (2001). Nonverbal immediacy in the physician/patient relationship. *Communication Research Reports, 18,* 211–216.

Riley, K. E., & Park, C. L. (2014). Problem-focused vs. meaning-focused coping as mediators of the appraisal adjustment relationship in chronic stressors. *Journal of Social and Clinical Psychology, 33,* 587–611.

Sarid, O., Anson, O., Yaari, A., & Margalith, M. (2004). Coping styles and changes in humoural reaction during academic stress. *Health and Medicine, 9,* 85–98.

Schiffrin, H., Liss, M., Miles-McLean, H., Geary, K., Erchull, M., & Tashner, T. (2014). Helping or hovering? The effects of helicopter parenting on college students' well-being. *Journal of Child Family Studies, 23,* 48–557.

Scott, E. (2015). Cognitive reframing and stress management. Retrieved April 1, 2015 from http://stress.about.com/od/positiveattitude/a/reframing.htm

Seaward, B. L. (2012). *Managing stress: Principles and strategies for health and well-being.* Burlington, MA: Jones & Bartlett.

Servaty, H. L., Krejci, M. J., & Hayslip, B. (1996). Relationships among death anxiety, communication apprehension with the dying, and empathy in those seeking occupations as nurses and physicians. *Death Studies, 20,* 149–161.

Smith, D. L. (2013). The relationship of age and satisfaction with physician-patient communication from the 2009 Medical Expenditure Panel Survey (MEPS). *Journal of Communication in Health care, 6,* 44–60.

Thompson, T. L. (1986). *Communication for health professionals.* Lanham, MD: University Press of America.

Wanzer, M., Booth-Butterfield, M., & Gruber, K. (2004). Perceptions of health care providers' communication: Relationships between patient-centered communication and satisfaction. *Health Communication, 16,* 363–384.

index

Page reference in *italics* refer to figures and tables.

A

ABCX model, 428–430, *429, 430*
abstract symbols, 137
accenting, 181
acceptance
    acceptance function, 397, *397*
    of death/dying, 492
    intercultural communication, overview, 388
    intercultural communication and, 388
    organizational communication and, 451
accounts, 280
acronyms, 188
action-oriented listening, 119, 120
active participation, in mediated communication, 344–345
active strategies, for intercultural communication, 386
activity jealousy, 282
acute stressors, 430
adaptation traits, 65–67, *66*
adaptors, 173

advice, 243
affect displays, 172
affection
    Affectionate Communication Index, 285
    decreased affection, 314
    defined, 9
    expressing, 140
    nonverbal expression, 183
affective orientation, 65–66, 494
affiliation needs, 444
affinity, 239
affinity-seeking strategies, 36–37
agape lovers, 285
Age Discrimination in Employment Act (ADEA), 396
age issues
    ageism, 395–396
    language and, 152–156
    nonverbal communication, 187
    organizational communication and, 460–461
    perception and, 114
    relationship initiation and, 207
agent, 280
aggressive traits, 67–71
Agnew, C. R., 306–307

Albada, K. F., 16–17, 21
alternating, 462
Altman, I., 220
ambiguous boundaries, 420
ambivalents, 456
ambushers, 123
American Institute of Stress, 478
analytical listening style, 120
Anderson, P. A., 283
anger, about death/dying, 492
anticipatory socialization phase, 459
antisocial behaviors, 244
anxiety, about death/dying, 490–491
anxious ambivalent attachment style, 42
anxious attachment style, 42
apologies, 280
apprehension traits, 59–62
appropriateness, 66, 157
argumentativeness, 67–68, 291
Argumentativeness Scale, 67
Aron, Arthur, 31
arousal relief theory, 281
artifacts, 178–179
assertive communication, 488
assertiveness, 68–69
assessment, of relationship problems, 304–306
assimilation, 459
assistance, requesting, 463
assurances, 242
asynchronous communication, 348
attachment security, 214
attachment theory, 41–44. *see also* relationship initiation
    attachment security hypothesis, 44
    overview, 40
    rebound relationships, 325
    styles of attachment, 41–43, 244
attending, 117
attitudes, of stereotyping/prejudice, 394–396
attitude similarity, 213
attraction
    Facebook and physical attraction, 351
    humor and, 211, *211*
    interpersonal attraction, 205
    perception and physical attractiveness, 209

    relationship initiation and, 205–212, *206, 209, 211,* 226, *226*
    relationship initiation and physical /social attraction, 351–354
    social attractiveness, 210–211
    task attractiveness, 211–212
attributions, assessing relationship problems, 304–306
attribution theory, 18, 110–113
authenticity/authentic self, 33–35
avoidance
    avoidance style conflict management, 255
    avoidant attachment style, 42
    avoidant strategy of relationship maintenance, 244
    avoiding stage of relationship dissolution, *309,* 309–312, *312*
    purposeful, and relationship termination, 315–316
Avtgis, T., 58
awareness, 66

B

back-channeling cues, 181
background similarity, 213
bargaining, about death/dying, 492
Beavin, J., 19
behavioral confirmation, 45
behavioral uncertainty, 350
beliefs, 391
believability, 167
Bell, R. A., 36–37
Berger, P. L., 141
betrayal, 315
bias
    biased information search, 103
    biased language, 149–150, *150*
    communicating prejudice, 396–398, *397*
    prejudice attitudes, 394–396
    prejudiced communication, 396–398, *397*
BIG EARS strategy for listening, 124
Bippus, A., 58
birth stories, 426
Bodie, G. D., 119–121
body piercings, 178

body size, 176–177, *177*
bonding stage, of relationship development, 222–224, *223*
boomerang children, 414
Booth-Butterfield, M., 63–65, 317–318, 488, 493
Booth-Butterfield, S., 63–65
boundaries, 420
Bowlby, John, 41, 44, 47
brain
    cognitive function of verbal communication, 140–141
    retention and, 118
breadth, relationship initiation and, 218
buffer effect, 32
Buller, D. B., 273
Burgoon, J. K., 168, 181, 273
Burleson, B., 240–241, 493

C

Cahill, D. J., 451
calibration, 420–421
Campbell, L., 211
Canary, Dan, 242–243, 355
Career Builder, 453
career decisions, stress and, 477
catfishing, 351
cell phones, *357,* 358
Chaffee, S., 421
character, 149
"Check Yo Nutz" campaign, 105
cheerleader mentors, 452
CHILE (clarity, humor, introductions, immediacy, listening, empathy), 489
chronemics, 179–180
chronic stressors, 430, 477
Cialdini, Robert, 101–102
circumscribing stage, of relationship dissolution, *309,* 309–312, *312*
Civil Rights Act of 1964, 454
clarity, 147–148, 275
classical theories, organizational communication and, 443
closure, following relationship termination, 325–326
co-cultures, within U.S., 375–378, *377, 380*
"codes," 143

coercive power, 288
cognitive arousal, 168
cognitive function, 140–141
cognitively complex individuals, 494
cognitive uncertainty, 350
collaborative/integrative conflict management, 256–258
collectivism, 114–115, 393
Collins, N. L., 218
comforting communication, about death/dying, 493–496
comforting skills, 241
commitment, 239, 306, 319
communication accommodation theory, 154
communication apprehension (CA), 60, 187
communication competence, 8, 40, 385–389, *386, 388*
communication predicament of aging model, 154
Communication Style Inventory, *63,* 63–65
communication traits
    adaptation traits, 65–67, *66*
    aggressive traits, 67–71
    apprehension traits, 59–62
    overview, 58–59, *59*
    presentation traits, 58, 62–65, *63*
communicator style, 62–65
compensatory restoration, 283
competence, 149
competing relationships, 315
competitive/distributive style conflict management, 255–256
complementarity hypothesis, 214
complementing, 180
completeness, 274
compliance, 289
concealment, 274
concreteness, 104, 157
concrete symbols, 137
confessions, 277
confirmation, 417
confirming communication, 428
confirming messages, *151,* 151–152, *152*
conflict management
    avoidance style, 255
    collaborative/integrative, 256–258
    competitive/distributive style, 255–256

conflict, defined, 250
conflict, overview, 249
conflict as productive or unproductive, 253–254, 261
conflict types, *250,* 250–252
perpetual conflict, 57
reasons for conflict, 252–253
styles of, overview, 254–255
conformity orientation, 421–422
connected individuals, 12
connecting, 462
connotative meaning, 138
consensual families, 423
constitutive rules, 136, 168
constructive communication, 67
constructivism, 106
Consumer Reports, 486
content, 15
content expectations, 410
content level of meaning, 139
content-oriented listeners, 120
context
    defined, 12
    relationship initiation and, 204, 225, *225*
    social *versus* workplace, 454
    verbal communication and, 139–140, 152–156
continuous nature, of nonverbal communication, 167
contradictory expressions, 180
control, 9
control mutuality, 238
conventional logic, 72–74
convergence, 154
conversation orientation, 421
conversations, starting, 216–217, *217*
coping skills. *see also* health communication; stress
    coping strategies, 479–480
    coping with death/dying, 492–493
    coping with stress, overview, 479–480
    for jealousy, 286–288, *287*
    relationship termination, 323–325
costs, 222
coup de foudre, 360
courtship stories, 426
Coyle, C. L., 354
credibility, 149

critical listening style, 120
Croskey, J. C., 61
culture, defined, 373–375. *see also* intercultural communication
culture, organizational, 457–458, *458*
Cupach, W, R, 8, 40
cyberbullying, 69, 356

D

Daly, J. A., 16–17, 21, 36–37, 58
dark side of communication, defined, 272. *see also* relationship problems
Dark Side of Interpersonal Communication, The (Cupach, Spitzberg), 272
dating. *see* romantic relationships
Dawson, E. J., 181
death/dying, communication about, 489–496
deception
    analyzing messages of, 278
    defined, 273
    detecting, 276–278
    in interpersonal relationships, 272–275
    mediated communication and, 362
    reasons for lying, 275–276
decoding, 181–182
decreased affection, 314
de-escalation messages, 313
de-escalatory conflict spirals, 254
defensive listening, 123
deidentification, 417
deindividuation theory, 347
Dekovic, M., 44
demographic similarity, 213
demographic trends, *382, 384,* 384–385
demonstrating openness, 355
denial, about death/dying, 491–492
denotative meaning, 138
depression, about death/dying, 492
depth, 218
destructiveness, 68–69
developmental approach, to interpersonal communication, 11
developmental definitions, 11
differentiating stage, of relationship dissolution, *309,* 309–312, *312*

direct communication style, 145–146
direct definitions, 43–44
direct methods, 317
directness, 274
direct request, for relationship termination, 316
disapproved behavior, 315
disconfirming communication, 428
disconfirming messages, 122–123, 151
discrimination, 397
dissimilarity, in relationships, 320–321
dissolution stages, of relationship termination, *309,*
    309–312, *312,* 358, *359*
distributive conflict management style, 255–256
diversity. *see also* intercultural communication
    defined, 373–375
    emotion and, 78–79
    levels of, *373*
divorce, parent-child relationship and, 414–416. *see*
    also family communication
dominance, 290
DoSomething.org, 347
Duck, S. W., 307–309, 358
duration, relationship initiation and, 204
dyadic communication, 11
dyadic process, relationship termination and,
    307–309
dynamic nature
    of culture, 379–380
    of interpersonal communication (IPC), 14–15

E

ectomorphs, 177, *177*
Edelmann, R. J., 280
educational settings
    email to instructors, 347
    emotion in classroom, 77–78
ego-defensive function, 397, *397*
ego support, 241
Ekman, P., 180–181
electronic paralanguage, 187–189, *188*
email read receipts, 346
embarrassment, 278–281, *279*
emblems, 171
emoticons, 188, 346

emotion. *see also* nonverbal communication
    effect on communication, 72–74, *73, 74*
    emotional intelligence (EI), 73, 74–75
    emotion work, 74–75
    overview, *71,* 71–72
    protecting feelings of others, 276, 277
    in relational contexts, 75–79
Emotional Expressivity Scale (EES), 182
emotional infidelity, 286
emotional response theory (ERT), 77
emotion-focused coping, 479
empathy, 77, 241–242
encoding, 181–182
encounter phase, 459
endomorphs, 177, *177*
environmental adornment, 178
environmental factors, 179
Equal Employment Opportunity Commission
    (EEOC), 454–455
equality, 450
equifinality, 421
equity
    assessing relationship problems, 304–306
    equity theory, 239–240, 305
    retailiation and, 284
equivocation, 147, 274
ERA (empathy, rationale, action), 318, 488
eros lovers, 285
errors, attribution, 111–113
escalatory conflict spirals, 254
escape, 418
essential skills, 6
esteem needs, 390
ethnicity, intercultural communication and, 375,
    376, *377*
ethnocentrism, 388
evading, 464
evocation, 73, 74
exit responses, 259
experimenting stage, of relationship development,
    222–224, *223*
expert power, 288
explicit learning, 379
expressed struggle, *250,* 250–252
expressive logic, 72–74
external attributions., 111
external stressors, 429

F

Facebook
- for family communication, 423
- humor, 64
- physical attraction and, 351
- relationship maintenance with, 248–249

face-management, 242

face-to-face communication, mediated communication compared to, *343,* 344–349, *348*

facial communication, *170,* 170–171

facilitative cognitive meaning, 180–181

fade-away method, of termination, 315

fair fighting, 261

false homophily, 214

falsification, 274

family, balancing work and, 461–464, *463*

family communication, 407–437. *see also* conflict management; relationship initiation; relationship maintenance
- consequences of relationships, 427–428
- co-parenting after relationship termination, 323
- defined, 408–409
- development of self and, 40–44
- difficulty of, 428–430, *429, 430*
- family communication patterns theory, 421–423, *422*
- family events, 417–418
- family identity and, 425–427, *427*
- family jealousy, 282
- family metaphors, 427
- family myths, 426
- family stories, 425
- family systems theory, *419,* 419–421
- family themes, 427
- "helicopter parenting," 482
- overview, 407–408
- relationship maintenance, 247
- skill similarity in, 241
- symbolic interaction theory, 423–425
- types of family relationships, 409–418, *411, 413, 418*
- verbal communication and, 153–155

Family First (McGraw), 412

favoritism, 450

Fehr, B., 107

feminine traits, 394

Festinger, L., 45

file sharing, 346–347

first dates, goals of, 216

Fitzpatrick, M. A., 410–412, 422

flaming, 73, 189

flat structures, 441–442

"Flight from Conversation, The" (Turkle), 3–4

flirting, 217, *217,* 453, 454

Floyd, K., 285

forgiveness, following relationship termination, 325–326

formal communication style, 146

formal mentoring, 452

friendship
- diversity in, 396 (*see also* intercultural communication)
- friend jealousy, 282
- friendship-warmth touch, 174
- organizational communication and, 449–451
- relationship termination of, 314–318
- stress and, 477–478

Friesen, W. V., 180–181

functional-professional touch, 174

fundamental attribution error, 112, 304

Furler, L. A., 184

G

Gallup, 460

Gearhart, C., 119–121

gender. *see also* relationship termination; sexism
- conflict management, 260
- emotion, 78–79
- feminine/masculine traits in cultures, 394
- language and, 143, 148, 152–156
- language and sexism, 149–150, *150*
- nonverbal communication, 184–185
- perception and listening differences, 104, 121–123
- relationship initiation and, 207, 208–209, *209*
- relationship problems and, 272, 284, 285–286
- relationship termination and, 315
- sexism, 149–150, *150, 396*

Global Language Monitor (GLM), 144
goals
    incompatible, *250,* 250–252
    relationship initiation and, 215–216
Goffman, Erving, 66
Gold, J. M., 415
Goleman, Daniel, 7, 77
goodwill, 149
Gottman, John, 57
granting forgiveness, 325
grave dressing, relationship termination and, 307–309
Greenfield, D. N., 360
groom mentors, 452
Gross, E., 279
group identification, 143
Guerrero, L. K., 283
guilt-trip producers (mentors), 452–453

H

Hall, Edward T., 18, 174–176, 179, 392
Hamilton, D. L., 108–109
Handbook of Family Communication, The, 409
Handbook of Interpersonal Communication (Knapp, Daly, Albada, Miller), 16–17, 21
haptics, 173–174
Harvard Dialect Survey (2003), 377, *377*
hate speech, 150
health communication, 475–502. *see also* stress
    communication about death and dying, 489–496
    communication between health care providers and patients, 482–487
    defined, 482
    emotion and, 75–76
    "helicopter parenting" and, 482
    improving communication between health care providers and patients, 487–489, *488*
    overview, 6–8, 475–476
    social support, 480–481
    stress, overview, 476–478
    stress and coping, 479–480
hearing, 116–117
Heider, Fritz, 18, 110–113

"helicopter parenting," 482
hierarchy, in workplace, 441–447, *444, 445*
hierarchy, of families, 420
hierarchy of needs, 17–18, *18,* 389–390, *390, 444,* 444–445
high aggression, 291
high-context cultures, 392
high power distance, 394
Hill, Reuben, 428–430
Hofstede, G., 393, 394
homophily, 176, *213,* 213–214, 378
honesty, 361
Horan, S. M., 184
hostile interaction, relationship termination and, 316
hostile work environment, 455
Houck, G. M., 35
Houser, M. L., 184
human relations, 445
human resources, 445
humor
    attraction and, 211, *211*
    humor orientation (HO), 62–65
    joking and, 280
    relationship maintenance and, 243
    in sibling relationships, 417
Hunsaker, F. G., 181
hyperpersonal model of CMC, 353

I

ideal-self similarity, 214
identity. *see also* self
    family identity, 425–427, *427*
    identification and power, 290
    identity management and nonverbal expression, 183–184
    identity scripts, 44
    studying identity formation, 30–31
illustrators, 172
immediacy, 150–152, *151, 152,* 185–186
impartiality, 450
implicit learning, 379
impression formation, 183–184
impression management
    impression construction, 37

impression motivation, 37
    overview, 37–38
    relationship initiation and, 210
improvisation action/strategies, *463,* 463–464
inclusion, 9
incompatible goals, *250,* 250–252
"indifferents," 456
indirect communication style, 145–146
Indirect methods, 316
individual differences. *see* personality
Individualism, 393
Individualistic cultures, 114
inequality, 450
Infante, D., 67, 68–69, 70
infidelity, 318–319
informal communication style, 146
informal mentoring, 451–452
information processing theory, 102
information seeking, 349–351
in-group status, 445
initiation of relationships. *see* relationship initiation
inner self, 33
inquisitiveness, 361
instructors, communication with, 347
integrating stage, of relationship development, 222–224, *223*
integrative communication, 286
integrative conflict management, 256–257
intensifying stage, of relationship development, 222–224, *223*
intentionality, 14, 111
interactional approach, to interpersonal communication, 11–12
interaction involvement, *66,* 66–67
interactive strategies, for intercultural communication, 386–387
intercultural communication, 371–406
    characteristics of culture, 378–381, *379, 380*
    co-cultures within U.S., 375–378, *377, 380*
    communicating prejudice, 396–398, *397*
    communication competence, 385–389, *386, 388*
    culturally bound messages, 168
    culture and diversity, defined, *373,* 373–375
    diversity in organizations, 460–461
    effective interpersonal relationships for, 398–399

emotion, 78–79
    impact on interpersonal relationships, 381–385, *382, 383, 384*
    overview, 371–373
    perception and listening differences, 104, 121–123
    personal orientation system, 389–396, *390*
    relationship initiation and, 209–210, 226, *226*
    relationship maintenance, 247
    social support and, 480–481
interdependence, *250,* 250–252, 420
interference, *250,* 250–252
internal attributions, 111
internalization, 290
internal stressors, 429
Internet addiction disorder (IAD), 356
interpersonal attraction, 205–212, *206, 209, 211*
interpersonal communication (IPC), 3–28. *see also* emotion; listening; nonverbal communication; perception; personality; self; verbal communication
    approaches to, 10–12
    defined, 10
    for establishing personal relationships, 6–9
    forms of, 9
    history of, 16–19, *18*
    overview, 3–4
    principles of, 13–16
    study of, 4–6
    textbook overview, 21–22
    theory of, 20–21
interpersonal deception theory (IDT), 273
interpersonal goals, relationship initiation and, 215–216
interpersonal solidarity, 320
interpretation
    attribution errors, 111–113
    attribution theory, 110–113
    defined, 110
intiation stage, of relationship development, 222–224, *223*
intimacy. *see also* relationship initiation; romantic relationships
    development of self and, 46–47
    impression management, 184
    intimacy jealousy, 282

intimate communication, 220
 of mediated communication, 353
intrapsychic process, relationship termination and, 307–309
introverts, 62
investment model of relationship termination, 306–307, *307*
investment size, 306
involuntary relationships, 203, 408, 441
involuntary stressors, 430
irreversibility, 13–14
"I" statements, 309

J

Jackson, D. D., 19
jealousy, 281–288, *287*
joint activities, 243
joking, 280
judgment, 451
"just friends," remaining, 322–323
justification messages, 313

K

Kelly, G. A., 106
kinesics, 18, 171–173
KISS (Keep It Short and Simple), 156
Klohnen, E. C., 213–214
Kluckhohn, C., 392
Knapp, M. L., 16–17, 21, 225, 278, *309,* 309–312, *312*
knowledge, 8, 385–387
Koerner, A. F., 422
Kring, A. M., 182
Kubler-Ross, E., 490, 491–492, 494–495

L

lack of commitment, 320
laissez-faire families, 423
language. *see also* verbal communication
 organizational culture and, 457–458, *458*
 style of, and mediated communication, 347–348
launching stage, 414

leader-member exchange (LMX) theory, 445–447
leakage cues, 275
legitimate power, 288
liking, 239
liking, self-disclosure, 217–218
limited capacity processors, 102
linguistic determinism, 142
linguistic relativity, 142
listening
 BIG EARS strategy for listening, 124
 effectiveness of, 123–124
 gender, culture, personality differences, 104, 121–123
 listening and hearing, defined, 116–117
 listening style, 119
 overview, 115
 skills for, 115–116
 steps of, 116–117
 styles of, 119–121
Listening Styles Profile (LSP-16), 119
looking glass self, 40
love and belonging, 390
love-intimacy touch, 174
low aggression, 291
low-context, 392
low power distance, 393
loyalty, 260
ludus lovers, 285
Luo, S., 213–214
lurking, 345
lying. *see* deception

M

mania, 285
marital relationships, communication in, 409–412
markers, 175
Martz, J. M., 306–307
masculine traits, 394
Maslow, Abraham, 17–18, *18,* 389–390, *390,* 444–445
mass communication, 10
Maxwell, John, 59–60
Mayer, J. D., 75
McCroskey, J. C., 68, 186, 187
McGraw, Phil, 412
McLeod, J. M., 421

McLuhan, M., 381

Mead, G. H., 423

media richness theory, 349

mediated communication, 341–370
    defined, 10, 243, 342
    face-to-face communication compared to, *343,
        344–349, 348*
    forming safe and meaningful online
        relationships, 358–362, *359*
    initiating online relationships, 349–353
    maintaining online relationships, *354,* 354–
        355, *356, 357,* 358
    overview, 341–344, *344*
    terminating online relationships, 357–358

medical care. *see* health communication

Medina, John, 118

Meeus, W., 44

Mehrabian, A., 150

mentor relationships, 451–453, *453*

mesomorphs, 177, *177*

message-centered approach, to interpersonal
        communication, 11, 12

message design logic (MDL), 72–74, *73*

"me" statements, 309

metacommunication, 16, 139

metamorphosis, 460

Miller, G. A., 102

Miller, G. R., 16–17, 21

Miller, K. S., 154

Miller, L. C., 218

moderate aggression, 291

monochronic characteristics, 179

monopolizing, 122

Morman, M. T., 285

motivation, 9, 77. *see also* hierarchy of needs

multi-channeled communication, 167

N

narrative paradigm theory, 457

National Council of Teachers of English (NCTE),
        150

Neale, J. M., 182

needs, 389. *see also* hierarchy of needs

negative affect expression, 286

negative identity management, 313–314

neglect, 259

no flirting relationship maintenance, 243

non-normative stressors, 429–430

non-verbal comforting strategies, 494

nonverbal communication, 165–197
    artifacts, 178–179
    best practices, 184–187
    characteristics, 167
    chronemics, 179–180
    cultural norms, 378–379, *379*
    defined, 166
    electronic paralanguage, 187–189, *188*
    facial, *170,* 170–171
    functions of, 180–184, *182*
    haptics, 173–174
    kinesics, 171–173
    mediated communication compared to face-
        to-face communication, *343,*
        344–349, *348*
    nonverbal expectancy violation theory, 168
    nonverbal messages, 12
    overview, 18, 165–166
    paralanguage and, 175–176
    physical appearance, 176–178, *177*
    proxemics, 174–175, *175*
    similarity to verbal messages, 168–169
    uncertainty reduction theory, 221

normative stressors, 429

Norton, R. W., *63,* 63–65

novelty, 104

Nussbaum, Jon, 153

O

objective self-awareness (OSA), 33

obligatory/involuntary relationships, 203

observers, 280

oculesics, 171

Olson, Loreen, 258

"onion" model, of social penetration, 220, *220*

online relationships. *see also* social networking sites
        (SNS)
    attraction and humor, 211, *211*
    cyberbullying, 69
    forming safe and meaningful online
        relationships, 358–362, *359*

honest descriptions of physical attributes, 207
initiating, 203, 349–353 (*see also* relationship
    initiation)
maintaining, *354,* 354–355, *356, 357,* 358
relationship initiation and technology, 225–226
self and, 34–35
technological transformation and intercultural
    communication, 381–384, *382*
terminating, 357–358
online self-disclosure, 352
openness, 242, 355
organization, of perception, 106–110
organizational communication, 439–473
    balancing family and work relationships, 461–
        464, *463*
    contemporary issues in workplace relationships,
        460
    diversity in organizations, 460–461
    educational settings, 77–78, 347
    emotion and work, 76
    friendship in organizations, 449–451
    gender bias in workplace, 208–209
    impact of technology on work relationships,
        464
    intercultural communication and, 384
    interpersonal effectiveness in work
        relationships, 455–456, *456*
    mentor relationships, 451–453, *453*
    organizational culture and, 457–458, *458*
    organizational jargon, 140
    organizational orientation, 456, *456*
    overview, 10, 439–440
    romantic relationships at work, 453–455, *454*
    socialization and, 458–460, *459*
    types of relationships in workplace, 443–449,
        111, 445, 447
    unique nature of workplace relationships,
        440–442
    workplace bullying, 294 (*see also* relationship
        problems)
    workplace communication, overview, 4–5
out-group status, 445
outside pressure, 321
overaccommodation, 154
overbenefited feelings, in relationships, 240
overinvolved parenting, impact of, 416

P

paralanguage
    defined, 175–176
    electronic para-language, 187–189, *188*
parent-child relationships, overview, 412–416, *413.*
    see also family communication
parent mentors, 452
partner uncertainty, 393
passive behavior, 344
passive strategies, for intercultural communication,
    386
peer relationships. *see also* friendship
    development of self and, 44–46
    trust in childhood peer relationships, 239
    at work, *447,* 447–449
peer-to-peer file sharing, 346–347
people-oriented listening, 119–120
people skills, 6
perception, 99–134
    defined, 100–101
    individual differences of, 113–115
    interpretation of, 110–113
    limitations of, 101–102
    listening, overview, 115–118
    listening and gender, culture, personality
        differences, 121–123
    listening effectively, 123–124
    listening styles, 119–121
    nonverbal communication and, 188–189
    organization and, 106–110
    overview, 99–100
    partner uncertainty, 393
    perceived scarce resources, 251
    perceptiveness, 66
    physical attractiveness and, 209
    selectivity processes, 102–106
    self-perception, 202
    self-system (self-concept, self-esteem, self-
        regulation), *35,* 35–40 (*see also*
        self)
    verbal communication and, 148–150, *150*
perpetual conflict, 57
personal adornment, 178
personal communication, 220
personal constructs, 107–108

personality, 55–97
    adaptation traits, 65–67, *66*
    aggressive traits, 67–71
    apprehension traits, 59–62
    defined, 55
    emotion, overview, *71,* 71–72
    emotion and communication, 72–74, *73, 74*
    emotion in relational contexts, 75–79
    emotion work and emotional intelligence (EI),
        74–75
    impact of individual differences on social
        interaction, 56–58
    overview, 55–56
    perception and listening differences, 121–123
    presentation traits, 58, 62–65, *63*
    trait and state approaches, overview, 58–59
personalization of information, 275
personal orientation system, 389–396, *390*
Personal Report of Communication Apprehension
        (PRCA), 60
Personal Report of Intercultural Communication
        Apprehension (PRI-CA), 375
person-centered comforting, 493
Pew Internet and American Life Survey, 352
Pew Research Center, 414
Pew Research Internet Report, 342
physical appearance, 176–178, *177*
physical arousal, 168
physical attractiveness, relationship initiation and,
        206, 351–354
physical evidence, 277
physician-patient communication. *see also* health
        communication
    improving, 487–489, *488*
    overview, 482–487
physiologial needs, 390. *see also* hierarchy of needs
pluralistic families, 422
polychronic, 179
positiveness, showing, 355
positive relational deceptive strategies, 277
positive tone messages, 313
positivity, 242
power
    power distance, 393–394
    powerful/powerless language, 147–148, *148*
    power jealousy, 282

verbal aggression and interpersonal power,
        288–290, *290*
pragma lovers, 285
Pragmatics of Human Communication (Watzlawick,
        Beavin, Jackson), 19
predicted outcome value theory, 221–222
prejudice
    attitudes about, 394–396
    communicating, 396–398, *397*
prepping, 462
presentation traits, 58, 62–65, *63*
primacy, 105
principles of interpersonal communication (IPC),
        13–16
    dynamic, 14–15
    intentionality, 14
    irreversibility, 13–14
    relational, 14–15
private communication, 220
proactive attribution, 183
problematic Internet use (PIU), 356
problem-focused coping, 479
process, defined, 12
process model of relationship termination, 307–309
protective families, 423
prototypes, 107–108
proximity
    listening and, 103
    organizational communication and, 447–448
    proxemics and nonverbal communication, 18,
        174–175, *175*
    relationship initiation and, 212
    relationship termination and, 314, 315
pseudo de-escalation, 316
pseudo-listening, 122
public self, 33

Q

quality, of relationships, 322
quality of alternatives, 306
quid pro quo, 455

R

race
    friendship diversity, 396
    intercultural communication and, 375, 376,
        377
    physical attractiveness and perception, 209
    racial profiling, 395
    racism, 395
Rancer, A. S., 58, 67
rapid-onset stressors, 477
rapport talk, 113, 156
read receipts, 346
re-assessment, of relationship, 283–284
rebound relationships, 325
recency, 105
recipients, 280
reciprocal self-disclosure, 218
reciprocating strategies, 463
reciprocity, of disclosure, 218–219
Recording Industry Association of American
        (RIAA), 346–347
reduced social cues theory, 345–346
referent power, 288
reflected appraisal, 40
reframing, 326, 479–480
regional differences, intercultural communication
        and, 375–378
regulate (regulation), 181
regulative rules, 137
regulators, 172
reinforcement, 104
rejection, 428
relational component, 15
relational expectations, 410–411
relational level of meaning, 138
relationally oriented listeners, 119
relational nature, of interpersonal communication
        (IPC), 14–15
relationship contexts and environments. *see
        also* conflict management; family
        communication; friendship; health
        communication; intercultural
        communication; mediated
        communication; organizational
        communication; peer relationships;

relationship initiation; relationship
        maintenance; relationship problems;
        relationship termination; romantic
        relationships
    emotion in relational contexts, 75–79
    self and, 34–35
    self-system (self-concept, self-esteem, self-
        regulation), *35,* 35–40 (*see also*
        self)
    types of, 202–203
relationship initiation, 201–233
    initiating online relationships, 349–353
    initiation, overview, 204–205
    interpersonal attraction and, 205–212, *206,*
        209, 211
    interpersonal communication for establishing,
        6–9
    interpersonal goals, 215–216
    nature of relationships, *203,* 203–204
    overview, 201–203
    proximity and, 212
    relationship, defined, 202, 203
    similarity/homophily and, *213,* 213–214
    stages of relationship development, 222–224,
        223
    theories about, 216–226, *223, 225*
relationship maintenance, 235–269
    communication skills for, 240–242
    conflict in, 249–261 (*see also* conflict
        management)
    in different types of relationships, 245–248
    Facebook and, 248–249
    maintaining online relationships, *354,* 354–
        355, *356, 357,* 358
    overview, 235–236
    reasons for, 238–240
    in sibling relationships, 417–418
    significance of, 236–238
    strategies, 238, 242–245, *244, 245*
relationship problems, 271–302
    assessment of, 304–306
    dark side of communication, defined, 272
    deception and, 272–278
    deception and analyzing messages, 278
    deception and reasons for lying, 275–276
    deception detection, 276–278

embarrassment, 278–281, *279*
jealousy and, 281–288, *287*
overview, 271–272
verbal aggression and interpersonal power, 288–290, *290*
verbal aggression strategies, 290–294
relationship termination, 303–337
assessing problems and, 304–306
closure and forgiveness for, 325–326
coping after, 323–325
Duck's process model of, 307–309
of friendship, 314–318
of homosexual relationships, 321–322
investment model, 306–307, *307*
overview, 303–304
relationship maintenance as alternative to, 237
remaining "just friends," 322–323
of romantic relationships, overview, 318–321
stages of relationship dissolution, *309,* 309–312, *312*
strategies, 312–314
terminating, defined, 311
terminating online relationships, 357–358
relevance, 274
remembering, 118
repetition, 180
report talk, 113, 156
requesting assistance, 463
resilience, death/dying and, 492–493
responding, 118
resurrection, relationship termination and, 307–309
retention, 118
retirement, 461
retroactive attribution, 183
reward power, 288
rewards, 222
rhetorical logic, 72–74
Richmond, V. P., 61, 68
rituals, organizational communication and, 458
roles
defined, 12
relationship initiation and, 204
Rollie, S. S., 307–309, 358
romantic jealousy, 282
romantic jealousy-induction, 285
romantic relationships

dating websites, 343
maintenance of, 245–248 (*see also* relationship maintenance)
marital relationships and family communication, 409–412 (*see also* family communication)
relationship termination of, 318–323
in workplace, 453–455, *454*
roommate communication challenges, 477
routine maintenance behaviors, 237–238
routinizing actions, 462–463, *463*
rules, 12
constitutive, 168
relationship initiation and, 204
of verbal communication, 136–137
Rusbult, Carl, 259, 306–307

S

SADFISH facial expressions, 170
safety and security needs, 390. *see also* hierarchy of needs
Salovey, P., 75
Samter, W., 240–241
Sapir, Edward, 142–143
Sapir-Whorf hypothesis, 142–143
satisfaction, assessing relationship problems, 304–306
scarce resource, *250,* 250–252
schema
personal constructs, 107–108
schemata, 106–107
scripts, 109–110
stereotypes, 108–109
schemata, 106–107
scientific management theory, 443–444
scripts, 109–110
script theory, 110
secure attachment, 41
security
hierarchy of needs and, 390 (*see also* hierarchy of needs)
of mediated communication, 350–351, 352, 358–362, *359*
selective listening, 123
selectivity processes (perception), 102–106
selection, defined, 102

INTERPERSONAL COMMUNICATION: Building Rewarding Relationships

selective attention, 104
selective exposure, 102–103
selective retention, 105
utility, 103
self, 29–53
  defined, 31
  interpersonal communication and development
    of, 40–47
  lying to protect self, 276
  overview, 29–30
  as process, 31
  self-actualization, 390 (*see also* hierarchy of
    needs)
  self-awareness, 33–35, 77
  self-complexity, 31–33, 32
  self-concept, 35
  self-disclosure, 141, 217–218, 219, 352, 386
  self-esteem, 38, 183
  self-forgiveness, 325
  self-monitoring, 210–211
  self-perception, 202
  self-regulation, 39, 77
  self-serving bias, 112
  self-system (self-concept, self-esteem, self-
    regulation), *35*, 35–40
  studying identity formation, 30–31
  understanding, for intercultural
    communication, 381, *382*
self-determination theory, 321
self-fulfilling prophecy, 45, 253
self-promoter mentors, 452
semantics, 138
Seventeen Essential Qualities of a Team Player, The
    (Maxwell), 59–60
severe aggression, 291
sexism
  attitudes of, 396
  biased language and, 149–150, *150*
sexual-arousal touch, 174
sexual harassment, 454
sexual infidelity, 286
sexual orientation
  relationship maintenance, 247–248
  termination of homosexual relationships, 321–322
shared meaning, 12
sharing tasks, 242

Sharkey, W. F., 279
Sheldon, W. H., 177
Sherman, J. W., 108–109
showing positiveness, 355
Sias, P. M., 451
sibling relationships, overview, 416–418, *418. see also*
    family communication
silence, 175–176
similarity
  defined, 36
  dissimilarity in relationships, 320–321
  relationship initiation and, *213*, 213–214
  similarity hypothesis, 47
  similarity to current self, 214
situational approach, to interpersonal
    communication, 11
situational definitions, 11
size, of stimuli, 104
skills, 8, 389
skill similarity model (SSM), 240–241
small group communication, 10
smartphones, *357, 358*
Smith, D. A., 182
social attraction, 351–354
social attractiveness, 210–211
social change, 144–145
social class, intercultural communication and, 378
social comparison theory, 45
social connections
  connected individuals, 12
  overview, 4
social exchange theory, 222, 316
social goals, relationship initiation and, 215–216
social identity model of deindividuation effects
    (SIDE), 347
social identity theory, 109
social influence, nonverbal messages and, 184–186
social information processing theory, 348
socialization
  intercultural communication and, 375
  organizational communication and, 458–460,
    459
social networking sites (SNS)
  computer-mediated communication for,
    342, *343* (*see also* mediated
    communication; online
    relationships)

development of self and, 45–46
Facebook and relationship maintenance, 248–249
personality and, 62, 64
relationship initiation and, 214
social networks, defined, 242
social penetration theory, 220
social-polite touch, 174
social process, relationship termination and, 307–309
social reality, 142
social referencing, 172–173
social skill, 77
social support, 417, 480–481
Socio-Communicative Orientation Scale, 68
soft skills, 5–6
solicited confessions, 277
Spegman, A. M., 35
Spitzberg, B. H., 8, 40
Stafford, Laura, 242–243, 279, 355
stagnating stage, of relationship dissolution, *309*, 309–312, *312*
state approach, to personality differences, 58
status, 149, 441–447
stepfamilies, parent-child relationship and, 414–416. *see also* family communication
stereotypes, 108–109
stereotyping, 394–396, *395*
Stevens, S. S., 177
Stone, G. P., 279
storge lovers, 285
stories of survival, 426
strategic maintenance behaviors, 238, 242–245, *244*, *245*
stress
coping with, 479–480
in families, 428–430, *429*, *430*
overview, 476–478
reducing, in relationships, 292
self-complexity and, 32
signs and symptoms of, 478
stressors, 429–430, 477
types of, 477
Strodbeck, F., 392
subjectivity, of verbal communication, 138–139
subtweeting, 99

superficial communication, 220
superior-subordinate relationships, 443–445
support, nonverbal expression, 183
suppression, 74
surveillance, 355
symbols
symbolic interaction theory, 17, 423–425
symbolism of verbal communication, 137–138
synchronous communication, 348

T

tall structures, 441
Tannen, Deborah, 113–114, 155–156
task attractiveness, 211–212
task goals, 215
task-oriented listeners, 120
tasks, sharing, 242
tattoos, 178
Taylor, D. A., 220
technological transformation, 381–384, *382*, 464
technology, for communication. *see* mediated communication; online relationships; social networking sites (SNS)
temporary relationships, at work, 441
terminating stage of relationship dissolution, *309*, 309–312, *312*
theory, 20
third-party information, 276–277
time-oriented listening, 119, 120–121
trading off, 463
traditional couples, expectations of, 410, 411, *412*
Trafford, A., 360
trait approach to personality, 58–59, *59*. *see also* communication traits
trust, 238–239
Turkle, Sherry, 3–4
turn-denying, 181
turn-maintaining, 181
turn-requesting behaviors, 181
turn-yielding, 181
two-function model of coping, 479

U

uncertainty, jealousy and, 283
uncertainty avoidance, 394
uncertainty reduction theory
    intercultural communication, 385–389, *386, 388*
    mediated communication and, 349–351
    relationship initiation and, 220–221
    verbal communication and, 141
underbenefited feelings, about relationships, 240
understanding, 117, 387–388
unintentionality, 111
United States, co-cultures within, 375–378, *377, 380*
United States Hostile Workplace Survey, 294
unsolicited confession, 277
upward mobiles, 456
U.S. Bureau of Labor Statistics, 440–441
U.S. Census, 383
utility, 103, 106

V

values, 391
Vangelisti, Anita, 205, 225, 278
Vaughn, H., 354
verbal abuse, 396
verbal aggression
    family communication and, 418
    interpersonal power and, 288–290, *290*
    relationship maintenance and conflict management, 258
    strategies of, 290–294
verbal aggressiveness, 69–71, 291
Verbal Aggressiveness Scale, 70
verbal communication, 135–164
    best practices, 156–157
    context of, 139–140

defined, 136
face-to-face communication compared to mediated communication, *343,* 344–349, *348*
factors affecting, 152–156
functions of, 140–145
immediacy of, 150–152, *151, 152*
overview, 135–136
perception and, 148–150, *150*
rules of, 136–137
similarity to nonverbal messages, 168–169
styles of, 145–148, *148*
subjectivity of, 138–139
symbols of, 137–138
verbal immediacy, 151
verbal messages, 12
veridicality, 275
violence, 397
voice responses, 260
voluntary relationships, 203, 408, 440–441
voluntary stressors, 430

W

Washington Post, 380, *380*
Watzlawick, P., 19
Whitaker, D. J., 154
white coat effect, 483
wholeness, 420
Whorf, Benjamin Lee, 142–143
Wigley, C. J., 69, 70
Wilbur, C. J., 211
willingness to communicate (WTC), 61
withdrawal, 313, 316
Wood, Julia, 20
workplace. *see* organizational communication
Workplace Bullying Survey, 294
work spouse, 453
Worthington, D. L., 119–121